The Waite Group's
MS-DOS®
Developer's Guide

HOWARD W. SAMS & COMPANY
HAYDEN BOOKS

Related Titles

**The Waite Group's MS-DOS®
Bible, Second Edition**
Steven Simrin

**The Waite Group's
Understanding MS-DOS®**
Kate O'Day and John Angermeyer

**The Waite Group's Tricks of
the MS-DOS® Masters**
*John Angermeyer, Rich Fahringer, Kevin
Jaeger, and Dan Shafer*

**The Waite Group's
Discovering MS-DOS®**
Kate O'Day

**The Waite Group's MS-DOS®
Papers**
The Waite Group

**C Programmer's Guide to
NetBIOS**
W. David Schwaderer

**Portability and the C
Language**
Rex Jaeschke

**Hard Disk Management
Techniques for the IBM®**
Joseph-David Carrabis

**The Waite Group's C++
Programming (Version 2.0)**
Edited by The Waite Group

**The Waite Group's Microsoft®
C Bible**
Naba Barkakati

**The Waite Group's Modem
Connections Bible**
Carolyn Curtis, Daniel Majhor

**The Waite Group's Printer
Connections Bible**
Kim G. House, Jeff Marble

Micro-Mainframe Connection
Thomas Wm. Madron

**IBM® PC AT User's Reference
Manual**
Gilbert Held

**IBM® PC & PC XT User's
Reference Manual, Second
Edition**
Gilbert Held

IBM® PS/2 Technical Guide
*James A. Shields and Caroline M.
Halliday*

*For the retailer nearest you, or to order directly from the publisher,
call 800-428-SAMS. In Indiana, Alaska, and Hawaii call 317-298-5699.*

The Waite Group's
MS-DOS®
Developer's Guide
Second Edition

JOHN ANGERMEYER   KEVIN JAEGER
RAJ KUMAR BAPNA   NABAJYOTI BARKAKATI
RAJAGOPALAN DHESIKAN   WALTER DIXON
ANDREW DUMKE   JON FLEIG   MICHAEL GOLDMAN

fff

HOWARD W. SAMS & COMPANY

A Division of Macmillan, Inc.
4300 West 62nd Street
Indianapolis, Indiana 46268 USA

International Standard Book Number: 0-672-22630-8
Library of Congress Catalog Card Number: 88-62227

From The Waite Group:
Development Editor: James Stockford
Technical Reviewers: Blair Hendrickson, David Blossom,
    and John Ferguson
Managing Editor: Scott Calamar
Content Editors: James Stockford and Mark Haas

From Howard W. Sams & Company:
Acquisitions Editor: James S. Hill
Development Editor: James Rounds
Manuscript Editor: Diana Francoeur
Cover Artist: Kevin Caddell
Illustrator: T. R. Emrick
Indexer: Ted Laux
Technical Reviewer: Mark Adler
Compositor: Photo Comp Corporation

Printed in the United States of America

To our families

Summary of Contents

Part I   Coding and Programming

Part II   Devices

Part III   Recovery

Part IV   Compatibility

Part V   Appendixes

Contents

Part I   Coding and Programming

ix

Part II   Devices

Part V   Appendixes

Preface
to the Second Edition

The Waite Group's MS-DOS Developer's Guide presents powerful programming techniques and an in-depth examination of the MS-DOS operating system. This edition has been newly revised to cover

- MS-DOS 4.0 compatibility, including all disk and file formats and the way in which the file allocation table (FAT) manages hard disk partitions greater than the 32-megabyte limit
- The LIM EMS 4.0 standard for expanded memory capacity, including its incorporation in MS-DOS 4.0
- New material on hardware control, including EGA and VGA programming techniques, as well as programming the serial port
- Detailed, completely updated explanation of terminate-and-stay-resident (TSR) programming
- Updated treatment of interrupts, functions, and error codes, with new material on undocumented functions
- Revised material on memory management, installable device drivers, disk layout and file recovery, real-time programming, and structured programming, with examples of MASM 5.0 programming techniques, as well as new tables, listings, appendixes, and an up-to-date quick reference card

A great deal has changed since the release of the first edition of this classic book on MS-DOS programming. At that time, MS-DOS 3.2 had just appeared, the standard display was still the monochrome or Hercules monochrome graphics, and the typical machine contained from 256K to 512K with a 10- or 20-megabyte hard disk. The hot available software included WordPerfect 3.x, dBASE III, Lotus 1-2-3 version 1.1, SideKick version 2.0, Microsoft's C compiler version 4.0, and MASM version 4.0. AT-class machines were selling in relatively small numbers, the term OS/2 had not appeared, EGA displays were rare and expensive, and Lotus/Intel/ Microsoft were about to release the LIM 3.2 Enhanced Memory Specification.

Today the MS-DOS operating system has reached its 4.0 incarnation. AT-class machines are the dominant platform, running at 10 to 16 megahertz with at least 640K memory, often with 1 or 2 megabytes of EMS RAM, and hard disks ranging from 40 to 100 megabytes. The EGA is the standard display, and IBM's model PS/2 machines have introduced the VGA standard, similar to the EGA in design but with better resolution. WordPerfect, dBASE, Lotus 1-2-3, and Side-Kick are still prominent in their latest versions, but the competition has stiffened from the likes of a revived WordStar and Microsoft Word; Paradox, Revelation, and Oracle; Twin, Lucid, and Excel; and a host of terminate-and-stay-resident programs.

In a world of fiercely competing operating systems such as UNIX, Macintosh, and OS/2, MS-DOS survives partly due to its huge installed base of users and feature-laden application programs, partly due to extensions such as Quarterdeck's DesqView and Microsoft's Windows, and partly due to much more powerful development software such as Microsoft's C Compiler and Macro Assembler, both in version 5.1 states, and Borland's new Turbo C and Turbo Assembler. But MS-DOS survives chiefly due to the army of MS-DOS programmers who have matured as well as MS-DOS has aged, squeezing systems to performance levels that two years ago would have been unbelievable.

Acknowledgments

The Waite Group wishes first to thank the authors for their patient, knowledgeable contributions to the revision of *The Waite Group's MS-DOS Developer's Guide*. Readers familiar with the first edition will recognize the huge changes this book has seen. Thanks to Michael Goldman for a creative approach to teaching the use of macros and structures. Thanks to Walter Dixon for your skillful unraveling of the I/O mysteries of TSRs. Thanks to Raj Bapna and Raj Dhesikan for a clear explanation of real-time programming issues. Thanks to Jon Fleig for an exhaustive examination of the EMS standard in all its incarnations. Thanks to Naba Barkakati for a complete lesson in communications and control of the serial port. Thanks to Andrew Dumke for your EGA and VGA drawing in C and your detailed explanations. Thanks to Kevin Jaeger for brilliant, accurate revisions of device drivers and memory managment discussions. Thanks to John Angermeyer for your care of the entire book project, your willingness to dig into any level for any detail, and your sensitive interleaving and explanations throughout the book.

The Waite Group wishes to thank Blair Henderson for your knowledgeable technical reviews of the revised material. Thanks to John Ferguson for the technical review of Chapter 4. Thanks to David Blossom for an excellent, detailed review of the disk layout and recovery material. Thanks to Mark Haas for content and copy editing during the development phase. Thanks to Diana Francoeur for deft and careful copy editing and skillful managment of the production of this book. Thanks to Joyce Smith of Automated Business Services whose unrivalled speed and accuracy in word processing allowed the editing to be completed on schedule. Thanks to Tom Emrick whose professional eye streamlined and clarified the art presentation. Thanks to Jim Rounds for advice and good-natured support during the turbulent conclusion of development. Thanks to Jim

Hill and Richard Swadley for pushing this project with the vision of what it should be. Thanks to Scott Calamar for your constant, caring help during a sea of crises. Thanks to Mitchell Waite for all that you have taught us—we have come a long way.

—James Stockford

Preface
to the First Edition

He felt like somebody had taken the lid off life and let him look at the works.
Dashiell Hammett, *The Maltese Falcon*

In one sense, this book is about the technical aspects of programming in a particular manner within a specific environment. In another sense, this book is about discovery and the process of discovery.

Too often we accept the circumstances that we see before us as absolute limits on our world. This is especially true of devices of great complexity such as computers. What we have worked to accomplish in this book is the removal of some of those limits and, more importantly, to give you, the reader, the confidence to go on to lift the barriers even further.

Some of the topics we have addressed are

- The fictitious conflict between structured programming and the use of assembly language

- Effectively using those elusive, poorly documented, "advanced" assembly language features, such as macros and conditional assembly

- Getting the best of two worlds by combining high-level languages with assembly language for easy programming and readability without sacrificing speed and compactness

- Customizing your system to take advantage of that old peripheral from your previous system or that new gadget you like but nobody supports

- Writing your own "magic" functions like SuperKey and SideKick through the use of memory resident programs

- Accessing the power of the 8087 and 80287 math coprocessors without the expense or limitations of high-level languages or manufacturer-specific libraries

- Recovering valuable data after the program crashes

- Rescuing erased files that you thought were gone forever

Each of these topics addresses an area that is usually left to experts, but with the aid of this book you can become the expert. This is no empty promise, for once you know how to learn about your system, you can continue to uncover new mysteries.

The collection of discussions in this book is organized in a manner similar to a compendium of articles. Each discussion is presented in its own chapter and may be read and referenced independently of the other chapters. Each chapter covers a topic that relates directly to program development within the MS-DOS environment. Because of the informative nature of this book and the way it is organized, it can also be read from beginning to end, thus yielding a greater confidence in your programming endeavors.

Although we assume that readers have some familiarity with the MS-DOS operating system, with the 8086 family of microprocessors, and with assembly language programming, this book, with its reference style, is appropriate for computer users with a variety of programming experience.

This book is by no means a complete presentation of application development, nor do we necessarily have the "right" way to program. Rather, we have tried to introduce some of the more immediate topics of programming that can be readily applied to actual problems. Should you decide to pursue the study of these topics, check the numerous references that can be found in some of the more specialized technical works. These references provide all the detail you desire, and some of them are listed in the bibliography at the end of this book.

Acknowledgments

The authors would like to thank Kim House and Robert Lafore for their many helpful comments, criticisms, and suggestions during the editing of our manuscript. Their valuable input helped in the fine-tuning of this book. We would also like to thank Larry Skene for his valuable information about IBM PC-DOS.

Special thanks are also due to Alan Stacy for his valuable knowledge, research, and writings on networking environments for MS-DOS systems.

We would also like to thank ComputerHouse of San Rafael, California, for answering our many questions and providing MS-DOS for our CompuPro system.

The Authors

JOHN ANGERMEYER is a design engineer specializing in word processing and telecommunications software and hardware. The former technical writer is also the coauthor of *CP/M Bible, MS-DOS Primer,* and *Tricks of the MS-DOS Masters.*

He is the author of Chapter 10, "Programming the Intel Numeric Processing Extension," Chapter 11, "Disk Layout and File Recovery," Chapter 12, "Recovering Data Lost in Memory," Chapter 13, "Differences between MS-DOS Versions," the appendixes, and the Quick Reference Card. He is the coauthor of Chapter 1, "Structured Programming 1: Tools for Structured Coding," and Chapter 2, "Structured Programming 2: The Design and Implementation of Modular Programs."

KEVIN JAEGER is a computer systems design engineer specializing in software architecture. He holds a degree in computer science and has worked in the telecommunications, graphics display, and process control industries.

He is the author of Chapter 3, "Program and Memory Management," and Chapter 6, "Installable Device Drivers." He is the coauthor of Chapter 2, "Structured Programming 2: The Design and Implementation of Modular Programs."

RAJ KUMAR BAPNA is a software engineer, with BSEE and MSCS degrees from BITS and ITT in India. His current interests include operating systems, software engineering, and real-time programming. He has experience in the fields of networking, DBMS, and continuous system simulation languages. He has worked for Intel Corporation in Hillsboro, Oregon.

He is the coauthor of Chapter 5, "Real-Time Programming."

NABAJYOTI BARKAKATI works as an electronics engineer for a well-known research laboratory. He began his programming career in 1975, and has worked extensively with FORTRAN, C, and several assembly languages (PDP-11, 80x86). He remains an avid programmer, primarily interested in developing communications and graphics software on the IBM PC and the Macintosh. He has a Ph.D in electrical engineering from the University of Maryland.

He is the author of Chapter 8, "Programming the Serial Port."

RAJAGOPALAN DHESIKAN has an M.S. from IISc, India. His areas of interest include networking software development and real-time programming. He has experience working with Intel's real-time operating system, RMX, and is currently working as a software engineer at International Software, Ltd. in India. He is also a consultant to Intel Corporation in Hillsboro, Oregon.

He is the author of Chapter 5, "Real-Time Programming."

WALTER DIXON holds degrees in both mechanical and electrical engineering. He is employed at General Electric Corporate Research and Development Center in Schenectady, where he works in the areas of distributed systems and computer networks. Mr. Dixon also teaches graduate computer science at Union College in Schenectady. He has written more than ten device drivers for PC-DOS.

He is the author of Chapter 4, "Terminate and Stay Resident Programming."

ANDREW DUMKE is the author of an EGA-based desktop publishing program, Laser GT, and an EGA print screen utility, Laser PR, both released by Sterling Pacific Inc. Mr. Dumke is currently a San Francisco–based fulltime computer industry investor with interests in microcomputers. He has owned a variety of microcomputer systems since 1978, and has programmed in C since 1983.

He is the author of Chapter 9, "Programming the EGA and VGA."

JON FLEIG is a software engineer with ten years of experience in programming mainframe, personal, and minicomputers. The coauthor of a popular LIM EMS 4.0 emulator product, he is currently developing real-time software for controlling high-performance machine tools. He lives in Rochester, New York.

He is the author of Chapter 7, "Using Expanded Memory."

MICHAEL GOLDMAN wrote his first program in 1964 when response time was days. He wrote his second program in 1972. While waiting for response time to improve, he received a B.S. in physics and an M.A. in mathematics from the University of Wisconsin. He now writes systems-level programs in C and assembly language in Silicon Valley. Only assembly language feeds his insatiable appetite for ever-faster response time.

He is the coauthor of Chapter 1, "Structured Programming 1: Tools for Structured Coding."

CODING AND PROGRAMMING PART I

Structured Programming 1: Tools for Structured Coding

1

WHEN hackers gather 'round their electronic campfires to discuss the mysteries of structured programming, comments are likely to center on a small set of language constructs like the IF-THEN-ELSE statement. A devotee of Pascal or C may lecture on the structured benefits of a higher-level programming language versus those of assembly language. Heated arguments about the use of GOTO may possibly ensue. In spite of all the earnest discussion, however, the complete story is not being told. Such discussion is really focused only on structured coding. As you will soon learn, structured programming is possible in any language. Even some assembly languages support all those nifty high-level control structures. One of them is Microsoft's Macro Assembler for MS-DOS, affectionately known as MASM.

The Need for Shorthand Statements

Before beginning our presentation of high-level control structures in assembly language, we first look at some of the advantages of higher-level languages. At the most basic level, anything that can be done in a higher-level language also can be done in assembly. Everything ends up at the assembly language level anyway. What then is gained from the use of a high-level language? Terseness! The ability to express a programming idea in a form that is readily understood by the coder or reader. Consider that each assembly language statement more or less corresponds to one machine instruction. On the other hand, a single higher-level statement may expand to tens or even hundreds of machine code instructions. (For anyone who doubts the hundreds, check a FORTRAN subroutine call with embedded argument calculations.)

Figure 1-1 shows the same fragment coded in both FORTRAN and 8086 assembly language. This fragment computes the sum of 1 . . . NUM for a given NUM. No doubt the assembly language routine could be further optimized to reduce either the amount of object code produced or the execution time. But no matter how you look at it, it is easier to write the routine in FORTRAN than in assembly. To code the assembly language routine, many more decisions need to be made. Because of the extra work involved in assembly, coding mistakes are more likely. I may know for a fact that the FORTRAN routine will run perfectly, but I may still harbor doubts about the assembly routine. Why do these doubts

FORTRAN	Assembly Language

```
        FORTRAN                      Assembly Language
      SUM = 0                              mov   sum,0
      DO 100 I = 1, NUM                    mov   ax,1
  100 SUM = SUM + I           loop1:       cmp   ax,num
                                           jg    loop1_end
                                           add   sum,ax
                                           inc   ax
                                           jmp   loop1
                              loop1_end:
```

Figure 1-1. Fortran versus assembly language.

exist? Because each line of the FORTRAN routine is an entire thought, whereas the assembly language routine requires many lines to complete the same thought.

In short, using higher-level constructs results in easier coding and more reliable code. These constructs make coding less complicated, which allows the programmer to concentrate on the logic of the program while assuming that the actual implementation is correct. Programmers would like to have faith in their work. Tools that support this faith make for better programmers.

Introduction to Macros

Assembly language coding thus would be greatly enhanced if there were a way to create a shorthand for commonly used statements. MASM provides this with the *macro* facility. *Macros* are "super-instructions" that off-load to MASM a lot of the tedious and repetitive work in assembly language programming. With macros, programmers define blocks of assembly statements, and then, with individual references, direct MASM to include the respective blocks in the assembled program. In this chapter we will introduce some of these macros and gradually build up your ability to write your own tools. This will enable you to combine the execution speed of assembly language with the power of a higher-level language.

Here are the two steps required to create and use a macro:

Step 1, Defining the Macro

```
;; Define     "Function Request" as @DosCall
@DosCall      MACRO
              int 21h                  ; call MS-DOS to perform function
              ENDM
```

Step 2, Using the Macro

```
              @DosCall       ←the macro call
```

What Appears in the Listing

```
        @DosCall        ←the macro call
1               int 21h                 ; call MS-DOS to perform function
```

When the program is assembled, the statement *DosCall* is replaced by the statement *int 21h*, including the comment. The listing file contains the line *DosCall* as a reference, but the object file contains only the code for *int 21h*. This operation is known as *macro substitution* or *macro expansion*.

Note in the previous example that the assembler inserts in the listing file a symbol denoting the expanded macro code. In MASM version 4 and higher, a *1* is placed on the lines pertaining to the first level of macro expansion, a *2* is used for the second level, and so on. In MASM version 3 and prior versions, all macro expansion lines, regardless of the level, are marked with the plus (+) character.

When processed by the assembler, the macro reference is replaced by the code that the macro represents. The macro does not generate a CALL instruction to the macro code, although macro references are sometimes referred to that way.

Like everything else in programming, macros have to follow strict formulas. The form for defining macros is

```
mname      MACRO       argument_list
           •
           •
           •         ←body of the macro code
           ENDM
```

The name of the macro is defined as *mname*, and *argument_list* is a list of arguments, separated by commas. The argument list may be blank if the macro contains no arguments (as in our example *@DosCall*).

This was a simple demonstration. If that were all that a macro could perform, it would be a sorry creature indeed. Luckily, macros may be tailored by using the arguments section. The next macro shows an example of this tailoring.

```
;; Define "Print Character" as PRINT_CHR
@PrintChr MACRO       char
          mov ah,05
          mov dl,&char
          @DosCall
          ENDM
```

Now, when we use this macro

```
@PrintChr 'A'     ←the macro call
```

the following appears in our listing file:

```
@PrintChr 'A'     ←the macro call
```

```
1   mov ah,05
1   mov dl,'A'
2   int 21h              ; call MS-DOS to perform function
```

The *&char* in the macro has been replaced with the 'A' in the macro call. (Yes, we refer to using macros as *calls*. It's okay as long as you remember that no CALL instruction is involved.) The number that appears at the beginning of the line is MASM's way of informing the programmer that the code is the result of a macro expansion. Note too that the macro *@PrintChr* contains a reference to the previously defined macro *@DosCall*, which was expanded into the *int 21h* statement that *@DosCall* represents. MASM continues to evaluate macro calls to any level to which they are nested until the symbol table storage area of MASM overflows. Nesting is another way of saying that macros may call macros that call macros and so on.

The name *char* in the *@PrintChr* macro is called a *dummy argument*. Whenever the dummy argument *char* appears in this macro, *char* is replaced with the value that was used in the call to the macro. In the *@PrintChr* example, replacing *char* means that any place in the macro that *char* appears, it was replaced with the character *A*.

Note that any name chosen for a dummy argument is used exclusively for that argument in the macro. Thus, if you were to choose a dummy argument with the name *AX*, you would not be able to refer to the AX register in that macro!

The same warning about naming dummy arguments applies to naming the macro itself. Should you choose to define a macro with the name *add*, you would find that all references to the op-code ADD in the program would generate an expansion of the macro *add*. You can even redefine MASM directives if you wish. It is therefore very important not to create a conflict of names.

The & in front of *char* in the *@PrintChr* macro is used to append the value of *char* to the string *mov dl,*. The & is not needed to evaluate the dummy argument, which happens anyway, but to tell MASM that *char* is a dummy argument, not just part of the larger string *mov dl,char*. The & operator is especially important when dummy arguments are contained in larger strings, as this next example demonstrates.

```
The Macro Definition          The Macro Expansion
@Example MACRO arg            @Example Y
    mov   dl,arg              1   mov   dl,Y        ←correct
    mov   dl,&arg             1   mov   dl,Y        ←correct
    mov   dl,argZ             1   mov   dl,argZ
    mov   dl,&argZ            1   mov   dl,argZ
    mov   dl,arg&Z            1   mov   dl,YZ       ←correct
    mov   dl,Xarg             1   mov   dl,Xarg
    mov   dl,X&arg            1   mov   dl,XY       ←correct
    mov   dl,XargZ            1   mov   dl,XargZ
    mov   dl,X&argZ           1   mov   dl,XargZ
    mov   dl,Xarg&Z           1   mov   dl,XargZ
    mov   dl,X&arg&Z          1   mov   dl,XYZ      ←correct
ENDM
```

Strictly speaking, the & is not required in the *@PrintChr* macro. MASM was able to detect that *char* is a dummy argument because *char* stands alone following a comma. However, it is a good habit to use & even when not required because it highlights the dummy argument when you read the macro and it makes clear to MASM just what is intended.

LOCAL Labels

So far, the macros we have used have been confined to generating simple assembly instructions. However, let's assume that we want to design a macro to choose between the smaller of two numbers and to place that result into another location. Such a macro might look something like this:

```
min       MACRO     result,first,second
          mov       &result,&first
          cmp       &first,&second
          jl        order_ok
          mov       &result,&second
order_ok:
          ENDM
```

When we invoke *min*, it produces the proper code, but we have a problem: Even though the macro evaluates perfectly, it can be used only once. Because the label *order_ok* can be defined only once in a program, when the macro is used in two places MASM complains that **Symbol is multidefined**.

We can make a small change in the macro to allow us to specify a label parameter in addition to the others:

```
min       MACRO     result,first,second,order_ok
          mov       &result,&first
          cmp       &first,&second
          jl        &order_ok
          mov       &result,&second
order_ok&:
          ENDM
```

When we invoke the new *min*, as shown in the following example, we can specify the name to be used for the jump label. Now *min* can be reused again when needed, but we still have to think of a new name for the jump label each time. However, the actual name is quite unimportant to us because the label is private to the *min* function.

```
          min       ax,bx,cx,jmp1        ←the macro call
1         mov       ax,bx
1         cmp       bx,cx
1         jl        jmp1
1         mov       ax,cx
1    jmp1:
```

There's a better way to create a new name each time that *min* is called. MASM provides the LOCAL directive for just this purpose. When MASM encounters LOCAL, a unique label is automatically generated for that name. To put it another way, it's as if the LOCAL parameter were included in the MACRO parameter list, but MASM filled in the actual argument. A word of caution. LOCAL statements must be placed directly after the MACRO definition line! After the LOCAL directive is included, the new *min* macro appears like this:

```
min       MACRO    result,first,second
          LOCAL    order_ok
          mov      &result,&first
          cmp      &first,&second
          jl       order_ok
          mov      &result,&second
order_ok:
          ENDM
```

When we invoke *min* this time, the expanded listing appears as shown in the following example. The value of *order_ok* has been replaced by *??0000*. Every time we call it, *order_ok* is replaced by a new value generated by MASM.

```
          min      ax,bx,cx        ; first call
1         mov      ax,bx
1         cmp      bx,cx
1         jl       ??0000
1         mov      ax,cx
1 ??0000:
          min      ax,bx,cx        ; second call
1         mov      ax,bx
1         cmp      bx,cx
1         jl       ??0001
1         mov      ax,cx
1 ??0001:
```

Of course, it is still possible to encounter a label conflict if you decide to use labels that begin with *??*. If you avoid using labels beginning with *??*, you can call the *min* macro as many times as you like.

The use of LOCAL labels is not restricted to jump addresses alone. LOCAL labels can also be used with data, as the following macros demonstrate. In this case the macros are used to insert text strings into the data segment and simultaneously create a reference to the string in the code segment. By comparing the source code with the macro expansion in Listing 1-1, you can see how much clearer it is to use macros.

Listing 1-1 also contains a few other useful macros to ease the task of writing .EXE programs. Once you define these macros, you need never again worry about getting the syntax of .EXE programs correct!

Listing 1-1. Hello World Program

```
; ***********************************************************
;   M A C R O   D E F I N I T I O N   S E C T I O N
; ***********************************************************
;
@DosCall MACRO
        int     21h             ; call MS-DOS function
        ENDM
;
@InitStk MACRO                  ; define stack size
stk_seg SEGMENT stack
        DB      32 dup ('stack   ')
stk_seg ENDS
        ENDM
;
@InitPrg MACRO   segment        ; initialize data segment
        ASSUME ds:segment
start:                          ; main entry point
        mov     ax,segment
        mov     ds,ax           ; set up data segment
        mov     es,ax           ; set up extra segment
        ENDM
;
@Finis  MACRO
        mov     ax,4C00h        ; terminate process
        @DosCall
        ENDM
;
@DisStr MACRO    string         ; display string from memory
        mov     dx,offset string
        mov     ah,09h
        @DosCall
        ENDM
;
@TypeStr MACRO   string         ; define and display a string
        LOCAL   saddr           ; set up a local label
cod_seg ENDS                    ; stop code segment
dat_seg SEGMENT                 ; change to data segment
saddr   DB      string,'$'      ; define string in data segment
dat_seg ENDS                    ; stop data segment
cod_seg SEGMENT                 ; return to code segment
        @DisStr saddr           ; display string
        ENDM
```

continued

Listing 1-1. *continued*

```
;
;
; ****************************************************************
; P R O G R A M   S E C T I O N
; ****************************************************************
;
        @InitStk                ; set up stack
cod_seg SEGMENT                 ; define code segment
main    PROC    FAR             ; main (and only) procedure
        ASSUME  cs:cod_seg       ; assign code segment to CS
register
        @InitPrg dat_seg         ; initialize data segment
        @TypeStr 'Hello world!' ; say "hi" to the folks at home
        @Finis                   ; terminate program
main    ENDP                     ; end procedure
cod_seg ENDS                     ; end code segment
        END     start            ; end program and ...
                                 ; ... define starting address
```

You can enter the program exactly as it appears and then assemble and run
it. The words *Hello world!* are displayed. Not a very impressive outcome in itself, but if the macros used are stored in an *include* file, writing .EXE programs
becomes much easier. Let's look at the expanded program listing, shown in Listing 1-2.

Listing 1-2. Macro Expansion for Hello World Program

```
; ****************************************************************
; P R O G R A M   S E C T I O N
; ****************************************************************
;
        @InitStk                ; set up stack
1       stk_seg SEGMENT stack
1               DB      32 dup ('stack   ')
1       stk_seg ENDS
cod_seg SEGMENT                 ; define code segment
main    PROC    FAR             ; main (and only) procedure
        ASSUME  cs:cod_seg       ; assign code segment to CS
register
        @InitPrg dat_seg         ; initialize data segment
1       start:                   ; main entry point
1               mov     ax,dat_seg
```

```
1                 mov     ds,ax           ; set up data segment
1                 mov     es,ax           ; set up extra segment
        @TypeStr 'Hello world!'  ; say "hi" to the folks at home
1       cod_seg ENDS                      ; stop code segment
1       dat_seg SEGMENT                   ; change to data segment
1       ??0000  DB      'Hello world!','$'      ; define string ...
1       dat_seg ENDS                      ; stop data segment
1       cod_seg SEGMENT                   ; return to code segment
2                 mov     dx,offset ??0000
2                 mov     ah,09h
3                 int     21h             ; call MS-DOS function
        @Finis                            ; terminate program
1                 mov     ax,4C00h        ; terminate process
2                 int     21h             ; call MS-DOS function
main    ENDP                              ; end procedure
cod_seg ENDS                              ; end code segment
        END     start                     ; end program and ...
```

The first point to notice is that the use of the *LOCAL saddr* in the *@TypeStr* macro worked fine as a label for the data statement. When using labels with data, do not use the colon (:). Next, notice how the macro expansion uses the reserved word *segment* in the macro *@InitPrg*. No problem! Remember that the dummy argument names in the argument list override any other MASM definitions.

Note that a number of lines weren't included in the listing file. For one example, the statement *ASSUME ds:data_seg* is missing from *@InitPrg*. The statement was assembled, but MASM suppressed the complete expansion.

Both of these exceptions occur because of the way MASM processes macros. The default condition suppresses listing source lines that do not generate code. The *ASSUME* statement is a MASM directive and generates no code of its own; therefore it is not listed. On the other hand, the *ENDS* segment end directives are listed and produce no code either. There are still mysteries in MASM for all of us to ponder.

Please don't take the code presented as a model for good programming. Although the idea of using macros for the prelude and postscript of .EXE programs is a good one, it is poor practice to embed the names of important symbols in the macros themselves. If the name of the data segment were other than *dat_seg*, unnecessary confusion would be created within the program. Either *@TypeStr* should be passed the name *dat_seg* as an argument, or *@InitPrg* should always assume that the data segment is *dat_seg*.

Macro Listing Directives

If you wish to see the complete listing of a macro, place the MASM directive .LALL in the assembly file. Then generate a .LST file, and compare it with the original listing in our example. You will see that the *ASSUME ds:data_seg* is now shown. To change the listing mode back, use the .XALL directive. This restores MASM to the default mode. If you wish to suppress all macro expansions, use the .SALL directive.

Macro Libraries

The term *macro library* is actually something of a misnomer. Macro libraries are not really libraries at all in the sense that Microsoft LINK or Microsoft LIB would understand. Macros must be included at compile time because they are directives for MASM and MASM only. LINK and LIB do not know what to do with them. Instead, macro libraries are really *include* files. They can be defined in a separate file, called MYLIB.MAC or STANDARD.MLB or whatever (you can choose any valid file name you like) and included in the assembly by placing an *include* directive in the source file, such as:

```
INCLUDE C:\MASM\LIB\STANDARD.MLB
```

The rules regarding the file name and drive specification are the same as for the rest of the system. Within the listing file, lines obtained from an *include* file begin with a *C*, just as macro expansion lines begin with a + (in versions of MASM below 4.0) or with a macro expansion level number. Of course, if you have a large library and don't want to clutter your .LST file with macro definitions, turn off the listing with the .XLIST directive before the *include* and then turn the listing back on with .LIST after the *include*.

The use of macro libraries provides justification for the next macro directive introduced. Although you very rarely define a macro in a program and then want to "undefine" it (you would just delete it!), you quite commonly may include a macro library for the purpose of using just a few of the defined macros. The rest of those macro definitions take up valuable storage space in the MASM symbol table and macro storage area. The way to recover this space is with the PURGE directive. PURGE allows you to remove definitions for specified macros. To remove the macros defined in our previous example, we would issue the directive:

```
PURGE    @DosCall,@InitStk,@InitPrg,@Finis,@DisStr,@TypeStr
```

This frees all the space occupied by the macro definitions and leaves us with a clean slate.

Macro Repeat Directives—REPT

Another macro facility provided by MASM is the ability to loop through a block of macro code. Three loop varieties are provided, each with specific uses.

For our first example, let's assume that we wish to create an area in the data segment for handling files. We use the file handle method of accessing files, and, because we may want to use more than one file, we write our routine to give unique names to each block.

```
file_head        MACRO      fnum
file_hand_&fnum     dw    ?               ; file handle
file_nmax_&fnum     db    49              ; maximum size of file name
file_nlen_&fnum     db    ?               ; actual length of file name
file_name_&fnum     db    50 dup (?)      ; file name buffer
                 ENDM
```

Why didn't we use the LOCAL directive for *fnum*? Because the labels are not local to the macro itself. They must be accessed from other parts of the program to set the file name, access the file handle, etc. This macro could still be improved. What if we want to use two files at once, say, in a file-to-file copy program? We would need to call *file_head* twice:

```
file_head        1          ; 1st file block
file_head        2          ; 2nd file block
```

Instead, we can write *file_head* to define as many blocks as we need, using the REPT directive. The macros appear in Listing 1-3.

Listing 1-3. Define File Access Block

```
fcnt            =          0             ; initialize and define symbol
file_head2      MACRO      fnum
file_hand_&fnum     dw    ?             ; file handle
file_nmax_&fnum     db    49            ; maximum size of file name
file_nlen_&fnum     db    ?             ; actual length of file name
file_name_&fnum     db    50 dup (?)    ; file name buffer
                ENDM
file_head       MACRO      fnum
                REPT       fnum          ; repeat block "fnum" times
                file_head2      %fcnt    ; create block #"fcnt"
fcnt            =    fcnt + 1
                ENDM                     ; end of repeat block
                ENDM                     ; end of file_head macro
```

As the expansion in Listing 1-4 demonstrates, when we call the *file_head* macro, it calls macro *file_head2* twice, each time using a different value of *fnum*. Of course, this macro expansion with the default listing status doesn't show the intermediate calls to *file_head2*. However, we can see the effects of the REPT in the two file control blocks that were created. Notice that the REPT directive must be terminated with ENDM, just like the MACRO directive. All repeat blocks must end with ENDM. Another ENDM must also appear at the end of each macro definition.

Listing 1-4. Define File Access Block Macro Expansion

```
            file_head   2
3           file_hand_0    dw    ?            ; file handle
3           file_nmax_0    db    49           ; maximum size of file name
3           file_nlen_0    db    ?            ; actual length of file name
3           file_name_0    db    50 dup (?)   ; file name buffer
3           file_hand_1    dw    ?            ; file handle
3           file_nmax_1    db    49           ; maximum size of file name
3           file_nlen_1    db    ?            ; actual length of file name
3           file_name_1    db    50 dup (?)   ; file name buffer
```

In addition to the REPT directive, we also used a counter. *Counters* are symbols that have a numeric value. They must be defined using the equate (=) operator so that they may be changed. (In MASM, *equ* is used to define static symbols that are never changed, whereas an equal sign (=) is used to define dynamic symbols that have values which may be changed.) The counter used with the *file_head* macros is *fcnt*. The counter *fcnt* is incremented for each pass in *file_head*. But why were the labels in *file_head2*, *file_hand_0*, etc., rather than in *file_hand_fcnt*? How did the name *fcnt* get replaced with its value? The answer is in the percent sign (%) operator preceding *fcnt* in the call to *file_head2*. The percent sign forces the replacement of a symbol with its numeric value. Because we used the percent sign, we needed two macros. If we had tried to evaluate and substitute *fcnt* in a single macro, as with:

```
          REPT       fnum         ; repeat block "fnum" times
file_hand_&%fcnt     dw    ?       ; file handle
```

the operation would fail, resulting in the symbol:

```
file_hand_fcnt       dw    ?       ; file handle
```

The percent sign operator (%) operates only on macro *arguments* in a macro call! In addition, the symbol's value must be an absolute (nonrelocatable) constant.

Another important aspect of our macros is that the counter *fcnt* is initialized outside the macro block. This is because we don't want to reset *fcnt* to zero each time we call *file_head* (which would cause duplicate labels). However, *fcnt* must be initialized somewhere, or the statement:

```
fcnt         =          fcnt + 1
```

would cause the error message **Symbol not defined**.

More about Macro Repeat Directives—IRP and IRPC

MASM supports two other macro repeat directives in addition to the REPT directive. These directives are IRP (indefinite repeat) and IRPC (indefinite repeat character). Neither really repeats indefinitely. Instead, each one repeats as long as arguments remain in the argument list. Listing 1-5 shows a simple repeat macro called *test_mac* that is designed to add items to the data segment.

Listing 1-5. Simple IRP Repeat Macro and Expansion

```
test_mac    MACRO       args                    ; define "test_mac"
            IRP         dummy,<&args>
            db          dummy               ; add item
            ENDM                            ; end of "IRP"
            ENDM                            ; end of "test_mac"


            test_mac    'one'                                   ←1st call
2           db          'one'               ; add item
            test_mac <'two','three','four'>                     ←2nd call
2           db          'two'               ; add item
2           db          'three'             ; add item
2           db          'four'              ; add item
```

On each pass through the repeat block, the next value in the argument list is used for the value of *dummy*. By using the IRP directive, we were able to use one macro call to do the work of three. On the second call to *test_mac*, the IRP block repeated the *db* once for each of the three strings in the argument list.

We've also introduced two special symbols for macros, the angle bracket (< and >) operators. The *test_mac* expects only one argument, but we want to send it a list of arguments. The angle brackets accomplish this by making the text inside of them into a single literal. So *'two','three','four'* becomes one argument rather than three. However, MASM does not send the angle brackets to the receiving macro. Inside *test_mac*, *args* has the value *'two','three','four'*, not <*'two','three','four'*>. This is why additional angle brackets were added in the IRP directive.

This reasoning does not apply to strings! The quotes that enclose strings are not stripped, and adding an extra layer really confuses things. If we use the *define byte* statement as

```
db          'dummy'             ; add item
```

MASM evaluates the line as

```
2           db          'dummy'             ; add item
```

which would give us quite a few dummies but not what we want. We could force the use of the actual argument through

```
db        '&dummy'           ; add item
```

but MASM would be trying to evaluate

```
2        db        "one"           ; add item
```

This causes a special error known as ***Text area read past end***. This error also occurs if you accidentally create an endless recursive macro call. Essentially, MASM runs out of places to store all the symbols in use. Beware! This error message repeats endlessly until you abort MASM by pressing Control-C.

Macro Summary

From what you've learned, you can see that macros use a type of programming shorthand. Thus, once you've defined a block of code, you may include it repeatedly through a simple macro call. You've seen that macros are defined with a MACRO statement that gives the macro its name, and optionally provides for macro arguments. The macro definition is then ended with an ENDM statement. After the definition has been completed, the macro call is made using the macro's name, followed by any parameters the macro requires.

You've also seen how MASM can generate unique labels using the LOCAL directive and how repeat directives are used. Your knowledge of repeat directives and some of their uses is expanded in the next section.

The Microsoft *Programmer's Reference Manual for the MS-DOS Operating System* contains macro definitions for each of the system calls. In addition, it also contains some general macros for common tasks, such as moving a string. This manual is a good place to study the use of macros and gain some additional experience in structuring macros. You will find the following three tables useful. Table 1-1 summarizes the macro directives that MASM uses, Table 1-2 lists the special macro operators, and Table 1-3 summarizes macro listing directives.

We're halfway to our structured control macros now. To complete the job of creating macros for structured control, we need to control just when and what is assembled into the program. That is the topic of the next section.

Conditional Assembly

When writing assembly language programs, it would be nice to be able to optionally include certain sections of code. When using macros, it also would be nice to be able to choose different code depending on the arguments passed to the macro. MASM provides these capabilities through the use of *conditional assembly*.

When can conditional assembly work for you? Assume that you are writing a rather large program, and, like most large programs, it has some bugs. You

Table 1-1. Macro Directives

Directive	Variable	Explanation
mname MACRO	*parameter_list*	**MACRO DEFINITION** Signals the start of a *macro* definition block; *parameter_list* defines the dummy arguments to be used within the block.
ENDM		**END MACRO** Signals the end of a MACRO definition or of a REPT, IRP, or IRPC repeat block. *Required!*
EXITM		**EXIT MACRO** Exits a macro expansion when encountered. Used most often with conditional assembly.
LOCAL	*symbol_list*	**LOCAL SYMBOL** Defines the symbols in *symbol_list* as unique symbols to the assembler. Expanded into *??xxxx* where *xxxx* is a hexadecimal number.
PURGE	*macro_list*	**PURGE MACRO DEFINITION** Deletes the definitions of the macros listed in *macro_list*.
REPT	*expression*	**REPEAT** Repeats the block of instructions between REPT and ENDM *expression* number of times.
IRP	*dummy,<parameter_list>*	**INDEFINITE REPEAT** Repeats the block of instructions between IRP and ENDM for each value in the *parameter_list*, replacing *dummy* with the value of the parameter on each expansion.
IRPC	*dummy,string*	**INDEFINITE REPEAT CHARACTER** Repeats the block of instructions between IRPC and ENDM for each character in the *string*, replacing *dummy* with the character on each expansion.

decide to place some debugging statements in the program to let you know what is happening. However, once the program seems to be running right, you want to remove the statements so that the program executes more smoothly. Of course, because the program probably contains still more bugs, back go the debugging statements. Adding and deleting statements can get rather tedious. Conditional assembly can be used to solve this problem. Listing 1-6 shows the effect of a switch called "DEBUG" on the statements in a conditional assembly block. A good deal of the program has been edited and the .SALL switch used to suppress some of the *@TypeStr* macro expansion. Our interest lies only in those lines related to conditional assembly.

Table 1-2. Special Symbols for Macros

Symbol	Explanation
&argument	Concatenates dummy arguments or symbols with text. Especially required to substitute dummy arguments within quoted strings.
;; comment text	Indicates a macro comment. These comments are never listed in the macro definition.
!char	Indicates that the next character is a literal. Used to include &, %, etc., in macro expansions where these symbols would otherwise be interpreted as special.
%symbol	Used to convert a symbol or optionally an expression to a number in the current radix.
<text>	The angle brackets (< and >) are used to define the text between them as a literal. Everything within the brackets may be passed as a single argument to a macro.

Table 1-3. Listing Directives for Macros

Directive	Explanation
.XALL	List source and object code for macro expansions, except source lines that do not generate code. The default condition is .XALL.
.LALL	List all lines for macro expansions, except comments preceded by two semicolons (;;).
.SALL	List none of the code produced by macro expansion.
.LIST	List source lines. Reverses .XLIST but does not change the state of macro listing as determined by .XALL, .LALL, or .SALL.
.XLIST	Suppress all listing. Overrides all other directives.

Listing 1-6. DEBUG Statements Conditional Assembly—FALSE

```
                         ; Part A--Source Listing
          FALSE    EQU    0
          TRUE     EQU    0FFFFh
          DEBUG    EQU    FALSE
  .
  .
  .
          @TypeStr  'hello world!'
          IF        DEBUG                      ←begin conditional block
          @TypeStr  'Hi - I made it to this point in the program'
```

```
        ENDIF                                    ←end conditional block
  •
  •
  •
                        ; Part B--MASM Listing

        @TypeStr 'hello world!'
1               mov     dx,offset ??0000
1               mov     ah,09h
1               int     21h              ; call ms-dos function
        ENDIF
```

This example was assembled with the value of the DEBUG switch set to FALSE. As a result, all that appears of the conditional block in the MASM listing is the ENDIF statement after the @*TypeStr* expansion. That is how MASM indicates that there was a conditional block there but that it wasn't assembled. When the value of the DEBUG switch is changed to TRUE, MASM produces a different program, as shown in Listing 1-7.

Listing 1-7. DEBUG Statements Conditional Assembly — TRUE

```
                        ; MASM Listing

        DEBUG      EQU     TRUE
  •
  •
  •
        @TypeStr   "hello world!"
1               mov     dx,offset ??0001
1               mov     ah,09h
2               int     21h              ; call ms-dos function
        IF         DEBUG
        @TypeStr   'Hi - I made it to this point in the program'
1               mov     dx,offset ??0002
1               mov     ah,09h
2               int     21h              ; call ms-dos function
        ENDIF
```

This time, the debugging statements are included. MASM also includes in the listing the line that caused the statements to be assembled. If you would like to see all conditional assembly directives in the listing file, whether or not they evaluate TRUE or FALSE, use the .LFCOND (list false conditions) directive. You can later suppress the listing of FALSE conditions with the .SFCOND (suppress false conditions) directive. Basically, a conditional assembly block begins with some type of IF statement (see Table 1-4 for a complete listing) and terminates with an ENDIF statement.

A common use of TRUE/FALSE switches in conditional assembly occurs in *systems programming* (programming the operating system of a computer). If you have a copy of the source assembly for your computer, take a quick look at it. You will most likely find that conditional assembly has been used extensively. Conditional assembly allows the designer to write one operating system and,

Table 1-4. Conditional Assembly Directives

Directive	Variable	Explanation
IF	*expression*	IF TRUE If *expression* evaluates to a nonzero number, the statements in the conditional block are assembled.
IFE	*expression*	IF FALSE If *expression* evaluates to 0, the statements in the conditional block are assembled.
ELSE		ELSE If the conditional assembly directive evaluates FALSE (does not assemble the conditional block), the alternative statements in the ELSE block are assembled. Terminates the IF*xxxx* block but must be followed by ENDIF. Only valid after an IF*xxxx* statement.
ENDIF		END of IF BLOCK Terminates an IF*xxxx* block or ELSE block.
IF1,IF2		IF MASM PASS 1, IF MASM PASS 2 Assembles the conditional block if the MASM assembler is in the pass indicated. See text for the relationship of IF1 and IF2 to IFDEF and IFNDEF.
IFDEF IFNDEF	*symbol* *symbol*	IF *symbol* DEFINED IF *symbol* NOT DEFINED Evaluates whether *symbol* is defined or declared external. IFNDEF is the opposite of IFDEF. See text for relationship to assembler passes.
IFB IFNB	*<argument>* *<argument>*	IF *argument* BLANK IF *argument* NOT BLANK Evaluates whether the *argument* is blank. Used with macro arguments to see whether an argument has been provided. IFNB is the opposite of IFB. The angle brackets are required.
IFIDN IFDIF	*<str1>,<str2>* *<str1>,<str2>*	IF *str1* IDENTICAL TO *str2* IF *str1* DIFFERENT FROM *str2* Evaluates whether string *str1* is identical to string *str2*. IFDIF is the opposite of IFIDN. The angle brackets are required.

through the use of conditional assembly "switches," to configure the system to a particular set of equipment. These switches, like the DEBUG switch in our example, can cause the proper system to be generated (proper configuration to be made) for a given type, number, or configuration of memory, boards, peripherals, drivers, and so forth.

For the purposes of the MASM assembler, any expression that evaluates to zero, or has a value of zero, is considered to be FALSE. A nonzero expression is considered TRUE. The value FFFF (hexadecimal) is commonly used for the symbol TRUE. This allows TRUE to be used in any bit operation. For example, the bitwise AND of 0001 and 1000 is 0000 so that, although both are true, the AND of them would be false. Remember that MASM uses the same operators for both logical and bit operations.

Relational Operators

In addition to using symbols with preassigned values or arithmetic expressions, MASM supports relational operators, which may be used to control conditional assembly statements. *Relational operators* are those that express the relationship between two values. *Less than, greater than, equal to,* and *not equal to* are all examples of relational operators.

These operators allow such things as range checking and special actions and in fact support what amounts to a programming language. Through the use of relational operators, you can create quite complex program structures that automatically adjust themselves to a particular environment (for example, sizing a data area to fit a reserved area of memory). However, when using relational operators, MASM doesn't always do the expected thing.

If you are used to working with signed integers, you may think of 0FFFFh and −1 as the same value. With some exceptions, MASM also uses the values interchangeably. Although earlier versions of MASM had some problems dealing with negative numbers, the newer versions (1.2 and later) do know that −1 is equal to 0FFFFh. However, when comparing the magnitude of two numbers, MASM treats them differently. A simple test illustrates:

True	FFFF	dw	1 gt −1	Obvious
False	0000	dw	1 gt 0FFFFh	65535, not −1
True	FFFF	dw	−1 ge 0FFFFh	−1=−1
False	0000	dw	−1 gt 0FFFFh	−1 not gt −1

What is demonstrated here is that MASM considers 0FFFFh to be a positive number, 65535 to be exact, except when it is being compared with −1, at which time 0FFFFh is treated as −1. Confusing as this is, forewarned is forearmed.

The full list of relational operators in MASM appears in Table 1-5. An example use of these operators is contained in the structured coding macros appearing at the end of this chapter. Table 1-6 shows the listing directives for conditional assembly.

**Table 1-5.   Relational and Logical Operators
for Conditional Assembly**

Operator	Syntax	Explanation
EQ	*exp1 EQ exp2*	TRUE if *exp1* equals *exp2*
NE	*exp1 NE exp2*	TRUE if *exp1* not equal to *exp2*
LT	*exp1 LT exp2*	TRUE if *exp1* is less than *exp2*
LE	*exp1 LE exp2*	TRUE if *exp1* is less than or equals *exp2*
GT	*exp1 GT exp2*	TRUE if *exp1* is greater than *exp2*
GE	*exp1 GE exp2*	TRUE if *exp1* is greater than or equals *exp2*
NOT	*NOT exp*	TRUE if *exp* FALSE, else FALSE
AND	*exp1 AND exp2*	TRUE only if both *exp1* and *exp2* are TRUE
OR	*exp1 OR exp2*	TRUE if either *exp1* or *exp2* is TRUE
XOR	*exp1 XOR exp2*	TRUE if *exp1* equals logical NOT of *exp2*
FALSE	(0000 hex)	For IF TRUE, any ZERO expression is FALSE
TRUE	(FFFF hex)	For IF TRUE, any NONZERO expression is TRUE

Table 1-6.   Listing Directives for Conditional Assembly

Directive	Explanation
.LFCOND	List conditional assemblies that evaluate to FALSE condition.
.SFCOND	Suppress listing of conditional assemblies that evaluate to FALSE condition. The default setting is .SFCOND.
.TFCOND	Toggles the listing of FALSE conditional assembly as determined by the MASM /X switch. Operates independently of the .LFCOND and .SFCOND switches.
.LIST	List source lines. Reverses .XLIST but does not change the state of conditional assembly listing as determined by .LFCOND, .SFCOND, or .TFCOND.
.XLIST	Suppress all listing. Overrides all other directives.

Conditional Assembly Summary

From a quick overview of conditional assembly, we see how it is possible to control which code is included in the assembled program. So far, we have investigated the use of conditional assembly to ease the task of including optional code. But we have only scratched the surface. Only one of the ten possible forms of conditional operators was used in our examples. What of the rest of these operators? They are intended primarily for use with macros. To that topic, we now turn.

Conditional Assembly and Macros

Although conditional assembly is frequently used with explicitly defined switches, conditional assembly's greatest potential is realized when it is combined with the MASM macro facility. There are a number of features of conditional assembly that are intended specifically for operation with the macro facility. Let's lay some groundwork to explain the possibilities of these features.

Macros may be classified into two groups. First, there are those macros designed to create a definite structure depending upon some input, where the structure is well defined and the input is of an expected class. The *file_head* macro, designed to insert a file definition block, is an example of this classification of macro.

The second class of macro is intended to generate a structure that is dependent on information that is unavailable to programmers or that they consider trivial and desire to ignore. These macros often must be able to process many classes of arguments and must determine the argument's class. At other times, these macros may maintain private data or counters in order to release the programmer from bookkeeping chores. The structured control macros contained in the last part of this chapter are prime examples of the latter. Of course, some overlap usually exists between these classes of macros.

To explain further, in one type of macro, the programmer uses the macro facility to avoid some typing or other drudge work. In the other type, the programmer uses the macro facility as a kind of higher-level structure, depending on the assembler to supply the missing information. The programmer intentionally hides the details of implementation for the purpose of simplifying the programming job.

One example of a higher-level macro is using macros to simplify the use of assembler mnemonics. Although most of the 8086 processor's instructions may be used with either register or memory operands, quite a number do not allow immediate operands. The PUSH instruction is one example, although the 186/188 and 286 do allow pushing immediate data onto the stack.

It is quite simple to design a *pushi* (push immediate) macro that transfers the desired argument to a register and pushes the register. However, if a macro were to be used to implement a more general push operation, it is not only desirable that the macro be able to push immediate data, but also desirable that the macro be able to decide whether such an operation is even required. In other words, the programmer would use a general *pseudo-opcode* that would apply to all cases. The pseudo-opcode would actually be a macro that would evaluate the operands and generate either a standard or extended instruction as required.

The first step in being able to write such a general-purpose macro is to be able to determine just what the macro operands are. MASM provides a number of special-purpose operators to accomplish this task.

Determining Operand Types

In the 8086/8088 environment there are four basic types of operands. These are *register, immediate, memory*, and *addresses*. For those that are data oriented, a number of subtypes are possible. Registers include the special cases of the accumulator (general register A) and the segment registers. All three data types may be subclassified as either 8-bit or 16-bit data. Addresses may be either *near* (offset only) or *far* (offset and segment).

How do we go about distinguishing among all these types? We use the MASM operators .TYPE and TYPE. Table 1-7 shows the results of using these operators with various classes of operands.

Table 1-7.   The .TYPE and TYPE MASM Operators

Rules for .TYPE and TYPE

Operator	Result	
.TYPE bits 5 and 7	8x	Defined external
	2x	Defined local
	0x	Invalid reference
.TYPE bits 0 through 2	x0	Absolute mode
	x1	Program related
	x2	Data related
TYPE used with data variable	01	Byte variable
	02	Word variable
	04	Double word variable
	08	Quad word variable
	10	Ten-byte variable
	xx	Structure of size *xx*
TYPE used with program label	FFFF	*Near* program label
	FFFE	*Far* program label

.TYPE and TYPE Examples

Variable Type	.TYPE	Definition	TYPE	Definition
Immediate	20	Defined local	0	Invalid
Register	20	Defined local	0	Invalid
Data label	22	Defined local	x	Number of bytes
Near label	21	Defined local	FFFF	*Near* label
Far label	21	Defined local	FFFE	*Far* label
MASM op-code	00	Invalid	0	Invalid
Nonsense	00	Invalid	0	Invalid

Some further examples may be constructed. Although .TYPE recognizes the names of the various registers, it does not recognize a register construct such as [BX] or ARRAY[BX][SI]. Single character constants, such as A, are recognized as locally defined variables by the .TYPE operator.

Nothing recognizes a forward reference during the first pass of the assembler. IFDEF returns a **not defined** result, .TYPE returns an **invalid**, and TYPE returns a zero length. Only one rule may be applied to forward references: Avoid them if at all possible.

Phase Errors and Other MASM Eccentricities

An important warning is associated with the use of MASM operators. MASM is a two-pass assembler that assigns values to symbols on the first pass and then evaluates the symbols on the second pass. Program labels and data labels are symbols. Their values are determined during the first pass and then used during the second pass to generate the code.

Consider the following chain of events. If a forward reference occurs, MASM does not recognize the label on the first pass and is not able to determine its type. Attempting to reference this symbol produces the error message ***Symbol is not defined***. MASM encounters this error when processing the first pass but suppresses it and continues the assembly. MASM is able to cover up by assuming the type of the symbol from the context in which the symbol appears. If this guess is wrong, MASM may end up producing the message ***Phase error between passes***, or MASM may shorten the instruction and place NOP instructions after it as place holders.

There are two ways that phase errors may be avoided during normal use of MASM. In the majority of cases, MASM is able to determine the operand type from the context. Programmers rarely jump to locations in the data segment and don't usually add program addresses. For those special cases where MASM makes a wrong guess, the programmer may set the assembler straight by using the PTR (pointer) override operator. With PTR the programmer may explicitly specify the type of a forward reference so that MASM does not guess incorrectly.

However, by attempting to produce multipurpose instructions with macros, we greatly increase the chance of guessing wrong in these cases. If our multipurpose instruction is intended to be able to process any operand class, exact meaning becomes more difficult to determine from context. In addition, although the use of PTR may aid in some of these cases (as we shall see in the *@PushOp* macro), its use defeats the purpose of using macros to relieve the programmer of burdensome detail.

By examining how a wrong guess produces a phase error, we may more easily avoid its occurrence. Because phase errors are the result of certain symbols (such as labels) changing value between passes, it is important that macros produce the same amount of code on each pass. This preserves the values of those labels located after the macro and is also why MASM pads shortened instructions with NOP instructions. Program labels generated by the macros must also remain constant from pass one to pass two.

String Matching—An Example

Unfortunately, the .TYPE operator's readiness to recognize immediate operands as well as registers, etc., greatly reduces its usefulness in detecting the type of a macro operand. Because it is especially useful to know whether an argument to a macro is a register, we must construct a method for determining this. Knowing whether the argument is a register usually is useful only when combined with the implicit assumption that if it's not a register and not a defined memory reference, the argument is assumed to be an immediate data reference.

A common use of conditional assembly with the IRP or IRPC directives is matching. The purpose in these cases is to see whether a macro argument is a member of some set. In this case, string matching is used to solve the problem of determining whether an argument is a register. Because all that the .TYPE operator can determine is that registers are both locally defined and absolute, a string-matching macro is used to explicitly check for a register name. The *?reg* macro shown in Listing 1-8 accomplishes this function.

Listing 1-8. Register Name Match *?reg* Macro

```
FALSE   EQU     0
TRUE    EQU     0FFFFh
;;
;; **** ?REG - Test to see if an argument is a register
;;
?reg    MACRO   arg
?isr8 =         FALSE
?isr16 =        FALSE
        IRP     reg,<ax,bx,cx,dx,bp,sp,si,di,cs,ds,es,ss>
        IFIDN   <&&reg>,<&arg>
        ?isr16 =        TRUE
        EXITM
        ENDIF
        ENDM    ;; end IRP section
;; If match then stop here
        IF      (?isr16)
        EXITM
        ENDIF
;; If not match yet, try the rest
        IRP     reg,<ah,bh,ch,dh,al,bl,cl,dl>
        IFIDN   <&&reg>,<&arg>
        ?isr8 =         TRUE
        EXITM
        ENDIF
        ENDM    ;; end IRP section
;; If match then stop here
        IF      (?isr8)
        EXITM
        ENDIF
;; If not match yet, try uppercase
        IRP     reg,<AX,BX,CX,DX,BP,SP,SI,DI,CS,DS,ES,SS>
        IFIDN   <&&reg>,<&arg>
        ?isr16 =        TRUE
        EXITM
```

```
        ENDIF
        ENDM        ;; end IRP section
;; If match then stop here
        IF          (?isr16)
        EXITM
        ENDIF
;; If not match yet, try the rest
        IRP         reg,<AH,BH,CH,DH,AL,BL,CL,DL>
        IFIDN       <&&reg>,<&arg>
        ?isr8   =          TRUE
        EXITM
        ENDIF
        ENDM        ;; end IRP section
        ENDM        ;; end macro definition
```

The heart of this macro, as with any matching macro, consists of the three lines:

```
IRP     reg,<ax,bx,cx,dx,bp,sp,si,di,cs,ds,es,ss>
IFIDN   <&&reg>,<&arg1>
?isr16  %       TRUE
```

These lines may be interpreted as performing the following function:

> For *reg* equals *ax* to *ss* do . . .
> > If *reg* equals the argument arg . . .
> > > The argument is a register!

There are two interesting points to note here. One, it is necessary to explicitly check for the register name in both lower- and uppercase. The IFIDN conditional assembly directive compares strings for an exact match. Even with the extra effort, the *?reg* macro is not foolproof. It does not match a register name that has one uppercase character and one lowercase character ("aL," for example). Second, two separate checks are performed: one for 16-bit registers and one for 8-bit registers. In the current implementation, having separate checks doesn't gain us anything, but it will be used in the next example.

The *?reg* macro has two additional syntax elements. One is the EXITM exit macro directive. This directive is used to stop processing of the *?reg* macro when a match is found.

Less obvious is the use of the double ampersand in the IFIDN statement. According to the Microsoft MASM manual, the user must "supply as many ampersands as there are levels of nesting." This rather laconic pronouncement doesn't do justice to the complexity of the problem. The "levels of nesting" doesn't apply to how many blocks deep the reference occurs but rather to how many blocks deep the definition occurs. Thus, *arg1* gets away with only one &, whereas *reg*, which is defined in a nested block, requires the double ampersand, &&. Microsoft does not state whether there is a limit to the allowed number of nesting levels or the number of ampersands that may be required. In cases where multiple ampersands seem indicated, the extra effort of trying a few examples to ensure proper operation is worth it.

The demonstration of the *?reg* macro in Listing 1-9 shows that this macro does function as expected. Do note that the register *bP*, which MASM would recognize, is rejected by *?reg*. This could be construed as a coercive argument for consistency in typing.

Listing 1-9. Test of the *?reg* Register Name Match Macro

```
          ?reg    ax      ; is "AX" a register?
FFFF      dw      ?isr16                              ←TRUE
          ?reg    cs      ; is "CS" a register?
FFFF      dw      ?isr16                              ←TRUE
          ?reg    zork    ; is "ZORK" a register?
0000      dw      ?isr16                              ←FALSE
0000      dw      ?isr8                               ←FALSE
          ?reg    01234h  ; is "1234" a register?
0000      dw      ?isr16                              ←FALSE
0000      dw      ?isr8                               ←FALSE
          ?reg    bP      ; is "BP" a register?
0000      dw      ?isr16                              ←FALSE—case change
0000      dw      ?isr8                               ←FALSE
```

Parsing Macro Arguments

With a macro that can recognize register names, you can now implement a general PUSH macro, which we'll call *@PushOp* (push operand). (*Note*: We considered the name *pusha* for "push all," but *PUSHA* is a defined op-code in the Intel 186, 188, and 286 chips. Its use as a macro could restrict upward compatibility. Of course, you can always implement the PUSHA instruction via a *pusha* macro for 8086 or 8088 processors and be ahead of the game.)

As mentioned previously, it is necessary to make some assumptions about the operand type in those cases where it is not defined and not a register. In the *@PushOp* macro, we assume that unknown operands are immediate data references. *@PushOp* references the macro *?reg*, and *?reg* must be included in the program for *@PushOp* to function. See Listing 1-10 for the *@PushOp* macro.

@PushOp makes use of the *?reg* macro's ability to distinguish between 16-bit and 8-bit registers. Because the PUSH instruction does not accept an 8-bit register, the IRPC macro directive is used to obtain the first character of the register name. *@PushOp* then appends an *x* to form the name of the 16-bit

Listing 1-10. @*PushOp* Generalized PUSH Macro

```
;; **** @PushOp Generalized Push Operand Macro
;; If the operand is defined then it may be one of:
;;      register
;;      data reference
;;
;; If the operand is NOT defined, then it will be assumed to
;; be an immediate reference.
@PushOp MACRO arg
        .SALL
        IFDEF   &arg                    ;; operand IS defined ...
          ?argtyp = .type &arg          ;; ... then get type
          IF      ((?argtyp and 3) EQ 2)  ;; operand is DATA
            ?argsiz = ((type &arg) + 1)/2 ;; ... get size in words
            ?argoff = 0                 ;; ... set offset to 0
            REPT  ?argsiz               ;; ... repeat each word
              ?argadd = word ptr &arg + ?argoff ;; get type ptr
              .XALL
              push    ?argadd           ;; ... push memory direct
              .SALL
              ?argoff = ?argoff + 2     ;; ... next word of data
            ENDM
          ENDIF
          IF      ((?argtyp AND 3) EQ 1)  ;; operand is PROGRAM
            @PushImOff    &arg          ;; ... push label offset
          ENDIF
          IFE     (?argtyp and 3)       ;; operand is ABSOLUTE
            ?reg  &arg
            IF    (?isr16)              ;; operand is REGISTER 16
              .XALL
              push    &arg              ;; ... push direct
              .SALL
            ELSE
              IF  (?isr8)               ;; operand is REGISTER 8
                IRPC chr1,&arg1
                  .XALL
                  push    &&chr1&&x     ;; save short register
                  .SALL
                EXITM
                ENDM
```

continued

Listing 1-10. *continued*

```
        ELSE                            ;; assume immediate
           @PushIm &arg                 ;; ... push immediate
        ENDIF
     ENDIF
   ENDIF
ELSE                                    ;; ... push immediate
   @PushIm &arg
ENDIF
ENDM                                    ;; end macro definition
```

register, which PUSH accepts. Note that the use of double ampersands is required again in this statement and that they are required on both sides of the dummy argument since string concatenation occurs at each end.

For those cases that are assumed to be immediate data, the *@PushIm* macro is called. This macro is more complicated than absolutely necessary because it assumes that no registers are available for use in transferring the immediate data to the stack. Instead, the macro uses the base pointer (BP) to address the stack. After saving the BP and AX on the stack, *@PushIm* slides the immediate data under the AX contents, swapping it with the contents of the old BP. After restoring the BP contents to its previous location in the BP, the macro retrieves the contents of the AX by popping them off the stack. The *@PushIm* macro is shown in Listing 1-11.

Listing 1-11. *@PushIm* **Immediate Data PUSH Macro**

```
;; **** @PushIm Immediate Data Push Macro
@PushIm MACRO arg
        .XALL
        push    bp                 ;; save base pointer
        mov     bp,sp              ;; move stack pointer to BP
        push    ax                 ;; save accumulator
        mov     ax,&arg            ;; get immediate data
        xchg    [bp],ax            ;; swap old BP and immediate data
        mov     bp,ax              ;; restore old BP from AX
        pop     ax                 ;; restore accumulator
        .SALL
        ENDM                       ;; end macro definition
```

This rather convoluted operation also may be adapted to swapping items on the stack. However, playing with the stack can be dangerous. If your computer supports interrupts, this operation should be done only with the interrupts disabled so that the integrity of the stack is preserved.

For those cases that attempt to push program locations on the stack, we assume that the programmer desires to save the actual offset of the label. Thus, the *@PushImOff* macro was created to push the offset of the label as immediate data. It differs from the *@PushIm* macro solely in its use of the instruction

```
mov     ax,offset &arg
```

as opposed to the simple move that appears in *@PushIm*. See Listing 1-12 for the *@PushImOff* macro.

Listing 1-12. *@PushImOff* Offset of Immediate Data PUSH Macro

```
;; **** @PushImOff Offset of Immediate Data Push Macro
@PushImOff MACRO arg
        .XALL
        push    bp                  ;; save base pointer
        mov     bp,sp               ;; move stack pointer to BP
        push    ax                  ;; save accumulator
        mov     ax,offset &arg      ;; get offset of immediate data
        xchg    [bp],ax             ;; swap old BP and immediate data
        mov     bp,ax               ;; restore old BP from AX
        pop     ax                  ;; restore accumulator
        .SALL
        ENDM                        ;; end macro definition
```

The last discrete case that *@PushOp* recognizes is an attempt to push memory data onto the stack directly. Here the difficulty lies in the fact that the stack accepts only 16-bit data. By using the PTR override directive, you can convince MASM to save the desired data one word at a time. *@PushOp* contains a loop that repeats the operation for each word of the data element being saved, incrementing the address by two on each pass. Thus double word, quad word, ten-byte, and structured variables may be saved onto the stack.

Finally, note that the *@PushOp* macro still does not process any references that contain complex addressing (such as 2[BP], etc.). If it proves necessary, you can implement such checks by using the IRPC macro directive to check the argument for brackets, base plus index addressing, and base plus offset addressing.

The final test of the *@PushOp* macro appears in Listing 1-13, which shows the code that results from a few example calls of the *@PushOp* macro.

This expansion shows everything as expected. The last operation in the listing, where *@PushOp* is used on a quad word variable, may not be clear. Each

**Listing 1-13. Example Expansion of @*PushOp* Generalized
PUSH Macro**

```
dat_seg SEGMENT
datq    dq      4040414142424343h
dat_seg ENDS
        .
        .
        .
start:
        @PushOp ax              ; general register save
1       push    ax
        @PushOp cs              ; segment register save
1       push    cs
        @PushOp al              ; short register save ...
2       push    ax...           ; becomes general reg.
        @PushOp 01234h          ; word constant save
2       push    bp
2       mov     bp,sp
2       push    ax
2       mov     ax,01234h
2       xchg    [bp],ax
2       mov     bp,ax
2       pop     ax
        @PushOp 'A'             ; byte constant save
2       push    bp
2       mov     bp,sp
2       push    ax
2       mov     ax,'A'
2       xchg    [bp],ax
2       mov     bp,ax
2       pop     ax
        @PushOp start           ; program label offset save
2       push    bp
2       mov     bp,sp
2       push    ax
2       mov     ax,offset start
2       xchg    [bp],ax
2       mov     bp,ax
2       pop     ax
        @PushOp datq            ; quad word variable save
2       push    ?argadd ; 1st word
2       push    ?argadd ; 2nd word
2       push    ?argadd ; 3rd word
2       push    ?argadd ; 4th word
        .
        .
        .
```

push has the same argument. What isn't visible from this trimmed listing is that each line has a relocatable address, 0000 for the first word, 0002 for the second word, and so forth. Unfortunately, we can't squeeze a 132-column listing into this book, so you'll just have to try it out if you want to check on it.

This example is especially useful because it demonstrates one area where macros are nearly always preferred over subroutines. When dealing with stack manipulations (as in *@PushIm* and *@PushImOff*), macros are able to perform the operation without "worrying" about the effects of the CALL instruction on the stack. This is especially important when placing or removing data from the stack because a subroutine cannot alter the top of the stack and return without causing major problems.

Warnings about Conditional Assembly and Macros in MASM

When using macros, we tend to forget that macros generate in-line code and not calls to routines. Although this has the advantages of generating fast code and of freeing us from some restrictions in using the stack, production of in-line code results in larger code. As a designer, your responsibility is to judge when a macro, with its quick execution, is called for and when a subroutine, with its space-saving ability and greater structure, is called for. Generally, use macros when the code is small and time is critical, or when you need to configure the routine to the individual circumstance. Use subroutines when the code is larger, is of a general nature that can be reused, or would be convenient to have in one place (so that it can be verified easily).

Another confusing issue with macros concerns the use of symbols. You remember that symbols are defined through the use of the *equ* or = operators. These symbols are then evaluated by MASM and replaced by their values. It sometimes happens that we programmers forget that macro arguments are not symbols and vice versa. According to the MASM manual, macro arguments are replaced by the actual parameters using one-for-one text substitution. Macro arguments may be created by one macro and, using the text substitution ability, passed as a complete text string to another macro. This is not possible with symbols. Indeed, symbols may only be assigned text values using the *equ* operator, which does not allow them to be modified. The = operator only allows symbols to be given numeric values or TYPE attributes. An example of this limitation, and of one way to overcome it, appears in our presentation of structured control statements that follows.

Structured Control Statements in Assembly Language

Now that we have all of the tools necessary to build our structured control statements, let's do it. The most common and useful control statements are shown in Table 1-8.

The statements in Table 1-8 are those that are used most frequently to implement structured control in structured programming. Some languages have an abundance of them; others have few. It was only recently that FORTRAN gained use of the IF-THEN-ELSE structure in FORTRAN-77. Out-of-the-box assemblers almost never have these structures implemented for coding

Table 1-8. Structured Control Statements

Statement	Structure
IF-THEN	IF *<condition>* (execute if *condition* TRUE) ENDIF
IF-THEN-ELSE	IF *<condition>* (execute if *condition* TRUE) ELSE (execute if *condition* FALSE) ENDIF
DO-WHILE	WHILE *<condition>* (execute if *condition* TRUE) END_WHILE
REPEAT-UNTIL	REPEAT (execute if *condition* FALSE) UNTIL *<condition>*
FOR-DO	FOR *<var>* = *<begin>* to *<end>* (execute for each integer value of *var* between *begin* and *end*, inclusive, incrementing or decrementing *var* by one each loop) END_FOR
CASE-OF-*<var>*	CASE *<var>* OF *<case A>* (execute if *var = A*) *<case B>* (execute if *var = B*) . . . *<case N>* (execute if *var = N*) *<default>* (execute if no match) END_CASE

purposes, even though many support IF-THEN-ELSE for conditional assembly. The reason is simple: Assemblers are supposed to be at a lower level than high-level languages. Because we have decided that these structures can make our programming life easier, we can implement them, using the tools that we've just learned about.

There is one structure that we have left out. This is the CASE statement. The structure that we have presented is taken from PASCAL syntax but is nevertheless similar to that used in C and other languages. The problem with the CASE statement is that you must check the key variable *var* against each case that appears in the list. If the initial statement and the cases are not contained in the same macro, you can't know what the key variable was. Remember that MASM does not allow strings to be used with the = symbol assignment operator.

You can create a variation of a CASE statement by listing all the possible cases and their destination labels as arguments to one macro. This pseudo *case* macro is discussed in a following section of this chapter.

The complete listing for the rest of the definitions of our structured control macros appears in Listing 1-14. Note the heavy use of macro comments (;;) to save room in the macro storage areas. These macros generate many symbols. They may be used in any legal order to a theoretical limit of 89 nesting levels. However, MASM runs out of storage long before that limit is reached. No initialization is required. All symbols are self-initializing.

Listing 1-14. Structured Control Macros

```
PAGE   50,132                  ; set listing to full screen
;;****************************************************************
;; M A C R O   D E F I N I T I O N S
;;****************************************************************
;;
FALSE   EQU    0               ; define "FALSE"
TRUE    EQU    OFFFFh          ; define "TRUE"
;;
;;** @TestSym ***************************** SUPPORT MACRO *****
;; Test to see if nesting level has been defined. If not,
;; then set "?SYMDEF" to initialize the counter for that level.
;; All processes normally on Pass #1 start counters at 0.
;; All symbols must be reset on the beginning of Pass #2.
;; Note that "?p2sw..." symbols stand for "Phase 2 SWitch".
;; Check that nesting level 10 is first level to be re-init.
;; Note: The value of 10 is chosen for the initial level to
;; reserve 2 digits for the nesting level.
;;
@TestSym MACRO p1,p2
        IF1               ;; if 1st pass then check for defined
        IFNDEF &p1&p2
?p2sw&p1&p2    = TRUE  ;; set pass two redefine switch
?symdef        = FALSE ;; cause counter initialization
        ELSE
?symdef        = TRUE  ;; allow counter increment
        ENDIF ;; end symbol definition check
        ENDIF ;; end 1st pass check
        ;;
        IF2               ;; if 2nd pass then reinitialize
        IF     (?p2sw&p1&p2) ;; if not reinitialized then ...
?p2sw&p1&p2    = FALSE ;; clear 2nd pass redefine switch
        IF     (?p2sw&p1&10) ;; ... and check level 10 for init
        .ERR ;; exit with error message
        %OUT @TestSym macro: &p1 nesting level not closed
        %OUT                 on 2nd pass
        ENDIF ;; end level 10 for init check
?symdef        = FALSE ;; force reinitialize of counter
        ELSE
?symdef        = TRUE  ;; allow counter increment
```

continued

Listing 1-14. *continued*

```
        ENDIF   ;; end "if not reinitialized" check
        ENDIF   ;; end 2nd pass check
        ENDM    ;; end macro definition
;;
;;** @ZeroSym ***************************** SUPPORT MACRO *****
;; Initialize the nesting sequence counter on 1st use
@ZeroSym        MACRO   p1,p2
&p1&p2 =        0
        ENDM
;;
;; ** @IncSym ***************************** SUPPORT MACRO *****
;; Increment nesting sequence counter
@IncSym MACRO   p1,p2
&p1&p2 =        &p1&p2  + 1
        ENDM
;;
;; ** @DecSym ***************************** SUPPORT MACRO *****
;; Decrement nesting sequence counter
@DecSym MACRO   p1,p2
&p1&p2 =        &p1&p2  - 1
        ENDM
;;
;; ** @MakeJmp2 **************************** SUPPORT MACRO *****
;; Insert actual JMP instruction and destination into code
@MakeJmp2 MACRO   p1,p2,p3
        jmp     &p1&p2&p3
        ENDM
;;
;; ** @MakeJmp ***************************** SUPPORT MACRO *****
;; Reformat symbols for evaluation for JMP instruction
@MakeJmp  MACRO   p1,p2,p3
??tmp  =        &p3&p2
        @MakeJmp2  p1,p2,%??tmp
        ENDM
;;
;; ** @MakeJmpLabel2 ********************** SUPPORT MACRO *****
;; Insert actual JMP destination label into code
@MakeJmpLabel2 MACRO   p1,p2,p3
&p1&p2&p3:
        ENDM
;;
;; ** @MakeJmpLabel *********************** SUPPORT MACRO *****
;; Reformat symbols for evaluation of JMP destination label
@MakeJmpLabel  MACRO   p1,p2,p3
```

```
??tmp    =         &p3&p2
         @MakeJmpLabel2  p1,p2,%??tmp
         ENDM
;;
;; ** @IfTrue ******************** STRUCTURED CONTROL MACRO *****
;; Structured "IF" Macro - IF True
@IfTrue    MACRO    p1
         LOCAL    iftrue
         j&p1     iftrue            ;; jump to "IF" section of code
         IFNDEF   ?if_level         ;; set up new level of nesting
?if_level      =         10
         ELSE
?if_level      =         ?if_level + 1
         ENDIF
         @TestSym ?if_nest,%?if_level        ;; set up new sequence #
         IF       (?symdef)
         @IncSym  ?if_nest,%?if_level
         ELSE
         @ZeroSym ?if_nest,%?if_level
         ENDIF
;; Insert jump to "ELSE" or "IF NOT" section into code
         @MakeJmp  ?if_,%?if_level,?if_nest
iftrue:
         ENDM
;;
;; ** @IfElse ******************** STRUCTURED CONTROL MACRO *****
;; Structured "ELSE" macro
@IfElse MACRO
         IFNDEF   ?if_level
; ERROR - "@IfElse" without opening "@IfTrue" statement
         EXITM
         ENDIF
         IF (?if_level LT 10)
; ERROR - "@IfElse" without opening "@IfTrue" statement
         EXITM
         ENDIF
;; Generate "@IfElse" code
         @IncSym  ?if_nest,%?if_level
         @MakeJmp  ?if_,%?if_level,?if_nest
         @DecSym  ?if_nest,%?if_level
         @MakeJmpLabel   ?if_,%?if_level,?if_nest
         @IncSym  ?if_nest,%?if_level
         ENDM
;;
;; ** @IfEnd ******************** STRUCTURED CONTROL MACRO *****
```

continued

Listing 1-14. *continued*

```
;; Structured "END" macro for use with "@IfTrue"
@IfEnd  MACRO
        IFNDEF  ?if_level
; ERROR - "@IfEnd" without opening "@IfTrue" statement
        EXITM
        ENDIF
        IF (?if_level LT 10)
; ERROR - "@IfEnd" without opening "@IfTrue" statement
        EXITM
        ENDIF
;; Generate "@IfEnd" label
        @MakeJmpLabel   ?if_,%?if_level,?if_nest
?if_level       =       ?if_level - 1
        ENDM
;;
;; ** @DoWhile ****************** STRUCTURED CONTROL MACRO *****
;; Structured "DO_WHILE" macro
@DoWhile        MACRO   p1,p2,p3
        LOCAL   iftrue
        IFNDEF  ?do_level       ;; set up new level of nesting
?do_level       =       10
        ELSE
?do_level       =       ?do_level + 1
        ENDIF
;; Set up new sequence number for nesting level
        @TestSym ?do_nest,%?do_level
        IF      (?symdef)
        @IncSym ?do_nest,%?do_level
        ELSE
        @ZeroSym ?do_nest,%?do_level
        ENDIF
;; Insert top-of-loop label for jump
        @MakeJmpLabel   ?do_,%?do_level,?do_nest
;; Insert condition check into code
        cmp     &p1,&p3
;; Jump to "DO_WHILE_TRUE" section of code
        j&p2    iftrue
;; Step to next label in sequence
        @IncSym ?do_nest,%?do_level
;; Insert end-of-loop jump into code
        @MakeJmp        ?do_,%?do_level,?do_nest
;; Begin the "DO_WHILE_TRUE" section of code
iftrue:
        ENDM
```

```
;;
;; ** @DoExit ******************** STRUCTURED CONTROL MACRO *****
;; Structured "DO_EXIT" macro for use with "@DoWhile"
@DoExit MACRO
;; Insert end-of-loop jump into code
        @MakeJmp    ?do_,%?do_level,?do_nest
        ENDM
;;
;; ** @DoEnd ******************** STRUCTURED CONTROL MACRO *****
;; Structured "DO_END" macro for use with "@DoWhile"
;; @DoEnd macro generates the code for a structured ENDDO
@DoEnd  MACRO
        IFNDEF  ?do_level
; ERROR - "@DoEnd" without opening "@DoWhile" statement
        EXITM
        ENDIF
        IF (?do_level LT 10)
; ERROR - "@DoEnd" without opening "@DoWhile" statement
        EXITM
        ENDIF
;; Back step to previous label in sequence
        @DecSym  ?do_nest,%?do_level
;; Generate jump to beginning-of-loop
        @MakeJmp    ?do_,%?do_level,?do_nest
;; Step to next label in sequence
        @IncSym  ?do_nest,%?do_level
;; Generate "@DoEnd" label
        @MakeJmpLabel    ?do_,%?do_level,?do_nest
?do_level       =       ?do_level - 1
        ENDM
;;
;; ** @Repeat ******************** STRUCTURED CONTROL MACRO *****
;; Structured "@Repeat" macro
;; @Repeat generates the code for a structured REPEAT-UNTIL
@Repeat MACRO
        IFNDEF  ?rep_level       ;; set up new level of nesting
?rep_level      =       10
        ELSE
?rep_level      =       ?rep_level + 1
        ENDIF
;; Set up new sequence number for nesting level
        @TestSym ?rep_nest,%?rep_level
        IF      (?symdef)
        @IncSym  ?rep_nest,%?rep_level
        ELSE
```

continued

Listing 1-14. *continued*

```
        @ZeroSym ?rep_nest,%?rep_level
        ENDIF
;; Insert top-of-loop label for jump
        @MakeJmpLabel    ?rep_,%?rep_level,?rep_nest
        ENDM
;;
;; ** @Until ******************** STRUCTURED CONTROL MACRO *****
;; Structured "@Until" macro for use with "@Repeat"
@Until  MACRO    p1,p2,p3
        LOCAL    iftrue
        IFNDEF   ?rep_level
; ERROR - "@Until" without opening "@Repeat" statement
        EXITM
        ENDIF
        IF (?rep_level LT 10)
; ERROR - "@Until" without opening "@Repeat" statement
        EXITM
        ENDIF
;; Insert condition check into code
        cmp      &p1,&p3
;; Jump to "@Until" .TRUE. section of code
        j&p2     iftrue
;; Insert beginning-of-loop jump into code
        @MakeJmp    ?rep_,%?rep_level,?rep_nest
iftrue:
?rep_level    =        ?rep_level - 1
        ENDM
;;
;; ** @For ********************** STRUCTURED CONTROL MACRO *****
;; Structured "@For" macro. Use of this macro as follows:
;;      @For       counter,begin,end,dir,step
;;
@For    MACRO    p1,p2,p3,p4,p5
        LOCAL    first
        LOCAL    iftrue
        IFNDEF   ?for_level        ;; set up new level of nesting
?for_level    =        10
        ELSE
?for_level    =        ?for_level + 1
        ENDIF
;; Set up new sequence number for nesting level
        @TestSym ?for_nest,%?for_level
        IF       (?symdef)
        @IncSym  ?for_nest,%?for_level
```

```
        ELSE
        @ZeroSym ?for_nest,%?for_level
        ENDIF
;; Insert counter initialization into code - (bypass 1st step)
        mov     &p1,&p2         ; initialize Count
        jmp     first           ; begin FOR loop
;; Insert top-of-loop label for jump
        @MakeJmpLabel   ?for_,%?for_level,?for_nest
;; Insert step calculation into code - check for proper step at
;; same time
        IFIDN   <p4>,<+>
        inc     &p1             ; increment count
        ELSE
        IFIDN   <p4>,<->
        dec     &p1             ; decrement count
        ELSE
; ERROR - Improper Step Specification in "@For" Statement
        EXITM
        ENDIF
        ENDIF
first:                          ; check for continuation
;; Insert condition check into code
        cmp     &p1,&p3         ; reached end yet?
;; Jump to "FOR_TRUE" section of code
        IFIDN   <p4>,<+>
        jl      iftrue          ; no - continue FOR loop
        ELSE                    ;; default to "-" step
        jg      iftrue          ; no - continue FOR loop
        ENDIF
;; Step to next label in sequence
        @IncSym   ?for_nest,%?for_level
;; Insert end-of-loop jump into code
        @MakeJmp   ?for_,%?for_level,?for_nest
iftrue:
        ENDM
;;
;; ** @ForEnd ******************** STRUCTURED CONTROL MACRO *****
;; Structured "FOR_END" macro for use with "FOR"
;; @ForEnd generates the code for a structured FOR loop
@ForEnd MACRO
        IFNDEF  ?for_level
; ERROR - "@ForEnd" without opening "FOR" statement
        EXITM
        ENDIF
        IF (?for_level LT 10)
```

continued

Listing 1-14. *continued*

```
; ERROR - "@ForEnd" without opening "FOR" statement
        EXITM
        ENDIF
;; Back step to previous label in sequence
        @DecSym  ?for_nest,%?for_level
;; Generate jump to beginning-of-loop
        @MakeJmp  ?for_,%?for_level,?for_nest
;; Step to next label in sequence
        @IncSym  ?for_nest,%?for_level
;; Generate "FOREND" label
        @MakeJmpLabel  ?for_,%?for_level,?for_nest
?for_level     =     ?for_level - 1
        ENDM
;;**********************************************************************
```

How the Structured Control Macros Work

The complexity of these macros results from the need to support nested control structures. Consider the example illustrated in Figure 1-2. Each IF-THEN-ELSE structure requires three jump statements with three unique labels. Because we cannot use symbols to store the unique labels generated by the LOCAL directive, we must resort to creating our own labels from counters. This provides the direct control required for the task.

For single levels of nesting, a simple counter would suffice. In Figure 1-2, note how the IF-THEN-ELSE associated with condition *b* uses the labels in the sequence 3,4,5. This would be easy to implement because the labels are used in the same order in both jump instructions and destination labels. However, a simple counter becomes "confused" as soon as we nest the control structures. A glance at the sequence of labels for all three IF-THEN-ELSE statements shows a distressing lack of order. This problem is overcome by using a separate counter for each nesting level.

Unique labels are ensured by including three pieces of information in each label. First, there is an identifier for the type of structure, such as *?if_us*, *do_*, and *?rep_*. The question marks are used to reduce conflicts with user-defined symbols or labels. The second piece of information is the nesting level, which is used to distinguish between label number *n* at one nesting level and label number *n* at another nesting level. Lastly, the value of the counter is included to provide a unique label for each jump at a particular nesting level.

For comparison, Listing 1-15 shows these unique three-part labels as generated by our structured control macros. The first two digits of the number are

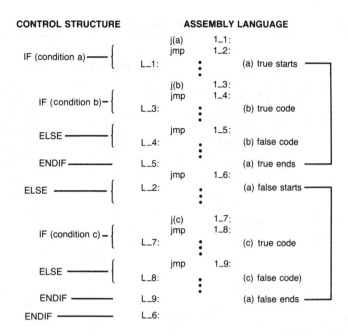

Figure 1-2. IF control structure and corresponding assembly language.

the nesting level, which starts at 10 so that two digits are always reserved for the nesting level. This prevents level one, counter eleven (1-11) from being confused with level eleven, counter one (11-1).

The condensed source corresponds exactly to that presented in Figure 1-2. By taking a close look, you will see that the expanded macros created the same structure as the assembly language section in Figure 1-2.

Because of the three-part labels, each type of structured control macro has to maintain a set of counters. This set includes a counter symbol to indicate the current nesting level. In order to generalize the task of maintaining these counters, we have created the following macros: *testsym*, *zerosym*, *incsym*, and *decsym*. These macros are passed their arguments, which they then append to create each counter, consisting of the type identifier (*?if_*) and the current nesting level.

Tricks and Warnings

When the time comes to create the actual jump instructions or jump destination labels, we use the macros *mkjmp*, *mkjmp2*, *mklbl*, and *mklbl1*. The actual labels consist of the type identifiers and *numbers*. The only way to evaluate a symbol to its numeric value in MASM is through the percent sign operator (%),

Listing 1-15. Nested IF-THEN-ELSE Structure

```
                            ; Condensed Source Code

        @IfTrue e                           condition (a)
          @IfTrue e                         condition (b)
          @IfElse                           "else" for condition (b)
          @IfEnd                            end of condition (b)
        @IfElse                             "else" for condition (a)
          @IfTrue e                         condition (c)
          @IfElse                           "else" for condition (c)
          @IfEnd                            end of condition (c)
        @IfEnd                              end of condition (a)


                          ; Expanded Listing


        @IfTrue e                           condition (a)
1       je      ??0000
3       jmp     ?if_100
1 ??0000:
  ; execute if condition (a) is true
        @IfTrue e                           condition (b)
1       je      ??0001
3       jmp     ?if_110
1 ??0001:
  ; execute if condition (b) is true
        @IfElse                             "else" for condition (b)
3       jmp     ?if_111
3 ?if_110:
  ; execute if condition (b) is not true
        @IfEnd                              end of condition (b)
3 ?if_111:
        @IfElse                             "else" for condition (a)
3       jmp     ?if_101
3 ?if_100:
  ; execute if condition (a) is not true
        @IfTrue e                           condition (c)
1       je      ??0002
3       jmp     ?if_112
1 ??0002:
  ; execute if condition (c) is true
        @IfElse                             "else" for condition (c)
3       jmp     ?if_113
3 ?if_112:
```

```
      ; execute if condition (c) is not true
              @IfEnd                              end of condition (c)
3 ?if_113:
              @IfEnd                              end of condition (a)
3 ?if_101:
```

---

which is valid only when applied to an argument of a macro call. We want to evaluate the symbol defined by the two pieces of the counter, such as:

```
mkjmp2   p1,p2,%&p3&p2
```

However, the MASM manual informs us that the ampersand operator (&) may not be used in macro calls. We are thus required to create a temporary variable and use that.

```
??tmp =       &p3&p2
          mkjmp2 p1,p2,%??tmp
```

This brings up an interesting point. The first form, which contains the ampersands in the macro call, does work. Choosing to use a "hidden" feature involves trading off ease of use against future compatibility or even future support. In addition, you must always ask whether an unsupported or illegal feature can be depended on to perform consistently. The resolution of this dilemma is left up to the reader.

The authors used this illegal feature in a program that generates no code but solves the famous "Towers of Hanoi" problem in a recursive manner. In addition to gaining generality, our method of creating counter symbols from their various parts allows creation of new counters as needed. These counters must be initialized before use, or the first attempt to increment or decrement them results in a *Symbol is not defined* error. Using the IFDEF conditional operator, a check is made to see whether initialization is required on each use of a symbol.

Initialization brings up yet another warning associated with MASM. As we have stated, MASM is a two-pass assembler that defines symbols on the first pass and uses them on the second. This implies that symbol definitions are preserved from pass one to pass two. Thus, when MASM begins its second pass, all of the counters from pass one are defined already and contain their last value. If the symbols are not reinitialized at the beginning of the second pass, a phase error results because the starting counter values are different.

Now, IFDEF is required to initialize the symbols on the first pass because we have no idea just how many counters we will require, but the use of IFDEF is insufficient for the second pass. We have solved this problem by creating the *?p2sw* . . . symbols, which are checked on the second pass to see whether the counters must be reset to their zero values. The name is derived from *Phase 2*

SWitch. This checking process also provides an opportunity to check that the nesting levels are at the outermost level, indicating that the IF-IFEND, DOWHILE-DOEND, etc., are properly paired.

Listing 1-16 contains sample expansions for the structured control macros defined above. As you can see, we have suppressed those portions of the expansion that do not produce code or jump labels. If you want to see the workings of these macros in more detail, use the .LALL directive. Use only a short example because many steps are involved in processing these macros. The number of steps also explains why the time required to assemble a program increases. Don't expect fast assemblies with these macros, just fast coding.

Listing 1-16. Expanded Use of Structured Control Macros

```
          @IfTrue e
1         je      ??0000
3         jmp     ?if_100
1  ??0000:
   ; Execute if true
          @IfElse
3         jmp     ?if_101
3  ?if_100:
   ; Execute if not true
          @IfEnd
3  ?if_101:
   ; -------------------------------------------------
          @DoWhile ax,le,bx
3  ?do_100:
1         cmp     ax,bx
1         jle     ??0001
3         jmp     ?do_101
1  ??0001:
   ; Execute while ax <= bx
          @DoExit
3         jmp     ?do_101
   ; Break out of code
          @DoEnd
3         jmp     ?do_100
3  ?do_101:
   ; -------------------------------------------------
          @Repeat
3  ?rep_100:
   ; Execute until condition met
          @Until  ax,e,bx
1         cmp     ax,bx
1         je      ??0002
```

```
3          jmp      ?rep_100
1      ??0002:
       ; ----------------------------------------------------
           @For     ax,10,20,+
1          mov      ax,10          ; initialize count
1          jmp      ??0003         ; begin FOR loop
3      ?for_100:
1          inc      ax             ; increment count
1      ??0003:                     ; check for continuation
1          cmp      ax,20          ; reached end yet?
1          jl       ??0004         ; no - continue FOR loop
3          jmp      ?for_101
1      ??0004:
       ; Execute for ax = 10 to 20 by 2's
           @ForEnd
3          jmp      ?for_100
3      ?for_101:
```

The Pseudo Case Macro

The last macro that we present in this chapter is the pseudo *case* macro, shown in Listing 1-17. Because the macro must have "foreknowledge" of the structures that it supports, we don't consider this a structured control statement. Our *case* macro functions more like a dispatch block, something like FORTRAN's computed GOTO.

Listing 1-17. Pseudo *case* Macro Definition

```
@Case   MACRO    key,case_list,jmp_labels
        ??tmp_1 = 0
        IRP      match,<&case_list>     ;; sequence through cases
          ??tmp_1 = ??tmp_1 + 1         ;; set index number
          cmp    key,&&match            ; case match?
          ??tmp_2 = 0
          IRP    retl,<&jmp_labels>     ;; sequence through jumps
            ??tmp_2 = ??tmp_2 + 1       ;; ... until index matches
            IF   (??tmp_1 EQ ??tmp_2)
              je &&&retl                ; Yes!
              EXITM
            ENDIF                       ;; end condition check
          ENDM                         ;; end 2nd IRP block
        ENDM                           ;; end 1st IRP block
        ENDM                           ;; end macro definition
```

This macro does provide a good example of the ability to parse two lists simultaneously. The outer loop, *irp match,< &case_list>*, sequences through the elements in the case list, whereas the inner loop, *irp retl,<&jmp_labels>*, selects the corresponding jump label. This technique may also be used to implement substitution macros.

In substitution macros, the outer loop sequences through elements of a list and looks for a match. Once a match is found, say, at the *xth* element, the macro enters the inner loop and sequences to the *xth* element of that list. One possible use of this would be to implement a jump-on-not-condition macro where the selected jump would be replaced by its opposite. Once again, remember that additional ampersands are required in nested macro blocks.

The expansion of the *@Case* macro in Listing 1-18 gives the expected results. The programmer is responsible for ensuring that the same number of elements appears in each list. Otherwise, an invalid control structure could be created.

Listing 1-18. Pseudo *@Case* Macro Expansion

```
    @Case      al,<'A','B','C','D'>,<subA,subB,subC,subD>
2              cmp     al,'A'              ; case match?
3              je      subA                ; yes!
2              cmp     al,'B'              ; case match?
3              je      subB                ; yes!
2              cmp     al,'C'              ; case match?
3              je      subC                ; yes!
2              cmp     al,'D'              ; case match?
3              je      subD                ; yes!
    subA:
               jmp     merge
    subB:
               jmp     merge
    subC:
               jmp     merge
    subD:
               jmp     merge
    default:
    merge:
```

Data Macros

Macros can be used to generate data or code. The ideas and methods are the same in either case, but for instructional purposes we'll start by looking at macros that generate only data.

The simplest example of an instruction to MASM that generates data is

```
TenBytes  DB   10 DUP 4          ; reserve 10 bytes with the
                                 ; number 4 in them
```

This instruction is of limited use, since it is more likely that we want a sequence of numbers as in an indexing set. As an example, let's reserve *N* words of data with the set of the numbers from *1* to *N* as follows:

```
@FirstTry MACRO N                ;; define macro with parameter N
     NUMB = 0                    ;; initialize the number
       REPT N                    ;; repeat the following N times
       NUMB = NUMB+1             ;; increment index
       DW    NUMB                ;; define word with NUMB
       ENDM                      ;; end REPT command
     ENDM                        ;; end macro
```

Note that we have an ENDM for every MACRO directive. The first variable, *NUMB*, is set to a value using = instead of *EQU* in order to allow changing the value within the REPT block.

The REPT directive is a looping structure like *do . . . while* in higher-level languages. It repeats the action between the REPT and the ENDM *N* times. In this case, it increments *NUMB* and then creates a word with that number. (Just bear in mind that you are programming MASM to create constants that will be assembled. You are not programming the computer to loop at execution time.)

If we put the *FirstTry* macro definition at the top of our program and then use it in our data segment with *N* equal to 4, we have

```
@FirstTry 4
```

which means that MASM will assemble four words of numbers from 1 to 4.

This is a pretty boring example of the use of macros, so let's make it more interesting by creating a table of binary-coded decimal numbers that could serve as a look-up table for hex to BCD translation.

```
@BCDtable MACRO N                ;; define macro with parameter N
     NUMB = 0                    ;; initialize the numbers
     HIGHBYTE = 0
       REPT N                    ;; repeat the following N times
       NUMB = NUMB+1             ;; increment index
         IF (NUMB GT 9)
         NUMB = 0
         HIGHBYTE = HIGHBYTE + 10H
         ENDIF
         IF (HIGHBYTE GT 90H)
         EXITM
         ENDIF
       BCDNUMB = (NUMB OR HIGHBYTE)
       DW BCDNUMB                ;; define word with NUMB
```

```
        ENDM                    ;; end REPT command
        ENDM                    ;; end macro
```

This is a bit more sophisticated but nothing too surprising for an experienced programmer. Before we do a line by line analysis of these directives (we use the term "directive" to indicate that it is an instruction to MASM and not to the CPU), let us look at the result when we put this in our assembly program with the parameter *N* set at 20:

```
38                          @BCDtable   20
39 0004  0001               2 DW    BCDNUMB ;
40 0006  0002               2 DW    BCDNUMB ;
41 0008  0003               2 DW    BCDNUMB ;
42 000A  0004               2 DW    BCDNUMB ;
43 000C  0005               2 DW    BCDNUMB ;
44 000E  0006               2 DW    BCDNUMB ;
45 0010  0007               2 DW    BCDNUMB ;
46 0012  0008               2 DW    BCDNUMB ;
47 0014  0009               2 DW    BCDNUMB ;
48 0016  0010               2 DW    BCDNUMB ;
49 0018  0011               2 DW    BCDNUMB ;
50 001A  0012               2 DW    BCDNUMB ;
51 001C  0013               2 DW    BCDNUMB ;
52 001E  0014               2 DW    BCDNUMB ;
53 0020  0015               2 DW    BCDNUMB ;
54 0022  0016               2 DW    BCDNUMB ;
55 0024  0017               2 DW    BCDNUMB ;
56 0026  0018               2 DW    BCDNUMB ;
57 0028  0019               2 DW    BCDNUMB ;
58 002A  0020               2 DW    BCDNUMB ;
```

The first column is the line of our assembly listing, the second column is the address offset from the beginning of the module, and the third column is what we wanted—a table of BCD numbers from 1 to 20.

Let us now go through the macro line by line. First we initialize two variables. *NUMB* will cycle through the digits from 1 to 9, for the low byte, while *HIGHBYTE* will have the high-order byte. The REPT directive governs the remainder of the macro. Within the repeat block the first thing we do is increment the *NUMB* variable. Then, we have counted to 10, and, if so, we reset *NUMB* to 0 to start the cycle again. Then we add 10h to *HIGHBYTE*, thereby incrementing the tens digit of the BCD number. Then we end the IF statement.

Next we check to see if we've built a BCD number bigger than one word can hold and, if so, quit the macro. Penultimately, we create the BCD number by bit ORing the ones digit with the tens digit. Finally, we create the word with the desired BCD number. The first ENDM ends the REPT loop; the second one ends the macro. We need a label to refer to this list of BCD numbers. We don't want to type a label every time we use the macro, so we'll use the substitute operator & to have MASM make our label for us:

```
@BCDtable MACRO N              ;; define macro with parameter N
        BCD1to&N label word    ;; define a label
        NUMB = 0               ;; initialize the numbers
        HIGHBYTE = 0
          REPT N               ;; repeat the following N times
          NUMB = NUMB+1        ;; increment index
            IF (NUMB GT 9)
            NUMB = 0
            HIGHBYTE = HIGHBYTE + 10H
            ENDIF
            IF (HIGHBYTE GT 90H)
            EXITM
            ENDIF
          BCDNUMB   = (NUMB OR HIGHBYTE)
          DW      BCDNUMB       ;; define word with NUMB
          ENDM                  ;; end REPT command
        ENDM                    ;; end macro
```

Now the list file shows our macro as follows:

```
31                        @BCDtable  20
32 0004            1      BCD1to20 label    word ;define a label
33 0004  0001      2          DW    BCDNUMB          ;
34 0006  0002      2          DW    BCDNUMB          ;
35 0008  0003      2          DW    BCDNUMB          ;
etc.
```

The & in the macro definition told MASM to substitute the value of *N* used in the macro invocation. But still we're not satisfied (we never are!). Having only one label for the list of BCD numbers will force us to use an index to access the list, since there is only one access point. What we would like is a label for every item. The expression operator % will enable us to take the value of each of our numbers and use it as part of a label. We rewrite our macro as the two macros shown here:

```
@BCD    MACRO   NAME,NUMBER    ;; NAME for label,
                               ;; ... NUMBER for the data
        BCDof&NAME DW NUMBER   ;; define word with bcd NUMBER
        ENDM                   ;; end macro
;;
@BCDtable MACRO N              ;; define a macro with parm. N
        NUMB          = 0      ;; initialize the numbers
        INDEX         = 0
```

```
HIGHBYTE          = 0
  REPT  N                     ;; repeat the following N times
  INDEX = INDEX + 1
  NUMB  = NUMB + 1            ;; increment index
    IF (NUMB GT 9)
    NUMB        = 0
    HIGHBYTE =  HIGHBYTE + 1OH
    ENDIF
    IF (HIGHBYTE GT 9OH)
    EXITM
    ENDIF
  BCDNUMB = (NUMB OR HIGHBYTE)
  @BCD %INDEX,BCDNUMB    ;; INDEX for label
                         ;; ... BCDNUMBER for data
  ENDM                   ;; end REPT command
ENDM                     ;; end macro
```

Now when we look at the listing file, we find that each byte in our table of BCD numbers has an appropriate label for our use, as shown in the following:

```
          @BCDtable  20
0004  0001   3  BCDof1  DW   BCDNUMB  ; define word with bcd NUMBER
0006  0002   3  BCDof2  DW   BCDNUMB  ; define word with bcd NUMBER
0008  0003   3  BCDof3  DW   BCDNUMB  ; define word with bcd NUMBER
000A  0004   3  BCDof4  DW   BCDNUMB  ; define word with bcd NUMBER
 .
 .
 .
```

We can create sophisticated tables in this way. If we have a formula such as $(N * M)/((P+Q) MOD T)$, we can let MASM create our table for us instead of doing it by hand and typing in the results.

We should check for overflow by including in our macro code something like the following

```
IFE (BCDNUMB LE 0FFFFh)     ;; bigger than a word can hold?
DW      BCDNUMB             ;; ok, small enough for a word
ELSE
%OUT ERROR IN @BCD MACRO
```

The OUT writes your message to the screen at assembly time—in this case *ERROR IN @BCD MACRO.*

So far, we have always used parameters as individual items separated by commas. It is also possible to have a set of items be a single parameter to the macro for repetitive data creation. For example, if we want to set up a list of strings of messages to display, we could code a macro set as follows:

```
@OptDisp MACRO OptType,Options  ;; OptType = label,
                                ;; ... Options = list
```

```
        OptType&List    db   Options
        ENDM                          ;; end macro
```

Then we could use it in the data segment as follows:

```
@OptDisp LineSpeed,<'1200sq],'2400','4800'>
```

LineSpeed will be substituted in the label, and each string in the angle brackets will be put in a *db* directive, just as if we'd typed in

```
LineSpeedList   db       '1200'
                db       '2400'
                db       '4800'
```

This is of limited use, since to access a string we have to rely on the knowledge that each string is 4 characters long. Much more often we have variable-length strings terminated by an ASCII zero. So here is a macro to make such strings:

```
@MakeList MACRO Name2,messag
        MESSAGE&Name2    db         CR,LF,messag,CR,LF,0
        ENDM
;;
@OptDisp MACRO Options  ;; OptType = label, Options = list
        Name3 = 0
          IRP msg,<Options>
          Name3 = Name3 +1
          @MakeList %Name3,msg
          ENDM
        ENDM            ;; end macro
```

We can use the strings in the data segment as follows:

```
@OptDisp <'Error','Waiting','Computing'>
```

Each string in the angle brackets will be put in a *db* directive, as shown in the following listing fragment:

```
                       @OptDisp <'Error','Waiting','Computing'>
OD OA 45 72 72 6F 72  3 MESSAGE1  db  CR,LF,'Error',CR,LF,0
OD OA 57 61 69 74 69  3 MESSAGE2  db  CR,LF,'Waiting',CR,LF,0
OD OA 43 6F 6D 70 75  3 MESSAGE3  db  CR,LF,'Computing',CR,LF,0
```

The instructive point in this macro is that we have used the literal-text operator (< >) in an IRP (Indefinite RePeat) directive to repeat the string creation as many times as necessary to use up our strings. Still, we are left with the problem of how to access this list of strings. We need a list of addresses. The following macro provides the answer.

```
@MakeList MACRO Name2,messag
        MESSAGE&Name2    db        CR,LF,messag,CR,LF,0
        ENDM
;;
@MakeNames MACRO Name5
        dw       MESSAGE&Name5
        ENDM                              ;; end REPT
;;
@OptDisp MACRO Options   ;; OptType = label, Options = list
        Name3 = 0
          IRP    msg,<Options>
          Name3 = Name3 +1
          @MakeList   %Name3,msg
          ENDM
        Name4 = 0
        MessageList Label  WORD
          REPT Name3
          Name4 = Name4 + 1
          @MakeNames   %Name4
          ENDM                        ;; end REPT
        ENDM                          ;; end macro
```

When the macro is used in the data section, we get the same result as if we had typed

```
@OptDisp <'Error','Waiting','Computing'>
MESSAGE1    db    CR,LF,'Error',CR,LF,0
MESSAGE2    db    CR,LF,'Waiting',CR,LF,0
MESSAGE3    db    CR,LF,'Computing',CR,LF,0
MessageList Label  WORD
dw        MESSAGE1
dw        MESSAGE2
dw        MESSAGE3
```

There is much more that we can do with macros to generate data, but we have given you a good idea of the possibilities. The same techniques can be used to generate code as well as data. Let's move on to code macros.

Code Macros

Macros are a very powerful way of getting the assembler to do some programming for you. Just as you can write a BASIC program to make the computer do work for you, so you can write a MACRO program to make the assembler program, MASM, do some of the tedious aspects of programming for you. A simple example of what we mean is the following macro designed to write a character to a file:

```
@WritToFil MACRO                  ;; define macro
        mov      ah,40h           ;; DOS function to write to a file
        int      21h              ;; DOS call
        ENDM                      ;; end macro
```

Now, instead of retyping the MOV and INT instructions whenever we want to write a character to a file, we can use *WritToFil* where we would otherwise have written the code.

Macros vs Subroutines

You can do the same thing with a subroutine that you do with a macro, but making short pieces of code into subroutines is inefficient. The difference between a macro and a subroutine is that the macro inserts the desired code right where the macro is placed in the source file, while a subroutine resides elsewhere and we have to jump to that location to execute the code. In other words, use of macros to create repetitive in-line code avoids the execution overhead involved in calling and returning from subroutines.

We use a macro instead of a subroutine for the same reason we call someone on the phone for a short conversation instead of going across town to visit—the time lost in going to another location isn't justified by the brevity of our task. Thus, code macros tend to be very short because they add to the size of the program every time they are used. If they get too long, they should be recoded as a subroutine. How long is too long? That depends on the overhead needed to invoke the subroutine, on how often you use the function, and on the relative value of memory versus speed for your application.

Macros are faster because they don't require saving registers, pushing parameters, etc., but a lot of repetitions of short macros can take up space in your object and executable files. Make the code a macro at first, and if it seems to be getting out of hand, recode it as a subroutine. Later we'll see how you can even code the subroutine call as a macro.

Conditional Macros

The code macro example given is fairly straightforward, so let's dress it up a little. Suppose that for debugging we would like to write our characters to the screen instead of to a file. We could rewrite the macro as follows:

```
@WritToFil MACRO EKOFLAG          ;; define INCHRIF with
                                  ;; ... argument EKOFLAG
```

```
        IFIDN <EKOFLAG>,<EKO>    ;; if argument EKOFLAG is
                                 ;; ... IDENTICAL to
                                 ;; the 3 letters EKO, assemble
                                 ;; ... next line
        mov     ah,06h           ;; DOS function to write to
                                 ;; ... standard output
        ELSE                     ;; if EKOFLAG is NOT IDENTICAL
                                 ;; ... to the 3 letters EKO,
                                 ;; ... assemble the next line
        mov     ah,40h           ;; DOS func. to write to a file
        int     21h              ;; DOS call
        ENDM                     ;; end macro
```

In this case, MASM looks at the argument EKOFLAG to determine whether to insert *mov ah,06h* or *mov ah,40h*, as shown in the following:

```
@WritToFil EKO     ; MASM substitutes MOV AH,06 & INT 21H here
    .
    .              ; because the argument is identical to EKO
@WritToFil NOEKO   ; MASM substitutes MOV AH,40H & INT 21H here
    .
    .              ; because the argument is NOT identical to EKO
```

Note that instead of *NOEKO* in the preceding example we could have used *PHUBAH* or anything else, since the important thing is that the argument not be *EKO*. The spelling of our parameter is highly arbitrary. This leaves open the possibility that we could forget our odd spelling and mistakenly write *@WritToFil ECHO*. This would give us no screen echo because we wrote *ECHO* instead of *EKO*. We can eliminate this error possibility by limiting ourselves to either *EKO* or *NOEKO* as follows:

```
@WritToFil MACRO EKOFLAG         ;; define INCHRIF with argument
                                 ;; ... EKOFLAG
        IFIDN <EKOFLAG>,<EKO>    ;; if EKOFLAG = EKO, assemble
                                 ;; ... next line
        mov     ah,06h           ;; DOS function to write to
                                 ;; ... standard output
        ELSE                     ;; otherwise ...
        IFIDN <EKOFLAG>,<NOEKO>  ;; if EKOFLAG = NOEKO, assemble...
        mov     ah,40h           ;; DOS func. to write to a file
        ELSE                     ;; if argument doesn't match
                                 ;; ... either then
        .ERR                     ;; generate an assembly error
        ENDIF                    ;; end condition testing
        int     21h              ;; DOS call
        ENDM                     ;; end macro
```

Nested Macros

The macros we have been defining use the DOS function to write characters to the standard output or to a file. But we may want to check to see if a key has been struck to interrupt the output, and, if not, we continue on. DOS function 0B hex will check to see if a key has been struck, returning AL = 0FF hex if a character is available and AL = 00 if a character is not available. We can write a macro *chkchr* and then call it from our macro *WritToFil* as follows:

```
@ChkChr MACRO                  ;; define macro @ChkChr
        mov     ah,0Bh         ;; check standard input
        int     21h            ;; DOS call
        ENDM                   ;; end macro
;;
@WritToFil MACRO WAITFLAG,EKOFLAG ;; 2 arguments
        LOCAL   bye            ;; define a dummy address
        IFNB    <WAITFLAG>     ;; if field for WAITFLAG is not
                               ;; ... blank, assemble the
                               ;; ... following
        @ChkChr                ;; see if a character is waiting
        cmp     al,0           ;; al = 0 => no character waiting
        je      bye            ;; if no character, continue on
        ENDIF                  ;; end condition testing
        IFIDN   <EKOFLAG>,<EKO> ;; if EKOFLAG = EKO, assemble ...
        MOV     AH,06h         ;; DOS function to write to
                               ;; ... standard output
        ELSE                   ;; otherwise ...
          IFIDN <EKOFLAG>,<NOEKO> ;; if EKOFLAG = NOEKO, assemble
          MOV   AH,40h         ;; DOS func. to write to a file
          ELSE                 ;; if arg. doesn't match either
          .ERR                 ;; ... generate an assembly error
        ENDIF                  ;; end condition testing
        int     21h            ;; DOS call
bye:
        ENDM                   ;; end macro
```

This newest version of *WritToFil* has several features to discuss. The LOCAL directive tells MASM that the label *bye* is a dummy label that MASM is to replace with a different label every time the macro is invoked within a program. This is to avoid the problem of the same label being used twice in one program, which would generate an assembly error. MASM will assemble the macro using *??0000* the first time in a module, *??0001* the second time the macro is used, etc., through *??FFFF* (hex), should you care to invoke the macro 65,536 times in one program. The LOCAL directive must be the very first thing after the MACRO directive—not even comments can be placed before it! The *IFNB WAITFLAG* tells MASM to assemble the next three lines only if the argument *WAIT-FLAG* is Not Blank. Otherwise, the code is not included and the first line assembled will be one of the IFIDN governed lines. This gives us the option of generating code that will either write output or just check the keys and go on if nothing is there. The IFNB checks for the existence of *WAITFLAG*, not for spelling, so we could invoke the macro by any of the following

```
@WritToFil WAIT,EKO
@WritToFil WAITE,EKO
@WritToFil NoWate,EKO
@WritToFil FOOBAH,EKO
```

and still generate code that does *not* wait for input. Note also that we have nested our macros, one macro invoking another.

More Macro Features

Instead of using only the *WAITFLAG* to determine whether to assemble the code for writing, we might also make it a global option that we can choose at assembly time. For example, we might like it to check for a key if we're debugging or if the *WAITFLAG* is set, but not wait otherwise. While we are extending this macro, we'll throw in some other new stuff. The new macro definition is

```
@WritToFil MACRO   WAITFLAG,EKOFLAG
       LOCAL    bye     ;; define a dummy address
       ;; macro to get a character from the standard input
       ;; 2 arguments: WAITFLAG & EKOFLAG determine whether to
       ;; wait for a character and whether to echo the input
       .XCREF           ;; suppress cross-referencing of local
                        ;; ... labels, etc.
       x = 0            ;; x will be our indicator
       IFNDEF   DEBUG   ;; if parameter DEBUG is not defined,
       x = 1            ;; flag = 1
       ENDIF            ;; end condition testing
       IFNB <WAITFLAG>  ;; if the field for WAITFLAG is not blank
       x = 2            ;; flag = 2
       ENDIF            ;; end condition testing
       IF (x EQ 1) or (x eq 2) ;; if either DEBUG is not
                        ;; defined, or WAITFLAG is not
                        ;; blank
       @ChkChr          ;; see if a character is waiting
       cmp      al,0    ;; al = 0 => no character waiting
       je       bye     ;; if no character, continue on
       ENDIF            ;; end condition testing
       IFIDN <EKOFLAG>,<EKO>   ;; if EKOFLAG = EKO,
                        ;; ... assemble next line
       mov      ah,06h  ;; DOS func. to write to standard output
```

```
        ELSE                ;; otherwise ...
          IFIDN <EKOFLAG>,<NOEKO> ;; if EKOFLAG = NOEKO, assemble
          mov    ah,40h  ;; DOS function to write to a file
          ELSE                ;; if argument doesn't match either then
            .ERR              ; ... generate an assembly error
            %OUT Error in @WritToFil MACRO - EKOFLAG not found
          ENDIF             ;; end condition testing
        ENDIF             ;; end condition testing
        int      21h      ;; DOS call
bye:
        .CREF             ;; restore cross-referencing
        ENDM              ;; end macro
```

Now at assembly time we can use the /*d* option to define DEBUG:

```
MASM  myprgm,,,; /dDEBUG
```

and all the invocations of *WritToFil* will generate code to check for input.

We have used a flag (with = instead of *equ* since we redefine it in the next two IF statements) to determine whether we wait for a character. Instead of *(x eq 1)* or *(x eq 2)*, we could have coded *x gt 0* or *x NE 0*, since any value other than our initial value of 0 is valid. Note that we also added a few new directives. The ;; tells MASM the comment should not be in the assembly listing. The .XCREF saves assembly time and cross-reference listing space by telling MASM not to clutter up our cross-reference listing with the names used only in the macro. The .CREF restores cross-referencing, or it would be off for the rest of the listing. We have also added the %OUT directive, which will write to the screen the error message given. Although there is plenty more that we could do to this macro, it has become pretty fearsome, so we'll leave it here and encourage you to experiment with additional features.

A Macro That Calls Subroutines

One of the more powerful uses for macros is as a generalized subroutine call, similar to the subroutine calls in higher-level languages. The task is to push some parameters on the stack and call the subroutine. Pretty simple, except that to be of general use the macro needs to accommodate a variable number of parameters, and it needs to allow for variable-size parameters (byte, word, double word, quad word, and 10-byte floating point). To handle these requirements, we use the .TYPE and TYPE operators (note the period before the first operator). Using .TYPE allows the macro to handle a register such as BX as well as a data word or byte. Using *.TYPE x* returns a byte with the bits set according to the following scheme:

Bit 0   = 1 if x is code related, 0 otherwise

Bit 1   = 1 if x is data related, 0 otherwise

Bit 5 = 1 if x is defined, 0 otherwise

Bit 7 = 1 if x is external, 0 local or public

All other bits are zero

For example, if x is data related, defined, and local, then *.TYPE x* returns 00100010b (22 hex); i.e., bit 1 is set, and bit 5 is set. Since we want to allow the use of registers (which are code related) as parameters, we will use the .TYPE operator to tell us if we have data-related parameters. Since we have to handle data for differing lengths differently, we use the TYPE operator, which returns the byte length of its argument, for example:

TYPE N = 1 if N is a byte

TYPE N = 2 if N is a word

TYPE N = 4 if N is a double word

TYPE N = 8 if N is a quad word

TYPE N = 10 if N is a ten-byte word (e.g., floating point)

TYPE N = xx if N is an xx-byte structure,

TYPE N = FFFF if N is a *near* program label

TYPE N = FFFE if N is a *far* program label

The following macro illustrates the use of the TYPE and .TYPE directives:

```
@FcnCall MACRO  Fnctn,ParmList      ;; subroutine & parameter list
     IRP    N,<ParmList2>           ;; indefinite repeat (see below)
     BYTELENGTH = TYPE N            ;; get length in bytes of the
                                    ;; ... "PUSHed" items
       IF ((.TYPE N) NE 22H)        ;; is N data-related and defined?
       push  N                      ;; no, assume 16-bit register
       ELSE                         ;; otherwise, it's data ...
         IF (BYTELENGTH EQ 2)       ;; so, if 2-byte parameter ...
         push N                     ;; then just push it
         ELSE                       ;; otherwise, ...
         IF (BYTELENGTH EQ 1)       ;; if 1-byte parameter,
                                    ;; ... assume AX is available
           mov       ah,0           ;; clear upper part of AX
           mov       al,N           ;; make parameter a word ...
           push      ax             ;; ... so we can push it
           ELSE                     ;; otherwise, ...
             IF (BYTELENGTH EQ 4)   ;; if 4-byte parameter,
             push   word ptr N      ;; push 1st and
             push   word ptr N + 2  ;; ... 2nd words
             ELSE                   ;; otherwise, ...
               IF (BYTELENGTH EQ 8) ;; if 8-byte parameter,
               push  word ptr N     ;; push 1st,
```

```
        push   word ptr N + 2     ;; ... 2nd,
        push   word ptr N + 4     ;; ... 3rd, and
        push   word ptr N + 6     ;; ... 4th words
        ELSE                      ;; otherwise, ...
          IF (BYTELENGTH EQ 10)   ;; if 10-byte param.,
          push   word ptr N       ;; push 1st,
          push   word ptr N + 2   ;; ... 2nd,
          push   word ptr N + 4   ;; ... 3rd,
          push   word ptr N + 6   ;; ... 4th, and
          push   word ptr N + 8   ;; ... 5th words
          ELSE
          .ERR
          ENDIF
        ENDIF
      ENDIF
     ENDIF
    ENDIF
   ENDIF
  call Fnctn
  ENDM                            ;; end IRP
  ENDM                            ;; end macro
```

The nice thing about this macro is that we don't have to specify in advance how many parameters we wish to send to the subroutine until we call it. We could call one routine with three parameters and another routine with two parameters, for example:

```
@FcnCall Fcn1,<word1,word2,byte3>
@FcnCall Fcn2,<word1,byte3>
```

We could have a virtually unlimited number of parameters for any subroutine call we wish.

There are numerous deficiencies in the macro. Some of these deficiencies are that we haven't covered all the possible values of *BYTELENGTH*, such as those for program labels or structures; we rather blithely assumed that the AX register was available for our 1-byte parameter, etc. There are fixes for many of these deficiencies—a loop based on *BYTELENGTH* might handle every possible length of data—but other problems would remain and we haven't even looked at the inverse macro we should write to pop the data for the called routine! The example served to illustrate the TYPE and .TYPE directives, but we need something better for a real general-purpose function calling routine. Before continuing with this macro, we take a short diversion to introduce the important subject of structures.

Using the STRUC Directive

Structures are assembler directives that enable you to build complex data formats composed of bytes, words, etc., in ways that make them much more meaningful and accessible to you. They are very similar to C structures and Pascal records. They differ in that indexing is harder in MASM, and nesting is not allowed. For an example that we can use in a parameter-passing macro, let's suppose you are writing a program that does mathematical routines. Here's a structure you might create:

```
MathNumbers      STRUC
Boolean1         DB      (0)     ; 1 byte
Boolean2         DB      (0)     ; 1 byte
ShortInteger1    DW      (0)     ; 1 word
ShortInteger2    DW      (0)     ; 1 word
LongInteger1     DD      (0)     ; 1 double word
LongInteger2     DD      (0)     ; 1 double word
Float1           DT      (0)     ; 1 ten-byte word (for 8087)
Float2           DT      (0)     ; 1 ten-byte word (for 8087)
MathNumbers      ENDS
```

MathNumbers defines a type of structure. STRUC and ENDS delimit the beginning and end of the structure definition. We can now use *MathNumbers* to declare some data as in the following:

```
TrueFalse      MathNumbers      <1,0,,,,,,>
MaxMinShort    MathNumbers      <,,32767,-32768,,,,>
MaxMinLong     MathNumbers      <,,,,2147483647,-2147483648,,>
e              MathNumbers      <,,,,,,,2.718281828>

ListLength     = 100
MathList       MathNumbers      ListLength dup <,,,,,,,>
```

Space is reserved for 104 numbers. At 34 bytes/number, this is 3536 bytes for our list of numbers. The structures are initialized first to 0 in the definition of the structure and then reset to various values in the data section. Structures can be considered as a user-defined data directive. The names of the structure elements are converted by MASM to byte displacements from the beginning of the structure. You can now refer to the numbers in a structure by the field names, just as you might in C or Pascal. For example,

```
cmp      MaxMinShort.ShortInteger1,ax
```

is equivalent to

```
cmp      [MaxMinShort + 2],ax
```

As an example, if we wish to scan the entire list of numbers for the first floating-point number less than 0, we would code

```
        mov     di,MathList         ; get address of list
        mov     cx,ListLength       ; length of list for looping
        mov     bx,(TYPE TrueFalse) ; length of structure
CmpLup: cmp     [di].Float1,0       ; floating point number > 0?
        jl      ExitLup             ; no, search done
        add     di,bx               ; point to next structure
        loop    CmpLup              ; scan entire list of members
ExitLup:...
```

Multiple Structures to Address Data

One very useful feature of using structures is that you can rearrange or add to the structure definition at any time and the names you gave the elements will be automatically updated when you reassemble. For example, let's change the preceding *MathList* structure so that it interchanges the Boolean and floating point numbers and adds the element *LibraryPtr*.

```
MathNumbers     STRUC
Float1          DT      (0)     ; 1 ten-byte word (for 8087)
Float2          DT      (0)     ; 1 ten-byte word (for 8087)
ShortInteger1   DW      (0)     ; 1 word
ShortInteger2   DW      (0)     ; 1 word
LongInteger1    DD      (0)     ; 1 double word
LongInteger2    DD      (0)     ; 1 double word
Boolean1        DB      (0)     ; 1 byte
Boolean2        DB      (0)     ; 1 byte
LibraryPtr      DD      (?)     ; 1 double word
MathNumbers     ENDS
```

The advantage of using structure names in our code is that, after reassembly of all the code and data elements, our new structure definition *[di].Float1* still points to the first of the floating point numbers, even though we've rearranged the data. So, code that refers to data by structure name needn't be rewritten. Note, however, that if we have data in our file using the old structure definitions, then we must realign the existing data to conform to our new structure. Rearranging the structure doesn't rearrange the existing data, only the relative positions declared for it. We have to ensure that the actual data corresponds to the data structure declaration.

Unlike C structures, MASM structures cannot contain other structure definitions (there's no reason they couldn't, so maybe a later version of MASM will allow it). However, there is no reason a structure can't contain the address of another structure, which is why we included *LibraryPtr* in the structure. Suppose we have another structure called *Library* defined as follows:

```
Library STRUC
FloatLib        DD      (0)     ; pointer to floating point lib.
ShortIntLib     DD      (0)     ; pointer to short integer lib.
LongIntLib      DD      (0)     ; pointer to long integer lib.
BooleanLib      DD      (0)     ; pointer to Boolean lib.
Library ENDS
```

We can now set up a set of library routines with their addresses organized in the structures, for example:

```
AddLibs   Library       <FloatAdd,ShortAdd,LongAdd,BooleanAdd>
SubLibs   Library       <FloatSub,ShortSub,LongSub,BooleanSub>
MultLibs  Library       <FloatMult,ShortMult,LongMult,BooleanMult>
  .
  .
  .
```

This combination of structures might be used as shown in the following code segment:

```
lds     si,MathList[bx]         ; addr of particular structure
push    ds                      ; save address of data structure
push    si
lds     si,LibraryPtr           ; addr of library addresses
call    [ds:si].LongIntLib      ; go do operation
```

The appropriate pointers have been loaded into the structures either at assembly time or at run time. The beauty of using a structure address to pass parameters and pointers to subroutines is that the calling code is always the same, regardless of how many additions to the structure you have to make in the life of the program. By putting into the structure pointers to other data structures, we make it unnecessary for the program code to have too much knowledge of the details of the data and/or operations involved. This "data hiding" is developed and employed much more in object-oriented programming languages such as C++ or Smalltalk, but you can do almost the same thing with the proper use of structures. You can also apply a structure you define to a data set that you had no hand in creating. For example, the first 22 bytes of the PSP (program segment prefix) that MS-DOS puts at the beginning of executable files could be accessed via the following structure:

```
PSP       STRUC
INT32     DB      2 DUP (?)     ; 2 bytes
MemSize   DW      (?)           ; 1 word
Reserved  DB      (?)           ; 1 byte
DOSCall   DB      5 DUP (?)     ; 5 bytes
```

```
TermVctr        DW      2 DUP (?)       ; 2 words
BreakVctr       DW      2 DUP (?)       ; 2 words
ErrorVctr       DW      2 DUP (?)       ; 2 words
PSP     ENDS
```

The PSP can now be accessed as in the following code fragment:

```
mov     di,0                    ; PSP begins at offset zero
push    cs                      ; PSP segment is in cs
pop     ds                      ; PSP segment -> ds
mov     si,[di].MemSize ; program mem. size -> extra seg.
```

Structures as Subroutine Parameters

We introduced structures as a way of simplifying the task of writing a generalized subroutine calling procedure. Let's return to this problem. The best way to pass parameters to a subroutine is via a structure address. As an example, let's pass to our subroutine the data in one of the elements of the math list defined in our discussion of structures. Addresses are always the segment and offset. So the macro to make subroutine calls and pass parameters is now simple:

```
@FcnCall MACRO Fnctn,StrucAddr  ; subroutine & structure addr.
        push    offset StrucAddr
        push    segment StrucAddr
        call    Fnctn
```

It sometimes happens that you need to assemble an instruction that the assembler will not handle. This came up in one of the earlier versions of MASM with a bug that would not assemble a particular type of jump instruction. This problem also will crop up if you are working on a new processor before MASM has been rewritten to accommodate the new instructions. One way of solving this problem uses macros to assemble data that would be the same as the opcode from the Intel handbook, like the following macro that creates a short jump instruction.

```
@JmpShort MACRO destin
        db      0EBh                    ; first byte of jump instruction
        n = destin - *                  ; calc distance to jump
        IFE     (n LE 255)              ; too big for a byte?
          db    n                       ; distance to jump
        ELSE
          .ERR                          ; generate an assembly error
          %OUT Error in @JumpShort macro.
        ENDIF                           ; end condition testing
        db      90h                     ; 3rd byte of short jump
                                        ; ... instruction
        ENDM
```

This example was chosen for simplicity. To make more complex instructions, you need more complex macros. As a word of encouragement, note that people have made full cross-assemblers using little more than this method.

Summary

Our presentation of the world of MASM macros, conditional assembly, and structures is completed. From the examples contained in this chapter, we hope that you have gained a feel for the design and use of the usually frustrating, often complex, but ultimately rewarding features of the Microsoft Macro Assembler.

In this chapter, we have presented a variety of examples of each feature, from the simple to the complex, so that some measure of the usefulness of these features has been conveyed. By using these examples and doing some experimentation on your own, you can define the boundary between the possible and the impossible in the MASM assembler.

But you shouldn't lose sight of the reason for exploring macros and conditional assembly. We contend that the proper use of these features can help you program in a more organized manner, thus enhancing the readability and reliability of your programs and reducing the amount of time you spend debugging your programs. We hope that the examples presented, along with friendly tips, comments, and some warnings, have given you a sense of how to apply these two features to advance your programming skills.

Structured Programming 2: The Design and Implementation of Modular Programs

2

HE discussion in Chapter 1 focused on the tools of structured programming as they can be applied to the MASM environment. In Chapter 2, we present the methods of structured programming as they apply to MS-DOS and the 8086/8088.

Our presentation consists of two separate yet interrelated topics. These topics deal with the design of modular programs in assembly language and with the implementation of that design using MASM, macros, and whatever else may be at hand. Both these topics affect the writeability, readability, reliability, and maintainability of your programs. In short, these methods, separately and together, can be used to structure your programs to produce better programs.

Principles of Modular Programming

When impartial analysis is made of assembly language programs, the most glaring deficiency usually discovered is lack of recognizable structure. Despite the best intentions of most assembly language programmers, their programs tend to be intricately connected, unwieldy conglomerations of code that require almost divine insight to fully understand. This statement is not intended as a slight upon these dedicated people. The lack of structure is the result of their having to simultaneously deal with a large number of details. There are two directions in which to approach this problem. One is to simplify the code, replacing long complicated instruction sequences with more understandable structures. The techniques developed in Chapter 1 go a long way toward relieving the burden of detail implicit in assembly language programming. However, the programmer is still left to cope with a sometimes staggering number of functional details.

The way out of this rat's maze is to apply the same techniques that rescued higher-level languages a decade ago. The concepts of decomposition and modular design should be applied to assembly language programming. These concepts, referred to under the collective heading of *structured design*, allow the programmer to segment the total programming task so that he or she need only deal with a manageable number of details at one time. This is the topic for our next discussion.

Designing Options

Modular design and *decomposition* refer to the process of breaking a large problem into smaller, more manageable, subproblems. The first design step is deciding where to draw the lines between these subproblems.

In order to derive the maximum benefits from the use of modular programming, each subproblem or *module* must have a single entry and a single exit. The flow of control in a program then may be readily traced. At any place in the module it should be possible to look at the module's entry point and say, "I know the values of registers X, Y, and Z at this point because they are specified as . . . ," and then trace the operation of the module without worrying about the intrusion of rogue program flows. The single exit ensures that when a module is invoked, the flow of control returns to the point of invocation. For this reason, modular programs are nearly always implemented with a CALL-RET structure.

Using multiple RET statements in a module does not violate this rule of single exit because all the RET instructions return to the same point. Similarly, jumping to a common RET at the end of a module does not add to the structure of the module but adds only code and complexity. On the other hand, jumping into or out of a module is strictly against the rules, for it negates the greatest advantage of modular programming: clean, maintainable program structure.

There is an exception to the rule of not jumping into a module. This arises when *jump tables* are used to decide the flow of control within a program. A jump table is used by pushing a return address of the stack, calculating the index of the desired jump address in the table, and performing a jump through memory. An example of this technique appears in the device driver program listings given in Chapter 6.

When practicing modular decomposition, you will find that a number of alternatives present themselves. Before we are able to intelligently choose, we must know the alternatives. The goal is to choose among alternatives those that give the most workable design.

Designing for Functional Separation

When approaching a problem in the design stage, the first alternative chosen should be functional decomposition, that is, the breaking up of a problem into small, manageable, functional units where each unit performs a complete, readily identifiable task.

There are many ways of determining what should be contained in a task. Some common examples are units that perform an explicit function, such as obtaining the square root of a number; units that perform all operations relating to a specific device, such as disk or keyboard I/O; units that perform a common group of actions at a specific time, such as initializing data areas; and units that are related in sequence or their use of common data elements, such as reading and converting keyboard data to integers.

In today's world of high-level language programming, value judgments often are made about which is the best method to use for segmenting programs.

In assembly language programming, we usually cannot afford to be so critical. Each of the preceding methods listed gives at least a starting point for breaking up the problem. Often, you find that some modules are related by one set of criteria and other modules by another set. As long as each module encompasses a section of code that can be readily understood (usually of two pages or less), you're off to a great start.

Designing to Minimize the Number of Parameters Passed

Sometimes, you find that after defining the modules for your program, you have created something unwieldy. This is often the case when a module requires access to an extensive amount of data in order to accomplish its task. This might easily occur if you're writing an integrated package that supports many options. The module must accept many different variables to know the state of the program at a given time. If this happens and you find yourself with a module that accepts a large number of parameters, you must then ask two questions.

First, are you attempting to perform more than one function in that module? Does the module require parameters that are used in unrelated sections of the module? If either applies, you must segment the module again. Second, are you cutting across functional lines? Are the calling module and the called module actually part of the same function? If so, put them together even if the result looks too large. Try to segment them again in a different way.

Segmenting modules across functional lines often occurs when the programmer notices that two sections of code are identical or strongly similar. The programmer then attempts to create from them a single module. This is not modular programming because the resulting module has no functional cohesion.

If you find that you can do nothing to avoid using many common data references or passing scores of parameters, go back to the original design and check to see if you have specified the problem correctly.

Designing to Minimize the Number of Calls Needed

One of the great advantages of modular programming is that the main-level program can often be constructed to read as a sequence of procedure calls. This enhances understanding of the program because the reader can become familiar with its basic flow and operation after reading only a page or two of code. However, this feature can also have drawbacks. One of the most overquoted statistics of programming is that typical programs spend 90 percent of their execution time in 10 percent of the code. The implications are that if this 10 percent contains a large number of chained procedure calls, the amount of time spent in program flow control can be a handicap to a program with severe time constraints.

Before giving up on modularizing your programs, examine just what these time-related statements mean. First, most programs spend the majority of execution time waiting for something to be entered from the keyboard. Once a key has been typed, the required functions are not usually time-consuming in a way that humans think of time. The difference between 100 microseconds and 100 milliseconds (a 1000 times difference) is not going to be noticeable to the average user.

Contrary to some beliefs, the actual mechanism of the CALL-RET pair is not overly time-consuming. When compared to the jump instructions, the CALL takes about 30 to 50 percent longer and the RET averages 1 cycle longer. Only when the overhead of pushing parameters, saving registers, and what is euphemistically called *housekeeping* is considered, do modular programs begin to look slow by comparison. In addition, because the modules of a modular program are usually more general than their unstructured counterparts, modules may use memory or stack references with greater frequency. The additional time required by effective address calculations may result in the body of the module executing more slowly than a linearly coded specific routine.

The advantages of housekeeping and generality are that the module may be used virtually anywhere in the program. When writing nonmodular programs, you may spend hours attempting to discover whether a register is in use, or worse, just what its contents are supposed to be. In modular programming, the programmer is not concerned with which registers are currently in use as long as the called module takes its parameters off the stack and saves the entire register set on entry. With these kinds of advantages, it makes sense to use these modular techniques initially to speed coding and then rework the program to remove bottlenecks.

For those areas that are speed-sensitive, the best recommendation is to selectively mainline the code. If a module is referenced only in the speed-sensitive section of the code, the module may be included "in-line" within the calling module. If other sections use the module, it may be copied to the calling module and fit into place. Because the main calling module grows larger, you should add comments that mark the included module as a block of its own. A future reader may then read the comments to determine the module's function and skip past it to resume reading the main code.

Rules for Modularization

We can summarize the more notable concepts of modular programming in the following rules:

- *Divide and conquer.* Divide the problem into smaller functional tasks, each one independent of the others except for its necessary parameters.
- *Single entry – single exit.* The module should have only one entry point where all calls begin. It should return control to the point in the program flow where control was invoked. (The return address may be modified as discussed in the following section on parameter passing.)
- *KISS—keep it sweet and simple.* Avoid complexity in coding. Handle complex logic in a well-documented way that explains each step and why it was designed that way.
- *Hide details.* Confine the details of register usage, local data structure, etc., to the internals of the modules. Don't let a module's implementation spill over into the rest of the program.

- ***If a module uses a particular variable, make that variable a documented parameter.*** Document all effects that a module has on global data.

- ***Plan for error detection and the actions to be taken if errors occur.*** Responsibility for *exception processing*, as it is known, must be assigned to the individual modules. Normally, lower-level modules report errors to the calling module. The responsibility for decisions about those errors normally is reserved to the upper-level modules.

References

What we have presented here has been a quick overview of the concepts of structured programming and modular design. We do not have the space to provide a full treatment of the subject. However, a wealth of literature is available. If your goal is to be a software professional, purchase some of these books and read them. The following titles are classic works on the subject and reflect a small sample of the excellent professional-level works available.

DeMarco, T. *Structured Analysis and System Specification.* New York: Yourdon, 1978.

Kane, G., D. Hawkins and L. Leventhal. *68000 Assembly Language Programming*, Berkeley: Osborne/McGraw-Hill, 1981.

Tausworthe, R.C. *Standardized Development of Computer Software.* Part I. Englewood Cliffs, N.J.: Prentice-Hall, 1977.

Yourdon, E.U., and L.L. Constantine. *Structured Design.* Englewood Cliffs, N.J.: Prentice-Hall, 1977.

Yourdon, E.U. *Techniques of Program Structure and Design.* Englewood Cliffs, N.J.: Prentice-Hall, 1975.

Implementing Modular Programs in Assembly Language

So far, we have been speaking in the abstract about modules, parameter passing, and other such terms. Now is the time to begin relating this information to the concrete world of MS-DOS, MASM, and 8086 assembly language.

Modules in the MASM environment are best handled by the MASM PROC directive. We have been using this all along as a method of defining the entry and exit points of the program. We now extend its use to define the boundaries of the individual modules. PROC is used by MASM to define a label in the code and to give that label either a *near* or *far* attribute. This attribute is used to generate both the correct type of CALL instruction and the correct type of RET instruction. A detailed presentation of these types of instructions is given in a later section, "Types of Coding." What we are concerned with here is that the PROC directive is a convenient way to denote a block of code with a single unique entry and constant exit that forms the basis of the module.

Definition of Parameter, Argument, Variable, and Constant

We have been tossing around the words *parameter*, *argument*, and *variable* like so many ping-pong balls. For the most part they have had interchangeable meanings. Now we need to start drawing some distinctions (although some will undoubtedly call this splitting hairs). After this chapter, we can all return to our slothful ways, but for the moment we need to be clear-headed and clear-thinking.

The dictionary sense of *parameter* is "a characteristic element." In common use, *parameter* is a reference to any piece of data used by a module that is not totally contained within that module. Why the added words, *reference to*? Because a parameter is not the data itself nor even an address of the data. Rather a parameter is a place holder (the characteristic element). For example, consider the equation $Y + 1$. No module can be written to evaluate that equation because Y is not a value! Y is a parameter that is replaced by an actual value when it is time to evaluate it. The actual value is called an *argument*.

We still have not defined *variables*. Strictly speaking, variables are register or memory locations that hold a piece of changeable data. In the preceding example, Y is also a variable because it changes to fit the required circumstances. Thus, parameters are automatically variables (but not vice versa).

To recap, if a data object can be modified, it is a variable. If that variable is required for a module to perform its task, it's also a parameter. The argument is the actual value that the variable takes on when the module is invoked.

We also need to consider the special case of constants. A *constant* is a data object whose value never changes. In assembly language, constants can appear in two ways. They may be part of the immediate data for an instruction (as in *mov al,4*), or they can be located in memory like other data. When constants are placed in memory, they differ from variables solely because they are only read, never written.

Can a parameter also be a constant? If the constant is of the memory type, unequivocally yes. But you encounter a problem when you try to use immediate data constants as parameters. Immediate data may not be passed by itself to a subroutine. Immediate data must be contained in something, either a register, memory location, or the stack. In higher-level languages, the compiler takes care of converting constants to locations. In assembly language you have to do it yourself.

Parameters and Modules

We have determined that a parameter is any data that a module requires to accomplish its task and that is located outside the module. We have also determined that parameters are by definition variables. This brings up the second great strength of modules. Because the inputs to a module are variables, they may be changed to fit the specific case at hand. This gives great generality to modules, enabling them to be reused in many places and in many programs.

In reality, parameters are an optional component of modular programming. You can have a module that accepts no outside parameters and operates solely on internal data. A simple routine to beep the console would have no parameters. A more common example is a simple routine to read numbers from the keyboard. Although the number reading routine would return a value, that routine would not necessarily need any arguments passed to it.

In combination, requiring input parameters and producing output values form four types of modules:

1. Modules that accept no inputs and produce no outputs.
2. Modules that accept inputs and produce no outputs.
3. Modules that accept no inputs and produce outputs.
4. Modules that accept inputs and produce outputs.

We typically call the first two types, which produce no output data, *subroutines*, and the last two types, which do produce output data, *functions*. Note that no distinction is made as to whether they require input parameters, although as a programmer, you are aware of the difference.

Parameter Passing Options

For those routines, be they subroutines or functions, that accept input parameters, the problem of passing data to them must be resolved. When programming in a high-level language, the programmer typically has no choice in the matter. In assembly language, many options exist. We have presented all options for consideration, although the use of some is strongly discouraged.

Passing through Registers

The most common method for passing data in assembly language programming is via the registers. Instant accessibility and high speed make them prime candidates for this task, for no matter what the program environment, registers are always an op-code away. Nearly all MS-DOS function calls pass their data in this manner. Short assembly language routines that interface to MS-DOS often use the same registers to manipulate data as those required by the MS-DOS functions they call. It makes sense to create a parameter in the same register that MS-DOS expects it.

One disadvantage of this method is that there are a limited number of registers. If you have a routine that requires more variables than you have registers, you're in trouble. Newer microprocessors have fewer restrictions than older ones, but the number of registers is still finite. In addition, if you ever think of *porting* your code, that is, moving it from one type of processor to another, a situation in which the two processors could share the same register set is very unlikely. You could end up redesigning all the module interfaces.

Another drawback is that you must continually keep track of the use to which each register is put. This game of "who's on first" can tire even the most dedicated bit pusher. Especially frustrating is the case when you decide that register X is free and code your module accordingly. Later you decide you can use the same module in another place, only register X is no longer free. So PUSH goes X, in goes the value, the call is made, and POP goes X. Whoops, X contained a returned value. Let's see, what's free now? And so it goes.

A practical limitation of passing parameters in registers is that the information is usually limited to 16 bits, the size of the largest register. Because most variables tend to be either bytes or words, size isn't a big problem. When the data to be passed exceeds the size of a register, the calling routine may pass the address of the data instead. Of course, the called routine must know what type of data is being pointed to in order to use it properly. MS-DOS function calls use this pass-by-address technique whenever they require large amounts of data.

Passing through Common

The next choice for most programmers is using a prearranged data area. We use *prearranged* in the sense that both the calling and called routine have "agreed" that their data is passed in some area of general memory. Routine A knows to put last month's receipts in the area labeled *FOO*, and routine B knows to go look for them in *FOO*. *FOO* is then known as a *common area*.

Passing through common has at least one thing going for it. Within the physical limits of your computer, you can put as much data as you want into memory. Passing through common puts an end to the shell game of free registers and allows data of any size, from one byte to kilobyte buffers, to be passed.

In addition, passing through common makes the data available to any module that needs it. This is a great advantage when the data in question is being passed from a high-level module through many intervening modules to a low-level module. Each module doesn't have to handle data that it does not use.

On the negative side, depending on common memory can restrict the generality and reusability of the modules. Consider a series of modules designed to read and write files. If the modules are coded to use a common block of memory for a data buffer, having two files open at the same time can be a problem. If the program were designed to do a compare, the program would have to copy one set of data from the buffer into a storage area to prevent the buffer from being overwritten. Granted, the example is simplistic, but we trust that the implications are clear.

The last drawback to common memory results from one of its strengths. Because the area is available to any module, it is in a way "fair game." Protecting the data from accidental destruction is nearly impossible. This is not normally a great risk (unless program errors are common) but becomes a factor in the consideration of reentrant programming (covered in a subsequent section, "Types of Coding").

Passing through Program Memory

Passing through program memory is a variant of passing data through common data memory. The differences are, one, the data resides in program space (code segment); and, two, the location of the data is determined by the CALL instruction because the data is located directly after the call.

The called routine takes the return address off the stack, uses that as a pointer to the memory area, adds the size of the memory area to the return address, and places it back on the stack. When the routine returns to the calling program, the return address is the first location after the data area.

This seems convenient until we consider that the 8086 is specifically designed for separate code and data areas. Passing through program memory requires that the code segment and the data segment be set to the same value, as the return address is code-segment relative.

The worst problem with this method of passing data is that it requires manipulation of the stack in what comes very close to being self-modifying code. One rule that you should always remember is *never, never modify program memory!* If you succumb to the temptation, you will find that your program becomes nearly impossible to debug without expensive hardware logic analyzers.

Passing on the Stack

The method used by most high-level languages for implementing procedure calls is passing the data on the stack. In this method all required parameters are pushed onto the stack before the call is made. After the call is made, the calling routine accesses the data without removing it. The designers of the 8086 family encouraged this method by providing the BP (base pointer) register. The BP has the wonderful feature of addressing its operands relative to the stack segment. This means that by setting the value of the BP to the proper location the contents of the stack may be addressed using indexed addressing.

What is the proper location to load into the BP? This is not the SP (stack pointer) itself because the SP is pointing to the return address on the stack. The data actually starts at either location SP + 2 or location SP + 4. Why plus two or plus four? Because for *near* procedure calls, the processor stores only the current offset (instruction pointer) on the stack (2 bytes), whereas for *far* procedure calls, the processor stores the offset and the code segment on the stack (4 bytes). The called routine may be coded to start access at the proper location (depending on the type of routine) by using the following addressing:

```
NEAR                            FAR
mov bp,sp                       mov bp,sp
mov <1st arg>,[bp+2]
mov                             <1st arg>,[bp+4]
  :                               :
  :                               :
```

Note that if the contents of the BP register must be saved, as is normally the case, the called routine must also push the BP onto the stack, changing the address of the first parameter to [BP + 4] for *near* routines and to [BP + 6] for *far* routines. One means of avoiding this change in addresses is to give the calling routine the responsibility for saving the BP, before the parameters are placed on the stack. However, for compatibility reasons this is *not* recommended. Instead, the structure shown in Listing 2-1 is the preferred method of passing parameters. Using this structure, which has been adopted by many high-level languages, will assist you in producing portable, reusable routines. These routines can be gathered into a "toolkit" that may be used in many places to reduce your coding burden and increase your productivity.

When the called routine returns, the parameters that were pushed onto the stack must now be removed. The calling routine can remove the parameters by either POPping them from the stack or by simply adding the size of the stored parameters to the SP register, as in *add SP,N*, where *N* is the number of bytes occupied by the parameters. This method, shown in Listing 2-1, effectively cuts off the stack at the original location. Alternatively, the called routine may be assigned the responsibility of clearing the stack via the RET *N* instruction, where *N* is again the number of bytes occupied by the parameters. In either method, *N* is equal to the number of words PUSHed times two.

The difference between these two methods is that when the RET *N* instruction is used, the routine must be called with exactly the proper number of parameters. If there are not *N* bytes of parameters, the RET *N* instruction will misalign the stack and crash the system. Alternatively, if the calling routine clears the stack by using the *add sp,N* instruction, then each call to the target routine may pass a different number of parameters. As long as the caller clears

Listing 2-1. Passing Parameters on the Stack

```
              ; The Calling Procedure

      :        :
      push   <argument_N>   ; push last argument
      :        :
      push   <argument_2>   ; push second argument
      push   <argument_1>   ; push first argument
      call   <myproc>       ; call procedure
      add    sp,<2N>        ; clear stack
      :        :


              ; The Called Procedure

<myproc> PROC  NEAR         ; near calling example
      push   bp             ; save old BP
      mov    bp,sp          ; reference point in stack
      :        :
      mov    <dummy>,[bp+4] ; access to first parameter
      mov    <dummy>,[bp+6] ; access to second parameter
      :        :
      mov    <dummy>,[bp+2+2N] ; access to last parameter
      :        :
      mov    sp,bp          ; restore SP
      pop    bp             ; discard saved BP
      ret                   ; return to caller
<myproc> ENDP
```

up properly, there will be no problem. (Of course, this dodges the issue of whether the called routine can make use of a different number of parameters being supplied from call to call.)

This seems like a lot of extra coding, what with PUSHes, MOVes, POPs, etc., in place of a simple call. This is one place to put our knowledge of macros to use and write a simple macro to perform these chores. The macros in Listing 2-2 help the calling program maintain the stack during parameter passing. Similarly, the macros in Listing 2-3 assist the called program in accessing and returning parameters on the stack. All registers used in these macros must be wordlength because the PUSH and POP instructions do not operate on 8-bit registers.

Listing 2-2. @*CallS* and @*FCallS* Macros for Parameters on the Stack

```
;; **** @PushIm Macro: Push Immediate Data through BP register
@PushIm MACRO   arg
        mov     cs:mem_16,&arg
        push    cs:mem_16
        ENDM
;; **** CALL SUBROUTINE Macro:   calls    name,<arg1,arg2,...>
@CallS  MACRO   routine_name,arg_list
?count  =       0
        IRP     argn,<&arg_list>
        push    &&argn          ; push parameters
?count  =       ?count + 1
        ENDM
        @PushIm %?count         ; push number of parameters
        call    &routine_name   ; call routine
        add     sp,2*(1+?count) ; clear stack
        ENDM
;; **** CALL FUNCTION Macro: @FCcallS name,<arg1,arg2,...>,ret
@FCallS MACRO   routine_name,arg_list,return_val
?count  =       0
        IRP     argn,<&arg_list>
        push    &&argn          ; push parameters
?count  =       ?count + 1
        ENDM
        @PushIm %?count         ; push number of parameters
        call    &routine_name   ; call routine
        pop     &return_val     ; get returned value
        IF      ?count          ;; if nonzero ...
        add     sp,2*?count     ; clear stack
        ENDIF
        ENDM
```

**Listing 2-3. @*Accept*, @*RetVal*, and @*CRet* Macros for Taking
and Returning Parameters on the Stack**

```
;; **** @RetVal Macro: @RetVal register
@RetVal MACRO   return_value
        mov     [bp+4],return_value      ; return word result
        ENDM
;; **** @Accept Macro:    pnum,<reg1,reg2,...>
@Accept MACRO   reg_list
        push    bp                ; save base pointer
        mov     bp,sp             ; set BP to access parameters
        mov     &pnum,[bp+4]      ; get number of parameters
?count  =       0
        IRP     reg,<&reg_list>
?count  =       ?count + 1
        push    &&reg             ; save register for new value
        mov     &&reg,[bp+4+?count*2]    ; get parameters
        ENDM
        ENDM
;; **** @CRet    Macro: <reg1,reg2,...>
@CRet   MACRO   reg_list
        IRP     reg,<&reg_list>
        pop     &&reg             ; restore the saved registers
        ENDM
        pop     bp                ; restore base pointer
        ret                       ; return from program
        ENDM
```

The @*PushIm* macro allows the 8086/8088 user to push immediate data on the stack. To use the macro, you must first define somewhere in the code segment the word location *mem_16*. Although using a memory location to transfer immediate data to the stack is slower and takes more code, doing so allows more freedom of register use.

In the @*CallS* and *FCallS* macros, the symbol *?count* is used to inform the called routine of the number of parameters provided and to keep track of the number of bytes pushed on the stack for use in clearing the stack after the call. If the target, or called, routine already knows how many parameters are being passed to it (which is usually the case), these macros may be modified to dispense with pushing and clearing the parameter count. Note that the parameter count also serves as a way of returning a value for function calls (the @*FCallS* and @*RetVal* macros).

The @*RetVal* macro is for use with the @*FCallS* macro and replaces the parameter count pushed on the stack by @*FCallS* with a 16-bit value to be returned to the caller.

The target routine macro @*Accept* works with either @*CallS* or @*FCallS* to transfer the parameters from the stack to registers. This macro saves the registers it uses as it progresses. The *?count* symbol is used here to determine the offset of the next parameter within the stack. Because @*Accept* works its way up the stack (increasing offsets), this macro removes the parameters from the stack in the reverse order from which they were pushed! Note also that both @*Accept* and @*RetVal* expect a *near* call because they allow for only a 2-byte return address.

The last target macro @*CRet* restores the registers that were saved by @*Accept*. Because POPs must be in reverse order from PUSHes, the argument list for @*CRet* must be in reverse order from that in @*Accept*. The last action that @*CRet* takes before RET is to restore the base pointer saved by @*Accept*.

These macros are presented more as examples than as working copies and can be enhanced to provide more general coverage. For example, the parameter PUSH, *push &&argn*, can be replaced with the more general @*PushOp* macro from Chapter 1 to handle immediate data parameters. One limitation of the current version is that the *mov [bp + 4],return_value* instruction in macro @*RetVal* cannot return memory variables on the stack because the 8086 family does not support a memory-to-memory move instruction. This macro could be enhanced to recognize a memory-to-memory move and generate a transfer through an intermediate register.

You should note, however, that the macros presented in Listings 2-2 and 2-3 implement a calling procedure that is *not* compatible with any known high-level language. Specifically, these macros pass the number of arguments to the called procedure as an additional argument, and they return a value to the calling procedure directly on the stack.

For the called routine, MASM provides some tools to simplify accessing the data on the stack. By defining a *structure* that represents the data on the stack and aligning the base pointer (BP) with the beginning of the structure, data on the stack may be accessed symbolically, that is, by name. This helps prevent disastrous coding errors, which result from specifying an incorrect offset. Listing 2-4 demonstrates the use of the MASM STRUC directive in this context.

Listings 2-1 and 2-4 differ in three important respects. The first difference is in the order that each example pushes its parameters onto the stack. In Listing 2-1, the calling program pushes its parameters from last to first, while in Listing 2-4 they are pushed in the order of first to last. For the *StackFrame* structure to work with Listing 2-1, the order of *params* must be reversed. (Assigning an order of "first to last" to the parameters may appear arbitrary at this point. The parameters are actually assigned an order from left to right, as they would appear in a subroutine call expressed in a high-level language.)

The second difference between the examples is in the way they each clear the passed parameters from the stack. In the example in Listing 2-1, the calling routine clears the parameters by means of the *add SP,<2N>* instruction. In Listing 2-4, the called routine clears the stack by using the *ret (2N)* instruction.

The last difference is that Listing 2-1 shows a *near* routine, while in Listing 2-4 the called routine is declared *far*. If *StackFrame* is used with a *near*

Listing 2-4. Accessing the STACK Symbolically
with the STRUC Directive

```
                          ; The Calling Procedure
        :           :
        push    <argument_1>    ; push first argument
        push    <argument_2>    ; push second argument
        :           :
        push    <argument_N>    ; push last argument
        call    <myproc>        ; call procedure
        :           :


                          ; The Called Procedure

StackFrame  STRUC               ; define a template for the stack
        dw      ?               ; saved BP
        dd      ?               ; return address (use "dw" for NEAR)
paramN dw      ?               ; last parameter
        :           :           :
param2 dw      ?               ; 2nd parameter
param1 dw      ?               ; 1st parameter
StackFrame  ENDS                ; end of template definition
;
base    EQU     [bp]            ; template base
;
<myproc> PROC   FAR             ; near calling example
        push    bp              ; save old BP
        mov     bp,sp           ; reference point in stack
        :           :
        mov     <dummy>,base.param1 ; access to first parameter
        mov     <dummy>,base.param2 ; access to second parameter
        :           :
        mov     <dummy>,base.paramN ; access to last parameter
        :           :
        mov     sp,bp           ; restore SP
        pop     bp              ; discard saved BP
        ret     (2N)            ; return to caller
<myproc> ENDP
```

procedure, the *dd* directive must be converted to a *dw* directive. This reserves only 2 bytes in the template for the caller's return address, rather than the 4 bytes required for a *far* call. On the other hand, if the structure is to be used in an interrupt routine, then an additional *dw* directive must be added after the *dd*, to reserve space for the processor flags that are placed on the stack by an interrupt.

The STRUC directive does not add any code to the finished program. This directive only defines offsets that are used with the BP to ease the task of referencing the parameters.

The stack also provides a convenient place to store returned values, but we delay discussion of that topic until we have discussed the differences between functions and subroutines, which we do in later sections of this chapter.

Summary of Parameter Passing Options

There are three proper ways to pass data to modules. These are

1. *Passing through registers*—few parameters are allowed; best for simple interfaces and for exception handling or returning values.

2. *Passing through common*—limited flexibility and generality but has the advantage of making the data available to all modules.

3. *Passing on the stack*—preferred method for handling data; excels in generality (reusable modules) and production of modular code; necessary for interfacing with most high-level languages; demonstrates that you're a member of the "in" crowd.

Additionally, when data is passed by any method other than common, each module must accept as parameters the data it needs not only for itself but for any modules that it calls in turn. This can sometimes lead to large parameter lists for upper-level modules.

In actual use, you probably want to use a combination of these techniques (with the exception of passing data in program memory).

Passing Parameters by Value or Address

Once a decision on how to pass the parameters has been made, you must answer the question of what form of argument to use. You remember that "argument" is what we have decided to call the *value* that is given to the parameter. This value may be either the data itself or the address of the data.

Pass by Value

Most parameter passing in assembly language is done with *pass by value*. In this method, the actual data (its value) is passed to the calling routine. The target routine receives a number, either stored in a register or pushed onto the stack.

Data that is stored in common memory is something of a special case. In one sense, it is passed by address because the calling and called routine access the data by means of a common address. In another sense, the data in the common area may be either values or addresses, and the problem is simplified by basing the decision on the nature of the data in the common block. If the data is a value, data is passing by value. If it is an address, data is passing by address.

If parameters consisting of immediate data are to be passed on the stack, users of the 8086 or 8088 face some additional effort when transferring the value to the stack. Users of the 80x86 advanced processors can use the PUSH

<immediate> instruction, but for users of the older processors, the data must be transferred to the stack through an intermediate register. The *@PushIm* macro presented in Chapter 1 could be used, but its complexity is not called for in this application. If the calling procedure shown in Listing 2-1 is used, the BP register is available for transferring immediate data to the stack. In almost all conventions for the 8086 architecture, the AX register is dedicated for this purpose. Any immediate data that must be moved to the stack is transferred with the following two lines of code:

```
mov     ax,<immediate_data>
push    ax
```

Passing parameters by value inherits the limitations of register and stack passing—restriction of the value to 16 bits. Indeed, 8-bit data may not be pushed onto the stack at all. There are ways around this, of course, of which the *@PushOp* macro from Chapter 1 is one example. Data belonging to large structures may be pushed a word at a time, but unless the called routine must receive its parameters from the stack, to pass the address of the data is much easier.

Pass by Address

In *pass by address*, the called routine receives only the address of the data. All accesses to the data are made using this address. There are a number of immediate advantages. One, unless the data resides in a different segment, all addresses may be contained in one 16-bit value, which is convenient for using registers or the stack. Two, the routine becomes completely general because specifying a different address yields a new set of data. Three, the data may be directly manipulated by the called procedure to return a value to the calling routine in the same location that contained the original value.

Sometimes a problem is encountered if the values to be passed are not located in memory (that is, immediate data). For this case (or if you find it simply inconvenient to push all the required addresses onto the stack), a type of hybrid parameter can be used: the argument block.

The *argument* or *parameter block* is a special form of pass by address. In this case, the required arguments are contained in a contiguous piece of memory. However, unlike passing through common, the called procedure has no implicit knowledge of this block. When the procedure is called, it is passed the address of this block as a parameter. It still may not be convenient to place all the required arguments into the block, but this does avoid the necessity of pushing all those values onto the stack. If the block already exists for another purpose, passing parameters through an argument block makes a lot of sense.

Protecting the Integrity of Passed Data

There is another aspect of the *pass by . . .* option that is just as important as ease of use. This aspect relates to the integrity of the data or its protection from unintentional change or corruption.

In typical use, data that is passed by value is a copy of the actual data. As such, the called routine may manipulate the data in any way without changing the data in the calling routine. On the other hand, if the called routine receives the address of the data, that routine may then alter the data, possibly changing the operation of the calling routine. Data that is passed by value is then considered to be protected, whereas data that is passed by address is considered to be at risk.

Surprisingly, variables that are passed in a register are sometimes considered to be passed by address because registers are simply specialized addresses in hardware. This distinction is made because the data in the register is at risk if the subroutine or function alters the data in the register and that alteration has an effect on the main routine.

There are no hard and fast rules regarding the degree of exposure of the data. Concepts such as pass by value and pass by address may help us to evaluate the situation, but the actual decisions of the type of passing to use depend on how valuable the data is to the calling routine (the degree of risk) and whether the called routine has access to the original data. This in turn determines how much protection is required for that data.

Functions versus Subroutines

It is often desirable for the called routine to return new data to the caller. As indicated earlier, those routines that return values are called *functions*; those that don't, *subroutines*. In high-level languages, functions are usually restricted to returning only one value. Any other information that must be returned to the calling procedure is passed back by modifying one or more of the parameters. In assembly language no such restrictions apply. Let's examine the options.

Returning Values in Registers

Once again, the simplest way to return a value is in a register. As with passing parameters, this option can be limited by the number of available registers and by the size of the data to be returned. On the positive side, the data is readily accessible and can be tested or manipulated quite easily.

For frequently called functions, returning values in the registers makes sense. It requires no special setup and no anticipation of memory buffers or such. Most MS-DOS functions return their values this way. However, if all functions in a program returned their data via the registers, you would be faced with a major bookkeeping and shuffling task. In addition, because the registers are where most computations take place, there is fierce competition for their use.

Rather, the registers should be used for those small, frequently called routines that return only a few values and for routines whose returned value must undergo immediate calculations. A function to read character values for transformation into a number would be one example of the latter case.

Most high-level languages use the technique for returning values. The AX register is usually used for returning byte or wordlength values. If a double word value must be returned, such as a *far* pointer, the least significant word (or offset portion) is returned in the AX register, and the most significant word (or segment portion) is returned in the DX register. In those cases where more than two words must be returned to the calling program, the data is placed in a memory buffer, and a *pointer* to the buffer is returned to the calling routine. Just how this pointer is managed depends on the individual language.

Returning Values in Common

When a routine returns values in common, no one thinks of it as a function. Nevertheless, this "side effect" method provides a reasonably simple means for returning large amounts of data. We call it a *side effect* method because the transfer operation is not readily apparent from reading the "call" section of the calling routine and appears to take place as an incidental result of the procedure. Because this is not readily apparent from the call, clear documentation must be added describing what values are returned and why.

However, if the address of the common area is instead passed in a parameter in either a register or the stack, the fact that returned values are expected in that particular memory area is made more apparent to the reader. In addition, the benefits of generality are gained because the procedure may be directed to return its values in any buffer location.

Returning Values on the Stack

The last method of returning values is to place them in the stack (as opposed to on the stack). This operation requires use of the BP to address the stack (in the same manner as passing parameters on the stack). To return a value, the value is loaded onto the stack in one of the memory locations above the return address. If the procedure is called with parameters, one of the parameter locations may be used to store the return value. If the procedure is called without parameters, the calling procedure must push a dummy argument on the stack in order to make room for the returned value.

When values are returned on the stack, the called routine should not clear the stack with a RET *N* instruction. Instead, the calling procedure should be used to clear the stack, retrieving the returned values through simple POPs.

If the returned values are too large to conveniently fit on the stack, the called routine may return a pointer to a memory location where the returned values may be found. Then that memory location would contain the actual returned values. In these cases, the calling routine should decide the location of the buffer area.

Exception Reporting

During this discussion, we have alluded to returning status indications or detecting and reporting errors. In many applications, a desirable option is to have called procedures, functions, and subroutines provide some type of error indication or status code. You probably have noticed that many MS-DOS function calls return a status code upon completion. Frequently the carry bit is used to indicate the presence of an error with one or more of the registers, usually the AX, containing detailed information on the type of error.

The carry bit is used for a number of reasons. It is easy to check (with JC or JNC); easy to set, complement, or clear (with STC, CMC, and CLC); and easy to save and restore (with PUSHF and POPF). Access to the carry flag is more complete than for any other status bit in the 8086/8088 architecture. This combination provides an ideal mechanism for indicating the presence of an exception. Of course, the programmer must remember to clear the carry bit to indicate a proper completion if no errors occurred because the carry bit may be already set by a normal operation.

Once the calling routine has determined that an error exists, the routine must discover the nature of the error. Sometimes no further information is required. When more information is needed, a dedicated register for completion codes is helpful. A logical choice is the AX register, but because so many other operations depend on it (MUL and DIV for example), it may not be available. Whatever choice is made, the register should contain not only error codes but also a normal completion code. This way, if the original error indication is lost, the program may retest the register to discover the completion status. If the information is critical, choose a value for normal completion that is not a normal result. What this implies is that you should not use a value of zero for normal completion because another error could easily clear the status codes.

MS-DOS provides an error reporting service for use with programs that run other programs. If a subprocess wishes to return an error code to the process that invoked that subprocess, it may do so as part of the Terminate Process function call, function 4Ch. The parent process then may obtain that return code through MS-DOS function 4Dh, Retrieve the Return Code of a Child. This mechanism is for use only with programs run under the Load and Execute Program function, 4Bh, which is introduced in Chapter 3.

Types of Coding

For most basic programming in any language, the programmer is rarely concerned with the details of how the processor is executing the program. Details of I/O handling, memory management, and where in memory the program is executing are left to the operating system to manage. However, there are times when more direct control of the program environment is desired. At these times the programmer may need to know about, and take responsibility for, the mechanism used to load, position, and execute the program. Examples of this occur when writing stand-alone programs that operate without MS-DOS present, supporting program overlays to fit large programs into limited physical memory, and writing interrupt driven or recursive programs.

During execution, a program's position in memory is reflected in two ways. One of the segment registers is used to relate the program counter (also known as the instruction pointer) or memory reference address to a block of physical memory. Then, within that block, the actual memory reference is formed, using an offset from the beginning of the block. This offset appears in the program counter, in memory references, and within indirect memory references through registers.

What does this have to do with different types of coding? These types of references and the way that they are used determine how a program is loaded into memory, what types of features it can use, and how the program may be structured. We examine how these references are created and how to use the right ones to allow us to write the best possible programs.

Program Code Positioning

Understanding the alternatives in positioning program code requires a clear understanding of both program flow control instructions (CALL, RET, and JMP) and memory accesses in the 8086 processor. Both of these can restrict the options available to the programmer in locating code in the available memory space.

Program flow control instructions, often called *control transfer* instructions, come in two basic forms: the CALL and the JMP. Each causes the program to begin executing code from a new place in memory, called the *destination*. Each of these instructions has three implementation options for specifying the destination location. They are: current location relative, current segment relative, and absolute addressing.

Location Relative

Current location relative, sometimes called *PC relative* (program counter relative), calculates the destination address from the current address and a displacement. The displacement is added to the current location to form the destination address. Because the entire operation is totally independent of the absolute location of the code in memory, the resulting address is position independent. If the entire block of code is moved in memory, the new destination address created correctly points to the new location of the destination instruction.

This method of calculating transfer addresses is used with all conditional jumps, all intrasegment (*short* or *near*) direct JMPs, and all intrasegment (*near*) direct CALLs. *Direct* means that the CALL instruction contains a displacement as immediate data. The alternative, *nondirect*, is a CALL to an address contained in a 16-bit register (offset only) or to an address contained in a 16-bit or 32-bit memory location (offset or offset and segment).

Because direct transfers involve no actual addresses, they may be located anywhere in memory and may even be moved about within a segment as long as both the source instruction (JMP or CALL) and destination routine are moved together.

Segment Relative

Current segment relative addressing specifies an actual offset value to be loaded into the instruction pointer (as in the nondirect CALL) or to be used as a pointer to data. References made using this method always point to the same location within the block of memory addressed by the relevant segment register.

As such, the code or data may not be moved within the segment. However, such code may be moved in memory if the segment register for that block is also updated. Because segments must be aligned on paragraph boundaries (address XXXX0 hex), the code may be moved only by increments of 16 bytes (one paragraph).

This type of addressing is used by intrasegment (*near*) indirect JMPs and CALLs where a new destination instruction pointer value is fetched from a register or memory location. This addressing is also used with all data references, regardless of the segment used (DS, ES, or SS). Code that uses this type of reference is still considered relocatable as long as the segment registers are updated to reflect the position of the code.

Absolute Addressing

Absolute addressing occurs when the entire physical memory address is explicitly specified. To accomplish this in the 8086 family, both the segment address and the offset may be explicitly specified. These references point every time to the same location in memory. Absolute addresses in the 8086 are rare. Only a few instructions have the ability to generate absolute addresses in the 8086. These instructions are intersegment (*far*) JMPs and CALLS and the LDS and LES instructions (load pointer using DS or ES). The JMP and CALL instructions, either direct or indirect, update not only the offset (instruction pointer) but the code segment (CS) register as well. This specifies a physical address in memory. Likewise, the LDS and LES instructions not only load an offset into a 16-bit register but load either the data segment (DS) register or the extra segment (ES) register. Once again, this is a physical address.

One other way to create an absolute address is to use a MOV or POP instruction to directly load one of the segment registers with a constant. However, note that POPping a value into the CS register is not allowed in the iAPX186, iAPX188, or iAPX286 processors and should not be done if only for compatibility reasons.

Types of Program Code

When discussing the properties of a program, we refer to it by the least flexible type of addressing that it contains. If only a single absolute reference is contained in a program, that program is said to have absolute addressing or to be nonrelocatable. It may not be moved in memory.

Attentive readers may believe that an error has been made. After all, the entry point of a MASM program is specified as *far*, and all .EXE programs load the DS and ES with a MOV instruction. Both of these facts would seem to imply a nonrelocatable program, yet MS-DOS does load our programs into memory at different addresses as required. The key to this dilemma is that the values used are not constants in MS-DOS. MASM and LINK treat segment and *far* procedure names in a special way, producing what is called a *relocation map*. When a program is loaded into memory, MS-DOS reads the relocation map, and changes the values of those references that contain segment addresses. The important note for us as programmers is that MS-DOS does not extend such courtesies to standard data values, and loading one of the segment registers with a constant is not the same as using a segment or *far* procedure name.

Relocatable Code

MASM and LINK normally produce relocatable code. That is, in normal use, they create programs that may be moved in memory by MS-DOS and still operate correctly. Only the contents of the segment registers change. This has uses in a number of applications. Programs may load other programs into any area of memory using MS-DOS function 4Bh (useful for program overlays). Multiple programs may be loaded into memory concurrently (useful for multitasking systems or memory resident programs, such as print spoolers).

As indicated, MS-DOS accomplishes this feat by changing only the values of the segment registers and any locations in the program code that reference the segment name or a *far* procedure. We can also extend these concepts of flexibility to the data areas used by a program. Normally, relocatable programs contain relocatable data areas. When the MS-DOS loader brings a program into memory, the loader assigns values to all segment references rather than just code segment references. Listing 2-5, which is taken from a standard .EXE type program file, shows the data segment reference used to load the data segment register. Listing 2-6 shows the equivalent code produced by MASM.

Listing 2-5. Source for .EXE Program Header

```
data_seg SEGMENT                ; define the data segment
         :                      ; data area & values
data_seg ENDS
code_seg SEGMENT                ; define the code segment
         ASSUME cs:code_seg
         ASSUME ds:data_seg
main     PROC    FAR            ; entry point for the program
start:
         mov     ax,data_seg    ; transfer data segment address
         mov     ds,ax          ; ... to AX and thence to ...
         mov     es,ax          ; ... segment registers
         :       :
         :       :
```

In standard use, the variable *data_seg* is not a constant. Rather, this variable is a segment relocatable value, which is indicated in the MASM listing by four dashes and the letter *R*. As it loads the program, MS-DOS inserts in the program the actual value to be used during execution. This value is the address of the location in memory where *data_seg* was loaded. So with the help of MS-DOS, a program's code and data areas may be moved around in physical memory.

Listing 2-6. Listing for .EXE Program Header

```
0000                          code_seg  SEGMENT
                                        ASSUME   cs:code_seg
                                        ASSUME   ds:data_seg
0000                          main      PROC     FAR
0000                          start:
0000 B8 ---- R                          mov      ax,data_seg
0003 8E D8                               mov      ds,ax
0005 8E C0                               mov      es,ax
```

Separate Data Area

If more than one data segment is defined in the program (using corresponding ASSUME directives), it is possible for routines to have separate data areas. But in typical programming style, each routine is limited to accessing the same data area every time that routine is called. The data area is dedicated to the routine and vice versa.

In normal use, dedicated areas are not a handicap because most routines execute in a sequential manner, one after the other. But what happens when we try to execute the same procedure more than once at the same time? Wouldn't the later call overwrite the earlier call's data because the routine uses only one data area? At this point, you may be wondering why the same procedure would be invoked more than once simultaneously.

There are at least three cases where this occurs. First, multitasking systems may have multiple programs running, sharing common libraries of code called *run-time libraries* (because the code is accessed at run-time instead of being included during link-time). Run-time libraries have only one copy of the code, located in memory, instead of having multiple copies located in the program file. (See Chapter 3 for a more complete discussion of run-time libraries.) Although they may all run the same code at the same time, run-time libraries must have separate data areas to avoid inadvertent sharing and corruption of data.

The second case where the same procedure may be invoked by two parties simultaneously occurs in interrupt-driven systems. Assume that a routine is executing but is interrupted by some external event. The program that services the interrupt starts executing but needs to call the routine that was interrupted. Unless they have separate data areas, the interrupt procedure destroys the data that belongs to the interrupted routine. For this reason, interrupt service routines need to have separate data areas.

Recursive Code

The third use for separate data areas occurs when a routine needs to call itself. This is a common tool for problem solving and is given the name *recursion*.

Calculating factorials is a good example of this technique. A sample recursive solution for calculating the value of a factorial appears in Listing 2-7. The solution is not very elegant and contains no overflow checks on the multiplication, but it suffices for values of *N* up to 7.

Listing 2-7. Recursive Solution for Calculating Factorials

```
factor  PROC    NEAR        ; find factorial N
        cmp     ax,2        ; reached end yet?
        jne     subfact     ; no, calculate (N - 1)!
        mov     ax,2        ; yes, start at the beginning
        ret
subfact:
        push    ax          ; save current value of N
        sub     ax,1        ; get N - 1
        call    factor      ; request (N - 1)!
        pop     bx          ; restore value of N
        mul     bx          ; N x (N [min] 1)! = N!
        ret
factor  ENDP
```

Reentrant Code—Local Storage Requirements

For all these cases, a routine's data must be preserved separately from its code in such a way that more than one procedure, each with its own data areas, may be executing the code at the same time. If this criterion is met, the routine is said to be *reentrant*. That is, the routine may be invoked (entered) by one program flow while another program flow is still executing it. We say *program flow* because we don't really care whether the routine is called by another program, by another routine, or even by itself (recursion).

In *factor*, the data to be preserved is saved on the stack by the calling routine. This is possible only in recursion because the programmer knows when control is given to the new routine and may anticipate the need to set up a new data area. For multiuser and interrupt handler applications, this is not sufficient, and the routines must have their data protected at all times. Control may be taken away at any time. In these cases, set up a local data area when the routine is first entered. This storage may be allocated in one of two ways: on the stack or in memory.

Local Storage on the Stack

A block of the stack may be reserved for local storage by decrementing the stack pointer. Then any interrupts or calls that occur continue to build on the stack, preserving any local data belonging to the routine that was interrupted. This is the easiest method but requires that all local variable access take place through the BP register. (See the preceding section entitled "Passing on the Stack" for a discussion of this.) Listing 2-8 contains an annotated example of this method.

Listing 2-8. Using the Stack for Local Storage

```
                    ; The Calling Procedure

        :           :
        push    <argument_3>    ; push third argument
        push    <argument_2>    ; push second argument
        push    <argument_1>    ; push first argument
        call    Example         ; call procedure
        add     sp,6            ; clear stack
        :           :


                    ; The Called Procedure

StackFrame      STRUC           ; define stack structure template
LocWord dw      ?               ; local word variable
LocChar db      14 dup (?)      ; local character array
LocIndx dw      ?               ; another local word variable
XamplBP dw      ?               ; saved BP
        dw      ?               ; return address (NEAR call)
Param1  dw      ?               ; 1st parameter (pushed last)
Param2  dw      ?               ; 2nd parameter
Param3  dw      ?               ; 3rd parameter (pushed first)
StackFrame      ENDS            ; end of template definition
;
base    EQU     [bp-offset XamplBP] ; aligns BP with template
;
Example PROC NEAR               ; start of procedure
        push    bp              ; save old base pointer
        mov     bp,sp           ; align StackFrame with stack
        sub     sp,offset XamplBP   ; reserve space on stack
        push    si              ; save any registers used
        push    di
        :       :               :
        mov     si,base.Param1 ; access to passed parameters
        mov     al,base.LocWord; access to local variables
        :       :               :
        pop     di              ; restore saved registers
        pop     si
        mov     sp,bp           ; discard local variables
        pop     bp              ; restore original BP
        ret                     ; return and DON'T clear
Example ENDP                    ; end of example procedure
```

Because the structure *StackFrame* is defined in the current segment, no segment overrides are necessary. If offsets from another segment are used, as in attempting to use a template from the data segment, you have to use the *SS: override* in the references. Failure to do so results in the MASM error message **Can't reach with segment reg**. If you ever see this message, an explicit segment overrides to define which segment you are accessing and see whether this solves the problem.

If local storage is allocated on the stack, that storage must be freed prior to returning from the routine. This may be accomplished by either adding the size of local storage to the stack (reversing the *sub sp,offset bp_* or restoring the SP from a saved value (*mov sp,bp*). It may not be freed by using the RET *N* because the current top of stack does not contain the return address!

In most high-level language compilers, the preferred method of storing local data is by using this "temporary" storage on the stack. Variables that are placed in this type of storage are sometimes referred to as *local, dynamic,* or *automatic* variables. Listing 2-8 contains the typical sequence of events that is expected to take place upon entry to a typical high-level language program. The procedure sets up a new stack frame (saving BP and setting BP to the current SP), allocates local storage (subtract from the SP), and saves any registers that it might destroy.

Figure 2-1 represents the arrangement of the stack as it would appear within the *Example* routine and shows how the *StackFrame* template is aligned with the stack. Note that it is our definition of *base* as "[BP−offset XamplBP]" that accomplishes the alignment. Since *XamplBP* is to align with the location of the saved BP on the stack, we chose the definition such that *base.XamplBP* is equal to [BP − offset XamplBP + offset XamplBP], which is the same as [BP+0]. The other important point is that the stack template structure must start with the declarations of those items that will be located in *lower* memory.

The ENTER and LEAVE Instructions for Local Stack Storage

In the more advanced members of the 8086 family, Intel has provided two new instructions to aid in using local storage on the stack. The iAPX186, iAPX188, and iAPX286 processors all support the ENTER and LEAVE instructions. *ENTER* is used to set up local storage on the stack when first entering a routine, and *LEAVE* deallocates this local storage when exiting the routine. In addition, ENTER and LEAVE has the capability of maintaining frame pointers, which are used in certain block structured high-level languages such as Pascal.

Because of the complexity of these instructions, we have presented their macro equivalents in Listing 2-9. This also allows 8086/8088 users to take advantage of these instructions in anticipation of an upward migration to one of the more advanced processors. Note that the *enter* and *leave* macros deviate from our unofficial standard of prefixing macros with an @ because they are intended to stand in for the ENTER and LEAVE instructions when using the 8088/8086.

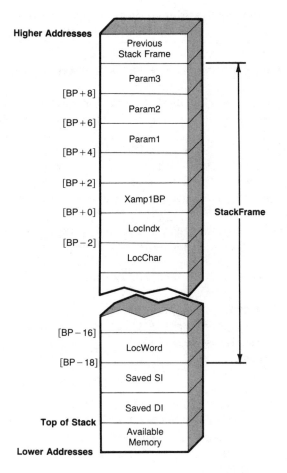

Figure 2-1. Local stack storage and parameter access.

The ENTER instruction performs three actions on the stack when the instruction is executed. It always pushes the value on the BP onto the stack. If the value of *level* is 1 or greater, the instruction copies the previous values of the BP onto the stack. If the value of *local* is 1 or greater, the instruction opens up space for local storage on the stack by subtracting *local* from the stack pointer. The BP is always set to the location of the old BP on the stack (the first PUSH).

The LEAVE instruction reverses the action of ENTER as long as the BP is left at, or reset to, the original value of the BP as set by ENTER.

The most confusing phase of this operation is that relating to the frame pointers. Figure 2-2 shows the state (and contents) of the stack for a series of operations that consisted of four successive ENTER instructions.

Listing 2-9. Macro Equivalents for the ENTER and LEAVE Instructions

```
;; MACRO DEFINITIONS FOR ENTER & LEAVE INSTRUCTIONS
;;
;; Base addressing definitions for use in accessing
;; elements in the stack frame created by ENTER.
;;
pbase equ      [BP + 4]          ;; access to parameters
lbase equ      [BP - ??tsize]    ;; access to locals
fbase equ      [BP - ??fsize]    ;; access to frame pointers
;; Form: ENTER     local <immediate 16>, level <immediate 8>
;;
;; ENTER--Create stack frame and allocate local storage
;; Copies stack frame pointers from previous routine into
;; a new stack frame for this routine and opens up space
;; on the stack for new local storage.
;;
enter  MACRO   local,level
       ??tsize = local + level * 2
       ??fsize = level * 2
       push    bp
       IF (level NE 0)
         IF (level GT 1)
           REPT level - 1
             sub        bp,2
             push       [bp]
           ENDM
         ENDIF
           mov bp,sp
         IF (level GT 1)
           add bp,(level - 1) * 2
         ENDIF
         push bp
       ELSE
         mov    bp,sp
       ENDIF
       sub        sp,local
       ENDM
;; Form: LEAVE
;;
;; LEAVE--Execute procedure return removing stack frame
;; and local storage set up by ENTER instruction.
;;
```

```
Leave   MACRO
        mov     sp,bp
        pop     bp
        ENDM
```

Each stack entry in Figure 2-2 symbolizes 2 bytes. (For this reason, all *local* parameters for ENTER are multiples of 2 bytes. This is not a restriction of the ENTER instruction.) The arrows in the figure symbolize that an entry points to another entry (contains the address of that entry).

The first ENTER (level one) sets up a single frame pointer, pointing to its own frame, and opens up space on the stack for 4 bytes of storage. The second ENTER (level two) not only creates its own frame pointer (FP #2) but copies the frame pointer from the previous frame (FP #1). The second ENTER creates only 2 bytes of local storage. The last ENTER (level three) carries the operation one step further, copying the frame pointers of the previous two levels (FP #1 and FP #2).

Why does the example sequence start with a level one ENTER rather than a level zero ENTER? A level zero ENTER simply pushes the BP onto the stack and subtracts the value of *local* from the stack pointer, setting the BP to point to the value of the BP just pushed. No frame pointers are copied. A level zero ENTER is thus ideal for creating local storage on the stack. When used in conjunction with the STRUC directive, ENTER can almost automatically create local stack storage that is easy to access. Listing 2-10 demonstrates further.

This program fragment defines, allocates, and uses local storage from the stack. ENTER is instructed to reserve the proper amount of space through the MASM SIZE operator. The percent mark (%) is required only with the macro implementation of ENTER. When using the machine code version (supported by MASM 2.0 and higher by specifying the .286C switch), the % should be omitted.

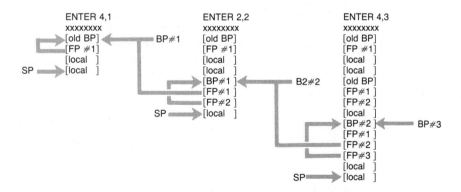

Figure 2-2. Effects of ENTER on the stack.

Listing 2-10. Creating and Referencing Local Stack Storage with ENTER

```
?data_1        STRUC
my_var dw      ?
?data_1        ENDS
test   PROC    NEAR
       ENTER   %(size ?data_1),0   ; allocate localstorage
       mov     lbase.my_var,10     ; store a value in local
```

The symbol *lbase* is defined in Listing 2-9 as the base address for all local variable accesses. The actual reference created in the MOV instruction is

```
mov    [BP - ??tsize].my_var,10
```

The symbol *??tsize* is set by the macro implementation of ENTER to the number of bytes added to the stack by the ENTER instruction, not including the BP. This symbol is calculated as *local* + *level* ∗ *2*. When *??tsize* is subtracted from the contents of the BP, the result is the address of the top of the stack. All structure references are thus positive offsets from *lbase*. Even if you use the machine code version of ENTER, you can easily write a macro that calculates *??tsize* and creates the ENTER instruction so that this technique can be used on the 186/188/286 processors as well.

Another symbol defined in Listing 2-9 is *pbase*, the base address for all access to variables passed on the stack. The value of *pbase* is [BP+4] to cover the 2 bytes pushed on the stack as part of a *near* CALL instruction and the 2 bytes required for the BP pushed on the stack by the ENTER instruction. Once a structure has been defined for the stack parameters, *pbase* can be used with their field names for symbolic access as in *pbase.my_param*.

Having described the simpler uses of ENTER, we return to the question of the frame pointers. What are they for? Each frame pointer points to the beginning of the previous routines' stack frames. By loading the BP with the contents of one of the frame pointers located in the current frame, access can be gained to the previous level's local variables. This is primarily designed for implementing high-level languages, such as Pascal, where a routine has automatic access to the parent routine's variables. Unless you are very serious about high-level structured programming in assembly languages, you probably pass by using the frame pointer capabilities of ENTER. If you decide to try using ENTER with frame pointer anyway, a little experimentation should give you a feel for the operation.

Code Positioning Summary

Note that reentrant routines are not necessarily relocatable, nor are relocatable routines necessarily reentrant. *Relocation* applies to the ability to position the program in memory. *Reentrant* applies to a routine having secure local data storage. *Recursive* routines are a type of reentrant routine with the relaxed restriction that the programmer knows at what point data must be preserved in preparation for the next call.

In addition, when writing reentrant routines, don't forget that the routines' parameters must be reentrant also. Data must be passed to the called routine in an area that either is protected (such as the stack) or is always saved when a new procedure or task takes control (for instance, all interrupt service routines save all registers when invoked).

You also should remember that there are two types of relocatable code. The first type is MS-DOS relocatable where MS-DOS, using the relocation map, alters the values of segment variables in order to relocate the program. The second type is self-relocatable, which simply means that no relocation map is required. Only programs that use only displacement addressing in CALLs and JMPs may be self-relocatable.

Interfacing to High-Level Languages

The most common use of assembly language today is as an adjunct to a high-level language. During development a program will typically be coded using a high-level language, with only a few modules being written in assembly language. Assembly language is used where either speed or code size is a critical concern, or because the high-level language does not support access to certain features or hardware.

There are three main areas of concern when interfacing an assembly language module to a high-level language program. These are: reconciling names between the two modules, handling any special setups that the language and compiler may require, and adjusting the assembly language module to the proper calling sequence and parameter passing techniques used by the particular high-level language compiler.

In the past there were few rules governing the naming conventions and calling sequences for high-level languages. Today the situation is much improved, with many compilers following standards laid down by the American National Standards Institute (ANSI). Because the high-level language compilers offered by Microsoft are widely used and because they adhere to the ANSI standard, we have chosen Microsoft's BASIC, C, FORTRAN, and Pascal compilers to illustrate common calling conventions.

The Microsoft C Calling Conventions

The calling conventions illustrated in Listing 2-8 represent a typical C program. Were the *Example* program translated into C, its opening statements would appear something like this:

```
void Example (Param1, Param2, Param3)
    int Param1, Param2, Param3 ;
    {
    int  LocIndx ;
    char LocChar [14] ;
    int  LocWord ;
     :    :
```

In the C language all subroutines are also functions; any routine can return a value to its caller. Because our function does not return a value, we have declared it as function type *void*.

C makes use of *automatic* variables for the storage of local data. Note, however, that there is no standard that dictates the order to be assigned to local variables as they are placed on the stack.

Listing 2-8, Figure 2-1, and the preceding code fragment all show how the C language pushes its arguments in the *reverse* order that they are declared. The purpose of this method is so that if a variable number of parameters are to be passed, the called routine can always find the leftmost parameters at a fixed position on the stack. *Param1* will always be located at [BP+4], regardless of how many parameters were actually passed. C programs that make use of this feature usually use the leftmost, or first, parameter to pass the total number of parameters passed to the called routine. In this manner the called routine can determine how many additional parameters it needs to read.

Another feature to note in the C language is that parameters are almost always passed by *value*. If we call *Example* with the variable *Foo*, the contents of *Foo* are placed on the stack. The called routine thus manipulates a copy of the variable passed, rather than the variable itself. The exception to this method is that arrays are typically passed by address. (In the C standard, an array's identifier is its address, so this apparent exception is actually consistent with C syntax.) However, C also allows the programmer to pass the address of any variable, if desired.

The Microsoft C compiler supports one of the richest programming environments, allowing the experienced programmer complete control over the memory module to be used. Our example represents the default C environment, composed of *near* program calls and *near* references to data.

In spite of all of the effort just presented, we would still be unable to substitute our assembly language version of *Example* for the C language routine. The obstacle to be surmounted lies in reconciling the names used between the calling C routine and the called assembly language routine. The problem is that the C compiler prefixes all names with an underscore (_). When the compiler generates a call to *Example*, it is really expecting that the destination routine's name is *_Example*. Possibly this nomenclature is designed to prevent collisions between the compiler's name space and the assembler's name space. If both the calling and called routines are in the C language, then the compiler translates both references, and there isn't any trouble. When one of the references is in assembly language, we must perform the translation ourselves. This translation applies to names given to global data variables as well as program labels.

Two items to note are that the C language limits names to 8 characters and that in C all names are case sensitive. In C, *Example* and *example* are two separate names. The assembly language routine should be assembled with the */mx* switch, to preserve the case of any names used.

The final requirement for a C program to be able to call an assembly language routine is that the function be declared *public* in the assembly language routine and *extern* in the C routine. Table 2-1 summarizes the calling conventions for Microsoft C.

Table 2-1. Microsoft C Calling Conventions

Convention	Description
Code references	*Near* or *far*
Data references	*Near* or *far*
Stack cleared by	Caller
Parameters passed in	Reverse order
Parameters passed by	Value
Values returned in	AX or DX:AX
Name length:	8 characters
All names are:	Preceded by an underscore (_)

The Microsoft Pascal Calling Conventions

Where Listing 2-8 approximates the C calling syntax, the calling conventions for Microsoft's Pascal compiler are best expressed by the example shown in Listing 2-4. The Pascal equivalent of *myprog* could be coded somewhat like this:

```
procedure MyProc ( Param1, Param2, Param3 : integer ) ;
begin
   :
```

The major difference between the C and the Pascal languages is that Pascal performs much more stringent checks. These checks ensure that the proper number and types of parameters are passed in calls, that function values are used in a manner appropriate to their type, and so forth. Thus, unlike C, in Pascal a routine must be declared either a procedure (a subroutine that returns no values) or a function.

Pascal also makes use of automatic variables for the storage of local data. As with C, there is no standard to dictate the assigned order of the local variables in the stack. Also, as with C, space for local variables is allocated on the top of the stack upon entry to the called routine. If the *MyProg* procedure used the local variables *LocIndx*, *LocChar*, and *LocWord*, they would be referenced as shown in the *StackFrame* structure of Listing 2-8. The Pascal equivalent code would be something like:

```
procedure MyProc ( Param1, Param2, Param3 : integer ) ;
var
    LocIndx, LocWord: integer ;
    LocChar[1..14] : character ;
begin
    :
```

From Listing 2-4 we can see that unlike C, Pascal pushes its arguments in the order that they are declared, left to right. The reason that this method is possible is that the Pascal compiler ensures that all calls to a given routine provide the proper number and type of arguments. Pascal simply does not allow a variable number of parameters to be passed, so the passing order used in C is not required in Pascal.

A consequence of the strict call checks performed by Pascal is that the called routine *always* receives the same number of arguments, allowing the called routine to use the RET *N* instruction to clear the stack, rather than depending on the caller.

In another similarity to C, the Pascal language usually passes its variables by *value* but also allows variables to be passed by address if desired, using the *var* declaration.

In a departure from C, the Microsoft Pascal compiler uses the LARGE memory module, expecting *far* calls and *far* memory references. Also unlike C, Pascal recognizes names in any case, although the assembly language function must still be declared *public* and the Pascal reference must be declared *extern*. Table 2-2 summarizes the calling conventions for Microsoft Pascal.

Table 2-2. Microsoft Pascal Calling Conventions

Convention	Description
Code references	*Far*
Data references	*Far*
Stack cleared by	Called (RET *n*)
Parameters passed in	Declared order
Parameters passed by	Value
Values returned in	AX or DX:AX
Name length	8 characters
All names are	Case-insensitive

The Microsoft BASIC and FORTRAN Calling Conventions

The standards followed by Microsoft's BASIC and FORTRAN compilers closely resemble those of Microsoft Pascal. Table 2-3 shows just how much similarity there is in the calling standards. However, in a major digression from the C and Pascal conventions, both BASIC and FORTRAN pass their arguments by *reference*. Because these languages pass the address of a variable, any manipulation of a variable that is performed by the called routine also alters the value of the variable in the caller routine.

In fact, the similarities between all four interfaces mean that it is just as easy to write assembly language routines for BASIC or FORTRAN as it is for Pascal, or even C for that matter. However, more effort is required within the BASIC or FORTRAN program to set up the proper interface.

The BASIC equivalent of the *extern* statement is DECLARE, while FORTRAN requires the INTERFACE statement. Each of these statements informs its respective compiler that the associated routine name is to be found outside the current module. Additional parameters may be needed to inform the compiler how to format and generate the proper call.

Table 2-3. Microsoft Calling Conventions for BASIC and FORTRAN

Convention	BASIC	FORTRAN
Code references	*Far*	*Far*
Data references	*Far*	*Near* or *far*
Stack cleared by	Called (RET *n*)	Called (RET *n*)
Parameters passed in	Declared order	Declared order
Parameters passed by	*Far* address	*Near/far* address
Values returned in	AX or DX:AX	AX or DX:AX
Name length	40 characters	6 characters
All names are	Uppercase	Case-insensitive

The Microsoft Segment Model

Microsoft's MASM version 5.0 allows the programmer to quickly specify the proper segment names and setup for a given language with the MODEL directive. Even without version 5, setting up the proper assembly language template is relatively easy. All four languages use the same primary segment names. The code segment is _TEXT, and the data segment is _DATA. Additional segments may be required for particular interfaces, and many Microsoft compiler models also require that the stack be placed in the data segment. However, a simple assembly language routine need not worry about such issues because it can operate off of the caller's stack, and the high-level language main routine will handle all necessary setup.

Allocation and Use of Local Storage in Memory

There is a third method of allocating storage for variables. We have seen storage in global memory and storage on the stack. Now we will see storage in allocated memory. Allocated memory must come from the unused memory of the system (often called the *memory pool*). MS-DOS supplies functions that may be used to allocate, deallocate, and size memory-system blocks. Once memory has been allocated, the programmer can implement a personal memory management scheme to manage the memory in smaller units. For now, however, we will concentrate on MS-DOS's features, beginning with function 48h, Allocate Memory.

Once the block of memory has been obtained, the program must be able to address it. Memory that has been allocated through MS-DOS comes in 16-byte chunks called *paragraphs*. MS-DOS returns a pointer to this memory that contains the high 16 bits of the block's memory address. Segments are also addressed as paragraphs, so the pointer should be loaded into one of the segment registers (but not the CS register!). Usually either the data segment or the extra segment is used to gain access to the block of memory. If the routine that allocated the memory is not the main routine of the program, the old segment register value must be saved and restored before the routine exits. In addition, the memory that was allocated should be returned to the system before the routine exits. MS-DOS function 49h, Free Allocated Memory, is used to return an allocated memory block to the system. Listing 2-11 shows how a routine from an .EXE type program would allocate, use, and free memory for use as local storage.

Listing 2-11. Allocating Local Storage through MS-DOS

```
              common    SEGMENT            ; common data used by all
              com_1   dw      ?
              com_2   db      14 DUP (?)
              common    ENDS
              dummy_dat   STRUC            ; structure definition ...
              dummy_1 dw      ?            ; ... used with the ...
              dummy_2 db      14 DUP (?)   ; ... allocated memory
              dummy_dat ENDS
                        ASSUME  ds:common  ; access to COMMON data
              local_example   PROC    NEAR; example procedure
              push    ds                   ; save previous DS
B8 ---- R     mov     ax,common            ; COMMON is MS-DOS relocatable
              mov     ds,ax
              push    es         ; save previous ES
              mov     ah,048h    ; allocate memory
              mov     bx,1       ; request 1 block (16 bytes)
              int     21h        ; call MS-DOS
              jc      not_alloc  ; carry means allocate failed
              mov     es,ax      ; if allocated, address it
              ;
              ; Three examples of addressing
              ;
A1 0000 R     mov     ax,com_1             ; proper seg.--DS assumed
B8 0000       mov     ax,dummy_1           ; wrong seg.--immediate
26: A1 0000   mov     ax,es:dummy_1        ; proper seg.--overridden
              ;
              mov     ah,049h              ; free allocated memory
              int     21h                  ; call MS-DOS
              jnc     free_ok              ; no carry means worked
              not_alloc:
```

```
; Error messages, if failed, allocate or deallocate
free_ok:
pop      es                    ; restore ES
pop      ds                    ; restore DS
ret
local_example    ENDP         ; end of example
```

Listing 2-11 contains both the Allocate Memory and Free Allocated Memory MS-DOS function calls. Instead of using the DS register to point to the newly allocated memory, we have used the ES register, reserving the DS for access to an area of common program variables. Note that unlike the stack example, accesses using the structure defined here do require the segment override operator (:). Without a segment override, *mov ax,dummy_1* does not generate a memory reference involving the ES but instead generates an immediate load of the offset (zero here) into register AX. When the segment override is added to the instruction, *mov ax,es:dummy_1*, MASM generates a memory transfer from offset *dummy_1* in the extra segment. The segment override is shown in Listing 2-11 with the prefix byte *26:*.

When using multiple data segments in a program, the programmer's responsibility is to manage the data areas in use. For example, if routine *X* allocates local storage and updates the DS register to access this area, the programmer must remember that this data area is now the default data area for all routines called by *X*. Common data areas that have been defined in the program are still accessible by loading either the DS or ES registers from a segment variable as shown in Listing 2-6. Those routines that modify their segment registers must save and restore the original segment registers to prevent their parent routines from being confused.

Whenever more than one data or extra segment is used by a program, the programmer must pay careful attention to the ASSUME directives used in the program. In assembling a typical memory reference, MASM first searches its internal symbol table for the name of the variable being accessed. If MASM finds the variable in the symbol table, MASM tries to create the reference using the segment in which the variable was defined. If that segment isn't present (through an ASSUME), MASM generates the error message ***Can't reach with segment reg***.

If MASM can't find the variable in the symbol table, MASM assumes that it's in the data segment. If this turns out to be wrong, MASM attempts to fix the error during pass two by attaching a segment override prefix to the instruction. Unfortunately, inserting this byte causes another error message, ***Phase error between passes***.

In case of confusion or of a forward reference where the variable name is not yet in the symbol table, the programmer must use the segment override operator (:) to more clearly define to MASM which segment is to be used. The SEG operator is also useful for controlling accesses in a routine. This operator allows the programmer to obtain the segment value (base address of the segment) for any defined variable. The references that SEG creates are MS-DOS relocatable and are useful for creating relocatable references in place of absolute ones.

Introduction to MS-DOS Memory Management

Our example in Listing 2-11 depends on there being free memory available within the system. Unfortunately, the default MS-DOS process allocates all memory for itself when it is loaded. The Allocate Memory call will fail because the process already has all the memory, even though it doesn't know it. If a program wants to use the Allocate Memory function, some of the memory that it received during the load must be returned to the system. Typically a process will wish to return all memory that is not occupied by the program's code, data, or buffers.

The function that MS-DOS provides to allow a process to return *part* of its allocated memory to the system is function 4Ah, Modify Allocated Memory Block. This allows the process to trim memory from its default allocation block.

Note that there are methods to prevent a process from allocating all memory when it is loaded, but their presentation is delayed until Chapter 3, where the topics of program loading and MS-DOS program files are covered in more detail.

The parameters required for the Modify Allocated Memory Block function are the segment address of the block to be modified and the new size of the block. The segment address of the block that contains the program (whose size we wish to modify) is given by the PSP (program segment prefix). The PSP is a section of memory that begins every program in the MS-DOS environment. The details of the PSP's contents are described in Chapter 3. For now, our only concern is that the segment address of the PSP is the segment address of the block to be modified, and we need that address.

Just how we go about determining these parameters is different for .COM type files and .EXE type files. Figure 2-3 shows the arrangement of memory for both .COM and .EXE files. The PSP is the first entry for each type. In the .COM type program, the PSP is contained in the first 256 bytes of the program segment, and the program's segment address (in all segment registers) is the segment address of the PSP.

For .EXE files, the PSP resides in its own segment. However, whenever an .EXE program is loaded and receives control from MS-DOS, both the DS and ES registers contain the segment address of the PSP. So for either type of program, the PSP address may be obtained from at least the DS and ES registers. In addition, users of MS-DOS version 3.0 (or higher) may use the Get Program Segment Prefix Address, function 62h, to determine the PSP address. MS-DOS returns the value in the BX register.

Because the Modify Allocated Memory Block function expects the block address in the ES register, the function may be called immediately upon the program starting execution, since the ES already has the PSP address.

Once the memory block address is found, we must determine the amount of memory to be saved. The difference between .COM programs and .EXE programs becomes much more marked here. For .EXE programs the size can be determined by subtracting the starting segment address of the PSP from the segment address of a dummy segment located at the end of the program, as

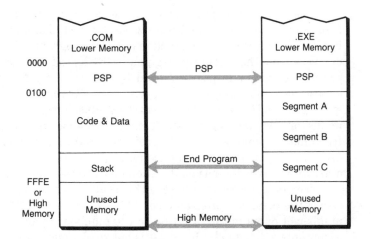

**Figure 2-3. MS-DOS program memory map and the program
segment prefix.**

shown in Listing 2-12. Why are segment addresses used? Function 4Ah expects
the size in paragraphs, and segment addresses are actually paragraph addresses.

**Listing 2-12. Function 4Ah, Modify Allocated Memory
Block—RESIZE for .EXE Programs**

```
resize PROC NEAR
        mov     ax,es               ; get PSP address
        mov     bx,SEG end_addr     ; get next segment address
        sub     bx,ax               ; difference is prog size
        mov     ah,04Ah             ; modify allocated memory
        int     21h                 ; ... MS-DOS call
        jnc     short resize_ok     ; no carry => resized okay
        mov     ax,04C00h           ; carry => failed--abort
        int     21h
resize_ok:
        ret
resize ENDP
;
; The remainder of the code goes here with END_ADDR as the last
; entry in the program file before the END statement. Take care
; to ensure that END_ADDR is linked as the last segment if more
; than one source file is used.
;
end_addr SEGMENT
end_addr ENDS
        END
```

For .COM type programs, a little forethought is required. Unlike .EXE programs, which have a definite size set by the linker, .COM programs can vary in size. The location of the stack in a .COM program, which is set by MS-DOS, can vary from the end of the segment (FFFE) to 256 bytes longer than the program (the minimum size required by MS-DOS for the stack). The user can choose between, one, accepting what MS-DOS has provided and resizing the stack provided by MS-DOS (set size 64K [1000 hex paragraphs]) or whatever remains; or, two, moving the stack and resizing based on that. The second choice frees more memory and so is preferred and recommended by Microsoft and IBM. Listing 2-13 contains an example of a .COM program that sets up its own stack and resizes its initial allocation block to the more moderate size.

The only interesting part of this routine is the way that it determines the size of the resultant program. The MASM operator SHR is used to convert the number of bytes in the program to the number of paragraphs through what is essentially a division by 16. What is not so obvious is why *seg_org* is subtracted from the offset of *last_byte*. The SHR operator doesn't work when applied to an offset, and it produces the error message ***Constant was expected***. However, the difference between two offsets is considered a constant, making the expression palatable to MASM. Note that *seg_org* must have an offset of zero so that the size is relative to the beginning of the segment. Were *start* used instead, the last 100 hex bytes of the program would be lost. (Note that *last_byte:* works just as well as *last_byte equ $* for calculations.)

In addition to being useful for freeing memory, the trick of subtracting two offsets (either Label or Number) to get a constant can be useful for all types of operations where sizes are required in expressions that demand constants. We'll see this applied to the task of aligning a data buffer on a paragraph boundary in Chapter 6.

Memory Allocation from within High-Level Languages

Most high-level languages handle the problems associated with allocating or resizing memory blocks. You will not need to add code to resize the initial allocation block in order to make use of a language's memory management functions. The *malloc* and *calloc* functions in the C library, for example, will work regardless of a process's initial memory allocation.

Protecting Data and Controlling the Scope of Data

The techniques used in reentrant coding lead us into another aspect of modular programming: protecting the data in the program from accidental alteration. Destruction of important data most often occurs when one part of the program mistakenly alters the data that belongs to another part of the program. The possibility of this happening can be reduced by following some basic rules. The foremost rule is to modularize the program data as well as the code, that is, control the range of data that a routine may access. This is often called the *scope of the data*. Let's review what we have just learned and see how it may be applied to our new problem.

**Listing 2-13. Function 4Ah, Modify Allocated Memory
Block—RESIZE for .COM Programs**

```
code_seg  SEGMENT
          ASSUME   cs:code_seg
          ORG      0000h
seg_org   EQU      $
          ORG      0100h
main      PROC     FAR
start:
          mov      sp,offset stack
          call     resize
;
; The remainder of the program can go here.
;
main      ENDP
resize    PROC     NEAR
          mov      bx,(offset last_byte - seg_org + 15) shr 4
          mov      ah,04Ah               ; modify allocated memory
          int      21h                   ; ... MS-DOS call
          jnc      short resize_ok       ; no carry => resized okay
          mov      ax,04C00h             ; carry => failed--abort
          int      21h
resize_ok:
          ret
resize    ENDP
          db       32 DUP ('stack    ')
stack:
last_byte EQU      $
code_seg  ENDS
          END      start
```

Local Storage versus Global Storage

The human mind can deal with only a limited number of concepts at any given time. The implication of this for programmers is that as the number of elements to be manipulated and remembered grows, so does the number of errors. By using local storage for subroutines, the programmer reduces the number of data elements that must be remembered. Rather than dealing with data areas containing hundreds of variables, the programmer can now deal with a data area that contains only a handful of variables. Many small data areas may exist, each one may be verified with the routine that uses it because each is secure in the knowledge that no other routine interferes with it. Either of the methods presented for reentrant routines serves for the allocation of temporary local data storage.

Global storage areas, also known as common areas, may be modularized. In this case, a number of smaller data areas are created in place of a monolithic one. Routines then can access only those portions of global data that they require. This necessitates careful attention on the part of the programmer to ASSUME directives in the contents of the segment registers, but such explicit handling of common data also makes clearer what is accessing and thus altering critical data. For example, a common data area containing text strings and character constants need not be part of a numerical calculation routine, just as a table of sine and cosine values is not needed by a terminal input routine.

Parameters should be passed on the stack as much as possible, reducing the number of interroutine data accesses. Whenever multiple routines must access common data areas for parameter passing purposes, the likelihood of a mistake increases.

Common data usually should be defined with DEFINE DATA directives so that the contents of the area are static and not subject to accidental deletion if a routine makes a mistake with Free Allocated Memory.

Using Segment Registers

The segment registers allow the programmer to restrict the range of possible data references. By changing the base of the segment that contains the data, the architecture of the machine automatically constrains the program to a 64K access window. If more sensitive data is located in the lower areas of memory, then as the segment register is changed to point to a higher addressed block of memory, the data in the lower area is totally protected against any unauthorized access.

Controlling the Size of Data Access

The programmer may further constrain this window on the data by setting up *bounds-checking* on array accesses. One of the most typical data errors occurs when an array access runs across its boundaries. Whatever data happens to border on the array is lost. Bounds-checking may be accomplished by a simple macro as shown in Listing 2-14. For those programmers who are working with an 80x86 processor, the BOUND instruction has been provided to accomplish this checking. The *bound* macro shown in Listing 2-14 has been written for compatibility with the BOUND instruction.

Listing 2-14. Checking Array Bounds with Macros

```
;; BOUND-Check the contents of the general register REG
;; against the two consecutive values located in memory at
;; address MEM32. This is a signed integer compare.
bound   MACRO   reg,mem32
        LOCAL   out_bound,in_bound
        pushf                               ; save flags
        cmp     reg,word ptr mem32          ; check lower limit
        jl      out_bound                   ; index underflow
```

```
        cmp     reg,word ptr mem32 + 2  ; check upper limit
        jle     in_bound                ; index is okay
out_bound:
        popf                            ; clean up stack
        INT     5                       ; ACTION TO BE TAKEN
in_bound:
        popf                            ; restore flags
        ENDM
```

The *bound* macro compares the contents of a general register containing the array index against two successive memory locations. The first memory location is assumed to contain the lower limit of the index, and the second memory location is assumed to contain the upper limit of the index. The BOUND instruction executes an interrupt type 5 (int 5) if the index tested is out of bounds. Macro version users may modify *bound* to take whatever action they desire.

Protecting the Integrity of the Stack

The other area that is susceptible to destruction is the stack. Because the stack mixes code and data, an error here undoubtedly will result in total failure of the program as the processor attempts to use data as an instruction reference.

The two most common ways to destroy the stack involve problems of faulty alignment. One way is caused by mismatching PUSH and POP operations, and the other is through attempting to POP data that was PUSHed on the other side of a CALL or RET. These problems may be avoided only by paying close attention to pairing the PUSHes and POPs used in a program and making sure that such pairings do not cross routine boundaries. When reading source code, remember that macros often contain PUSH and POP instructions that must be taken into account.

In the case of parameter passing, the question of which routine clears the stack arises. Normally the rule for such occasions is that the routine that pushed the data gets to pop the data from the stack. If this rule is followed, the programmer can verify that the stack is aligned by reading one routine's listing rather than two. However, rigidly following this rule prevents use of the 8086's RET *N* instruction. If the interface between two routines is fully debugged and dependable, an acceptable risk is to use the RET *N* instruction.

Whenever a routine must be coded to accept a variable number of parameters, the RET *N* instruction should not be used. There are various ways to get around the limitation of being able to clear the stack only of a set number of variables, but all of them involve tricky manipulations of the stack that are difficult to understand and even more difficult to debug. If a routine must take a variable number of parameters, the calling routine should clear those parameters from the stack. In addition, the calling routine must clearly indicate to the called routine the number of parameters that have been passed to it.

All operations performed on the stack, except PUSH and POP, should take place under the umbrella of the stack pointer and use the BP register to access the stack. What this means is that the stack pointer should be set to a value below the elements being manipulated. Should an interrupt take place, the data being manipulated remains untouched. For the same reason, the stack pointer should not be directly manipulated unless switching stacks or opening storage on the stack. If an interrupt takes place at a time when the stack pointer is not pointing at the true top of stack, data on the stack could be lost. What this all adds up to is a warning not to use clever manipulations of the stack.

Summary

In this chapter, we have covered a variety of topics ranging from the theoretical nature of structured programming to the details of MASM, MS-DOS, and 8086 family processor operation. We have tried to give you some alternative approaches for your structured programming needs. Although it is most unlikely that all or even most of these techniques will appear in your small assembly language programs, we think that many of them will find uses in your larger projects. And if only one point is remembered, let it be this: think first, code later.

Most of the more practical points about MASM and MS-DOS resurface in subsequent chapters. Try out the examples in our sample programs and get comfortable with their use. You'll need many of them. Most particularly, our introduction to MS-DOS memory management forms the stepping stone for Chapter 3, "Program and Memory Management."

Program and Memory Management

3

I N the previous chapters we explored the tools for creating DOS programs and the various ways in which DOS programs can be internally structured. Now we will examine how MS-DOS programs exist within the MS-DOS environment. In the course of this examination, we will backtrack to more fully explain some of the topics hinted at in the previous chapters: the program segment prefix, the working of MS-DOS's memory allocation, and the mechanism used to load MS-DOS programs. Lastly, we will introduce the mechanism for installing memory resident programs, a topic that is followed up in Chapter 4, which discusses terminate and stay resident programs (TSRs).

MS-DOS Memory

The easiest way to understand the MS-DOS operating environment is to examine the MS-DOS *memory map*, the pattern used by MS-DOS to allocate its limited memory to all of its competing purposes. Although generic MS-DOS does not dictate a particular memory map, the immense popularity of the IBM standard, and its consequent adoption, provides us with a *de facto* memory map.

MS-DOS Physical Memory Map

MS-DOS was developed on the 8086/8088 central processing unit (CPU), which can address a total of 1 megabyte of memory. The typical uses and locations of this memory are shown in Figure 3-1. The first ten *segments* (64-Kbyte "chunks") of this memory are referred to as the *user area*. This 640-Kbyte area is where MS/PC-DOS itself and the user's application programs reside. The remaining six segments, which total 384 Kbytes, are called the *system area*, and are reserved for use by the ROM-BIOS, for the various device drivers contained within the BIOS, and for communication with other boards in the system. Note that Figure 3-1 simplifies the uses of the system area considerably. Actually, there are many types of boards that use this area for many purposes, but we are concerned only with the general layout.

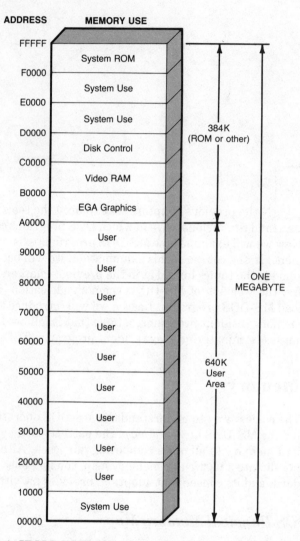

Figure 3-1. IBM PC/XT/AT standard memory map for MS-DOS.

Expanded and Extended Memory

Since the introduction of MS-DOS, more powerful central processing units have been developed. The 80286 and 80386 have each expanded the limits of addressable memory, allowing megabytes of memory to be placed in a single system. What use, if any, does MS-DOS make of this additional memory? None directly, but in many cases this additional *extended memory* (because it "extends" above the 1-megabyte boundary) can often be used as a RAM disk or, more commonly, as another type of additional MS-DOS memory, called *expanded memory* (because it "expands" on the basic 640-kilobyte limit of MS-DOS).

For MS-DOS versions 3.3 and earlier, expanded memory products are available in three varieties. The first Expanded Memory Specification was developed jointly by Lotus, Intel, and Microsoft, and is called LIM EMS version 3.2. Soon afterward, Ashton-Tate, Quadram, and AST developed an improved standard, AQA EEMS (the Enhanced Expanded Memory Specification). Lotus, Intel, and Microsoft incorporated the AQA EEMS improvements in LIM EMS version 4.0. All EMS systems consist of memory (on the motherboard or on an expansion card) and the Enhanced Memory Manager (EMM), an installable device driver. MS-DOS interrupt 67h is reserved for the set of EMS functions. MS-DOS versions 4.0 and above, as part of the operating system, support the LIM EMS 4.0 standard. Hardware implementations vary between manufacturers. The MS-DOS 4.0 EMS software consists of an installable device driver, and, in fact, any EMS device driver and compatible hardware combination can be substituted for those supplied with the operating system.

Expanded memory results from the introduction to the MS-DOS world of the established tradition of using *paged* or *bank-switched* memory. In this process a large section of memory that lies outside the processor's address space is "mapped" in small pieces into a much smaller section of memory that lies within the processor's address space. While the processor cannot address the entire large section of memory directly, it can select and reach any individual part, much like selecting a page in a book.

Under the MS-DOS *Expanded Memory Specification*, or EMS, the larger physical memory is mapped into the MS-DOS memory space in 16-Kbyte sections, called *pages*. The corresponding 16-Kbyte address space in the MS-DOS memory space is called a *page frame*. The number of page frames supported, and the locations of the page frames within the MS-DOS system, vary with the type of expanded memory board used and the existing configuration of the system.

Chapter 7 is dedicated to the topic of EMS memory, describing methods of access, the EMS standard, and much more. For the purpose of our discussion, we acknowledge the existence of EMS memory, but it does not greatly affect us. We are concerned with how MS-DOS itself uses memory, and for us it is sufficient to note that EMS memory must be mapped into the standard memory address space in order to be accessible by MS-DOS. (There is speculation that future versions of MS-DOS may utilize EMS memory directly, effectively breaking through the 640-Kbyte boundary.)

MS-DOS Memory Utilization

By this time we have established that under the current *de facto* standard, MS-DOS has 640 kilobytes of memory to utilize for itself and the user's application programs. In a typical MS-DOS system, this memory will be allocated as shown in Figure 3-2. You should note that most of the addresses given in Figure 3-2 are only approximate and depend on the version of MS-DOS, the physical configuration of the system, and the options specified by the user in the CONFIG.SYS and AUTOEXEC.BAT files. In addition, the sizes of the segments given in

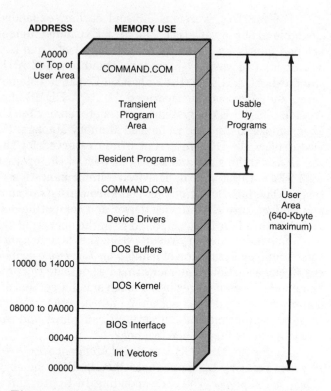

ADDRESS | MEMORY USE

A0000 or Top of User Area

COMMAND.COM

Transient Program Area

Resident Programs

COMMAND.COM

Device Drivers

DOS Buffers

10000 to 14000

DOS Kernel

08000 to 0A000

BIOS Interface

00040

Int Vectors

00000

Usable by Programs

User Area (640-Kbyte maximum)

Figure 3-2. MS/PC-DOS user memory utilization.

Figure 3-2 are not to scale but are provided to give the relative position of the various components.

Within Figure 3-2 there are a few areas that require further explanation. First, note that COMMAND.COM appears twice in the memory map. Are there two copies of COMMAND.COM loaded? No, it is rather that COMMAND.COM is loaded in two separate pieces. The piece located just above the device drivers is kept permanent in memory and is called the *resident* portion. This portion is responsible for handling program termination and any user program errors that result in program termination. This section is the *parent program* of any user programs that are run. The other section of COMMAND.COM, located at the top of memory, is the piece that provides the user's interface to DOS. This piece is called the *transient* portion because it is present only when there are no user programs running or when the user program is attempting to load another program. The transient portion processes MS-DOS's *internal commands* (DIR, COPY, SET, etc.) and contains the program loader. It is used to load programs either from the COMMAND.COM prompt (in response to *external commands*) or upon request by the user program. Later in this chapter you will see how one program can make use of this feature to load other programs or program overlays.

The section of Figure 3-2 labeled "Resident Programs" refers to *terminate and stay resident* programs, such as Borland's Sidekick. The memory location shown in the figure applies to TSRs that are loaded from the AUTOEXEC.BAT file, or directly upon system initialization. Chapter 4 covers TSR programs in greater depth.

The "Device Drivers" section refers to *installable* device drivers, those that are specified by the DEVICE= command in the CONFIG.SYS file. Installable device drivers are the topic of Chapter 6. The default device drivers supplied with the system are located in the section labeled "BIOS Interface," where they are used during the process of loading or "bootstrapping" the MS-DOS system.

The "DOS Kernel" is the section of MS-DOS that processes the various MS-DOS functions, such as the int 21h functions. It provides the bridge between the user's program or COMMAND.COM and the various device drivers and hardware.

The "int Vectors" section contains the system's 256 interrupt vectors.

The remaining area is the one that we are really interested in—the "Transient Program Area," or TPA. (The name TPA dates back to the days of CP/M, the progenitor of MS-DOS.) It is within the TPA that the user's program is located and where the remainder of our attention will be focused.

In some ways Figure 3-2 is misleading. Not all of the elements shown in the figure have their own memory block, and there are a number of elements that are not shown that have their own discrete memory blocks. We will start by examining the TPA in more detail, beginning with the method that MS-DOS uses to organize its sections.

MS-DOS Memory Chains

MS-DOS's memory control begins when DOS is loaded. All MS-DOS memory blocks, either free or allocated, begin with a *memory control block*, or MCB. These control blocks, shown in Figure 3-3, identify the type and size of the memory block, and the program (or *process*) that owns it.

The two types of memory control blocks are *chained blocks*, whose type is 4D hex, and the final block of the chain, whose type is 5A hex. The type is stored in the first byte of the MCB.

The next two bytes in the MCB are a word that identifies the owner of the memory block. A value of zero indicates that the block is unallocated, or free. If the owner field is nonzero, indicating that the block is allocated, then this word contains the *process identifier*, or PID, of the owner process. The PID for a user process is normally taken from the segment address of the process's *program segment prefix*, or PSP.

The fourth and fifth bytes in the MCB are a word that contains the size of the memory block that follows. This size is expressed in paragraphs (16-byte blocks), and does not include the size of the MCB itself. The remaining eleven bytes of the MCB are undefined.

Although the complete list of memory control blocks is often referred to as the memory allocation *chain*, the MCBs are not actually linked together, nor does the MCB point to the allocated memory block. Rather, each MCB is directly followed in memory by the block that it controls. If an MCB and its associated memory block are not the last in the chain, then another MCB and memory block directly follow.

Starting from a given MCB, the segment address of the next MCB in the chain is located by adding the size (in paragraphs) of the current block to the current MCB's segment address, plus one more. In this manner the entire chain of MCBs may be traversed, but only in the forward direction. Starting from a given MCB, it is impossible to determine the address of the preceding MCB. How then can we find out which blocks are in memory?

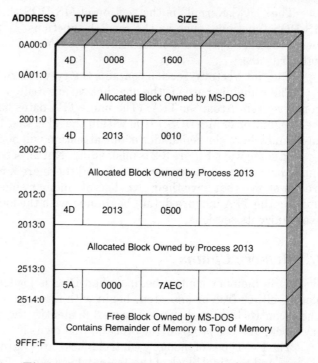

Figure 3-3. MS-DOS memory control blocks.

MS-DOS function 52h (int 21h) is an undocumented function that returns a pointer to a list of DOS's internal values. The pointer is returned in the ES:BX register pair. Just before this list, at the word pointed to by ES:[BX– 2], is the segment address of the first MCB. From this starting point the entire MCB chain may be determined.

These methods are used in the SHOWMEM program, shown in Listing 3-1. The listing contains both the SHOWMEM.ASM source file and the header file PSP.INC (of which we'll see more). Figure 3-4 depicts a sample result from the SHOWMEM program. Within SHOWMEM.ASM, the *ShowMCBInfo* routine displays the contents of the MCB. The *main* procedure contains the code to locate the initial block and, after the label *show_mem*, the arithmetic for finding the next block in the chain. The additional code in *ShowMCBOwner* may not make sense just yet. This code is used to display the name of the process that owns that block of memory and is explained in subsequent sections.

There are a number of very interesting items that can be learned from examining Figure 3-4. We can see that the author has loaded three memory resident programs: RETRIEVE, MODE, and SWITCH. We can see that SHOWMEM has a *very* large block of memory allocated to it: 555 kilobytes! And we can see that every program that was loaded has two memory blocks allocated to it. It is this last phenomenon that we will explain first.

```
SM-ShowMem, Version 1.00, © Copyright 1988

MCB     Size    Owner   Command Line
-----------------------------------------------------------
0A01    08D7    0008    DOS
12D9    00D3    12DA    [ SHELL ]
13AD    0003    0000    [ available ]
13B1    0032    12DA    [ SHELL ]
13E4    0004    13EA    c:\bin\RETRIEVE.COM
13E9    00A9    13EA    c:\bin\RETRIEVE.COM
1493    000F    14A4    S:\MODE.COM
14A3    0017    14A4    S:\MODE.COM
14BB    0010    14CD    c:\ws2000\SWITCH.COM
14CC    0018    14CD    c:\ws2000\SWITCH.COM
14E5    0011    14F8    C:\GUIDE\EXAMPLES\SHOWMEM.EXE
14F7    8B08    14F8    C:\GUIDE\EXAMPLES\SHOWMEM.EXE

<<< ------------ End Of Memory Block List ------------ >>>
```

Figure 3-4. Sample display from SHOWMEM.

**Listing 3-1. SHOWMEM MS-DOS Memory Block
Display Program**

```
                        SHOWMEM.ASM

PAGE    60,132
; **** SHOWMEM *****************************************************
; ShowMem - Display MS-DOS Linked Memory Control Blocks
; This file creates the program SM.EXE
;
; ***** INCLUDES & EQUATES ****************************************
;
INCLUDE stdmac.inc
INCLUDE psp.inc
```

continued

Listing 3-1. *continued*

```
;
BlocMCB EQU 4Dh                         ; type of chained MCB
LastMCB EQU 5Ah                         ; type of last MCB
FreeMCB EQU 0000h                       ; owner of free MCB
;
NameSig EQU 0001h                       ; signature of process name
;
; **** DGROUP (DATA) COMPONENT SEGMENTS ****************************
;
_DATA   SEGMENT BYTE PUBLIC 'DATA'
_DATA   ENDS
;
STACK   SEGMENT PARA STACK
        dw      1024 dup (?)            ; 2K stack
STACK   ENDS
;
DGROUP GROUP    _DATA, STACK
;
; **** DATA STORAGE & TEMPLATES ***************************************
;
_DATA   SEGMENT BYTE PUBLIC 'DATA'
;
; Text Messages for Display: Format as Follows:
;
; "MCB    Size   Owner  Command Line"
; "-----------------------------------------------------------"
; "xxxx   xxxx   xxxx   cccccccc..."
; "<<< ------------ End of Memory Block List ------------ >>>"
;
$Title db  CR,LF
       db  'SM-ShowMem, Version 1.00, © Copyright 1988'
       db  CR,LF,CR,LF
       db  'MCB    Size   Owner  Command Line'
       db  CR,LF
       db  '-------------------------------------------'
       db  '------------------'
       db  CR,LF,'$'
$Space db  '   $'
$Free  db  '[ available ]$'
$DOS   db  'DOS$'
$Shell db  '[ SHELL ]$'
$MCBad db  CR,LF
       db  '********** Error in MCB Chains : Aborting List'
       db  ' **********'
```

```
$End    db   CR,LF
        db   '<<< *********** End of Memory Block List'
        db   ' ------------ >>>'
$Crlf   db   CR,LF,'$'
;
; Structure Templates
mcb     STRUC                            ; memory control block structure
        TypeMCB  db    ?                 ; block type
        OwnerMCB dw    ?                 ; block owner
        SizeMCB  dw    ?                 ; block size
mcb     ENDS
;
_DATA   ENDS
;
; **** PROGRAM CODE STARTS HERE ****************************************
;
_TEXT   SEGMENT byte public 'code'
        ASSUME  cs:_TEXT, ds:DGROUP, es:DGROUP, ss:DGROUP
;
        EXTRN   bin2hex:NEAR             ; hexadecimal display
main    PROC    FAR
        mov     ax,DGROUP                ; set up data segment
        mov     ds,ax
;
; Display title for memory block list
        @DisStr $Title
;
; Find start of the memory block queue
        mov     ah,52h                   ; get DOS parameters
        int     21h                      ; return pointer in ES:BX
        sub     bx,2                     ; point to 1st MCB address
        mov     ax,word ptr es:[bx]      ; get starting block
        mov     es,ax
        xor     di,di                    ; clear index
        cmp     byte ptr es:[di].TypeMCB,BlocMCB
        jne     bad_chain                ; exit if not start
                                         ; ... of chain
;
; Loop to find and display each memory block
show_mem:
        call    ShowMCBInfo              ; dump MCB contents
        cmp     byte ptr es:[di].TypeMCB,LastMCB
        je      done                     ; exit if end of chain
        mov     ax,es                    ; calculate next address
        add     ax,es:[di].SizeMCB       ; add block size
        inc     ax                       ; plus one for ourselves
```

continued

Listing 3-1. *continued*

```
        mov     es,ax                       ; start of new block
        cmp     byte ptr es:[di].TypeMCB,LastMCB
        je      show_mem                    ; continue if proper type
        cmp     byte ptr es:[di].TypeMCB,BlocMCB
        je      show_mem                    ; continue if proper type
;
bad_chain:                                  ; error in MCB "chains"
        @DisStr $MCBad                      ; terminating message
        @DisStr $Crlf
        mov     al,1                        ; terminate w/ error
        @ExitToDOS                          ; terminate program
;
done:   @DisStr $End                        ; terminating message
        @DisStr $Crlf
        mov     al,0                        ; normal terminate
        @ExitToDOS                          ; terminate program
;
main    ENDP
;
; **** ShowMCBInfo ****************************************************
; ShowMCBInfo displays the block addressed by ES:DI as an MS-DOS
; Memory Control Block. Format for the display is shown above.
;
ShowMCBInfo PROC    NEAR
        mov     ch,04                       ; display numeric data
        mov     ax,es                       ; MCB address
        call    bin2hex
        @DisStr $Space
        mov     ax,es:[di].SizeMCB          ; associated block
        call    bin2hex
        @DisStr $Space
        mov     ax,es:[di].OwnerMCB         ; owner
        push    ax                          ; save owner
        call    bin2hex
        @DisStr $Space
        pop     ax
        cmp     ax,FreeMCB                  ; is block free?
        je      is_free                     ; yes, don't need name
        call    ShowMCBOwner                ; no, display owner
        jmp     Info_Exit
;
is_free:
        @DisStr $Free                       ; note block as free
Info_exit:
```

```
        @DisStr $Crlf
        ret
ShowMCBInfo ENDP
;
; **** ShowMCBOwner **************************************************
; ShowMCBOwner extracts and displays a DOS MCB owner from an
; associated environment string. ES:DI points to a valid MCB,
; with a nonzero owner field.
;
ShowMCBOwner PROC    NEAR
        push    es                      ; save MCB address
        push    di                      ; save for cleanup
;
; Obtain the PID (PSP address) that owns this memory block
        mov     ax,es:[di].OwnerMCB     ; get owner's PSP address
        mov     es,ax
        cmp     es:[di].PSPExitInt,PSPSignature ; valid PSP ?
        je      Owner_PID               ; yes, owner has PID
;
; Without a PSP the owner must be the DOS kernel
Owner_DOS:
        @DisStr $DOS                    ; owner is MS-DOS
        jmp     Owner_Exit              ; all done
;
; Extract the process's Environment Segment from the PSP
Owner_PID:
        mov     ax,es:[di].PSPEnvironment ; yes, get envir. addr
        push    ax                      ; save environment seg.
;
; Get the Size of the Environment Segment
        dec     ax                      ; environment MCB
        mov     es,ax
        mov     cx,es:[di].SizeMCB      ; get size of environ.
        shl     cx,1                    ; convert paragraphs ...
        shl     cx,1                    ; ... to bytes
        shl     cx,1
        shl     cx,1
;
; Proceed to search for the process name at ES:DI, length CX
; Each environment variable is terminated with a zero byte.
; The list of variables is terminated with a(nother) zero byte.
        cld                             ; forward search
        pop     es                      ; restore environment
        xor     al,al                   ; search value
search:
        repne   scasb                   ; search for ASCIIZ
```

continued

Listing 3-1. *continued*

```
        jne     Owner_DOS               ; stop if overrun
        scasb                           ; end of string list
        jne     search                  ; continue if more
;
; Check to see if a "Signature" preceeds the (possible) name
        mov     si,di                   ; transfer to SI
        push    ds                      ; save string seg
        push    es                      ; transfer ES to DS
        pop     ds
        lodsw                           ; read word preceding
        cmp     al,NameSig              ; check for real name
        je      show_name               ; valid name
;
; Without a real name, the owner must be the SHELL
        pop     ds
        @DisStr $Shell                  ; owner is shell
        jmp     Owner_Exit
;
; ES:DI points to a valid (0 terminated) process name
show_name:
        lodsb                           ; read Name char at a ...
        cmp     al,0                    ; ... time, checking ...
        je      Owner_POP               ; ... for end, and ...
        @DisChr al                      ; ... displaying
        loop    show_name
Owner_Pop:
        pop     ds
Owner_Exit:
        pop     di
        pop     es
        ret
ShowMCBOwner ENDP
;
; ***** END OF PROGRAM : END OF FILE *******************************
;
_TEXT   ENDS
        END     main


                                        ; PSP.INC


;*********************************************************************
; PSP DEFINITIONS INCLUDE FILE
;*********************************************************************
;
```

```
PSPSignature        EQU      020cdh  ; word begining all PSPs
;
ProgramSegmentPrefix         STRUC
PSPExitInt          dw       ?       ; int 20h exit interrupt
PSPMemTot           dw       ?       ; top of memory
PSPResvr1           db       ?
PSPDOSCall          db       5 dup (?) ; call to MS-DOS
PSPTerminate        dd       ?        ; terminate address
PSPControlC         dd       ?        ; control-C address
PSPCritical         dd       ?        ; critical error address
PSPParent           dw       ?        ; parent PSP
PSPHandleTable      db       20 dup (?) ; default handle table
PSPEnvironment      dw       ?         ; environment address
PSPStack            dd       ?         ; initial stack values
PSPHandleSize       dw       ?         ; handle table size
PSPHandlePntr       dd       ?         ; address of handle table
PSPResvr2           db       24 dup (?)
PSPDOSInt           db       3 dup (?) ; interrupt 21h & ret
PSPResvr3           db       9 dup (?)
PSPFCB1             db       16 dup (?) ; file control block
PSPFCB2             db       16 dup (?) ; file control block
PSPResvr4           db       4 dup (?)
PSPCommandLen       db       1         ; length of command line
PSPCommandBuf       db       127 dup (?) ; command line text
ProgramSegmentPrefix         ENDS
```

The Program Environment Block

When MS-DOS loads a program, it always prefixes the program with an *environment block*, stored in its own memory block. In Figure 3-4, this appears as the first, smaller block that is associated with each program. The program's environment block contains the program's personal copy of the MS-DOS environment. The MS-DOS environment, in turn, is the area in MS-DOS where the PATH, COMSPEC, and PROMPT settings are stored, along with any variables assigned with the SET command. The generic form of an environment variable is *NAME*=string. The format of an environment block is given in the example shown in Figure 3-5.

From Figure 3-5 you can see that each entry in the environment block is made of an ASCII string terminated with a zero byte. (This format has been named *ASCIIZ* by Microsoft.) The entire list of entries is terminated with another zero byte, shown as the seventh entry in Figure 3-5. The entries preceding this list-end marker are those that are displayed whenever you use the SET command. But what of the two entries following the list-end marker?

An undocumented feature of MS-DOS versions 3 and later is that, whenever a process is loaded by COMMAND.COM, either directly or in response to

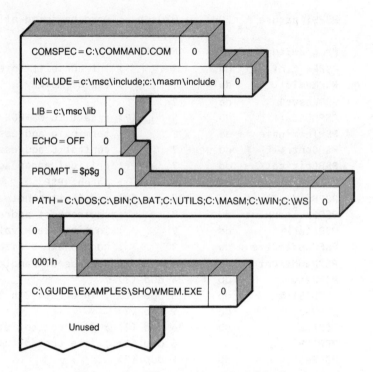

Figure 3-5. The environment block.

the EXEC function, the process's name is placed in the process's environment block. The last two entries in Figure 3-5, before the "Unused" portion, are this undocumented process name. The process name is prefixed with the word *0001* hex. The name contains both the name and the path of the process, and is stored in ASCIIZ format. From Figure 3-5 you can see that this environment block belongs to the process SHOWMEM.

One item that Figure 3-5 does not give us is the total size of the environment block. Unlike DOS's master environment, whose size can be controlled by parameters set in CONFIG.SYS, the process's environment block is sized at program load time to contain only the current valid portion of the environment.

Compare, in the sample SHOWMEM display of Figure 3-4, the 800-byte size of DOS's environment (the second "SHELL" entry) to the environments of RETRIEVE and SHOWMEM, at 64 and 272 bytes, respectively. Although DOS had reserved 800 bytes, the environment contained less than 64 bytes when RETRIEVE was loaded towards the front of the AUTOEXEC.BAT file. After the AUTOEXEC.BAT file had finished setting up the PATH, PROMPT, and various other variables, the environment had grown by around 200 bytes.

There are two reasons why each process receives its own environment block when it is created. One, this reduces the probability that a process will corrupt its parent's environment—a crucial requirement if the parent process is COMMAND.COM. Two, because the parent process has control over the environment given to the child, this allows a parent process to control the behavior of the child. We will return to this topic again when we confront the issues of loading and executing programs.

We have also left unresolved the question of SHOWMEM's large memory block. Keep that problem in mind, as we will return to it after a little more groundwork has been laid.

MS-DOS Processes

We started this chapter with a description of how the entire memory space of a system is mapped into sections for MS-DOS and for the BIOS and hardware system functions. We then saw how the section managed by MS-DOS is organized into different areas, including the transient program area, or TPA. We have also seen how the TPA is managed through use of the memory control blocks and how each process consists of two memory blocks: an environment block and what we will call a *process block*. We are now ready to expand our view of the process block and examine the individual components that make up an MS-DOS process.

The MS-DOS Process Context

Figure 2-3 in Chapter 2 gave us one view of the internal layouts of MS-DOS processes for both an .EXE and a .COM type process. We can now combine that with what we have just learned to produce a more detailed image of an MS-DOS process in memory. This new view is shown in Figure 3-6.

There are many features illustrated by Figure 3-6 that we need to consider. We'll start with the program segment prefix, or PSP.

The Program Segment Prefix (PSP)

The program segment prefix, introduced in Chapter 2, is in some ways the keystone of an MS-DOS process. The segment address of the PSP provides the process identifier and serves as the identifier for a process's memory block. Always located at the start of a process block, the PSP also serves as the repository for a large number of invaluable pieces of information.

The PSP is presented here in three forms: as a graphic representation in Figure 3-7; as detailed definitions in Table 3-1; and as a MASM *STRUC* definition in PSP.INC, appearing in Listing 3-1. The figure enables quick location, the table provides in-depth information, and the listing provides offsets for use in your programs.

A quick glance at Figure 3-7 and Table 3-1 reveals a wealth of information that can be useful to the programmer. However, a little more explanation is required for a few of the items.

The PSP Terminate Addresses

Table 3-1 shows three *terminate addresses* stored in bytes 0A through 15 (hex) of the PSP. As explained, these copies of the program terminate address, Control-Break exit address, and critical error exit address are taken from the actual interrupt vectors located in int 22h, int 23h, and int 24h. In order to affect the behavior of the system during a terminate situation (such as trapping the

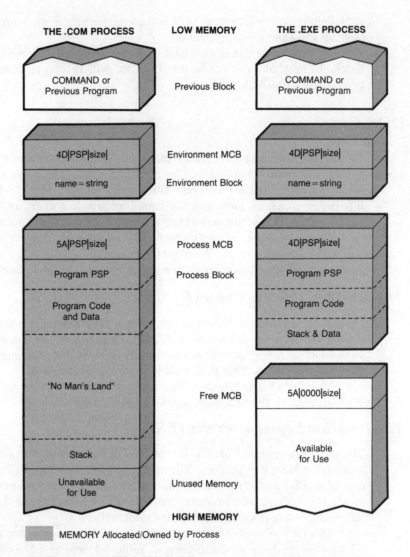

THE .COM PROCESS   LOW MEMORY   THE .EXE PROCESS

COMMAND or Previous Program — Previous Block — COMMAND or Previous Program

4D|PSP|size| — Environment MCB — 4D|PSP|size|

name = string — Environment Block — name = string

5A|PSP|size| — Process MCB — 4D|PSP|size|

Program PSP — Process Block — Program PSP

Program Code and Data — Program Code

"No Man's Land" — Stack & Data

Stack — Free MCB — 5A|0000|size|

Unavailable for Use — Unused Memory — Available for Use

HIGH MEMORY

MEMORY Allocated/Owned by Process

Figure 3-6. The MS-DOS process context in memory.

Control-Break/Control-C exit), the programmer is required to alter the master interrupt vectors. This can be accomplished using the Set Vector (code 25h) and Get Vector (code 35h) functions to obtain and change these addresses.

The PSP's File Handle Table
Three of the "undocumented" entries in the program segment prefix deal with file handles: the *handle table address*, the *handle pointer*, and the *handle count*. These three are related, as you will see.

The handle table address contains a long pointer to a byte-wide table in memory, the size of which is given by the handle count. Each byte entry in this

Table 3-1. Contents of the Program Segment Prefix

Offset (hex)	Size (hex)	Contents
00	2	*Int 20h.* Contains an int 20h instruction (bytes CD 20 hex). Archaic use. Programs should instead terminate using function 4Ch, int 21h.
02	2	*Top of memory.* Contains the address of the segment following the program's memory. This can be either the address past DOS memory (such as A000) or the address of the next available memory control block.
04	1	*Reserved.*
05	5	*Long call to MS-DOS function dispatcher.* Contains a long jump to the MS-DOS function dispatcher, for use with CP/M type programs. Archaic use. Programs should instead call MS-DOS using int 21h.
06	2	*Available Memory.* The offset portion of the long call also contains the number of bytes available in the program's code segment.
0A	4	*Program terminate address.* A copy of the int 22h address (IP,CS), to which control is transferred when the program terminates.
0E	4	*Control-Break exit address.* A copy of the int 23h address (IP,CS), to which control is transferred when Control-Break or Control-C is entered.
12	4	*Critical error exit address.* A copy of the int 24h address (IP,CS), to which control is transferred when a critical error is detected in processing.
16	2	*Parent program segment prefix.* This is the segment address of the parent process's program segment prefix. This is the current PSP address for processes that have no parent.
18	14	*File handle table.* Contains 20 single-byte "handles" (indices) into the system's file table. The first 5 are dedicated to STDIN, STDOUT, STDERR, AUXIO, and LSTOUT. See text for details.
2C	2	*Environment address.* Segment address of the process's environment block.
2E	4	*Stack switch storage.* Used to store the process's stack segment and pointer (SS:SP) when the process is operating on the MS-DOS stack.
32	2	*Handle count.* Maximum number of entries allowable in the file handle table. The default value is 20.
34	4	*Handle table address.* Long pointer to the file handle table. Default value is offset 18 (hex) in the current PSP.
38	18	*Reserved.*
50	3	*Function dispatcher interrupt.* Contains code for an int 21h to call the MS-DOS function dispatcher, followed by a *far* RET.
53	2	*Reserved.*
55	7	*File control block extension.* Extension fields for file control block #1. Archaic use. Programs should instead use file handles. Refer to the MS-DOS manual for detailed information on FCBs.

continued

Table 3-1. *continued*

Offset (hex)	Size (hex)	Contents
5C	10	*File control block number one.* Contains unopened FCB #1. Use is archaic and can result in possible destruction of FCB #2 and the command line length. File name paths are not supported. Programs should instead use file handles. Refer to the MS-DOS manual for detailed information on FCBs.
6C	10	*File control block number two.* Contains unopened FCB #2. Use is archaic and can result in possible destruction of the command line parameters. Programs should instead use file handles. Refer to the MS-DOS manual for detailed information on FCBs.
7C	4	*Reserved.*
80	80	*Default disk transfer area.* Overlays the command line text string when used.
80	1	*Command line length.* Length of the text string that was typed following the program name, minus any redirection characters or parameters.
81	7F	*Command line buffer.* Text string that was typed following the program name. Redirection characters (< and >) and their associated file names do not appear in this area, since redirection is transparent to the application.

table is a handle that can be opened to a file or device. Once opened, the handles store indices into the system file table. Unused entries in the table are marked with the value 0FF (hex). The first five handles in a file handle table are reserved for the STDIN, STDOUT, STDERR, AUXIO, and LSTOUT devices, and are already opened when the process is started. All indices are calculated from an origin of zero.

Figure 3-8 shows the state of the default file handle table following a successful open to the file *myfile*. The default file handle table is a 20-byte table located at offset 18 (hex) in the PSP. This address is stored in the handle table address when a process is started. Because the first five handles are reserved for standard devices, this leaves only fifteen handles available for files or other devices.

In Figure 3-8 the value of the handle returned by the successful function call to OPEN is 0005, which signifies that *myfile* was assigned the sixth entry in the process's file handle table. The sixth entry in turn contains the value 03, which means that *myfile* has been assigned the fourth entry in the system file table. Figure 3-8 also demonstrates, using the first three handles, that multiple handles may be assigned to the same entry in the system file table. The maximum number of entries in the system file table is set by the *FILES=* statement in the CONFIG.SYS file.

In most situations the user need never be aware of these arrangements, but there are two situations where this knowledge becomes useful.

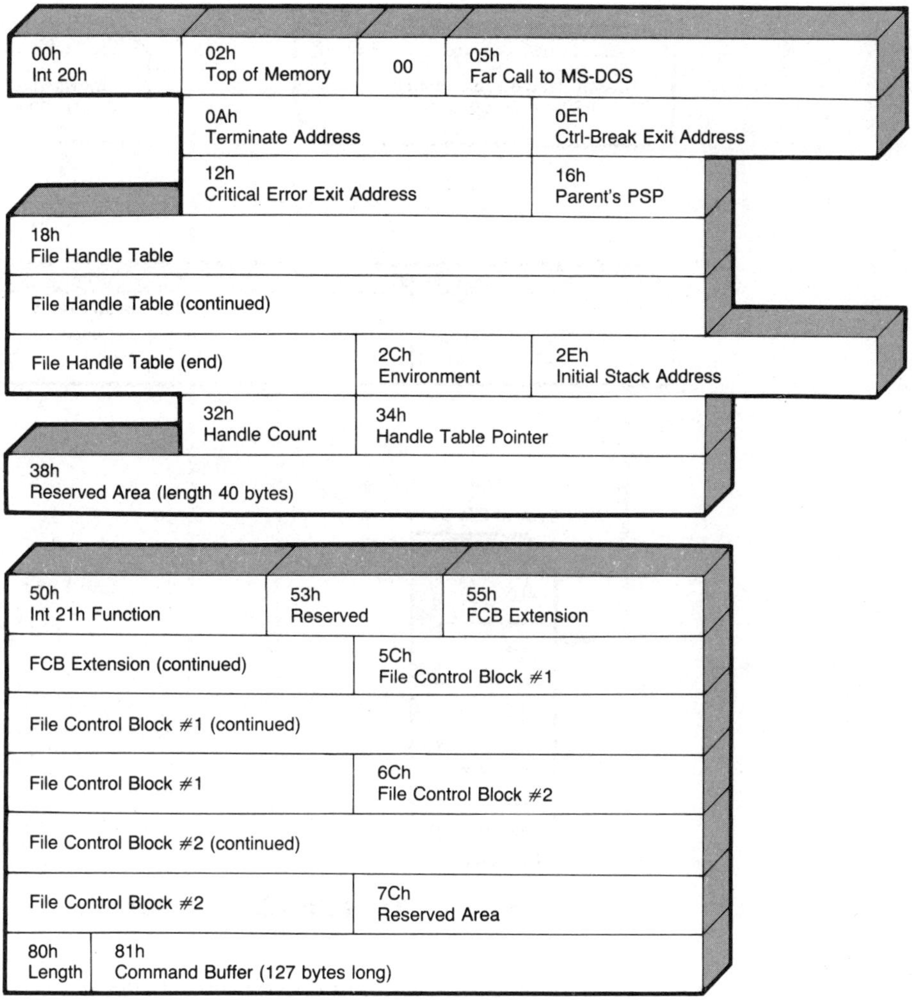

00h Int 20h	02h Top of Memory	00	05h Far Call to MS-DOS	
0Ah Terminate Address			0Eh Ctrl-Break Exit Address	
12h Critical Error Exit Address			16h Parent's PSP	
18h File Handle Table				
File Handle Table (continued)				
File Handle Table (end)		2Ch Environment		2Eh Initial Stack Address
32h Handle Count		34h Handle Table Pointer		
38h Reserved Area (length 40 bytes)				

50h Int 21h Function	53h Reserved	55h FCB Extension
FCB Extension (continued)	5Ch File Control Block #1	
File Control Block #1 (continued)		
File Control Block #1	6Ch File Control Block #2	
File Control Block #2 (continued)		
File Control Block #2	7Ch Reserved Area	
80h Length	81h Command Buffer (127 bytes long)	

Figure 3-7. Structure of the PSP (program segment prefix).

One situation arises when the user's program requires more handles than can be opened at a given time. Since the default file handle table supports only twenty handles, and since five handles are already assigned, this may not be such a far-fetched proposition. In order to overcome this restriction, the program must set up its own expanded file handle table, as the code fragment in Listing 3-2 shows.

In the second situation, Listing 3-2 assumes that the location of the new table is supplied to it, and it also assumes that the table has been preloaded with 0FFh, the code for an unused handle. The code first determines the location of the PSP, using function 62h. From the PSP, the size and location of the existing file handle table are found, and the old table is copied into the new table. The

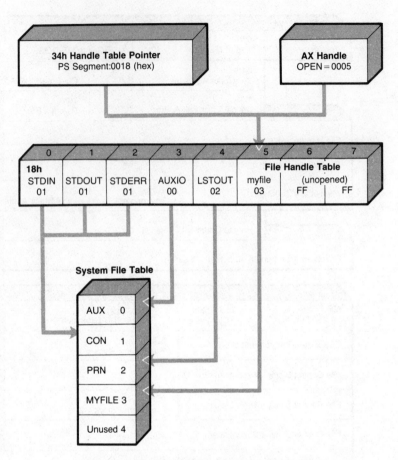

Figure 3-8. The PSP's file handle table.

new table's address and size are stored in the proper fields of the PSP, and the exchange is complete.

Another feature made possible by this mechanism is that the programmer now has control over redirection of the program's input and output. In MS-DOS, redirection is accomplished by simply changing the handle associated with a particular device. This method even works to redirect input and output performed with the older, nonhandle input and output calls (such as function 09h, Display String).

Listing 3-3 demonstrates how *StdOut* is redirected to the file or device *my-file*. The program first opens the name *myfile* and saves the handle. It then obtains the PSP's address, and from within the PSP it obtains the address of the file handle table. Using *myfile* as an index into the file handle table, the program obtains *myfile's* system file table index and stores it in the index assigned to *StdOut*, accomplishing the redirection. The remainder of the program reverses the process and finishes by closing *myfile's* handle.

Listing 3-2. Code Fragment for Switching the File Handle Table

```
; This listing transfers the default File Handle Table to an
; area specified in ES:DI. The new table size is assumed in CX.
; MS-DOS version 3.xx is assumed (for "Get PSP Address").
; The AX and BX registers are destroyed.
;
        push    ds              ; save DS
        push    si              ; save SI
        push    di              ; save new table offset
        push    cx              ; save new table size
        mov     ah,62h          ; get program segment prefix
        int     21h             ; returns PSP in BX
        mov     ds,bx           ; address the PSP
;
; Obtain current table address and size
        mov     bx,032h         ; address of table size
        mov     cx,[bx]         ; obtain table size
        push    ds              ; save PSP address
        lds     si,[bx]2        ; obtain current table address
;
; Copy the old table from DS:SI to the new location at ES:DI
        cld                     ; forward direction move
        rep     movsb           ; move table to new location
;
; Restore new table location and size and update PSP
        pop     ds              ; restore PSP address
        pop     cx              ; restore new table size
        pop     di              ; restore new table offset
        mov     [bx]2,di        ; store new table offset
        mov     [bx]4,es        ; store new table segment
        mov     [bx],cx         ; store new table size
        pop     si              ; restore original SI
        pop     ds              ; restore original DS
```

Listing 3-3. Code Fragment for Redirecting *StdOut* to a File

```
; This listing opens a handle to the file or device "myfile",
; and replaces the StdOut handle with the newly opened handle.
; Entry is assumed with DS and ES pointing to the data segment.
; The following data variables are assumed to be defined:
```

continued

Listing 3-3. *continued*

```
;
StdOut  equ     1                       ; code for StdOUT handle
Handle  dw      ?                       ; new handle variable
Outhand db      ?                       ; StdOut handle variable
MyFile  db      'filename.ext',0
;
; Open a handle to the file/device found in myfile.
        lea     dx,MyFile       ; name
        mov     al,2            ; read/write access
        mov     ah,03dh         ; open function
        int     21h
        jc      OpenError
        mov     Handle,ax       ; save handle
;
; Transfer the file/device handle to the StdOUT handle.
        push    es              ; save ES
        mov     ah,62h          ; get program segment prefix
        int     21h
        mov     es,bx           ; ES points to PSP
        les     bx,es:[bx].PSPHandlePntr
;
; ES:BX now points to the File Handle Table
        mov     al,es:[bx].StdOut       ; read StdOut handle
        mov     Outhand,al              ; ... and save
        mov     di,Handle               ; read handle.s index
        mov     al,es:[bx+di]           ; read handle.s entry
        mov     es:[bx].StdOut,al       ; store as StdOut handle
        pop     es
;
; Restore StdOut.s original handle
        push    es              ; save ES
        mov     ah,62h          ; get program segment prefix
        int     21h
        mov     es,bx           ; ES points to PSP
        les     bx,es:[bx].PSPHandlePntr
;
; ES:BX now points to the File Handle Table
        mov     al,Outhand              ; read StdOut Handle
        mov     es:[bx].StdOut,al       ; store as StdOut handle
        pop     es
;
; Close the redirected file
        mov     bx,Handle       ; handle for file or device
```

```
        mov     ah,03eh         ; close function
        int     21h
```

SHOWMEN and the PSP's Environment Address Pointer

Another of the useful values stored in the PSP is the segment address of the process's environment block. We are returning to this entry not because it requires further explanation but because we are now in possession of all the information necessary to understand the entire SHOWMEM program, including the *Show-MCBOwner* routine:

- Find the initial memory control block using int 52h.
- Use the owner field of an MCB as the address of a PSP.
- Verify the PSP by checking the first 2 bytes for an int 20h.
- If the MCB's owner is a PSP, extract the environment address. If the owner is not a PSP, then the owner must be MS-DOS.
- Subtract one from the environment's segment address to get the environment's MCB, and extract from it the environment's size.
- Search the environment for the double zero that signals the end of the ASCIIZ strings.
- Check for the user process "signature" of 0001. If found, print the following name. If not found, then the process must be COMMAND.COM or equivalent shell.
- If the current MCB is not the last one, find the next MCB by adding the block's size (plus one) to the MCB's address.
- Repeat from the second step.

The SHOWMEM program demonstrates the interrelationships that exist within the DOS world and shows how we can move from memory control block to program segment prefix, to environment block, and back to the environment's MCB, gathering data as we progress.

Functions for Manipulating the PSP

MS-DOS contains a number of functions that directly relate to the program segment prefix. These functions are listed in Table 3-2. For those functions that get and set the PSP, the current PSP is determined by DOS, not by which program segment is executing at the time.

For example, let us assume a program MYPROG is running when an installed memory resident routine (TSR, if you will) receives control and issues the Get PSP call (function 62h). In this case MS-DOS returns the PSP value for the interrupted program MYPROG. This happens because once a memory resident routine has executed a Keep Process or Terminate and Stay Resident function it is no longer considered active. MS-DOS considers the last program loaded to be the currently active program.

If it is important that a TSR have access to its own PSP, the undocumented function Set PSP (function 50h) can be used. When the TSR is first loaded, it must save the value of its PSP. Then, when the TSR receives control at a later time, the interrupted program's PSP can be determined with function 62h, Get PSP. This value should be saved, and the TSR's own PSP activated with function 50h, Set PSP. After the TSR is done executing, it should restore the original PSP with the Set PSP function.

Table 3-2. Int 21h Functions for the Program Segment Prefix

Function	Purpose
26h	*Create PSP block.* Archaic use.
50h	*Set current PSP.* Undocumented. BX contains the segment address of a valid PSP. This function causes the new PSP (BX) to be made the MS-DOS active PSP. Subsequent calls to DOS that reference PSP data, such as the file handle table, will use the new PSP.
51h	*Get PSP segment.* Undocumented. Returns the current PSP's segment address in the BX register. This is the same as function 62h, but is also available in versions of MS-DOS prior to 3.00. Not safe to call from a TSR. Recommended that function 62h be used instead.
55h	*Duplicate PSP.* Undocumented. Functions almost identical to function 26h. DX contains segment address of the new PSP. However, this function will also set the parent PSP field of the new PSP to the segment address of the current PSP. Since this is undocumented, and useful only when loading a new program, it is recommended that function 4Bh, EXEC, be used instead.
62h	*Get current PSP.* MS-DOS version 3.00 or later. Returns the current PSP's segment address in the BX register.

The MS-DOS Process File: .EXE versus .COM

As you know, executable program files in MS-DOS come in two flavors, *.COM* files and *.EXE* files. Figures 2-3 (in Chapter 2) and 3-6 have illustrated some of the differences between these two formats. To MS-DOS, the differences appear in other forms.

The .EXE type is actually the "native" mode file for MS-DOS. The MS-DOS system and language tools have been designed to work with this type. .COM type files were originally provided for compatibility with CP/M processes, and the type just doesn't seem to die. Even under today's MS-DOS, .COM type files are simply stripped down versions of .EXE files, with some of the flexibility of the .EXE format replaced by .COM format default values. As a result of this simplicity, .COM type files do load faster, but the speed differences are trivial on modern machines.

When a process is being built, MASM does not know or care what type of file is being assembled. During the link, LINK will detect that .COM format files have no stack segment, but LINK will otherwise not complain. It is when EXE2BIN is run to convert the .EXE type file into a .COM type file that the differences begin to show up.

All object files produced by MASM and .EXE files made by LINK can contain *segment relocatable references*. These files contain tables that list where in the program explicit references are made to a program or code segment *by its address*. Because the segment addresses in a program will depend on where it is loaded in memory, when an .EXE program is loaded, MS-DOS must somehow update the locations in the program where these segment references are made, changing the values to point to the current segment. This process is called *relocating*. Before examining how relocation is performed, let's see how this process differs from the way a .COM type file is loaded.

When EXE2BIN converts an .EXE type file to a .COM type file, it scans the .EXE file looking for these segment references. If it finds any explicit segment references in the code, or an implicit reference to a segment other than the base, it produces an error message stating that the file cannot be converted. In addition, EXE2BIN checks to make sure that the code starts at address 100 (hex), relative to the base segment. If all these conditions are met, EXE2BIN strips the file of all relocation information and produces a .COM file. The differences between these two program formats are summarized in Table 3-3.

Table 3-3. Differences between the .COM and .EXE Formats

Attributes	.COM Type	.EXE Type
Number of segments allowed	ONLY ONE	Multiple segments
Segment references	NONE	References allowed
Stack segment	NONE specified	Must be defined
Program code origin	ORG at 100h	No ORG required
Program size	Less than 64K	May be any size
PSP address found in	All segment regs	ES and DS registers
Initial allocation block	All of memory	Can be sized

Loading a .COM Type File

The initial steps taken in loading and executing a .COM type program file are identical to those in loading an .EXE type program file. In setting up the process's "context," MS-DOS first initializes the environment block, taking the information either from the current system environment (the default case) or from an environment specified by the parent process.

Once the environment has been set up, MS-DOS allocates a memory block for the program. For .COM type programs, this memory block occupies all of remaining memory. The minimum size required is the size of the .COM program file, plus space for the PSP. Once the memory block is obtained, MS-DOS proceeds to build the program segment prefix for the program at the beginning of the block. At this point the loading process used differs markedly from that used with an .EXE type program.

The .COM file is read into memory directly above the PSP, at offset 0100 hex in the memory block, and without relocation. The segment registers are all initialized to PSP's segment address, the instruction pointer is set to 0100 (hex), and the stack pointer is set to 0FFFE (hex), or lower if there is less that 64K of memory available for the process. (The minimum stack pointer value is 0100 hex.) Control is turned over to the process, and the .COM program begins running.

Some .COM programs have trouble operating with the minimum stack provided by MS-DOS. If a program runs with a stack that's too small, it can result in the stack growing downwards into the code or data sections of the program; this is almost surely fatal. If you have a .COM program that requires more than the minimum stack of 256 bytes, you can build your own minimum stack into the program's file image by reserving large amounts of space at the end of your program. (Remember that MS-DOS will automatically add at least 256 bytes to your stack when it loads the .COM program.) That way, if there isn't enough memory available for the stack needed, MS-DOS won't be able to load the program.

The .EXE Program File Format

Unlike the .COM type program file, which contains only a program image, the .EXE type program file must contain all the information necessary to relocate the embedded segment references. Also, because an .EXE type program is not constrained to have a particular stack or particular starting point, the .EXE program file must contain the information for the loader to properly initialize the program.

An .EXE program file is made up of three sections: the .EXE file header, the *relocation map*, and the program image. The .EXE file header is shown in Table 3-4. Some entries in the header provide the initial state of the program image. These are *MinAlloc*, *MaxAlloc*, and the initial SS:SP and CS:IP values. Other entries, *relocation entries* and *relocation table offset*, allow the loader access to the process's relocation map.

Each entry in the relocation map allows the loader to resolve one segment reference within the program image. Each entry consists of a long pointer (segment and offset) to a segment reference within the load image. The pointer itself is relative to the start of the program's load image. During relocation, the initial segment references contained in the load image are updated to contain the actual segment values. We will see this process in more detail as soon as we cover one more aspect of the .EXE program file: the initial allocation values.

Table 3-4.   .EXE Type Program File Header

Offset (hex)	Contents
00	*Signature.* .EXE program file type marker: 4D5H (hex).
02	*Remainder.* Number of bytes in last page of file (the load image size modulus 512).
04	*Pages.* Number of 512-byte pages in the file, including the header.
06	*Relocation entries.* Number of entries in the relocation table.
08	*Header size.* Size of the header in 16-byte paragraphs.
0A	*MinAlloc.* Minimum number of memory paragraphs required beyond the end of the program.

0C	*MinAlloc.* Maximum number of memory paragraphs required beyond the end of the program.
0E	*Stack segment.* Initial value for the stack segment (relative to the start of the program load image).
10	*Stack pointer.* Initial value for the stack pointer.
12	*Checksum.* Two's complement checksum of the program file.
14	*Instruction pointer.* Initial value for the instruction pointer.
16	*Code segment.* Initial value for the code segment (relative to the start of the program load image).
18	*Relocation table offset.* Relative byte offset from beginning of the program file to the relocation table.
1A	*Overlay number.* Number of the overlay generated by LINK.

The .EXE Initial Memory Allocation Block

The examples presented so far have taken for granted that when MS-DOS loads a program into memory, *all* of remaining memory is allocated to that program. This is what was shown by SHOWMEM in Figure 3-4: the last, and largest, memory block was assigned to SHOWMEM. It was to overcome this phenomenon in Chapter 2 that the Modify Allocated Memory Block function (function 4Ah) was used in the programs shown in Listings 2-12 and 2-13. But, we have been hinting at other methods of obtaining free memory for .EXE type programs. Figure 3-6 shows an .EXE program that has a large block of free memory available, and the last entry of Table 3-3 says that an .EXE program's initial allocation block can be *sized*. How is this accomplished?

The .EXE type file header contains two entries that control exactly how much memory a program is given when it is loaded. These two entries are *MinAlloc*, the minimum memory allocation (at offset 0A hex), and *MaxAlloc*, the maximum memory allocation size (at offset 0C hex). *MinAlloc* tells the loader how much memory (in 16-byte paragraphs) the program must have to be run, i.e., how much memory the program actually uses. *MaxAlloc*, on the other hand, tells the loader the number of memory paragraphs the program *desires* to be allocated to it.

The DOS linker normally sets the *MaxAlloc* value to 0FFFF hex, which indicates that the program wants almost 1 megabyte of memory. Since DOS doesn't have a megabyte, it does the next best thing: it gives the program all of memory. However, if we were to set the value of *MaxAlloc* to *MinAlloc*, then the program would get the memory it required, and the rest would be available. There are two very simple ways to accomplish this.

Microsoft's languages, including MASM, come with a utility called *EXEMOD*. This utility can be used both to display and to modify an .EXE program's header. Figure 3-9 shows how we would go about using EXEMOD to first dump and then modify the *MaxAlloc* parameters.

You may be surprised to see that the example changes *MaxAlloc* to a 1, but from looking at Figure 3-10 you can see that the modified SHOWMEM does indeed run, and that the goal of freeing up memory has been accomplished. The modified SHOWMEM's program image looks in memory just like the .EXE

```
C> exemod c:\guide\examples\showmem.exe

Microsoft ® EXE File Header Utility Version 4.02
Copyright © Microsoft Corp 1985-1987. All rights reserved.

c:\guide\examples\showmem.exe          (hex)          (dec)

EXE size (bytes)                        CC5            3269
Minimum load size (bytes)               AC5            2757
Overlay number                            0               0
Initial CS:IP                      0093:0000
Initial SS:SP                      0013:0800            2048
Minimum allocation (para)                 0               0
Maximum allocation (para)              FFFF           65535
Header size (para)                       20              32
Relocation table offset                  1E              30
Relocation entries                        1               1

C> exemod c:\guide\examples\showmem.exe /max 1

Maximum allocation (para)              FFFF           65535
```

Figure 3-9. Using EXEMOD with .EXE program files.

program image in Figure 3-6, including the free block. You may also be surprised to see that the *MinAlloc* values are zero. If this is the case, then the actual minimum allocation for the program will be the size of the program itself. No additional space is allocated.

You could resize all of your .EXE programs this way, even to the extent of adding EXEMOD to your build batch files. However, when building .EXE files there is another way to control the *MaxAlloc* parameter—by using the LINK switch "/CPARMAXALLOC:*nnn*" (which can be abbreviated as "/CP:*nnn*"), where *nnn* is the *MaxAlloc* value in paragraphs. For example, SHOWMEM can be built with a maximum allocation value of 1 by using the command:

```
C> link /cp:1 showmem,,,stdlib.lib;
```

The MS-DOS .EXE Process Loader

Knowing all of the pieces that go into the .EXE type program file, let us now look at how the .EXE program is loaded and executed. As with the .COM type program, the first step is to set up the process's context, beginning with the environment block.

After the environment is established, from either the system or the parent tables, the .EXE program file header is read into a work area. Using the *MinAlloc*, *MaxAlloc*, and program image size (from *pages* and *header size*) values, MS-DOS determines the size of the required memory block and allo-

```
SM-ShowMem, Version 1.00, © Copyright 1988

MCB     Size    Owner   Command Line
------------------------------------------------------------
0A01    08D7    0008    DOS
12D9    00D3    12DA    [ SHELL ]
13AD    0003    0000    [ available ]
13B1    0032    12DA    [ SHELL ]
13E4    0004    13EA    c:\bin\RETRIEVE.COM
13E9    00A9    13EA    c:\bin\RETRIEVE.COM
1493    000F    14A4    S:\MODE.COM
14A3    0017    14A4    S:\MODE.COM
14BB    0010    14CD    c:\ws2000\SWITCH.COM
14CC    0018    14CD    c:\ws2000\SWITCH.COM
14E5    0011    14F8    C:\GUIDE\EXAMPLES\SHOWMEM.EXE
14F7    00D1    14F8    C:\GUIDE\EXAMPLES\SHOWMEM.EXE
15C9    8A36    0000    [ available ]
<<< ------------ End Of Memory Block List ------------ >>>
```

**Figure 3-10. Sample display from SHOWMEM, with *MaxAlloc*
set to *MinAlloc*.**

cates it. If the *MaxAlloc* value is 0FFFF hex, then all of memory will be
allocated.

Once the block has been allocated, the program segment prefix is created
at the start of the process block. The PSP for an .EXE type program is no different than that of a .COM type program. MS-DOS then reads the program image into memory directly above the PSP, reads the *relocation table* into a work
space, and proceeds to relocate the program image. Figure 3-11 shows how the
entries in the relocation map relate to the program image. All numbers and
arithmetic in the figure are in hex.

The first step in relocation is to calculate the *starting segment address*.
This is the address in real memory that corresponds to the starting address of
the program image in the file. In Figure 3-11 the process memory block was allocated at segment address 1000. The PSP occupies 100 bytes, or 10 segments.
The program's starting segment address in memory is then segment 1010:0000,
and this is where the loader will place the program's image.

Once the program image has been loaded, the loader must update, or relocate, every segment reference. When LINK first builds the program image, it
uses an assumed base segment of 0000. In actual fact, the program was loaded at
segment 1010, so every segment reference must have 1010 added to it. The
loader finds all these references by using the *relocation map*, which contains a
pointer to every segment reference in the program.

Figure 3-11 contains two references to segment values. Let us trace the
relocation process for the *far* call located at 0003:1234. The actual segment reference is in the fourth and fifth bytes of this instruction, at address 0003:1237.

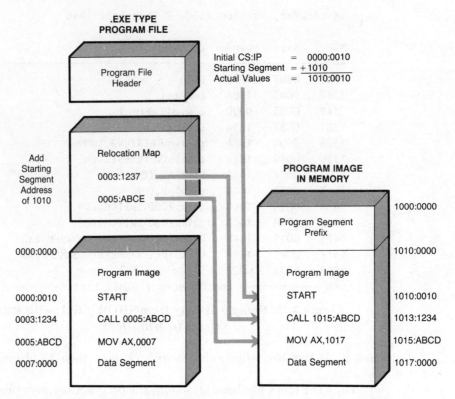

Figure 3-11. The relocation process for loading .EXE type programs.

However, this address is relative to an imaginary base segment of zero, and not to the actual program image in memory. To find the actual segment reference in memory, the relocation map pointer itself must be updated by the starting segment address. The actual segment reference is at address 1013:1237.

The words pointed to in memory are then incremented by the starting segment address. The *far* call to segment 0005 now becomes a *far* call to segment 1015—the actual location of the routine.

After relocation has been completed, the process's ES and DS registers are set to the segment address of the PSP, and the CS:IP and SS:SP registers are initialized from the values given in the .EXE program file header. Both the CS and the SS registers are incremented by the program image starting segment address. For example, in Figure 3-11 the address of *START*, 0000:0010, is offset by the actual starting segment address, 1010, to form the actual CS:IP values, 1010:0010, used in starting the program.

Overlays

Sooner or later you will write a program that is too large to fit into whatever space you have for it. When this happens, one of the possibilities is to create overlays. An *overlay* is a section of a program that does not need to be in memory all the time. It is loaded into memory when it is needed; but, when it is not needed, its memory space can be used by some other overlay. The remainder of the program that cannot be placed in an overlay is called the *root*. All data must go into the root, since data in an overlay is lost when the overlay is overlaid. Overlays are, after all, read only.

Overlays are useful entities, and MS-DOS fully supports them. One of the uses for the EXEC function is to load overlays. But before looking into that option, you should note that the MS-DOS linker has the ability to create overlays and an overlay manager *automatically*!

The rules for using MS-DOS's overlay manager are simple. The overlay modules may not contain any global or static data, although constant data is allowed. The other rule is that the overlay can be called only by *far* calls, by either the root or another overlay. The overlay can call the root via *near* calls.

The method for creating an overlay is very simple: when invoking the LINK command, the object files that make up an overlay are enclosed in parentheses. That's all there is to it. The following command line creates a program file that uses three overlays.

```
C> link root + (init + read) + (work) + (save + exit) , myprog ;
```

This example uses one set of routines to read in some data and initialize the program, another set to process the data, and yet another to save the processed data and exit. Since none of these operations occurs simultaneously, each was made into an overlay, and thus the hypothetical memory problem was avoided.

Memory Resident Programs

In typical use, MS-DOS is a single-task operating system. Only one program executes in memory at one time. In fact, MS-DOS is capable of supporting multiple programs in memory at any given time. Only one program is actually executing at a time because the processor can execute instructions only one at a time, but programs may be configured so as to give the appearance of executing simultaneously. These multiple programs are created by having MS-DOS load a program into memory and then return control to MS-DOS without removing the program from memory. Because the program doesn't leave memory when control is returned to the operating system, the program is called *memory resident*. The first step in the implementation of a memory resident program is the installation of the program in memory. One of the simplest types of memory resident programs is the run-time library, and we use that as our first example.

Defining a Run-Time Library

What is a run-time library? You know that *libraries* are collections of useful routines that may be called from a program. Most libraries are link libraries in which the desired routines are included in the program file (.EXE or .COM) at link time. Because they are part of the program file, the linked library routines are loaded with the program when the program file is loaded. An RTL (run-time library) is not linked with a program but is included at execution time, also called *run-time*. The RTL must already be in memory or it must be brought into memory when needed, but an RTL is not part of the program file itself.

An RTL is not directly connected to a program, so how does the program call it? The program must somehow signal either the operating system or an RTL support process that the program has a request for the library. This signaling can take place via calls, traps, exceptions, or interrupts, depending on the complexity of the hardware and operating system. In the MS-DOS/8086 environment, the most convenient way is through interrupts.

Why use RTLs if they require the additional effort of loading, calling, etc.? First, RTLs are often used to develop applications that have a large number of programs sharing common routines or to provide a common resource to all users of a particular language. By using RTLs, the developers need store a copy of the library only once instead of making sure that each program contains a copy. As long as the interface between the programs and the RTL remains the same, the routines in the RTL may be updated without modifying or relinking the programs that call them. Thus, an RTL may be viewed as an extension of the operating system because an RTL provides those facilities that the developers deem necessary but that the system does not support. Second, RTLs have additional benefits of reduced disk storage and faster program load time because the RTL doesn't have to be loaded with each program.

Loading Memory Resident Routines from the Command Line

There are a variety of methods that may be used to load a program image in MS-DOS. The methods range from using MS-DOS to load a program from the command line to the lower-level boot routines that transfer program code from absolute disk locations to fixed locations in memory. The easiest method to use is the MS-DOS command line loader, which is simply a request to run a program. Memory resident programs, such as RTLs, are loaded like any other program. However, once a memory resident program has been loaded and after it runs through its initialization sequence, the program terminates by using a special exit: MS-DOS function code 31h (Keep Process) or interrupt vector 27h (Terminate But Stay Resident). The recommended procedure is to use function code 31h of int 21h, which is demonstrated in Listing 3-4.

Function code 31h has two parameters: an optional return code used to signal the exit status and a required value indicating the size of the memory block, in paragraphs, that remains allocated to the process. When the function is called, MS-DOS reserves the requested amount of space, starting at the address of the PSP (program segment prefix). This is almost exactly what happens when the Modify Allocated Memory Block function is called with the PSP address and desired size. In the case of the Keep Process function, MS-DOS knows that the block to be resized has to start at the PSP address, so that parameter is not needed.

Listing 3-4. Keep Process—Function Code 31h

```
                        ; .COM Type Use

program      segment
             ORG     0
seg_org      equ     $
             ORG     0100h
start:
                 .
                 .
                 .
             mov     dx,(offset last_byte - seg_org + 15) shr 4
             mov     ah,31h              ; keep process
             int     21h                 ; call MS-DOS
                 .
                 .
                 .
last_byte:
program      ends
             end     start

                        ; .EXE Type Use

                 .
                 .
                 .
             mov     ax,es               ; get PSP address
             mov     dx,seg end_addr     ; get last segment address
             sub     dx,ax               ; difference is program size
             mov     ah,31h              ; keep process
             int     21h                 ; call MS-DOS
                 .
                 .
                 .
program      ends
end_addr     segment
end_addr     ends
             end     start
```

In Chapter 2 we presented a set of formulas for calculating the size of a program in paragraphs. Those formulas can be used with the Keep Process function as well as with the Modify Allocated Memory Block function. When we use them in memory resident programs, the proper equations appear as shown in Listing 3-4. Note that even though the Keep Process function doesn't require the PSP address, .EXE type programs need to save the PSP address until the exit call. These programs need to save the PSP address for the purpose of calculating the size of the program.

Because space is reserved from the start of the PSP, memory resident routines must not be loaded into the upper part of a memory block (by using MS-

LINK switch /*high*, for example). If the routine is loaded into high memory, that routine is left unprotected when the memory resident routine terminates because the block of memory saved is located at the start of the memory block. The routine itself would be located above the reserved memory space. When routines are thus unprotected, MS-DOS could load another program or the transient part of COMMAND.COM in the same space, overwriting the memory resident routine.

In any case, the MS-LINK switch /*high* affects only .EXE programs. When converting a program to a .COM file, EXE2BIN removes the "load high" marker. MS-DOS then loads the program at the beginning of the PSP.

The other method for installing memory resident programs, the Terminate and Stay Resident interrupt, int 27h, is a holdover from earlier versions of MS-DOS. Int 27h has a number of disadvantages that make it a poor choice. Unlike Keep Process, int 27h *does* require the memory block address (given by the PSP address), and int 27h requires this address in the CS register. Only .COM type files have the PSP address in the code segment register, making this function difficult to use in .EXE type programs. (How do you change the CS and still execute code?) In addition, the size parameter is specified in bytes rather than paragraphs, which limits the size of program that can be saved to 64 Kbytes (the maximum size of a .COM program). The only advantage to this function is that the offset of the last address can be used as a parameter with no conversion as shown here:

```
        .
        .
        .
mov         dx,offset last_byte     ; get number of bytes
int         27h                     ; terminate & stay resident
        .
        .
        .
last_byte:
program     ends
            end     start
```

Microsoft recommends that this interrupt be converted to function code 31h for all new programs written and for all existing program upgrades. When performing the conversion, remember to modify the size parameter from bytes to paragraphs.

Accessing Memory Resident Routines via Int

If you were to run the program shown in Listing 3-4, you would install a memory resident program on your system. Unfortunately, as this program now stands, all it would do is take up space in memory. To turn this program into an RTL, we need to give it a purpose, and we must make it available to other programs.

An RTL may contain any function and make any call to MS-DOS (for example, int 21h) as long as the library is called only by the currently executing program. This restriction is intended to prevent inadvertent reentering of MS-DOS, which causes system failure. The next program, shown in Listing 3-5, contains an example interface to an RTL that could support many separate functions, much like the MS-DOS int 21h handler.

As shown in Listing 3-5, this sample framework can be extended to support math routines, table lookups, I/O conversions, or even a common area for multiple programs, all by adding the necessary "personality" code. We have attempted to include some examples of the techniques outlined in Chapter 2, such as stack parameters, error reporting, etc. If this routine is used to support a large number of functions, you may wish to replace the *case* macro with a jump table as demonstrated in the RDISK ram disk driver in Chapter 6.

The MACRO library referenced in the EXRTL program contains the *case* macro introduced in Chapter 1 and the *dis_chr* (display character) and the *dis_str* (display string) macros as presented in the *MS-DOS Technical Reference Manual*. @DosCall is, of course, a macro for interrupt 21h.

Listing 3-5. Example Run-Time Library Installation

```
;====== RTL.ASM - This file produces a .COM file ================
V_NUM    EQU     40h               ; this RTL uses vector 40 hex
;
INCLUDE STDMAC.INC                 ; include macro library file
;====== PROGRAM CODE SECTION ====================================
;
frame    STRUC                     ; layout caller's stack structure
old_bp   dw      ?                 ; pushed base pointer
ret_IP   dw      ?                 ; return address (IP)
ret_CS   dw      ?                 ; return address (CS)
flags    dw      ?                 ; caller's flags
funct    dw      ?                 ; function number to perform
frame    ENDS
;
code_seg SEGMENT
         ASSUME cs:code_seg
         ASSUME ds:code_seg
main     PROC    FAR
         ORG     0
seg_org  EQU     $
         ORG     2Ch
env_adr  LABEL   WORD              ; offset of environment in PSP
         ORG     0100h
start:   jmp     install
entry:   push    bp                ; save base pointer
         mov     bp,sp             ; get stack address
         push    ds                ; save data segment
         push    ax                ; save register
```

continued

Listing 3-5. *continued*

```
            push    bx
            mov     ax,cs              ; set up data segment
            mov     ds,ax
            mov     ax,[bp].flags      ; transfer caller's flags to AX
            sahf                       ; ... and to my flags
            clc                        ; clear carry (no error)
            pushf                      ; and save copy of flags
            mov     bx,[bp].funct      ; get function code
            @Case   bl,<1,2>,<f1,f2>
            popf                       ; get copy of flags
            stc                        ; set carry - illegal function
            pushf                      ; save copy of flags
            jmp     short exit
f1:         @DisStr f1msg
            jmp     short exit
f2:         @DisStr f2msg
exit:       pop     ax                 ; put flags back in stack
            mov     [bp].flags,ax      ; ... through AX
            pop     bx                 ; restore registers
            pop     ax
            pop     ds                 ; restore data segment
            pop     bp                 ; restore base pointer
            iret                       ; return from interrupt
main        ENDP
;
f1msg       db      'Function # 1 performed',CR,LF,'$'
f2msg       db      'Function # 2 performed',CR,LF,'$'
lst_byt:                               ; last byte to save
;
; This is the installation code. All code following this point
; is thrown away after installation is complete.
;
; See the section on "MEMORY MANAGEMENT TIDBITS" for an
; explanation of why the Environment Block is being removed.
;
; Remove Environment Block - DS points to current segment
; Set ES to point to Environment Block
;
install:
            mov     es,env_adr         ; get address of environment
            mov     ah,49h             ; free allocated memory
```

```
        @DosCall                 ; call MS-DOS
        jnc     setvect          ; branch if no error
        @DisStr fail49           ; inform if was error
        mov     ah,4Ch           ; terminate process
        @DosCall                 ; abort on error
;
; Set Vector - DS points to current segment
setvect:
        mov     dx,offset entry  ; get RTL entry point
        mov     al,V_NUM         ; set vector number
        mov     ah,25h           ; set vector
        @DosCall                 ; call MS-DOS
;
; Terminate & Stay Resident
        mov     dx,(offset lst_byt - seg_org + 15) shr 4
        mov     ah,31h           ; keep process
        @DosCall                 ; call MS-DOS
;
fail49  db      'Failed to Free Environment Block',CR,LF,'$'
code_seg ENDS
        END     start
```

A peculiarity of the EXRTL routine is that no memory for a local stack is provided when the Keep Process executes. This would be a fatal mistake were EXRTL a program because the program stack would then be totally un-protected and subject to destruction. EXRTL, however, is not a stand-alone program but is called by other programs, which do have local stacks. The EXRTL routine performs all of its operations using the calling routine's stack.

Once we have written the RTL, we must provide some means of accessing it. Because it is impossible to determine in advance where MS-DOS will load the procedure in memory, we cannot CALL the library directly from a program that wishes to access it. The 8086 family provides one solution in the form of interrupt vectors. By setting an interrupt vector to point to the address of the library, any program that wishes may access the library by the use of the INT instruction.

The 8086 family supports 256 interrupt vectors, of which at least 64 (00h through 39h) are reserved for the use of the system hardware or MS-DOS. Table 3-5 contains a partial listing of interrupt vector use for Intel, IBM standard, IBM BIOS, and MS-DOS. A variety of vendors have used other interrupts throughout the remaining range. Usually, higher-numbered vectors are safe to use, although only a test can tell. We have chosen to use vector 40h for our RTL because the test system didn't crash when we tried it.

```
                          CAUTION

Some systems may use interrupt vectors other than those defined for MS-DOS.
Check your system's manual before using any of the vectors. Complete system
failure may result from altering a vector that is already in use.
```

Table 3-5.   IBM Standard Interrupt Vectors, Processor, Hardware, BIOS, and MS-DOS Interrupts

Interrupt (hex)	Defined by	Used for
Int 0	Intel	Divide-by-zero-error interrupt
Int 1	Intel	Single step "trace" interrupt
Int 2	Intel	Nonmaskable hardware interrupt
Int 3	Intel	Breakpoint interrupt
Int 4	Intel	Multiply overflow interrupt
Int 5	Intel	80x86 BOUND exception
	BIOS	Print screen function
Int 6	Intel	Undefined op-code exception
Int 7	Intel	ESC op-code exception
Int 8 /IRQ 0	IBM	System timer hardware
Int 9 /IRQ 1	IBM	Keyboard hardware
Int A /IRQ 2	IBM—XT	Spare hardware request
Int A /IRQ 2	IBM—AT	IRQ 8—IRQ F
Int B /IRQ 3	IBM	Serial port 2 hardware
Int C /IRQ 4	IBM	Serial port 1 hardware
Int D /IRQ 5	IBM—XT	Fixed disk hardware
Int D /IRQ 5	IBM—AT	Parallel port 2
Int E /IRQ 6	IBM	Disk controller hardware
Int F /IRQ 7	IBM	Parallel port 1 hardware
Int 10	BIOS	Video and screen services
Int 11	BIOS	Read equipment list
Int 12	BIOS	Report memory size
Int 13	BIOS	Disk I/O service
Int 14	BIOS	Serial I/O services
Int 15	BIOS	Cassette and extended services
Int 16	BIOS	Keyboard I/O services
Int 17	BIOS	Printer I/O services
Int 18	BIOS	BASIC loader
Int 19	BIOS	Bootstrap loader
Int 1A	BIOS	System timer and clock services
Int 1B	BIOS	Keyboard Control-Break (from int 9)
Int 1C	BIOS	User timer tick (from int 08)
Int 1D-1F	Intel	Reserved
Int 20	MS-DOS	OLD program terminate function
Int 21	MS-DOS	MS-DOS function call
Int 22	MS-DOS	Program terminate address
Int 23	MS-DOS	Control-C exit address
Int 24	MS-DOS	Fatal error abort address
Int 25	MS-DOS	Absolute disk read function

Int 26	MS-DOS	Absolute disk write function
Int 27	MS-DOS	Terminate & stay resident function
Int 28	MS-DOS	Keyboard busy/DOS idle (reserved)
Int 29	MS-DOS	Fast console output (reserved)
Int 2A	MS-DOS	MS-NET interface (reserved)
Int 2B–2D	MS-DOS	Reserved for MS-DOS (IRET)
Int 2E	MS-DOS	Execute command (reserved)
Int 2F	MS-DOS	Printer control MS-DOS version 3
Int 30–3E	MS-DOS	Reserved for MS-DOS
Int 3F	MS-DOS	LINK overlay manager (reserved)
Int 4A	BIOS	Real time clock (from int 70)
Int 67	EMS 4.0	Expanded Memory Specification
*Int 70 /IRQ 8	IBM	Real time clock hardware
*Int 71 /IRQ 9	IBM	IRQ 2 hardware interrupt
*Int 72 /IRQ A	IBM	Reserved hardware
*Int 73 /IRQ B	IBM	Reserved hardware
*Int 74 /IRQ C	IBM	Reserved hardware
*Int 75 /IRQ D	IBM	Coprocessor hardware
*Int 76 /IRQ E	IBM	Fixed disk hardware
*Int 77 /IRQ F	IBM	Reserved hardware

*AT-type bus only

Under MS-DOS, interrupt vectors may be set through the use of MS-DOS function code 25h, Set Interrupt Vector. The installation operation is very simple: the vector number is provided in the AL register, and the address to be loaded into the vector is provided in the DS:DX register pair (segment:offset). Because the DS register is set to the same value as the CS register in .COM programs, the DS register's contents are already correct for the call. The remaining registers are loaded, and the call is made with the following code:

```
mov     dx,offset entry     ; get RTL entry point
mov     al,v_num            ; set vector number
mov     ah,25h              ; set interrupt vector
doscall                     ; call MS-DOS
```

Once the EXRTL routine has been installed in memory and its access interrupt vector installed in the interrupt vector table, the RTL is ready for use. To call it, a routine uses the *int 40h* instruction, and control is transferred to the EXRTL routine. The program RTL_TEST, shown in Listing 3-6, is one example of a routine that accesses this particular RTL.

The interface between EXRTL and RTL_TEST is all through the stack. RTL_TEST pushes a function code on the stack and executes the int 40h instruction. Note that the stack layout in RTL differs from that of a CALL interface in that the interrupt pushes the flags on the stack as well as the return segment and offset.

The flow of control between the two sections is illustrated in Figure 3-12. The *int 40h* instruction transfers control through the interrupt vector table to the EXRTL routine. The EXRTL routine then extracts the function code from the stack, assisted by the stack structure definition *frame*. EXRTL

Listing 3-6. Exercise Program for RTL

```
;====== RTL_TEST.ASM - This file produces a .COM file ==========
V_NUM    EQU     40h             ; this RTL uses vector 40 hex
;
INCLUDE STDMAC.INC               ; include macro library file
;====== PROGRAM CODE SECTION ===================================
;
code_seg SEGMENT
         ASSUME  cs:code_seg
         ASSUME  ds:code_seg
main     PROC    FAR
         ORG     0100h
start:   mov     cx,3            ; start at illegal value
loop:    push    cx              ; function code
         int     V_NUM           ; call RTL
         pop     cx              ; clear return param
         jnc     nxt             ; branch no error
         @DisStr caserr          ; show error
nxt:     dec     cx
         jge     loop            ; loop through 0
         mov     ah,4Ch          ; terminate process
         @DosCall
;
caserr   db      'Case Error - Illegal Function Code',CR,LF,'$'
main     ENDP
code_seg ENDS
         END     start
```

analyzes the function code to check whether it is legal and, if it is, branches to the proper function handler through use of the *case* macro. Once the function has been performed, EXRTL returns control to RTL_TEST with an IRET (Return from Interrupt) instruction.

The stack structure *frame* also provides EXRTL access to the caller's flags, which are stored on the stack by an int. By copying the flags from the stack into its own flags register, EXRTL can change the value of the carry bit; then, before exiting, it can copy the flags back into the stack (including the new value of the carry flag). This operation allows EXRTL to use the carry flag to signal error conditions to the calling routine, using the IRET instruction to restore the flags from the stack.

The last point is that EXRTL may make full use of MS-DOS as control is passed directly to it by a program. This isn't the case in some of the other memory resident programs presented in following sections of this book. Those programs receive control via hardware or MS-DOS interrupts.

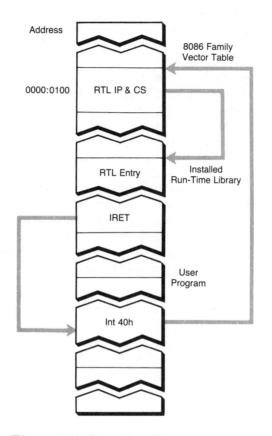

Figure 3-12. Run-time library access.

Determining Whether a Memory Resident Program Is Installed

So far we have assumed that the RTL would be loaded into memory and then the programs that use it would be started. In some circumstances, the RTL may already be present in memory. Rather than loading two copies of the RTL, the loader should first determine whether the RTL is loaded and then load it only when it is not present. There are two ways to determine whether an RTL is present, both of which depend on using a preassigned int vector to access the RTL.

The first method involves reading the interrupt vector contents via function code 35h, Get Interrupt Vector, to determine the starting address of the interrupt service routine. The next step is to place into the DS and SI registers the starting address of the existing routine to be installed. A CMPS instruction is executed for some number of bytes (in CX) to compare the two sections of code. If a match results, the routine is already present. If the compare fails, the routine hasn't been installed. The effectiveness of this method is greatly decreased if all of your RTLs (or memory resident routines) begin with the same sequence of instructions. Conversely, the effectiveness can be greatly increased if all memory resident routines contain the header block shown in Listing 3-7, which uniquely identifies each memory resident routine.

The second method for checking to see whether an RTL or memory resident routine is present requires that all unused vectors (vectors 40h through 0FFh on most systems) be set to a known state. This known state can be either high or low memory (0000:0000 or FFFF:FFFF) or the address of an IRET instruction. In MS-DOS version 2.0 and higher, vector 28h seems to always point to the location of the IRET instruction, although this is not guaranteed! A more elegant solution is to install a pseudo-device driver to handle unsolicited interrupts and to initialize all unused interrupt vectors to point to this routine. (See Chapter 6 on installable device drivers.) This driver can then contain an IRET instruction, report an error to the console, or do whatever else is desired. By permanently allocating one vector to always point to the unsolicited interrupt handler (for example, vector 40h), an installation program can read and compare that vector and the vector of the memory resident routine to see whether the memory resident routine has yet been installed in memory.

Listing 3-7. In-Line Routine Identification

```
enter:   jmp     start             ; bypass the data area
         db      '< routine name >' ; your routine's name goes here
         :       :                 ; data area ...
start:   < beginning of the code >
         :       :
```

Removing Memory Resident Routines

When a program is through using an RTL or when a memory resident routine is no longer needed, you want to be able to recover the memory that was allocated to that routine. The simplest way to remove a memory resident routine is to reboot your system. This restores all the vectors that the system requires and returns all allocated memory to the system. However, this is a rather drastic step and is best reserved for desperate situations.

Without rebooting, removal of the routine should take place in two steps: (1) disable the routine and (2) recover the memory.

The first step is to reset to a null state the vector that points to the routine. The null state indicates to any potential users that the routine is no longer available. If you have patched the memory resident routine to a preexisting vector, the vector must be restored so that it points to the original location. You can write a program to restore the vector if the value of the old vector is stored somewhere in the memory resident routine where the restore program can find it. Programs INIT28 (Listing 3-12) and REMOVE (Listing 3-13) demonstrate this process of saving the vector for later restoration.

If the memory resident routine is driven by its own hardware interrupt (not patched), you must be sure to disable interrupts from that device before you remove the memory resident routine. You can change the value of the vector in the table or leave the vector as it is.

Once the memory resident or RTL routine has been disabled, step two is to recover the memory. Memory is recovered from MS-DOS through the Free Allocated Memory function, function 49h. MS-DOS doesn't seem to care whether you deallocate memory that doesn't really belong to the program, so if the starting address of the block of memory occupied by the memory resident routine can be determined, the memory can be freed and recovered. The installed routine can usually determine this address, so one option is to provide a function code to call the routine and tell it to disable and remove itself. For routines that have been installed through the use of the interrupt vectors, a second interrupt vector may be allocated for the purpose of instructing the routine to remove itself.

If you know that the routine's interrupt vector segment address and the routine's memory block segment address are the same, another method is to write a program to read the vector, determine the memory block segment address from it, and instruct MS-DOS to free the memory.

For some reason, neither of these methods always works because MS-DOS may not recover all of the memory. The problem seems to be internal to MS-DOS, so we can give you no advice at present for doing something about the inconsistency.

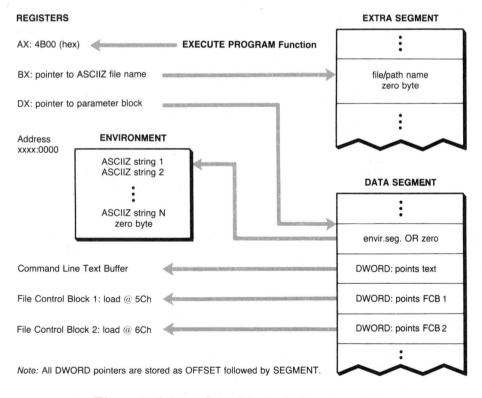

Figure 3-13. Parameter block for function 4Bh (AL = 0)—EXECUTE.

Function 4Bh—Load and Execute Program

Memory resident routines and RTLs often are initiated by a user entry or batch file, but on occasion a program may need to load another program into memory, either for use as a program overlay or as part of a memory resident routine installation process. In either case, the original program is called the *parent* and the other program is called the *child*.

MS-DOS provides for these occasions through the Load Program and Execute function, function code 4Bh. This function can operate in either of two modes. The first mode, Execute Program, is designed to load a program file into memory and execute that program. The child program runs without control from the parent program. This mode is chosen by setting register AL equal to zero and setting the appropriate parameters in the parameter block. The parameters required for this operation are shown in Figure 3-13, and an example of loading and executing a program is contained in the LOAD program, shown in Listing 3-8. The macro library referenced in LOAD is the same one that was used for the EXRTL program (Listing 3-5).

Listing 3-8. Loading Programs with MS-DOS Function 4Bh (AL = 0)

```
;====== LOAD.ASM - This file produces a .COM file ==============
; LOAD has the ability to load and execute another program.
; LOAD is invoked by typing:
;       "LOAD <file name> <program arguments>
; There must be only one space between the LOAD and file name,
; and between the file name and arguments. The file name must
; include the extension.
;
NEWPROG EQU     82h       ; addr of load command line in PSP
NEWSTR  EQU     81h       ; addr of string in PSP (blank 20h)
NEWLEN  EQU     80h       ; addr of command line length
;
INCLUDE STDMAC.INC        ; include macro definitions
;====== PROGRAM SECTION =======================================
;
code_seg SEGMENT
        ASSUME  cs:code_seg
        ASSUME  ds:code_seg
        ORG     0
SEG_ORG EQU     $
        ORG     0100h
main    PROC    FAR
start:
        mov     sp,offset TOP_STK       ; set the top_of_stack
;
```

```
; Parse the command line looking for the end or a space.
; Convert the program name into an ASCIIZ string.
        mov     bx,0                ; clear upper BX
        mov     bl,NEWLEN[bx]       ; get length of command string
        or      bl,bl               ; check length of string
        jnz     cmd_ok
        @DisStr bad_cmd             ; command line error
        jmp     exit
cmd_ok:
        dec     bx                  ; subtract 1 for leading space
        mov     cx,bx               ; copy length into count
        mov     di,NEWPROG          ; search address (1st nonblank)
        mov     al,' '              ; search value (blank)
        repne   scasb               ; search for file extension
        pushf                       ; save results of search
        sub     bx,cx               ; get remaining count
        popf                        ; ... and get search results
        jz      set_zb              ; zero flag => params.
                                    ; ... (found space)
        inc     bx                  ; not zero flag implies end of
                                    ; ... string
set_zb:                             ; convert command line to ASCIIZ
        mov     byte ptr NEWSTR[bx],0
        mov     cmd_buf,cl          ; set length of parameter string
        cmp     cl,0                ; check if end of string reached
        jle     free_mem            ; no command parameters
;
; Take the remainder of the line and transfer it into the
; command line text buffer for the called program.
        inc     cl                  ; transfer the CR also
        mov     si,di               ; transfer source index
        mov     di,offset cmd_txt   ; & set destination index
        rep     movsb               ; transfer remainder of line
        add     cmd_buf,1           ; inc. length for leading space
;
; Free system memory for the Loader and the invoked program.
; Cut down allocation block to minimum necessary
free_mem:
        mov     bx,(offset LST_BYT - SEG_ORG + 15) shr 4
        mov     ah,04Ah             ; ES contains address of PSP
        @DosCall                    ; modify allocated memory
        jnc     modify_ok
        push    ax                  ; (push expected by error)
        @DisStr fail4A              ; error message & terminate
                                    ; ... if fail
        jmp     error
```

continued

Listing 3-8. *continued*

```
;
; Set up the parameter block and register parameters for the
; Load & Execute Program Function call.
modify_ok:
        mov     ax,cs           ; set all parameter segments to
        mov     p1,ax           ; this segment.
        mov     p2,ax
        mov     p3,ax
        mov     dx,offset NEWPROG
        mov     bx,offset param_block
        mov     spoint,sp       ; save stack pointer
        mov     ax,4B00h        ; load & execute program func.
        @DosCall
;
; Restore the Segment Registers and Stack Pointer after call
        mov     cx,cs           ; duplicate CS into all segs.
        mov     ss,cx           ; stack restored first
        mov     sp,cs:spoint    ; restore stack pointer
        mov     ds,cx
        mov     es,cx
        jnc     exit            ; exit program if all okay
        push    ax              ; save error code
        @DisStr fail4B          ; display error if failed
;
; Parse the error code returned from the system and
; display the corresponding text message
error:
        pop     ax              ; get back error code
@Case   ax,+,2,7,8,9,10h,11h>,<em1,em2,em7,em8,em9,em10,em11>
        mov     dx,offset err0  ; bad error code - no match
        jmp     merge
em1:    mov     dx,offset err1  ; invalid function
        jmp     merge
em2:    mov     dx,offset err2  ; file not found
        jmp     merge
em7:    mov     dx,offset err7  ; memory arena trashed
        jmp     merge
em8:    mov     dx,offset err8  ; not enough memory
        jmp     merge
em9:    mov     dx,offset err9  ; invalid memory block
        jmp     merge
em10:   mov     dx,offset err10 ; bad environment
        jmp     merge
em11:   mov     dx,offset err11 ; bad .EXE file format
        jmp     merge
```

```
merge:    mov      ah,09h           ; display string
          @DosCall
exit:     mov      ax,04C00h        ; terminate when finished
          @DosCall
main      ENDP
;
bad_cmd db         'Error in Command Line',CR,LF,'$'
fail4A  db         'Failed to Modify Allocated Memory Blocks'
        db         CR,LF,'$'
fail4B  db         'Failed to Load Program Overlay',CR,LF,'$'
err0    db         '>>> UNKNOWN ERROR CODE <<<',CR,LF,'$'
err1    db         '>>> invalid function <<<',CR,LF,'$'
err2    db         '>>> file not found <<<',CR,LF,'$'
err7    db         '>>> memory arena trashed <<<',CR,LF,'$'
err8    db         '>>> not enough memory <<<',CR,LF,'$'
err9    db         '>>> invalid memory block <<<',CR,LF,'$'
err10   db         '>>> bad environment <<<',CR,LF,'$'
err11   db         '>>> bad .EXE file format <<<',CR,LF,'$'
;
spoint  dw         ?                ; space for stack pointer
param_block        label word
        dw         0                ; use parent environment
        dw         offset cmd_buf
p1      dw         ?                ; cmd. line segment
        dw         5Ch              ; FCB #1 segment & offset
p2      dw         ?
        dw         6Ch              ; FCB #2 segment & offset
p3      dw         ?
cmd_buf db         ?                ; length of command string
        db         ' '              ; space always expected
cmd_txt db         80 dup (?)       ; 80 characters
;
; Local Stack Definition
EVEN                               ; word align the stack
stack   db         32 dup ('stack   ')     ; local stack
TOP_STK EQU        $-2              ; set top stack address
LST_BYT EQU        $                ; last byte in program
;
code_seg ENDS
        END        start
```

The second mode is called Load Overlay. Although it loads a program file, Load Overlay does not invoke the program. Instead, control is immediately returned to the calling program. This mode is selected by setting register AL equal to three, and its parameter block is shown in Figure 3-14.

In either mode of operation, before the Load and Execute Program function may be executed, the initial allocation block of the calling program must be

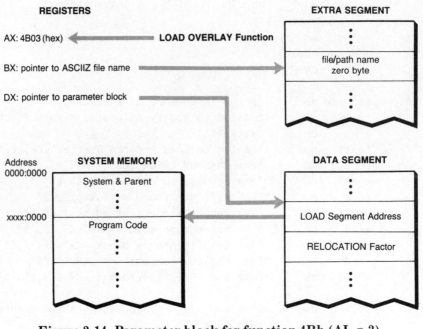

**Figure 3-14. Parameter block for function 4Bh (AL = 3)—
LOAD OVERLAY.**

reset to free up memory space. The reason is that MS-DOS loads programs by
using the COMMAND.COM program loader, which is not in the memory resident part of COMMAND.COM. Instead, the program loader must itself be read
into memory from the disk before it can load a user's program or program overlay. (This also implies that a disk containing the file COMMAND.COM must be
in the system for this function to work.)

There is an important difference between loading program overlays and
loading and executing programs. Program overlays are loaded under control of
the parent program, at an address determined by the parent program, and are
considered part of the parent program. Program files that are to be executed
(function 4Bh with register AL equal to 0) are loaded at an address of the system's choosing and are considered a separate program.

Loading and Executing Programs via MS-DOS (Code 4Bh with AL = 0)

When using the Load and Execute function, MS-DOS requires not only enough
free memory to load the COMMAND.COM program loader but also enough free
memory to contain the new program. This memory is used to create an initial
allocation block for the new program also.

Remember that the initial allocation block of the parent program must be
set large enough to preserve the current program, or MS-DOS overwrites the
block when the new program is loaded. In addition, most of the memory resident

routines or RTLs are written in .COM format. For .COM programs, MS-DOS sets the stack to start at the highest available memory address in the common segment that is used for code, data, and the stack. Unless the top of the stack is relocated downward in the segment, up to 64K of the parent program must be preserved. If the stack is relocated downward, whatever was on the stack (such as the return to MS-DOS) is lost. Of course, the return to MS-DOS on the stack is not needed if you exit from your programs by using function code 4Ch.

Inheritance and Control of the Child Program

Even though the child program is autonomous, the parent program still has a measure of control over the child's behavior. This control is accomplished through *inheritance*, the ability of the parent process to affect how the child process interacts with the rest of the system.

From Figure 3-13 we can see that the parent process supplies the child with a command line, an environment block (or the parent's block if a block is not specified in the EXEC call), and file control blocks. In addition, when a process is loaded, it automatically inherits the majority of its parent's program segment prefix, including the parent's file handle table. By controlling these items, the parent controls the three primary items that control a program: its command line, its file handles, and its environment block.

There are some differences between the command line as it is passed to a child process and as it is used at the system prompt. For one thing, it becomes the responsibility of the parent process to set up any redirection, a task normally handled by COMMAND.COM. Because a child process inherits the file handles of its parent, a parent can easily redirect the I/O of its child. By changing the values of handles stored in the parent's *stdin* or *stdout* devices, the parent will change what the child perceives as *stdin*, *stdout*, or any other valid device. The parent can change these by using the techniques shown earlier in Listing 3-3 (in the section on the PSP's file handle table) or by using the MS-DOS functions for manipulating files and devices. (MS-DOS function 46h, int 21h, Force a Duplicate of a Handle, is one method that may be used to override a handle.)

Note that certain handles can be excluded from being inherited. When a file or device is opened, an *Open Mode* must be specified (see MS-DOS function 3Dh, int 21h, Open File or Device). Bit 7 of the Open Mode is the inheritance bit. When this bit is 0 (the default), the handle will be inherited by any child process. If this bit is set to 1 during the open call, then the returned handle will be exempt from inheritance.

One other way exists in which the parent process can control the child's view of the system. The first entry in the Load and Execute parameter block is a pointer to the child's *environment block*. If the pointer in the Load and Execute parameter block is a zero, the parent's environment is duplicated for the child. If it is nonzero, the block that it points to is loaded as the child's environment.

What does this mean for you? You can write a program to search the environment block for particular entries amd then use those values to establish the program's run-time parameters. Entries may be inserted in the system environment block with the SET command to control the actions of programs that read and act on their environment block. Because the parent process can change the block, the parent process can change the behavior of a child process that reads the block.

An executing process can access its environment block through a pointer stored at offset 2Ch in the PSP. The pointer is used as a segment address with an offset of zero pointing to the start of the block. If this address is transferred to the extra or data segment register, the program can do a string search to find those parameters that the program requires. Be careful when you do this so that you don't lose the PSP address.

The information contained in the PSP is equally valid for the .COM and .EXE format files, and either type may be used with the Load and Execute Program function.

Executing MS-DOS Commands with Function 4Bh

One of the Load and Execute function applications is loading COMMAND.COM. If you consider that COMMAND.COM may be given commands through the command line text buffer, you can see that you can invoke built-in MS-DOS commands from within a user's program. In addition, the command line passed to COMMAND.COM may contain redirection, pipes, and filters. The format of the command text used with this method is nearly the same as that used on the initial command line, except that when invoking COMMAND.COM from a program, the text must begin with /c.

Loading two files (COMMAND.COM and the application program) to execute just one is not a terribly efficient way of running programs. However, the flexibility and power gained by using this method are worth considering.

An Important Warning

The implementation of the Load and Execute Program function in version 2.0 of MS-DOS has a serious bug. It causes the function to "trash" all the segment registers (with the exception of the Code Segment), to destroy the stack pointer, and to destroy the majority of the general registers. If this function is used with any of the subversions of MS-DOS version 2.0 (that is, 2.00 or 2.10), you must save the stack pointer and any needed general registers in memory before the call; and you need to restore the segment registers, stack pointer, and needed general registers after the call. The code sequence appearing in Listing 3-9 seems to do the job for .COM programs.

For .EXE files, you can recover the proper segment values from the values established by LINK (for example, *mov ss,stack*) or from memory located within the Code Segment. To protect the stack, remember to restore the stack segment and stack pointer in that sequence, one right after the other.

Beginning with version 3.0 of MS-DOS, this problem appears to have been corrected. The Load and Execute function returns with all registers intact.

Listing 3-9. Recovering from the Load and Execute Program Function in MS-DOS Versions 2.XX

```
        .
        .
        .
    < set up calling parameters >
        .
        .
        .
    mov     spoint,sp       ; save stack pointer in memory
    mov     ax,4B00h        ; load & execute program function
    int     21h             ; call MS-DOS
; Registers are unchanged if the load fails--don't recover
    jc      error           ; jump if error
    mov     ax,cs           ; get common segment ...
    mov     ds,cx           ; ... for data segment ...
    mov     es,cx           ; ... for extra segment ...
    mov     ss,ax           ; ... and for stack segment
    mov     sp,spoint       ; stack is now realigned
        .
        .
        .
    < recover general registers >
        .
        .
        .
```

Loading Program Overlays via MS-DOS (Code 4Bh with AL = 3)

The ability to execute one program from within another is indeed powerful but has the disadvantage of having the invoked program run once and then terminate. On many occasions, the developer wants to invoke another program to perform some sort of function but in addition wants greater control of the child program or a higher degree of communication with the child, or the developer just wants to be able to call the child program repeatedly without having it reloaded each time. For these circumstances, MS-DOS provides the Load Overlay option for function 4Bh.

One difference between the Load and Execute function and the Load Overlay function is that when loading overlays, the parent program has no means to modify the parameters of the child program. This is because the parent and child are really part of the same program. All that the Load Overlay function accomplishes is to load additional program code (and/or program data) into memory.

Another way in which Load Overlay differs from Load and Execute is that Load Overlay does not require a memory block of its own. It is not given an environment or initial allocation block, as with the Load and Execute Program function. Load Overlay simply loads the requested file in memory, relocating the program's segment values based on the parameters that are provided in the Load Overlay function call (as shown in Figure 3-14). The resulting code may be run as a subroutine but should not be executed as a separate program.

If the overlay terminates through one of the MS-DOS Terminate Program functions, both the overlay and the parent program are terminated. If either function 31h or interrupt 27h (Terminate and Stay Resident) are used to exit, the initial allocation block of the parent routine is modified and the parent program stays in memory. The child stays resident only if the requested memory block is large enough to cover both parent and child. If one of the other Terminate Program functions is executed, both programs are removed from memory.

Figure 3-14 shows that the relocation factor specified as part of the Load Overlay function does nothing to affect the load address of the overlay. Instead, the relocation factor is used to modify offset references within the code being loaded. If the overlay to be loaded is in .COM format, the relocation factor has no effect on the loaded overlay and should be set to 0.

For .EXE files, the relocation factor is added to the values of the segment references that appear in the load file. When loading most .EXE format overlays (which usually default to origin 0000:0000), the relocation factor should be set to the same value as the load address.

Accessing Program Overlays from the Parent Program

Once the program overlay has been loaded, the parent program must access it. Because the parent knows the address at which the overlay was loaded, it can either CALL the overlay or JMP to it. Calling is recommended for the reason that the overlay may then return to the parent by using the RET instruction rather than having to know the return address to JMP to in the parent. If control doesn't need to be returned to the parent program, a JMP is recommended. The overlay then contains the Terminate Program function call.

All accesses, by either CALL or JMP, to the overlay must be *far* references. The code that has been loaded in the overlay is relative to its own segment address and may not be run in the same segment as the parent routine (although it can be loaded into the same memory space). In addition, no PSP is built by the Load Overlay function. Because there is no additional information placed in memory by the loader, the code and data are loaded from the overlay file beginning at the exact load address specified.

Let's consider the simplest case: overlays that are loaded from .COM format files. All .COM files have origins of 100 hex. That is, their code starts at address 100 hex relative to their segment. All references contained in the program are relative to that address. Because the .COM file is loaded right on the load address, you would be incorrect to use the load address as the segment value for the overlay. Figure 3-15 shows that if the load address is used as the segment, the offset values in the code are misplaced by 100 hex. The correct program segment address to use is the load address minus 10 (hex), which translates the code offsets by 100 hex.

A different problem exists for .EXE format programs. When an .EXE file is loaded for execution, MS-DOS initializes the Code Segment and Stack Segment to point to the proper segments and the Instruction Pointer to point to the first instruction of the program. When an .EXE file is loaded as an overlay, MS-DOS doesn't provide these values. How then does the parent program know where to enter the program?

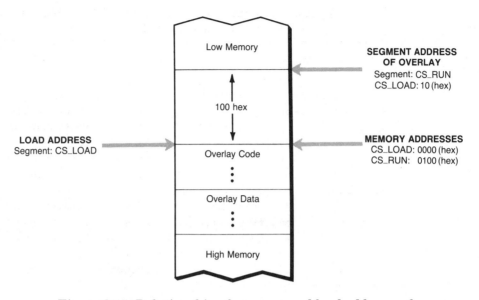

Figure 3-15. Relationship of segment and load addresses for .COM format overlays.

Because .EXE files usually have an origin of zero, couldn't we just call or jump to the load address? That would depend on how the program was written. For .EXE files created from a single source file, LINK and MS-DOS load the segments in memory in the same order in which they appear in the source program! A common order for defining segments is stack segment, then data segment, then code segment. (The reason is to minimize forward references in the code segment.) For an .EXE program to be callable at its load address, the code segment must be the first segment in the .ASM file, and the entry point must be the first instruction in the code segment. MASM and LINK have no problems handling this, although in some cases you may need to use override directives to resolve forward references for MASM.

Listing 3-10 shows how the load and call sequence could appear when using the Load Overlay function for a .COM file. The sequence for an .EXE type program is simpler. No translation from load address to run address is needed. We have assumed that all segment registers in the parent program are already initialized and that Modify Allocated Memory has already been called to free enough memory for the COMMAND.COM loader. The sample program allocates the memory that is to contain the overlay code. This reserves that area of memory so that if the overlay also allocates memory, a virgin area is provided. Otherwise, the overlay could allocate the memory that it already occupies and overwrite itself. The actual space reserved can be adjusted for the true size of the overlay.

The overlay may be changed as often as necessary for the execution of the program. The only warning that applies to all uses of the Load Overlay function

**Listing 3-10. Loading and Accessing a .COM Program with
MS-DOS Function 4Bh (AL = 3)**

```
                    .
                    .
                    .
; Allocate memory for Overlay
        mov     ah,48h              ; allocate memory function
        mov     bx,1000h            ; assume 64K segment for now
        int     21h                 ; call MS-DOS
        jc      error               ; branch if error occurred
        mov     params,ax           ; save memory address
; Load overlay
        mov     dx,offset params    ; access parameter block
        mov     bx,offset filename  ; access ASCIIZ file name
        mov     ax,4B03h            ; load overlay function
        int     21h                 ; call MS-DOS
        jc      error               ; branch if error occurred
; Call overlay
        mov     ax,params           ; get load address
        sub     ax,10h              ; translate to run address
        mov     run_seg,ax          ; and save it
        push    ds                  ; save data segment
        call    dword ptr run_adr   ; call overlay
; Free memory that was used for overlay
        pop     ds                  ; restore data segment
        mov     ah,49h              ; free memory function
        mov     es,params           ; get memory block address
        int     21h                 ; call MS-DOS
        jc      error               ; branch if error occurred
                    .
                    .
                    .
params  dw      ?                   ; load address
        dw      0                   ; relocation value
run_adr dw      0100h               ; new instruction pointer
run_seg dw      ?                   ; new code segment value
```

is that MS-DOS does nothing to prevent you from loading the overlay on top of
the currently executing program or anywhere else in memory, including the
system itself! Although someone might find such a trick useful, it is definitely
not recommended procedure, and care should be taken to prevent its inadvertent occurrence.

Loading Memory Resident Programs

Memory resident routines and RTLs to be installed from another program are
best loaded through the Load and Execute Program function so that the new

routine has its own memory block. In these cases, the calling program (the parent) receives control after the memory resident program's initialization section executes its Terminate and Stay Resident request.

If a stand-alone memory resident routine was loaded, the parent program terminates, leaving the memory resident program in place. This breaks up memory free space, but there is no risk of MS-DOS loading a subsequent program over the memory resident routine. If an RTL were loaded, the parent program would be ready to call the RTL as needed. When the parent routine terminates, it has the option of leaving the RTL in memory for subsequent use or of removing it by resetting its interrupt vector and freeing its memory block.

Because the Load and Execute Program function does not inform the calling routine of the load address of the memory resident routine and because that address cannot be passed back to the parent in the single byte reserved for the program's exit code (see Terminate and Stay Resident, function 31h), the parent routine must resort to the tactics discussed in preceding text to determine the location of the memory block to be removed.

A Special Case: Part-Time Run-Time Libraries

One of the many features that can be implemented with the functions presented is a part-time run-time library. Part-time RTLs are resident only when required and the rest of the time reside on disk. A part-time RTL is implemented by installing the header part of an RTL exactly as described in this chapter. However, this header contains none of the code for executing the library functions; that is, it doesn't contain the library routines themselves, which are left on disk in another file. Flowchart 3-1 shows the sequence of events in the life of a part-time RTL.

When one of the routines in the library is accessed (via an int), the header portion of the routine loads the library file into memory using function code 4Bh with AL = 3 (Load Overlay) and locks it into its own memory. The desired library routine is then called to execute the requested function. Either the header or the individual library routines can contain the IRET to return to the caller. From this point on, all subsequent calls access the library without having to wait for the load because the RTL stays resident in memory.

When the main program terminates or requires the RTL's space, it signals the RTL entry point with a code to release the memory allocated to the RTL. Because the header portion specified the load address of the library routines when it loaded them and because the memory block they occupy is "owned" by the header, freeing the memory is no problem. After this is accomplished, the header goes back into hibernation and waits for the next call.

Context Switching and Switching Stacks

Because so many of the topics that have been discussed in this chapter relate to operations between separate programs with separate stacks, the process of switching deserves some attention. Stack switching, or changing from one stack to another, is part of a broader topic called *context switching*.

Flowchart 3-1. Part-time RTL load sequence.

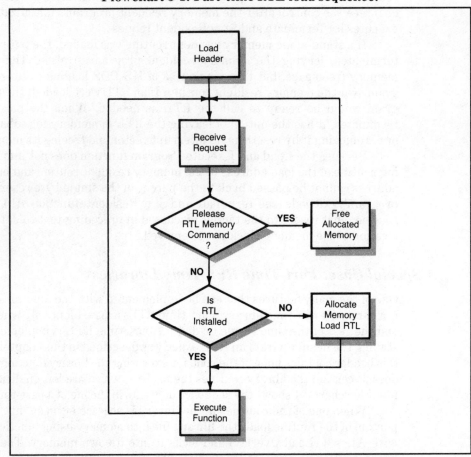

If you view the segments in which a program executes as its context, you can see that in many instances you need to change the entire context of a program. Examples of such instances are when invoking memory resident routines, calling RTLs, and using some types of overlays or co-routines. (A *co-routine* is a sort of special overlay where there is no parent-child relationship.) In these cases, when one routine receives control, it wishes to set up its own data, extra, and stack segments for execution. At the time that it receives control from the other program, the only thing that is known for sure is that its code segment and instruction pointer are set to the proper values. Refer to Listing 3-9. We had to reset the program context after calling the Load and Execute Program function, and this listing shows one way to establish a context for a program. The example in Listing 3-9 unfortunately does not preserve the context of the previous program but simply overwrites it.

When you need to save the entire register set on receipt of control, the easiest way is to set up the new program's stack first and then proceed to stack the other registers. Because the values of the stack segment and stack pointer cannot be saved on the caller's stack (there would be no way to retrieve them) and because they cannot be saved on the new stack (which hasn't been set up yet), the stack's parameters must be saved in memory. If you can stand mixing code and data in the same segment just this once, the sequence shown in Listing 3-11 can be used to store the old stack segment and pointer and set up the new stack segment and pointer.

Listing 3-11. Stack Switching for an .EXE Program

```
enter:   mov     cs:old_stk_seg,ss      ; save old stack values
         mov     cs:old_stk_ptr,sp
         mov     ss,cs:new_stk_seg      ; load new stack values
         mov     sp,cs:new_stk_ptr
         push    ds                     ; stack segment registers
         push    es
         push    ax                     ; start stacking general regs.
          :       :
         push    bp
         push    si
         push    di
          :       :
body: < body of the program >           ; your code goes here
          :       :
         pop     di                     ; start recovering general
         pop     si
         pop     bp
          :       :
         pop     ax
         pop     es                     ; recover segment registers
         mov     ss,cs:old_stk_seg      ; restore old stack values
         mov     sp,cs:old_stk_ptr
         jmp     exit                   ; bypass data storage
;
old_stk_seg   dw      ?                 ; caller's stack segment
old_stk_ptr   dw      ?                 ; caller's stack pointer
new_stk_seg   dw      segment stack     ; this routine's stack segment
new_stk_ptr   dw      top_of_stack      ; this routine's stack pointer
exit:                                   ; exit position
         ret                            ; return to calling program
```

The code in Listing 3-11 depends on having the values for the stack segment and stack pointer already located in memory. This could be accomplished for a memory resident or run-time routine by the initialization process. For an

.EXE program, MS-DOS places the proper values in memory during the relocation process.

Because .COM routines cannot contain segment values, these routines require another method for switching stacks. Embedding the value for the top of stacks in memory causes no problem, except with determining the starting segment address. Because .COM routines share the same segment for all purposes, the stack segment value may be obtained from the code segment register. Unfortunately, the 8086 family does not support moves from segment register to segment register, so the value must be passed indirectly. Because none of the registers have been saved as yet, the value is passed through memory using the code segment. To implement this modification, start the routine with the instruction:

```
mov      cs:new_stk_seg,cs ; get new stack segment
```

If you intend doing a fair amount of stack switching in your programs, you can set up two macros to include the necessary code. The first macro includes the code from *enter* to *body*, and the second macro contains the code from *body* to *exit*. Both macros must agree on the names of the stack variables in the data area, and the second macro must accept the label *top_of_stack* as a parameter to include in the *dw* statement for *new_stk_ptr*. The RET instruction should not be part of the macros. This allows them to be used with JMP and IRET exits as well as RET exits.

For .EXE files, the second macro must also accept the name of the stack segment as a parameter. Listing 3-12 (INIT28), found later in this chapter, contains an example in a .COM format of the two macros just described.

Additional Considerations for Stack Switching

When swapping stacks or otherwise manipulating the stack segment, the program is vulnerable to interrupts. Should an interrupt occur when the stack segment but not the stack pointer has been changed, the system could very well crash. In the 8086 family, this is prevented by changing the stack pointer *immediately* following the instruction that loaded the stack segment. When an 8086 family processor loads a segment register (through either a MOV or POP instruction), interrupts are prevented from occurring until after the next instruction executes. This feature allows both the stack segment and the stack pointer registers to be safely updated. This also explains why DEBUG appears to skip one instruction when tracing a MOV to a segment register. DEBUG single-steps the program by setting the trap flag, which generates a type #1 interrupt following most instructions. Because interrupts are disabled following a MOV to a segment register, DEBUG does not regain control until two instructions following the MOV.

In any case, you don't always have to go to the lengths demonstrated in Listing 3-11. Many times some registers may be pushed onto the caller's stack, allowing the registers to be used in the program or at least to transfer new values into the stack register. The individual programmer must decide how much of the current context should be saved in a particular program.

If context switching is used with co-routines, each routine ends up saving the other routine's context. Although this is redundant, because only one routine needs to save the other's context, it is not really harmful. Co-routines that use this structure should exit only via function code 4Ch, Terminate Program, so that MS-DOS correctly terminates the program regardless of the state of the stack.

If parameters are to be passed from one program to another and each program maintains its own stack, the BP register cannot be used to access parameters on the stack. Instead the programmer needs to extract the caller's stack segment value and move it into either the DS or ES segment registers and perform the memory access relative to that register. The parameters may then be read from the caller's stack even though the called routine is using its own stack.

Underpinnings for Memory Residency

In some ways, MS-DOS itself is implemented as a memory resident program. Look back at Figure 3-15 to see the memory layout for a typical MS-DOS system that is running version 2.0 or higher. (Note that this does not necessarily apply to versions higher than 3.1.) All of these parts, with the exception of a transient piece of COMMAND.COM, are resident in memory at all times. User programs access MS-DOS through interrupts or jumps to interrupts, just as we did for our memory resident routines.

Certain parts of this system are common to all MS-DOS systems and are compatible even among systems of different version numbers. Other parts of the system are unique to the particular version number or particular hardware that is running MS-DOS. Table 3-6 lists the different sections that make up the MS-DOS system and the attributes that are associated with each part. The names may change from system to system, but the functions are equivalent. Your user's manual tells you what files are for what part of the system. Note that some of the files may be hidden files that do not appear in a directory listing. These files are still on disk.

Table 3-6. Components of the MS-DOS System

Name	Attributes	Function
COMMAND.COM	Compatible	Command processor
IBMDOS.COM or other	Compatible	System services
IBMBIO.COM or other	System-dependent	ROM-BIOS interface or BIOS
ROM-BIOS	System-dependent	ROM-based BIOS (some)

ROM-BIOS versus a Loadable BIOS

There are two main areas of difference that may occur within the realm of MS-DOS systems. These differences drastically affect what can be done and what cannot be done in the way of memory resident systems. One of these differences is whether your particular hardware has its BIOS (basic input/output system) in ROM (read-only memory) or in a file that must be loaded from the disk. The effect of these alternatives is that a ROM-based BIOS (often called a ROM-BIOS) provides a set environment for that particular machine, whereas a loaded BIOS is often inaccessible to the programmer. (Unlike CP/M systems, MS-DOS suppliers don't seem to be as willing to provide source listings for a loadable BIOS.)

The importance of this option lies in the fact that MS-DOS is not *reentrant!* That is, if you have written a memory resident routine that either is interrupt driven or patches into the MS-DOS interrupt vectors, that routine may not call MS-DOS! MS-DOS apparently maintains only one set of internal data buffers, and any attempt at reentering that set results in a total failure of the system. Because MS-DOS isn't reentrant, it cannot be used to perform I/O or support functions for interrupt-driven memory resident programs. This restriction may be lifted whenever Microsoft releases a concurrent version of MS-DOS, which we hope will provide some method for handling such events. Until then, programmers who wish to write memory resident routines most likely will have to rely on a ROM-BIOS or will have to write their own driver routines. All of these options result in nonportable code, but sometimes that is the price one pays for desired features.

If the BIOS is actually loaded from the disk during boot, you almost certainly will have to write your own routines to interface with the hardware. Unlike communications between normal programs and MS-DOS, which use the interrupt vectors, MS-DOS communicates with the BIOS through CALLs and JMPs. There is no MS-DOS standard jump table for the BIOS (á la CP/M) that can be used by the application programmer, so you can see that having a ROM-based BIOS can be a great asset in writing memory resident routines that need to access the hardware.

Interrupt versus Polled Systems

The second area of difference is whether the hardware is interrupt driven or polled. By *interrupt driven*, we mean a system that uses hardware interrupts to notify the BIOS of events that have occurred. By *polled*, we mean a system that must repeatedly ask, or poll, the hardware to check for the occurrence of events. Interrupt-driven systems provide more flexibility and greater opportunity for installing some types of memory resident programs.

One of the temptations of interrupt-driven systems is to use one of the hardware interrupts to drive a memory resident routine. This sometimes can be an easy way out and sometimes can be a nightmare. As long as you use a local stack and don't trash the system's stack, MS-DOS itself is usually insensitive to the presence of interrupts. However, your BIOS may not be so forgiving. Often the BIOS is not written with interrupts in mind, or at least not ones that the authors of the BIOS were expecting. Should an interrupt occur in a time-sensitive portion of the BIOS, as in reading or writing to a disk drive, the interrupt service routine could disrupt the operation of the BIOS, with the result that the entire system may fail and hang.

Patching into the Interrupt Vectors

Memory resident routines are activated in one of two ways: they are initiated by hardware interrupts (event-driven), or they must patch into the existing system (trap-driven). A combination of these methods is also possible, where the patch point is one of the hardware interrupts. If the system that you are using does not support hardware interrupts, you must use the patch method.

Hardware interrupts that are unused by MS-DOS can be used to access with few complications a memory resident routine. As long as the program doesn't call MS-DOS, no system conflicts should occur. If the hardware of the system is accessed by the memory resident routine, it should check to make sure that no one else is accessing the hardware at that time and be careful to restore the hardware to its original state. An example of a minimal impact interrupt-driven routine is a program to save all the registers of a currently running program in a reserved section of memory when an outside interrupt occurs. Such a routine is useful when debugging a program in real time. However, if the interrupt that is to be used is also used by the system, the routine should be considered trap driven because the memory resident routine is installed with a patch.

The *patch method* is a way of inserting a memory resident routine into the normal system flow at a given point so that all accesses to that point of the system pass through the memory resident routine. An example of patching that also involves a hardware interrupt is found when a keyboard-driven memory resident routine is installed. To accomplish this, the keyboard interrupt vector is changed to point to the memory resident routine. The value of the previous keyboard vector is stored in the destination address of a *far* jump instruction that is used to exit the memory resident routine. When a keyboard interrupt occurs, the memory resident routine is entered. When the interrupt completes, the memory resident routine jumps to the keyboard handler. If the memory resident routine actually uses the keyboard input in some way that does not continue to the keyboard handler, the memory resident routine must service and clear the interrupt itself and then return to the calling program with an IRET instruction. In all cases, the memory resident routine must preserve the context of the interrupted program.

Other possible patch points that do not use hardware interrupts are patches into one of the software interrupt vectors or into a jump address. Patching into MS-DOS is usually done via the software interrupt vectors because there is no recognizable jump table in the MS-DOS system. In addition, because no standard interface exists between MS-DOS and its BIOS interface, patching between MS-DOS and the BIOS is extremely difficult. Using software interrupts remains the solution.

One of the common places to patch into the MS-DOS interrupt vectors is at int 28h. This is apparently an auxiliary interrupt used internally by MS-DOS. This also seems to be one patch point where frequent access is assured. A memory resident routine patched at this point must not call the MS-DOS function handlers, or a system failure results. The memory resident routine should also use its own context to prevent altering the existing stack and registers. Listing 3-12 shows the code necessary to install a memory resident routine at interrupt 28h and the accompanying memory resident routine.

Listing 3-12. Program INIT28—Patching into System Interrupt Vectors

```
; ==== INIT28 - This file produces a .COM program ================
; ==== Install Memory Resident Routine by patching into int 28 ==
PAGE    60,132
; ==== EQUATES FOR INSTALL INTERRUPT ============================
VECT_NUM EQU    28h             ; vector number to install
OFF     EQU     0h              ; routine inactive
ON      EQU     0FFFFh          ; routine active
;
INCLUDE STDMAC.INC              ; include macro definitions
; ==== BEGIN PROGRAM SECTION ====================================
init28  SEGMENT
        ASSUME  cs:init28
        ASSUME  ds:init28
        ORG     0
SEG_ORG EQU     $
        ORG     0100h
main    PROC    FAR
start:  jmp     init            ; skip "old vector" storage
old_v   dd      ?               ; space to store old vector
entry:  jmp     first           ; skip "identification"
        db      'TEST ROUTINE'
first:  @SwapNewStack           ; MACRO to swap to new stack
        cmp     go_switch,ON     ; test if I am active
        jne     bypas           ; yes - continue to exit
        mov     go_switch,OFF    ; no - set active switch
;
;       < YOUR MEMORY RESIDENT ROUTINE GOES HERE >
;
        mov     go_switch,ON     ; set inactive
bypas:  @SwapOldStack TOS       ; restore stack (& include data)
        jmp     cs:exit         ; goto interrupt service Routine
exit            dd      ?
go_switch       dw      ?
                db      32 dup ('stack  ')
```

```
TOS             EQU     $
LAST_BYTE       EQU     $
;
; ===== INITIALIZATION SECTION - THROWN AWAY AFTER LOAD =========
;
init:   mov     go_switch,OFF           ; prevent activation
        mov     ah,35h                  ; get vector address
        mov     al,VECT_NUM
        @DosCall
        mov     word ptr exit,bx        ; save pointer IP for exit
        mov     word ptr exit+2,es      ; save pointer CS for exit
        mov     word ptr old_v,bx       ; save pointer IP for remove
        mov     word ptr old_v+2,es     ; save pointer CS for remove
        mov     ah,25h                  ; set new pointer
        mov     al,VECT_NUM
        mov     dx,offset entry         ; set pointer IP
                                        ; ... (CS & DS same)
        @DosCall
        mov     go_switch,ON
        mov     dx,(offset LAST_BYTE - SEG_ORG + 15) shr 4
        mov     ah,31h                  ; terminate & stay resident
        @DosCall
;
main    ENDP
init28  ENDS
        END     start
```

Other possible patch points depend on the type of memory resident routine and the frequency with which it must be called. For example, a print spooler routine (which prints files while allowing other programs to be run at the same time) not only must trap an interrupt to activate it to send characters to the printer, but must also trap any accesses to MS-DOS that use the printer so that conflicts do not occur. Figure 3-16 shows a print spooler trapping int 28h to activate itself and trapping int 21h to guard itself against printer access conflicts. Your particular system may require additional traps if it provides other means of accessing the printer.

In any use of trap vectors to implement some semblance of concurrency, there is a risk of running afoul of programs that access the hardware directly. For example, if a keyboard trap vector is installed to provide some feature and if another program bypasses the keyboard vector and instead reads the hardware directly, the memory resident routine is bypassed. These effects can occur quite easily if multiple memory resident programs are installed because each program must bypass MS-DOS to perform I/O. For example, if both a print spooler and a memory resident routine to print the contents of the video display are installed and both are activated at the same time, a conflict occurs. These

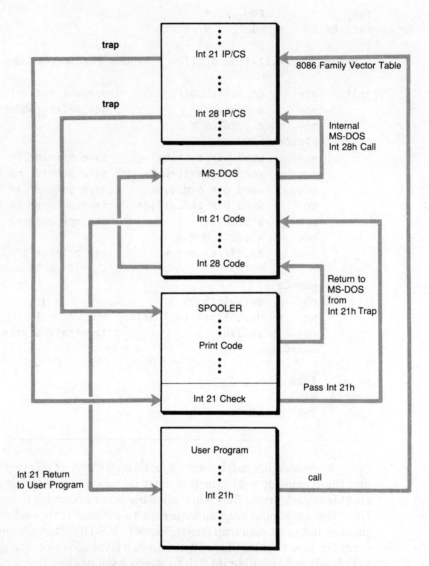

Figure 3-16. Print spooler using trap vectors.

problems can occur with commercially available memory resident routines also. The only way for users to protect themselves is to install one routine at a time, checking for conflicts.

REMOVE—An Integrated Program Example

The REMOVE program (see Listing 3-13) is intended to "uninstall" a memory resident program, based on the example given in INIT28 (Listing 3-12). REMOVE attempts to identify the memory resident program by dumping the bytes following the entry point, and it displays the 4 bytes preceding the entry point as a previous vector address. In addition, REMOVE assumes that the program is in a .COM format and attempts to locate the addresses of the PSP and environment block. REMOVE presents all this information to the user and prompts the user to decide to attempt removal or not.

Listing 3-13. REMOVE—Remove Memory Resident Routines Patched into Interrupt Vectors

```
PAGE    60,132
;===== REMOVE - This file generates a .COM program ==============
;===== Removes a memory resident program that has been patched ==
;===== into an interrupt vector. ===============================
; (ISR refers to Interrupt Service Routine)
OLD_IP  EQU     -4              ; possible IP location in ISR
OLD_CS  EQU     -2              ; possible CS location in ISR
ID      EQU     0               ; location of 1st byte in ISR
IRETOP  EQU     0CFh            ; IRET op-code
;
;====== MACRO DEFINITIONS FOR UTILITIES =======================
;
INCLUDE STDMAC.INC              ; include macro definitions
;
remove  SEGMENT
        ASSUME cs:remove
        ASSUME ds:remove
; Define needed addresses within the Program Segment Prefix
        ORG     2Ch
env_adr LABEL   WORD            ; address of environment pointer
        ORG     80h
cmd_len db      ?               ; command line string length
new_len db      ?               ; buffered read string length
cmd_buf db      ?               ; command line string
;====== BEGIN PROGRAM CODE ====================================
        ORG     0100h
main    PROC    FAR
start:
        mov     ch,byte ptr [cmd_len]
        cmp     ch,0            ; was argument provided ?
        jnz     have_cmd
; Argument not provided - prompt user to supply one
get_cmd:
        @DisStr request         ; ask for vector number
        mov     byte ptr [cmd_len],80
```

continued

Listing 3-13. *continued*

```
          mov     dx,offset cmd_len
          mov     ah,0Ah            ; perform buffered read into
          @DosCall                  ; the command line buffer
          @DisChr LF                ; new line
          mov     ch,new_len        ; get size of text entered
          cmp     ch,0              ; see if user responded
          jz      abort             ; if not then assume exit
          inc     ch                ; adjust response to conform
have_cmd:
          cmp     ch,3              ; check for proper # characters
          je      ok_cmd
          @DisStr bad_cmd           ; if incorrect flag error
abort:    jmp     finis
ok_cmd:   mov     bx,offset cmd_buf
          mov     ch,2              ; parse 2 characters
          call    get_hex           ; convert # in buffer to binary
          jc      abort             ; exit if error in parse
          mov     vec_num,al        ; save vector address
          mov     ah,35h            ; get vector pointer from MS-DOS
          @DosCall
          mov     vec_ip,bx         ; store the vector IP
          mov     al,vec_num        ; restore vector number
          call    show_vector       ; display contents of vector
          @DisStr askresv
          call    yesno
          jc      no_restore        ; don't wish vector restored
;
; RESTORE THE VECTOR FROM ADDRESS IN ROUTINE
          mov     bx,vec_ip         ; get address of routine
          mov     dx,es:OLD_IP[bx]; get old vector IP
          mov     cx,es:OLD_CS[bx]; get old vector CS
          mov     al,vec_num        ; get the vector number
          push    ds                ; save current DS
          mov     ds,cx             ; set vector destination
          mov     ah,25h            ; set vector address
          @DosCall
          pop     ds                ; restore data segment
;
; Display environment address and ask if wish removed.
; The environment address will be valid only if this is a .COM
no_restore:
          @DisStr askremb           ; display environment address
          mov     ax,es:env_adr     ; get address of environment
          mov     ch,4
```

```
        call    bin2hex         ; display possible envir. seg.
        @DisStr ipO
        call    yesno
        jc      no_env          ; bypass removing the environment
;
; REMOVE ENVIRONMENT BLOCK
        push    es              ; save main routine segment
        mov     cx,es:env_adr   ; get address of environment
        mov     es,cx           ; and prepare to remove
        call    rem_mem         ; attempt to remove block
        pop     es              ; restore address of main routine
;
; Display Main Routine Segment Address and ask if want removed
no_env:
        @DisStr askremm         ; display main block address
        mov     ax,es           ; address of main block
        mov     ch,4
        call    bin2hex
        @DisStr ipO
        call    yesno
        jc      finis           ; don't want to remove main block
;
; REMOVE MAIN MEMORY RESIDENT ROUTINE MEMORY BLOCK
        call    rem_mem         ; attempt to remove block
;
finis:  mov     ax,4C00h        ; terminate program
        @DosCall
;
vec_num db      ?               ; space to store vector number
vec_ip  dw      ?               ; space to store vector IP
;
request db      'Vector number to remove: $'
bad_cmd db      'Command line format error - aborting',CR,LF,'$'
askresv db      'Restore Vector from Old? $'
askremb db      'Remove Environment Block: $'
askremm db      'Remove Main Program Block: $'
ipO     db      ':0000 $'
;
main    ENDP
;
; ===== REM_MEM uses MS-DOS Function 49 (hex) to attempt to    ==
; ===== deallocate the memory block addressed by ES.          ==
;
rem_mem PROC    NEAR
        push    ax              ; save registers
```

continued

Listing 3-13. *continued*

```
        push    cx
        push    dx                  ; used by @DisStr & @DisChr
        mov     ah,49h              ; free allocated memory
        @DosCall
        jnc     free_ok             ; no errors - give success msg
        push    ax                  ; save error code
        @DisStr fail                ; inform that it failed
        pop     ax                  ; and give the error code
        mov     ch,4                ; (all 4 digits)
        call    bin2hex
        @DisChr CR
        @DisChr LF
        jmp     rem_exit
free_ok:
        @DisStr pass
rem_exit:
        pop     dx                  ; restore registers
        pop     cx
        pop     ax
        ret
pass    db      'Successful Free Allocated Memory',CR,LF,'$'
fail    db      'Failed to Free Allocated Memory - Error Code: $'
rem_mem ENDP
;
; ===== YESNO prompts the user for a Y or N. If Y is entered  ==
; ===== YESNO returns w/o carry (NC). If N or <RET> is entered =
; ===== then YESNO returns w/ carry (CY).                     ==
yesno   PROC    NEAR
        push    ax
        push    dx
        @DisStr prompt              ; prompt user for input
retry:  mov     ah,08h              ; get response (no echo)
        @DosCall
        @Case   al,<'y','Y','n','N',CR>,<yes,yes,no,no,no>
        @DisChr 07h                 ; illegal response - beep
        jmp     retry               ; and wait some more
no:     @DisChr 'N'
        stc
        jmp     yn_exit
yes:    @DisChr 'Y'
        clc                         ; clear carry
yn_exit:
        @DisChr CR
        @DisChr LF
```

```
            pop     dx
            pop     ax
            ret
prompt  db          ' (Y/N): $',
yesno   ENDP
;
; ===== SHOW_VECTOR displays the contents of location pointed ==
; ===== to by ES:BX in both HEX and ASCII format. Since it is ==
; ===== intended for use in displaying vectors, it also shows ==
; ===== AL in hex as a vector number, and informs the user if ==
; ===== the first byte pointed to is an IRET instruction.    ==
; ===== SHOW_VECTOR also displays the two words located before =
; ===== the vector address as CS:IP in case the user has      ==
; ===== stored the old vector address there on installation.  ==
;
show_vector     PROC    NEAR
            push    cx              ; save registers
            push    dx
            push    ax              ; used by @DisChr & @DisStr
            @DisStr vmsg1           ; start displaying messages
            pop     ax              ; restore value of AL
            push    ax
            mov     ah,al
            mov     ch,2            ; display 2 digits of hex
            call    bin2hex
            @DisStr vmsg2           ; show potential restore address
            mov     ax,es:OLD_CS[bx]; get possible CS value
            mov     ch,4
            call    bin2hex         ; display possible old CS
            @DisChr ':'
            mov     ax,es:OLD_IP[bx]; get possible CS value
            call    bin2hex         ; display possible old CS
            cmp     byte ptr es:ID[bx],IRETOP
            jne     noiret          ; is this an IRET instruction?
            @DisStr vmsg3
noiret: @DisChr CR
            @DisChr LF
            mov     cl,16           ; dump 16 bytes
            call    dump            ; show HEX and ASCII values
            pop     ax
            pop     dx
            pop     cx
            ret
vmsg1   db          'Vector # $'
vmsg2   db          '  Old Vector: $'
```

continued

Listing 3-13. *continued*

```
vmsg3    db      ' IRET$'
show_vector      ENDP
;
; ===== DUMP displays the contents of location pointed to by  ==
; ===== ES:BX in both HEX and ASCII format. CL contains the # ==
; ===== of bytes to display.
dump     PROC    NEAR
         push    ax              ; save registers
         push    dx              ; used by @DisChr & @DisStr
         push    bx
         push    cx
         @DisStr dmsg1           ; start displaying messages
         mov     ch,2            ; 2 hex digits per byte
h_dump:  mov     ah,es:[bx]      ; get byte
         inc     bx              ; next byte
         call    bin2hex
         @DisChr ' '
         dec     cl              ; loop count - 1
         jnz     h_dump          ; repeat until count 0
         @DisStr dmsg2           ; next section
         pop     cx              ; restore values of
         pop     bx              ; ... BX (index) ...
         push    bx              ; ... and ...
         push    cx              ; ... CX (count)
t_dump:  mov     al,es:[bx]      ; get byte
         inc     bx              ; next byte
         cmp     al,' '          ; check for printable range
         jb      no_prnt         ; ? < space
         cmp     al,7Eh          ; DEL is not printable either
         ja      no_prnt
         @DisChr al              ; is printable - do so ...
         jmp     nxt_txt
no_prnt:
         @DisChr '.'             ; use "." for nonprintable
nxt_txt:
         dec     cl              ; loop count - 1
         jnz     t_dump          ; repeat until count 0
; All done - clean up & exit
         @DisChr CR
         @DisChr LF
         pop     cx              ; restore registers
         pop     bx
         pop     dx
         pop     ax
```

```
        ret
dmsg1   db      'HEX: $'
dmsg2   db      ' ASCII: $'
dump    ENDP
;
; ===== GET_HEX parses the buffer pointed to by BX for a hex  ==
; ===== number, returning the number in AX. The # of digits   ==
; ===== to parse is contained in CH, and BX is incremented by ==
; ===== the # of digits processed.                            ==
;
get_hex PROC    NEAR
        push    dx              ; save DX register
        push    cx              ; save CX register
        mov     ax,0            ; clear accumulated #
        mov     dh,0            ; clear upper workspace
        mov     cl,4            ; set shift count for later
nxt_digit:
        mov     dl,[bx]         ; get character
        sub     dl,'0'
        jb      bad_digit       ; ? < '0' - illegal
        cmp     dl,0Ah
        jb      ok_digit        ; '0' through '9' - ok
        sub     dl,'A'-'0'
        jb      bad_digit       ; '9' < ? < 'A' - illegal
        add     dl,0Ah
        cmp     dl,10h
        jb      ok_digit        ; 'A' through 'F' - ok
        sub     dl,'a'-'A'-0Ah
        jb      bad_digit       ; 'F' < ? < 'a' - illegal
        add     dl,0Ah
        cmp     al,10h
        jae     bad_digit       ; 'f' < ? - illegal
ok_digit:
        add     ax,dx           ; accumulate digits in AX
        inc     bx              ; next digit
        dec     ch
        jnz     more_digit      ; more digits to accumulate
        clc                     ; no error - clear CY
        pop     cx
        pop     dx
        ret
more_digit:
        shl     ax,cl           ; open room for next digit
        jmp     nxt_digit       ; loop for next digit
bad_digit:
```

continued

Listing 3-13. *continued*

```
        @DisStr digit_error      ; inform of entry error
        stc                      ; error - set carry
        pop     cx
        pop     dx
        ret
digit_error db 'A two-digit hex number was expected',CR,LF,'$'
get_hex ENDP
;
; ===== BIN2HEX displays the value contained in AX as a hex #.==
; ===== No registers are destroyed. CH contains the # of     ==
; ===== digits to display, taken left to right in AX. (AH is ==
; ===== displayed if CH equal 2.)                            ==
;
bin2hex PROC    NEAR
        push    ax               ; save all registers
        push    bx
        push    cx
        push    dx
        mov     cl,4             ; set rotate count
        mov     bx,ax            ; copy AX for work
; Begin DIGIT loop to process digits
moredig:
        rol     bx,cl            ; convert binary to hex
        mov     al,bl
        and     al,0Fh
        add     al,90h
        daa
        adc     al,40h
        daa
; Display the digit & check for more - restore if done.
        @DisChr al
        dec     ch
        jnz     moredig
        pop     dx
        pop     cx
        pop     bx
        pop     ax
        ret
bin2hex ENDP
;
remove  ENDS
        END     start
```

The section that displays the contents of the location addressed by the vector may be extracted and made into a program. This program can be used to display the contents of any of the interrupt vectors and their possible service routines.

REMOVE serves as an example of many of the topics discussed in this chapter and helps to demonstrate recommended installation and removal techniques.

Summary

In this chapter we have presented material about many separate topics. In addition to the promised material on program and memory management, we have also included material on organizing programs and on the structure and contents of MS-DOS programs. More examples of the way MASM operates have been given.

Although some of the material covered may seem only occasionally useful, we think that you will find applications for most of it. Especially important to the systems and applications programmers are the PSP and the organization of programs in memory.

Terminate and Stay Resident Programming

4

ERMINATE and stay resident (TSR) programs are useful tools, but their operation remains a mystery to most users. The MS-DOS architecture and the PC hardware impose constraints on the things a TSR may do and when it may do them. Some of these limitations manifest themselves only when a TSR writes to the screen or makes a BIOS request from an interrupt service routine; others demand our attention when the TSR installs itself.

This chapter will explain how to write a TSR. You will learn about the services (documented and otherwise) that DOS provides and how TSRs interact with DOS. You will also learn about several of the technical issues that confront a TSR author. But first a few words of caution.

Much of the material covered in this essay is undocumented, obtained by disassembling PC-DOS version 3.10. Many services discussed here are not available in versions of PC-DOS below 3.00, and there is no guarantee that they will be present in future versions of DOS. Some features may be specific to PC-DOS 3.10. Software that uses these features may not be portable to different DOS environments and may break in the future.

It is possible for conflicts to exist among various TSRs (including the examples presented here). The severity of these conflicts can range from annoying to catastrophic. More serious conflicts can cause data loss or can corrupt disks.

Additionally, this chapter describes the programming of the 6845 CRT controller, which drives both the MDA and the CGA. Errors in programming this device can result in severe damage to your system.

Overview

TSRs have become common. They are available as commercial programs, shareware, and even as part of MS-DOS. Borland's Sidekick is probably the best-known commercial offering. The commands PRINT and ASSIGN and several other DOS utilities are TSRs.

All TSRs begin life as ordinary programs. After a while the program exits, leaving part of its code behind. The code that runs first is called the *initialization code*, and that which remains behind is known as the *resident code*. The main task of the initialization code is to prepare the resident code for later use.

There are no restrictions on what the initialization code may do, but programming the resident code can be tricky.

TSRs may be grouped into three categories based on what the resident code does. Members of the first group have no user interface to their resident portion. Once loaded, these TSRs sit quietly in the background, performing their tasks without making any BIOS requests. The DOS ASSIGN command is one such TSR; its resident portion monitors and redirects disk requests from one drive to another. Adequate documentation and numerous examples make writing this type of TSR an easy task.

The members of the second group of TSRs remain dormant until specifically activated by a user request. Normally, this request comes as a specific key or key combination (e.g., Alt-Shift) called a *hot key*. Again, their resident code makes no BIOS requests; they must obtain any DOS services, such as reading a file, only during initialization.

A small telephone-database TSR might fall into this second group. Initialization code would read the entire phone directory into memory. In response to a hot key, the resident code must save the current display, get one or more names, look up the associated phone numbers, and display the search results. When there are no more names to look up, the TSR must restore the original screen and deactivate itself.

The services needed by these TSRs are reasonably well documented, but there are a number of technical issues in dealing with hot key activation and in interacting with the display hardware.

The final group of TSRs makes asynchronous BIOS requests. These requests may be triggered by a hot key or some other hardware interrupt (e.g., a timer). The resident code does not necessarily have a user interface. The DOS PRINT utility falls into this category. These TSRs are difficult to write because DOS is basically a single-user/single-program operating system. Microsoft has retrofitted support for programs such as PRINT, but these services are undocumented and require an in-depth understanding of DOS for proper use.

Before you can write a TSR, you will need some background information. For instance, you must know how the keyboard and display work in order to understand the issues involved in supporting hot keys. As another example, the DOS software architecture imposes some very real constraints on what a TSR may do; you must know about the workings of the various DOS modules that affect a TSR. Once you understand the hardware and operating system mechanisms, you will be ready to learn what a TSR needs to do when it initializes and reactivates. Finally, you will learn how to write a TSR that runs in the background.

Dealing with PC Hardware

The keyboard, timer, and several other devices generate interrupts to get the processor's attention. PC/XT systems provide eight distinct hardware interrupts, and AT systems support more. Many of these interrupts belong to the realm of device drivers, and a TSR must be careful not to interfere with them. Of all the hardware interrupts, it is the clock and keyboard interrupts with which most TSRs interact.

Part of the appeal of TSRs is the hot-key user interface. With a single keystroke, you can wake up a TSR and ask it to do something. If a TSR is well written, it springs to life quickly, does its job, and slips into the background without missing a beat or disrupting any other programs. But implementing a hot key requires quite a bit of work and a good understanding of how the display and keyboard hardware work.

Some TSRs must perform their tasks periodically. Every PC has a timer that generates an interrupt 18.2 times per second and provides a mechanism for scheduling periodic events. The DOS PRINT utility uses the timer to keep the printer busy regardless of what else is happening on the system.

Hot keys and timers interrupt the CPU when they need its attention. The CPU deals with this interrupt and then returns to its original task. The PC has special hardware to deal with interrupts. Both the keyboard and the timer interact with this hardware; you'll need to understand how both the hardware and the software interrupt system work if you want to support a hot key or make use of the timer.

Hardware Interrupts

At the hardware level supporting MS-DOS is a scheme of hardware interrupts, each of which is associated with a particular device. Each device wanting the processor's attention sends an *interrupt request*, or IRQ, to the 8259A interrupt controller, which schedules the interrupt for service. Each device has a priority. Higher-priority devices get first crack at the processor and can preempt less important devices. (The 8259A interrupt controller can be programmed differently, but these other operating modes are not of interest to us.) When the interrupt controller decides that an interrupt can be serviced, it sends an "interrupt acknowledged" message to the device, disables all interrupts, and generates an interrupt.

In response to a particular hardware interrupt, the processor looks up the address of an interrupt service routine in the *interrupt vector table* (IVT). This table occupies the first 256 *double words* (1024 bytes) of memory. Each entry contains the address of an *interrupt service routine* (ISR). The processor pushes the current flags and program counter (CS:IP) onto the stack and begins executing this ISR.

The ISR does whatever is required to service the interrupt. At some point, the ISR sends an end of interrupt (EOI) message to the 8259 controller, indicating that it is ready to accept another interrupt service request. The interrupt controller will not recognize interrupts from this or any lower-priority devices until it receives this EOI. After the ISR does its job, it executes an IRET instruction that restores the flags and the original CS:IP.

Software Interrupts

The INT instruction of the 80x8x processors provides a software interrupt mechanism. The processor treats software- and hardware-generated interrupts in the same way. Execution of an INT instruction transfers control to the ISR specified by the instruction operand. For example, the instruction *int 60h* invokes the ISR whose address is recorded at offset 180h (4*60h) of the IVT. The interrupt controller is not involved, and the software ISRs should not send an EOI to the interrupt controller. DOS uses software interrupts extensively. Since all access to an ISR occurs through its IVT entry, it is a simple matter to replace an interrupt service routine. You will often have occasion to modify the IVT when you write TSRs.

The Timer Interrupt

The PC uses one channel of an 8253 counter/timer chip to request an interrupt 18.2 times per second. The 8259A controller generates an int 8h in response to this request. This clock interrupt has the highest priority and will preempt any other interrupt as long as the processor has not disabled all interrupts with a CLI (CLear Interrupts) instruction.

Code within ROM-BIOS normally responds to this interrupt. After updating the time of day and performing some other housekeeping tasks, the ROM-BIOS code executes an *int 1ch* instruction. Programs that run periodically can set up their own *int 1ch* ISR (we'll explain this shortly). The default ROM-BIOS *int 1ch* service routine consists of an IRET instruction.

The Keyboard

The standard PC keyboard contains its own microprocessor (an Intel 8048 or equivalent). Pressing or releasing a key sends an IRQ1 signal to the interrupt controller, which invokes the int 9 interrupt service routine to process this request. The priority of the keyboard interrupt is second only to that of the clock.

ROM on the system board contains the default int 9 ISR. This code is quite complicated. It reads and decodes the scan code, tracks the state of special keys (Control, Shift, Alt, etc.), and maps scan codes into key codes. Each keystroke produces two scan codes, one for key press-down and one for key release-up. Keyboard state information affects these mappings. For instance, pressing the A key produces a scan code of 1eh. The keyboard ISR normally translates this scan code to a key code of 61h (the ASCII code for lowercase *a*). If the control key is down at the key-press, the scan code translates to a 01h (ASCII for Control-A). If the shift key is down, the same scan code becomes a 41h (ASCII for uppercase *A*).

In response to keys such as Shift and Alt, the int 9 ISR updates a keyboard status byte within the BIOS data segment and then exits with an IRET. The BIOS data segment begins at paragraph 40h and contains many dynamic variables manipulated by various ROM-BIOS routines. Listing 4-1 describes part of this data area.

Listing 4-1. The BIOS Data Segment

```
KB_M_RShift       EQU     01h     ; right shift being held down
KB_M_LShift       EQU     02h     ; left shift being held down
KB_M_Control      EQU     04h     ; control key being held down
KB_M_Alt          EQU     08h     ; alt key being held down
KB_M_Scroll       EQU     10h     ; scroll lock key down
KB_M_Num          EQU     20h     ; num lock key down
KB_M_Caps         EQU     40h     ; caps lock key down
KB_M_InsState     EQU     80h     ; insert state is active

KB_C_BufSize      EQU     10h     ; size of keyboard buffer

BIOS              SEGMENT         at 40h
                  ORG     17h     ; not interested in other BIOS data
KB_B_Flag         DB      0       ; keyboard status flag
                  ORG     1ah     ; not interested in 18h and 19h
KB_W_BufHead      DW      0       ; head of keyboard buffer
KB_W_BufTail      DW      0       ; tail of keyboard buffer
KB_T_Buffer       DW      KB_C_BufSize DUP(0)
BIOS              ENDS
```

Certain key combinations have special meaning. The keyboard ISR executes an *int 1bh* instruction when it sees the scan code corresponding to the break key. The default *int 1bh* ISR consists of an IRET, but the console driver normally sets up its own *int 1bh* ISR. This ability to process breaks makes the console driver special. (This discussion is extended in the section on break handling.)

The dreaded Control-Alt-Delete eventually produces an *int 19h*. Further discussion of the *int 19h* and the Control-Alt-Delete key combination is unnecessary.

If the key code does not have any special meaning, the int 9 ISR saves it in a type-ahead buffer. This buffer begins at offset 1eh within the BIOS data segment and is arranged as a 16-word circular buffer. Offsets 1ah and 1ch in this segment point, respectively, to the buffer head and tail. If the buffer is full, the int 9 ISR beeps and discards the character; otherwise, it inserts the character at the tail of the buffer.

Each buffer entry is 2 bytes long; its format depends on how the int 9 ISR interprets the keystroke. Certain key combinations (e.g., Alt plus a letter or number) and special keys (e.g., function keys) produce an "extended ASCII" character; other keys produce "normal ASCII." The int 9 ISR records a zero byte followed by a numeric identifier for extended ASCII characters, and records the ASCII character code and scan code for all others.

Software accesses the keyboard hardware through ROM-BIOS. Int 16h lets you remove characters from the keyboard buffer, peek at the first character in the buffer, and check keyboard status. Virtually all access to the keyboard occurs through int 16h. Even the console driver uses int 16h to retrieve input characters and check keyboard status.

The Display Hardware

There are a number of different displays available for computers in the PC family. The Monochrome Display Adapter (MDA) and the Color Graphics Adapter (CGA) are the most common. Some of the other hardware emulates one or both of these adapters, as well as providing added capability (more colors, better resolution, etc.). This discussion is limited to the MDA and CGA hardware.

The PC display hardware has analog and digital components. The screen and its associated control logic make up the analog part. The surface of the screen is coated with a phosphor that glows when struck by an electron beam. The analog control circuits sweep a beam of electrons across and down the screen; each sweep is known as a scan line. Other parts of this circuit turn the beam on and off.

The process begins at the upper left corner of the screen. The beam moves horizontally across the screen from left to right. When it reaches the right side of the screen, the control electronics turn it off and move it back to the left edge and down one position. The time that the beam is off is known as the *horizontal blanking interval*. This process continues until the beam sweeps the lowest line of the screen. When the electron beam reaches the bottom of the screen, the control circuit turns it off and returns it to the top left corner of the screen to repeat the entire process. The time required for this motion is called the *vertical retrace interval*. The horizontal and vertical retrace periods are important to managing a CGA display.

As the beam sweeps horizontally to the right, a representation of the display saved in display memory causes the necessary signals to turn the beam on and off and control its position. The base address of this memory varies with the adapter type. MDA screen memory begins at b000:0000h, and CGA memory at b800:000h. Both the CPU and the CRT controller can access this memory.

Some fancy electronics make this arrangement work, but, as far as you are concerned, you can read and write to screen memory without worrying too much about what the 6845 CRT controller is doing. The 6845 CRT controller is a general-purpose chip that can support many different monitors. It has a status register that contains information about retrace cycles; several other registers control scan rates, cursor position, cursor mode, and display page.

CAUTION

You should be very careful when programming the 6845. Certain registers contain critical values that, if not properly set, will destroy your monitor. Consult the *IBM Hardware Technical Reference Manual* for a more complete description.

The MDA and the CGA

There are some electronic differences between the MDA and the CGA. The MDA operates fast enough that the CPU can access display memory whenever it wants, even as the scan line is active. Attempts to access CGA graphics memory produce *snow* unless they occur during retrace intervals. The slowest IBM processor (8088 CPU at 4.77 MHz) can move only 1 byte in the horizontal retrace period, and it can move approximately 100 bytes during vertical retrace. Both the CGA and the MDA provide vertical retrace status, but only the CGA indicates horizontal retrace.

There are some functional differences between the MDA and the CGA as well. The MDA can display only text; the CGA can display both text and graphics. In text mode, both adapters use 2 bytes of screen memory to display one character. The lower byte contains the character to be displayed, and the higher byte describes the character attributes (bold, blink, color, underline, etc.). Location of graphics data is slightly more complex. Refer to the *IBM Hardware Technical Reference Manual* for details.

Writing to Display Memory

Display memory is mapped into the PC address space. Listing 4-2 shows how easy it is to write to MDA display memory.

Listing 4-2. Writing Directly to MDA Display Memory

```
; Write Hello on MDA screen in normal video starting at (0,0).
; The 7 following each letter in Hello is the video attribute. A
; value of 7 describes normal mode (white letter on dark background,
; normal intensity)

Hello       DB      'H',7,'e',7,'l',7,'l',7,'o',7
HelloLength EQU     $-Hello

            mov     ax,0b000h
            mov     es,ax               ; es <== MDA base
            xor     di,di            ; di <== offset into screen memory
            mov     si,OFFSET Hello   ; si <== string to write
            mov     cx,HelloLength/2  ; cx <== words to write
            rep     movsw             ; do the write
```

Writing to the CGA is a little tricky. The previous program will run on a CGA (provided the screen base address is changed to 0b800h), but it will cause snow on the screen. Because adapter memory is dual-ported, it can be accessed by both the CPU and the display processor (the Motorola 6845 CRT controller). The snow is due to memory contention—both the processor and the controller trying to access memory at the same time. Accessing display memory only during retrace cycles eliminates this unsightly effect.

The MDA and many CGA clones are fast enough to obviate the restriction of using only retrace intervals. With the IBM CGA, you can either ignore the snow, turn the display off during screen updates (more ugly than the snow), or sync with the retrace signals. Listing 4-3 illustrates how to avoid snow by using the least-significant bit of the 6845 status register at address 03dah to coordinate with the horizontal retrace signal.

Listing 4-3. Writing to CGA Screen Memory

```
; Write Hello on CGA screen in normal video starting at (0,0).
; The 7 following each letter in Hello is the video attribute. A
; value of 7 describes normal mode (white letter on dark
; background, normal intensity). The CGA is assumed to be in
; text mode.

Hello       DB      'H',7,'e',7,'l',7,'l',7,'o',7
HelloLength EQU     $-Hello

HRetrace    EQU     1

            mov     dx,3dah              ; dx <== CGA status register
            mov     ax,0b800h
            mov     es,ax                ; es <== CGA adapter memory
            xor     di,di              ; di <== offset into screen memory
            mov     si,OFFSET Hello      ; si <== string to write
            mov     cx,HelloLength/2     ; cx <== words to write
_nextbyte:
_sync:      in      al,dx                ; al <== 6845 status
            test    al,HRetrace          ; horizontal retrace?
            jz      _sync                ; if z -- not yet
            stosb                        ; write 1 byte in retrace
            loop    _nextbyte            ; wait for next retrace
```

Although it is not obvious with a short string, this program is not terribly efficient. To move big blocks of text, you must take advantage of the much longer vertical retrace interval as well.

ROM-BIOS Video Support

ROM-BIOS provides fairly complete video support through int 10h. For many applications, these services provide adequate performance. The screen switching needed to support a hot key severely taxes the capabilities of the ROM code, especially on the slower 8088 machines. The extra memory and dual modes of the CGA compound this problem. ROM-BIOS supports CGA access in both text and graphics modes and provides services for switching modes. You should note that a side effect of mode change is the erasure of display memory.

Capturing an Interrupt

The process of changing an IVT entry is known as *capturing an interrupt*. TSRs rely on interrupts for hot-key activation. Those that run periodically also depend on the timer interrupt. TSRs frequently alter the IVT to monitor DOS activity and hardware status and to locate previously loaded copies of themselves. The timing of these interrupts is unpredictable in that certain DOS operations (int 21h functions) cannot be interrupted.

To capture an interrupt, the initialization code of the TSR reads the IVT entry, stores its contents safely away in a data area, and inserts a new address in the IVT table. Control will pass to this new ISR the next time the interrupt occurs. Your new ISR code should usually call the original ISR first. When the old ISR has completed, its IRET instruction will return control to your code, which then issues its own IRET to return control to the program that originally called the interrupt.

DOS provides two functions to help us capture an interrupt vector. To find the contents of a specific IVT entry, place its interrupt number in the AL register, place the value of 35h in the AH register, and execute an int 21h instruction. This BIOS service returns the contents of the IVT entry in the ES:BX register pair.

After you record this value, you can modify the IVT entry. Load the DS:DX with the location of the new ISR, specify an interrupt vector number in the AL register, place 25h in the AH register, and execute an int 21h instruction. Listing 4-4 illustrates the use of these services to capture the timer (1ch) interrupt.

The specific actions taken in the new ISR depend on which IVT entry you are replacing and what you are trying to accomplish by replacing it. Notice that our new ISR "chains" to the old ISR. This technique is quite common. The *pushf/call* sequence simulates an INT instruction. Note that the *call* must be an intersegment (*far*) call because *OldInt1c* is a double word (DD pseudo op).

Setting up a Hot Key

Implementing a hot-key feature in a TSR imposes some unique demands on program design. The hot key should wake up the TSR without sending the keypress to the foreground program. The basic approach is to examine each keystroke before the foreground program reads it. You can capture interrupt 16h to inspect input to the keyboard buffer, or you can poll the keyboard buffer by using the timer tick (int 1ch), or you can monitor the contents of the type-ahead buffer by trapping interrupt 9. Quite often you will find it useful to choose a hot key that affects keyboard status but does not result in an addition to the type-ahead buffer. Each of these approaches has certain advantages and a number of problems. You will have to decide which technique is best for your application.

Capturing Int 16h
The simplest way to look for a hot key is to capture int 16h. Most well-behaved applications use this interrupt for keyboard input. Installing your own int 16h

Listing 4-4. Capturing the Timer Interrupt Int 1ch

```
OldInt1c    DD      0

            mov     ax,351ch                    ; get int 1c
            int     21h
            mov     WORD PTR OldInt1c,bx         ; save it
            mov     WORD PTR OldInt1c+2,es
            push    ds                          ; save ds
            mov     ax,cs
            mov     ds,ax
            mov     dx,OFFSET NewInt1c           ; ds:dx <== new isr
            mov     ax,251ch                    ; set new isr
            int     21h
            pop     ds                          ; recover ds
;           ...                                 ; whatever
NewInt1c    PROC    FAR
            pushf                               ; push flags to simulate
            call    cs:OldInt1c                 ; an interrupt
;           ...                                 ; whatever
            iret
NewInt1c    ENDP
```

ISR gives you a chance to examine each character and divert any hot keys. Listing 4-5 shows a typical replacement for the int 16h ISR.

The new int 16h ISR looks at the results of every read (AH = 0) and buffer status (AH = 1) request but does not intervene in shift status requests (AH = 2). If the ROM-BIOS code returns a hot key, the new ISR removes the key code from the type-ahead buffer, wakes up the TSR, and then repeats the request. As long as the first character in the type-ahead buffer is a hot key, the replacement ISR does not return to its caller. This example makes the simplifying assumption that reactivation will be safe. (See the section titled "Reactivation and DOS Architecture and Services" for a complete discussion of this topic. *The code in Listing 4-5 is therefore only a general model and is not strictly correct.*)

The limitation to this technique is that the only time you get to look for hot keys is when the foreground program issues a read. If this program is compute-intensive, there may be lengthy delays between the time a hot key is entered and your TSR responds.

Polling the Keyboard Buffer with Timer Interrupt Int 1ch

You can ensure frequent keyboard checks by capturing the timer interrupt and checking the keyboard buffer from within your timer ISR. Listing 4-6 checks for a hot key on every timer tick. If the first key code in the type-ahead buffer corresponds to a hot key, the new ISR removes the key code and activates the TSR. In either case, the new ISR chains to the previous timer ISR code.

Listing 4-5. Replacing Int 16h to Look for a Hot Key

```
OldInt16    DD          0               ; initialization code saves
                                        ; original isr address here
HotKey      DW          (?)             ; define hot key here

NewInt16    PROC    FAR
            cmp     ah,1                ; look at function
            jg      DoShift             ; if g -- shift status
            jl      DoRead              ; ah=0 ==> read

DoStatus:                               ; ah=1 ==> check for status
            pushf                       ; simulate an int 16
            call    cs:OldInt16         ; pass request to BIOS
            pushf                       ; save flags
            cmp     ax,HotKey           ; did we find a hot key?
            jnz     Done1               ; not the hot key
            xor     ax,ax               ; ah <== 0 (read request)
            call    cs:OldInt16         ; remove the hot key
            call    ActivateTSR         ; hot key activates TSR
            mov     ah,1                ; ah <== 1 (status request)
            jmp     SHORT DoStatus      ; repeat request

DoRead:
            pushf                       ; simulate an int 16h
            call    cs:OldInt16
            cmp     ax,HotKey           ; did we find a hot key?
            jnz     Done0               ; if nz -- no hot key
            call    ActivateTSR         ; hot key activates TSR
            xor     ah,ah               ; ah <== 0 (read request)
            jmp     SHORT DoRead        ; repeat request
DoShift:                                ; pass this request along to
            jmp     cs:OldInt16         ; old ISR. Ignore results

Done0:                                  ; ax has character
                                        ; flags are not used
            iret                        ; return to caller

Done1:                                  ; ax has character
            popf                        ; recover flags from int 16h
            ret     2                   ; discard flags pushed by
                                        ; int instruction and return

NewInt16    ENDP
```

Listing 4-6. Using Int 1ch to Poll the Keyboard

```
HotKey      DW           (?)           ; define hot key here
                                       ; NB cannot be extended ascii
OldInt1c    DD           0             ; old timer ISR stored here

NewInt1c    PROC   FAR                 ; new timer isr
            push   ax                  ; needed for int 16h
            xor    al,al               ; xor,inc combo faster than
            inc    al                  ; mov al,1
            int    16h                 ; check type-ahead buffer
            jz     NoHotKey            ; if z--buffer empty
            cmp    ax,HotKey           ; not empty--1st char hot key?
            jnz    NoHotKey            ; if nz--not hot key
            xor    al,al               ; al <== read request
            int    16h                 ; remove hot key
            call   ActivateTSR         ; wake up the TSR
NoHotKey:   pop    ax                  ; restore ax
            jmp    cs:OldInt1ch        ; pass timer tick
NewInt1c    ENDP
```

If you use this technique, you can access only the first character in the type-ahead buffer. The presence of an ordinary character will hide subsequent hot keys from this poll routine. Assuming that a user never anticipates program input requests, frequent polling would provide adequate response to a hot key. But because user actions are unpredictable, this technique is not a reliable way to detect a hot key. *Again, please note that the example does not check to determine if it is safe to reactivate the TSR.*

Trapping Int 9

Another approach to monitoring the keyboard is to trap int 9h. When a key is pressed or released, the keyboard hardware generates an int 9. The new int 9 ISR calls the ROM keyboard ISR and then uses int 16h to peek at the first character in the type-ahead buffer. The disadvantage of this approach is that a nonempty type-ahead buffer hides hot keys. If you can guarantee that no TSR loaded afterward will move the buffer, you can use this technique to scan the entire buffer on every key-press.

TSRs that extend the type-ahead buffer are quite common. They work by replacing both the int 9 and the int 16h ISRs. Their int 9 code calls the old int 9 ISR to service the keyboard interrupt and then invokes the old int 16h ISR to drain the type-ahead buffer. The new int 9 ISR saves these characters in its own buffer. The replacement int 16h ISR removes characters from this new buffer.

TSRs that redefine or bind macro definitions to keys also use this technique. If your TSR loads before any TSR that moves the type-ahead buffer, your

TSR will always find the buffer empty. It is not a good idea to write a TSR that depends on load order to work correctly.

Monitoring Keyboard Status

An alternative to checking the type-ahead buffer is to monitor the keyboard status byte. This technique eliminates the need to know the location of the ROM-BIOS type-ahead buffer but requires that the user select character combinations that alter keyboard status (e.g., Alt-Shift, etc.) as a hot key. This technique will work as long as any TSRs loaded afterward do not alter the keyboard status bytes. Because the keyboard status affects scan code processing, TSRs should not fool around with this variable, so this technique is very reliable.

Listing 4-7 shows a replacement for the ROM-BIOS keyboard ISR. Some of the things that this code does may seem a little confusing right now because the process involves looking for hot keys in an interrupt service routine. As you will see later, you cannot safely interrupt some DOS operations. Part of the challenge of writing a TSR is coding around this limitation.

In this example, the new ISR runs whenever a key is pressed or released. Its first action is to call the old keyboard ISR to read and process the keyboard scan code. The new ISR examines the *PgmState* variable maintained by the TSR to determine if the TSR is a foreground application. If the TSR is not running in the foreground and the ISR detects a hot key, it attempts to bring the TSR to the foreground. If the TSR is currently in the foreground, the interrupt requires no further processing.

If the keyboard status bits corresponding to the hot key are set, the ISR increments the *PopupPending* flag and checks to see if it is safe to bring the TSR to the foreground. The section entitled "Reactivation and DOS Architecture and Services" describes the mechanics of this process. If it is safe, the ISR calls *BKGResume* to reactivate the TSR. *DOSSafe* increments the *BusyFlag* to prevent the TSR from being reentered; the ISR must decrement this variable before returning to the interrupted program.

Listing 4-7. Sample Replacement Keyboard ISR

```
FGCombo            EQU     KB_M_Alt OR KB_M_LShift

BKG_C_FG           EQU     1
BKG_C_BG           EQU     2

BIOS        SEGMENT     at 40h
            ORG     17h
KB_B_Flag              DB   0
BIOS        ENDS

_text       SEGMENT     BYTE PUBLIC 'code'-
```

continued

Listing 4-7. *continued*

```
PgmState         DB    0
BusyFlag         DB    -1              ; protects against interrupting
                                       ; non-reentrant code section
OldInt9          DD    0               ; initialization saves original
                                       ; int 9 ISR here
PopupPending     DB    0               ; incremented if popup requested
                                       ; but couldn't be honored


                 ASSUME ds:NOTHING
Int9ISR          PROC  FAR
NewInt9:
                 pushf                 ;;; simulate an interrupt
                 call  cs:OldInt9      ;;; dispatch to original ISR
                 cmp   cs:PgmState,BKG_C_BG ;;; are we in background now?
                 jz    i9_0            ;;; if z -- yes
                 iret                  ;;; ignore popup if not
                                       ;;; currently in background
i9_0:            pushr <ax,ds>         ;;; so we can access B_FLAG
                 mov   ax,SEG BIOS
                 mov   ds,ax
                 ASSUME ds:BIOS
                 mov   al,KB_B_Flag    ;;; al <== current KB flags
                 and   al,FGCombo      ;;; mask all unneeded bits
                 cmp   al,FGCombo      ;;; popup being requested?
                 popr  <ds,ax>
                 ASSUME ds:NOTHING
                 jnz   Int9Exit1       ;;; if NZ -- not a popup
                                       ;;; request
                 inc   cs:PopupPending ;;; say a popup was requested
                 call  DOSSafeCheck    ;;; can we do it now?
                 jc    Int9Exit0       ;;; if c -- no
                 call  BKGResume       ; bring to foreground
Int9Exit0:
                 dec   cs:BusyFlag     ; release our lock
Int9Exit1:
                 iret                  ; and dismiss interrupt
Int9ISR          ENDP
_text            ENDS
```

An Alternative to Capturing Int 1ch

It is important to note that the int 1ch ISR is nested within the int 8 ISR because the clock interrupt has the highest priority—no other interrupts will be serviced until the interrupt controller receives an EOI. Any operations that depend on interrupts will not work. Another potential problem is that DOS will lose clock ticks if it takes too long to traverse the int 1ch chain. *PRINT.COM* solves this problem by sending an EOI in its int 1ch ISR.

   An alternate strategy is to capture int 8. The new int 8 ISR immediately calls the old ISR, which sends an EOI to the interrupt controller before returning. No interrupts are blocked when the old ISR returns. The ISR shown in Listing 4-8 works together with the one in Listing 4-7. If a hot key is pending or if 1 second has elapsed since the last activation, the int 8 ISR calls *BKGResume* to reactivate the TSR.

Listing 4-8. Sample Replacement of the Clock Interrupt Int 8 ISR

```
OldInt8         DD      0       ; initialization code saves
                                ; original int 8 isr address here
BusyFlag        DB      -1      ; protects against interrupting
                                ; non-reentrant code sections
PopupPending    DB      0       ; nonzero if hot key encountered
Ticks           DB      18      ; runs once a second

Int8ISR   PROC  FAR
NewInt8:
          pushf                          ;;; simulate an int
          call  cs:OldInt8               ;;; dispatch to ROM code
          cli                            ;;; not really needed
          cmp   cs:PopupPending,0        ;;; pop request pending?
          jnz   i8_0                     ;;; if nz -- yes
          cmp   cs:Ticks,0               ;;; tick counter reached 0?
          jz    i8_0                     ;;; if z -- yes
          dec   cs:Ticks                 ;;; otherwise decrement it
          jnz   Int8Exit1                ;;; if not at 0 yet, continue
8_0:      call  DOSSafeCheck             ;;; safe to (re)enter OS?
          jc    Int8Exit0                ;;; if c -- no
                                         ;;; NB that ticks remains at 0
                                         ;;; we'll keep trying to
                                         ;;; dispatch on every tick
          call  BKGResume                ; dispatch to background code
          mov   cs:Ticks,18              ; reset timer
Int8Exit0:
          dec   cs:BusyFlag              ; release our lock
Int8Exit1:
          iret                           ; and return
Int8ISR   ENDP
```

Managing the Display

Because of the previously discussed limitations in the ROM-BIOS video support, a TSR frequently needs to manipulate the display hardware directly. Direct screen reads and writes speed up the process of switching displays when a hot key activates a TSR. Direct access to the 6845 CRT controller can eliminate the problems associated with changes between text and graphics modes.

CAUTION

Direct access to the display hardware can be dangerous. Mistakes in this process can destroy your monitor.

Before you attempt to program the display, you should understand how it works. The following discussion is an overview; consult the *Hardware Technical Reference Manual* for further details.

There are two techniques for changing the screen contents. One technique is to maintain two buffers: one buffer contains an image of the TSR screen, and the other contains the image of the DOS/application screen. The second technique is to substitute video memory for one of these buffers; this saves some memory at the expense of slightly slower response.

Listing 4-9 shows the dual buffer technique. When the hot key is invoked, the current screen is copied to a DOS/application buffer and then the contents of the TSR buffer are moved to display memory. You can move a large block of data at this time, so use the string MOVE instruction. Counting clock cycles suggests that this routine should take about 21 ms to execute on a 4.77-MHz 8088. Actual measurements reveal an execution time of about 29 ms. Part of the difference is due to the crude method of counting clock cycles; memory contention accounts for the rest. The timing was done with the display turned on—a worst case.

Listing 4-9. Screen Switching Using Two Buffers

```
_text       SEGMENT       WORD PUBLIC 'CODE'
            ASSUME  cs:_text, ds:_text, es:_text
VideoSEG    DW      0b000h
DOSBuffer   DW      25*80         DUP   (0)
TSRBuffer   DW      25*80         DUP   (720h)

Switch      PROC    NEAR
            cld                         ; direction flag <== UP
            lea     di,DOSBuffer        ; di <== buffer offset
            mov     ax,cs
            mov     es,ax               ; es:di <== DOSBuffer
            xor     si,si               ; si <== video offset
            mov     ds,VideoSEG         ; ds:si <== video memory
```

```
                 mov      cx,25*80            ; cx <== words in display
                 rep      movsw               ; DOSBuffer <== video memory
                 mov      ds,ax
                 lea      si,TSRBuffer        ; ds:si <== TSRBuffer
                 mov      es,VideoSEG
                 xor      di,di               ; es:di <== video memory
                 mov      cx,25*80            ; cx <== words in display
                 rep      movsw               ; video memory <== TSRBuffer
                 ret
Switch           ENDP
```

The next listing uses only one buffer. Using a single buffer requires the slower *mov/xchg* sequence and takes approximately 45 ms to change screens with the display turned on. This performance is still acceptable. Note that forcing the buffer to be paragraph aligned will eliminate one *add* instruction, but this change has no significant effect on performance.

Listing 4-10. Screen Switching Using a Single Buffer

```
_text            SEGMENT      WORD PUBLIC 'CODE'
                 ASSUME cs:_text, ds:_text, es:_text
VideoSEG         DW       0b000h
TSRBuffer        DW       25*80       DUP   (720h)

Switch           PROC     NEAR
                 cld                          ; make sure we move up
                 lea      si,TSRBuffer        ; si <== TSR buffer offset
                 xor      di,di               ; di <== video memory offset
                 mov      bx,2                ; bx <== size of move
                 mov      es,VideoSEG         ; ds:si <== video memory
                 mov      cx,25*80            ; cx <== words in display
_nb:             mov      ax,[si]             ; ax <== word from TSRBuffer
                 xchg     ax,es:[di]          ; video memory <== TSRBuffer
                                              ; ax <== word from video memory
                 mov      [si],ax             ; TSRBuffer <== video memory
                 add      si,bx
                 add      di,bx
                 loop     _nb
                 ret
Switch           ENDP
```

Working with and around DOS

Many of the operations you will want your TSR to perform involve some interaction with DOS. DOS is basically a single-user/single-program operating system.

Although Microsoft has added some hooks to support TSRs, many of these hooks are undocumented and difficult to use. You often have to "stand on your head" to do things in a TSR that would be trivial in an ordinary foreground program. This section discusses several key features of DOS that are important to writing a TSR. You should be aware that most of this material is not formally documented and consequently may be changed.

The DOS I/O Data Structures

DOS maintains a number of data structures that are important to a TSR. Some of these are common to all resident programs. For instance, DOS maintains two *system file tables*, one for handle access and the other for *file control block* (FCB) operations; all programs access the same two system file tables. Other data structures are unique to each program. For instance, each program has its own program segment prefix (PSP).

When DOS loads a program, it records that program's PSP in a global variable. (In DOS 3.10 this variable is located at offset 02deh in the DOS segment.) A program whose PSP is recorded here becomes the *current program*. Once IBMBIO loads the shell, there is always one and only one current program.

When a program makes an I/O request, it gives DOS either a handle or a file control block. To process a handle request, DOS must locate a data structure known as the *job file table* (JFT). Each PSP contains a JFT address at offset 34h (Listing 4-15 "Structure of the PSP"). DOS looks in the PSP of the current program to find the current JFT. The JFT normally begins at offset 18h of the PSP (i.e., the JFT address points to another location within the PSP). DOS uses the handle as an index into the JFT to get a *system file number* (SFN) which, in turn, is an index into the system file table. One of the undocumented fields within an FCB contains a system file number; this SFN is an index into the FCB system file table. This SFT tells DOS how to find a device.

The "List of Lists"

DOS records the address of both the handle and the FCB system file table in a data structure known as the "list of lists." This data structure contains many other important pieces of information. Your TSR may need to look at the contents of this list or be aware of some of the data structures that it points to. Undocumented int 21h function AH = 52h returns the address of the list of lists in the ES:BX register pair. The code fragment in Listing 4-11 shows how to locate this list.

Briefly, here are the functions for the various entries in the list of lists. Block devices (usually disks) record information on file system structure in device control blocks (DCBs). DCB data includes disk size, number of entries in the root directory, number of FATs, etc. DOS records the address of the clock device as a performance optimization. In addition to processing time and date requests, DOS time-stamps every FCB write and then records the last access time for handle writes. DOS uses the saved address of the console device to check for break and to report divide-by-zero errors. DOS expects the console

Listing 4-11. Finding the List of Lists

```
ListAddr    DW      0,0

            mov     ah,52h          ; ask DOS where it's located
            int     21h             ; (undocumented function)
            mov     ListAddr,bx     ; address returned in es:bx
            mov     ListAddr+2,es
```

device to have an int 1Bh ISR so that the keyboard ISR can report breaks immediately. DOS uses the current directory for block device operations. DOS maintains a list of *cache* blocks used to process partial block read/write requests and to access directory and FAT blocks. Each cache block is *DOS_W_MaxSector* bytes long. *DOS_D_HDLSFT* and *DOS_D_FCBSFT* are the listheads for the handle and FCB system file tables, respectively. Listing 4-12 summarizes the contents of this list.

Listing 4-12. The Layout of the List of Lists

```
DOS                         STRUC
DOS_D_DCB         DD    0    ; list head for device control
                             ; block (DCB) chain
DOS_D_HDLSFT      DD    0    ; list head for handle SFT
DOS_D_Clock       DD    0    ; device header for CurClk device
DOS_D_Console     DD    0    ; device header for console device
DOS_W_MaxSector   DW    0    ; size of largest sector
DOS_D_Cache       DD    0    ; list head for cache control
                             ; blocks (CCB)
DOS_D_CDS         DD    0    ; address of current directory
                             ; structure
DOS_D_FCBSFT      DD    0    ; list head for FCB SFT
DOS_W_Unknown     DW    0    ; unknown
DOS_B_DriveCount  DB    0    ; max number of drives
                             ; (value set by lastdrive=)
DOS_B_LastDrive   DB    0    ; current number of drives
DOS               ENDS
```

The System File Table

Of all the data structures referenced in the list of lists, the system file table entries are the most important to a TSR. Information contained in these table entries affects the way a TSR must handle I/O requests. This data structure, which is located in DOS global data area, is made up of one or more blocks. Each block contains a header that points to a following block and several system file table entries. Each SFT entry is a data structure in its own right.

The header is 6 bytes long. The first field is a double word that contains the address of the next block in the system file table chain or a −1 to indicate the end of the list. The second field is a word that tells the number of system file table entries in this block. Listing 4-13 illustrates the structure of the SFT.

Listing 4-13. Header for a System File Table Block

```
SFTTBL                     STRUC
SFTTBL_D_Next              DD      0
SFTTBL_W_Count             DW      0
SFTTBL                     ENDS

SFTTBL_K_Size    EQU       SIZE SFTTBL  ; defined here for later use
```

Many fields in each SFT entry are important only for block devices, but values in the reference count and *ownerPSP* fields directly impact a TSR. When DOS opens a file, it allocates an SFT entry in the system file table and records the current PSP in the *OwnerPSP* field, which is the eighteenth field in the entry (offset 22h). Because only the owner of a file may actually close it, be sure that you have set up your PSP as the current program before asking DOS to close the file. Similarly, be sure to restore the PSP of the original foreground application as you terminate.

The *reference count* is the first field in the entry and contains a word that records the number of times a file or device has been opened. Before allocating a new entry, DOS checks all existing entries to see if the file or device making the request is already open. If an SFT entry already exists, DOS increments the reference count rather than allocating a new entry. DOS decrements the reference count when the file/device is closed but will not deallocate the entry until the reference count goes to zero.

When DOS processes an open or create request (either FCB or handle), it records the current PSP in the SFT owner field and records the mode bits (arguments to the open request such as exclusive access and read access) in the SFT mode field if the file was not opened previously. The mode bits determine what type of future access DOS will permit.

Listing 4-14. Structure of an SFT Entry

```
SFT   STRUC
SFT_W_RefCnt       DW      0     ; [00] reference count
SFT_W_Mode         DW      0     ; [02] open mode
SFT_B_DirAttrib    DB      0     ; [04]
SFT_W_Flags        DW      0     ; [05]
```

```
SFT_D_DCB              DD      0         ; [07] (FILE) device control block
SFT_W_Cluster1         DW      0         ; [0b] (FILE) initial cluster
SFT_W_HHMMS            DW      0         ; [0d] (FILE) Hour, Min, Sec/2
SFT_W_YYMMDD           DW      0         ; [0f] (FILE) Year, Month, Day
SFT_D_FilSiz           DD      0         ; [11] file size/EOF location
SFT_D_FilPos           DD      0         ; [15] Current file position
SFT_W_RelClstr         DW      0         ; [19] (FILE) clusters from beginning
SFT_W_CurClstr         DW      0         ; [1b] (FILE) current cluster
SFT_W_LBN              DW      0         ; [1d] (FILE) block number
SFT_W_DirIndex         DB      0         ; [1f] (FILE) directory index
SFT_T_FileName         DB      0bh  DUP  (0)  ; [20] (FILE) file name
SFT_T_Unknown          DB      04h  DUP  (0)  ; [2b] unknown
SFT_W_OwnerMach        DW      0         ; [2f] machine number of file owner
SFT_W_OwnerPSP         DW      0         ; [31] psp of task that initially
SFT_W_Status           DW      0         ; [33]
SFT    ENDS

SFT_K_Size             EQU     SIZE SFT
;
;MOde field
;
SFT_M_FCB              EQU     8000h     ; entry is for FCB
SFT_M_DenyNone         EQU     0040h     ; sharing bits (4-6)
SFT_M_DenyRead         EQU     0030h     ; "
SFT_M_DenyWrite        EQU     0020h     ; "
SFT_M_Exclusive        EQU     0010h     ; "
SFT_M_NetFCB           EQU     0070h     ; this is a network FCB
SFT_M_Write            EQU     0001h     ; file access bits (0-2)
SFT_M_Read             EQU     0000h     ; "
;
;FLags Field
;
SFT_M_Shared           EQU     8000h     ; network access
SFT_M_DateSet          EQU     4000h     ; date set (FILE only)
SFT_M_IOCTL            EQU     4000h     ; IOCTL support (DEVICE only)
SFT_M_IsDevice         EQU     0080h     ; entry is for a device
SFT_M_EOF              EQU     0040h     ; (DEVICE) end of file on input
SFT_M_Binary           EQU     0020h     ; (DEVICE) transparent mode
SFT_M_Special          EQU     0010h     ; (DEVICE) supports int 29H output
SFT_M_IsClock          EQU     0008h     ; (DEVICE) current
                                         ; clock device
SFT_M_IsNul            EQU     0004h     ; (DEVICE) current nul device
SFT_M_IsStdOut         EQU     0002h     ; (DEVICE) current stdout device
SFT_M_IsStdIn          EQU     0001h     ; (DEVICE) current stdin device
SFT_M_Written          EQU     0040h     ; (FILE) file written
SFT_M_DriveMask        EQU     003fh     ; (FILE) mask for drive bits (0-5)
```

The Program Segment Prefix (PSP)

When DOS loads a program, it creates a program segment prefix (PSP). The previous chapter discussed many of the fields in the PSP. DOS always locates the PSP on a 16-byte paragraph boundary, so that it can be described as a word-length value (a segment with an offset of zero). DOS function 62h returns the address of the current PSP in the BX register (undocumented function AH = 51h also returns the PSP in BX).

Listing 4-15 shows the PSP as a structure. In it, the *PSP_D_JFTAddr* and *PSP_W_JFTSize* fields contain the address and size of the job file table (JFT). The PSP also contains a copy of the default JFT beginning at location *JFT_T_JFT*. DOS uses some of the other PSP fields to process critical errors and termination requests; more about these fields later.

Listing 4-15. Structure of the PSP

```
PSP     STRUC
PSP_W_int20         DW      0cd20h          ; [00] int 20 instruction
PSP_W_MemSiz        DW      0               ; [02] top of memory (para)
PSP_B_Unused0       DB      0               ; [04] unknown
PSP_T_Call          DB      09aH,0f0h       ; [05] far call to DOS
                    DB      0feH,01dh,0f0h  ;dispatcher (CPM relic)
PSP_D_Term          DD      0               ; [0a] terminate address
PSP_D_Break         DD      0               ; [0e] break address
PSP_D_CritErr       DD      0               ; [12] critical error
PSP_W_Parent        DW      0               ; [16] parent PSP
PSP_T_JFT           DB      14h     DUP     (0ffh) ; [18] JFT table
PSP_W_Envron        DW      0               ; [2c] environment
PSP_D_SSSP          DD      0               ; [2e] User SS:SP at time of
                                            ; int 21
PSP_W_JFTSize       DW      14h             ; [32] size of JFT
PSP_D_JFTAddr       DD      0               ; [34] address of JFT
PSP_D_NextPSP       DW      0ffffH,0ffffh   ; [38] unused
PSP_T_Unused2       DB      14h     DUP     (0) ; [3c] unused
PSP_W_Int21         DW      0cd21h          ; [50]
PSP_B_Retf          DB      0               ; [52]
PSP_T_Unused3       DB      9       DUP     (0) ; [53]
PSP_T_Parm1         DB      10h     DUP     (0) ; [5c] formatted param 1
PSP_T_Parm2         DB      14h     DUP     (0) ; [6c] formatted param 2
PSP_T_DTA           DB      80h     DUP     (0) ; [80] default DTA
PSP     ENDS
```

The Job File Table (JFT)

In most cases the PSP will contain the job file table itself. The default JFT limits you to 20 simultaneously open files, but you can provide an alternate JFT to increase the maximum number of open files. DOS 3.3 provides a function for this purpose (int 21h AH = 67h). Prior to DOS 3.3 you could manually change the JFT address in the PSP. DOS would use the newly defined JFT for I/O but had problems cloning this JFT when processing a load (int 21h AH = 4bh) request.

The job file table (JFT) links handles to system file table entries. Each entry in the JFT is 1 byte. If an entry is not used, it will contain a 0ffh; otherwise, it contains a system file number (SFN), which is an index into the system file table. DOS uses the file handle as an index into the JFT.

Listings 4-16 and 4-17 illustrate the relationship among the PSP, JFT, SFN, and SFT. The first routine accepts a handle in BX and returns the corresponding system file number in AX. The routine uses a BIOS service AH = 62h to locate the current PSP, then gets the address of the JFT from the PSP, and finally uses the handle as an index into the JFT. The macros *pushr* and *popr* save and restore the registers listed as arguments. This routine returns with the carry flag set (CY = 1) if it encounters an error.

The second routine accepts an SFN in AX and returns the address of its corresponding SFT entry in ES:DI. It gets the "list of lists" address with function AH = 52h and then gets the handle SFT list head in ES:DI. Each block has a "next" field and part of a header that tells how many entries are in that particular block. This routine walks the chain of SFT blocks until it finds the block containing the SFT entry. If the handle is invalid or if the SFT is corrupt, these routines return with the carry set.

Listing 4-16. Using a Handle to Get a System File Number

```
GetSFN      PROC    NEAR
            pushr   <ds,es,di,bx>               ; macro to save some
                                                ; registers
            mov     ah,62h...                   ; get current PSP
            int     21h
            mov     ds,bx                       ; ds <== current psp
            pop     bx                          ; handle
            cmp     bx,0ffh                     ; check =the handle
            jz      BadHandle                   ; negative handle is not valid
            cmp     bx,ds:PSP_W_JFTSize
                                                ; handle too big?
            jge     BadHandle                   ; if ge -- yes
            les     di,ds:PSP_D_JFTAddr
                                                ; es:di <== JFT
            mov     al,es:[di][bx]              ; al <== SFN(Handle)
            cbw                                 ; ax <== SFN(Handle)
            clc                                 ; indicate success
Done: popr         <di,es,ds>                   ; macro to restore
                                                ; registers
            ret                                 ; and return
```

continued

Figure 4-16. *continued*

```
BadHandle: stc                         ; indicate error
           jmp    SHORT Done            ; take common exit
GetSFN     ENDP
```

Listing 4-17. Finding the System File Table

```
LocateSFT  PROC   NEAR
           push   ax                       ; save SFN
           mov    ah,52h                   ; request list of
           int    21h                      ; lists address
;
;          es:di <==1st block handle SFT list head
;
           les    di,es:[bx].DOS_D_HDLSFT
           pop    ax                       ; recover SFN
           xor    bx,bx                    ; bx <== 0
_l0:       cmp    di,0ffffh                ; at end of chain
           jz     _l2                      ; if z -- yes
;
;          bx <== first SFN in next block
;
           add    bx,es:[di].SFTBLK_W_Count
           cmp    ax,bx                    ; SFN in this block?
           jl     _l1                      ; if l --  yes
;
;          es:di <== next SFT block
;
           les    di,es:[di].SFTBLK_D_Next
           jmp    SHORT _l0                 ; continue searching
;
;          bx <== first SFN this block
;
_l1:       sub    bx,es:[di].SFTBLK_W_Count
           sub    ax,bx                    ; ax <== offset into block
           mov    bl,SFT_K_SIZE            ; bl <== entry size
           mul    bl                       ; convert offset to bytes
           add    di,ax                    ; di <== offset into block
                                           ; (almost)
           add    di,SFTBLK_K_Size         ; add overhead
           clc                             ; indicate success
           ret                             ; and return
_l2:       stc                             ; indicate error
```

```
          ret                                    ; and return
LocateSFT ENDP
```

The BIOS Dispatcher, Int 21h

When DOS boots, IBMDOS initializes the IVT entry for int 21h to point to code within the IBMDOS image. This ISR processes all int 21h requests. Because of the way this code switches stacks and uses static variables, it is not reentrant. If a TSR makes a BIOS request at the wrong time, it will corrupt information that DOS has saved about the foreground program. The effects of this corruption are normally disastrous. If you are lucky, your system will crash without corrupting your disk.

Int 21h processing begins with interrupts disabled as a result of the INT instruction. The dispatcher contains a table of action routines that complete processing of various BIOS requests. There is an entry in this table for each valid int 21h function. Immediately preceding this table is a byte containing the number of table entries. DOS ultimately uses the function code in AH as an index into this table and first checks the value passed in AH. The dispatcher returns an error if the request is not valid.

The int 21h dispatcher services requests for AH = 51h (undocumented Get Current PSP), AH = 62h (documented Get Current PSP), AH = 50h (undocumented Get Current PSP), and AH = 33h (Get/Set Break) immediately. Since the dispatcher doesn't switch stacks or save context information in static variables, these requests are always safe.

Here is what happens when the request is not for one of the four that can be immediately serviced (nearly all other int 21h functions). DOS saves all registers on the current stack, saves the current contents of DS:BX in a static variable, and increments the critical section (also known as InDOS) flag. The dispatcher needs the DS and BX registers to continue processing the BIOS request; DOS will reload these registers before it dispatches to the action routine, which will complete the request.

At this time the SS:SP registers still contain the address of the foreground program stack. DOS records in static variables the values of SS:SP for the current and previous entrance (i.e., the corresponding SS:SP value the last time through the dispatcher). The dispatcher also saves the current SS:SP values in the current PSP at offset 16h. DOS uses the stack values in the PSP to process critical errors; it uses the stack values in the global variables when it returns control and has to restore the original stack.

The dispatch routine uses three private stacks: the auxiliary stack, the user stack, and the disk I/O stack. Having saved the program stack, the dispatcher makes an unconditional switch to the auxiliary stack and enables the interrupts. If the request is in the range 01h to 0ch, and if the dispatcher is not processing a critical error, it switches to the user I/O stack. The dispatcher services all other requests except Get Extended Error (AH = 59h) on the disk I/O stack.

If the request is to be serviced on the disk I/O stack, and if breaks are enabled, the dispatcher checks for a break before completing the request. Functions 01h to 0ch make explicit break checks as appropriate. (Some of these functions explicitly ignore breaks; all others check for breaks. Refer to the *IBM Technical Reference Manual* for a complete description of these requests.)

The int 21h dispatcher uses the function code in AH as an index into the action routine table, restores DS:BX, and dispatches to the action routine. After the action routine completes, the dispatcher disables interrupts, decrements the critical section flag, restores the SS:SP registers, restores the pre-int 21 register values, and exits with an IRET. Action routines that need to return values in index registers modify the register values saved on the program stack.

Character I/O Routines

BIOS functions in the range 01 to 0ch are collectively known as character I/O functions because of the way they are used. Character I/O operations take a relatively long time to complete. BIOS may have to wait for input in order to satisfy a read request. Character output also takes a relatively long time. Most character input functions call a keyboard poll routine. The keyboard poll routine repeatedly checks both the console and the standard input for a break and then checks the input device for an available character. If no character is available, the keyboard poll routine always calls the background dispatcher. The display output function (AH = 2) calls the background dispatcher each time it writes four characters. The background dispatcher executes an int 28h.

Int 28h ISRs play an important role in background processing. It is safe for an int 28h ISR to make BIOS requests that will be serviced on the disk I/O stack. With the exceptions of the functions that are processed without any stack switch, DOS services all int 21h functions above 0ch on the disk I/O stack.

DOS Global Variables

DOS relies on many global variables to keep operating state information and to maintain the context of BIOS requests. DOS provides a work area for buffered input and keeps track of the current column to support buffered input line editing. Other variables control screen logging, the memory allocation algorithm, and current switch character. Global variables include the critical error and critical section flags, the current PSP, and the current disk transfer area (DTA). Many other global variables describe handle I/O operations; they record the SFN, JFT entry address, and many other important pieces of information about the request.

The *disk transfer area* (DTA) is an insidious data structure because DOS uses it in unexpected ways. DOS maintains its own internal DTA for parsing file names and directory searches; it copies the results of these operations to the user DTA. DOS replaces the DTA address with a buffer address for handle file reads and writes. Operations such as *find first/find next* write directly into the current DTA.

Requests made by the TSR may alter DOS global variables as a side effect. DOS is not expecting another program to walk all over its global variables and will probably get very confused if you allow these variables to change.

Break Processing

DOS checks for the presence of a break in two places. The int 21h dispatcher calls a *break check* routine if a request is to be processed on the disk stack and if break checks are enabled. The *keyboard poll* routine (called by the character I/O functions) checks for break while waiting for input and while writing to *stdout*.

The break check routine checks the current console device. DOS identifies the console device by examining the device attributes of drivers as it loads them (see Chapter 6). The current console device will have the IsStdIn and IsStdOut bits set in the device header. DOS records the address of the current console device in the list of lists. DOS will check the console device for breaks even if some program redirects *stdin*. There is an implicit assumption that the console device has declared an int 1bh service routine and can receive break notification asynchronously. A side effect of this design is that if *stdin* is redirected to a file and a program does its reads with int 21h functions greater than 0ch, then a Control-C has no special meaning.

The keyboard poll routine first calls the break check routine and then checks standard input. When character I/O operations are in progress, DOS will detect a break either from the console device or from standard input; but when DOS is operating on the disk I/O stack, it checks only the console device.

The DOS routine that processes breaks sets SS:SP to the value recorded by the int 21h dispatcher, restores all registers to their pre-int 21h values, resets the critical section and critical error flags, and executes an int 23h instruction. The int 23h ISR can return to the DOS break routine with either an IRET or a RET instruction. Executing an IRET instruction removes 6 bytes from the stack, but executing a *far* return removes only 4 bytes. By comparing the value in the SP before and after executing an int 23h instruction, the break routine can tell which instruction (i.e., RET or IRET) returned control.

If the int 23h ISR preserves any registers it uses, it can continue execution by executing an IRET instruction. If the ISR returns with a *far* return instead, the state of the carry flag determines whether or not execution will continue. If the carry flag is clear, execution will continue; otherwise, the program will be aborted. The DOS break routine forces an abort by loading 4c00h into the AX register. In all cases, control returns to the start of the int 21h dispatcher. The dispatcher then re-executes the int 21h request or executes the terminate request in the case of an abort.

The default int 23h ISR consists of an IRET instruction. COMMAND.COM sets up its own int 23h ISR, which aborts the current program. Other programs may set up their own int 23h service routines.

Critical Error Processing

Many int 21h requests cause an I/O operation. BIOS passes most I/O requests to a device driver. If the device driver has a problem completing the request, it reports the problem to BIOS. BIOS responds to device errors by declaring a critical error. Logic within DOS decrements the critical section flag and increments the critical error flag in response to a device error. Corrupt FAT blocks also cause critical errors.

DOS takes one of four different actions when it detects a critical error: ignore the error, retry the operation that caused the error, terminate the current program, or fail the current call. All four options are not always available. DOS contains a flag that defines acceptable actions.

If DOS is already processing a critical error, the critical error routine fails the call that caused the second error. The critical error routine checks a DOS global variable to see if a handle I/O request is in progress If it is, DOS retrieves the JFT entry address of this handle from another global variable and marks the handle invalid; this action prevents another critical error on the same handle.

With interrupts disabled, the DOS critical error routine increments the critical error flag, decrements the critical section flag, restores the SS:SP values saved by the int 21h dispatcher and executes an int 24h instruction. When the int 24h ISR returns, the critical error routine resaves the SS:SP pair (the int 24h ISR may change it), increments the critical section flag, and resets the critical error flag.

The critical error routine expects the int 24 ISR to return a processing action. If the ISR requests an acceptable action, the critical error routine honors it. If the critical error routine has marked a handle invalid, it restores the SFN from a DOS global variable before exiting. Termination requests pass through the break handler, which forces the int 21h dispatcher to execute a terminate request.

When COMMAND.COM initializes, it sets up its own int 24 ISR; it is this routine that prints the abort, retry, or ignore message. Other programs may declare their own int 24h ISRs.

Loading a Program

A common BIOS service loads all programs. The int 21H AH = 4bh action routine sets up an environment, allocates memory for the program image, loads the program from disk, and creates a PSP. It uses the largest available memory block to load the program. The .EXE files specify their memory requirements in the program header, and the load routine adjusts the memory block size accordingly. A .COM file's size determines its minimum memory requirements, but the load action routine does not adjust block size for .COM files. A .COM file will begin executing with the entire memory block allocated to it.

Normally, DOS loads a program because a user has invoked it from the shell prompt. The program being loaded is known as the *child* and the one requesting the load is known as the *parent*. The parent creates a parameter block containing the address of an environment table, the address of a command line, and the addresses of two file control blocks (FCBs). The parent passes the address of this parameter block and the address of an ASCIIZ file specification to the load action routine using an int 21h AX = 4b00h request. The parent may explicitly specify the location of the environment or may request that its environment be copied by specifying zero as the starting segment of the environment. If the parent does not have an environment and requests that its environment be copied, the child will have no environment.

The previous section discussed the details of loading a program. This process is important, but not terribly interesting as far as implementing a TSR is concerned. After loading the program image from disk, DOS builds a program segment prefix. The contents of this PSP are important to a TSR. The same code that services the Build PSP request (int 21h AH = 26h) completes the PSP for the load routine.

Prior to calling the Build PSP routine, the load routine sets a flag that forces the Build PSP routine to initialize the child's JFT. The Build PSP routine examines each entry in the parent's JFT, locates its corresponding SFT entry, and clones a reference unless the "NoInherit" bit is set in the SFT or unless the SFT entry corresponds to a network FCB. Cloning increments the SFT reference count and copies the SFN into the child's JFT. The child is said to "inherit" these files. COMMAND.COM uses inheritance to provide redirection of *stdin* and *stdout*. Because an application inherits these files, it does not have to open them explicitly. The JFT entries for these handles already contain valid system file numbers copied from the parent process. A second side effect of the flag being set is that the child PSP becomes the current PSP. The Build PSP routine fills in several other fields in the PSP; copies the contents of the current IVT entries for terminate (int 22h), break (int 23h), and critical error (int 24h) into the child's PSP; and then returns to the load routine.

The load routine fills in the address of the environment; initializes the two PSP FCB entries; copies the parent's return address to the termination vector (int 22h); sets the disk transfer address to child PSP:80h; initializes the ES, DS, SS, and SP registers; and passes control to the child process.

Program Termination

There are a number of different ways for a normal program to terminate. The two most common are int 21h AH = 4ch and int 21h AH = 00h. A common DOS routine processes all termination requests. When a program terminates, this routine copies the critical error (int 24) and break ISR (int 23) addresses saved in the PSP to the IVT, closes all files, and deallocates all memory belonging to the current process. Control returns to the terminate address (int 22h). Unless the terminating process modified the IVT entry for the termination address, the program that loaded the terminating program regains control at the instruction immediately following the load request. Normally, control then returns to COMMAND.COM. Critical errors cause aborts. The same code processes aborts and termination requests; the only difference between the two cases is a completion code saved in an internal DOS variable.

Memory deallocation is a simple process. DOS allocates memory in blocks. Immediately preceding each block is a 16-byte memory control block (MCB). This area contains the size of the following block and records the owning PSP. The word immediately before the list of lists contains the segment of the first memory control block. The DOS termination routine scans the MCB list looking for blocks owned by the current process. Whenever it finds one, the termination routine sets the owner field of the MCB to zero, indicating that the block is free. This MCB scan frees all blocks owned by the terminating process, including the environment. A program need take no special action to deallocate its environment.

The DOS termination routine gets the JFT address from the PSP of the current (terminating) process and scans the JFT, looking for open files. The termination routine closes every open file. The close routine decrements the SFT reference count for every open file. If the reference count goes to zero and the current program owns the file, the close routine deallocates the SFT entry. The entries corresponding to the inherited files will have reference counts greater than one; the SFT entries for these files remain. (Since the terminating program is still the current PSP, any attempt to close these entries would fail; the *OwnerPSP* field of these SFT entries lists COMMAND.COM as their owner.)

There are two terminate-and-stay-resident functions, int 27h and int 21h AH = 31h. The int 27h function is obsolete, and DOS internally maps it to an int 31h request. The same termination routine handles terminate-and-stay-resident requests. When a program makes a terminate-and-stay-resident request, the termination routine does not close any files or deallocate any memory blocks, but it does modify the size of the memory block containing the PSP. The terminating program specifies the new block size as an argument to the terminate-and-stay-resident request. Any handles that were valid before the terminate-and-stay resident request will be valid when the TSR reactivates.

Loading and Initializing a TSR

A TSR may be either a .COM or an .EXE file. DOS loads all programs the same way. Each program has a program segment prefix (PSP), code, and data. The difference between a TSR and standard applications is that the TSR has to perform a few basic tasks to prepare itself for reactivation at a later time.

At initialization, the TSR is the foreground program and the entire DOS system is fully available. Certain information is valid only while the TSR runs in the foreground. A TSR must record any of this information as part of its initialization. During initialization, a typical TSR

- Checks to see which DOS version is running
- Checks to see if another copy of itself is already loaded
- Locates important DOS data structures
- Captures one or more interrupt vectors
- Checks to see which display adapters and peripherals are present

- Performs some additional application-specific processing
- Calculates the memory needed by the resident code

Initialization completes when the program invokes the terminate-and-stay-resident function (int 21h, AH = 31h). It is important to stress that once the TSR terminates, it is no longer the foreground program. Background programs are unexpected guests; consequently, they must be very careful about the things that they do. The primary job of the initialization code is to record the state of the system so that the TSR can reactivate without corruption of the system.

In short, the initialization routine gets the program started, ensures that the TSR can run when it is called later, calculates memory requirements for the resident code, and finally issues a terminate-and-stay-resident request (int 21h, AH = 31h) to return control to DOS.

Checking for DOS Version

Many TSRs rely on version-specific, undocumented features of DOS and routinely check the current system version before doing anything else. If the version is not correct, the TSR should exit with an appropriate error message.

DOS records its version in a global variable and makes this value available through a BIOS request, function 30h. The int 21h dispatcher does not switch stacks or alter any global variables to satisfy this request. Although this request is always safe, good programming practice dictates that you make this request in your initialization code. Listing 4-18 shows how to determine the operating system version.

Listing 4-18. Checking the DOS Version

```
VersionID   EQU    0a03h            ; DOS 3.10 (note that minor
                                    ; version is in msb)

            mov    ah,30h           ; ah <== function to check
                                    ; DOS version
            int    21h              ; make the request
            cmp    ax,VersionID     ; version is returned in ax
            jnz    WrongVersion     ; version is wrong
```

Locating Resident Copies of a TSR

Monitoring some DOS action or hardware activity dictates which IVT entry to use. TSRs also use interrupts and IVT entries to locate resident copies of their code. You may not want multiple copies of your TSR in memory, or you may need to locate data recorded by the resident code. If a TSR takes over some IVT entry when it first runs, subsequent activations locate the resident code by executing an INT instruction or inspecting the code pointed to by the IVT entry.

Which IVT entry should you choose? It turns out that choosing an interrupt to locate resident code is one of the tricky problems confronting a TSR author. There are no absolutely foolproof techniques.

DOS and the PC hardware use only a few of the available IVT entries. Theoretically, any unused entry is a good candidate. If your TSR actually executes an INT instruction, the IVT entry must point to a valid ISR. There is no guarantee what an IVT entry contains if a TSR has not initialized it. One way out of this "Catch 22" dilemma is to inspect the IVT entry.

DOS loads all programs on a segment boundary. If a previous copy of your code has captured an interrupt vector, the offset value (lowest word) in the IVT entry must match the offset of the ISR in the current code. Since there is a slight possibility that ISRs for two different TSRs will use the same IVT entry and have the same offset, you should do some additional checking. Listing 4-19 illustrates this technique.

The previous example looked for an ASCII string (*UniqueID*); we could have also done a string comparison on the ISR code. One shortcoming of this technique is that it does not solve the problem of conflicting interrupts. If two TSRs decide to use the same IVT entry, there is no way to locate which TSR loaded first.

Beginning with DOS version 3.0, Microsoft documented the *multiplexed interrupt*, which is their first attempt at solving the problem of conflicting interrupts. The multiplexed interrupt provides a guaranteed valid IVT entry for int 2fh and a protocol for locating TSRs. The initial int 2fh IVT entry points to an IRET instruction. Each TSR that wants to use the multiplexed interrupt first looks for previously loaded copies of its code and then installs its own int 2fh ISR.

**Listing 4-19. Locating a TSR by Using an Arbitrary
Interrupt Vector**

```
NewISRVector     EQU    ??                 ; fill in the vector number

OldISRxx    DD    0                        ; init code saves old vector here

UniqueID    DB    'a unique string'        ; to help identify ISR
IDLength    EQU   $-UniqueID               ; length of string

NewISRxx    PROC  FAR                       ; installed by init code
;
;                 ...                        ; whatever the ISR does
;
            iret
NewISRxx    ENDP
```

```
LocateISR   PROC    NEAR
            mov     al,NewISRVector         ; al <== vector number
            mov     ah,35h                  ; ah <== get int vector function
            int     21h                     ; ask DOS for int vector
            ret                             ; es:bx has ISR address
LocateISR   ENDP

CheckISR    PROC    NEAR
            cmp     bx,OFFSET NewISRxx      ; existing offset OK
            jnz     done                    ; if nz -- no
            mov     si,OFFSET UniqueID      ; si <== offset UniqueID
            mov     di,si                   ; di <== offset UniqueID
            mov     cx,IDLength             ; cx <== length of ID
            cld
            repnz   cmpsb                   ; compare IDs
done:       ret                             ; return with results
                                            ; zr=1 ==> installed
CheckISR    ENDP                            ; zr=0 ==> not installed

TSRResdnt   PROC    NEAR                    ; determines if TSR resident
            call    LocateISR               ; gets ISR address
            call    CheckISR                ; validates ID
            ret                             ; and returns with results
                                            ; zr=1 ==> installed
                                            ; zr=0 ==> not installed
TSRResdnt   ENDP
```

A TSR looks for resident copies of itself by loading a unique identifier in AH and a zero in AL and by executing an int 2fh instruction. The int 2fh ISR examines the value in AH. If the ISR recognizes the ID, it sets AL = 0ffh and returns with an IRET; otherwise, it jumps to the previously saved int 2fh ISR. Eventually, either the end of this chain will be reached or some ISR will recognize the AH value.

Again, conflicts are possible. The TSR should make some additional checks to detect this possibility. You may extend the int 2fh protocol to help with these checks, but you should be aware that there are no standards for additional checks. You must program defensively. Listing 4-20 illustrates one approach.

The fact that you get a positive response to your AL = 0 int 2fh request means that some TSR has responded. The int 2fh ISR shown in the listing responds to an AL = 1 function by returning its code segment in ES. The TSR that made the initial request can use this value to locate a unique string. If the strings match, you can be sure that you have found the correct ISR.

This extension to the multiplexed interrupt protocol is not standard. You have no guarantee what some other TSR will do in response to an int 2fh AL = 1 request. By zeroing the ES register before making this second request, you can at least tell if the responding TSR is returning anything meaningful in ES. (You know that your TSR would not be loaded in segment 0.)

Listing 4-20. Locating a TSR by Using the Multiplexed Interrupt

```
OurID EQU        81h                     ; ah value selects TSR

OldISR2f    LABEL   FAR                  ; init code saves old int 2f vector here

UniqueID    DB              'a unique string'  ; to help identify ISR
IDLength    EQU             $-UniqueID          ; length of string

OldInt2f    DD              0       ; initialization code records original
                                    ; ISR address here
NewISR2f    PROC    FAR             ; new int 2f ISR
            cmp     ah,OurID        ; request for us?
            jz      ItsMe           ; if z -- for us
            jmp     cs:OldInt2f     ; pass request along
ItsMe:      or      al,al           ; loaded check?
            jnz     GetAddress      ; if nz -- no
            mov     al,0ffh         ; say we're loaded
            iret                    ; and return
GetAddress:
            cmp     al,1            ; address check?
            jnz     BadFunction     ; if nz -- no
            push    cs              ; return segment in es
            pop     es
            iret
BadFunction:
            stc                     ; indicate error
            iret
NewISR2f    ENDP
LocateISR   PROC    NEAR
            mov     ax,OurID SHL 8      ; anyone listening?
            int     2fh
            cmp     al,0ffh         ; check out reply
            jnz     NotFound        ; nz ==> no response
            xor     ax,ax           ; zap segment so we can
            mov     es,ax           ; check out reply
            mov     ax,(OurID SHL 8) OR 1
                                    ; ask for segment
            int     2fh
            jc      NotFound        ; if cy=1, it's not us
            xor     ax,ax           ; did es change?
            mov     bx,es           ; if es didn't change
            cmp     bx,ax
            jz      NotFound        ; es didn't change
            lea     bx,NewISR2f
```

```
                                        ; es:bx has ISR address
                clc                     ; indicate success
                ret                     ; and return
NotFound:       stc                     ; say we failed
                ret                     ; and return
LocateISR       ENDP


TSRResdnt       PROC    NEAR            ; determines if TSR resident
                call    LocateISR       ; gets ISR address
                jc      NotLoaded
                call    CheckISR        ; validates ID
                ret                     ; and returns
                                        ; zr=1 ==> installed
                                        ; zr=0 ==> not installed
NotLoaded:      or      al,1            ; force zr=0
                ret                     ; and return
TSRResdnt       ENDP
```

Note that the TSR cannot just grab the int 2fh. If some other TSR loads afterward and captures this vector, the IVT table entry will not point to your code but to the most recently loaded TSR.

Recording the PSP Address

The program segment prefix (PSP) is an important data structure. DOS uses the PSP address to manage programs and support many I/O services. DOS does not know how to manage multiple PSPs; it only knows about the current PSP. If your TSR is going to do anything that requires a PSP, you are responsible for managing the current PSP. Later you will see how to tell DOS which PSP to use. If your TSR will need the address of its PSP after initialization, it must record it now. Initialization is the only time you can be sure that the current PSP belongs to you. The following code illustrates how to determine the address of your PSP.

Listing 4-21. Getting the Address of Your PSP

```
MyPSP DW    0                           ; PSP address recorded here

        mov     ah,62h                  ; ask DOS to get the current PSP
        int     21h                     ; it belongs to us now
        mov     MyPSP,bx                ; save the PSP
```

Recording the Critical Section (INDOS) and Critical Error Addresses

After a TSR terminates with a stay resident request (function 31h), it waits for a captured interrupt to reactivate its code. When the TSR wakes up, you must have a way to test what the foreground program is doing or to see if any DOS or BIOS activity is in process. Since it is non-reentrant, DOS maintains critical error and critical section flags to help the resident code decide whether it is safe to make BIOS requests.

When the TSR reactivates, it must check both the critical error and the critical section flags to be sure that it is safe to continue. DOS makes the address of the critical section flag available through the undocumented int 21h AH = 34h request. In version 3.10 of DOS, there is no BIOS function to return the address of the critical error flag; this flag is located immediately before the critical section flag. DOS 3.3 int 21h, AX = 5d06h returns the critical error flag address in ES:BX.

Because of the way DOS processes int 21h requests, you may not safely ask DOS for these addresses within an ISR. The only reliable way to access these flags is to record their address during initialization. The following code fragment illustrates capturing the addresses of the critical section and critical error flags.

Listing 4-22. Locating the Critical Section and Critical Error Flags

```
CSectFlg     DW      0,0              ; address of DOS critical section
CErrflg      DW      0,0              ; and critical error flags


GetCritFlags         PROC    NEAR

             mov     ah,30h           ; ah <== check DOS version
             int     21h
             cmp     al,03h           ; at least version 3.00?
             jnz     WrongVersion     ; if nz -- no
             push    ax               ; save version
             mov     ah,34h           ; to get address of critical
             int     21h              ; section flag
             mov     CSectFlg,bx      ; es:bx has address
             mov     CSectFlg+2,es    ; remember address
             dec     bx               ; assume critical error flag
                                      ; precedes critical section flag
             pop     ax               ; recover version
             cmp     ah,1eh           ; version 3.30?
             jnz     v3xx             ; if nz -- no
             mov     ax,5d06h         ; get critical error address
             int     21h              ; (DOS 3.3 only )
```

```
v3xx:           mov     CErrflg,bx          ; store critical error address
                mov     CErrflg + 2,es      ; es:bx has address
                clc                         ; indicate success
                ret                         ; and return

WrongVersion:                               ; bad version
                stc                         ; indicate failure
                ret                         ; and return

GetCritFlags    ENDP
```

Capturing Interrupt Vectors

At some point in its initialization sequence, the TSR may want to declare its own int 2fh ISR so that future program activations can locate its resident code. The TSR may need to modify other IVT entries as well. Int 25h (absolute disk read) and int 26h (absolute disk write) make blind stack changes. By its very nature, int 13h (low-level disk I/O) cannot be interrupted. Imagine what would happen if the int 13h code were interrupted between a seek and a transfer. If another disk I/O operation occurred as a result of this interrupt, the first transfer would probably do serious harm to the disk structure.

DOS does not expect any interruptions while it is servicing one of these requests. It is the TSR's responsibility to protect DOS at these times. Capturing these interrupts lets a TSR manage disk activity. These ISRs are tricky to write because of the way they use the processor flags. The original int 13h ISR returns the results in the flags register; the new ISR must return these results rather than the flags pushed by the int 13h instruction. The original int 25h and int 26h ISRs add yet another twist by leaving the flags pushed by the INT instruction on the stack. Note that the *NewInt25* and *NewInt26* ISRs do not execute a *pushf* before calling the original routine and that all these ISRs use a *far* return. Listing 4-23 shows what you might want to do when you capture these interrupts.

Be very careful when you capture an interrupt. Once you modify an IVT entry, the processor will dispatch to the new ISR even if the ISR address no longer points to valid code. You have to watch out for breaks and critical errors. If either of these conditions occurs after you have captured an interrupt, they can force your program to terminate. DOS will reuse the memory occupied by your program and its ISRs. Once this happens, the IVT entries no longer point to valid ISRs.

> **CAUTION**
>
> Before you modify any interrupt vectors, you must set up your own break and critical error ISRs. Do not attempt to restore either of these vectors. DOS will fix the IVT entries for these functions when your program terminates. If you try to restore either the critical error or the break address and have other vectors captured, your code will become vulnerable to premature termination.

Listing 4-23. Typical Replacement Disk I/O ISRs

```
DiskIO      PROC    FAR

OldInt13    DD      0           ; initialization code records
OldInt25    DD      0           ; addresses of original int 13h,
OldInt26    DD      0           ; 25h, and 26h here

BusyFlag    DB      -1          ; protects against interrupting
                                ; non-reentrant code

DiskIOExit0:
            pushf               ; save disk I/O flags
            dec     cs:BusyFlag ; release lock
            popf                ; restore disk I/O flags
            ret     2           ; return, removing flags
                                ; pushed by int
DiskIOExit1:
            pushf               ; save disk I/O flags
            dec     cs:BusyFlag ; release lock
            popf                ; restore disk I/O flags
            ret

NewInt13:
            inc     cs:BusyFlag     ; take out lock
            pushf                   ; simulate an int
            call    cs:OldInt13     ; dispatch to real code
            jmp     SHORT DiskIOExit0
                                    ; take common exit

NewInt25:   inc     cs:BusyFlag     ; take out lock
            call    cs:OldInt25     ; dispatch to real code
            jmp     SHORT DiskIOExit1
                                    ; take common exit
```

```
NewInt26:       inc     cs:BusyFlag         ; take out lock
                call    cs:OldInt26         ; dispatch to real code
                jmp     SHORT DiskIOExit1
                                            ; take common exit
DiskIO          ENDP
```

Checking the Display Type

Initialization code should test for the display type and other peripherals as necessary. A TSR needs to know quite a bit about the display if it is going to support hot keys. It is relatively easy to determine whether the display is an MDA or a CGA. Other display types are possible. Many of these other types emulate either an MDA or a CGA. Because the MDA and CGA are by far the most common, this discussion is limited to these two types. The following listing shows how to tell the difference between an MDA and a CGA.

Listing 4-24. Determining the Display Type

```
C40         EQU    1                ; CGA 40 x 25 display
C80         EQU    2                ; CGA 80 x 25 display
M80         EQU    3                ; MDA 80 x 25 display

DisplayType DB     0

            int    11h              ; equipment check interrupt
            and    al,30h           ; isolate video bits
            mov    cl,4             ; shift video mode bits to bits
            asr    al,cl            ; 0 and 1
            mov    DisplayType,al   ; remember video mode
```

Freeing the Environment

The environment contains character strings. Each string has a variable name followed by a value. (See Chapter 3 for a more complete description of the environment.) DOS sets up the environment when it loads your TSR. Programs are free to interpret the meaning of these variables. COMMAND.COM uses the PATH variable to specify which directories to search when loading a program or a batch file.

Since COMMAND.COM asks DOS to pass a copy of the environment when it loads a program, a TSR will not notice any posttermination changes to the environment. The only time that the environment is valid is during initialization. Whether or not your TSR uses the environment for any reason is application-dependent. Because the environment is not valid after termination and the environment does take up memory, there is no reason to keep it (although failing to free the environment does not adversely affect a TSR).

The PSP contains the starting segment of the environment at offset 2ch (see Listing 4-15, "Structure of the PSP"). To free your environment, use the int 21h AH = 49h Free Memory Block service. Under some circumstances, there will be no environment. You must check for this case before attempting to free the environment. If there is no environment, the PSP will contain a zero at offset 2ch (function 49h will have trouble freeing the memory block at location 00000h). Listing 4-25 shows how to free the environment.

Listing 4-25. Freeing the Environment

```
;
;       Frees the environment
;       Note: PSP_W_Envron is part of PSP STRUC in
;             Listing 4-15

FreeEnv     PROC    NEAR

            pushr <ax,bx,es>              ; save some registers
            mov     ah,62h               ; request PSP address
            int     21h
            mov     es,bx                ; es <== PSP
            xor     ax,ax                ; ax <== 0

            xchg    ax,es:PSP_W_Envron     ; zap environ segment in PSP
                                           ; ax <== environment segment

            or      ax,ax                ; is there an environment?
            jz      NoEnv                ; if z -- none
            mov     es,ax                ; es <== environment
            mov     ah,49h               ; free the block
            int     21h
NoEnv:      popr  <es,bx,ax>             ; restore registers
            ret                          ; and return

FreeEnv     ENDP
```

Program Termination

The last task of initialization is to invoke the DOS terminate-and-stay-resident function, int 21h, function 31h. When you make a terminate-and-stay-resident request, you must tell DOS how much memory to keep. You load the number of segments needed into the DX register and issue the int 21h AH = 31h terminate-and-stay-resident request. DOS frees all but the first DX segments of the memory owned by your program. It is common to locate initialization code at the end of a TSR so that it can be discarded at this time. The following listing illustrates how to use this service. This code starts with an address (*EndOfCode*), rounds it up to the next segment boundary, and finally converts the result to paragraphs by dividing by 16.

Listing 4-26. Making a Terminate-and-Stay-Resident Request

```
mov     dx,OFFSET EndOfCode   ; dx <== end of resident code
add     dx,0fh                ; round up to next segment
mov     cl,4                  ; convert offset to segment
shr     dx,cl                 ; dx <== resident paragraphs
mov     ah,31h                ; DOS TSR function
int     21h
```

As a result of the termination request, control passes to DOS, and DOS returns control to the shell (normally COMMAND.COM). The shell becomes the foreground application until the user invokes another program.

Reactivation and DOS Architecture and Services

When the TSR gets a reactivation request, it must determine if it is safe to run. Actions taken by the initialization code simplify this task. The TSR must check the critical error and critical section flags and verify that no uninterruptable operation is in progress. If it is safe to continue, the TSR must save current register values, switch to its own stack, set up its own critical error and break routines, record information saved in various DOS global variables, and finally set up its own run-time environment that includes the current PSP and DTA addresses. Note that the order of these operations is very important.

Other actions may also be needed. If the TSR needs to use the display, it must save the contents of screen memory. PRINT.COM checks the interrupt summary register in the 8259 interrupt controller. If any interrupts other than the ISR that woke it up are active, it ignores the reactivation request. Presumably, PRINT.COM makes this check to avoid losing characters on the serial port and other slow devices.

After the TSR completes its work, it must undo these steps and slip quietly into the background, waiting to be called again. The TSR must restore the PSP, DTA, stack, and other register values of the interrupted program. Once the TSR completes these steps, it can safely restore the critical error and break handlers and return to the interrupted program.

Determining Whether Reactivation Is Safe

There is no way to predict when the interrupt reactivating a TSR will occur. Sections of DOS are non-reentrant, and a TSR cannot always reactivate when

asked. The DOS architecture section explained the details of this problem. You must respect these limitations, or your code surely will crash the system and possibly corrupt the disk in the process.

Listing 4-27 illustrates the minimal checks that your TSR must perform. This code is designed to run with interrupts disabled. When the processor responds to an interrupt, it disables the interrupts. Unless your interrupt service routine enables interrupts before calling *DOSSafeCheck*, you do not have to explicitly manipulate the interrupt flag.

This code begins by incrementing the same *BusyFlag* used by the new disk I/O routines (Listing 4-23, "Typical Replacement Disk I/O ISRs"). This flag has an initial value of −1. If the INC instruction in *DOSSafeCheck* produces a zero, it is safe to continue. A nonzero result means that one or more disk operations are in progress (an int 13h ultimately gets executed as a result of int 25h and int 26h) or that a previous invocation of the TSR has not completed. Because of the stack switch made by the reactivation code, the TSR is not reentrant. (Later, the reactivation sequence will be described in detail.)

Next, this code checks the critical section and critical break flags. Note that you must check both flags. The DOS critical error handler decrements the critical section flag and increments the critical error flag before it begins processing a critical error. A side effect of calling this routine is that it prevents the TSR from being reentered. Before the TSR goes back to sleep, it must decrement this *BusyFlag*.

Listing 4-27. Determining Whether It Is Safe to Reactivate

```
BusyFlag:   DB          -1              ; manipulated by disk ISRs
                                        ; as well
CSectFlg    DW          0,0             ; critical section flag address
                                        ; stored here (initialization)
CErrFlg     DW          0,0             ; critical error flag address
                                        ; stored here (initialization)


DOSSafe     PROC    NEAR
DOSNotSafe:
            stc                         ;;; indicate that it's not safe
            ret                         ;;; and return

DOSSafeCheck:
            inc     cs:BusyFlag         ;;; try to take out a lock
            jg      DOSNotSafe          ;;; if g -- some one already
                                        ;;; has lock
            pushr <ds,si,ax>            ;;; save so we can get at
                                        ;;; INDosFlag

            lds     si,DWORD PTR cs:CSectFlg  ;;; ds:si <== address
                                              ;;; critical section flag
```

```
          lodsb                                 ;;; al <== value of critical
                                                ;;; section flag
          lds     si,DWORD PTR cs:CErrFlg       ;;; ds:si <== address
                                                ;;; critical error flag

          or      al,BYTE PTR [si]              ;;; account for nonzero critical
                                                ;;; error flag
          popr    <ax,si,ds>
          jnz     DOSNotSafe                    ;;; if nz either critical
                                                ;;; error
                                                ;;; or int 21 in progress
          clc                                   ;;; indicate safe
          ret                                   ;;; and return
DOSSafe   ENDP
```

Stack Switching and Saving Register Contents

The stack is an important part of a program's environment. Since reactivation occurs as the result of an interrupt, there is no way of knowing which stack is in use or how much stack space is available. The stacks used by the int 21h dispatcher are large enough to record all the processor registers. Any interrupted program must also be assumed to have this much space left; otherwise, it could not make BIOS requests. The BIOS dispatcher saves all registers on the current stack.

Before reactivating a TSR, an ISR should save all registers and switch to the TSR's private stack. It is reasonable to save register values on the stack that was in use when the interrupt occurred. Both the stack and register values are part of the same program context, and the stack should have room for these values.

Trapping Breaks and Critical Errors

The next step in the reactivation sequence involves changing the state information that DOS has recorded about the current program. At this point, your TSR is about to become the current program. Since critical errors and breaks can terminate the current program, you must be sure that you get a chance to put things back the way you found them. Establishing its own critical error and break handlers lets a TSR deal with these events in an orderly and safe manner.

Since you have no way of knowing what the foreground program is up to, setting up break and critical error handlers from within an ISR is tricky. If you use int 21 to manipulate the IVT, you risk causing a break check. The safest technique is to manipulate the IVT directly. Note that you must disable interrupts while you are changing table entries. Although it is not likely, another program could interrupt your code in the middle of making your change and could modify the IVT entry that you are working with. Listing 4-28 shows how to accomplish this task.

What you do in your newly established break and critical error handlers depends on your TSR. It is reasonable for a TSR to ignore breaks, but it usually must do something when a critical error occurs. If your TSR can deal with failed int 21h requests (you really should check the results of every request and be prepared to deal with errors), the simplest approach is to fail the call. There are times when other actions would be more appropriate. If a disk-write fails because the drive door was open, you should print an error message and retry the operation.

Listing 4.28. Trapping Critical Errors and Breaks from an ISR

```
IVT             SEGMENT AT 00h              ; note absolute address
                ORG          23h*4          ; we don't care about 0 to 22h
IVT23 DW             0,0                     ; reference entries for int 23h
IVT24 DW             0,0                     ; and 24h
IVT             ENDS


_text           SEGMENT      BYTE PUBLIC 'code'
OldInt23        DW       0.0                 ; we'll save current critical
OldInt24        DW       0,0                 ; error and break address here
                ASSUME ds:_text
BKGNewErrHndlr       PROC  NEAR

                pushr   <ax,di,si,ds,es>    ; save all modified registers
                cld                         ; put direction flag in known
                                            ; state for movsw and stosw
                mov          ax,cs          ; make es point to segment
                mov          es,ax          ; containing OldInt23
                xor          ax,ax          ; make ds point to IVT
                mov          ds,ax
                ASSUME ds:IVT,es:_text              ; tell masm what to expect
                mov          si,OFFSET IVT23    ; set up to copy IVT
                mov          di,OFFSET OldInt23 ; entries with movsw
                mov          cx,4               ; each entry is 2 words
                cli                             ; IMPORTANT!!!
                rep          movsw          ;;; copy current ivt entries
                mov          es,ax          ;;; es now points to IVT
                ASSUME es:IVT                ;;; tell masm about change
                mov          ax,OFFSET NewInt23 ;;; enter new values in
                stosw                           ;;; IVT
                mov          ax,cs
                stosw
                mov          ax,OFFSET NewInt24
                stosw
                mov          ax,cs
                stosw
```

```
                sti
                popr        <es,ds,si,di,ax>
                ASSUME ds:_text
                ret

BKGNewErrHndlr      ENDP

NewInt23    PROC    FAR              ; new break handler
            iret                     ; ignore breaks
NewInt23    ENDP

NewInt24    PROC    NEAR             ; new critical error handler
            iret                     ; probably should do something
NewInt24    ENDP                     ; about error
                                     ; (maybe fail the call)

_text       ENDS
```

Dealing with DOS Global Variables

As a minimum, your TSR will have to record the current DTA and PSP, establish a private DTA, and make itself the current program. Both the DTA address and the current PSP are recorded in DOS global variables. You can access the variables directly, but their location may vary with DOS version. There are BIOS services to get and set both the DTA address and the current PSP. At this point in the reactivation sequence, you have determined that it is safe to make BIOS requests, and you have protected yourself against breaks and critical errors. Using BIOS services for these functions insulates you from changes in the locations of these global variables.

Listing 4-29. Dealing with DOS Global Variables

```
BKGDTA      DB      80h DUP(0)       ; minimum size for DTA
BKGPSP      DW      0                ; initialization code stores PSP
                                     ; value here
DOSPSP      DW      0                ; we'll save PSP and DTA of
DOSDTA      DW      0,0              ; interrupted program here

BKGSetPSP   PROC    NEAR
            pushr <ax,bx>            ; save nonvolatile registers
            mov     ah,62h           ; ask DOS for current PSP
            int     21h
            mov     DOSPSP,bx        ; save current PSP
            mov     ah,50h           ; tell DOS to use new PSP
            mov     bx,BKGPSP        ; let it be us
```

continued

```
               int     21h                  ; (undocumented)
               popr    <bx,ax>
               ret
BKGSetPSP     ENDP


BKGSetDTA PROC  NEAR
               pushr   <ax,bx,dx,es>
               mov     ah,2fh
               int     21h
               mov     DOSDTA,bx            ; record DTA address
               mov     DOSDTA+2,es
               lea     dx,BKGDTA            ; ds:dx <== new DTA
               mov     ah,1ah
               int     21h
               popr    <es,dx,bx,ax>
               ret
BKGSetDTA ENDP
```

Background Processing Using Int 28h

The final piece of the TSR puzzle is background processing. This capability is undocumented and consequently poorly understood. Under the right conditions, a TSR can make BIOS requests while another program is running. PRINT.COM uses this feature to read blocks from a file. A word processor might use this capability to save a file concurrent with foreground editing, or a spreadsheet might perform a lengthy calculation in the background.

DOS provides some hooks to help you, but you still must do a lot of work to use this feature. The critical section, critical error, and int 28h ISR are all hooks for background processing. Programs quite frequently spend much of their time waiting for input. By capturing int 28h, a TSR can use CPU cycles that would otherwise be wasted waiting for input. Since other TSRs may also use this feature, an int 28 ISR should chain to the previous ISR when it is done.

The int 28 ISR gives a TSR a chance to run only if the foreground application uses DOS character I/O functions. A TSR that wants to run in the background normally captures one of the two timer interrupts as well. The timer ISR ensures that the TSR will get access to the processor even if the foreground program is compute-intensive or does not use the character I/O functions.

Writing an int 28h ISR is a fairly simple matter. The new ISR first calls the old ISR and then increments the same *BusyFlag* used by the int 8, int 9, and disk I/O ISRs. If the result is not zero, some uninterruptable function is in progress. Since this ISR should get control only when disk access is safe, the increment should always produce a zero result. Nonetheless, you should be prepared for errant int 28s. After reactivating the TSR, the int 28h ISR decrements the *BusyFlag* and returns to DOS. Note that you do not have to check the critical section flag: Because an int 21h request is in progress, you know it is set; but it is still always safe to make int 21h requests whose function is greater than 0ch. You must increment the *BusyFlag* to prevent the TSR from being reactivated by hot key or timer interrupts.

Listing 4-30. Interrupt Service Routine for Int 28h

```
OldInt28    DD      0           ; initialization code records old
                                ; ISR address here
BusyFlag    DB      -1          ; protects no-reentrant sections of
                                ; code


Int28ISR    PROC    FAR
Int28Exit0:
            dec     cs:BusyFlag ; release our lock
            iret                ; and return


NewInt28:
            pushf               ; simulate an int
            call    cs:OldInt28 ; dispatch to original code
            inc     cs:BusyFlag ; try to take out lock
            jg      Int28Exit0  ; if g -- someone beat us to it
            call    BKGResume   ; dispatch to background task
            dec     cs:BusyFlag ; release lock
            iret                ; and return
Int28ISR    ENDP
```

The process of reactivating a TSR is fairly simple: Save all the registers on the current stack and switch to the TSR's private stack. Most background TSRs run for a short time and then suspend themselves. Typically they will save all their registers on their own stacks and then return to the interrupted program. As part of the reactivation sequence, restore the registers saved on the TSR's stack when it suspended itself.

PRINT.COM increments the critical section flag during its reactivation sequence. This utility does some pretty unusual things. It bypasses DOS and calls the printer device driver directly. Presumably, incrementing the critical section flag eliminates potential reentrancy problems in the device driver. If your TSR accesses a driver directly, it's probably a good idea to mimic PRINT.COM.

Next, set up your own break and critical error handlers, make your TSR the current PSP, and switch to a private DTA. The TSR from which the following routine was taken supported both background processing and hot-key activation. If the reactivation is in response to a hot key, you should save the contents of the current display and flush the type-ahead buffer. The assumption made here is that any keys in the type-ahead buffer were for the previously current program and would only confuse the reactivating TSR. The return instruction dispatches to the TSR code. When the TSR is done, it will call *BKGSuspend*.

The suspension code is a little strange. The TSR that used this code periodically calls *BKGSuspend*. Under certain conditions, *BKGSuspend* actually sends the TSR into the background; at other times, it does nothing. You might like to be able to send a TSR activated by a hot key into the background. If a TSR running in the foreground calls *BKGSuspend*, this routine checks the type-ahead buffer for the specific key that sends it into the background (*BGCombo*). If this key is not at the head of the type-ahead buffer, *BKGSuspend* ignores the suspension request. If the *BGCombo* key is found or if the TSR is currently running in the background, it is deactivated.

Deactivation reverses the steps taken in activation. *BKGSuspend* restores the saved DTA and PSP, restores the critical break and critical error handlers, saves the current TSR registers, restores the screen (*SCRBackground*), decrements the critical section flag, switches stacks, restores index registers, and updates the *PgmState* variable. The RET instruction at the end of *BKGSuspend* returns control to the ISR that activated the TSR. The *SCRBackground* does not switch screens if the TSR had been running in the background.

Listing 4-31. Suspending and Resuming a TSR

```
SuspendResume        PROC  NEAR

AltF10               EQU   113                    ; extended ascii for ALT F10
BGCombo              EQU   AltF10 SHL 8 ; LSB of extended ascii = 0

BKG_C_FG             EQU   1
BKG_C_BG             EQU   2

SaveStack            STRUC
rSP                  DW    0
rSS                  DW    0
SaveStack            ENDS

switch      MACRO    sstack,dstack              ;; switches stacks
            cli                                 ;; disable ints during switch
            mov      sstack.rSS,SS              ;; record current stack
            mov      sstack.rSP,SP
            mov      SS,dstack.rSS              ;; set new stack
            mov      SP,dstack.rSP
            sti                                 ;; ints ok now
            ENDM

_text                SEGMENT      BYTE PUBLIC 'code'
```

```
PgmState         DB      0           ; keeps track of program state
InDosFlag        DD      0           ; initialization code saves address of
                                     ; critical section flag here
OldStack         SaveStack    <>     ; stack of interrupted program
BKGStack         SaveStack    <>     ; stack of TSR. Set up by
                                     ; initializaiton code

BKGResume:
        call    BKGSaveAll           ; save all reg on current
                                     ; stack
        cld                          ; init direction flag
        mov     ax,cs
        mov     ds,ax                ; ds <== code segment
        switch OldStack,BKGStack     ; switch to background stack
        call    BKGRestoreAll        ; restore background registers
        pushr <es,di>
        les     di,InDosFlag         ; es:di <== indos flag
        inc     BYTE PTR es:[di]     ; set indos flag
        popr    <di,es>
        call    BKGNewErrHndlr       ; set up own critical error and
                                     ; break handlers
        call    BKGSetPSP            ; now change PSP
        call    BKGSetDTA            ; change DTA
        cli
        cmp     PopupPending,0       ;;; popup pending?
        jz      _br0                 ;;; if z -- no
        dec     PopupPending         ;;; one less popup pending
        mov     PgmState,BKG_C_FG    ;;; bring program to
                                     ;;; foreground
        call    SCRForeground        ;;; bring up screen
        call    BKGBufFlush          ;;; flush keyboard buffer
_br0:   sti
        ret


BKGSuspend:
        cmp     PgmState,BKG_C_FG    ; running in foreground?
        jl      _bs0                 ; if l -- background
        jg      _bs2                 ; if g -- initializing
                                     ; (ignore suspend)
;
;       Currently running in foreground. Check for keystrokes
;
        push    ax                   ; save current ax value
        xor     ah,ah                ; ah <== 1 (status check)
        inc     ah
        int     16h                  ; make request
```

continued

Listing 4-31. *continued*

```
              jz     _bs1              ; if z -- no character available
              cmp    ax,BGCombo        ; is this the character to push
                                       ; us into the background?
              jnz    _bs1              ; if nz -- no
              xor    ah,ah             ; ah <== 0 (read request)
              int    16h               ; remove character from buffer
              pop    ax                ; recover ax
;
;      Running in background and asked to suspend. Do it.
;
_bs0:         call   BKGRestoreDTA     ; restore DTA
              call   BKGRestorePSP     ; restore PSP

              call   BKGRestoreErrHndlr ; restore old critical error
                                        ; and break handlers

              call   SCRBackground     ; restore screen
              call   BKGSaveAll        ; save background registers
              les    di,InDosFlag      ; es:di <== indos address
              dec    BYTE PTR es:[di]   ; decrement indos flag
              switch BKGStack,OldStack  ; change stacks
              call   BKGRestoreAll     ; restore registers
              mov    cs:PgmState,BKG_C_BG  ; program in background
              ret                       ; and return

_bs1:         pop    ax                ; recover original ax
_bs2:         ret                       ; and return

SuspendResume    ENDP
_text            ENDS
```

Removing a TSR from Memory

Because of the limited physical memory available on the PC, you may need to remove a TSR from memory when you no longer need it. Removing a TSR from memory appears easy, but there are some problems. A TSR frequently captures interrupt vectors, and before releasing a TSR's memory, you must restore these vectors.

When the TSR initializes, it should record the initial contents of any vectors it modifies. If no other TSR loaded after yours captured these vectors, you can restore the interrupt vectors to their original values and release the memory occupied by your TSR. If the vectors of interest still point to your code, it is a safe assumption that no other TSR has captured them. But suppose your TSR shares an interrupt vector with a TSR that loaded after it. Each should have recorded the original vector contents and inserted an IVT entry pointing to its own code. The existing IVT entry points to the TSR loaded last, which should have saved the vector to the first TSR, which should have saved the vector to the original ISR.

If you replace the current IVT entry with the value you saved, you have effectively removed the other TSR from the ISR chain. If the second TSR could be entered only by this one vector, all you have done is wasted memory. If the second TSR has another entry point and tries to chain to the saved interrupt vector that you have altered, this reference points to a block of deallocated memory.

The cleanest solution to this problem is to implement a TSR that manages other TSRs. There is an excellent public domain package called *Mark/Release* available on many bulletin boards. The *Mark* TSR runs before any other programs are loaded and makes a copy of the IVT and records the current state of memory. The user loads other TSRs as necessary. Running *Release* restores memory and the IVT to the values recorded by the *Mark* program, effectively unloading any TSRs loaded after *Mark*. It is possible to nest *Mark* invocations.

Mark/Release works in most, but not all, cases. It restores the IVT and memory. If a TSR has altered some other DOS data structure, that data structure will remain changed after the TSR is evicted from memory.

Summary

This chapter has described the technical details of writing TSRs. It has explained what you must do and why you must do these things. These techniques have many other applications. You can use them to add background saves to a word processor or background calculations to a spreadsheet. You can implement many simple functions as background TSRs. The code fragments presented here are a good starting point for writing more sophisticated TSRs.

Real-Time Programming 5

REAL-TIME systems are used in many applications, and there are few people who do not interact with one every day. For example, applications like telephone switching systems, power generation and distribution, and automatic teller machines use real-time systems.

MS-DOS is widely used for personal and business computing applications, but its use for real-time applications is less popular. In this chapter, we will discuss what real-time systems are and how to use MS-DOS for many simple yet useful real-time applications.

Overview of Real-Time Systems

Before discussing real-time systems, let us briefly discuss other types of computer systems. This will help us gain a better understanding of real-time systems.

In the early days of computers, the cost of computers was very high as compared to the cost of salaries for computer professionals. As a result, the goal was to maximize the use of every computer. This resulted in *batch-processing* computer systems, where the computer was supplied a constant backlog of work, and the computer waited for no one. All human activities were done *off-line* so that the inevitable human delays did not waste expensive computer time.

As the cost of computers came down, it was no longer economical to have highly paid professionals wait for computer time. Therefore, more computers were purchased and people worked interactively with the computers. This is called *on-line* processing. Still, however, the computer was too fast for human beings; it wasted time waiting for human responses. This led to the development of *time-sharing* systems. Time-sharing systems allow more than one user to work at a time, each user getting a small slice of time. Time-sharing often gives the user the impression that the computer system is dedicated only to that user.

In addition to batch-processing, on-line, and time-sharing systems, there is another important type of computer system called *real-time*, and that is the topic we shall discuss in the rest of this chapter.

What Is Real-Time?

To understand what real time is, let us consider a simple example of a scene generation system in which a computer is used to produce video effects. A scene generation system may produce a frame of movie film every few minutes. It would give an effect of ultra-slow motion. But, ideally a movie maker would like to see the scene at full speed, just the way the audience would see it. If the computer could produce 24 frames per second, which is the speed of movie film, then the scene would appear in a nonstretched time frame or in "real time."

This suggests that a real-time computer system is one that:

- Deals directly with the environment external to the computer.
- Is fast enough to keep up with the external environment.

With this understanding of real time, the field of real time in a broad sense could include all computer systems. For example, a batch-processing system is capable of real-time performance if the response criteria are long enough. If the Internal Revenue Service says that refund checks will be delivered within 60 days, and if their batch-processing computers can manage the work, they have a real-time system. However, the term *real-time systems*, as used in computer literature, usually includes only those systems with time constraints in the order of seconds or less. It is in this sense that we are going to study real-time systems in this chapter. To summarize: When a computer is used to deal with an external environment having certain time constraints (usually less than a few seconds) that must be met without fail, it is called a real-time system.

Batch-processing, on-line, and time-sharing systems are not real-time systems because they are not guaranteed to meet absolute time constraints. For example, time-sharing systems are usually fast enough for interactive use, but they can sometimes slow down, and one user's computing task may be blocked by another user's computing task.

Characteristics of Real-Time Systems

Real-time systems have many unique characteristics. The external environment of a real-time system usually contains input/output devices that act as the *senses* of the system. In general, any computer system can be said to sense the environment because it performs input/output. Usually, the input and output happen at discrete, distinct points of time. However, real-time systems have input/output devices (such as thermocouples, optical scanners, valves, motors, etc.) that collect and output data continuously. The continuous output usually overlaps the continuous input. For example, a real-time system may continuously sense the temperature of a chemical process and take action to maintain it at a desired value.

The real-time systems usually require *concurrent* handling of multiple inputs/outputs. In real-time systems, the requirement for concurrency involves correlated processing of two or more inputs/outputs over the same time interval. This requirement for concurrency is different from the overlapped processing of independent transactions in time-sharing systems. For example, a real-time system for a chemical process control may need to simultaneously monitor temperature, pressure, level, concentration, flow, etc., and adjust valves, heaters, etc., to maintain the process in a desired state.

The timing constraints for real-time systems typically range from several nanoseconds to seconds. This range is fast compared to human standards.

The precision of the required response is greater for real-time systems than for other systems. For example, in a payroll processing system, salary checks need to be ready three days before the date of payment. Occasionally, a delay of one or two days is acceptable. However, for a chemical process control system requiring adjustment of temperatures within a second, a delay of another second may result in a disastrous chemical reaction.

Note that not all the characteristics just explained need to be present in a real-time systems.

Basic Types of Real-Time Systems

Real-time systems can be divided into three types based on the direction of data flow, as shown in Figure 5-1:

- *Unidirectional*
- *Bidirectional stable*
- *Bidirectional potentially unstable*

Any real-time system can be viewed as one of these three basic types.

Unidirectional Systems

Unidirectional systems are those real-time systems in which the data flow is in only one direction, i.e., either from the external environment to the computer or from the computer to the external environment, but not both. Such systems are primarily *data generation* or *data collection* systems.

The movie scene generation system mentioned before is an example of a data generation system. The only requirement is that the frames must be produced at the rate of 24 frames per second. This means that it should not take more than $\frac{1}{24}$ of a second to generate a frame. Even a slight delay will be noticed and thus will be unacceptable. If most frames can be generated within $\frac{1}{24}$ of a second, and a few take a little longer than that, then a buffer can be used as shown in Figure 5-2 to get a real-time effect. The computer can actually generate a few frames before starting the display. New frames are put in the buffer as they are generated, and one frame from the buffer is displayed every $\frac{1}{24}$ of a second. Even if the computer takes longer for a frame, it is acceptable because the output from the buffer is still 24 frames per second.

Data collection systems are the opposite of data generation systems. In data collection systems, the environment dictates how fast the computer must be. If the computer is a little slow, then some data will be lost. A buffer cannot help to smooth out short-term delays in data collection as it does in data generation. A laboratory measurement system that collects data is such a system. After collecting data, it may also analyze it and display it in a graphical or text

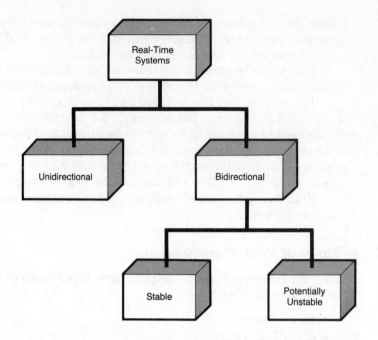

Figure 5-1. Types of real-time systems based on direction of data flow.

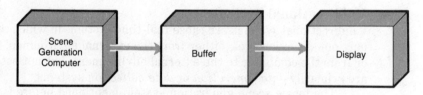

Figure 5-2. Buffered data generation.

form. Thus, it also performs output. But the output phase is usually separate from the data collection phase. Thus, a laboratory measurement system may predominantly be a data collection system.

Bidirectional Stable Systems

Unidirectional systems input to or output from the computer, but not both. However, many real-time systems require both input and output. Such systems are called *bidirectional* systems. A bidirectional system may be *stable* or *potentially unstable*. Let us first discuss bidirectional stable systems with the help of a home control system.

A home control system can be used for heating, ventilation, air-conditioning, lighting, watering the lawn, etc. To maintain the temperature at some value, the system needs to read the temperature and take appropriate corrective action every few minutes. The temperature is acceptable even if it is left unchanged for 10 or 20 minutes. Thus, occasional delays are acceptable because no disaster results and the temperature can still be maintained. The system still remains under control. This is what we mean by a stable system. Another example is an automatic teller machine. Most transactions should take only a few seconds, but it is acceptable if occasionally a transaction takes longer because of overload. Note that there is no fixed absolute time constraint (e.g., that responses must come within x seconds). But still there is a time constraint (e.g., a customer will get annoyed if he or she does not receive money for 5 minutes after entering the request).

Bidirectional Potentially Unstable Systems

Consider balancing a broomstick on your fingertip as shown in Figure 5-3. To maintain balance, you must be quick enough to constantly move your fingertip. This system is bidirectional because you must sense the position of the broomstick and take corrective action accordingly. If you are a bit too late, the broomstick may move too far and fall out of balance. Thus, there is some "absolute" time constraint that must always be met. Even an occasional delay is not acceptable. This is what we mean by an unstable system. Another example is rocket flight control as shown in Figure 5-4. A rocket is balanced on its exhaust, just like a broomstick on a fingertip. Like the broomstick, if the rocket gets too far out of balance, it is not possible to control it anymore.

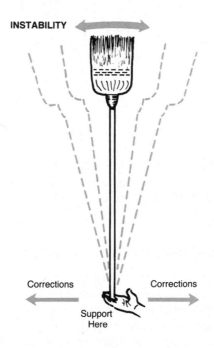

Figure 5-3. Balancing broomstick on fingertip: potentially unstable.

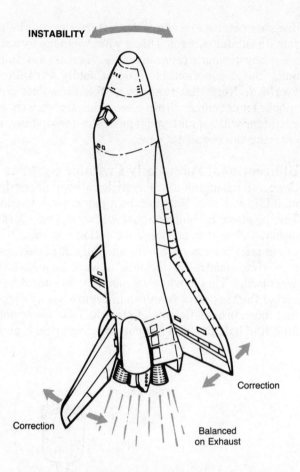

INSTABILITY

Correction

Correction

Balanced
on Exhaust

**Figure 5-4. Rocket balanced on its exhaust:
potentially unstable.**

In bidirectional potentially unstable systems, the computer makes decisions about how to control the external environment. Such systems are most demanding on the part of the computer action because even a small delay can have disastrous results.

Typical Timing Requirements and Real-Time Solutions

The *response time* is the most important timing requirement for understanding how fast the external environment requires responses. The response time is the elapsed time between the input to the computer system and the completion of its processing or sending an output in response. The response time is thus the total time a transaction or activity remains in a computer system.

For example, if the automatic teller machine system (ATM) has only one terminal, then the response time is simply the time from when the customer makes a request to the time when the computer executes it to completion. In actuality, however, the ATM system has many terminals. Therefore, the response time also includes the delays involved because the computer is handling several requests at a time.

The range of response times for some applications is shown in Figure 5-5. For ATM or airline reservation systems, the response time required may be in the order of seconds. For some database query systems, a response time of 20 seconds may be acceptable. On the other hand, the required response times for applications such as rocket flight control, radar readings, and scientific data collection may be in milliseconds.

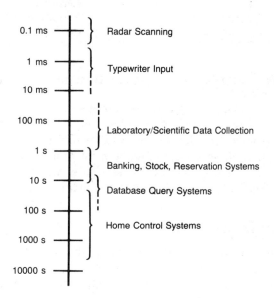

Figure 5-5. Range of typical response times.

Another important timing requirement is *interval time*, the time interval between two transactions. It determines how frequently the transactions may come for processing. The interval time may be *random* or *periodic*. It is random when it is determined by events in the external environment (such as a clerk pressing a key or an interrupt from some device). It is periodic when it is determined by a clock or some other device in the computer. When determining the required interval time, we must consider the maximum possible load at any time. Otherwise, there will be loss of data during the peak load periods, which is not acceptable.

Like response time, interval time may vary from a fraction of a millisecond (or smaller) to several minutes. A savings bank system with several branches may have one transaction per second during the busy lunch hours. A keyboarder may type 5 to 10 characters per second. A scanning radar system may send data every millisecond. A database inquiry system may have only an occasional inquiry.

Table 5-1 gives the types of real-time solutions popularly used for real-time applications, depending on the response time required. Note that MS-DOS is not included in the table because it is not popular for real-time applications.

Table 5-1.   Response Times and Popular Real-Time Solutions

Range of Response Time	Popular Real-Time Solutions
10 ns–100 ns	Dedicated ECL logic, fixed program
100 ns–1 μs	Dedicated standard logic, programmable
1 μs–100 μs	Fast processor with dedicated program
100 μs–1 ms	Microprocessor with real-time kernel (os)
1 ms–1 s	Microprocessor with real-time (os)
1 s–upward	Anything

MS-DOS for Real-Time Applications

As we have already discussed, real-time systems span a wide range of applications, from a simple data collection system to a complex and elaborate rocket control system. Real-time systems differ not only in the basic type (unidirectional, bidirectional stable/potentially unstable) but also in their timing requirements. Before we can investigate when to use MS-DOS for real-time applications, we need to understand how fast MS-DOS is.

How Fast Is MS-DOS?

The speed of a computer running MS-DOS depends on the processor as well as the methods of data transfer used. We will discuss several issues that determine the speed of MS-DOS and thus help determine whether it can be used for a real-time application.

MS-DOS Clock Frequencies

At the time of writing this book, MS-DOS is available on six members of the Intel 8086 family of processors: 8088, 8086, 80188, 80186, 80286, and 80386. Of these, the 8088 is the slowest, and the 80386 is the fastest (and most powerful). The 8086 family processors are available at different clock frequencies, as shown in Table 5-2. The clock frequency of 4.77 MHz means that 4.77 million "clock ticks" are generated per second. The clock frequency determines the speed of the processor: the higher the clock frequency, the faster the processor. Note, however, that the 80286 is faster than the 8086 running at the same clock frequency.

Because the 8088 processor is the slowest in the 8086 family, all timing information given in this chapter is for an 8088 processor running at 4.77 MHz. If your computer has a faster processor, you will be able to get faster response. Because all 8086 family processors have pre-fetch queues, the actual execution time of any sequence of instructions may be different from that calculated solely on the basis of individual instruction execution time.

Table 5-2. Clock Frequencies for MS-DOS Computers

8086 Family Processor	Computer Name	Clock Frequencies
8088	IBM PC	4.77, 8 MHz
8086	IBM PC Compatible	8, 12 MHz
80188/186	IBM PC Compatible	8, 10 MHz
80286	IBM PC AT (8086 real mode)	8, 10 MHz
80386	IBM PC AT (386) (8086 real mode)	16, 20, 25 MHz

MS-DOS maintains a real-time clock. This real-time clock provides the date and time, and can be accessed by any program. The time of the real-time clock is accurate up to 10-millisecond intervals. Thus, if our application requires a resolution time less than 10 ms, we cannot use the real-time clock.

The following program reads the date from MS-DOS. For reading the date, software interrupt 21h is used. As a matter of fact, when any service is requested from MS-DOS, this int 21h is used, with the AH register holding the code for the function to be performed. Later, we will discuss some more example programs using software interrupts to make calls to MS-DOS or the ROM-BIOS.

```
mov     ah,2ah          ; function to read date
int     21h             ; call DOS
mov     year, cx        ; year in CX (1980 through 2099)
mov     month, dh       ; DH has month (1 through 12)
mov     day, dl         ; DL has day (1 through 31)
```

In the preceding program, the day of the week (0 = Sunday, 1 = Monday, etc.) is also returned in AL.

As seen in the program, the following steps are performed in making a function call to MS-DOS or the ROM-BIOS:

- Set up registers to contain appropriate function codes and parameters.
- Make an interrupt corresponding to the function call.
- On return, read the return parameters and status information from the registers.

To read the time from MS-DOS, int 21h with a function code of AH = 2ch is used as in the following program:

```
mov     ah, 2ch         ; function = read time
int     21h             ; call DOS
mov     hours, ch       ; CH has hours (0 through 23)
mov     mins, cl        ; CL has minutes (0 through 59)
mov     secs, dh        ; DH has seconds (0 through 59)
mov     msec, dl        ; DL has 10 ms (0 through 99)
```

The program reads the time from the system and stores it in variables named appropriately. We can also set the time and date by using function calls in MS-DOS.

Data Transfer in MS-DOS

For real-time systems, the MS-DOS computer needs to transfer data with the external environment. The data to be transferred falls into the following three categories:

- Data represented by single bits indicating the current state of a two-state device.
- Data representing the digitized value of analog signals produced by analog-to-digital converters.
- Digital information sent from another piece of equipment (which could have obtained the data in one of three ways).

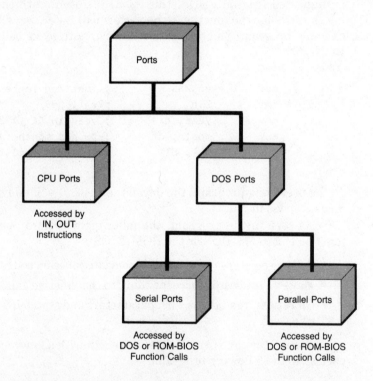

Figure 5-6. Types of ports and methods of access.

Ports are used by MS-DOS for data transfer. The data read from a port represents the external environment. The data written to a port affects (controls) the external environment. There are two types of ports in MS-DOS: *CPU ports* and *DOS ports*. Figure 5-6 shows the two types of ports and methods used for accessing them. Physically, these ports may be the same. It is the method of access that distinguishes them. CPU ports are also called logical ports.

CPU ports represent low-level data transfer and are accessed directly by the processor. Each CPU port is identified by its address; there may be as many as 65,536 different ports. MS-DOS uses some of the CPU ports for the programmable timer and for specific purposes like talking to the keyboard and data transfer with the disk drive. Other CPU ports can be used for other purposes by a user. The basic method of accessing these ports is to use the assembly instructions IN and OUT. The IN instruction reads one byte or one word from a port. The OUT instruction writes a byte or a word to a port.

In MS-DOS, the CPU port 61h is used for the speaker. The second least-significant bit (bit 1) is used for controlling the sound from the speaker. If the bit is set, the speaker is turned on; otherwise it is turned off. The other bits in this port control other functions. The following program in Listing 5-1 uses the speaker port to generate sound:

Listing 5-1. Sound Generation with the Speaker Port

```
            in      al, 61h     ; 61h is speaker port address
            mov     bl, 0fch    ; mask to reset bits 0 and 1
            and     al, bl      ; mask al
noise_on:
            or      al, 2       ; bit 1 in al is set
            out     61h, al     ; turn speaker on
            mov     cx, 0ffh    ; spend time
time_1:
            loop    time_1
noise_off:
            and     al, bl      ; reset bits 0 and 1
            out     61h, al     ; turn speaker off
            mov     cx, 0ffh    ; smaller value in cx means
                                ; higher frequency of sound
time_2:
            loop    time_2
            push    ax          ; save ax
            mov     ah, 1       ; read keyboard status
            int     16h         ; call BIOS keyboard services
            pop     ax          ; restore ax before jumping
            jnz     exit        ; a character has been typed
            jmp     noise_on    ; no character is typed
exit:
            ret
```

In the preceding program, the speaker is repeatedly turned on and off by writing a byte to port 61h. After turning on the speaker, a LOOP instruction is executed for spending some time before turning it off. The sound continues until a character is typed from the keyboard. The int 16h function is used for reading the status of the keyboard.

Table 5-3 gives the CPU port numbers used in MS-DOS for specific purposes.

Table 5-3.   CPU Ports Used for Specific Purposes

CPU Port	I/O Address	Interrupt Vector
Clock	040=043	8
Secondary RS 232	2F8=2FF	11
Keyboard	060=063	9
Hard disk	320=32F	13
Printer	378=37F	15
Monochrome display	380=3BF	—
Color display	3D0=3DF	—
Floppy disk	3F0=3F7	14
Primary RS-232	3F8=3FF	12

DOS ports are for high-level data transfer; that is, they are not controlled by the processor directly but are accessed by function calls to DOS and the ROM-BIOS. There are two types of DOS ports, commonly known as *serial ports* and *parallel ports*.

Parallel ports are basically designed for printers. They transfer data in parallel; that is, all 8 bits of a byte are transmitted to the printer at the same time. DOS supports parallel port data flow in only one direction (i.e., from computer to printer), although the hardware itself is capable of both input and output. The following piece of code outputs to a parallel port a string pointed to by DS:DX. The DOS function int 21H with AH = 40H (write file) is used for this purpose. The BX register contains the file handle for the standard list device (4). After execution of the call, the AX register will contain the count of the characters actually written to the parallel port.

```
        mov     ah, 40h             ; function = write file
        mov     bx, 4               ; handle for standard printer
        mov     cx, 20              ; count of characters
        mov     dx, seg OUTSTR      ;
        mov     ds, dx              ;
        mov     dx, offset OUTSTR   ; ds:dx points to OUTSTR
        int     21h                 ; call DOS to print
        jc      failed              ; carry set means print failed
```

Serial ports are commonly used for connecting to modems as well as for interfacing with a serial mouse. Serial ports transfer data one bit at a time on the same wire. DOS supports data transfer bidirectionally, i.e., into and out of the computer.

Serial ports transfer data asynchronously. As a result, a set of communication parameters must be negotiated between both ends. The *baud rate* of a serial port is the number of bits transferred per second. Baud rates supported by MS-DOS 3.3 range from 110 to 19,200 bits per second. *Word length* is the number of bits that constitute a character. This could be 7 or 8. *Parity* is a simple mechanism for error detection in the communication line. According to RS-232 standards of serial communication, parity could be odd or even (two ways of checking errors) or no parity. Each character is delimited by bits known as *stop bits*. One or two stop bits can be specified. These parameters have to be initialized before beginning data transfer.

BIOS function int 14h is used for data transfer with a serial port. Initializing a serial port is performed by a function code of 0 in the AH register. The communication parameters are encoded in the AL register as shown in Table 5-4. The *port number* is specified in DX. There are four serial ports in MS-DOS, known as COM1 through COM4. In the following program, a serial port is initialized to 9600 baud, 8-bit word, 1 stop bit, and no parity. After execution of the function call, the AH register contains the status of the port.

```
mov     ah,0        ; initialize serial port
mov     al,0e3h     ; 9600 baud, 8-bit word,
                    ; no parity, 1 stop bit
mov     dx,0        ; COM1 is initialized
int     14h         ; call ROM-BIOS
```

Table 5-4. Communication Parameter Encoding in AL

Baud Rate		Parity		Stop Bits		Word Length	
Bits 7, 6, 5	Rate	Bits 4, 3	Parity	Bit 2	Stop Bit	Bits 1, 0	Length
000	110	x0	None	0	1 bit	10	7 bits
001	150	01	Odd	1	2 bits	11	8 bits
010	300	11	Even				
011	600						
100	1200						
101	2400						
110	4800						
111	9600						

The following program code writes a character 'x' to a serial port. On return, if bit 7 of the AH register is set to 0, then the function call is successful. A value of 0 in bit 7 of the AH register indicates failure.

```
mov     ah,1        ; function 1 = write character
mov     al,'x'      ; AL contains the character
mov     dx,0        ; write to COM1
int     14h         ; ROM-BIOS call
```

The time taken for data transfer with ports usually depends on external devices. For example, the time taken for writing/reading 1 byte to/from a hard disk depends on several factors: the type of hard disk, hard disk parameters such as the number of heads and the number of cylinders, granularity of I/O to the hard disk, file structure, number of files, etc. If your real-time system uses external devices, you should experiment and find out the timings of the operations needed. Since the resolution of the system clock in MS-DOS is 10 ms, the experiment should repeat the operation many times in order to get accurate time estimates.

There are three methods of data transfer, as shown in Figure 5-7:

- *Polled*
- *Direct memory access (DMA)*
- *Interrupt-driven*

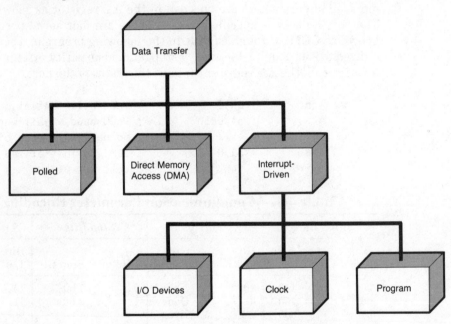

Figure 5-7. Methods of data transfer.

Polled Data Transfer

Polled data transfer can be used virtually for any device. In this scheme, the ports are checked in some fixed sequence to determine if data is available at the port. If data is available, it is transferred. Thus, a lot of computer time may be wasted if ports are inactive most of the time. Moreover, the processor remains busy during data transfer and no polling occurs at this time.

To understand how fast polled data transfer is, consider the following program code which inputs data from a CPU port into memory. The DX register contains the address of the port.

```
read:       in    ax, dx     ; read data -- 12 cycles
            add   di,2        ; next destination -- 4 cycles
            mov   [di],ax     ; store data -- 18 cycles
            loop  read        ; loop until done -- 17 cycles
                                    ; total  --  51 cycles for 8088
                                    ; total  --  43 cycles for 8086
```

For an 8088 running at 4.77 MHz, the 51 clock cycles take 10.69 micro-seconds, resulting in a *transfer rate* of 93 kHz. This transfer rate means that the computer can read data a maximum of 93,000 times from the port.

The following program checks to see whether data is ready in a serial port. Int 14h with AH = 03 (serial port status request) is used for this purpose. On return, if bit 0 of AH is set, it indicates that data is ready. The program waits until data is ready, and the data is returned in AL.

```
wait:
            mov     ah, 3     ; read serial port status
            mov     dx, 0     ; status of COM1 is required
            int     14h       ; call ROM-BIOS
            and     ah, 1     ; is data ready?
            jz      wait      ; no, wait until ready
            mov     ah, 2     ; function = read data
            mov     dx, 0     ; read from COM1
            int     14h       ; call ROM-BIOS
```

DMA Data Transfer

DMA data transfer is used when large quantities of data are to be transferred and the processor has other tasks to do during the data transfer. Usually, only the processor accesses the memory. But in DMA, the external device can also access the memory. The external device puts the processor on hold and initiates data transfer with the memory. During data transfer, the processor cannot access the memory, but it is free to do something else. Once the data transfer is completed, the processor can access the memory.

Interrupt-Driven Data Transfer

Interrupt-driven data transfer is used when the data transfer is asynchronous (the time of data transfer is not predetermined). And usually the data transfer is relatively infrequent. An interrupt indicates the occurrence of some external event to the processor, and can be generated by an external device, a clock, or a program. When an interrupt occurs, the processor suspends the current program, reads the address of an *interrupt service routine* (ISR) from the *interrupt vector table*, and executes it.

The main functions performed by an ISR are:

1. Enable interrupts, so that higher-priority interrupts can be serviced.

2. Save those registers that the ISR will use.

3. Do the processing associated with the interrupt as quickly as possible.

4. Restore the registers saved.

5. Execute an IRET instruction to resume the interrupted program.

The following program shows the skeleton of an ISR.

```
sti                         ; enable interrupts
push      ax                ; save only those registers
push      bx                ; that are used by
push      cx                ; the ISR
push      dx
.
.
.
mov       ax,cs             ; local data to be accessible
mov       ds,ax             ; using DS
.
.
.                           ; process the interrupt
pop       dx                ; restore registers in the
pop       cx                ; reverse order
pop       bx                ;
pop       ax                ;
iret                        ; resume interrupted program
```

When an interrupt occurs, the processor saves three words (CS, IP, flags) and reads two words (address of ISR). Thus, the overhead on serving an interrupt takes 71 cycles for an 8088 processor and 51 cycles for an 8086 processor. There is no overhead for setting up the interrupt or clearing it because the act of servicing the interrupt clears it (called *automatic end of interrupt mode*).

Comparison of Data Transfer Methods

A comparison of timings and maximum rates of non-DMA data transfer is presented in Table 5-5. The timing overheads (cycles and time) in the table are calculated for just the loops, with no actual data transfer. The timing information is given for the purposes of approximate comparison only. For example, the "software loop" timing is obtained by the following assembly language instruction:

```
again:    loop again
```

The CX register is loaded with a particular count and no data is transferred in this loop.

The timing cycles for polling are based on the following program, which reads the status from a port, checks for a ready bit, and loops if not ready.

```
again:
          in        ax,dx         ; port is specified in DX
          test      ax,bx         ; register/register comparison
          jnz       again         ; loop until ready
```

Table 5-5. Data Transfer Rates for Non-DMA
Interfaces

Data Ready Determined by	Timing Overhead		Data Transfer		Maximum Data Transfer Rate
	Cycles	Time	Cycles	Time	
Software loop (8088, 4.77 MHz)	17	3.564 μs	—	—	—
Polling (8088, 4.77 MHz)	27	5.660 μs	51	10.692 μs	61 kHz
Interrupt (8088, 4.77 MHz)	115	24.109 μs	43	9.015 μs	30 kHz
Interrupt (8086, 8 MHz)	83	10.375 μs	43	5.375 μs	63 kHz

The data transfer rates that can be achieved in practical applications are lower than the maximum data transfer rates in Table 5-5 because of the time required to set up the timers, receive the data, etc. If a data acquisition board is used, then the rate of data transfer also depends on the data transfer rate of the board.

Techniques for Writing Faster Programs

Many software techniques and boards (standard and custom) can be used for faster execution of MS-DOS programs. You should consider them only if your real-time system design requires a faster response from your computer. Although an exhaustive discussion of all these is beyond the scope of this chapter, we will discuss a few such techniques in this section.

If an application requires computation with floating point math, the use of a math coprocessor 8087 (or 80287/80387) can improve the speed of calculations by orders of magnitude. Intel, the manufacturer of the 8087, has benchmarks showing over a thousand times speed increase in certain math operations when the 8087 is used in place of software math routines. An 8087 provides the system with instructions for *fast* floating point calculations such as number conversions, basic mathematics, and some transcendental functions (e.g., sine, cosine, log). Because these math routines are contained in the 8087 rather than in program memory, use of the 8087 can also result in smaller programs. Refer to Chapter 10, "Programming for the Intel Numeric Processing Extension," for programming details.

If an array is to be looked up, the XLAT instruction can be used in all processors except the 8088. The XLAT instruction has a quick way to index into a 256-byte table and obtain the contents of that location, as shown in Figure 5-8. By chaining XLAT instructions together, larger table lookups can be handled.

Instead of using an IN/OUT instruction in a loop to transfer a number of bytes, REP INS/OUTS can be used for 80188, 80186, 80286, and 80386.

Using DMA techniques for data transfer can considerably increase the speed of a system. The data transfer takes place at the full speed of the bus and

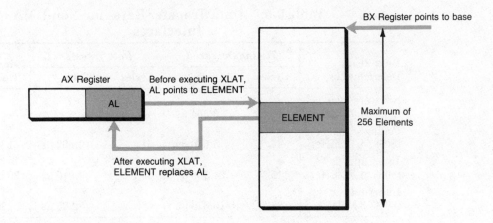

Figure 5-8. Operation of XLAT instruction for table lookup.

the memory because the processor is not involved. Another advantage is that transfer is not limited to the data bus width of the processor.

Using a *macro* in place of a subroutine call makes a program faster. This is because a macro expands code in-line whereas a subroutine call has to store the return address in a stack, usually save registers, and make a jump. Refer to Chapter 1, "Structured Programming 1: Tools for Structured Coding," for details on writing macros.

When to Use MS-DOS for Real-Time Applications

The decision to use MS-DOS for a particular real-time application depends on several considerations. These considerations include

- Response time
- Interval time
- Number of inputs
- Number of outputs
- The processor used
- The clock frequency
- The system design

Of all these considerations, only the design of the real-time application depends on the designer. The clock frequency is sometimes under the direct control of the designer: a faster MS-DOS system can be selected. All other considerations are dictated by the external environment and cannot be changed by the designer.

We need to calculate the required response time for the application as well as calculate the response time that MS-DOS can support in the application environment. It is usually easy to determine the required response time for the application. Consider a simple example of data collection. Assume that in 1 second you need to collect 50,000 bytes of data and process them. This means that you have 1/50000 = 20 microseconds to collect and process each byte.

In another example, suppose you require a response time of 10 ms to monitor and take corrective action to control the temperature of a chemical process. (This may be based on factors such as timings of equipment that control the temperature as well as the nature of the process.) Thus, the response time required by the application is inherent to the application as well as the existing environment.

It is more difficult to determine the response time that your real-time system can support. To determine the response time that can be supported by MS-DOS, first consider the existing MS-DOS and existing equipment (if any), as well as some simple software design method (different design methods are discussed later). Now compute the response time, which is the time it would take for the necessary input, processing, output, and all associated delays. If this response time is less than the required response time, then you have an acceptable design using MS-DOS.

Consider again the example of data collection, with the required response time of 20 microseconds. MS-DOS could provide a response time of 20 microseconds if there is enough primary memory to store the required amount of data. But if there is not enough memory, you may need to store data in the secondary memory. In that case, 20 microseconds may not be sufficient to store the data.

If the response time supported by MS-DOS is not less than the required response time, you need to experiment with other techniques for faster programs (discussed already), standard or custom-made boards, a faster processor, other system designs, and use of a faster environment (maybe more expensive devices). This is the most difficult part of a real-time system design, and a complete discussion of all these techniques is beyond the scope of this chapter.

The required interval time determines how frequently transactions will be processed. Depending on the processing required, MS-DOS can handle a certain maximum number of transactions per second. If the total number of transactions can be greater than what MS-DOS can handle, then obviously MS-DOS cannot be used. For example, if a real-time system needs to get 1 million transactions per second, MS-DOS cannot be used for such a system.

Whether or not MS-DOS can be used also depends on the need for multitasking. In general, MS-DOS cannot be used if multitasking is required. For example, MS-DOS cannot be used in a savings bank system with eight terminals. However, MS-DOS for the IBM PC AT provides some features to permit very simple multitasking. This is discussed later. Also discussed later is the concept of *cyclic schedulers* as a design method to achieve a very simple form of multitasking.

In general, we can say that MS-DOS can be used for most of the unidirectional systems, several of the bidirectional stable systems, and very few of the bidirectional potentially unstable systems. There are several relatively simple but useful real-time applications in which MS-DOS can be used. Such applications include home control systems, laboratory measurement systems, simplified robot systems, etc.

Designing Real-Time Systems Using MS-DOS

Design of real-time systems using MS-DOS is difficult because there is no formal methodology for design, implementation, and testing. This results in common problems such as:

1. Working designs may have mysterious crashes, or produce strange results because of timing problems.

2. The existing implementations become nonmaintainable because of changes and extensions.

3. When coding is completed, you don't know if it will ever work.

Figure 5-9 shows the methods of designing real-time systems. *Synchronous* methods require a single task for implementation. The synchronous methods are of three types:

- *Polled (no interrupts)*
- *Main loop with interrupts*
- *Cyclic scheduling*

We will use examples and assembly code to explain these design methods. We shall limit the discussion to design without worrying about timing considerations which we have already discussed. *Multitasking* is explained in the next section.

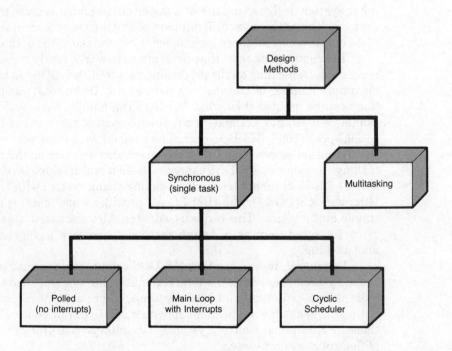

Figure 5-9. Methods of designing real-time systems.

Simplified Home Control System—An Example

Let us consider a simplified home control system for controlling the heat, fire alarm, and the lawn watering, as shown in Figure 5-10. The temperature is sensed by a temperature-sensing device. A transducer converts the temperature from an analog to a digital value. This value can be read from a port and compared with a reference temperature. The reference temperature value can be set by the user. For simplicity, let's assume it to be a constant *ref_temp*. The program *adjust_temp* to control the temperature is given in Listing 5-2. Note that the program shows only the important parts of the code. Less important details, such as declaration and initialization of variables, are not shown.

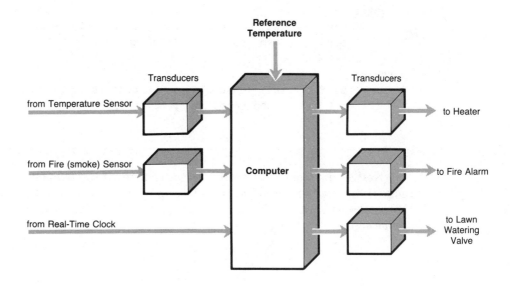

Figure 5-10. A simplified home control system.

Listing 5-2. The *adjust_temp* Program

```
adjust_temp:
        ; delta - to avoid oscillation of temperature
        ; ref_temp - reference temperature value
        ; temp_port - port where temperature control
        ;                  information is output
        ; inc_code - code to increase temperature
        ; dec_code - code to decrease temperature
        ; read_port - port from where current
        ;                  temperature is read
        in      al, read_port  ; read temperature into AL
        mov     bl, ref_temp   ; get ref_temp to BL
        mov     cl, bl         ; BL will be used again later
```

continued

Listing 5-2. *continued*

```
        sub     cl, delta       ; ref_temp - delta in CL
        cmp     al, cl          ; is current temperature less
                                ; than (ref_temp - delta)?
        jl      increase        ; then increase temperature
        add     bl, delta       ; ref_temp + delta in BL
        cmp     al, bl          ; is current temperature more
                                ; than (ref_temp + delta)?
        jg      decrease        ; then decrease temperature
        ret                     ; done
decrease:
        mov     al, dec_code    ; dec_code is to be output
        out     temp_port, al   ; to temp_port
        ret
increase:
        mov     al, inc_code    ; inc_code is to be output
        out     temp_port, al   ; to temp_port
        ret
```

Notice that the heater setting is not changed if the temperature is in the range from (*ref_temp − delta*) to (*ref_temp + delta*), as shown in Figure 5-11. Here *delta* is a small tolerance value (e.g., 1° F), and it is used to avoid oscillation.

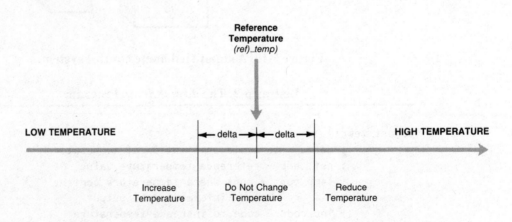

Figure 5-11. Use of a small-tolerance *delta* to avoid oscillation.

To understand the concept of oscillation, consider the value of *delta* to be zero. In such a case, the temperature needs to be changed when it is not exactly equal to *ref_temp*. Suppose the temperature is slightly less than *ref_temp*. So, when the procedure is called, action will be taken to increase the temperature.

As a result, the temperature will go beyond *ref_temp*. When the procedure is called again, it will take action to decrease the temperature. As a result, the temperature will be increased and decreased alternately. This is called *oscillation*. Thus, use of *delta* (small but nonzero) avoids oscillation because the temperature is not changed in the small range around the *ref_temp*.

Now consider the program to activate the fire alarm. We just need to send a signal that will set off the fire alarm. This procedure, *initiate_alarm*, is shown in Listing 5-3.

Listing 5-3. The *initiate_alarm* Program

```
initiate_alarm:
        ; alarm_port - port to send the alarm signal
        ; activate_signal - signal to activate alarm
        mov     al, activate_signal
        out     alarm_port, al
        ret
```

Next consider the procedure for watering the lawn. Assume we need to water the lawn in the evening every day for two hours from 1830 hours to 2030 hours. This dictates the need to use a real-time clock. Listing 5-4 shows the procedure *water_lawn*.

Listing 5-4. The *water_lawn* Program

```
water_lawn:
                        ; start_hours - hours component of start time
                        ; start_mins - minutes component of start time
                        ; stop_hours - hours component of stop time
                        ; stop_mins - minutes component of stop time
                        ; water_port - port to control watering lawn
                        ; start_code - code to start watering
                        ; stop_code - code to stop watering
                        ; watering - state variable indicating whether
                        ; or not watering is started
        mov     ah, 2ch         ; function to read time
        int     21h             ; call to DOS, on return
                                ; CX has hours and minutes
        mov     bl, watering    ; is watering started?
        test    bl, 1           ;
        jz      start_or_not    ; no, then start watering
        mov     dh, stop_hours  ; is it time to stop?
        mov     dl, stop_mins   ; to be compared with stop time
```

continued

Listing 5-4. *continued*

```
        cmp     cx, dx              ; time to stop watering?
        jl      exit                ; no, let watering continue
        mov     watering, 0         ; watering stopped
        mov     al, stop_code       ; output stop code
        out     water_port, al      ; through the water port
        ret                         ; done
start_or_not:
        mov     dh,start_hours      ; start time is in DX
        mov     dl, start_mins      ;
        cmp     cx, dx              ; is it time to start watering?
        jl      exit                ; not yet
        mov     watering, 1         ; yes, watering started
        mov     al, start_code      ; output start code
        out     water_port, al      ; through the water port
exit:
        ret                         ; done
```

In this program it is assumed that the stop time (*stop_hours:stop_mins*) is greater than the start time (*start_hours:start_mins*). A global boolean variable *watering* is used so that the signal to start or stop watering need be given only once every day.

Now that we have individual procedures to control heating, fire alarm, and watering of the lawn, let us investigate the requirements of the whole system. The temperature needs to be adjusted repeatedly once every few minutes. The fire alarm must ring soon after a fire (or smoke) is detected; delay is not acceptable. The lawn needs to be watered daily for two hours from 1830 hours onwards. We have assumed that appropriate devices and transducers for input/output are interfaced with the processor.

Now we are ready to discuss the overall design of the real-time system for simplified home control. We will consider three synchronous methods: polled (no interrupts), main loop with interrupts, and cyclic schedulers. As we have already mentioned, the synchronous methods require only a single task for implementation.

Polled System

A *polled* system design has a main loop in which all the devices are polled (or required procedures are called) one time each. The program for the simplified home control system using this design is shown in Listing 5-5.

Here the *wait_loop* is a software loop to wait for a certain amount of time. In general, there may be a need to sleep in polled systems. To understand why there may be a need to sleep, consider the example of computer-controlled steering in a car. Assume that the computer decides to turn right and issues the com-

Listing 5-5. The *ref_level* Program

```
        ; ref_level - danger level of smoke
forever:
        call    adjust_temp      ; subroutine call
        in      al, smoke_port   ; read smoke level
        cmp     al, ref_level    ; compare to check danger
        jl      no_danger
        call    initiate_alarm   ; start fire alarm
no_danger:
        call    water_lawn       ; subroutine call
        call    wait_loop        ; sleep (do nothing)
        jmp     forever
wait_loop:
        mov     cx, 0ffh         ; the value in cx determines
                                 ; the wait time
wait:
        loop    wait
        ret
```

mand *turn right*. The wheels begin to turn, but suppose the computer is sampling input data at its own much higher rate. It decides that the car is not turning and resends the command *turn right*. Before realizing that the car *is* turning, the computer issues enough *turn right* commands to put the car in a skid. To avoid this, the computer must be programmed to respect the slower pace of the physical world, and there is a need to let the computer wait. But, in the case of our home control example, sleep delays the detection of fire, which is not acceptable.

The advantages of this approach are

- Simple system design.
- Fast response time.

The disadvantages are

- The processor is always busy because it is dedicated to polling ports.
- The loop time may become excessive as the number of devices increases.
- Time is wasted in polling ports that are inactive most of the time, e.g., the smoke sensor in our example.

Main Loop with Interrupts

The *main loop with interrupts* design approach can be viewed as a polled system with interrupts. As in a polled system, this design uses a main loop. The loop does nothing or does something that can be interrupted as frequently as needed by the devices or the clock. As soon as some event occurs, an interrupt is sent to the processor. An interrupt service routine (ISR) is associated with each interrupt.

Let us return to the example of the simplified home control system. In our example, the interrupts are designed so that the processor is interrupted when

1. Temperature goes beyond the range (*ref_temp* – *delta*) to (*ref_temp* + *delta*).

2. Smoke level goes beyond the safe limit.

The procedures *adjust_temp* and *initiate_alarm* are the ISRs corresponding to the two interrupts.

An interrupt cannot be associated with the *water_lawn* procedure because the procedure uses the MS-DOS function int 21h to find the time of day. As the MS-DOS code is not reentrant, an ISR cannot make another interrupt in MS-DOS. So the procedure *water_lawn* is not designed as an ISR, but it is called from the main program loop, *main_loop*:

```
forever:
        call        water_lawn      ;
        call        wait_loop       ; to spend some time before
                                    ; calling water_lawn again
        jmp         forever
```

The interrupt service routines are *adjust_temp* and *initiate_alarm*. The code for the ISRs is the same as the code for procedures already described, with the difference that

1. An ISR uses IRET in place of RET in ordinary procedure. The IRET returns to the main program when the ISR is completed.

2. You must save the registers used by the ISR. The registers have to be restored before executing the IRET instruction.

3. Interrupts must be enabled/disabled.

The program *adjust_temp* must enable the interrupts. Otherwise the smoke signal may go undetected, which is not acceptable. Similarly, *initiate_alarm* must disable the interrupts because it is the highest priority procedure and must not be interrupted before setting off the fire alarm.

These ISRs have to be associated with the corresponding interrupt levels. This can be achieved by the function Set Interrupt Vector in MS-DOS. Int 21h with the function code of AH = 25h is used for this purpose. DS:DX points to the ISR before making the call.

```
        mov         ah, 25h             ; function=set interrupt vector
        mov         al, int_level       ; interrupt level in AL
        mov         dx, seg adjust_temp
        mov         ds, dx              ; address of ISR in DS:DX
        mov         dx, offset adjust_temp
        int         21h                 ; call to DOS
```

Similar function calls have to be executed for the other ISRs in the system. The advantages of this approach are

- No time wasted in polling devices that are not active.
- Very quick response to any number of asynchronous external events (if most are inactive).
- Simpler code because each ISR is written independently of others.

The disadvantages are

- Tricky interaction between ISR and main program.
- Difficult main program flow because of the asynchronous nature of events.

Cyclic Schedulers

To understand cyclic schedulers, consider a process control system. It is required that the temperature of the process be monitored and controlled once every 100 ms. The other factors to be controlled are pressure, moisture content, and chemical content. These factors need to be controlled less frequently than the temperature of the process.

Suppose that the procedure *temp_control* takes 10 ms to monitor and control the temperature. The procedure *temp_control* must be executed once every 100 ms because the temperature must be controlled once every 100 ms.

Similarly, procedures B, C, and D monitor and control the other three factors, as shown in Table 5-6. Further assume that it is acceptable if procedures C and D are executed once every 300 ms, and if procedure B is executed twice every 300 ms.

Table 5-6. Procedures Required for the Example

Procedure Name	Controls	Execution Time	Required Repetition	
			Time	Comment
temp_control	Temperature	20 ms	100 ms	Variation not acceptable
B	Pressure	40 ms	about 150 ms	Variation acceptable
C	Moisture	60 ms	about 300 ms	Variation acceptable
D	Chemical	38 ms	about 300 ms	Variation acceptable

Such a real-time system can be accomplished by using the cyclic scheduler design in Flowchart 5-1. There are three cycles: 0, 1, and 2. The execution sequence of the cycles is 0, 1, 2, and 0, 1, 2 repeatedly.

Note that procedure *temp_control* is executed once in each cycle. Each cycle takes 100 ms to execute, which is the time needed for the main loop, the time required to execute *temp_control*, and the time for a sleep loop at the end of each cycle. The sleep loop is provided to synchronize the execution of cycles to the timing requirement of the most frequently executed procedure (*temp_control* in our example).

Flowchart 5-1. The cyclic scheduler design.

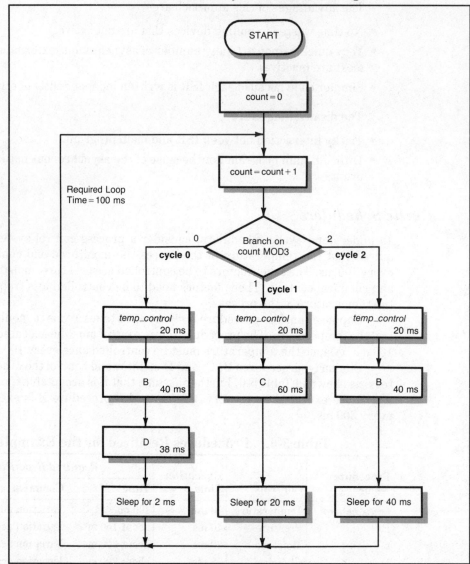

Flowchart 5-1 illustrates the concept of a cyclic scheduler without interrupts. In many applications, it may be necessary to use interrupts to signal an external event requiring immediate attention. A cyclic scheduler can also be designed with interrupts, as shown in Figure 5-12.

Figure 5-12(A) shows that we can guarantee that the main loop will take 100 ms to execute for each cycle if there are no interrupts. Figure 5-12(B) shows what happens in the presence of interrupts. Suppose an interrupt occurs while the procedure *temp_control* is being executed. The procedure *temp_control* is completed, and then the interrupt is processed. After processing the interrupt,

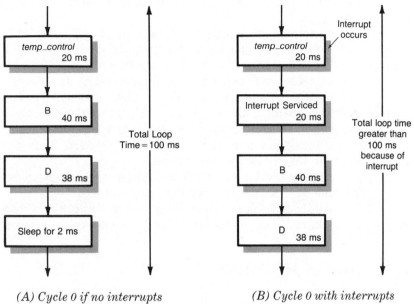

*(A) Cycle 0 if no interrupts
(deterministic).*

*(B) Cycle 0 with interrupts
(nondeterministic).*

**Figure 5-12. Cyclic scheduler with interrupts:
nondeterministic loop time.**

procedure B is executed. Since the occurrence of interrupts cannot be predicted, the total execution time of each cycle cannot be predicted. Thus, the loop execution time of a cyclic scheduler with interrupts is nondeterministic.

The advantages of the cyclic scheduler design are

- Simple form of multitasking.
- Deterministic operation except when interrupts are present.

The disadvantages are

- Inefficient—all cycles must run to completion.
- Loop time increases with number of cycles.
- Difficult to modify and stay within time constraints.

Deciding on a Design Method

The choice of a design method depends on the external environment/hardware as well as the timing requirements of the system. It also depends on whether already available hardware is to be used or new hardware is to be procured. If new hardware is to be procured, then we may consider an interrupt-driven device or a device without interrupts. However, if the hardware already exists, we may not have a choice whether to use an interrupt. For example, a device may not have provisions for an interrupt; then we must use a polled design for that device.

In some applications, the choice may be dictated by the timing requirements, as the following simple example shows. Decisions in a practical application design are, of course, more involved.

Suppose that we need to use MS-DOS with an 8088, 4.77-MHz processor. Assume that we need to collect data at the rate of 35,000 bytes per second. Note from the previous Table 5-5 that with interrupts the maximum rate of data transfer is 30 kHz. So we cannot use interrupts. However, polled systems can have a maximum rate of data transfer of 60 kHz. Moreover, the data can be stored in the primary memory itself.

Finally, if it is required that different procedures be executed at different frequencies, then cyclic schedulers may be used.

All three design methods discussed so far are synchronous (requiring only one task, i.e., nonmultitasking). Next we will explore multitasking in MS-DOS.

Multitasking in MS-DOS

In general, MS-DOS does not support multitasking, although MS-DOS for the IBM PC AT computers has provisions for simple multitasking. Multitasking is a very powerful technique for real-time system design. It simplifies system design and makes it possible to design large, complex systems.

A real-time system is aimed at processing several independent events that occur at random times. The events can be asynchronous and concurrent. This means that an event can occur while one is already being processed.

Multitasking can be used in such systems to simplify software design. Instead of writing a single program to monitor all the events, you can write several programs, each monitoring a single event. All the programs can be executed concurrently by the computer supporting multitasking. These individual programs are known as *tasks*. Because they coexist and coexecute in the computer, the design is known as *multitasking*. Multiple tasks are executed by the computer at the same time conceptually, in much the same way as a juggler keeps many balls in the air at a given time. However, in actuality, only one task is executed at a given time.

Multitasking Provisions in the IBM PC AT

The BIOS of the IBM PC AT provides "hooks" to implement a scheduler. The functions supported are very primitive but can be used to design and implement a program to support simple multitasking features (a discussion that is beyond the scope of this chapter). Designing a general-purpose scheduler in MS-DOS is very difficult, so we recommend that you design a scheduler specific to your application.

Interrupt 15h is provided for supporting a multitasking scheduler. The scheduler initially sets up the service routine for interrupt 15h. The scheduler can support primitive functions such as *task switching* and nonbusy wait loops.

One provision in the IBM PC AT is to implement a nonbusy wait loop. A task that needs to execute a nonbusy wait loop issues an interrupt 15h with a function code of 90 hex in AH. At this point, the scheduler should save the status of the current task and initiate another task. This allows overlapped execution of tasks when a nonbusy wait is executed.

The waiting task can later be resumed by the scheduler when an interrupt 15h with a function code of 91 hex occurs in AH. At this point, the scheduler should remember that the task is ready to be resumed at a later time.

This concludes our discussion of multitasking in MS-DOS. We have kept it short and simple because multitasking in MS-DOS (AT) is very limited in scope as well as difficult to implement.

Summary

A real-time system deals with its external environment directly and must always meet certain timing constraints. We classified real-time systems into three categories based on the direction of data flow:

- Unidirectional systems
- Bidirectional stable systems
- Bidirectional potentially unstable systems

We discussed speed as a requirement of MS-DOS to be used in a real-time application. In addition to clock frequency, the speed of MS-DOS depends on data transfer. Using examples, we illustrated the use of CPU ports and serial and parallel ports for data transfer with the external environment. We also discussed three basic methods of data transfer into and out of the computer:

- Polling
- DMA
- Interrupt-driven

We explained the importance of response time in deciding whether MS-DOS can be used for a real-time application. Three synchronous (nonmultitasking) methods of designing real-time systems were described:

- Polling
- Main loop with interrupts
- Cyclic scheduling

With the help of examples and assembly code, we demonstrated that MS-DOS can be used for relatively simple yet useful real-time applications. Finally, we explored the multitasking support in MS-DOS.

Bibliography

Allworth, S.T. *Introduction to Real-Time Software Design.* New York: Springer-Verlag, 1981.

Savitzky, Stephen. *Real-Time Microprocessor Systems.* New York: Van Nostrand Reinhold, 1985.

DEVICES PART

Installable Device Drivers 6

THE primary requirement of any computer system is not only the ability to compute but also the ability to communicate with the outside world through its peripherals. Without communications the computer becomes an expensive paperweight at best. The responsibility of any operating system is to provide communications facilities for application programs and the internal needs of the operating system itself.

An operating system must meet two separate requirements to enable an application program to communicate with an external device. First, a defined interface between the application program and the operating system must exist and must be flexible enough to allow the program to specify what is desired of the device. Second, the operating system must have the capability of transferring data to and from the device and controlling the device's operation. This system-to-device interface is provided by sections of the operating system called *device drivers*.

Although mainframe and minicomputer operating systems have a tradition of extensive device support, microcomputer operating systems are generally lean in this area. They usually contain support for the primary disk drives, the system's terminal, a printer port, and possibly an auxiliary device. Support beyond that level has been an unexpected plus. In previous operating systems, including MS-DOS version 1.0, adding this support after purchase has been difficult. The operating systems did not contain applications-level function requests for nonstandard devices, and the drivers themselves were embedded deep in the BIOS (basic input/output system). Adding or changing a device driver required editing the BIOS source (if it was available), reassembling it, and copying it to the system disk's boot track (for which task all too often no utility was provided). Computers such as the IBM Personal Computer did not even allow that much. Because its BIOS is in ROM (read-only memory), modifying the BIOS required the use of a PROM programmer (a device that writes to a programmable ROM, which isn't an everyday piece of equipment). After all this effort, no way was available for the application program to talk via the operating system to the driver.

MS-DOS version 2.0 changed all that. In what is probably the most significant advance in microcomputer operating systems since the inception of CP/M, MS-DOS versions 2.0 and later provide not only the ability to install device drivers without arcane measures but also a standard extensible interface that allows programs to communicate with the drivers. The result has been an explosion in the number of devices that MS-DOS now supports and in virtual devices that supply MS-DOS systems with such features as RAM disks, high-level graphics interfaces, and the like.

The MS-DOS device driver is a subprogram that is called by MS-DOS on one side and communicates with the actual device on the other. The middleman between the system and the hardware, the MS-DOS device driver passes data between the subprogram and the device.

Why Have Device Drivers?

Device drivers serve two purposes. The first is to provide a standard interface to all programs that desire to use a particular device, irrespective of the idiosyncrasies of that device. A program that does text processing or spreadsheet calculations does not care exactly what type of terminal is connected to the system. The program desires to accomplish functions such as Display Character or Read Keyboard. The terminal device driver takes care of the details of accomplishing the transfers and thus provides the high-level interface desired by the application program. Change the terminal; change the device driver. No modifications to the application program should be necessary. Device drivers provided for disk drives should present a standard interface for all the different types of disks. A program that performs disk I/O should operate with a floppy disk of any format, a hard disk, and even a RAM disk. It should make no difference to the application program. So to sum up, the first purpose of device drivers is to provide a device-independent, uniform interface.

The second purpose of device drivers is that they serve as a type of RTL (run-time library). Device drivers provide the same measure of support to all programs. Each program is relieved not only of the necessity for supporting multiple device formats but also of the necessity for supporting any device formats. Support is handled by the device driver. Because all the device drivers are collected into the operating system, only one copy of each driver need be maintained. The result is that programs written to use the MS-DOS interface don't have to contain any driver code at all.

In the MS-DOS implementation, device drivers may be added to the system to replace the built-in drivers for nondisk devices. If you don't like the way that the system driver handles a certain device, you can write your own driver. The difference is once again transparent to application programs. It's not a trivial matter to write a driver, but at least the option is available.

Given this powerful ability to interface MS-DOS with diverse foreign devices, it is but one more step to conceive of device drivers without physical devices! In other words, device drivers can be written to support devices that don't really exist, such as the ubiquitous RAM disk. These types of devices are called *virtual devices;* and their drivers, *virtual device drivers.*

Virtual devices, or physical devices for that matter, are not limited to strictly input/output functions. Any transformation function that accepts and/ or returns data may be placed in a device driver. High-speed floating-point array processors are only one example of transformation devices. Beyond that, drivers can contain software with no external I/O to emulate the behavior of actual devices that the system does not yet contain, such as a software clock or the floating-point processor.

When to Use Device Drivers

At what point should a function be removed from a program and turned into a device driver? The rule of thumb is that a function performing I/O at a hardware level is a likely candidate for a device driver. Because of the nature of the 8086 processor family, this sort of function is usually an IN or OUT instruction (including the INS or OUTS instructions). If the system uses memory-mapped I/O, accesses to absolute memory addresses may also be indicative of hardware level I/O. (Reading and writing the interrupt vectors are also absolute memory accesses, but you should really use the MS-DOS functions Get Vector and Set Vector rather than a driver.)

Putting the I/O handlers into a device driver accomplishes four things: it makes the main program more transportable, makes the I/O handler available to other programs that desire to access that device, makes the system slightly larger in terms of memory used, and appreciably slows down the access time to the hardware. A slightly larger system should not be of any great concern, but the extended access time can be the critical factor in some applications. Whenever a decision is made to write a device driver, the speed constraints of the application must be weighed against the increase in program compatibility and accessibility of the driver. The increase in access time is more noticeable for a device that transfers data a word or a byte at a time because the overhead penalty is paid on each call of the driver. For device drivers that transfer an entire block of data on each call, the overhead is spread over more transfers and the resultant penalty decreased.

The Limitation of MS-DOS Being Non-Reentrant

Because device drivers are called by MS-DOS, they are subject to the same limitations as memory resident routines. To wit, they may not use MS-DOS to perform any functions. (The single exception to this is that certain MS-DOS function calls may be made during the initialization phase of the driver.) This severely limits the portability of virtual device drivers written to preprocess information intended for standard drivers.

For example, a virtual device driver written to provide graphics capability for a dot-matrix printer cannot use the standard MS-DOS print character functions for final output. The virtual device driver must contain all the necessary code to perform the actual output to the printer. (Note that the driver described for this example is considered a virtual device even though it communicates with a physical device. The reason is that the driver provides capabilities not inherent in the device; that is, this driver provides graphics operations on a dumb printer.)

Because MS-DOS is non-reentrant, DEBUG may not be used to debug an installed driver. DEBUG uses MS-DOS to handle its own I/O, and if DEBUG is used inside of a driver, the program destroys the context of the driver call, leaving it unable to return proper information to MS-DOS. One way to handle this shortcoming is to use any built-in I/O functions (for example, BIOS functions) that your system may contain to perform rudimentary output of debugging information. A more dependable method is to design a test jig to exercise the driver routine. A *test jig* is a small program that feeds test data to the driver and checks for expected returns. This program is then run by MS-DOS, allowing DEBUG to be used. Of course, if the device is speed dependent, some additional care must be exercised to avoid interfering with the driver's handling of the device.

Installing Device Drivers

As mentioned before, in the days before MS-DOS version 2.0, installing a device driver meant patching the BIOS. Although this method is still possible, the new method installs additional or replacement device drivers during the boot process itself.

The process of loading MS-DOS, called *bootstrapping*, begins with a system reset. Your system's hardware also provides a reset when the system's power is turned on. Following a reset, the system processor begins executing code at an address at the upper end of the processor's address range. For the 80386 processor, this address is FFFFFFF0 hex. For the 80286 processor, the initial address is FFFFF0 hex, and for the remainder of the 8086 family processors, the address FFFF0 hex is used. In each case there is a program contained in ROM that is located at the initial address. This program, called the *primary bootstrap*, is given the responsibility of reading the first portion of the boot disk into memory. It is interesting to note that the capabilities of the primary bootstrap have grown with time. The original IBM Personal Computer could boot only from the "A" floppy drive. The IBM XT computer introduced the ability to optionally boot from a fixed disk, and it appears likely that the ability to boot from a network connection in lieu of a disk is not far off.

The portion of the boot disk read into memory by the primary bootstrap is called the *secondary bootstrap*. In the case of an MS-DOS system running on IBM-compatible hardware, this portion is a single sector of 512 bytes. This small size is made possible by the fact that the BIOS of an IBM-compatible system is located in ROM. The secondary bootstrap of such a system need only call the BIOS already present in ROM in order to read into memory the rest of the system. For those systems that do not contain a BIOS in ROM, the primary bootstrap must also read from the boot disk sufficient code to enable the secondary bootstrap to read in the remainder of the system. This requires that a much larger portion be read from the boot disk.

It is not until the secondary bootstrap is read from the boot disk that MS-DOS *per se* is actually being loaded. (This is what allows many users to run non MS-DOS games or systems on the same hardware. The type of system run is

Flowchart 6-1. MS-DOS initialization process.

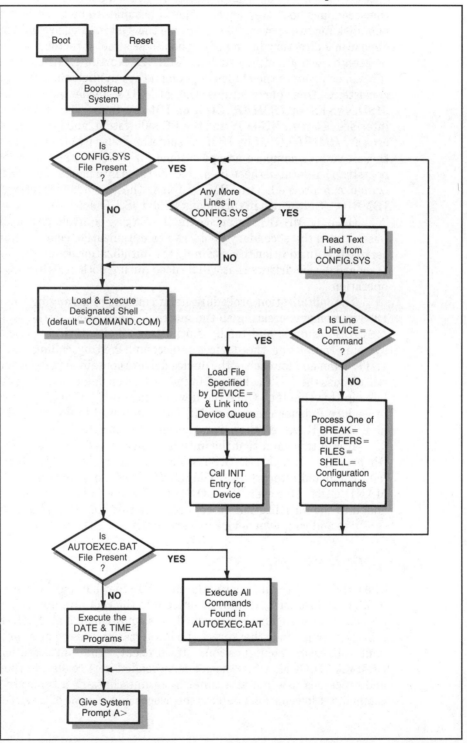

entirely dependent on what is loaded from the boot disk.) In loading MS-DOS, the secondary bootstrap checks what it assumes to be the root directory of the boot disk for two system files. Because the system files are hidden, they *do not* appear in a directory listing of the boot disk's root directory (although they can be seen by using a utility such as XTREE, Norton Utilities, or SDIR). While the names given to these files depend on the supplier, their functions are fairly consistent. One file contains the MS-DOS kernel and is usually named *MSDOS.SYS*, or *IBMDOS.COM* on IBM systems. The other file contains the interface between MS-DOS and the I/O subsystem, and is named *IO.SYS* by Microsoft, *IBMBIO.COM* by IBM, or something else by other suppliers. Together these two files compose an operational MS-DOS system. Once the secondary bootstrap has located these files, it loads them into memory and MS-DOS initialization can proceed. (In IBM systems, the secondary bootstrap loads only IBMBIO.COM, which in turn loads IBMDOS.COM.)

Once the MS-DOS interface file (IO.SYS or equivalent) is loaded, control is passed from the secondary bootstrap to initialization code contained in the interface file. In addition to containing the initialization code, this file contains the standard device drivers that will be used during both MS-DOS initialization and operation.

The initialization procedure itself consists of arranging the pieces of MS-DOS in memory; creating all the internal tables, work areas, and so forth that MS-DOS requires; and finally, initializing all the devices associated with the system. Initializing the devices is accomplished by calling the *Initialize*, or INIT, command for each of the device drivers contained in the interface file. (We will discuss the INIT command in the section on device driver commands, found later in this chapter.) Once the devices have been initialized, the initialization procedure finishes creation of MS-DOS's internal tables, and MS-DOS is now able to run. However, there remains one step to complete.

It is at this point that the initialization code asks *"Is there a CONFIG.SYS file present?"* If a CONFIG.SYS file is not found, then MS-DOS loads the default command interpreter, COMMAND.COM, and control is passed to COMMAND.COM. However, if a CONFIG.SYS file is found, then another step is added to the initialization procedure. It is this step that allows you the opportunity to add your own device drivers to the MS-DOS system.

The CONFIG.SYS File

The CONFIG.SYS file is a regular MS-DOS file that may be present in the boot disk's root directory. (If it is not present in the root directory, then as far as the initialization procedure is concerned, it is not present at all.) CONFIG.SYS contains text commands that direct the initialization code to alter or add to the default MS-DOS configuration. If present, the initialization code (not COMMAND.COM, which hasn't been loaded yet) reads the file into memory and processes it a line at a time. Each line contains a separate configuration command. Flowchart 6-1 depicts the processing of some of these commands. The most important to us at this time is the DEVICE command, which has the format

DEVICE = [*d:*][*path*]*filename*[*.ext*][*parameters*]

where the items enclosed in brackets are optional portions of the command. The DEVICE command instructs MS-DOS to install a new device driver. The driver program contained in the specified file is similar to an MS-DOS .COM program, but it has some significant differences that are explained in the upcoming section on writing device drivers. For the moment, we are concerned with how device drivers fit within the MS-DOS system as a whole.

In general, device drivers are a special form of memory resident programs. When the DEVICE command is encountered in the CONFIG.SYS file, the associated file is loaded into memory and analyzed. A *header block* in the file contains information about the type, name, and attributes of the device, and also specifies the program entry points within the driver. After the file has been loaded, MS-DOS calls the driver's entry point with the INIT command. The driver performs any required initialization and then returns to MS-DOS the *end-of-driver address*, which is the address of the next available byte of memory located after the driver. Installation of the driver is complete.

The end-of-driver address returned to MS-DOS by the driver's INIT command is similar to the *size* parameter specified by a memory resident routine in its Keep Process function call. Its purpose is to inform MS-DOS of where available memory begins. Then, if the CONFIG.SYS file contains another DEVICE command, the next device driver is loaded after the previous one. After MS-DOS has finished processing the CONFIG.SYS file, one more device driver is loaded—the NUL device. MS-DOS then completes its initialization by loading the permanent portion of COMMAND.COM, or a user-specified shell.

Internally, MS-DOS threads all of its device drivers onto a queue, with each driver pointing to the previously loaded driver. The driver "chain" thus begins with the last driver loaded—the NUL device—and ends with the first driver loaded, usually the default COM2 device. The driver chain is maintained in the first two words on the driver's header block, which begins each driver. These two words contain the segment and offset of the next driver or, in the case of the last driver, the value of minus 1, which is FFFF hex. An example of a device driver queue appears in Listing 6-6, near the end of this chapter.

When MS-DOS needs to access a particular device driver, it begins searching the driver queue starting with the NUL device, which is in the *reverse* order from the order in which the drivers were loaded. When the proper driver is located, MS-DOS calls it with the necessary command. The consequence of searching the queue in this order is that if a user-supplied driver having the same name as a standard driver (such as CON, AUX, or PRN) is loaded, MS-DOS will find the newer, user-supplied driver first. This allows user-supplied device drivers to supplant the standard device drivers (such as replacement of the standard CON driver with the ANSI.SYS CON driver).

The default device drivers are actually loaded and initialized by MS-DOS before the CONFIG.SYS file is read and parsed. This allows the initialization section of a device driver to use some of the MS-DOS function calls for the purpose of displaying messages or configuring the driver for a particular version of MS-DOS. The calls that may be safely used at this time are functions 01 through 0Ch, which support CON, PRN, and AUX I/O; and function 30h, Get DOS Version Number. Calls related to file I/O or memory management should be avoided, since the MS-DOS memory map is not yet stable. However, once the driver has been installed, all MS-DOS function calls are off limits, including MS-DOS interrupts 20h through 27h.

After the CONFIG.SYS file has been processed and the drivers initialized, the standard devices CON, PRN, and AUX are closed and then reopened by MS-DOS so that any replacement drivers for one of these units take effect. From that point on, any such new drivers are used exclusively.

Certain drivers may not be replaced by the user. One of these is the NUL device driver. This limitation results from the fact that MS-DOS uses the NUL device as the head of the device queue. Because the system-supplied NUL device is always the first device in the queue, the system-supplied device is always the first NUL device found. An example device queue is shown in Figure 6-1. Not all of the labeled areas will make sense immediately. They will be explained later. The device marked *last device* is actually the first device to be installed, and the device located directly after the NUL device is the last device to be installed.

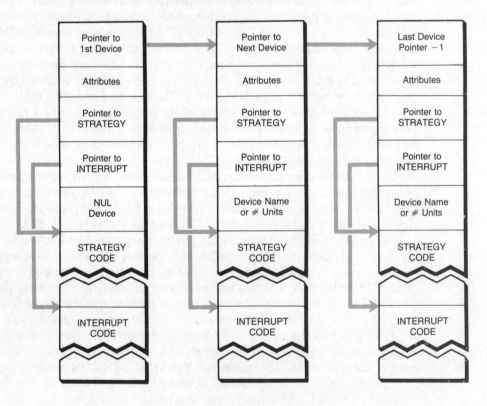

Figure 6-1. Device driver queue.

The NUL device is not the only device that cannot be replaced. Device drivers that deal with mass storage devices (that is, disks) are also not replaceable. You may add drivers for new disk devices but not remove or replace the old ones. This restriction arises because disk device drivers have identifying letters assigned by MS-DOS during the boot process (A, B, C, etc.) rather than unique names (such as CON and PRN). Because you can't name a particular disk device driver, you can't replace it.

Using ASSIGN to Replace Disk Device Drivers

However, don't despair if you don't like your existing disk device drivers. Although they can't be removed, they can be bypassed. After you have written (and tested) the new driver, add it to the CONFIG.SYS file. When MS-DOS is rebooted, the new driver is installed as the next device in the list. For example, if you already have three drives, the new driver is drive D. Now use the MS-DOS command ASSIGN to redirect all accesses of the old drive to the new drive. As an example, let's assume we want to replace the drive A driver. The ASSIGN command for this is

ASSIGN A = D

MS-DOS redirects all drive A accesses to the new device D driver, including absolute disk access interrupts 25h and 26h. If you have written the new device driver to access the same physical device as the old one, you have effectively replaced the old device driver. If you decide that you like the old one better, you can restore the original assignments by entering the ASSIGN command without any parameters.

CAUTION: When NOT to Use ASSIGN

Although the ASSIGN command does enable you to replace an existing disk driver with a newer, installed driver, this isn't always a good idea. Some commands, such as BACKUP and PRINT, and programs such as Lotus 1-2-3 become confused when asked to work with assigned drivers. Other commands, such as FORMAT, DISKCOPY, and DISKCOMP, ignore assigned drives and process the actual logical drive.

Types of Device Drivers

There are two types of device drivers, named and unnamed, called respectively *character* device drivers and *block* device drivers. The differences between the two types go much deeper than the issue of names and replaceability. Not only does MS-DOS provide block-oriented drivers to support disk devices, it expects a block-mode device driver to be controlling one or more disks. The I/O commands for block device drivers are structured to support sector accesses, and unless the *NONIBM attribute* (also known as the *NONFAT attribute*) is specified for a block device driver, the block device is assumed to support the standard MS-DOS disk structure, complete with FATs (file allocation tables) and directories.

Truthfully, the names *character* and *block* device drivers are somewhat misleading because the character device driver can support block-mode transfers just as well as the block mode driver. The actual relationship is something more akin to nondisk and disk drivers. It cannot even be said that character device drivers are sequential and block device drivers random access because character-mode drivers can be constructed to perform random access of the devices they support.

Leaving aside for the moment the question of what constitutes a block-mode device driver and what constitutes a character-mode device driver, here are some of the ways that device drivers can be accessed through MS-DOS. This will give you some idea of the type of device driver you may wish to write for a particular application.

Accessing Device Drivers from MS-DOS

MS-DOS supports four basic types of device I/O that may be used within an application program. Each of these types is suited for particular applications, and our intention is to present the strengths and weaknesses of each type of I/O so that you can judge which type is suited to your application. We have not presented the details of each of the function calls because that information may be found in the Microsoft *MS-DOS Programmer's Reference Manual* (or your system's equivalent manual). The following list classifies the four types.

- *CP/M-style dedicated I/O functions* for devices such as console, printer, and auxiliary. These are truly character-oriented devices. The functions in this group are

CON:	Functions 01, 02, and 06 through 0Ch
PRN:	Function 05
AUX:	Functions 03 and 04

- *CP/M-style file access using the FCB (file control block)*. This method may also be used to access character-style devices. FCB access functions are

Open/Close:	Functions 0Fh and 10h
Device/File Read/Write:	Functions 14h and 15h
File Only Read/Write:	Functions 21h, 22h, 27h, and 28h

- *MS-DOS—style file access using file handles*. As with the FCB-type I/O, character-style devices may be accessed as well as disk files. Those functions that are used with file handles are

Open/Close:	Functions 3Dh and 3Eh
Device/File Read/Write:	Functions 3Fh and 40h

I/O Control for Devices: Function 44h

- ***Direct disk I/O functions performing absolute disk reads and writes.*** These are not part of the MS-DOS function call int 21h but are supported instead by interrupts 25h (Absolute Read) and 26h (Absolute Write).

CP/M-Style Character Device I/O

The CP/M-style functions dedicated to the standard device CON are useful for most terminal I/O and offer the options of buffering, echoing, waiting for a character, and status checking. Support for the PRN and AUX devices is more limited but sufficient for most purposes. However, for nonstandard devices, either the FCB (file control block) or the file handle methods of access must be used.

Device Access Using the File Control Block

The FCB (file control block) method of device access is a mixed blessing. On one hand, FCB is more cumbersome to set up and use than the file handle method, although the use of macros and the STRUC directive can greatly ease the task of setting up the FCB data structure. On the other hand, FCB-type file access allows the programmer to directly specify the record number within a file, making it possible to perform random access I/O on a file. The file handle I/O functions 3Fh (read) and 40h (write) allow only sequential operations. To perform random I/O with file handles, the application program must use function 42h (Move File Pointer). This extra step is not required with FCB-type file accesses.

Using File Handles for Device I/O

Although random access is fine for files, it doesn't do much for nondisk-type devices. When performing I/O to a nondisk device, the file handle method is much simpler to use and doesn't require the programmer to set up an FCB. In addition, the file handle access method supports the IOCTL (I/O control for devices) function call (44h). As we shall soon see, IOCTL can be extremely useful for advanced control of the device.

When using file handles to access nondisk devices, the programmer is not limited to performing I/O 1 byte at a time. Up to 64 Kbytes may be transferred to or from the device in a single call of the File/Device I/O functions. As with disk devices, when these functions are used by themselves on nondisk devices, they perform sequential transfers, with each successive block of data following the previous one. However, by using the IOCTL function, additional parameters for the device can be specified. For example, if both the device and the device driver are set up to handle random mode transfers, the IOCTL function can be used to control the transfer source or destination within the device.

An example of this last point may help to illustrate the potential of I/O control for devices. Suppose that a particular system has associated with it a memory-mapped graphics display device. Using a device driver, data is transferred from system memory to the graphics memory. Because the device is not a mass storage device, its driver must be a character-mode device driver. If I/O is performed using only the file handle I/O functions, no way is available to specify where on the display the data is to be sent. However, if the driver supports the IOCTL function, the location of the data in the graphics memory may be specified through the control channel.

Function 44h — I/O Control for Devices

As we have implied, not all device drivers support the IOCTL function call. In those drivers that do support IOCTL, not all of the various features of the call are necessarily supported. However, IOCTL is such a powerful tool for controlling devices that it behooves the MS-DOS programmer to become familiar with its capabilities. The knowledge of what can be done through IOCTL calls surely influences the programmer's decisions on which features to incorporate in a device driver.

The I/O Control for Devices function has three basic modes of operation, which are determined by a function code passed in the AL register when the request is made. The three modes are: *device configuration* (codes 0, 1, and, in later versions of MS-DOS, codes 8, B, E, and F); *control channel I/O* (codes 2 through 5, and, in MS-DOS 3.2, codes C and D); and *device status requests* (codes 6 and 7). A list of the function codes supported by IOCTL appears in Table 6-1.

Examining these modes in reverse order, the device status requests return a simple ready (FFh) or not ready (0) indication. Microsoft includes a warning in the *MS-DOS Programmer's Reference Manual* to the effect that, in future versions of MS-DOS, the status code may not be valid by the time the system returns control to the calling program. Presumably the manual is referring to the future possibility of multitasking or multiuser MS-DOS. One can only hope that when future versions appear, Microsoft will have found a way to return the correct information. In any case, until concurrent MS-DOS arrives, the inaccuracy should not be a problem.

We have already mentioned the IOCTL device control channel I/O capability. Simply put, this is a means to transfer a buffer of data to or from an auxiliary channel. The mechanics of the call are identical to the file handle I/O calls (3Fh and 40h), except that the function code specified in the AX register is different. Whether the data is intended for an auxiliary channel on the device or for the driver itself is up to the implementor.

Don't, however, be misled by the simplicity of the call and dismiss it as just another I/O function. In the proper application, IOCTL can be a real blessing as a secondary channel to communicate with the device driver. Microsoft has provided a "trapdoor" function to accommodate unforeseen contingencies. They are saying, "You feel our device interface is too limiting? Need more configuration ability? Here, use this." This is a great improvement over the "We don't got it; you don't need it!" attitude taken by systems developers not too long ago.

Table 6-1.   I/O Control for Devices Function Operation

Code (AL =)	DOS Version*	Note	Description
0:	2.0	#1, 2	Get device information
1:	2.0		Set device information
2:	2.0	#3	Read from character device control channel
3:	2.0	#3	Write to character device control channel
4:	2.0	#3	Read from block device control channel
5:	2.0	#3	Write to block device control channel
6:	2.0	#1	Get input information
7:	2.0	#1	Get output information
8:	3.0	#2	Does block device support removable media?
9:	3.2		Is a block device local or remote (redirected)?
A:	3.2		Is a handle local or remote (redirected)?
B:	3.0	#4	Change sharing retry count
C:	3.3	#5	Generic IOCTL handle request (code page switch)
D:	3.3	#5	Block device generic IOCTL request
E:	3.3	#5	Get logical drive
F:	3.3	#5	Set logical drive

Note #1: Function supported for files as well as devices.
Note #2: Function not supported for network devices.
Note #3: Function enabled by bit 14 of driver attribute word, and support indicated by bit 14 of IOCTL configuration word.
Note #4: Function requires file sharing command (SHARE) to be loaded.
Note #5: Function enabled by bit 6 of driver attribute word.

*Earliest version of MS-DOS that supports the command.

Configuration via the I/O Control Commands

MS-DOS has also provided for configuration commands with the Get/Set Device Information functions supported by the IOCTL function. Figure 6-2 shows the 16-bit configuration word used by the Get/Set Device Information functions, codes 0 and 1. In current versions of MS-DOS, only the lower 8 bits of this word may be specified in the Set Device Information word. Those bits in the device configuration word that either have meaning for device drivers or affect the way a driver processes data are described next.

IOCTL Bit 14: CTRL

The CTRL bit is set to 1 if the device driver can process I/O control strings. This bit exactly reflects the value of the IOCTL bit in the associated device driver's attribute word. The IOCTL bit is used by the device driver to indicate to MS-DOS that the driver will accept I/O control strings. This bit applies to both files and devices.

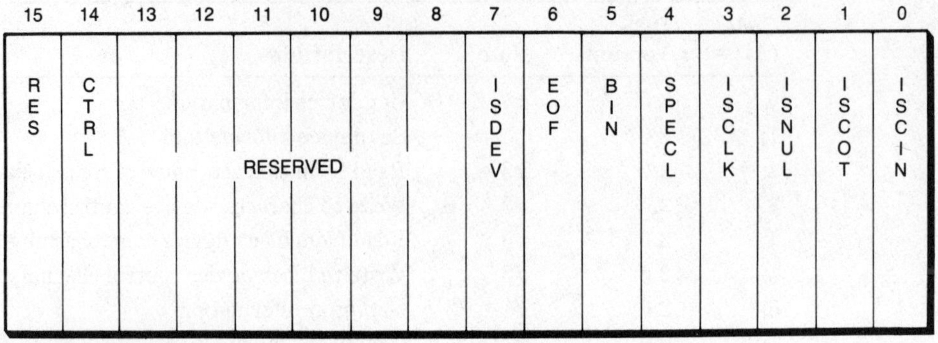

15	14	13	12	11	10	9	8	7	6	5	4	3	2	1	0
R E S	C T R L				RESERVED			I S D E V	E O F	B I N	S P E C L	I S C L K	I S N U L	I S C O T	I S C I N

BIT MEANINGS

CTRL   = 1: Supports control channel I/O
ISDEV = 1: Channel is a device
       = 0: Channel is a file

FILE

Channel has been written

BITS 0 through 5 are block device number

DEVICE

EOF   = 0: END-OF-FILE on input
BIN   = 1: Operating in binary mode
SPECL = 1: Device is special
ISCLK = 1: Device is the clock device
ISNUL = 1: Device is the NUL device
ISCOT = 1: Device is the console output device
ISCIN = 1: Device is the console input device

Figure 6-2. IOCTL device configuration word.

IOCTL Bit 7: ISDEV

The ISDEV bit is set to 1 if the channel (MS-DOS handle) is open to a device. If the channel is open on a file, then this bit is set to 0.

IOCTL Bit 5: BIN

The BIN bit is sometimes called the *raw* bit in MS-DOS documentation, since it reflects and selects between "raw" and "cooked" modes of operation. This bit indicates whether MS-DOS "cooks" the data as it is passed, or whether MS-DOS simply passes "raw" binary information between the device and the application program. Cooking the data implies checking for certain control characters, providing tab expansion, echoing characters, and so forth.

More traditional terms for these functions are the *binary* mode and the *ASCII* mode, corresponding to the "raw" and "cooked" modes. The *MS-DOS Programmer's Reference Manual* contains more detailed instructions on how to check and set this bit. For now, we'll examine what effect this bit has on the operation of character device drivers. (Note from Figure 6-2 that this bit does not apply to block-mode drivers.)

When a character device is in the cooked mode (the default mode), data is transferred to and from the device one character at a time; that is, one device driver call is made for each character to be transferred. This occurs regardless of the transfer count specified when the applications program called MS-DOS. For example, if an application requests that 128 characters be output to a character device, and the device is in the cooked mode, then MS-DOS will make 128 calls to the device driver with the Output or Output with Verify function, each call with a transfer count of one.

Single-byte I/O can be avoided by operating the device in raw mode. This mode must be explicitly set by using the IOCTL function. In raw mode, the transfer count specified in the application will also be used in the I/O call made to the device driver. Using our earlier example, if an application requests that 128 characters be output to a character device, and the device is in the raw mode, then MS-DOS will make one call to the device driver with the Output or Output with Verify function, and that call will specify a transfer count of 128.

IOCTL Bit 4: SPECL

Like the CTRL bit, the SPECL bit of the device configuration word exactly reflects the status of the SPECL bit in the associated device driver's attribute word. If set, this bit implies that the driver, which is almost always the console driver, is capable of performing high-speed output in *binary* mode through the use of interrupt 29h.

The BIN bit, specifying raw mode, is also required to enable the high-speed output mode associated with the SPECL attribute. When both the IOCTL word's BIN bit and the attribute word's SPECL attribute bit are set, then the device will be operated in the high-speed output mode. This output mode and the SPECL attribute bit are discussed in more depth in the upcoming section "The Device Header Attribute Word."

The Generic I/O Control Commands

The four IOCTL commands introduced with MS-DOS version 3.3−commands C, D, E, and F−are all optional, and are enabled only if bit 6 in the driver's attribute word is set. The name "Generic I/O Control" given to commands "C" and "D" is something of a misnomer, since the subfunctions supported under these commands are quite specific and rather esoteric. The generic I/O control commands are actually used to support particular, vendor-specific devices, with functions that allow font switching in printers, formatting for disk drives, and so forth. You should refer to your MS-DOS programmer's documentation for more information if you think that you need to use these commands.

Commands E and F allow an application programmer to manage logical drive assignments, such as those set up by the MS-DOS SUBST (substitute) command. Command E, Get Logical Drive, returns the drive assignment that was last used to access a physical device, and Command F, Set Logical Drive, is used to sequence through a driver's logical drive assignments.

Direct Disk Access with Interrupts 25h and 26h

At the other end of the spectrum from file handle device accesses are the absolute disk access interrupts: Absolute Disk Read (int 25h) and Absolute Disk Write (int 26h). As the name implies, the Direct Disk Access interrupts work solely with block-mode devices, for instance, disks. The purpose of absolute disk access is to allow I/O to disks without having to go through the MS-DOS file structure. This is useful in two cases.

In the first case, programmers can read or write selective parts of a standard MS-DOS disk that contains a file and directory structure. This is often required when part of the disk has gone bad, preventing the FCB or file handle methods from working. Direct disk I/O functions can then be used to "surgically" pick around the disk and recover what may be salvaged. Another use is to allow programs to read and write the FAT or directory on the disk, something not allowed through the other methods. Utilities that sort directories, patch files, etc., require this ability.

The second case for using absolute disk access is when the disk does not contain any FAT entries or directory structure. The disk is to be used purely as a data disk. This can also occur when reading disks that were written under a different operating system like CP/M or the UCSD-p System. In such cases, the disk configuration parameters returned to the system by the driver prevent MS-DOS from being able to access the disk in any other way. Any attempts to perform file I/O, including reading the directory, return garbage or the ***Non-DOS Disk*** error message. (For more information on how MS-DOS determines the format of a disk, refer to the "Build BIOS Parameter Block" driver command described in the Microsoft *MS-DOS Programmer's Reference Manual*, or in your system's equivalent manual.)

In return for providing direct access to the drivers, int 25h and int 26h do not perform blocking or deblocking for the disk. Blocking and deblocking are required when the physical sector size on the disk is different from the logical record size used within the system. When blocking, the system gathers together enough records to fill a physical sector before issuing a disk write. Deblocking is used when reading from the disk because one physical sector can contain many records. The system reads the entire sector and then extracts the requested record for the calling program. Absolute disk access functions read and write only entire sectors, so the programmer must know the sector size of the disk to determine just how many bytes are transferred.

Because the calling parameters used in these interrupts are passed directly to the device driver without conversion, reads and writes transfer data in units of the physical sector size on the device. This is contrasted with the FCB and file handle access methods in which I/O is specified in logical blocks and records and MS-DOS handles the conversion to physical sectors.

One last peculiarity of absolute disk access functions is that they return from the interrupt with a *far* RET rather than an IRET instruction, leaving the flags on the stack. Therefore, after checking to see whether the function has completed properly, you must pop the original flags from the stack.

The Verify Switch

There is one more ingredient in device I/O that has an effect on device driver behavior. This is the *verify* switch, which controls whether or not a driver is expected to verify the performance of an output command, e.g., perform a read after a write. The verify switch is set or reset in three ways:

1. At the DOS command line, the user can specify "VERIFY ON" or "VERIFY OFF" to turn the switch on or off.

2. For some MS-DOS commands, such as COPY, the /V switch will set the

verify mode ON for the duration of the command, as in the command *copy this that /v*.

3. The verify switch may be set or reset from within a program by using MS-DOS function 2Eh, Set/Reset Verify Switch.

I/O Summary

Now that we have a basic idea of the types of operations that may be requested of a device driver, we are ready to proceed with the actual construction of the driver. To summarize, all device drivers are asked to perform basic I/O. Device drivers may also support an optional separate I/O channel for device control, which is called the I/O Control for Devices channel.

Character-type device drivers may be asked to transfer from 1 to 64 Kbytes of data in a single call. Block device drivers are asked to transfer data in units of sectors only because MS-DOS takes care of conversion from sectors to records and back again. As we have hinted, block-mode drivers also are asked to return configuration information about the disk that they are currently using.

Writing Device Drivers

Writing device drivers in any operating system has a great advantage over writing standard programs. Device drivers must follow a fairly rigid structure, sort of a "cookbook," and once the structure is understood, the rest follows.

The basic parts of a device driver and a suggested structure are shown in Figure 6-3. The three required sections are the *device header*, the *strategy routine*, and the *interrupt routine*. The interrupt routine is not the same as an interrupt service routine, which can be an optional part of an interrupt-driven device driver. Instead, this routine is really the entry point to the driver for processing the request received from MS-DOS.

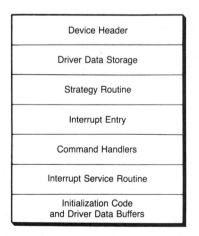

Figure 6-3. The parts of an MS-DOS device driver.

Listing 6-1 shows the skeletal structure of a minimal device driver. While the driver appears similar to the structure expected of a .COM type program, it is very important to note the following differences:

1. The program has its origin at *zero*, not 100 hex.
2. The program image begins with the data directives for the device driver's device header.
3. The program does not contain an ASSUME for the stack segment.
4. The program does not contain an END START directive.

Listing 6-1. Device Header, Strategy, and Interrupt Routines

```
;
; ===== DRIVER CODE STARTS HERE =====================================
;
DRIVER   SEGMENT PARA
         ASSUME  CS:DRIVER, DS:NOTHING, ES:NOTHING
         ORG     0
START    EQU     $                    ; start location of driver
;****** DEVICE HEADER **********************************************
         dw      -1,-1                ; pointer to next device
         dw      ATTRIBUTE            ; attribute word
         dw      offset STRATEGY      ; strategy entry point
         dw      offset INTERRUPT     ; interrupt entry point
         db      8 dup (?)            ; # units/name field
;****** RESIDENT DATA AREA *****************************************
req_ptr         dd      ?            ; pointer to request buffer
         •
         •
         •
******* STRATEGY ENTRY POINT FOR DEVICE DRIVER ********************
; Save the request header pointer for INTERRUPT in REQ_PTR.
; Entered with pointer contained in ES:BX registers.
;
STRATEGY PROC    far
         mov     cs:word ptr [req_ptr],bx
         mov     cs:word ptr [req_ptr + 2],es
         ret
STRATEGY endp
;****** INTERRUPT ENTRY POINT FOR DEVICE DRIVER *******************
; Process the command contained in the request header.
; The pointer to the request header is located in REQ_PTR
; in the form OFFSET:SEGMENT.
;
INTERRUPT PROC    far
         pusha                        ; save all registers
```

```
        lds     bx,cs:[req_ptr]     ; get DS & request header
          •
          •
          •
INTERRUPT endp
          •
          •
          •
DRIVER  ENDS
        END
```

The Device Header

The device header is an 18-byte block of data that must begin every device driver. This header must be located at origin 0 in the device driver segment. When a device driver is loaded, MS-DOS reads the device header to determine the type of device and the entry points into the device. The header contains four pieces of information critical to MS-DOS's use of the driver: the *chain pointer*, the *attribute word*, the *entry point vectors*, and the *unit/name field*.

The Device Chain Pointer

The first 4 bytes of the device header are a double word pointer (offset:segment) to the next device in the device chain. These bytes are normally set to FFFF:FFFF (−1) in the driver code. MS-DOS overwrites them with the address of the next driver when the system loads the new driver. An exception occurs when the device driver file contains more than one device driver, in which case, the first 2 bytes should contain the offset of the next driver's device header.

The Device Header Attribute Word

The next word in the device header is called the *attribute word*. It contains a number of single-bit fields that convey the type and capabilities of the device driver to MS-DOS. Figure 6-4 shows the layout and meanings of the bits in the attribute word. Some examples of attribute words for various devices are as follows:

IBM format disk device—0000

Standard console terminal driver—8003h

Standard character device (for example, PRN)—8000h

Attribute Bit 15: CHR. The CHR bit *must* be set to 0 if the driver is for a block device, and it *must* be set to 1 if the driver is for a nonblock device. (See the previous section "Types of Device Drivers.")

Attribute Bit 14: IOCTL. The IOCTL bit is an optional setting used to inform MS-DOS that the block or character device driver supports I/O control for devices by reading or writing to the device control channel. If this bit is set, the driver *must* support driver commands 3 (I/O Control for Devices Input) and

15	14	13	12	11	10	9	8	7	6	5	4	3	2	1	0
C H R	I O C T L	N O N I B M / O T B	N E T W O R K	O C R M		RESERVED			G I O C T L	R E S E R V E D	S P E C L	C L O C K	N U L	S T D O U T	S T D I N

BIT MEANINGS

CHR	= 1: Device is a character device
IOCTL	= 1: Driver supports I/O control for devices I/O
*OCRM	= 1: Device supports Open/Close/Removable Media calls

BLOCK DEVICES

NONIBM	= 1: Driver is for Non-IBM type disk
‡NETWORK	= 1: Driver is for a network device
**GIOCTL	= 1: Device supports generic I/O control and Get/Set logical device

CHARACTER DEVICES

**GIOCTL	= 1: Device supports generic I/O control
‡‡OTB	= 1: Device supports Output Til Busy
SPECL	= 1: Device has special attributes
CLOCK	= 1: Device is the clock device
NUL	= 1: Device is the NUL device
STDOUT	= 1: Device is the standard output device
STDIN	= 1: Device is the standard input device

* = MS-DOS version 3.00 or later
‡ = MS-DOS version 3.10 or later
‡‡ = MS-DOS version 3.20 or later
** = MS-DOS version 3.30 or later

Figure 6-4. Device driver attribute word.

12 (I/O Control for Devices Output). This bit *must* be set to 0 if these commands are not supported. If supported, these driver commands are accessed via MS-DOS function 44h, subcommands 2 and 3 (for character devices) or subcommands 4 and 5 (for block devices).

Attribute Bit 13: NONIBM/OTB. For block device drivers this is the NON-IBM or NONFAT bit. When this bit is set to 1, it indicates that the block device may not support the IBM/MS-DOS standard for disk structures. This bit has implications in the driver's processing of the INIT and Build BIOS Parameter Block commands. For character device drivers used under MS-DOS versions 3.2 or later, this bit is the OTB, or Output Until Busy, bit. When set to 1, it indicates that the driver supports the optional driver command Output Until Busy (command 9). This command is useful for character devices with large buffer capacities, such as some printers. Character device drivers used with versions of MS-DOS prior to 3.2 should set this bit to 0.

Attribute Bit 12: NETWORK. The NETWORK attribute is an optional attribute, introduced in MS-DOS version 3.10. Interestingly, it is *not* mentioned in any subsequent documentation for MS-DOS versions 3.2 or 3.3, leaving its current use in question. This bit is used to indicate to MS-DOS that the device is a network device. Network devices are marked as block devices in the attribute word. The assumption is made that a network device is a gateway onto the network, allowing entire system calls to be sent to a remote device for processing. However, in order to use the network, some facility for redirection must be provided, such as MS-NET.

Attribute Bit 11: OCRM. The Open/Close/Removable Media attribute (OCRM) is a semioptional attribute, introduced with MS-DOS version 3.0. It may be used with either character or block device drivers. We have called this attribute "semioptional" because, although it is not required, Microsoft *recommends* that it be set for all new device drivers. An explanation of the implications of setting this attribute will undoubtedly aid the programmer in deciding whether to use this attribute.

For both character and block device drivers, when this attribute bit is set to 1, it means that the driver supports the driver commands Device Open and Device Close (commands 13 and 14). Block device drivers with this attribute set must also support the driver command Check for Removable Media (command 15).

For block-type device drivers, the Device Open and Device Close commands are invoked only if *file sharing* is in effect. File sharing is enabled by executing the MS-DOS command SHARE.EXE. Once file sharing is in effect, the Device Open command is invoked by MS-DOS when function 0Fh (Open File via FCB) or function 3Dh (Open File via Handle) is called. The Device Close command is similarly invoked when function 10h (Close File via FCB) or function 3Eh (Close File via Handle) is called. For block-type drivers, the Device Open and Device Close commands may be used to maintain a count of the number of open accesses on a given device, such as the number of open files on a disk. This can be helpful in determining if there has been an illegal disk swap (e.g., a disk was changed with files open).

For character-type device drivers, the Device Open and Device Close commands are called whenever the associated device is opened or closed, regardless of file sharing. SHARE.EXE is not required. Only MS-DOS functions 3Dh (Open Device via Handle) and 3Eh (Close Device via Handle) can be used with devices because the FCB method of access will not work with devices. For character-type drivers, the Open and Close driver commands can be used to prevent simultaneous access to a device such as a printer or modem, or to invoke preprocessing and postprocessing routines, such as printer setup and shutdown.

Note that the CON, AUX, and PRN devices are *always* open because they are associated with handles 0, 1, and 2 (STDIN, STDOUT, and STDERR, all mapped to CON), handle 3 (STDAUX, mapped to AUX), and handle 4 (STDPRN, mapped to PRN).

The Check for Removable Media driver command is called when a user process issues MS-DOS function 44h (I/O Control for Devices) with subcommand number 8. The driver responds by informing the caller whether or not the media is removable.

The Open/Close/Removable Media attribute also has implications for the processing of the driver command, Build BIOS Parameter Block, abbreviated as Build BPB. Removable media are expected to support *volume identification*, an eleven-character name for the disk. If the device supports removable media, the volume name must be determined, reported, and maintained by the driver. Further details are given in the upcoming section on processing the Build BPB command.

Attribute Bits 10 through 7. These bits are reserved.

Attribute Bit 6: GIOCTL. Under MS-DOS version 3.3, the Generic I/O Control, or GIOCTL, bit is set to 1 to indicate that the block or character device driver supports the optional driver commands for Generic I/O Control Request (command 19). When this feature is enabled for block device drivers, the driver must also support the driver commands for Get and Set Logical Device (driver commands 23 and 24).

If the driver supports these commands, the user program may access the Generic I/O Control Request via MS-DOS function 44h (I/O Control), subcommands 0Ch and 0Dh. For block devices, the driver functions for Get and Set Logical Device are accessed via MS-DOS function 44h (I/O Control) and subcommands 0Eh (Get Logical Drive) and 0Fh (Set Logical Drive). (For more detailed information on these functions refer to the previous section "Function 44h—I/O Control for Devices" and to the later sections "Generic IOCTL Command" and "Get and Set Logical Device Commands".)

Attribute Bit 5. This bit is reserved.

Attribute Bit 4: SPECL. The SPECL bit is an optional bit used only by console device drivers (named "CON") to inform MS-DOS that the device driver has installed a special trap handler on interrupt 29h for the purpose of performing high-speed console output. If this bit is set, whenever MS-DOS needs to perform fast console output, it invokes int 29h, with the character to be output contained in the AL register. Fast output mode is both controlled by and indicated by bit 5 (binary mode) in the device's IOCTL device configuration word. (See I/O Control for Devices commands 0 and 1.)

When invoked by int 29h, the driver is expected to output the character in the AL register and return from the interrupt. Normal device I/O procedures are bypassed. Both the standard MS-DOS console driver and the standard ANSI.SYS replacement console driver support this feature. If the console driver in use supports the SPECL interrupt, as determined by reading the device's IOCTL device configuration word, then application programs can also perform fast console output by calling int 29h.

Note that the SPECL bit is marked "reserved" in IBM documentation and is ignored in Microsoft's recent documentation. Both of these facts tend to imply that future support of the SPECL bit is not guaranteed.

Attribute Bit 3: CLOCK. The CLOCK bit is set on the character device driver with the name "CLOCK$" to signify that this device is the system's real-time clock device. Since a clock device is nearly always provided with the system, there is rarely a need to use this bit.

The clock device driver is usually implemented as a standard character device without any optional attributes (attribute word 8008h). The time is read with the Input command and set with the Output command. All transfers are exactly 6 bytes, and are interpreted as follows:

Byte	Size	Meaning
0, 1	16 bits	Number of days since January 1st, 1980
2	8 bits	Minutes (past hour)
3	8 bits	Hour (since midnight)
4	8 bits	$\frac{1}{100}$ of a second (past second)
5	8 bits	Second (past minute)

Attribute Bit 2: NUL. The NUL bit designates the device as the *NUL* device. Since the NUL device cannot be replaced, there is no reason to ever create a NUL device driver.

Attribute Bits 1 & 0: STDIN & STDOUT. The STDIN and STDOUT bits designate the associated character device driver as the standard input and output device. These bits are almost always defined together on the console device, CON, which supports the system keyboard and system monitor. If a new console driver, such as ANSI.SYS, is installed in order to add features to the system, the device should have these bits set. These attributes should be set on only one *active* device per system. (Other copies of the CON driver may have these attributes, but they would be superseded by the latest driver installed.)

The Strategy and Interrupt Entry Pointers
The next two words in the device header contain the offsets of the strategy routine and interrupt routine, respectively. MS-DOS uses this information together with the segment address of the driver to find the entry points to the routine. MS-DOS knows the segment address, of course, because the system loaded the driver in the first place.

The Number of Units/Name Field
The last 8 bytes of the device header are used for two purposes. For character-type device drivers, this field contains the ASCII name of the device, padded with blanks. For example, the printer device field would appear as 'PRN   '.

For block-mode device drivers, only the first byte has any meaning. It indicates to MS-DOS how many separate units are supported by this device driver. This is necessary because many disk controllers support more than one physical drive. Because the remaining 7 bytes are unused, they may contain the name of the device to assist in finding the device in memory or in identifying the driver.

For example, the unit field of the RAM disk driver RDISK (shown in Listing 6-10) is defined as: *1, 'RDISK   '.*

The Strategy Routine

The next required section of the device driver is the strategy routine. The strategy routine in Listing 6-1 has only three lines of executable code. This section has the single task of saving the driver request block for later execution by the interrupt routine.

What is the driver request block? Listing 6-2 shows the structure definition for the request header. Every I/O request made to the driver begins with this request header. The request may sometimes require more information than that contained in the request header, which is why the length parameter is included. We will return to the request header, but first we must finish our coverage of the strategy routine.

Listing 6-2. Structure for the I/O Driver Request Header Block

```
request equ      ds:[bx]          ; base addr of request head
reqhdr  struc
length  db       ?                ; length of request block (bytes)
unit    db       ?                ; unit #
command db       ?                ; driver command code
status  dw       ?                ; status return
        db       8 dup (?)        ; reserved bytes
reqhdr  ends
```

The reason that the strategy routine must save the request block is because MS-DOS does not make a single call to a driver to perform a function. Instead, the system first calls the driver and tells the driver what it wants done and then recalls the driver and tells the driver to actually perform the action.

The reason for the two calls is that when MS-DOS eventually supports a multitasking or concurrent system, multiple driver requests may be outstanding at any given time. By separating the request and execution portions of the driver, multiple requests can be pending, even while the driver is still processing an earlier request.

MS-DOS passes to the strategy routine a pointer to the driver request block in the ES:BX register pair. As the following code fragment demonstrates, most drivers save the driver request block by simply saving the pointer to the block. This is because MS-DOS currently calls the interrupt routine immediately after the strategy routine returns. The data in the request block is still valid.

```
mov      cs:word ptr [req_ptr],bx
mov      cs:word ptr [req_ptr + 2],es
```

However, as soon as MS-DOS becomes multitasking, saving the pointer alone no longer suffices. The strategy routine will have to save the contents of the request block. In addition, drivers probably will have to be able to queue multiple request blocks unless MS-DOS handles this function for them. Until the day when MS-DOS becomes multitasking, we can get by with the easier method of saving just the pointer itself.

Both the strategy routine and the interrupt routine must be defined in MASM as *far* procedures and return to MS-DOS with a *far* RET. Because MS-DOS calls these routines with a *far* CALL, any other type of return would either return to the wrong location (*near* RET) or misalign the stack (IRET).

The Interrupt Routine

After the strategy routine saves the pointer to the request block and returns, MS-DOS calls the interrupt routine (also called the *request entry point* in IBM DOS documentation). This is the routine that actually performs the requested operation.

The first action that the interrupt routine must take is to save all registers! When a device driver is called, the stack has enough room for about 20 pushes. Pushing all of the registers, including the flags, takes 14 pushes. If the interrupt routine requires more than six words of stack storage for its own use, the interrupt routine should set up its own local stack.

After the state of the machine has been saved, the interrupt routine must retrieve the request block that was saved by the strategy routine. If the pointer to the block was saved, using the code fragment in preceding text, the pointer can be retrieved with an LDS instruction.

```
lds     bx,cs:[req_ptr]   ; get DS & request header
```

Now that the interrupt routine has access to the request block, processing may begin. The first step is to analyze the desired request. Accessing the individual fields of the request header is much simpler if a structure is defined for the header. The structure that we use in the RDISK driver to define the request header was shown in Listing 6-2.

If the driver supports a block-type device, the first element of the header checked should be the unit number, *request.unit*. After the unit number has been validated, the interrupt routine should fetch the command code, *request.command*, from the header to determine the action to be performed. Character-type device drivers can fetch the command code immediately because each driver supports only one unit.

Once the command code has been determined, the interrupt routine must transfer control to the proper function handler. Listing 6-3, which contains a sample INTERRUPT routine, shows one method for handling this: the *jump table*. The jump table itself is a list of the program offsets for each of the routines that may be called. In order to access a particular routine, the caller specifies an index, in this case the driver's command code. The index is converted into an offset into the table, and the program executes an *indirect* call or jump through the table to the destination routine:

```
call    word ptr cs:jumptab[bx]    ; invoke command
```

Because the index (driver command code) can often be much larger than the number of valid commands, the INTERRUPT routine must first check to ensure that the specified command code is within range. Rather than use a pre-set value, the INTERRUPT routine compares the command code with the maximum allowed code stored in *max_cmd*:

```
cmp     bl,[max_cmd]               ; is the command supported?
```

Listing 6-1 shows that *max_cmd* has a default value of 0C (hex), the highest command supported prior to MS-DOS version 3.0. However, since *max_cmd* is stored in memory, it can be modified during the driver's initialization to enable the use of higher-numbered commands if the driver is loaded under a newer version of MS-DOS. The different commands supported under the various versions of MS-DOS are given in Table 6-2.

Table 6-2.   Device Driver Command Functions

Command	DOS Version*	Block	Char	Attribute**	Function Meaning
0:	2.0	X	X		INITialization
1:	2.0	X			MEDIA CHECK
2:	2.0	X			BUILD BIOS Parameter Block (BPB)
3:	2.0	X	X	14: IOCTL	INPUT I/O Control for Devices
4:	2.0	X	X		INPUT (read)
5:	2.0		X		Nondestructive INPUT no-wait
6:	2.0		X		INPUT STATUS
7:	2.0		X		INPUT FLUSH
8:	2.0	X	X		OUTPUT (write)
9:	2.0	X	X		OUTPUT (write) with VERIFY
10:	2.0		X		OUTPUT STATUS
11:	2.0		X		OUTPUT FLUSH
12:	2.0	X	X	14: IOCTL	OUTPUT I/O Control for Devices
13:	3.0	X	X	11: OCRM	DEVICE OPEN
14:	3.0	X	X	11: OCRM	DEVICE CLOSE
15:	3.0	X		11: OCRM	REMOVABLE MEDIA
16:	3.1		X	13: OTB	OUTPUT (write) Until Busy
19:	3.2	X	X	6: GIOCTL	Generic IOCTL Request
23:	3.2	X		6: GIOCTL	Get Logical Device
24:	3.2	X		6: GIOCTL	Set Logical Device

*Earliest version of MS-DOS that supports command.
**Bit in device attribute word (if any) that enables command.

The final task of the INTERRUPT routine, after the driver function has returned, is to set the return status in the request block. In Listing 6-3, each function is expected to return its completion status in the AX register. After the called function has returned, the INTERRUPT routine transfers this status to the status word in the request block header, *request.status*. The INTERRUPT routine then ensures that the *done* bit is set, and returns to MS-DOS. Since the return to MS-DOS must be a *far* return, the INTERRUPT routine is defined as a *far proc*.

Listing 6-3. Sample Driver INTERRUPT Processing

```
; Device Driver Status Word Bit Definitions
;
ST_ERROR    equ    1000000000000000b    ; error has occurred
ST_BUSY     equ    0000001000000000b    ; device is busy
ST_DONE     equ    0000000100000000b    ; device is done
;
; Device Driver Error Code Definitions
;
WRITE_PROTECT      equ0
UNKNOWN_UNIT       equ1
NOT_READY         equ2
UNKNOWN_COMMAND    equ3
    .
    .
    .

;****** INTERRUPT ENTRY POINT ****************************************
;
INTERRUPT          proc  far
        pusha                          ; save all working registers
        push   ds
        push   es
        push   cs                      ; establish local data segment
        pop    ds
        les    di,[req_ptr]            ; obtain request block pointer
        mov    bl,es:[di.command]      ; obtain driver command code
;
; preset a command error in case the command is unrecognized
        mov    ax,(ST_ERROR or UNKNOWN_COMMAND)
        cmp    bl,[max_cmd]            ; is the command supported?
        ja     exit                    ; no - reject it
;
; Invoke designated command: Each handler is called with DS & CS
; set to segment DRIVER, and ES:DI pointing to the request block.
; Each handler must return with its status in the AX register.
        xor    bh,bh           ; adjust command to be table index
        shl    bx,1
        call   word ptr cs:jumptab[bx]    ; invoke command

; Transfer status from AX register to request block STATUS word
```

continued

Listing 6-3. *continued*

```
exit:   push    cs                          ; establish local data segment
        pop     ds
        les     di,[req_ptr]                ; obtain request block pointer
        or      ax,ST_DONE                  ; always set done bit
        mov     es:[di.status],ax           ; store return status
        pop     es                          ; restore context
        pop     ds
        popa
        ret
INTERRUPT       endp
        .
        .
        .

;****** COMMAND PROCESSING JUMP TABLE *********************************
;
JUMPTAB label   word
        dw      offset INIT                 ; 0--INITialization
        dw      offset MEDIA_CHECK          ; 1--MEDIA check
        dw      offset BUILD_BPB            ; 2--Build BIOS Parameter Block
        .
        .
        .
        dw      offset NO_COMMAND           ; 16
        dw      offset GET_LOGICAL          ; 17--Get Logical Device
        dw      offset SET_LOGICAL          ; 18--Set Logical Device
        .
        .
        .
```

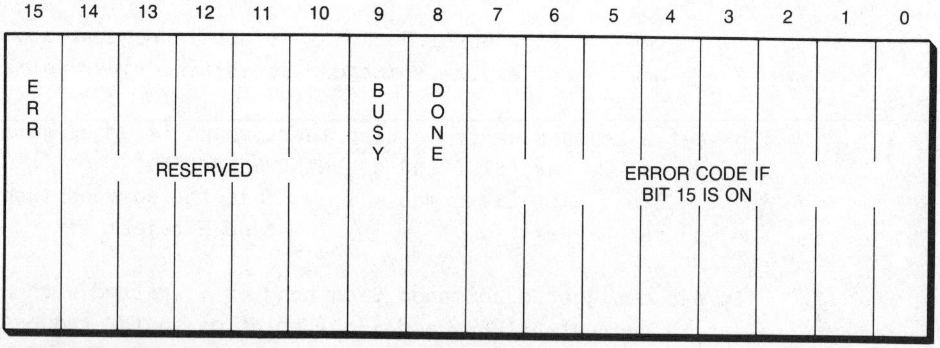

BIT MEANINGS

ERR = 1: Error has occurred on device. Error code in bits 0-7.
BUSY = 1: Set by Status and Removable Media calls.
DONE = 1: Operation is complete. Bit set on exit.

Figure 6-5. Device driver status word.

The status word, shown in Figure 6-5, is used to indicate error conditions for all commands (the error bit) and the status of the device for the Status and Removable Media commands (the busy bit). The error bit is set if an error occurs in processing the command or if the command is illegal for that driver. If the error bit is set, the driver must place the proper error code in bits 0 through 7 of the status word. The various error codes that can occur on a device are listed in Table 6-3.

The *done* bit must always be set in the status word before the driver returns to MS-DOS.

The Driver Commands

For most driver operations, the request header block doesn't contain all the information needed to process the command. Those few commands that do not require additional information are the Status commands and the Flush, Open, Close, and Removable Media commands. All of the other commands require more information than that contained in the request header. For each of these commands, the additional information required is appended to the request block. The length parameter, *request.length*, indicates the total size of the request block (in bytes).

Once again, structures can be used to ease the task of accessing the various elements of the request blocks. Listing 6-10, the RDISK listing (found at the end of the chapter), shows structure definitions for those commands that RDISK expects to process. Notice that because many of the different requests use similar request blocks, we don't need to define all of the fields in every block. This is convenient because MASM doesn't allow us to use the same name more than once, even in different structures.

Table 6-3. Driver Error Codes

Code	Error	Code	Error
0	Write protect violation	8	Sector not found
1	Unknown unit	9	Printer out of paper
2	Device not ready	A	Write fault
3	Unknown command	B	Read fault
4	CRC error	C	General failure
5	Bad request structure length	D	Reserved
6	Seek error	E	Reserved
7	Unknown media	*F	Invalid disk change

All error codes are given as hexadecimal numbers.
*Supported only under MS-DOS versions 3.0 and later.

INIT Command

```
INIT Command (0)                              ☑ BLOCK    ☑ CHARACTER

+00  __23__         Length
+01  _____       Unit
+02  __00__         Command
+03  _____       Status
     _____       Reserved        Read Write
+13  _____           ☐     ☑     Number of Units
+14  _____           ☐     ☑     End Address
+18  _____           ☑     ☑     Command/BPB* Pointer
+22  _____                       ☑     ☐     Device Number†

*BPB Table Pointer returned only for block devices.
†Device Number supplied only for block devices under DOS 3.10 and later.
```

The INIT, or initialize, command is *always* the first command called when a device driver is installed, and it is called only *once* for each driver. This function has the responsibility of informing DOS of the pertinent characteristics of the driver, and of performing whatever startup functions are necessary. The startup requirements depend on the type of device being controlled. Deciding which driver characteristics to return to DOS depends on the type of driver.

All device drivers must return the *break address* (memory address of the end of the driver) and the number of units controlled by the driver. Character device drivers may support a maximum of one unit. Block device drivers may support more than one unit, such as when the device contains multiple drives. A driver may also return *zero* units in order to abort the installation, as may be required in situations where the device is absent. If the driver does return a unit count of zero, it must also set the break address to the value CS:0 (current code segment, offset zero) to inform MS-DOS that the entire driver may be overwritten. In normal use, the break address is the address (segment and offset) of the next byte located after the last byte of the program. MS-DOS resumes loading the system at the next memory paragraph following the break address (or the paragraph *of* the break address if the address is on a paragraph boundary).

The third parameter specific to the INIT command is the *BPB table pointer*. This pointer, which is returned to MS-DOS by the INIT command, is the address of a table which is itself made up of pointers to BIOS Parameter Blocks. There is one pointer for each unit that the driver supports. A BIOS Parameter Block, or BPB as it is called, is a structure that defines the format of a block device (see Figure 6-6). Because BPBs apply only to block devices, this parameter is not returned by character device drivers. However, the BPB table pointer field has another feature which may be used by both types of device driver—it points to the driver's command line. We'll see more of this in a moment.

The last parameter unique to the INIT command is the *drive number*. This parameter, which is supported only under MS-DOS versions 3.10 and later, is

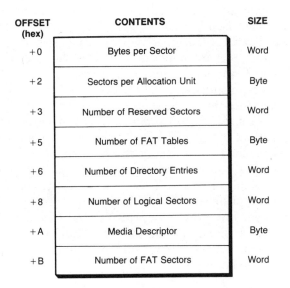

OFFSET (hex)	CONTENTS	SIZE
+0	Bytes per Sector	Word
+2	Sectors per Allocation Unit	Byte
+3	Number of Reserved Sectors	Word
+5	Number of FAT Tables	Byte
+6	Number of Directory Entries	Word
+8	Number of Logical Sectors	Word
+A	Media Descriptor	Byte
+B	Number of FAT Sectors	Word

Figure 6-6. Contents of the BIOS Parameter Block.

used to specify the starting drive number of the associated device(s). For example, if the driver is intended to control disks *C:* and *D:*, this field would be set to 2, and the number of units would be set to 2. If the driver is to control only disk *A:*, the drive number is set to 0, and the number of units is set to 1. This feature is important because it finally allows the default block device drivers to be replaced with user-installed drivers.

The INIT command is unique because, of all the commands used by a driver, INIT operates in an environment closest to that of a standard MS-DOS program. Unlike the other commands, the INIT command may make use of the int 21h function calls 01 through 0Ch (the CP/M-style I/O commands) and function 30h (Get MS-DOS Version Number).

The preceding I/O functions allow the driver to identify itself with a "sign-on" message during installation, possibly indicating configuration options or the like. The Get DOS Version function allows a device driver to adjust its behavior depending on the number and type of driver commands supported under a given version of MS-DOS. A developer can then write one driver that works with many versions of MS-DOS.

Another similarity between the INIT command and a standard DOS program is that the INIT function can read the driver's command line and use it to configure the driver. A driver is specified in the CONFIG.SYS file with the DEVICE command, such as:

DEVICE=[*d:*][*path*]*filename*[*.ext*][*parameters*]

When the INIT command is called, the driver is passed a pointer to the command line text buffer. This pointer, passed in the BPB table pointer field of the INIT command's request block, points to the first character after the = in the command line. In order to obtain configuration information from the command line, the initialization code would skip over the file specification portion of the command and proceed to parse the parameters. However, unlike a standard MS-DOS program, only the address of the command line is passed to the INIT command, and not a copy of the command line. The command line itself must only be read, and never written over. For block device drivers, the *address* of the command line is of course overwritten with the BPB table pointer parameter.

Because the INIT command is called only when the driver is first loaded by the system at boot time, and never called again, the code required to process this command is essentially "throwaway" code. To minimize memory use by the driver, the code to handle the INIT command can be located after the break address or can be colocated (having the same memory address) with an internal buffer in the driver. (The RDISK driver reuses the INIT code as part of a memory buffer.) In either case, the memory occupied by the INIT command's program code will be reused, either by MS-DOS or by the driver. All other code is required to process the various command functions and must be located before the break address.

Media Check

```
MEDIA CHECK Command (1)              ☑ BLOCK      ☐ CHARACTER

+00    19          Length
+01   unit #         Unit
+02    01          Command
+03  _____   Status
                   Reserved      Read Write
+13  _____                  ☑   ☐    Media Descriptor
+14  _____                  ☐   ☑    Media Status*
+15  _____                  ☐   ☑    Pointer to Volume Name†

*Media Status are: −1: is changed; 0: don't know; 1: not changed.
†Volume Names returned only if: DOS 3.00 and later; device has OCRM bit (attribute bit is 11); and
 if returning Media Changed status (−1).
```

The Media Check command is *always* required for block device drivers and is *never* required for character device drivers. This command is used by MS-DOS to remedy a problem that can occur with block devices using removable media: the media can be changed. Whenever a diskette or equivalent is exchanged, the physical format of the new disk may be different from the previous one, and the contents of the new disk will almost undoubtedly be different.

If the disk format has changed, MS-DOS will need to adapt to the new structure of the disk: sector size, number of sectors, and so forth. MS-DOS keeps track of a disk's format with the information contained in the BPB, and if the disk's format has changed, DOS will need a copy of the new BPB.

Even if a disk is exchanged with another of the same format, MS-DOS needs to know if the change occurred. Any time that a disk is changed, the directories and files on the new disk will most likely be different from the previous disk, and MS-DOS may have to decide what to do with any data in its buffers that was supposed to have been written out to the previous disk.

These questions are addressed with the Media Check command, which asks the driver if the disk has been changed. The driver must answer the question with one of these responses: "Yes" (Media Status: −1), "No" (Media Status: 1), or "I don't know" (Media Status: 0).

The importance of this question is reflected in the action that MS-DOS takes upon receiving the response. If the driver answers, "No, the media has NOT changed," MS-DOS proceeds with whatever disk access it was planning, without checking to see if the disk's contents are the same or not. If the driver responds with "Yes, the media HAS changed," MS-DOS throws out any data it may have in its buffers, and requests new disk parameters from the driver. Lastly, if the driver says that it just doesn't know, MS-DOS makes the choice itself. If there is data to be written to the disk, MS-DOS assumes that it is the same disk. Otherwise, it assumes that the disk has changed, and it proceeds as if the driver had answered in the negative (media HAS changed).

To assist the driver in making its decision, MS-DOS provides the driver with the current *media descriptor byte*, or MDB. This byte is one of the values that is returned to MS-DOS inside the Bios Parameter Block(s) returned by the INIT and Build BIOS Parameter Block driver commands. Each unique disk format should have a unique media descriptor byte, although this is not always possible. (The next section on the Build BIOS Parameter Block command covers this in more detail.)

The media descriptor byte is stored as the first byte of the disk's FAT, or file allocation table. This is also the low byte of the disk type value, as shown in Table 11-5 of Chapter 11. Chapter 11 supplies more information about the FAT and the disk type value.

The driver can now decide if the disk has been changed by using the following logic:

1. If the device does not support removable media (e.g., the device is a fixed or RAM disk), then the driver should answer "No: The media is NOT changed." Otherwise, go to step 2.

2. Microsoft states that a diskette cannot be exchanged in less than two seconds. With this reasoning, the driver should check the system clock and if less than two seconds have elapsed since the last access, the driver should answer "No: The media is NOT changed." Of course, this method requires that the driver always save the time of any access. If more than two seconds have elapsed, go to step 3. (If there is no system clock that can be read, skip this step entirely.)

3. Sometimes the disk drive itself may be able to inform the driver if a change has occurred. Some disk drives have door locks that report if the door has been opened since the last access. If the device is such a drive, and the drive reports that the door has not been opened, the driver should answer "No: The media is NOT changed." If the door has been opened, go to step 4.

   Other drives use disk drive motors that run only when a disk is accessed, with a timed delay before the drive motor shuts off. With these drives, if the motor status can be read by the driver, and the drive motor is still active from the last access, this would tend to imply that the disk was not changed, and the driver should answer "No: The media is NOT changed." However, some drive motors also turn on any time a disk is inserted, regardless of whether there was an access, which invalidates this test.

4. The driver should read the disk to obtain its media descriptor byte. If the media descriptor byte is different from that provided by MS-DOS in the call to the Media Check command, then the driver should answer "Yes: The media HAS been changed." Otherwise, proceed to step 5.

5. The driver should read the disk to obtain its volume identification. If the volume ID is different from that stored inside the driver from the last Build BPB command, then the driver should answer "Yes: The media HAS been changed." Otherwise, proceed to step 6.

6. The driver should answer, "Don't know if the media has changed."

It may not be possible to implement some of the steps in the preceding logic chain. If for any reason you cannot determine whether the disk was changed, it is best to answer, "Don't know if the media has changed." The exact method used will have to depend on the capabilities of the device itself, and the fortitude of the programmer.

There is one other piece of information that the Media Check command *may* have to return under MS-DOS versions 3.0 and later. If the driver supports the Open/Close/Removable Media calls (bit 11 in the driver attribute word), *and* if the Media Check command is going to answer "Yes, the media HAS changed" (media status: –1), then the driver *must* return a pointer to the volume name of the *previous* disk. (See Chapter 11 for the format and location of a disk's volume name.) The pointer is returned as shown in the preceding Media Check request header. If the driver does not know the volume name of the previous disk, such as on the first call to this command, then the driver should return a pointer to the string "NO NAME   ", terminated with a zero byte (i.e., "NO", one space, "NAME", four spaces, and a zero).

Build BIOS Parameter Block Command

```
BUILD BIOS PARAMETER BLOCK          ☑ BLOCK      ☐ CHARACTER
Command (2)

+00   22            Length
+01  unit #          Unit
+02   02           Command
+03                  Status
                    Reserved      Read Write
+13                                ☑    ☐    Media Descriptor
+14                                ☑    ☐    Pointer to FAT/Scratch*
+18                                ☐    ☑    Pointer to BPB

*Pointer to FAT if IBM/FAT Device (attribute bit 13 is 0). Pointer to scratch buffer if NONIBM/NONFAT Device
(attribute bit 13 is 1).
```

The Build BIOS Parameter Block command is *always* required for block device drivers and is *never* required for character device drivers. Whenever MS-DOS has been informed, or decides for itself, that the media in a block device has been changed, it must obtain new parameters for the device's media. It does this through the Build BIOS Parameter Block command, which requests the driver to return a pointer to a BIOS Parameter Block containing the new values. (The preceding Figure 6-6 shows the contents of the BPB.)

There is an important difference between the BPB pointer returned by the Build BPB command and the BPB table pointer returned by the INIT command. The Build BPB command returns a *pointer* to the BIOS Parameter Block itself, whereas the INIT command returns a pointer to a *table of pointers* to BIOS Parameter Blocks. Although the difference between a single pointer and a pointer to pointers is fairly obvious once recognized, it can be subtle enough to cause unnecessary grief.

Like the Media Check command, the Build BPB command may have to concern itself with a disk's volume name. Under MS-DOS versions 3.0 or later, if the device supports removable media, and the Open/Close/Removable Media bit (bit 11) of the attribute word is set to 1, then the driver will need to *read and save* the disk's volume name. This stored name may need to be returned in subsequent calls to the Media Check command.

Receiving a Build BIOS Parameter Block command may be taken by the driver as notification that as far as MS-DOS is concerned, the disk has legally changed. If the driver is maintaining a count of the number of "opens" and "closes" performed on the device (from the Open Device and Close Device driver commands), this is the time to reset the count to zero.

Obtaining the BIOS Parameter Block. With the mechanisms for returning BIOS Parameter Blocks behind us, we need to address the question of how to determine the contents of the BPB. These methods apply to processing the INIT command as well as to the Build BIOS Parameter Block command. In the simplest case, for device drivers that support only one type of media (such as a RAM disk driver), the contents of the BPB can be coded into the driver itself. Unfortunately, real disks, even fixed disks, aren't so obliging, and the driver must read the disk to determine the contents of the BPB.

Normally the BPB is part of the disk's boot record, as shown in Figure 6-7. In this case the driver must find and read the disk's boot record, extract the BPB, and return a pointer to it. In almost all cases the boot record is located at logical sector zero of the disk. (The translation from logical to physical sectors varies from device to device, and must be determined from the device's documentation.) The driver should examine the structure of the sector to verify if it is a valid boot record.

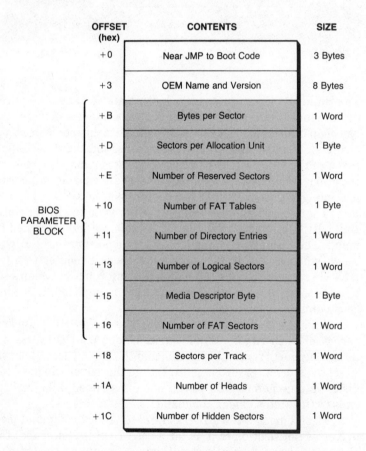

OFFSET (hex)	CONTENTS	SIZE
+0	Near JMP to Boot Code	3 Bytes
+3	OEM Name and Version	8 Bytes
+B	Bytes per Sector	1 Word
+D	Sectors per Allocation Unit	1 Byte
+E	Number of Reserved Sectors	1 Word
+10	Number of FAT Tables	1 Byte
+11	Number of Directory Entries	1 Word
+13	Number of Logical Sectors	1 Word
+15	Media Descriptor Byte	1 Byte
+16	Number of FAT Sectors	1 Word
+18	Sectors per Track	1 Word
+1A	Number of Heads	1 Word
+1C	Number of Hidden Sectors	1 Word

BIOS PARAMETER BLOCK (brackets +B through +16)

Figure 6-7. Contents of the first 30 bytes of the boot record.

If the first logical sector does not appear to be a valid boot record, such as occurs with disks formatted under versions of MS-DOS prior to 2.0, then the driver must read the first sector of the disk's file allocation table, or FAT. Luckily, pre 2.0 versions of MS-DOS support only a few formats, all of which store the first FAT sector in the *second* logical sector of the disk. The first byte of the first

FAT sector contains the disk's media descriptor byte, which can then be used to determine the proper contents of the BPB to be returned to MS-DOS. Versions of MS-DOS prior to 2.0 used only media descriptor bytes 0FEh or 0FFh. Chapter 11 lists the various disk type values from which the media descriptor byte is taken.

Throughout this process you should note that simply reading the disk must not be taken for granted. If the device and driver support multiple formats (e.g., different sector sizes), the driver may need to attempt the read with a number of formats before finding the correct one.

For removable media devices (attribute bit 11), after the disk's BPB has been located and the disk's format determined, the driver must obtain the disk's volume ID. This will be found by reading the disk's root directory, as explained in Chapter 11.

In summary, the sequence for processing the Build BIOS Parameter Block command is as follows:

1. The driver should read the disk's boot record (usually located at logical sector zero) and check the record for the BIOS Parameter Block. If the BPB is found, proceed to step 3; else proceed to step 2.

2. The driver should read the first sector of the disk's FAT to obtain the media descriptor byte. Based on the MDB, the driver must construct the appropriate BPB. (Refer to Chapter 11 for MDB to BPB correspondence.)

3. If the device supports Removable Media (attribute bit 11), the driver should read the disk's volume identification from the root directory sector, and store it.

To implement this strategy, the driver will need internal buffers to store a copy of the BIOS Parameter Block and volume ID, and an internal scratch buffer in which to read into a sector from the disk.

We have skipped over in this explanation the parameters that are passed to the driver when the Build BIOS Parameter Block command is invoked. Ignore them! One parameter is the previously described media descriptor byte, which has no meaning since the Build BPB command will provide MS-DOS with a new value. The second parameter is a pointer to a buffer that is either a scratch buffer (if driver attribute bit 13, the NONIBM bit, is set to 1) or a buffer that contains a copy of the first sector of the disk's FAT (if driver attribute bit 13 is 0). If the buffer contains the FAT sector, then it *must not be modified*. Since the driver must contain its own scratch buffer into which the boot record is read, the buffer passed with the call can be ignored.

The last point to note in the importance of the BIOS Parameter Block is that the media descriptor byte does not uniquely determine a disk's format. Only the BPB can do that. However, MS-DOS versions 3.0 and later will not update their internal device structures unless the media descriptor byte is different from the previous one. Even though MS-DOS versions 3.0 and later attach no importance to the actual *value* of the MDB, the driver should return a different MDB whenever the disk's format changes.

Input and Output Commands

INPUT & OUTPUT
Commands (3,4,8,9,12,16)   ☑ **BLOCK**   ☑ **CHARACTER**

```
+00    26          Length
+01   unit #       Unit (Block Device Only)
+02  command       Command   3:  I/O Control for Devices Input
+03                Status    4:  Input (Read)
                   Reserved  8:  Output (Write)
                             9:  Output (Write) with Verify
                            12:  I/O Control for Devices Output
                            16:  Output Until Busy (character device only)
```

	Read	Write	
+13	☑	☐	Media Descriptor
+14	☑	☐	Transfer Address
+18	☑	☑	Byte/Sector Count*
+20	☑	☐	Starting Sector (block only)
+22	☐	☑	Pointer to Volume Name†

*Contains *requested* transfer count on entry. The driver should always update this entry with the *actual* transfer count.
†Volume Name *returned only* if DOS is 3.00 and later and Invalid Disk Change Error (OF) is returned.

The Input, Output, and Output with Verify commands (4, 8, and 9) are *always* required for all device drivers. These commands support the transfer of data between MS-DOS and the device.

The I/O Control Input and I/O Control Output commands (3 and 12) are optional commands, required only if the I/O Control attribute (bit 14) is set in the device driver attribute word. These commands apply to both block and character device drivers and support the transfer of data between MS-DOS and the device *driver*.

The Output Until Busy command (16) is an optional command, used solely with character device drivers and required only if the NONIBM/OTB attribute (bit 13) is set in the device driver attribute word. This command supports the transfer of data from MS-DOS to the device. Note also that this command is not documented in IBM's *Technical Reference Manual* for version 3.30.

The commands Output and Output with Verify are selected by a combination of IOCTL bit 5 (the BIN or RAW mode bit) and the *verify* switch. In verify mode, all driver output uses the Output with Verify command. If verify mode is not set, then the normal Output command is used. Putting the device in binary mode (selected by IOCTL bit 5, the BIN bit) allows multibyte transfers to be performed.

There is one combination of modes that should cause the Output Until Busy command to be used, but doesn't. This setup consists of no verify (so the Output with Verify command won't be used), device in binary mode (to allow multibyte transfers), and a device that supports the Output Until Busy command. However, in testing this mode, the Output with Verify command was

never called, which may explain why IBM left this command out of its version
3.30 documentation.

All of these commands share a common request structure, but there are
differences based on the type of I/O requested and the type of device driver. The
basic parameters of an Input or Output call are as follows:

- The *command* itself specifies the source and destination entities for the
  transfer operation. It is important to note that I/O Control operations are
  intended to transfer command and configuration information to the
  driver, not to transfer data directly to the device. The four possible
  combinations of source and destination are then as follows:

Command(s)	Source	Destination
Input	Device	Buffer
Output, Output Verify, Output Until Busy	Buffer	Device
I/O Control Input	Driver	Buffer
I/O Control Output	Buffer	Driver

- The *transfer address* contains the full address of the MS-DOS buffer that
  either contains data to be written (an Output call) or is to be filled with
  data (an Input call).
- The *count* specifies the number of bytes (character device I/O and all I/O
  Control commands) or sectors (block device Input, Output, and Output
  Verify commands) that are to be transferred.
- For block device drivers only, the *unit* and *starting sector* parameters
  further identify the source (Input) or destination (Output) location.
- For block device drivers only, the *media descriptor byte* parameter may
  be useful in determining the device's format or in determining if the
  device has changed illegally.

Once the driver has identified the source and destination, it performs the
transfer. After the transfer operation has been completed, the driver must return, in the count parameter, the number of bytes or sectors that it was actually
able to transfer. Even if an error has occurred and the error bit was set in the
returned status, MS-DOS assumes that the returned count is valid. If the driver
fails to update the count parameter, then the returned value will be the same as
the *requested* value. You must also be aware that even if the transfer succeeds,
the count can still be wrong. This can happen if a "wrap" has occurred.

A *wrap* occurs in block device drivers when the number of bytes to be
transferred exceeds what is addressable from the buffer segment address. One
example of a wrap would be a transfer of 64 sectors of 512 bytes per sector from a
buffer with an offset address of 8002 hex. This transfer consists of 32,768 bytes
(8000 hex). Since the buffer's offset address is 8002 hex, the address of the last
byte will be 10002 hex, which is illegal. In the case of a wrap, the driver should
NOT transfer the unreachable portion.

Each command has somewhat different requirements for processing the
transfer and returning the status and count. These requirements are described
next for each command.

I/O Control Input and I/O Control Output Commands (3 and 12). These are the simplest commands, usually requiring only that data be transferred from or to the driver itself. The data has no meaning to MS-DOS itself, and can even be ignored by the driver if it so chooses. Whatever data is sent or received, and whatever meaning is attributed to it, is strictly up to the driver and the application that it is conversing with. Typically, this data is used for configuring the device, although other uses are possible. However, the driver must not forget to set the resulting transfer count.

Input and Output Commands (4 and 8). For most character device drivers, processing the Input and Output commands is fairly direct. If the transfer succeeds, then the *done* bit is set in the status word and the driver returns. If there is a problem, the appropriate error is set in the status word (see Table 6-3), the actual transfer count is set, and the driver returns.

For character devices, if the device has no data to be read on an input operation, the driver can either wait for data or return the Device Not Ready error. On Output, if the device cannot accept the data, the driver can also return Device Not Ready. However, the Device Not Ready error is usually reserved to mean that the device is off-line, or unreachable in some way. It is not normally used to indicate that the device is simply backed up, since returning the Device Not Ready error may very well cause MS-DOS to request operator intervention.

For block device drivers, the operation is more complicated. Typically, the driver will have to convert the starting sector number into a physical sector, usually consisting of cylinder (or track), head, and physical sector. The driver may have to "seek" the drive (move the read/write head to the proper track) before starting the transfer, and may have to perform further "seeks" between transferring sectors. (A more complete description of disk anatomy appears in Chapter 11.)

Furthermore, devices such as disk drivers are subject to a plethora of errors, as seen in Table 6-3, such as Write Protect Violation, CRC Error, Seek Error, Read and Write faults, and the ever descriptive General Failure. Usually, if an error does occur, the driver sets the appropriate error code in the status word, sets the count of sectors that were successfully transferred, and returns. However, there is one failure that requires further thought and processing—the Invalid Disk Change.

The error Invalid Disk Change is allowed only under MS-DOS versions 3.0 and later, and only then if MS-DOS knows that it is dealing with a Removable Media device, as determined by attribute bit 11, the OCRM bit. The difference between this error and the others is that if the driver informs MS-DOS that the disk change was invalid, MS-DOS wants to know what disk the driver had expected. This information is conveyed via the expected disk's volume name, and the driver must return a pointer to the proper volume name. As with the Media Check command, if the driver does not know the proper name, it should return a pointer to the name, "NO NAME   ".

How does the driver known when an Invalid Disk Change has occurred? If the driver is maintaining a count of the number of opens and closes performed on a disk (via driver commands 13 and 14), and the disk changes (detected by a different format, different media descriptor byte, or some such) with more opens than closes, then the disk is assumed to have changed illegally, and the Invalid Disk Change error is appropriate.

Output with Verify Command (9). The Output with Verify command applies only to devices where the data written to the device can be read back to ensure that the write was successful. For these devices, such as disk drives, the driver should write the data as with the Output command, read it back as with the Input command, and compare the data read back against the data written. If there is an error, the driver should not reattempt the operation but rather should report it to MS-DOS with the appropriate error code (Table 6-3) and the count of the data successfully transferred.

As with the Build BIOS Parameter Block command, processing this command requires that the driver have an internal buffer in which to read back the data. If the device does not allow data to be read back from it, this command should be processed by using the Output command, command 8.

Output Until Busy Command (16). Output Until Busy is another variant of the Output command. This command, which is called only for character devices that have attribute bit 13 set, allows programs to transfer large chunks of data to devices with internal buffers, such as printers. The driver should continue to send data to the device until there is no more data or until the device cannot accept any more data. It is most important that the driver correctly set the transfer count so that MS-DOS will know how much data was sent. Note that, for this command, transferring less than the requested amount is *not* an error.

Nondestructive Input without Wait Command

The Nondestructive Input without Wait command (5) is *required only* for character device drivers and is not used for block device drivers. Although this command is similar to a standard character Input command, it has some major differences:

- There is no transfer buffer or transfer count. The request count is always 1, and if a byte is available, then it is returned in the *byte read from device* field.

- *Without Wait:* If no input is available from the device, then the driver must set the busy bit in addition to the *done* bit in the status word, and return immediately.

- *Nondestructive:* If input is available, then the driver not only must return that byte but also must save the byte to be read by the next Input command. If input data is queued within the driver, as with an interrupt-driven driver, then the byte returned must remain in the queue.

This command is intended to allow MS-DOS to: (1) determine if data is available without having to do an Input operation, which could result in waiting for input, and (2) to look ahead in the buffer at the next character without having to accept and "consume" it.

Status and Flush I/O Commands

```
STATUS and FLUSH I/O                    □ BLOCK    ☑ CHARACTER
Commands (6,7,10,11)

+00    13          Length
+01   unit #       Unit
+02  command       Command      6:  Input Status
+03                Status       7:  Input Flush
                   Reserved    10:  Output Status
                               11:  Output Flush
```

The Input Status and Output Status commands (6 and 10) are *required* for character device drivers and are not used for block device drivers.

The Input Flush and Output Flush commands (7 and 11) are *required* for character device drivers and are not used for block device drivers.

The Input Status and Input Flush commands have meaning only for character device drivers that support interrupt-driven input queuing, although they may be called for any character device driver. The Input Status call is used to show the status of the queue as follows:

- If there is a queue and there are *no* available characters, the driver should set the done and busy bits in the status word, and return.

- If there is a queue, and there *are* available characters, the driver should set the *done* bit and should clear the busy bit in the status word, and return.

- If there is *not* an input queue, the driver should set the done bit and should clear the busy bit in the status word, and return. This seems like a contradiction, telling MS-DOS that there are characters available when there isn't even a queue. The reason for this is so that MS-DOS will call the Input command to read from the device. Were this not done, MS-DOS would continue to check for input with Input Status, which could never occur since there would be no queue to hold the character.

The Input Flush command is used to direct the driver to discard any characters that may be in its input queue. After clearing the queue, if there was one, the driver should set the *done* bit and return. No errors are expected on this call.

The Output Status command is used to check the status of an output queue or of a device. If the device does not have an output queue, then the driver should return the status of the device itself, if possible. The driver should set the status in the busy bit (busy meaning "output pending"), set the done bit, and return.

The Output Flush command is used to direct the driver to discard any characters that may be in its output queue, if there is one, and, if possible, *to abort any device output*. After completing these actions, the driver should set the done bit and return.

Device Open/Close and Removable Media Commands

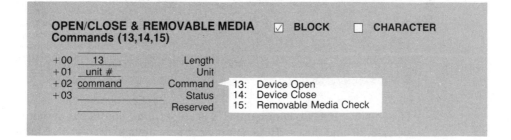

The Device Open and Device Close commands (13 and 14) are *optional* commands, supported under MS-DOS versions 3.0 and later, and are used only if device driver attribute bit 11, the OCRM bit, is set to 1. However, Microsoft recommends that new drivers implement these commands.

The Removable Media command (15) is an *optional* block device command under MS-DOS versions 3.0 or later, used only if device driver attribute bit 11, the OCRM bit, is set to 1. However, Microsoft recommends that new drivers implement this command.

The conditions under which the Device Open and Device Close commands are called, are explained in an earlier section "The Device Header Attribute Word," under the subheading "Attribute Bit 11: OCRM."

For block-type devices with removable media, these commands can be used to keep track of the number of open files on the device, with the intention of detecting if the media is changed illegally (e.g., if the media is changed while files are still open).

For character-type devices, these commands can be used to prevent simultaneous access to a device such as a printer, or to supply preprocessing and postprocessing capabilities such as printer setup or printer reset.

The Removable Media call can be invoked by application programs using the IOCTL subfunction for Check for Removable Media (subfunction 08h of function 44h). The application program specifies the drive number of interest in the call. In processing the Removable Media call, the device driver must first determine if the drive unit referenced in the call contains removable media and then return the status in the busy bit of the driver status word. If the drive *does not* contain removable media, then the driver must set the busy bit to 1. If the drive *does* contain removable media, then the driver should clear the busy bit to 0.

Generic IOCTL Command

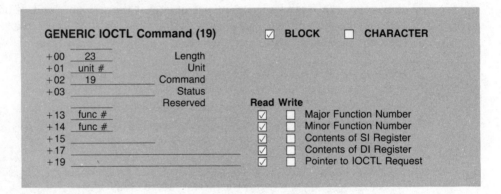

The Generic IOCTL command (19) is an *optional* command under MS-DOS versions 3.20 and later. It is enabled when device driver attribute bit 6, the GIOCTL bit, is set to 1.

The name "Generic IO Control" is really something of a misnomer because this command is used to implement what amounts to *extended* device driver functions. One group of extended functions (accessed by IOCTL subfunction 0Ch) supports *code page switching*, a means of supporting a run-time configurable driver. The other major group of functions (accessed by IOCTL subfunction 0Dh) provides a standard interface for hardware-dependent block device operations. The operations supported are reading, writing, verifying, and formatting entire tracks, and reading and changing the device's BIOS Parameter Block (BPB).

The extended operations of MS-DOS's Generic IO Control command are well documented in the *DOS Technical Reference Manual* in the section on function 44h, IOCTL for Devices, and since these functions are intended primarily for original equipment manufacturers, we refer the reader to the manual for more information.

Get and Set Logical Device Commands

```
GET & SET LOGICAL DEVICE              ☑ BLOCK       ☐ CHARACTER
Commands (23 & 24)

+00    21            Length
+01   unit #         Unit
+02  command         Command      ┌─────────────────────────────┐
+03  _____       Status       │ 23:  Get Logical Device     │
     _____       Reserved     │ 24:  Set Logical Device     │
                                  └─────────────────────────────┘
                                   Read Write
+13  _____                      ☑    ☐    Input (unit code)
+14  _____                      ☑    ☐    Command Code
+15  _____                      ☑    ☐    Status
+17  _____          ☐    ☑    Reserved
```

The Get Logical Device and Set Logical Device commands (23 and 24) are *optional* block-device driver commands, supplied under MS-DOS versions 3.20 and later. They are also enabled when device driver attribute bit 6, the GIOCTL bit, is set to 1.

These commands are used to keep track of the current drive reference for devices that have more than one logical drive name. Like the Generic IO Control command, these commands are accessed using MS-DOS's function 44h, IOCTL for Devices. Subfunction 0Eh is used to get the logical drive assignment, and subfunction 0Fh is used to set the logical drive assignment. Like the Generic IO Control command, these commands are really intended to support OEM devices, in this case MS-DOS's DRIVER.SYS device driver for the 3¼-inch micro floppy. A complete description of these commands can also be found in the *DOS Technical Reference Manual*, in the section on function 44h, IOCTL for Devices, and it is to that manual that we refer you.

Creating the Loadable Device Driver File

It has already been said that a device driver program bears much resemblance to a .COM type program. This is especially true in the method used to create the driver's .SYS file. (Note that there is no reason other than convention for using the extension ".SYS" to denote a device driver. Any extension name will do.) Listing 6-4 shows the dialogue for creating the device driver "DRIVER". The file is assembled and linked as normal, and then converted to a binary .SYS file. Note that it is quite normal for the driver to be without a stack segment, as it uses MS-DOS's own stack when invoked.

The example shown in Listing 6-4 also creates a .LST assembler listing file and a .MAP linker listing file. The .OBJ and .EXE files can be deleted, of course, after the .SYS file has been created.

Listing 6-4. Sample Device Driver Build Process

```
C> masm driver,driver,driver;

Microsoft Macro Assembler Version 4.00
Copyright Microsoft Corp 1981, 1983, 1984, 1985. All rights reserved.

   45976 Bytes symbol space free

       0 Warning Errors
       0 Severe  Errors

C> link driver,driver,driver;

Microsoft 8086 Object Linker
Version 3.00 Copyright Microsoft Corp 1983, 1984, 1985

Warning: no stack segment

C> exe2bin driver driver.sys
```

Debugging Device Drivers

Once a driver has been installed in the system, that driver cannot be debugged with MS-DOS (because of the reentrance problem). But there is still a need to be able to debug drivers because (like most things in programming) they cannot be expected to function properly the first time through. Three approaches can help to make simpler the task of debugging the driver.

First, build the driver a block at a time. Get the main routines working first and then move on to the more advanced features. Don't try to do the IOCTL handlers right away. The routines that you need to have operating before the driver loads properly are the strategy and interrupt routines and the INIT command handler. For block-mode devices, you also need the Media Check command and, unless you have specified the NONIBM bit in the attribute word, the Build BPB command. You won't be able to perform I/O with just these command handlers, but MS-DOS should at least be able to load your driver successfully.

Another approach that can help in debugging drivers is to use the BIOS functions to handle simple output that can inform you of the current state of the driver. It is helpful to know just how far the driver got before it crashed. If you don't have a ROM-BIOS to rely on, you can cobble together some sort of output routine and include it in the driver source. For example, when debugging the RDISK driver at the end of this chapter, the authors had the driver display a single character for each command that it processed (*I* for interrupt, *S* for strategy, *i* for INIT, and so forth). That was a real help when the driver loaded and could be accessed with the Absolute Disk Access functions but crashed the system when an attempt was made to read the device's directory. The interaction between the driver and the system can be one of the most complex problems to solve and, unfortunately, usually can be debugged only with the driver in place in the system.

If you decide to add debugging statements to your driver, be aware that such actions most likely will increase the depth of the stack required, and you may need to change your driver to use a local stack if the driver doesn't do so already.

When testing the individual pieces of the driver, you don't need to debug it in place. If you are willing to spend the time to write a simple test program that creates request blocks and passes them to the driver for processing, you will be able to use DEBUG to debug that test program and the driver, too. This enables you to at least get the driver to a state where it should boot. After that, you can continue with other types of debugging to flush out the final bugs.

When developing drivers, *always* use a copy of your system disk, not the original system disk. An error in the driver code can prevent the system from booting. An error in a disk driver may destroy valuable data on the disk. For these reasons, you should always have a copy of your system disk to return to in case of failures.

Displaying the Device Drivers in Your System

It is often helpful when debugging device drivers to know exactly which devices are present in your system. To this end, we have provided a small program named "SD," for Show Driver. A sample output of this program appears in Listing 6-5.

Most of the devices are standard MS-DOS devices, except for the topmost CON device, which is ANSI.SYS, and the topmost block device, which represents a Bernoulli Box device driver. The lower block device driver, with three drives, is the standard MS-DOS device driver, which interestingly enough supports both the hard disk and two floppy disks.

Attrib is the driver's attribute word; *Address* is its start address (found in the previous driver's link field); and *STRAT* and *INTRP* are the offsets of the strategy and interrupt routines within the device driver. The assembly language source for the SD program appears in Listing 6-6. Note that SD uses DRIVER.INC (Listing 6-7), STDMAC.INC (Listing A-7, Appendix A), and the BIN2HEX routine found in STDLIB.LIB (Listing A-8, Appendix A).

Listing 6-5. Sample Device Driver Chain from the Show Driver Program

SD-ShowDriv, Version 1.00, Copyright 1988 Kevin Jaeger

Device	Type	Units	Attrib	Address	STRAT	INTRP
NUL	Char	01	8004	0000:1898	1418	141E
CON	Char	01	8013	08A9:0000	00A2	00AD

continued

Listing 6-5. *continued*

```
SD-ShowDriv, Version 1.00, © Copyright 1988 Kevin Jaeger
```

Device	Type	Units	Attrib	Address	STRAT	INTRP
--------	Block	02	0000	083D:0000	00A7	00B2
CON	Char	01	8013	0070:0160	00A7	00B2
AUX	Char	01	8000	0070:01F1	00A7	00B8
PRN	Char	01	A000	0070:02A0	00A7	00C7
CLOCK$	Char	01	8008	0070:034A	00A7	00DC
--------	Block	03	0800	0070:0416	00A7	00E2
COM1	Char	01	8000	0070:0203	00A7	00B8
LPT1	Char	01	A000	0070:02B2	00A7	00C7
LPT2	Char	01	A000	0070:0B13	00A7	00CD
LPT3	Char	01	A000	0070:0B25	00A7	00D3
COM2	Char	01	8000	0070:0B37	00A7	00BE

```
<<< ------------- End Of Device Driver List ------------ >>>
```

Listing 6-6. SHOWDRIV.ASM Source File

```
PAGE    60,132
; ***** SHOWDRIV ********************************************
; ShowDriv - Display Installed Device Driver Chain for MS-DOS
; This file creates the program SD.EXE
;
; ***** INCLUDES ********************************************
INCLUDE stdmac.inc
INCLUDE driver.inc
;
; ***** DGROUP (DATA) COMPONENT SEGMENTS ********************
;
_DATA   SEGMENT BYTE PUBLIC 'DATA'
_DATA   ENDS
;
STACK   SEGMENT PARA STACK
        dw      1024 dup (?)             ; 2K stack
STACK   ENDS
;
DGROUP GROUP    _DATA, STACK
;
; ***** DATA STORAGE & TEMPLATES ***************************
;
_DATA   SEGMENT BYTE PUBLIC 'data'
```

```
;
; Search Parameters
;
nuldev  db      'NUL    '                   ; NUL device string
nulattr dw      AT_CHR OR AT_NUL            ; NUL attribute word
;
; Text Messages for Display: Format as Follows:
;
; "Device     Type   Units Attrib   Address     STRAT   INTRP"
; "----------------------------------------------------------"
; "xxxxxxxx   xxxx   xx    xxxx      xxxx:xxxx   xxxx    xxxx"
; "<<< ------------ End Of Device Driver List ------------ "
;
$title db   CR,LF
       db   'SD-ShowDriv, Version 1.00, Copyright 1988'
       db   CR,LF,CR,LF
       db   'Device        Type   Units Attrib      Address'
       db   '    STRAT   INTRP'
       db   CR,LF
       db   '-------------------------------------------'
       db   '------------------'
       db   CR,LF,'$'
$space db   '    $'
$block db   '--------   Block    $'
$char  db   'Char$'
$colon db   ':'
$end   db   CR,LF
       db   '<<< ------------ End Of Device Driver List'
       db   ' ------------>>>'
$crlf  db   CR,LF,'$'
;
; Structure Templates
devhead         STRUC               ; device header structure
       next    dd      ?           ; long pointer to next block
       attrib  dw      ?           ; attribute
       strat   dw      ?           ; offset to strategy
       intrp   dw      ?           ; offset to interrupt
       dname   db      8 dup (?)   ; name/number of units
       term    db      ?           ; terminating position
devhead         ENDS
;
_DATA  ENDS
;
; ***** PROGRAM CODE STARTS HERE *******************************
;
```

continued

Listing 6-6. *continued*

```
_TEXT   SEGMENT BYTE PUBLIC 'CODE'
        ASSUME  cs:_TEXT, ds:DGROUP, es:DGROUP, ss:DGROUP
;
        EXTRN   bin2hex:NEAR                ; hexadecimal display
main    PROC    FAR
        mov     ax,DGROUP                   ; set up data segment
        mov     ds,ax
;
; Find the NUL device by searching for the NUL name
        cld
        mov     cx,0FFFEh                   ; search count
        xor     ax,ax                       ; start after INT table
        mov     es,ax
        mov     di,0400h
        mov     al,[nuldev[rv]              ; beginning search value
search:
        repne   scasb                       ; search until match
        jne     exit                        ; no match
;
        push    cx                          ; possible match: ...
        push    di                          ; ... save search position
        mov     si,offset nuldev+1          ; remainder "NUL" string
        mov     cx,7                        ; remainder of count
        repe    cmpsb                       ; compare until no match
        jne     not_it                      ; didn't match
;
        sub     di,(offset term - offset attrib) ; adjust pointer
        cmpsw                               ; NUL's attribute word ?
        jne     not_it                      ; didn't match
        add     sp,4                        ; discard saved DI & CX
        sub     di,(offset strat - offset next)  ; adjust pointer
        jmp     found_nul                   ; found NUL device header!
;
not_it:         pop     di                  ; restore position & count
        pop     cx
        jmp     short search
;
; Have found NUL device header: continue to display entire chain
found_nul:
        @DisStr $title                      ; display title
show_driver:
        call    ShowDeviceInfo              ; display device header
        cmp     word ptr es:[di],-1         ; check for end of chain
        je      done                        ; if -1 then exit
        les     di,es:[di.next]             ; if not -1 then get next
```

```
        jmp     short show_driver   ; continue;
done:   @DisStr $end                ; terminating message
        @DisStr $crlf
;
exit:   mov     al,0                ; normal terminate
        @ExitToDOS                  ; terminate program
main    ENDP
;
; ***** ShowDeviceInfo *****************************************
; ShowDeviceInfo displays the block addressed by ES:DI as a
; device header. Format for the display is show in Data above.
;
ShowDeviceInfo PROC    NEAR
        test    es:[di.attrib],AT_CHR  ; device char or block?
        jnz     is_char
        @DisStr $block              ; unnamed block device
        xor     ah,ah
        mov     al,es:[di.dname]    ; number of units
        jmp     short dis_units
is_char:
        push    ds                  ; save program DS
        push    es                  ; make Src same as Dest
        pop     ds
        lea     si,es:[di.dname]    ; SI to name string offset
        mov     cx,8                ; # of char to display
show_name:
        lodsb                       ; read Name char at a ...
        @DisChr al                  ; ... time and display
        loop    show_name
        pop     ds                  ; restore program DS
        @DisStr $space
        @DisStr $char               ; show type
        @DisStr $space
        mov     ax,1                ; only one unit
;
dis_units:
        mov     ch,02               ; show number of units
        call    bin2hex
        @DisStr $space
        mov     ch,04               ; display numeric data
        mov     ax,es:[di.attrib]
        call    bin2hex             ; show attribute word
        @DisStr $space
;
        mov     ax,es
        call    bin2hex             ; show address segment
```

continued

333

Listing 6-6. continued

```
        @DisChr $colon
        mov     ax,di
        call    bin2hex                 ; show address offset
        @DisStr $space
;
        mov     ax,es:[di.strat]
        call    bin2hex                 ; show strategy address
        @DisStr $space
;
        mov     ax,es:[di.intrp]
        call    bin2hex                 ; show interrupt address
        @DisStr $crlf
;
        ret
ShowDeviceInfo ENDP
;
; ***** END OF PROGRAM : END OF FILE ***************************
_TEXT   ENDS
        END     main
```

Listing 6-7. DRIVER.INC Include File

```
; ***** DRIVER.INC *************************************************
; Driver.Inc: Contains definitions and equates for use with
; MS-DOS device drivers.
;
; ***** DEVICE DRIVER RELATED EQUATES *****************************
;
; Device Driver Attribute Word Bit Definitions
AT_CHR    EQU   1000000000000000b     ; character device
AT_IOCTL  EQU   0100000000000000b     ; supports IOCTL calls
AT_BUSY   EQU   0010000000000000b     ; supports Output Til Busy
AT_NOIBM  EQU   0010000000000000b     ; Non-IBM device
AT_NET    EQU   0001000000000000b     ; Network device
AT_OCRM   EQU   0000100000000000b     ; Open/Close Removable Media
AT_GIOCTL EQU   0000000001000000b     ; supports Generic IOCTL
AT_LOGICL EQU   0000000001000000b     ; supports Get/Set Logical
                                      ; ... device
AT_SPECL  EQU   0000000000010000b     ; Special device
AT_CLOCK  EQU   0000000000001000b     ; Clock device
AT_NUL    EQU   0000000000000100b     ; NUL device
AT_STDOUT EQU   0000000000000010b     ; Standard Output device
```

```
AT_STDIN    EQU    0000000000000001b   ; Standard Input device
;
; Device Driver Status Word Bit Definitions
ST_ERROR    EQU    1000000000000000b   ; error has occurred
ST_BUSY     EQU    0000001000000000b   ; device is busy
ST_DONE     EQU    0000000100000000b   ; device is done
;
; Device Driver Error Code Definitions
WRITE_PROTECT          EQU     0
UNKNOWN_UNIT           EQU     1
NOT_READY             EQU     2
UNKNOWN_COMMAND        EQU     3
CRC_ERROR             EQU     4
BAD_REQUEST           EQU     5
SEEK_ERROR            EQU     6
UNKNOWN_MEDIA         EQU     7
SECTOR_NOT_FOUND      EQU     8
OUT_OF_PAPER          EQU     9
WRITE_FAULT           EQU     0Ah
READ_FAULT            EQU     0Bh
GENERAL_FAILURE       EQU     0Ch
INVALID_DISK_CHANGE   EQU     0Fh
;
; Media Check Return Status Codes: Block Devices Only
IsChanged    EQU    -1    ; media has changed
DontKnow     EQU     0    ; unsure if media has changed
NotChanged   EQU     1    ; media has not changed
;
; ***** END OF FILE : DRIVER.INC ********************************
```

The Ubiquitous RAM Disk

The RAM disk program that is presented at the end of this chapter in Listing 6-10 is intentionally simplified. It is still 100 percent functional and may be used on any MS-DOS system running MS-DOS version 2.0 or higher. The RAM disk shown in Listing 6-10 uses 360 Kbytes of your system memory to emulate a standard 5¼-inch floppy drive. Your system should have at least 512 Kbytes of memory if you intend to use the RDISK program as supplied. If you have less memory, or simply want a smaller RAM disk, you can change the default parameters as they appear in the section of RDISK labeled "Description of the RAM Disk".

A more elegant solution to the task of changing the RAM disk's size is to utilize command line parameters. Remember that during the driver's INIT call the parameters *request.bpbtabo* and *request.bpbtabs* form a long pointer to the command line string. This string can be examined for switches or options that can be used to customize the driver. If this method is used, the INIT procedure should perform the check, adjust the appropriate parameters within the BPB, and also adjust the driver's ending segment address.

Once the program has been assembled and linked, rename the file to RDISK.SYS. Now create the file CONFIG.SYS if it does not already exist and put in the command line: *DEVICE = RDISK.SYS*.

The next time you reboot your system, the RAM disk will be installed as the next drive in your system (probably drive C if you don't have a hard disk). No additional operations are required to install the driver.

The RAM disk can be accessed with any MS-DOS function calls or programs, with the exception of the DISKCOPY and DISKCOMP commands. Both of those programs expect a particular type of disk and don't work with RAM disks.

The RDISK driver of Listing 6-10 contains sample code that can be used for debugging or exploring device drivers. It is written to use the BIOS level I/O routines provided in Listing 6-8. RDISK includes the source file BIOSIO.ASM (shown in Listing 6-9). This was required to ensure that the debugging code was located *before* the ending address of the RAM disk. Because library routines are the last piece of code to be linked into an image, it is usually not possible to use library routines with device drivers.

The debugging code can be activated by including in the RDISK file the statement *DEBUG equ 1* or, if using Microsoft MASM version 4 or later, it can be activated with the MASM command line statement */DDEBUG*.

During execution the debugging code uses the number of the driver command to index into the table *message_table*. The entries of *message_table* are the offset addresses of the command name strings, stored in the data area preceding *message_table*. These text strings are then displayed using the hardware-dependent routine *_biosprt*. In RDISK, *_biosprt* has been coded for an EGA with a color monitor, which allows the debugging text to be easily distinguished from normal MS-DOS messages.

Listing 6-8. The BIOSIO.INC Include File

```
; ***** BIOSIO.INC *************************************************
;
; BiosIO.Inc contains equates for using the BIOS level I/O
; routines contained within STDLIB.LIB
;
; @Video macro is for use with the Video functions listed below
;
@Video  MACRO    function
        mov      ah,function
        int      10h
        ENDM
;
```

```
; ***** BIOS I/O Equates ****************************************
;
; These definitions support the use of BIOS level I/O.
;
; BIOS Video Functions (10h) Function Definitions
SET_CURSOR_POS  EQU 02h ;; bh = page, dh => row, dl => column
GET_CURSOR_POS  EQU 03h ;; bh = page; row => dh, column => dl
SET_PAGE        EQU 05h ;; al => page;
SCROLL_UP       EQU 06h ;; al = # lines, bh => attr, ...
SCROLL_DOWN     EQU 07h ;; c(x) = upper left, d(x) = lower right
                        ;; ... (x)h = row, (x)l = column
READ_CHR_ATR    EQU 08h ;; bh = page; attr. => ah, char => al
WRITE_CHR_ATR   EQU 09h ;; bh = page, cx = 1;
                        ;; ... al => char, bl => attr.
WRITE_CHAR      EQU 0Ah ;; bh = page, cx = 1;
                        ;; ... al => char, no attr.
WRITE_TEXT      EQU 0Eh ;; bh = page; al => char;
GET_MODE        EQU 0Fh ;; mode => al. # columns => ah; page =>bh
;
; Video Color Attributes for Use with EGA Boards
BLINK           EQU     10000000b
BRIGHT          EQU     00001000b
BLACK_F         EQU     00h
BLUE_F          EQU     01h
GREEN_F         EQU     02h
CYAN_F          EQU     03h
RED_F           EQU     04h
MAGENTA_F       EQU     05h
YELLOW_F        EQU     06h
WHITE_F         EQU     07h
BLACK_B         EQU     00h
BLUE_B          EQU     10h
GREEN_B         EQU     20h
CYAN_B          EQU     30h
RED_B           EQU     40h
MAGENTA_B       EQU     50h
YELLOW_B        EQU     60h
WHITE_B         EQU     70h
;
; ***** End of BiosIO.Inc ****************************************
```

Listing 6-9. The BIOSIO.ASM Procedure File

```
PAGE    60,132
PUBLIC  _biosprt
; ***** BIOSIO.ASM *************************************************
; BIOSIO: Contains routines for performing BIOS level I/O,
; using PC standard BIOS calls. These routines are intended for
; debugging.
; This file is one of the modules within STDLIB.LIB
;
IFNDEF DEBUG            ; if not included as part of DEBUG
                       ; then must be part of LIBRARY, and
                       ; must include our own definitions.
; ***** INCLUDES ***************************************************
;
INCLUDE biosio.inc     ; BIOS I/O definitions
;
; ***** DGROUP (DATA) COMPONENT SEGMENTS **************************
_DATA   SEGMENT BYTE PUBLIC 'DATA'
_DATA   ENDS
;
DGROUP  GROUP   _DATA
;
;***** PROGRAM CODE STARTS HERE **********************************
;
_TEXT   SEGMENT BYTE PUBLIC 'CODE'
        ASSUME  cs:_TEXT, ds:DGROUP, es:DGROUP, ss:DGROUP
ENDIF
;
; Call Stack Frame Structure Template for _BIOSPRT routine
bpframe STRUC
                dw      ?               ; old bp
                dw      ?               ; return address
        p1      dw      ?               ; parameter #1
        p2      dw      ?               ; parameter #2
        p3      dw      ?               ; parameter #3
        p4      dw      ?               ; parameter #4
bpframe ENDS
prtbase EQU     [bp]
;
; _BIOSPRT
; This routine performs BIOS level screen I/O for use in
; debugging the device driver. This routine uses Video Mode
; 03h: 80x25 color text
;
; "C" Equivalent Call Syntax:    biosprt (string,color)
```

```
;
_biosprt        PROC     NEAR      ; print string using BIOS I/O
        push    bp
        mov     bp,sp
        push    si
        push    cx
        push    bx
;
        @Video  GET_MODE                    ; get current page number
        mov     si,word ptr [prtbase.p1] ; address of string
        mov     bl,byte ptr [prtbase.p2] ; attribute
        mov     cx,1
;
biosprtloop:
        lodsb                               ; read current character
        or      al,al                       ; terminate on NUL
        jz      biosprtdone
        cmp     al,'$'                      ; terminate on "$"
        jz      biosprtdone
        push    ax
        mov     al,020h
        @Video  WRITE_CHR_ATR               ; blank with attribute
        pop     ax
        @Video  WRITE_TEXT                  ; rewrite with TTY
                                            ; ... interpretation
        jmp     biosprtloop                 ; next character
;
biosprtdone:
        pop     bx
        pop     cx
        pop     si
        pop     bp
        ret
_biosprt        ENDP
;
IFNDEF DEBUG            ; if not included as part of DEBUG
_TEXT   ENDS           ; then will require our own ENDS
ENDIF
;
; ***** END OF FILE BIOSIO.ASM ***********************************
;       END                    ; remove leading ";" for library use
```

Listing 6-10. The RDISK Ram Disk Driver

```
PAGE    60,132
; *** RDISK.ASM : MS-DOS DEVICE DRIVER FOR RAM DISK *************
;
; This file contains the source code for a sample MS-DOS device,
; a RAM Disk that emulates a 360K floppy disk.
;
; This driver demonstrates the basic principles of a device
; driver, including one method that can be used for debugging
; device drivers. This driver is installed by inserting the
; following in your CONFIG.SYS file: "DEVICE=RDISK.ASM"
;
; ===== INCLUDE FILES FOR DEVICE DRIVER =========================
;
INCLUDE driver.inc            ; MS-DOS device driver equates
IFDEF   DEBUG
INCLUDE biosio.inc            ; BIOS IO definitions for debugging
ENDIF
;
; ===== EQUATES =================================================
;
; MS-DOS Version limitations
;
CMD_PRE_30       EQU      00Ch   ; highest command before DOS 3.00
CMD_PRE_32       EQU      00Fh   ; highest command before DOS 3.20
CMD_32           EQU      018h   ; highest command at DOS 3.2 & 3.3
;
IFDEF   DEBUG
CR               EQU      0Ah    ; used in debugging messages
LF               EQU      0Dh
ENDIF
;
PAGE
;
; ===== STRUCTURE TEMPLATES =====================================
;
request EQU     es:[di[rv]                    ; request block pointer
;
; Driver GENERIC REQUEST Header Structure
reqhdr  STRUC
        rlength db      ?              ; length of request block
        unit    db      ?              ; unit number for request
        command db      ?              ; command code
        status  dw      ?              ; return status
                db      8 DUP (?)      ; reserved
```

```
reqhdr  ENDS
;
; Driver INITIALIZE REQUEST Header Structure
inithdr STRUC
                db          (type reqhdr) DUP (?)
        units   db      ?       ; number of units
        endadro dw      ?       ; end address offset
        endadrs dw      ?       ; end address segment
        bpbtabo dw      ?       ; ptr. to BPB pointer table
                                ; ... (offset)
        bpbtabs dw      ?       ; ptr. to BPB pointer table
                                ; ... (segment)
        devnum  db      ?       ; device unit number
inithdr ENDS
;
; Driver MEDIA CHECK Command Header Structure
mchkhdr STRUC
                db          (type reqhdr) DUP (?)
        mdb     db      ?       ; media descriptor byte
        change  dw      ?       ; media change status
        volume  dd      ?       ; volume name returned on CHANGED
mchkhdr ENDS
;
; Build BIOS Parameter Block Header Structure
bpbhdr  STRUC
                db          (type reqhdr) DUP (?)
                db      ?       ; media descriptor byte
                dd      ?       ; pointer to FAT/scratch buffer
        bpbptro dw      ?       ; pointer to BPB (offset)
        bpbptrs dw      ?       ; pointer to BPB (segment)
bpbhdr  ENDS
;
; Read/Write Header Structure
iohdr   STRUC
                db          (type reqhdr) DUP (?)
                db      ?       ; media descriptor byte
        bufptr  dd      ?       ; pointer to Transfer Buffer
        count   dw      ?       ; byte/sector count
        start   dw      ?       ; starting sector (block only)
        nuvol   dd      ?       ; pointer to new volume name
iohdr   ENDS
;
; BIOS Parameter Block Structure
bpbstrc STRUC
        bps     dw      ?       ; bytes per sector
        spau    db      ?       ; sectors per allocation unit
```

continued

341

Listing 6-10. *continued*

```
          nrs     dw      ?        ; number of reserved sectors
          nft     db      ?        ; number of FAT tables
          nde     dw      ?        ; number of directory entries
          nls     dw      ?        ; number of logical sectors
          md      db      ?        ; media descriptor
          nfs     dw      ?        ; number of FAT sectors
bpbstrc ENDS
;
PAGE
;
; ===== DRIVER CODE STARTS HERE ===================================
;
_TEXT   SEGMENT BYTE PUBLIC 'CODE'
        ASSUME  CS:_TEXT, DS:_TEXT, ES:NOTHING
        ORG     0
ORIGIN  EQU     $
;
; ===== DEVICE DRIVER HEADER ======================================
;
          dw      -1,-1               ; next device pointer
          dw      AT_IOCTL OR AT_OCRM OR AT_NET
          dw      offset STRATEGY    ; offset to STRATEGY routine
          dw      offset INTERRUPT   ; offset to INTERRUPT routine
          db      1,'CDEVICE..       ; number of units/name
;
; ===== COMMAND PROCESSING JUMP TABLE =========================
;
JUMPTAB LABEL   WORD
          dw      offset INIT          ; 0--INITialization
          dw      offset MEDIA_CHECK   ; 1--MEDIA check
          dw      offset BUILD_BPB     ; 2--build BIOS parameter
                                       ;     block
          dw      offset IOCTL_INPUT   ; 3--IO control input
          dw      offset READ          ; 4--input from device
          dw      offset READ_NOWAIT   ; 5--nondestructive input
                                       ;     no-wait
          dw      offset INPUT_STATUS  ; 6--input status
          dw      offset INPUT_FLUSH   ; 7--flush input queue
          dw      offset WRITE         ; 8--output to device
          dw      offset WRITE_VERIFY  ; 9--output with verify
          dw      offset OUTPUT_STATUS ; A--output status
          dw      offset OUTPUT_FLUSH  ; B--flush output queue
          dw      offset IOCTL_OUTPUT  ; C--IO control output
          dw      offset DEVICE_OPEN   ; D--open a device
          dw      offset DEVICE_CLOSE  ; E--close a device
```

```
        dw        offset REMOVABLE     ; F--is the media removable
        dw        offset NO_COMMAND    ; 10
        dw        offset NO_COMMAND    ; 11
        dw        offset NO_COMMAND    ; 12
        dw        offset GENERIC_IOCTL ; 13--generic IOCTL request
        dw        offset NO_COMMAND    ; 14
        dw        offset NO_COMMAND    ; 15
        dw        offset NO_COMMAND    ; 16
        dw        offset GET_LOGICAL   ; 17--get logical device
        dw        offset SET_LOGICAL   ; 18--set logical device
;
; ===== DRIVER COMMAND DATA STORAGE ==============================
;
req_ptr dd        ?                    ; request block pointer
max_cmd db        CMD_PRE_30           ; highest command allowed
;
save_ss dw        ?                    ; entry stack segment value
save_sp dw        ?                    ; entry stack pointer value
;
PAGE
;
; ===== STRATEGY ENTRY POINT ====================================
;
STRATEGY          PROC    FAR
        mov       cs:word ptr [req_ptr],bx
        mov       cs:word ptr [req_ptr+2],es
        ret
strategy          ENDP
;
; ===== INTERRUPT ENTRY POINT ===================================
;
INTERRUPT         PROC    FAR
        push      ax                   ; save all working registers
        push      cx
        push      dx
        push      bx
        push      bp
        push      si
        push      di
        push      ds
        push      es
;
        push      cs                   ; establish local data segment
        pop       ds
;
        mov       word ptr save_ss,ss  ; save entry values of SS:SP
```

continued

Listing 6-10. *continued*

```
        mov     word ptr save_sp,sp
;
        mov     bx,cs               ; establish local stack
        mov     ax,offset local_stack - 2
        mov     ss,bx
        mov     sp,ax
;
        les     di,[req_ptr]        ; obtain request block pointer
        mov     bl,request.command  ; obtain driver command code
;
; preset a command error in case the command is unrecognized
        mov     ax,(ST_ERROR OR UNKNOWN_COMMAND)
        cmp     bl,[max_cmd]        ; is the command supported?
        ja      exit                ; no - reject it
;
; invoke the designated command
; each handler is called with CS & DS set to the driver segment,
; and ES:DI set to point to the request block each handler must
; return with its status in the AX register
        xor     bh,bh               ; adjust command to be table index
        shl     bx,1
IFDEF   DEBUG
        call    print_command   ; print name of invoked command
ENDIF
        call    word ptr jumptab[bx]    ; invoke command
;
; transfer status from AX register to request block STATUS word
exit:   push    cs                      ; establish local data segment
        pop     ds
;
        les     di,[req]ptr]            ; obtain request block pointer
        or      ax,ST_DONE              ; always set done bit
        mov     request.status,ax       ; store return status
;
        mov     ss,word ptr save_ss     ; restore entry values
                                        ; ... of SS:SP
        mov     sp,word ptr save_sp
;
        pop     es                      ; restore context
        pop     ds
        pop     di
        pop     si
        pop     bp
        pop     bx
        pop     dx
```

```
            pop     cx
            pop     ax
            ret
interrupt       ENDP
;
PAGE
;
; ===== DRIVER FUNCTION PROCESSING =================================
;
NO_COMMAND      PROC    NEAR        ; unimplemented command
            ret                     ; return with preset error code
NO_COMMAND      ENDP
;
MEDIA_CHECK     PROC    NEAR        ; 1--MEDIA check
            mov     request.change,NotChanged
            xor     ax,ax
            ret
MEDIA_CHECK     ENDP
;
BUILD_BPB       PROC    NEAR        ; 2--build BIOS parameter block
            mov     request.bpbptro,offset bpb
            mov     request.bpbptrs,cs
            xor     ax,ax
            ret
BUILD_BPB       ENDP
;
IOCTL_INPUT     PROC    NEAR        ; 3--IO control input
            xor     ax,ax
            ret
IOCTL_INPUT     ENDP
;
READ            PROC    NEAR        ; 4--input from device
            call    verify          ; verify & set up transfer params
            jc      rd_err          ; exit on error
            les     di,request.bufptr ; destination is buffer
            rep     movsw           ; transfer
            xor     ax,ax           ; no errors
rd_err: ret
READ            ENDP
;
READ_NOWAIT     PROC    NEAR        ; 5--nondestructive input
                                    ; ... no-wait
            xor     ax,ax
            ret
READ_NOWAIT     ENDP
;
```

continued

Listing 6-10. *continued*

```
INPUT_STATUS      PROC      NEAR ; 6--input status
        xor       ax,ax
        ret
INPUT_STATUS      ENDP
;
INPUT_FLUSH       PROC      NEAR ; 7--flush input queue
        xor       ax,ax
        ret
INPUT_FLUSH       ENDP
;
WRITE             PROC      NEAR ; 8--output to device
        call      verify         ; verify & set up transfer params
        jc        wr_err         ; exit on error
        push      ds             ; save "sector" segment
        lds       si,request.bufptr ; source is buffer
        pop       es             ; destination is "disk"
        xor       di,di          ; offset 0
        rep       movsw          ; transfer
        xor       ax,ax          ; no errors
wr_err: ret
WRITE             ENDP
;
WRITE_VERIFY      PROC      NEAR ; 9--output with verify
        call      write
        ret
WRITE_VERIFY      ENDP
;
OUTPUT_STATUS     PROC      NEAR ; A--output status
        xor       ax,ax
        ret
OUTPUT_STATUS     ENDP
;
OUTPUT_FLUSH      PROC      NEAR ; B--flush output queue
        xor       ax,ax
        ret
OUTPUT_FLUSH      ENDP
;
IOCTL_OUTPUT      PROC      NEAR ; C--IO control output
        xor       ax,ax
        ret
IOCTL_OUTPUT      ENDP
;
DEVICE_OPEN       PROC      NEAR ; D--open a device
        xor       ax,ax
        ret
```

```
DEVICE_OPEN     ENDP
;
DEVICE_CLOSE    PROC    NEAR ; E--close a device
        xor     ax,ax
        ret
DEVICE_CLOSE    ENDP
;
REMOVABLE       PROC    NEAR ; F--is the media removable?
        mov     ax,ST_BUSY   ; media is NOT removable
        ret
REMOVABLE       ENDP
;
GENERIC_IOCTL   PROC    NEAR ; 13--generic IOCTL request
        xor     ax,ax
        ret
GENERIC_IOCTL   ENDP
;
GET_LOGICAL     PROC    NEAR ; 17--get logical device
        xor     ax,ax
        ret
GET_LOGICAL     ENDP
;
SET_LOGICAL     PROC    NEAR ; 18--set logical device
        xor     ax,ax
        ret
SET_LOGICAL     ENDP
;
PAGE
; ----- RAM DISK PROCESSING SUBROUTINES ------------------------
; Called to process parameters of an I/O request
; Enter with ES:DI pointing to request block structure
;       Verify "sector" is within range
;       Transform "sector" into segment & offset
;       Clip count to prevent DTA "wraparound"
; Return with:  DS:SI pointing to RAM Disk Address
;               ES:DI pointing to request block
;               CX contains transfer count in words
;
verify  PROC    NEAR
; verify starting & ending sectors - sectors
; are indexed 0 through n
        mov     cx,request.start
        cmp     cx,bpb.nls   ; start sector vs. # logical
                             ; ... sectors
        jae     out_of_range
        add     cx,request.count ; find ending sector
```

continued

Listing 6-10. *continued*

```
        dec     cx
        cmp     cx,bpb.nls      ; end sector vs. # logical
                                ; ... sectors
        jb      in_range        ; continue if in range
; specified sectors are not contained on the disk
out_of_range:
        mov     ax,ST_ERROR OR SECTOR_NOT_FOUND
        mov     request.count,0 ; nothing transferred
        stc                     ; return with error
        ret
; calculate starting segment address of the "sector"
in_range:
        mov     ax,bpb.bps      ; obtain bytes per sector
        mov     cl,4            ; divide by 16 to get
                                ; ... paragraphs
        shr     ax,cl
        mul     request.start   ; paragraph offset relative
                                ; ... to disk
        add     ax,RPARA        ; paragraph offset relative
                                ; ... to CS
        mov     dx,cs
        add     ax,dx           ; absolute paragraph offset
        mov     si,ax           ; store segment in SI for now
; calculate and trim transfer count to proper values
        mov     ax,bpb.bps      ; sector size in bytes
        mul     request.count   ; transfer count in bytes
        cmp     dx,0            ; check for overflow
        jne     out_of_range
; clip transfer count in AX if required to prevent wraparound
        mov     cx,word ptr request.bufptr
        cmp     cx,0            ; offset of 0 is O.K.
        je      set_size
        neg     cx              ; 64K - buffer offset = remainder
        cmp     cx,ax           ; is remainder larger than count?
        jae     set_size        ; if yes then is O.K.
        mov     ax,cx           ; if no then only transfer
                                ; ... remainder
; set number of sectors transferred and transfer count
set_size:
        mov     cx,ax           ; transfer count
        shr     cx,1            ; converted transfer count to words
        div     bpb.bps         ; (DX was 0) sector count
        mov     request.count,ax ; save transfer count
; set DS:SI to point to memory address
        mov     ds,si
```

```
        xor     si,si
; set transfer direction & return without error
        cld
        clc
        ret
verify  ENDP
;
IFDEF   DEBUG
INCLUDE biosio.asm              ; include BIOS IO program code
PAGE
;
; ***** DEBUGGING DATA & CODE ***************************************
;
; Debug Message Storage
;
NO_COMMAND_msg          db      'NO COMMAND',CR,LF,'$'
INIT_msg                db      'INITialization',CR,LF,'$'
MEDIA_CHECK_msg         db      'MEDIA check',CR,LF,'$'
BUILD_BPB_msg           db      'Build BIOS Parameter Block'
                        db      CR,LF,'$'
IOCTL_INPUT_msg         db      'IO Control Input',CR,LF,'$'
READ_msg                db      'Input from device',CR,LF,'$'
READ_NOWAIT_msg         db      'Nondestructive Input no-wait'
                        db      CR,LF,'$'
INPUT_STATUS_msg        db      'Input Status',CR,LF,'$'
INPUT_FLUSH_msg         db      'Flush Input queue',CR,LF,'$'
WRITE_msg               db      'Output to device',CR,LF,'$'
WRITE_VERIFY_msg        db      'Output with verify',CR,LF,'$'
OUTPUT_STATUS_msg       db      'Output status',CR,LF,'$'
OUTPUT_FLUSH_msg        db      'Flush Output queue',CR,LF,'$'
IOCTL_OUTPUT_msg        db      'IO Control Output',CR,LF,'$'
DEVICE_OPEN_msg         db      'Open a device',CR,LF,'$'
DEVICE_CLOSE_msg        db      'Close a device',CR,LF,'$'
REMOVABLE_msg           db      'Is media removable',CR,LF,'$'
GENERIC_IOCTL_msg       db      'Generic IOCTL Request',CR,LF,'$'
GET_LOGICAL_msg         db      'Get Logical Device',CR,LF,'$'
SET_LOGICAL_msg         db      'Set Logical Device',CR,LF,'$'
;
PAGE
;
; ===== DEBUG MESSAGES ADDRESS TABLE ============================
;
message_table   LABEL   WORD
        dw      offset INIT_msg             ; 0--INITialization
        dw      offset MEDIA_CHECK_msg      ; 1--MEDIA check
        dw      offset BUILD_BPB_msg        ; 2--build BIOS parameter
```

continued

349

Listing 6-10. *continued*

```
                                         ;      block
        dw       offset IOCTL_INPUT_msg   ; 3--IO control input
        dw       offset READ_msg          ; 4--input from device
        dw       offset READ_NOWAIT_msg   ; 5--nondestructive
                                         ;    input no-wait
        dw       offset INPUT_STATUS_msg  ; 6--input status
        dw       offset INPUT_FLUSH_msg   ; 7--flush input queue
        dw       offset WRITE_msg         ; 8--output to device
        dw       offset WRITE_VERIFY_msg  ; 9--output with verify
        dw       offset OUTPUT_STATUS_msg ; A--output status
        dw       offset OUTPUT_FLUSH_msg  ; B--flush output queue
        dw       offset IOCTL_OUTPUT_msg  ; C--IO control output
        dw       offset DEVICE_OPEN_msg   ; D--open a device
        dw       offset DEVICE_CLOSE_msg  ; E--close a device
        dw       offset REMOVABLE_msg     ; F--is the media
                                         ;    removable?
        dw       offset NO_COMMAND_msg    ; 10
        dw       offset NO_COMMAND_msg    ; 11
        dw       offset NO_COMMAND_msg    ; 12
        dw       offset GENERIC_IOCTL_msg ; 13--generic IOCTL
                                         ;       request
        dw       offset NO_COMMAND_msg    ; 14
        dw       offset NO_COMMAND_msg    ; 15
        dw       offset NO_COMMAND_msg    ; 16
        dw       offset GET_LOGICAL_msg   ; 17--get logical device
        dw       offset SET_LOGICAL_msg   ; 18--set logical device
;
PAGE
; PRINT_COMMAND
;
; This routine invokes the BIOS print routine (_biosprt) with
; the address of a string name of the driver command that was
; just called. This routine is entered with the driver
; code * 2 in the BX register. Save all registers that will
; be used.
;
print_command   PROC    NEAR
        push     ax                       ; save AX register
        mov      ax,BLUE_F OR BRIGHT OR BLACK_B ; set color
        push     ax
        mov      ax,word ptr message_table[bx]  ; get string
                                         ; ... address
        push     ax                       ; and pass it
        call     _biosprt                 ; call BIOS print routine
        add      sp,4                     ; clean up & exit
```

```
            pop     ax
            ret
print_command   ENDP
ENDIF
;
PAGE
;
; ***** LOCAL STACK & END OF OPERATIONAL DRIVER *****************
;
            db      32 DUP ('stack   ')     ; local processing stack
local_stack     EQU     $                   ; depth 256 bytes
;
bpb_tab dw      offset  bpb                 ; pointer to BPB (stored
                                            ; ... outside)
LAST_USED   EQU     $                       ; last memory location
                                            ; ... used

;
; ***** DEFAULT DESCRIPTION OF THE RAM DISK **********************
;
; Parameters for a 5-1/4" Double side Double density 9 sectored
; disk
;
MTYPE   EQU     0FDh            ; media descriptor byte
TRACKS  EQU     40              ; 40 tracks
SECTORS EQU     9               ; 9 sectors/track
DSIZE   EQU     512             ; 512 bytes/sector
SIDES   EQU     2               ; 2 sides/disk
;
FSECS   EQU     2               ; # sectors/FAT
DIREN   EQU     112             ; # directory entries
DSECS   EQU     7               ; 7 directory sectors
CLSIZ   EQU     2               ; sectors/cluster
;
STOTAL  EQU     TRACKS*SECTORS*SIDES ; total number of sectors
PTOTAL  EQU     (DSIZE/16)*STOTAL    ; total number of paragraphs
;
; ***** BEGINNING OF RAM DISK DATA AREA *************************
;
; Paragraph Align the RAM Disk
;
        IF      ($-ORIGIN) mod 16
        ORG     ($-ORIGIN) + 16 - (($-ORIGIN) mod 16)
        ENDIF
RDISK   LABEL   BYTE                    ; start of RAM Disk
RPARA   EQU     ($-ORIGIN) / 16         ; code size in paragraphs
;
```

continued

Listing 6-10. *continued*

```
; ----- BIOS Parameter Block & Pointer --------------------------
        jmp     near ptr boot           ; 3 byte jump
        db      'IBM  3.1'              ; 8 byte name & version
;
; default BPB
bpb     bpbstrc <DSIZE,CLSIZ,1,2,DIREN,STOTAL,MTYPE,FSECS>
; compatibility information
        dw      SECTORS                 ; # sectors/track
        dw      SIDES                   ; # head
        dw      0                       ; # hidden sectors
boot:
        db      (DSIZE-30) DUP (?)       ; remainder of boot
                                        ; ... sector
; ----- FAT Entries ---------------------------------------------
FAT_1   db      MTYPE,0FFh,0FFh         ; 1st two FAT entries
        db      (DSIZE-3) DUP (0)        ; zero remainder of FAT
        db      ((FSECS-1) * DSIZE) DUP (0)
FAT_2   db      MTYPE,0FFh,0FFh         ; 1st two FAT entries
        db      (DSIZE-3) DUP (0)        ; zero remainder of FAT
        db      ((FSECS-1) * DSIZE) DUP (0)
; ----- Directory Sectors ***************************************
DIREC   db      'RAM_DISK    '          ; volume name (11 bytes)
        db      08h                     ; VID
        db      10 DUP (?)              ; reserved
        dw      0600h                   ; time 12:00:00 noon
        dw      021h                    ; data Jan 1, 1980
        dw      0                       ; start cluster 0
        dd      0                       ; file size 0
        db      (DSIZE-32) DUP (0)       ; zero remainder of
                                        ; ... directory
        db      ((DSECS-1) * DSIZE) DUP (0)
BUFFER  LABEL   BYTE                    ; beginning of data
                                        ; ... storage
;
; ***** INITIALIZATION CODE *************************************
;
; ===== INCLUDE FILES FOR INITIALIZATION =======================
;
INCLUDE stdmac.inc          ; DOS function allowed during init
;
; ===== INITIALIZATION DATA ====================================
;
$signon db      'RAM DISK Driver Version 1.00 Installed: Drive '
$desig  db      'A'
$crlf   db      0Dh,0Ah,'$'
```

```
;
; ===== INITIALIZATION CODE STARTS HERE =========================
;
INIT    PROC    NEAR                    ; 0--INITialization
;
; set end address, units, and pointer to BPB table
        mov     request.endadro,0       ; end of driver address
        mov     request.endadrs,cs
        add     request.endadrs,(RPARA+PTOTAL)  ; ending segment
        mov     request.units,1
        mov     request.bpbtabo,offset bpb_tab
        mov     request.bpbtabs,cs
        mov     al,$desig               ; update drive
        add     al,request.devnum       ; designation
        mov     $desig,al               ; letter
;
; display sign-on message
        @DisStr $signon
;
; update "max_cmd" from MS-DOS Version number
        @GetDOSVersion                  ; get the DOS version number
        cmp     al,3                    ; is this DOS 3.00 or higher?
        jb      init_done               ; no - return from init
        mov     [max_cmd],CMD_PRE_32 ; enable DOS 3.00 commands
        cmp     ah,2                    ; is this DOS 3.20 or higher?
        jb      init_done               ; no - return from init
        mov     [max_cmd],CMD_32 ; enable DOS 3.20 commands
;
init_done:
        xor     ax,ax                   ; no problems
        ret
INIT    ENDP
;
; ***** END OF DRIVER : END OF FILE ******************************
;
_TEXT   ENDS
        END
```

Summary

You're now ready to write and install device drivers on your own. Follow our guidelines and the information in the *DOS Programmer's Reference Manual* when you are presented with technical questions. You should have very few problems.

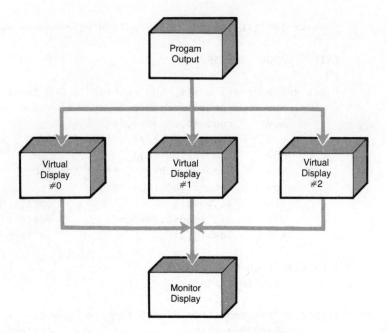

Figure 6-8. Virtual screen device driver.

Some ideas for useful device drivers are a driver for a dot matrix printer that accepts graphics commands (such as *draw line*) and converts them to the format required by the printer driver or a terminal driver (see Figure 6-8) that supports virtual screens. The terminal driver can have a number of memory buffers that contain copies of screen information. By sending commands to the driver's IOCTL channel, the driver can be told which memory buffer to update and which to display on the screen. Programs using this driver have a type of windowing capability. Initially, care must be taken not to use the standard MS-DOS console I/O functions, which know nothing of the virtual windowed device. If the driver is successful, you can use it to replace the existing console driver.

The list of ideas for device drivers is endless. You have probably already thought of a few of your own that you would like to implement. With a little patience and care, there's no reason why you can't, so go to it!

Using Expanded Memory

THE incorporation of the expanded memory specification in MS-DOS 4.0 has legitimized this standard as the technique for increasing memory in all MS-DOS systems. Despite the ever-growing speed and sophistication of DOS-based, IBM-compatible personal computers, their ultimate hardware and software performance has been subject to constraints imposed by the system design and 8088 processor architecture embedded within the original IBM Personal Computer. Until recently, one such limit, the 640K barrier, has been a steady source of frustration to both users and programmers of MS-DOS systems. Signifying the maximum amount of user RAM supported by MS-DOS, the 640K memory limit has loomed as a persistent obstacle to the relentless drive to develop and employ more capable and potent software solutions.

Users demanding sophisticated databases, spreadsheets, graphical interfaces, and resident utilities want to use these features simultaneously under the control of a multitasking windowing system. Developers have risen to meet this challenge armed with resident debuggers, on-line manuals, and user interface toolkits. Both groups had struggled forward under the 640K ceiling with no certain solution to the DOS memory crunch.

The entire PC industry has now cooperated to devise a workable solution to MS-DOS's memory limitations with a memory expansion scheme called *expanded memory,* which provides MS-DOS programs with access to a maximum of 32 megabytes of RAM memory beyond the 640K bytes managed by MS-DOS. Unfortunately, expanded memory cannot be used by MS-DOS applications automatically. Each program must be specifically written to recognize and use it. While the process of recognizing and using expanded memory is not automatic, it is not particularly difficult or mysterious. This chapter will provide you with the background and knowledge you need to add this powerful tool to your own base of programming expertise.

The performance and flexibility demands that PC users place on software almost dictate that programs directly manipulate the PC hardware, bypassing DOS and the BIOS, to wring maximum potential out of the PC family hardware. Building such programs is a laborious task for developers, who not only must master the hardware intricacies of the PC and its various I/O adapter boards, but also must take special care to accommodate the hardware diversity of the installed base of PC-compatible systems.

Fortunately, developers writing applications that use expanded memory need not submerge themselves in the obscure hardware details of expanded memory boards to obtain high performance and flexibility. Rather, complete access to expanded memory is provided by well-documented, hardware-independent programming interfaces that have been developed and supported by the personal computer industry's premier vendors of hardware and software.

The best-known of these programming interfaces is the *Lotus/Intel/Microsoft Expanded Memory Specification* (LIM EMS). An impressive variety of commercially available system and application software exploits LIM EMS expanded memory to relieve DOS memory constraints. Microsoft Windows 2.0 and Quarterdeck Office Systems DESQView utilize expanded memory to help multitask several applications. Lotus 1-2-3 and Symphony, Microsoft Excel, Autodesk AutoCAD, and a host of other popular software applications all employ expanded memory to provide users with the means to solve larger and more complex real-world problems. PC-DOS and MS-DOS 4.0 include drivers that support the LIM EMS standard as part of the operating system, although early releases of DOS 4.0 seemed not to support EMS function 19h, the Get/Set Handle Attribute function, and early system-supplied drivers were buggy. PC-DOS and MS-DOS 4.0 use LIM EMS 4.0 memory to buffer sectors from open files (controlled by the BUFFERS parameter in the CONFIG.SYS file) and to check directory entries (which the FASTOPEN command supplied with DOS 3.3 and above does). Early releases of DOS 4.0 seem not to use LIM EMS 4.0 multitasking features in any way. (Note that throughout this chapter whenever we refer to MS-DOS version 4.0, we are also including PC-DOS 4.0, unless specifically stated otherwise.)

This chapter will conduct an in-depth survey of the techniques needed to exploit expanded memory in your own programming projects. Expanded memory can be a potent, multifaceted tool empowering your programs to handle bigger problems, to quickly access large databases customarily stored on disk, to share data with other programs, or to reduce the amount of DOS memory they require.

You may be surprised to learn that your computer does not even need any special hardware or add-on memory boards for you to write, test, and run expanded memory applications. This chapter explains how expanded memory emulation software can provide you with a low-cost tool for developing expanded memory applications.

You will learn how expanded memory fits into the hardware and software architecture of PC-compatible computers. You will also learn the programming conventions and protocols that are necessary in order to use expanded memory without interfering with other applications, including:

- How to detect when expanded memory is present on a computer and, if so, how much is installed.

- How to allocate, deallocate, and manipulate up to 32 megabytes of expanded memory, using the *Expanded Memory Manager's int 67h interface* defined by the Lotus/Intel/Microsoft Expanded Memory Specification.

- How to exploit the functional and ease-of-use enhancements incorporated in the most recent version (4.0) of the LIM EMS.

- How to interpret and respond to error conditions returned by the expanded memory subsystem.

In this chapter we'll provide reference material detailing the specific interrupt mechanism and register usage conventions required to use the LIM EMS programming interface. We'll also help you determine the types of data structures that are best suited for storage in expanded memory.

We will review the history and motivation behind the Lotus/Intel/Microsoft Expanded Memory Specification and the AST/Quadram/Ashton-Tate Enhanced Expanded Memory Specification (AQA EEMS). You will see how various features of these standards evolved to help overcome DOS memory restrictions for nearly every type of program, including device drivers, terminate-and-stay-resident utilities, and operating system enhancements. This chapter will explore the technical and compatibility considerations relevant to each expanded memory specification, including EMS 4.0 support built-into MS-DOS 4.0, so that applications you write will be compatible with the widest variety of expanded memory implementations.

To get you started programming for expanded memory, this chapter includes a collection of low-level interface routines, written in Microsoft C version 5.0, and a sample application. The sample application, consisting of two complete, working programs, gives you a start-to-finish demonstration of the key LIM EMS programming techniques presented in the chapter. Some of the advanced techniques illustrated by the application include data sharing between two programs and the use of expanded memory inside an interrupt service routine.

We begin our exploration of memory expansion options by examining the history and events in the PC-compatible personal computer industry that spawned its development and use.

A History Lesson

In 1981, the typical personal computer could address no more than 64 kilobytes of main storage. Serious programmers of these machines spent an inordinate amount of time squeezing out those last few bytes, just to shoehorn in one extra feature. The introduction of the IBM Personal Computer, with RAM storage that was an order of magnitude more than its predecessors, seemed to offer the promise of long-term relief from the memory crunch.

Barely three years later, the computer memory analog of Parkinson's Law (work expands to fit the time available in which to do it) had done to the IBM PC what it had done to every previous generation of computers. Today, burgeoning spreadsheets, integrated applications, networks, and a flood of resident utilities render the IBM PC's memory space as cramped and limited as its ancestors'.

No perfect solution to the RAM limit exists. Even though the Intel 8088 microprocessor in the IBM PC supports a 1-Mbyte address space, the 384

Kbytes of the PC's address space between 640K and the 1-Mbyte addressing limit are reserved for video adapter buffers, system and BASIC ROM, and other I/O card ROM-BIOS modules. New PC-DOS applications are trapped within the bounds of the 640-Kbyte user RAM with which the IBM PC family was born.

One traditional solution to memory problems, the overlay, is frequently used by PC applications whose code components can be layered appropriately. For other types of applications, such as spreadsheets, this approach is not completely effective. The storage requirements for this type of application are driven primarily by the potentially unlimited size of their central data structures, rather than the size of their executable code.

LIM EMS

In the absence of a universal solution, Lotus Development Corporation, Intel Corporation, and Microsoft Corporation collaborated to produce a scheme allowing individual applications to work around the 640K RAM limit imposed by the IBM PC implementation of DOS. The result is called the Lotus/Intel/Microsoft Expanded Memory Specification, or LIM EMS. Intel produced a board to hold this memory, Lotus adapted their spreadsheet to use the memory, and Microsoft made sure that the specification would be responsive to the requirements of the operating system enhancements it was working on.

What LIM EMS actually defines is a new implementation of a popular, ancient maneuver around the address space crunch: memory-bank switching. In short, memory-bank switching schemes work by using electronic switches (in the form of software-addressable I/O ports) to dynamically alter how physical blocks of memory are mapped into part of the processor's address space. In this way, a computer system may access more bytes of physical memory than were provided for by its processor's memory architecture, though not all the bytes of physical memory may be accessed by a program at any given instant.

As a technical solution to the memory space problem, the LIM EMS is not all that more exciting or effective than the bank-switching schemes present in many machines built during the 6502 and 8080 microprocessor era. What the LIM EMS does have is the sponsorship of several market leaders in the PC industry and documentation that is readily available to software developers, free for the asking. This circumstance is something of a rarity these days, when major software vendors seem to focus their efforts selling application-building toolkits to developers at costs of $500 to $3000.

Until the release of PC-DOS version 4.0, IBM had remained neutral toward the LIM EMS, choosing to promote the adoption of Operating System/2 by application developers as a more permanent solution to the memory problem. While OS/2 definitely represents a longer-term solution, for most MS-DOS users the relative lateness of its introduction and its lack of total upward compatibility with much of the enormous existing base of PC-compatible hardware and software has limited its immediate potential as a solution.

Because the LIM EMS is a practical, immediately available, and upwardly compatible solution for the entire existing base of systems running MS-DOS, it has become a commercially and technically successful way for a DOS program to break the 640-Kbyte barrier. In fact, several industry observers have speculated that the effectiveness of the LIM EMS solution may actually extend the useful life of MS-DOS based systems for several years beyond the point of their supposed technological obsolescence.

LIM EMS 3.2

The first widely supported version of the LIM EMS, numbered 3.2, was published in September 1985. It defined a memory expansion protocol providing appropriately programmed applications with up to 8 megabytes of bank-switched memory for data or code storage. The specification included facilities that allow several active applications to use this memory concurrently without mutual interference.

The ability for multiple programs using expanded memory to coexist particularly benefits developers of terminate-and-stay-resident programs (TSRs) in at least two ways. First, a TSR program may store portions of its data or code in expanded memory, reducing the amount of conventional memory it occupies. Second, conflicts between TSRs and other programs over the use of expanded memory may be avoided, since the LIM EMS defines specific programming conventions that prevent such conflicts from occurring.

LIM EMS 3.2 Concepts and Terminology

The basic LIM EMS 3.2 scheme works as follows:

1. Up to 8 megabytes of RAM, on one or more memory cards, can be installed in a machine. Unlike the garden variety memory cards, storage on these cards is divided into 16 kilobyte *pages*. Expanded memory is not directly addressable by DOS applications, since it does not appear in the lower 640K of the PC's address space.

2. These memory cards also incorporate a set of mapping registers that are manipulated under software control to *map* any of the 16-Kbyte pages on the expanded memory card(s) into any of four 16-Kbyte slots in a 64-Kbyte portion of the PC's address space called the *page frame*. The page frame is located somewhere in the PC's reserved address space, above the 640K line, and below the 1-megabyte addressing limit of the 8086/8. Each slot in the page frame is called a *physical page* and is identified by a number, 0–3. The page frame constitutes a window through which a suitably written program can access the entire memory capacity of the expanded memory card(s). The process of altering the board's mapping registers to make an expanded memory page available to a program is called *page mapping*.

3. Control of the expanded memory system, including the page mapping process, is performed by a software component called the *Expanded Memory Manager*, or EMM, that is supplied by the expanded memory board manufacturer. Much as DOS and the BIOS provide a programming

interface between an application and the underlying computer system's hardware, the EMM provides a programming interface between an application and the underlying expanded memory system. The EMM is loaded into memory as a DOS character device driver at boot time, and communicates with programs via software interrupt 67h, using a parameter-passing mechanism comparable to DOS's int 21h interface.

4. Upon program request, the EMM allocates a set of one or more 16-Kbyte *logical pages* to the program. It also allocates a *handle* that the program uses, in subsequent expanded memory service requests to the EMM, to identify the set of expanded memory pages to be operated upon. In much the same way that DOS file handles are used by the operating system to keep track of each program's open files, expanded memory handles are used by the EMM to keep track of each program's set of active expanded memory pages. The format of the handle is unspecified, except for the fact that a handle is a 16-bit quantity. Logical page numbers associated with a handle are numbered zero relative, up to one less than the number of pages requested by the program.

5. When requesting a service from the EMM, the program identifies the particular 16K page of expanded memory it wishes to use by specifying a combination of a handle and a logical page number.

   Note: Earlier versions of the specification used the term *process ID*, rather than the term *handle*, to refer to a set of expanded memory pages. The designers of the LIM EMS originally assumed that each program would allocate only one set of pages, implying a one-to-one correspondence between programs and process IDs. In practice though, many programs requested more than one set of expanded memory pages. As you will see later, this is a legal and useful programming technique. However, the fact that one program could have more than one EMS process ID confused many developers, thus prompting the terminology change.

6. The EMM for a LIM EMS 3.2 expanded memory system provides 14 user-callable functions (plus 2 reserved functions) that applications use to obtain information about and manipulate expanded memory pages.

Enhanced Expanded Memory Specification

A second computer industry collaboration soon formed to promote an Enhanced Expanded Memory Specification. The result of this effort, which was sponsored by AST Research, Quadram, and Ashton-Tate Corporation, was an upwardly compatible (with the LIM EMS 3.2) expanded memory scheme called the AQA EEMS.

The Window Size Limitation
A major limitation of the LIM 3.2 scheme, from the AQA point of view, was the paltry 64-Kbyte page frame size. Through this small window into expanded memory, a program could access only 4 of the 16-Kbyte expanded memory pages

out of the 512 possible pages (8 megabytes) supported by the specification. The AQA EEMS allowed a program to access, in theory at least, up to sixty-four 16-Kbyte pages of expanded memory at any given time. A quick trip to the calculator (binary thinkers can shift bits) reveals that this works out to 1 megabyte of mappable memory! But wait, you ask, what about all the video buffers and the ROM-BIOS in the space above 640K, not to mention DOS and applications in the space below 640K? Are these summarily dealt with in a wink of the mapping registers?

No. The reality that EEMS deals with is the same one that the LIM EMS faces; the AQA EEMS just handles that reality more boldly. The LIM EMS 3.2 is an example of a conservative, worst-case design philosophy. For example, the designers calculated that a PC with an Enhanced Graphics Adapter (EGA) and a network card containing a ROM might have only 64K of unreserved, unused address space above 640K. DOS was already firmly in control of the address space below 640 Kbytes. Thus, LIM EMS 3.2's designers were left with a 64-Kbyte page frame.

AQA's designers evaluated the problem from a different perspective. They reasoned that a standard PC with a CGA or MDA had enough address space available above 640K to map in at least 12 EMS pages at a time. And Quarterdeck Office Systems, ceding nothing to DOS, had developed an operating system extender called DESQView that could swap programs in and out of the lower 640K. If DESQView were able to substitute a nearly instantaneous page mapping operation for the comparatively slow memory swapping process, its potential as a high-performance multitasking system for the IBM PC would be greatly enhanced.

AST designed and built a board capable of mapping memory throughout the 1-Mbyte address space, thus providing DESQView with the mechanism necessary to achieve rapid switching among several programs. Practical limitations, however, prevent remapping of those portions of the address space occupied by the ROM-BIOS, Display Adapter, and permanent planar board memory needed to boot the system.

The EEMS scheme enjoyed only limited market success. A combination of product marketing confusion generated by AST and Quadram, and lackadaisical support for its functional extensions by other major PC software developers limited its growth as a major alternative standard to the LIM EMS. Developers were glad that EEMS was at least upwardly compatible with LIM EMS, but many of them apparently did not think that the extensions it offered were worth pursuing if the extensions entailed a loss of downward compatibility with the LIM scheme.

LIM EMS 4.0

Regardless of the marketing results, someone in the LIM camp must have found things to like about the AQA EEMS. As Microsoft's Windows 2.0 product neared release (and the amount of memory required to run it edged ever upward), the idea of being able to switch tasks rapidly in memory below 640K must have gained considerable appeal. And maybe the space above 640K wasn't all that crowded, as even an IBM PS/2 with a Video Graphics Array (VGA) display controller had space for at least six 16-Kbyte pages.

In August of 1987, the Lotus/Intel/Microsoft group announced the LIM EMS 4.0 specification. The new specification incorporated essentially all the enhanced features of the AQA EEMS, and added several more of its own, all of which will be covered in detail later in the chapter. The AQA group was so impressed (or doubted the wisdom of engaging in another marketing battle) that they soon announced their public support for the 4.0 specification.

In 1988 IBM and Microsoft incorporated EMS drivers in version 4.0 of the PC-DOS and MS-DOS operating systems. EMS drivers in the early releases of this operating system were buggy, and technical specs explicitly defined lack of support for EMS function 19h, the Get/Set Handle Attribute function, although in all other respects the DOS version 4.0 EMS implementation complies with the LIM EMS 4.0 spec. This chapter refers to the LIM EMS 4.0 specification whether or not it resides in the DOS 4.0 operating system, for in all respects interfacing with EMS 4.0 systems is identical.

As of 1988, all major players in the MS-DOS domain have settled on the LIM EMS 4.0 specification. The unification of the expanded memory standard removes at least one worry from the minds of software developers, who no longer have to worry whether it is better to be safe with EMS or to get fancy with the EEMS extensions.

Figure 7-1 illustrates how up to 32 megabytes of expanded memory are addressed within two distinct regions of the 1-megabyte address space of the IBM Personal Computer. Depending on the ROM-BIOS and Video Display Adapter usage of the space between 640K and 1024K, from four to twelve 16-Kbyte pages of expanded memory can be mapped into this region. Mappable conventional memory (a feature of the AQA EEMS and the LIM EMS 4.0) can be used only by operating system extensions.

A few features of the new specification were not clearly documented in its August 1987 edition. And a couple of revised boundary conditions for some 3.2 functions introduced in the 4.0 specification created downward incompatibilities between versions. A revision of the 4.0 specification that clarified the new features and resolved the incompatibilities was published in October 1987.

The number of functions supported by the 4.0 specification doubled the number of user-callable functions available under the 3.2 specification to 28, and most of the new functions had several subfunctions. Thus, the whole subject of expanded memory is now several times larger than it used to be. The official specification document for the LIM EMS 4.0, whose appearance follows the style of the *DOS Technical Reference Manual*, has more than doubled in size relative to its version 3.2 predecessor.

While this chapter will present as many details as it can to illustrate expanded memory concepts, serious developers may find that it cannot serve as a complete substitute for the official specification. You can obtain a copy of the

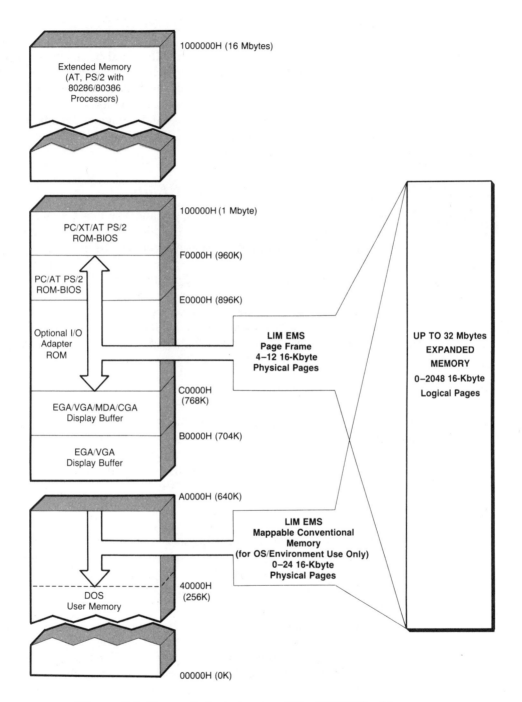

Figure 7-1. Expanded memory and the IBM PC address space.

specification directly from Intel by calling (800) 538-3373 in the USA and Canada or (503) 629-7354 elsewhere.

One possible approach to exploring EMS would be to study the EMS 3.2 compatible functions and then follow up with a discussion of functions added by the 4.0 specification. As you will soon see, the functions added by EMS 4.0 are more than upwardly compatible extensions: in many cases, the new functions offer much easier ways of accomplishing expanded memory management tasks than were possible with the old functions. Therefore, this chapter presents related 3.2 and 4.0 functions together.

LIM EMS 4.0 vs LIM EMS 3.2 vs AQA EEMS

Because each of these expanded memory standards has a significant market presence, developers who intend to write applications that use expanded memory must decide which version (or versions) of the specification to support in their programs. Since all versions of the expanded memory specification provide a function that allows the program to determine the level of the specification implemented by the EMM, your programs will have no trouble determining which expanded memory functions are usable on a given machine. The following discussion presents compatibility and technical factors that should help you select the expanded memory specification that best matches your programming inclination and target market.

Compatibility Considerations

If you intend to write expanded memory applications that can utilize the largest installed base of expanded memory systems, then you are unlikely to err by using only those EMM functions supported by the LIM EMS 3.2 specification. However, you should note that most major expansion board and software vendors strongly endorsed the LIM EMS 4.0 specification soon after its announcement. This degree of acceptance of the LIM EMS 4.0 practically assures its position as the primary expanded memory standard. The following factors support this assertion:

- The user does not have to buy *any* new hardware to use applications that are written to the LIM EMS 4.0 specification. Older expanded memory boards designed for the LIM EMS 3.2 specification can support the 4.0 specification—the manufacturer just has to write a new EMM to implement the 4.0 function calls.

- Intel Corporation provides owners of its Above Board expanded memory products with an EMM supporting the 4.0 specification free of charge. Other manufacturers of expanded memory hardware are likely to follow this bold action on the part of a market leader (and codeveloper of the LIM specification).

- Practically every new expanded memory hardware (and expanded memory emulator) product supports the LIM EMS 4.0.

- High-visibility software products, such as Microsoft's Windows 2.0 (presentation manager) and Excel (spreadsheet), and Quarterdeck Office

Systems' DESQView 2.0 (multitasking environment) all use features of the LIM EMS 4.0. Forthcoming upgrades to other major vendors' spreadsheet and database products are also expected to include support for the LIM EMS 4.0.

Since the codevelopers of the AQA EEMS specification announced that their new expanded memory products would conform to the LIM EMS 4.0 specification, it seems inadvisable for programmers to use EEMS functions in new programs. Therefore, no further details about the EEMS will be presented in this chapter. It is incumbent on the developer to write an EMS application such that it tests both for the presence of the EMM driver and for the EMS version installed, as well as testing for the MS-DOS and PC-DOS 4.0 EMS drivers.

Technical Considerations

From the viewpoint of the application developer, the decision to use LIM 4.0 functions in a program, rather than employing only the LIM 3.2 functions, may initially look like a matter of programmer preference.

This is true on one level, since it is possible for you to accomplish any reasonable application function requiring expanded memory by using functions that are available only in the LIM EMS 3.2 specification. However, by using the higher-level functions introduced by the 4.0 specification, you will be able to reduce the amount of code you must write to perform many common expanded memory manipulation tasks. In particular, later sections of this chapter will show you how LIM EMS 4.0 functions make it possible to transfer large blocks of memory between expanded memory and conventional memory, and to execute code in expanded memory with a single EMM function call.

The Expanded Memory Manager

Many PC programmers and users associate expanded memory with only a set of memory chips installed on a special type of memory board. This exceedingly narrow perception is unfortunate, as no part of the LIM EMS specifies anything about the hardware used to implement an expanded memory system. As was mentioned briefly in the chapter introduction, it is possible to have expanded memory on a computer with no special hardware whatsoever. We will present the support for this bold claim in a later section of the chapter describing several different types of expanded memory implementations.

Regardless of the expanded memory system's construction, each one must include a software component, called the *Expanded Memory Manager* (EMM), that provides the software interface defined by the LIM EMS between the application program and the underlying expanded memory system.

The EMM software itself is packaged within a DOS character device driver, defined in CONFIG.SYS, that is loaded and activated by DOS at boot time. It differs from other DOS device drivers in that communication between the application and the EMM device driver does not take place through the DOS file system in the form of opens, closes, reads or writes. Rather, it uses a software interrupt mechanism very similar to the one employed by DOS, passing function codes, parameters, and return codes back and forth in registers. The main reason that the EMM is packaged as a device driver is to permit it to be loaded early enough in the boot process so that device drivers (e.g., RAM disks and print spoolers) may use expanded memory.

EMM Functions

To satisfy the LIM EMS 4.0 specification, the EMM must implement 28 different user-callable functions, many of which have multiple subfunctions. The large number of functions and subfunctions defined by the specification presents a significant obstacle to the intelligent use of expanded memory.

The complexity of LIM EMS 4.0 almost demands that the developer obtain some higher-level understanding of the EMM's functions. Before we delve into the mechanics of using these functions from assembly and high-level language programs, we will approach the task by dividing EMM functions into five manageable categories:

Informational	Return the status of the EMM, as well as the quantities of expanded memory resources that are available and that are in use by EMS applications.
Data Management	Control the allocation, deallocation, movement, mapping, and sharing of data and code in expanded memory.
Context Management	Control the saving and restoring of the EMM mapping state by device drivers and terminate-and-stay-resident programs.
Operating-System— Oriented	Control the switching of the EMM mapping state among several concurrent applications by multitasking environments, such as Microsoft Windows or Quarterdeck DESQView.
Reserved	Hardware-dependent services that were removed from the documented specification when LIM EMS 3.2 was announced.

Table 7-1 presents the LIM EMS 3.2 and 4.0 functions belonging to each of the preceding classifications (also see Table 7-2). You should note that several functions combine informational, data management, and context management services into one function, and are listed in more than one category.

Table 7-1.   LIM EMS 3.2 and 4.0 Functions

	EMS 3.2 Functions	EMS 4.0 Additions
Informational	(1) Get Status (2) Get Page Frame Address (3) Get Unallocated Page Count	(21) Get Handle Directory (25) Get Mappable Physical Address Array

	EMS 3.2 Functions	EMS 4.0 Additions
	(7) Get Version (12) Get Handle Count (13) Get Handle Pages (14) Get All Handle Pages	
Data Management	(4) Allocate Pages (5) Map/Unmap Handle Page (6) Deallocate Pages	(17) Map/Unmap Multiple Handle Pages (18) Reallocate Pages (19) Get/Set Handle Attribute (20) Get/Set Handle Name (22) Alter Page Map and Jump (23) Alter Page Map and Call (24) Move/Exchange Memory Region
Context Management	(8) Save Page Map (9) Restore Page Map (15) Get/Set Page Map	(16) Get/Set Partial Page Map (22) Alter Page Map and Jump (23) Alter Page Map and Call
Operating-System—Oriented	None	(26) Get Expanded Memory Hardware Information (27) Allocate Standard/Raw Pages (28) Alternate Map Register Set (29) Prepare Expanded Memory Hardware for Warm Boot (30) Enable/Disable Operating System/Environment Function Set Functions
Reserved	(10) Reserved (11) Reserved	

Table 7-2. EMM Functions

Function No.	Function Name	Input Registers	Output Registers
1	**Get Status**	AH: 40h (function code)	None
2	**Get Page Frame Segment Address**	AH: 41h (function code)	BX—page frame segment address
3	**Get Unallocated Page Count**	AH: 42h (function code)	BX—no. of unallocated pages
4	**Allocate Pages**	AH: 43h (function code) BX: no. of pages to allocate	DX—handle

continued

Table 7-2. *continued*

Function No.	Function Name	Input Registers	Output Registers
5	**Map/Unmap Handle Pages**	AH: 44h (function code) AL: physical page no. BX: logical page no. (−1 to unmap physical page) DX: handle	None
6	**Deallocate Pages**	AH: 45h (function code) DX: handle	None
7	**Get Version**	AH: 46h (function code)	AL: BCD EMM version
8	**Save Page Map**	AH: 47h (function code) DX: handle	None
9	**Restore Page Map**	AH: 48h (function code)	None
10	**Reserved**		
11	**Reserved**		
12	**Get Handle Count**	AH: 4Bh (function code)	BX — no. of handles in use
13	**Get Handle Pages**	AH: 4Ch (function code) DX: handle	BX — no. of pages allocated to specified handle
14	**Get All Handle Pages**	AH: 4Dh (function code) ES:DI → handle page array	BX — no. of handles in use
15	**Get Page Map**	AX: 4E00h (function code) ES:DI → dest. page map array	Dest. page map array ← EMM mapping state
	Set Page Map	AX: 4E01h (function code) DS:SI → source page map array	EMM mapping state ← source page map array
	Get & Set Page Map	AX: 4E02h (function code) ES:DI → dest page map array DS:SI → source page map array	Dest. page map array ← EMM mapping state; EMM mapping state ← source page map array

Function No.	Function Name	Input Registers	Output Registers
15	**Get Size of Page Map Array**	AX: 4E03h (function code)	AL: no. of bytes required for source or dest. page map array
16	**Get Partial Page Map**	AX: 4F00h (function code) DS:SI → mappable segment array ES:DI → dest. partial page map array	Dest. partial page map array ← partial EMM mapping state
	Mappable segment array structure: *mappable_seg_count*	*dw ?*	No. of mappable segments to save
	mappable_seg_addr	*dw (mappable_seg_count) dup (?)*	Segment address of mappable segment to save
	Set Partial Page Map	AX: 4F01h (function code) DS:SI → source partial page map	Partial EMM mapping state ← source partial page map array
	Get Size of Partial Page Map Array	AX: 4F02h (function code) BX: no. of pages in the partial page map array	AL: no. of bytes needed to store partial page map array with specified no. of physical pages
17	**Map/Unmap Multiple Handle Pages**	AH: 50h (function code) AL: 00h—physical page specified as page no. 01h—physical page specified by segment address DX: handle CX: no. of entries in logical to physical map array DS:SI → logical to physical map array	None
	Logical to physical map array structure: *log_page_number*	*dw ?*	Logical page no.
	phys_page_number	*dw ?*	Physical page no. or segment address, depending on value specified in register AL

continued

Table 7-2. *continued*

Function No.	Function Name	Input Registers	Output Registers
18	**Reallocate Pages**	AH: 51h (function code) DX: handle BX: no. of pages handle should have after relocation	BX: no. of pages allocated to handle after reallocation
19	**Get Handle Attribute**	AX: 5200h (function code) DX: handle	AL: 0—handle is volatile 1—handle is nonvolatile
	Set Handle Attribute	AX: 5201h (function code) DX: handle BL: new handle attribute 00h, volatile 01h, nonvolatile	None
	Get Attribute Capability	AX: 5202h (function code)	AL: 0, nonvolatility not supported 1, nonvolatility is supported
20	**Get Handle Name**	AX: 5300h (function code) DX: handle ES:DI → 8-character handle name dest. buffer	Handle name dest. buffer ← handle name
	Set Handle Name	AX: 5301h (function code) DX: handle DS:SI → 8-character handle name source buffer	Handle name ← handle name source buffer
21	**Get Handle Directory**	AX: 5400h (function code) ES:DI → handle directory array	AL: no. of entries in the handle directory array
	Handle directory: *handle_value* *handle_name*	*dw ?* *db 8 dup (?)*	Active handle Handle name
	Search for Named Handle	AX: 5401h (function code) DS:SI → 8-character handle name search buffer	DX: handle with specified name
	Get Total Handles	AX: 5402h (function code)	BX: total no. of handles supported by EMM

Function No.	Function Name	Input Registers	Output Registers
22	**Alter Page Map & Jump**	AH: 55h (function code) AL: 0—physical pages specified by physical page no. 1—physical pages specified by segment address DX: handle DS:SI → map and jump structure	None
	Map and jump structure: *target_address*	*dd ?*	Entry point of target
	log_phys_map_len	*db ?*	No. of entries in page map structure → logical to physical map array structure as in function 17
	log_phys_map_ptr	*dd ?*	
23	**Alter Page Map & Call**	AH: 56h (function code)	None
		AL: 0—physical pages specified by physical page no.	1—physical pages specified by segment address DX: handle DS:SI → map and call structure
	Map and call structure: *target_addr*	*dd ?*	Far → target entry point
	new_page_map_len	*db ?*	No. of pages to map after call far → as in function 17
	new_page_map_ptr	*dd ?*	
	old_page_map_len	*db ?*	No. of pages to map after return far → as in function 17
	old_page_map_ptr	*dd ?*	
	Reserved	*dw 4 dup (?)*	Reserved for EMM
	Get Page Map Stack Space Size	AX: 5602h (function code)	BX: No. of bytes of stack space required by Alter Page Map and Call function

continued

Table 7-2. *continued*

Function No.	Function Name	Input Registers	Output Registers
24	**Move Memory Region**	AX: 5700h (function code) DS:SI → source/dest. region descriptor	None
	Exchange Memory Region	AX: 5701 (function code) DS:SI → source/dest. region descriptor	None
	Source/dest. region descriptor: *region_length*	dd ?	No. of bytes to move/exchange
	source_memory_type	db ?	Conventional memory: 0
	source_handle	dw ?	Conventional memory: 0 Expanded memory: source handle
	source_init_offset	dw ?	Conventional memory: initial offset within source segment Expanded memory: initial offset within source page Conventional memory: initial source segment
	source_page_seg	dw ?	Expanded memory: initial logical source page
	dest_memory_type	db ?	Conventional memory: 0 Expanded memory: 1
	dest_handle	dw ?	Conventional memory: 0 Expanded memory: dest. handle
	dest_init_offset	dw ?	Conventional memory: initial offset within dest. segment Expanded memory: initial offset within dest. page
	dest_seg_page	dw ?	Conventional memory: initial dest segment Expanded memory: initial logical dest. page
25	**Get Mappable Physical Address Array**	AX: 5800h (function code) ES:DI → mappable physical address array	CX: no. of entries in mappable physical address array
	Mappable physical address array:	(Array sorted in ascending segment order)	

Function No.	Function Name	Input Registers	Output Registers
25	*phys_page_segment*	*dw ?*	Segment address of mappable page corresponding to physical page no.
	phys_page_number	*dw ?*	
	Get Physical Address Array Entry Count	AX: 5801h (function code)	CX: no. of entries in mappable physical address array
26	**Get Hardware Configuration Array**	AX: 5900h (function code) ES:DI → hardware configuration array	Hardware configuration array ← hardware data
	Hardware configuration array: *raw_page_size*	*dw ?*	Raw page size in bytes
	alternate_reg_sets	*dw ?*	No. of alternate map register sets
	save_area_size	*dw ?*	No. bytes in context save area (also returned by function 15)
	DMA_reg_sets	*dw ?*	No. of register sets that can be assigned DMA channels 0: LIM standard DMA operation
	DMA_channel_op	*dw ?*	0: LIM standard DMA operation 1: only 1 DMA channel
	Get Unallocated Raw Page Count	AX: 5902h (function code)	BX: no. of unallocated raw pages
			DX: total no. of raw pages
27	**Allocate Standard/ Raw Pages**	AH: 5Ah (function code) AL: 00h—allocate standard pages 01h—allocate raw pages BX: no. of pages to allocate	DX: raw/standard handle
28	**Get Alternate Map Register Set**	AX: 5B00h (function code)	If BL <> 0 ← active alternate map register set If BL = 0—ES:DI ← map register context save area

continued

Table 7-2. *continued*

Function No.	Function Name	Input Registers	Output Registers
28	Set Alternate Map Register Set	AX: 5B01h (function code) BL: 00h ES:DI → map register context save area <> 00h—no. of alternate map register set	None
	Get Alternate Map Save Area Size	AX: 5B02h (function code)	DX: no. of bytes in map register context save area
	Allocate Alternate Map Register Set	AX: 5B03h (function code)	BL: 0—no alternate map register sets are available <> 0—no. of alternate map register set allocated
	Deallocate Alternate Map Register Set	AX: 5B04h (function code) BL: no. of alternate map register set	None
	Allocate DMA Register Set	AX: 5B05h (function code)	BL: 0—DMA register sets are not supported <> 0—no. of DMA register set allocated
	Enable DMA on	AX: 5B06h (function code)	None
	Alternate Map Register Set	BL: DMA register set no. DL: DMA channel no.	
	Disable DMA on	AX: 5B07h (function code)	None
	Alternate Map Register Set	BL: DMA register set no.	
	Deallocate DMA Register Set	AX: 5B08h (function code) BL: DMA register set no.	None
29	Prepare for Warmboot	AH: 5Ch (function code)	None
30	Enable OS/E Function Set	AX: 5D00h (function code) BX,CX: access key (required on all calls after the first)	BX,CX: access key (returned only on the first call)

Function No.	Function Name	Input Registers	Output Registers
30	**Disable OS/E Function Set**	AX: 5D01h (function code) BX,CX: access key (required on all function calls after the first)	BX,CX: access key (returned only on the first call)
	Return Access Key	AX: 5D02h (function code) BX,CX: access key (returned by first invocation of Enable or Disable OS/E Function Set)	None

Expanded Memory Manager Implementations

The original EMM was developed by Intel to provide a software interface to memory boards that are manufactured for LIM EMS memory. Other vendors produced EMMs that were tailored to expanded memory boards of their own manufacture. But EMM implementations are not limited in form to a software driver for a special type of memory board.

Our previous discussion of the EMM introduced the notion that the LIM EMS (at least since version 3.2) is basically hardware independent. Several system software developers took note of this fact and proceeded to build expanded memory managers that required no special expanded memory hardware whatsoever. These EMMs, which are usually referred to as expanded memory *emulators* or *simulators*, simulate expanded memory by swapping data from conventional memory to and from either disk storage or the extended memory present on many PC/AT compatible systems.

The introduction of PC/AT compatibles and PS/2 systems that use the Intel 80386 microprocessor has made it possible to build another type of expanded memory manager that uses the advanced memory management hardware inherent in each 80386. COMPAQ currently includes with each of its Deskpro 386 models an EMM based on this capability, called CEMM.

While every variety of EMM implements the LIM EMS specification, each type also presents a set of cost, performance, and compatibility trade-offs that are important to you as an EMS application developer. You need to be aware of the design and programming considerations that will affect the ability of your software to function correctly with acceptable performance on different types of expanded memory systems. If development cost is a major consideration, for example, investing in a relatively inexpensive expanded memory simulator program should permit you to build, test, and run programs that use expanded memory without investing hundreds of dollars in new hardware.

The following sections describe the specific advantages and disadvantages associated with each type of expanded memory implementation with regard to compatibility, performance, and cost.

Expanded Memory Hardware and Software

Regardless of the particular details of a board's construction, the EMM controls the dynamic switching of memory into and out of directly addressable memory through a set of mapping registers on the board. The mapping registers are implemented by a series of I/O ports somewhere in the computer's I/O space. The board and its supporting EMM must be configured at installation to accommodate the usage of the I/O address space and addresses above 640K by video and I/O adapters, as well as the ROM-BIOS.

Advantages

Speed—can map a page of expanded memory into the EMS page frame in approximately 100 microseconds.

Widely Available—Boards are available for PC, PC/AT, and IBM Micro Channel Architecture bus systems.

Disadvantages

Costly—Expanded memory boards with large amounts of memory can cost as much as an entire computer.

Space—Requires one or more bus slots in the computer chassis.

Compatibility—Not every EMS board will work in every computer system. Users of high-performance PC/AT compatibles must take care to purchase an EMS board capable of operating at the bus speed of their system.

80386 Hardware and Software

It is possible to use the memory management hardware present in every Intel 80386 microprocessor in combination with the 80386's virtual 8086 mode. The operational details of the 80386's memory management and *virtual 8086* mode are far too complex to explain here. Suffice it to say that they are capable of performing the mapping functions served by the page-mapping registers on a dedicated expanded memory board.

Advantages

Speed—Page maps can be performed in a few microseconds.

Inexpensive—This assumes that you already have an 80386 machine with a large amount of extended memory.

Disadvantages

Expensive—This assumes that you don't already have an 80386-based machine or that your 80386 machine doesn't have a large amount of extended memory.

Compatibility—Other software using the protected mode of the 80386, as several multitasking environments or "DOS extenders" do, can conflict with the EMM's use of protected mode features like paging and virtual 8086 mode. Testing of the 80386 EMM with the actual combination of hardware and software with which it will be used may be the only way to ensure success.

Software Only

On 8086-based machines, the EMM simulates EMS memory by swapping data between a page frame allocated in conventional memory and a floppy or fixed disk. On 80286-based machines with extended memory (PC/AT compatibles and PS/2 Models 50 or 60), the EMM can simulate expanded memory by swapping EMS pages between extended memory and the EMS page frame in conventional memory.

Advantages

Inexpensive—The EMM requires only the resources that are usually available on the base hardware.

Disadvantages

Performance—Moving data from conventional memory to and from extended memory takes tens to hundreds of times as long as it does to map pages on a real EMS board. A hard disk takes hundreds or thousands of times as long. If all you have is a floppy disk, it takes seemingly millions of times as long. Perhaps surprisingly though, there are certain uses of EMS memory that don't require the performance of a board, such as storing a text or graphics screen for later recall, or swapping TSRs to and from memory on demand.

Compatibility—On a real board (or 80386-type emulator), one logical EMS page can be mapped into more than one physical EMS page at a time, using a technique called *aliasing* (which will be explained in further detail later in the chapter). Because simulators copy pages of memory, rather than "mapping" them into different parts of the address space, applications that depend on data aliasing cannot work with this type of EMM. In practice, most applications that use EMS do not depend on aliasing to operate.

IBM PS/2 80286 Memory Expansion Option

A sketchily documented feature of the IBM 82086 Memory Expansion Option for the PS/2 Models 50 and 60 provides a set of subaddressing registers, accessible through the Programmable Option Select feature of the Micro Channel Architecture bus, that can be programmed to operate like the mapping registers on a real expanded memory board.

Ostensibly, these subaddressing registers were designed to allow the power-on-self-test (POST) routines in the ROM-BIOS to remap any failing physical memory blocks to the high end of memory (and map good blocks into the space left behind) so that the machine could operate even after one or more memory chips had failed.

It is also possible to map expansion board memory into the space below 640K, to furnish *mappable conventional memory* allowed by the AQA EEMS and LIM EMS 4.0. Unfortunately, the entire megabyte of memory present on the planar boards of the PS/2 Models 50 and 50 must be disabled to do so.

Advantages

Inexpensive—This assumes that you already have an IBM PS/2 Model 50 or 60 with the IBM Extended Memory Expansion Option. Other memory expansion boards for the PS/2's may or may not support the subaddressing feature.

Performance—An EMM written to use these registers can perform identically to a dedicated expanded memory board.

Disadvantages

Expensive—This assumes that you don't already have a PS/2 with the IBM Extended Memory Expansion Option.

The EMS Application Program Interface

Moving forward from a general discussion of the EMM's structure and function, we can now explain how to issue expanded memory requests to the EMM from your assembly and high-level language programs, and how to interpret the EMM's response to those requests.

Programs communicate requests to the EMM via software interrupt 67h, using the processor's registers to specify expanded memory function codes and arguments. Since the use of software interrupts and processor registers is least complex from assembly language, we will explore that interface first.

EMS Assembly Language Programming

Assembly language programmers accustomed to the DOS system-call interface will find that the Expanded Memory Manager presents a practically identical situation:

1. Place a function code for the desired EMS function in the AH register.
2. Place the other arguments needed by the selected function in other microprocessor registers and/or data structures in memory, as specified by the LIM EMS.

3. Transfer control to the EMM by issuing software interrupt 67h.

4. The EMM returns control to the requesting program after the interrupt instruction, overwriting the function code placed in register AH in step 1 with a status code for the requested operation. A status code of 00h signals successful completion of the function; any other value signifies that the EMM encountered some problem while attempting to execute the selected function. Error code values and their meanings are listed later in the chapter.

5. Depending on the EMS function, other information is returned in registers and/or data structures in memory.

Interrupt Conflict

Programmers should note that int 67h is not "officially" reserved for the LIM EMS; many other commercially available programs also use it. Conflicts in the usage of this interrupt often bewilder developers and users of EMS software when an application that works on one machine will fail to work on a machine with an identical hardware configuration. It is possible for int 67h to be shared cooperatively by more than one program, though EMMs are not programmed to do so. Even if the EMM is capable of sharing the use of int 67h with other software, one of the two documented methods for detecting the presence of the EMM will fail if another interrupt handler chains itself in front of the EMM's interrupt handler.

Because the use of int 67h is embedded in the LIM EMS specification, every application written to use expanded memory communicates with the EMM by issuing this interrupt. Thus, conflicts in the use of int 67h between the EMM and other software can be resolved only if the non-EMS software can be reconfigured or modified to use another interrupt vector.

High-Level Languages

As is the case with DOS system calls, there is no standard interface between high-level languages such as C, Pascal, or FORTRAN and the LIM EMS. However, developers who wish to access expanded memory from applications written in high-level languages ordinarily have several viable alternatives for doing so. EMS function libraries for several different language products are commercially available. Many popular language products include subroutines or functions that provide a general means for accessing the microprocessor registers and issuing software interrupts. Additionally, the high-level language must also provide some way to specify *far* pointers (a segment register plus offset) for the address of data structures passed to the EMM.

Programmers who know 808x assembly language, and who are familiar with the subroutine linkage and parameter-passing conventions of their high-level language, will find it easy to construct a collection of EMS interface routines. An example of such a collection, written in Microsoft C version 5.0, appears at the end of the chapter along with the sample programs.

Handling Error Conditions

Every programmer attempting to write reliable software should expect to handle the inevitable errors that will occur. The LIM EMS 4.0 defines 36 different error conditions that might be returned by the EMM, as well as a code that signals successful function completion. Listing 7-1 contains *equates* for LIM EMS 4.0 error codes, and Table 7-3 lists the error status codes.

The EMM returns this detailed completion status code in the AH register for each service request at the return from the interrupt. With respect to error detection and reporting, the EMM's programming interface is more consistent and less complicated than DOS's. To detect and report an error condition following a DOS call, the programmer must examine a register or the carry flag and then issue another system call to return a detailed error code.

Table 7-3. Lotus/Intel/Microsoft Expanded Memory Specification 4.0 Status Codes

Code	Description
00H	The specified function completed without error.
80H	EMM driver software failure.
81H	EMM driver detected hardware failure.
82H	EMM driver busy (doesn't happen any more).
83H	Cannot find the specified handle.
84H	The function code is undefined.
85H	No handles are currently available.
86H	A mapping context restoration error has occurred.
87H	Insufficient total pages for request.
88H	Insufficient unallocated pages for request.
89H	Zero logical pages have been requested from a LIM 3.2 compatible function.
8AH	Logical page out of range for specified handle.
8BH	Physical page out of range.
8CH	Mapping register context save area is full.
8DH	Mapping register context stack already has a context associated with the specified handle.
8EH	Mapping register context stack does not have a context associated with the specified handle.
8FH	Undefined subfunction was requested.
90H	The attribute type is undefined.
91H	The system does not support nonvolatility.
92H	Partial source overwrite occurred during move region.
93H	Expanded memory region is too big for specified handle.
94H	Conventional memory region and expanded memory region overlap.
95H	Offset within a logical page exceeds the length of a logical page.
96H	Region length exceed 1-Mbyte limit.
97H	Source and destination expanded memory regions have the same handle and overlap.

Code	Description
98H	Undefined/unsupported memory source and destination types.
9AH	Specified alternate map register set does not exist.
9BH	All alternate map/DMA register sets are in use.
9CH	Alternate map/DMA register sets are not supported.
9DH	Specified alternate map/DMA register set is not defined, not allocated, or is the current one.
9EH	Dedicated DMA channels are not supported.
9FH	The specified dedicated DMA channel does not exist.
A0H	No corresponding handle value could be found for the specified handle name.
A1H	A handle with the specified name already exists.
A2H	Attempt to wraparound 1-Mbyte address space during move or exchange.
A3H	The contents of the user data structure passed to the function were corrupt or meaningless.
A4H	The operating system denied access to the function.

Listing 7-1. EMMERR.H

```
/*

Product:      Above Disc
Version:      2.00
Name:         emmerr.h
Contents:     equates for LIM EMS Spec 4.0 Error Codes
Reference:    Lotus/Intel/Microsoft
Expanded Memory Specification
Version 4.0, pp A5 - A10
*/

#defineFRSTEMERR   0x80   /* first emm error number */
#defineLASTEMERR   0xA4   /* last emm error number */

#defineFUNCCOK     0x00   /* the specified function completed without error */
#defineEMDRVSWF    0x80   /* EMM driver software failure */
#defineEMDRVHWF    0x81   /* EMM driver detected hardware failure */
#defineEMDRVBSY    0x82   /* EMM driver busy (doesn't happen any more) */
#defineHANDLNFD    0x83   /* cannot find the specified handle */
#defineFUNCCUND    0x84   /* the function code is undefined */
#defineHANDLINS    0x85   /* no handles are currently available */
#defineMAPCXPRO    0x86   /* mapping context restoration error has occurred */
#defineTOTPGINS    0x87   /* insufficient total pages for request */
#defineUNAPGINS    0x88   /* insufficient unallocated pages for request */
```

continued

Listing 7-1. *continued*

```
#defineLPAGE2SM     0x89    /* zero logical pages have been requested from
                               LIM 3.2 compatible function */
#defineLPAGERNG     0x8A    /* logical page out of range for specified handle */
#definePPAGE2BG     0x8B    /* physical page out of range */
#defineMRCSAFUL     0x8C    /* mapping register context save area is full */
#defineMRCSTDUP     0x8D    /* mapping register context stack already has a
                               context associated with specified handle */
#defineMRCSTNFD     0x8E    /* mapping register context stack does not have a
                               context associated with the specified handle */
#defineSFUNCUND     0x8F    /* undefined subfunction was requested */
#defineATTRBUND     0x90    /* the attribute type is undefined */
#defineNVSTGUNS     0x91    /* the system does not support nonvolatility */
#defineMREGNOVW     0x92    /* partial source overwrite occurred during move
                               region */
#defineMREGN2SM     0x93    /* expanded memory region too big for specified handle */
#defineMREGNOVL     0x94    /* conventional memory region and expanded memory
                               region overlap */
#defineLPGOF2BG     0x95    /* offset within a logical page exceeds the length of
                               a logical page */
#defineMREGN2BG     0x96    /* region length exceeds 1-Mbyte limit */
#defineMREGNDUP     0x97    /* source and destination expanded memory regions
                               have the same handle and overlap */
#defineMREGNUND     0x98    /* undefined/unsupported memory source and destination
                               types */
#defineAMRSNFD      0x9A    /* specified alternate map register set does not exist */
#defineAMDRSINS     0x9B    /* all alternate map/DMA register sets are in use */
#defineAMDRSUNS     0x9C    /* alternate map/DMA register sets are not supported */
#defineAMDRSUND     0x9D    /* specified alternate map/DMA register set is not
                               defined, not allocated, or is current one */
#defineDDMACUNS     0x9E    /* dedicated DMA channels are not supported */
#defineDDMACNFD     0x9F    /* the specified dedicated DMA channel does not exist */
#defineHNDVLNFD     0xA0    /* no corresponding handle value found for
                               the specified handle name */
#defineHNDNMDUP     0xA1    /* a handle with specified name already exists */
#defineMREGNWRP     0xA2    /* attempt to wraparound 1-Mbyte address space during
                               move or exchange */
#defineUSRDSFMT     0xA3    /* contents of user data structure passed to
                               the function were corrupt or meaningless */
#defineOPSYSACC     0xA4    /* operating system denied access to function */
```

Since checking for EMM-detected errors is a simple matter of testing the
AH register for zero after every call, it is always a disappointment to discover
popular commercial software that doesn't take the care to do it. Save yourself

(and your users) the headache of tracking down mysterious hang-ups and failures by checking the error code after each call to the EMM.

A program's response to an error condition returned by the EMM depends on the nature of the error and on the ability of the program to adapt to conditions that the LIM EMS refers to as "recoverable." For example, there is very little a program can do if it receives an "Expanded Memory Hardware Failure" indication from the EMM, other than to report the problem to the user and to refrain from making additional use of EMM services.

Alternatively, an adaptable program might be able to recover from a condition such as "Insufficient EMS Pages Available," perhaps by using a disk file as a temporary storage area for the data that cannot be placed in expanded memory.

Other conditions, such as "Physical Page Out of Range," generally indicate that a design or programming error is present in the EMS application. Implement your EMS error-handling routines so that they report the location in your program where the error condition occurred, preferably in a way that relates to the source code.

Writing Programs That Use Expanded Memory

All programs using expanded memory must observe a certain protocol. Each program should perform the following steps in the order in which they are listed:

1. Detect the presence of the EMM.
2. Determine whether a sufficient number of expanded memory pages is available to your application.
3. Obtain the address of the start of the page frame.
4. Allocate expanded memory pages.
5. Map expanded memory pages into the page frame.
6. Read, write, or execute data in expanded memory.
7. Return expanded memory pages to the EMM before your application terminates.

General Programming Guidelines

The characteristics of expanded memory and the EMM impose relatively few restrictions on programs that use it. The following guidelines are relevant to all programs using expanded memory:

- **Programs using data aliasing must ensure that the expanded memory system supports it.** Data aliasing occurs when one logical page of expanded memory is mapped into more than one physical page of the page frame. With EMM implementations that use page-mapping hardware, the effect of this technique is that a 16-Kbyte page of expanded memory will appear in more than one 16-Kbyte block of the processor's address space. EMMs written for actual EMS boards, 80386 paging hardware, and the IBM PS/2 80286 Memory Expansion Option can all support this technique. However, software-only EMS emulators that simulate page mapping by copying blocks of data in memory cannot perform data aliasing.

Your program can perform the following test to determine whether the EMM supports data aliasing:

1. Map one logical page into at least two physical pages.
2. Write data to one of the physical pages.
3. If the data written to the physical page in step 2 also appears in each of the other physical pages into which the logical page has been mapped, then the EMM implementation supports data aliasing.

Figure 7-2 graphically illustrates data aliasing. Because a single logical page is mapped into the first and third physical pages within the page frame, the data element located at offset 2132H within the logical page may be accessed by the physical addresses CC00:2132 *and* D400:2132.

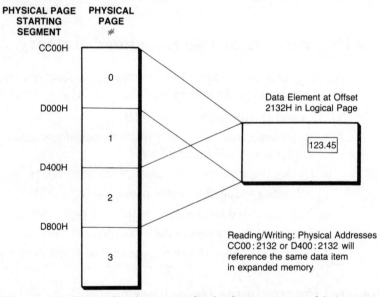

Figure 7-2. Data aliasing—one logical page mapped into more than one physical page.

- **Applications should return any allocated pages to the EMM before program termination.** Your program must return each expanded memory handle allocated by your program to the EMM prior to its normal or abnormal termination. Failure to return all pages to the EMM may cause subsequent application requests for expanded memory to fail for lack of sufficient pages or handles. Be sure your program's error or abort exit code frees expanded memory, as well as its normal termination code.

- **Map data only into conventional memory that your program has allocated from DOS.** The Move/Exchange Region function introduced in LIM EMS 4.0 made it possible to swap data to or from the address space managed by DOS. Prior to swapping any data into the DOS address space, your program must have allocated it from DOS, since the EMM does not manage conventional memory. Failure to observe this rule is likely to result in corrupted data and a system crash.

- **Any data structure whose address is passed to an EMM function call must not reside in mappable memory.** Except for the Alter Page Map and Jump and the Alter Page Map and Call functions, which were specifically designed to support the execution of code objects in expanded memory, data structures whose addresses are passed to the EMM must reside in memory that cannot be mapped out. For example, your program cannot store mapping context save areas in expanded memory.

- **Do not locate a program's stack in expanded memory.** If you use expanded memory to store and execute code, its stack must be located in conventional (nonmappable) storage. If an interrupt service routine using expanded memory gains control from a program whose stack resides in expanded memory, reading or writing data on a stack that has been mapped out would fail disastrously.

Using Expanded Memory in Transient Programs

DOS device drivers and terminate-and-stay-resident programs (TSRs) have to perform additional tasks in order to use expanded memory without interfering with other programs. A discussion of the extra requirements for using expanded memory in these programs will be postponed until we have gained a foothold in the programming techniques used to manipulate expanded memory in normal DOS programs.

Detecting the Presence of the EMM

The LIM EMS documents two techniques that can be used to detect the presence of expanded memory: the *open handle* technique and the *get interrupt vector* technique. For standard DOS programs, the method you choose is a matter of preference. An outline of the open handle technique is presented here; an example of the get interrupt vector technique will be presented in the section describing the use of expanded memory with resident programs.

Open Handle Method

To detect the presence of the EMM using the open handle method, a series of DOS file system calls is used to establish the presence of the EMM device driver and, if present, to determine whether it is capable of servicing requests for int 67h. The method operates as follows:

1. Perform a DOS open handle call (DOS function 3Dh), specifying read-only access (mode 0), with a path name of *EMMXXXX0*. This is the name of

the EMM character device driver that was installed at boot time if a *DEVICE=* entry for the EMM device driver was specified in the CONFIG.SYS file.

2. If the open handle call fails with a "file or path name not found" return code, you may assume that expanded memory is not present. The open call might also fail if all DOS file handles are in use prior to the presence test. To prevent this from occurring, your program should perform the expanded memory presence test before opening any other files.

3. If the open completes successfully, it indicates that a file or device with the name of the EMM exists. To determine whether the handle returned in step 1 refers to a device or a file, issue an I/O Control for Devices (IOCTL) call (DOS function 44h) with the Get Device Information subfunction (register AL = 00h) for the file handle returned in step 1.

4. If the handle belongs to a device, bit 7 of register DL will be 1, which indicates that an expanded memory manager is present. If bit 7 is 0, the handle is associated with a file, so you may assume that expanded memory is not present.

5. If the handle does refer to a device, issue an IOCTL call with the Get Output Status subfunction (register AL = 07h) for the handle, to determine whether the EMM is ready to process expanded memory service requests.

6. If the EMM is ready to process expanded memory service requests, the IOCTL call will return the value 0FFh in the AL register. Otherwise, the EMM is not present or is unable to process expanded memory service requests.

7. If the initial DOS open handle succeeded, close it by using the close handle call (DOS function 3Eh). The handle is no longer needed, since further communication between the EMM and your application takes place via the int 67h interface and does not use the DOS file system.

Checking the EMS Specification Supported by the EMM

If the EMM exists and is ready to service requests, issue function 7, *Get Version*, to ensure that the version of the EMM with which your program is communicating supports the version of the Expanded Memory Specification required by your program. This function returns a two-digit binary-coded decimal (BCD) number in the AL register. The upper 4 bits of this number indicate the major version number. The lower 4 bits or fractional part of this number may be used by vendors to signify enhancements or error correction to their memory managers. Therefore, your program to check the version should not depend on both digits matching. A much better strategy is to perform a "greater than or equal to" comparison.

In the case of MS-DOS version 4.0, the user may have installed third party drivers to compensate for deficiencies in those provided by early releases of the operating system, so it is not sufficient to test for MS-DOS 4.0 and assume the presence of EMS drivers. In fact, the MS-DOS 4.0 drivers may be installed and yet not control the hardware. As a simple test, invoke function 1, Get Status, by putting the value of 40h into the AH register and calling int 67h; if the hardware and software are working together, the function will return a value of zero in AH; if not, you will get a nonzero value. Any nonzero value indicates failure, but values of 80h or 81h indicate hardware failure typical of driver mismatch. In this case, display a message to the user that the drivers may not be operating correctly. If your application tests working operation for MS-DOS version 4.0 EMS, remember that the early DOS 4.0 versions do not support LIM EMS 4.0 function 19h, Get/Set Handle Attribute.

Determining the Amount of Expanded Memory Available

Before your program may use expanded memory, it must explicitly allocate it from the EMM. The first step toward doing this is determining if enough pages are available to satisfy your program's requirements by issuing EMS function 3, Get Unallocated Page Count. This function returns the total number of 16-kilobyte pages managed by the EMM, as well as the number of pages currently available to your program.

Allocating Expanded Memory

Depending on your program's dynamic behavior, you may choose to allocate all of the expanded memory it could possibly need at one time, or you could make separate allocation requests as run-time requirements vary. The first choice is most appropriate if the number of required pages does not vary significantly over time. The second choice is appropriate if you expect the program's expanded memory requirements to grow and shrink appreciably throughout its execution. This choice is also more cooperative in that it leaves more expanded memory available for other programs that may be executed concurrently. For example, one popular spreadsheet program retrieves the available amount of expanded memory and allocates ⅛ of that amount each time it needs more. Of course, there is another popular spreadsheet package that allocates the entire unallocated pool of expanded memory when it starts execution, leaving nothing for any other programs that may be subsequently invoked from inside itself.

Under the LIM EMS 3.2 specification, only one function was furnished to allocate expanded memory: Allocate Pages, which is EMS function 4. Each allocation request returns a separate handle that has to be used to reference pages associated with that particular allocation. The number of pages associated with that handle is fixed from the time the pages are allocated until the time they are returned to the EMM. This restriction discourages the dynamic allocation and deallocation of expanded memory, since it is impossible to return to the EMM just some of the pages belonging to a particular handle.

This limitation was relieved in the LIM EMS 4.0 specification by the Reallocate Pages function, EMS function 18. It allows the number of pages associated with a handle to be increased or decreased any time after allocation. The new function doesn't solve all the problems associated with dynamic management of data structures in EMS storage, since logical pages may be added or removed only from the back. For example, if you wanted to free the third logical page in a handle to which six pages had been allocated, you would have to release the fourth through sixth logical pages as well. This function also allows the return of all the pages associated with a handle to the EMM, without returning the handle itself, by specifying a new page count of zero.

To complete discussion of expanded memory allocation, the LIM EMS 4.0 specification also introduced the concept of *raw pages*. Raw pages—logical pages that are some submultiple of the *standard* EMS page size of 16 kilobytes—were introduced to provide additional flexibility for expanded memory hardware and software capable of supporting smaller page sizes. For example, an EMM based on the paging hardware of the Intel 80386 could support a raw page size of 4 kilobytes, providing suitably written software with the ability to manage expanded memory more efficiently than it could with a 16-Kbyte page size. EMS 4.0 EMMs written to support existing EMS board designs support the concept of raw pages in a hollow manner—the raw page size is identical to the standard page size.

Raw pages are allocated using EMS function 27, subfunction 1, Allocate Raw Pages. EMS function 27 also has a subfunction 0, Allocate Standard Pages, which provides identical service to the LIM EMS 3.2 Allocate Pages function, with one extension: it allows zero pages to be allocated to a handle. This extension also applies to subfunction 1.

Addressing Expanded Memory

Conventional memory addresses on Intel 80x86 processors (in real address mode) are specified by a pair of 16-bit components: a segment value, sometimes called a *selector*, and a byte offset value.

Forming the address of a data item in expanded memory is a little more complicated. To begin with, items of data in expanded memory have a three-part logical address: a handle number, a logical page number, and a byte offset within the logical page. Furthermore, unlike a data item in conventional memory, whose location remains constant once it has been allocated, the physical address of a data item in expanded memory can change, since it depends on the current mapping state of the expanded memory system.

These characteristics make the task of keeping track of data in expanded memory a two-fold problem: managing logical addresses and managing physical addresses.

Managing Logical Addresses

The LIM EMS defines a *handle* to be a 16-bit quantity (even though it supports a maximum of 255 handles) and a *logical page number* to be a 14-bit quantity (logical pages are numbered from 0 to 2047). The subaddressing of objects within a logical page is not of concern to the EMM, but it is a major concern to the expanded memory application developer. Specifically, what type of data should be stored in expanded memory and how should it be managed?

A general method of keeping track of a data item in expanded memory, without resorting to bit-twiddling tricks, requires your program to manage three 16-bit variables per item—a handle, a page number, and a byte offset within that page. This overhead makes the use of expanded memory most appropriate for storing data structures that are comparatively large with respect to the pointers used to access them. It makes little sense to store a 4-byte data item in expanded memory if it requires a 6-byte pointer to access it.

Another factor to consider is the dynamic behavior of the data structures that you intend to store in expanded memory. Maintaining a linked list consisting of variable-sized elements could be an interesting proposition if it resides in expanded memory. A fairly involved storage management scheme would be required to efficiently compact free space and handle spillover when the size of the list exceeds the size of a logical page.

Actually, effective techniques for managing expanded memory are quite similar to the file buffer and index management techniques employed by database management systems. The essential problem is one of managing variable-sized data elements (records, arrays, etc.) in a limited set of fixed-size buffers (16-Kbyte in the case of an EMS page). Not surprisingly, some database programs for IBM PC-compatibles take advantage of this similarity by keeping file indices, or even entire files, in expanded memory when it is available.

It would require a significant effort to use expanded memory as a general-purpose storage management tool within your programs. However, you can effectively employ expanded memory in many common data storage tasks with simple, ad-hoc approaches. The sample application listed at the end of this chapter shows how comparatively simple methods of managing expanded memory suffice for handling a dynamic memory management task. Later sections in this chapter will explain in detail several functions added by the LIM EMS 4.0 specification that greatly reduce the programming effort needed to manipulate code and data objects in expanded memory.

Managing Physical Addresses

In the LIM EMS 3.2 specification, the physical address of a data item in a logical page that is currently mapped into a physical page is calculated relative to the base of the 64-kilobyte page frame. The segment address of this page frame is obtained via EMS function 2, Get Page Frame Segment Address. Dividing the size of the page frame by the size of the standard logical page yields the four physical pages, numbered 0 through 3, that can be specified in EMS function calls. All four physical pages are contiguous in memory—the address of each page is 16 kilobytes higher than the address of the preceding page.

The LIM EMS 4.0 specification, incorporating the AQA EEMS concept of multiple, possibly discontiguous page frames, makes calculation of physical addresses either easier or more difficult, depending on your point of view. In addition to function 2 of the LIM 4.0 specification, the EMM can now provide your program with a table of physical page numbers and segment addresses corresponding to each physical page.

EMS function 25, subfunction 1, Get Physical Page Address Entry Count, returns the number of mappable physical pages supported by the EMM. Use this subfunction to determine the size of the array whose address is passed to EMS function 25, subfunction 0, Get Mappable Physical Address Array, which fills the array with the ascending segment addresses and the corresponding page numbers.

While the LIM EMS 4.0 does not require the EMM to provide any more than the four standard physical pages defined by the 3.2 specification, the EMM can provide up to thirty-six 16-Kbyte physical pages. Up to 12 pages can be located in the space between 768K and 960K (addresses C0000 to F0000 in hex), and up to 24 pages can be located between 256K and 640K (addresses 40000 to A0000 in hex).

Access to the page frame above 640K is available to any EMS application. Access to mappable memory below the 640K line, which the specification refers to as *mappable conventional memory*, is intended for developers of operating system extensions, such as Microsoft Windows 2.0.

The number of physical pages in the page frame above 640K can vary, depending on the layout of the ROM space on any particular machine. Video adapters of various types can take up a substantial portion of the ROM space for their display buffers. Many types of I/O adapters, including network cards and disk controllers, contain ROM-BIOS extensions that appear in the address space between C0000 and F0000.

Software emulators must usually allocate the EMS page frame out of the DOS address space, below the 640K line, because most PC-compatible systems do not have RAM present between 640K and 960K. Some EMS software emulators can take advantage of the capability of certain memory expansion boards to map 64K or more of RAM into the space above 640K.

It is hazardous to make any simplifying assumptions about the location and alignment of the page frame. Several existing EMS applications do make such assumptions, relying on the page frame alignment typically provided by EMS hardware, in order to save storage space for expanded memory pointers or to simplify calculation of data addresses in expanded memory. However, the page frame provided by software-only EMM implementations may not have the same alignment as an EMS board's page frame. To allow your EMS application to be used on systems with software-only EMMs, here are several simplifying assumptions that you should avoid making in your programming:

1. Because EMS hardware provides page frames aligned on 16-Kbyte boundaries, only the high-order byte of the segment address is significant in forming a physical address. As a result, some programs do not store the low-order byte of the page frame segment, assuming it to be zero. The LIM EMS does not specify that physical pages must be aligned on any boundary higher than a paragraph boundary.

2. Some EMS applications perform expanded memory address calculations assuming that the page frame is above 640K, or that its address in memory is greater than the address of the application itself. The page frame provided by a software EMM may not obey either assumption.

Reading and Writing Expanded Memory

While the LIM EMS 4.0 allows up to 32 megabytes of data to be managed by the EMM, the amount addressable by your program at any one time is limited by the number of physical pages present in the page frame.

Prior to reading data from or writing data to expanded memory, the logical page on which the data is located must be made accessible to a program by *mapping* the logical page into a physical page in the page frame. Page mapping is really the heart of EMS memory management; for most applications that use expanded memory, it is the most frequently used EMM function.

The LIM EMS 3.2 specification provided function 5, *Map/Unmap Handle Pages*, for this purpose. By supplying a handle, a logical page number, and a physical page number, a single logical page is mapped into a single physical page. Specifying −1, or 0FFFFH, as the logical page number makes any logical page that is mapped into the specified physical page inaccessible to the program. Of course, the contents of a page mapped out in this manner are not altered, and may be made accessible again by subsequently mapping that logical page into a physical page.

The LIM EMS 4.0 specification function 17, Map/Unmap Multiple Handle Pages, added a more concise and flexible means of mapping pages. In one invocation, this function can map or unmap logical pages into as many pages as the EMM supports. Programs that frequently map multiple pages at a time may realize visibly better performance because of the reduction in the fixed overhead associated with each call to the EMM.

As is the case with function 5, specifying a logical page number of −1 (0FFFFh) causes any logical page mapped into the specified physical page to be mapped out.

Two Ways to Specify Physical Pages

The initial discussion of physical pages in connection with LIM EMS 3.2 stated that physical pages are identified by an ordinal number (0 through 3 in the LIM EMS 3.2). The LIM EMS 4.0 specification provides an additional way to specify physical pages: by the actual segment address of the beginning of the physical page. For example, if the page frame address returned by Get Page Frame Address was CC00h, the third physical page within the page frame could be specified by its ordinal number, 2, or by its segment address, D400H. This segment address was calculated by adding three times the physical page size (in paragraphs) to the page frame base address.

Any LIM EMS 4.0 functions taking physical page numbers as parameters allow physical pages to be specified by either the ordinal number or the corresponding segment address. You can choose the method most convenient for your program by specifying a subfunction code in register AL for EMS 4.0 functions that accept physical page numbers. A subfunction code of 00h indicates that the physical page values are specified as ordinal physical page numbers, while a subfunction code of 01h indicates that physical page values are specified by their corresponding segment address.

As was described in a preceding section, the cross reference between physical page numbers and their segment address is obtained from the EMM via function 25, Get Physical Address Array.

Once a logical page is mapped into a physical page, your program can then address any data in that page with a *far* pointer. Language processors that generate only so-called small model programs may not support the use of 32-bit (*far*) pointers for named data items. In the absence of such support, some compilers provide a library routine that copies a block of data from an arbitrary segment and offset address to an area within a program's single 64-Kbyte data segment. Lacking even this, you may be able to write an assembly language interface routine to accomplish the same result.

Figure 7-3 shows a hypothetical 384K expanded memory configuration that is being used by two programs, a spreadsheet and a print spooler. It illustrates some of the dynamic relationships between programs, handles, logical pages, and physical pages, particularly:

- Two (or more) independent programs may use expanded memory simultaneously without interference.

- A single program may have more than one EMS handle allocated to it — the background task in the illustration has two handles.

- Sequentially numbered logical pages do not have to be mapped into sequential physical pages — the active foreground task has logical pages 6, 7, 2, and 1 mapped into physical pages 0 through 3.

The Move/Exchange Memory Region function (24), which was added as part of the LIM EMS 4.0, provides comprehensive facilities for managing the movement of data areas up to 1 megabyte in length between expanded memory and conventional memory. This function also allows data to be moved or exchanged when both specified regions are within expanded memory or when both regions are located within conventional memory.

The move subfunction (00h) copies the contents of the source region to a destination region. If the specified regions overlap, the EMM chooses the move direction so that the destination region receives an intact copy of the source region. When part of the source region has been overlaid by the target region during a move operation, a status code indicating that this has occurred will be returned by the EMM (as always, in the AH register).

The exchange subfunction (01h) exchanges two regions of memory; either or both regions can be either expanded memory or conventional memory. Unlike the move subfunction, the exchange subfunction does not allow overlapping regions to be specified.

A convenient feature of both subfunctions is that the current mapping context is not altered by the move or exchange operation. Any logical pages that your program may have mapped into the page frame will be unaltered by function 25, so there is no need for your program to save the mapping context prior to using this function.

The Move/Exchange Memory Region function relieves the programmer from several tedious programming chores associated with expanded memory

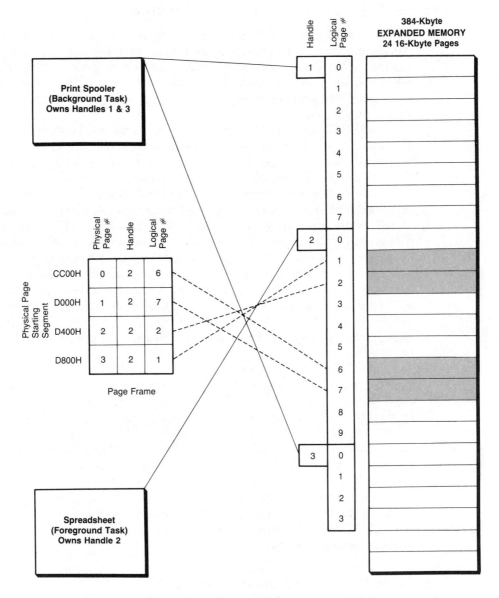

Figure 7-3. Snapshot of expanded memory with foreground and background tasks. Foreground task is currently active.

management that were a fact of life in earlier versions of the LIM EMS. None-theless, it is important to check the status code returned by this function. There are 13 different errors that could occur during either the move or the exchange operation.

Sharing Expanded Memory among Programs

Under LIM EMS 3.2, nothing prevented two programs from sharing data in expanded memory. A program needed to know only the handle and logical page number of the data it wanted to access. Since a program can't know *a priori* which handle(s) will be allocated to it by the EMM, two programs designed to share data in expanded memory had to arrange some means to pass handle numbers during execution.

LIM EMS 4.0 made the sharing of data in expanded memory a little easier by making it possible to associate an 8-character name with a handle. Two EMM functions were introduced to support this capability: Get/Set Handle Name, function 20, and Get Handle Directory, function 21.

Subfunction 00h of function 20, Get Handle Name, returns the 8-character name associated with a handle passed to the function. Subfunction 01h, Set Handle Name, associates an 8-character string with a specified handle number. There are no restrictions on the characters used to form the name, and all 8 characters are significant (the name is not a NULL-terminated ASCII string). A handle with no name would have a handle name consisting of 8 bytes of binary zeros (or ASCII NULLS, if you prefer). A handle's name is set to NULLS at EMM initialization, when the handle is allocated, and when the handle is deallocated. You can change a handle's name at any time, including resetting it to binary zeros. The only restriction is that no two handles are permitted to have the same name.

The EMM provides function 21, Get Handle Directory, to determine which handle is associated with a particular name or to provide a table of handle names associated with each active handle. Subfunction 00h, Get Handle Directory, returns this table to a user-supplied data area. Since the specification supports up to 255 handles, an 8-byte handle name plus a 2-byte handle value, the entire table could require as much as 2550 bytes to store. The actual number of handles supported by the EMM may be obtained from subfunction 02h, Get Total Handles. Multiplying this number by 10 yields the size of the area needed to contain the handle directory. Subfunction 01h, Search for Named Handle, is provided so that a program may look up the handle associated with a given name without having to scan the entire handle directory or without having to request the name associated with each handle number.

Executing Code in Expanded Memory

It has always been possible to use LIM EMS memory to store and run executable code, but it hasn't always been easy. In the first place, the 64-Kbyte maximum size of the pre-4.0 specification page frame limited the size of an overlay that could be active at one time. It was also up to each developer to work out the complete linkage mechanism that permitted the code in conventional memory to execute the code residing in expanded memory.

The LIM EMS 4.0 has the potential to alleviate some of these problems. Page frames larger than 64 Kbytes can now be supported, although EMMs written for boards designed for the 3.2 spec probably cannot provide a larger page frame. Two new functions, Alter Page Map and Jump (22) and Alter Page Map and Call (23), were introduced to assist the mapping and linkage of code objects in expanded memory.

Alter Page Map and Jump maps zero or more logical pages (up to the maximum number of physical pages supported by the EMM) into the page frame, and transfers control to a specified target address. Unlike every other EMM function, this one does not return control to the instruction following the int 67h (except when the EMM detects an error prior to jumping to the target address). The routine that receives control as a result of this function is responsible for establishing its own exit linkage. When the target address receives control, the contents of the processor registers and flags are as they were when the EMM interrupt was issued. Thus, programs may pass parameters to the target routine in registers. The mapping context that existed before this function was invoked is not preserved.

The Alter Page Map and Call function is an analog of the 80x86 *far* CALL instruction. Like the Alter Page Map and Jump function, this function maps zero or more logical pages (up to the maximum number of physical pages supported by the EMM) into the page frame, and transfers control to the target address. The pages mapped before the transfer of control occurs are called the *new* page map. Unlike the Alter Page Map and Jump function, the target routine returns control to the EMM (and eventually to the routine that issued the Alter Page Map and Call) by executing a *far* RETURN instruction. When the EMM receives control again from the target routine, a set of pages, called the *old* page map, is mapped into the page frame, and the EMM returns control to the original calling function. Both the *new* and *old* page map contents are specified by the calling program. The caller's registers are preserved throughout the process. The register contents at entry to the target routine are the same as they were at the time the calling routine issued the EMM interrupt.

This function is able to support nested calls—a routine entered via an Alter Page Map and Call may itself use this function. The EMM uses the invoking program's stack to keep track of the context at each call level. The number of stack bytes needed by the EMM to accomplish this is obtained by using subfunction 02, Get Page Map Stack Space Size, of the Alter Page Map and Call function.

Freeing Expanded Memory

Properly constructed programs close files and deallocate conventional memory that has been allocated from DOS before terminating. Likewise, expanded memory resources allocated by your program should be returned to the EMM before it terminates.

Since it acts completely independently of the operating system, the EMM has no way to determine when your program has ended. If your program does not explicitly deallocate all the expanded memory pages it has allocated before exiting, the next program that attempts to use expanded memory could find that expanded memory is full, even though the data in expanded memory is no longer being used.

If you intend to write robust applications using expanded memory, it will not be enough for your program to return resources to the EMM before normal terminations. A more thorough treatment must include code to clean up expanded memory resources in the Break (Control-C) handler, Critical Error handler, and the Zero Divide handler. Previously, handling these conditions required a significant amount of assembly language programming, along with the ability to decipher the *DOS Technical Reference Manual*. Recently, though, several high-level language products, including Microsoft C 5.0 and Borland's Turbo Pascal 4.0 and Turbo C, have included facilities for handling these conditions in the high-level language itself. Programmers using these products to write EMS applications no longer have a good reason to gloss over abnormal termination procedures.

System Software

The set of functions presented so far satisfies the expanded memory management needs of normal DOS (transient) programs. In the DOS environment, *transient* refers to programs that are executed from the DOS prompt or that are invoked from within another such program through the use of the DOS EXEC function. Memory occupied by such programs reverts to the operating system when the program is exited, and the program must be reloaded into memory before it is entered again.

As we mentioned earlier, device drivers, interrupt service routines (ISRs), and terminate-and-stay-resident programs (TSRs) that use expanded memory have additional responsibilities with respect to its use. These kinds of programs are classified as *resident*, since they remain in memory even after they are exited for the first time and since they may be reentered at any time — even while other programs are executing.

Transient vs Resident Programs

Memory residence or transience really isn't the important issue with respect to the use of expanded memory. The critical difference is that transient programs are executed *synchronously*, that is, explicitly at the request of the user. DOS manages the transition between programs so that the machine's state and operating-system–controlled resources are properly managed.

Hardware ISRs (including ISRs embedded inside device drivers and TSRs) obtain control *asynchronously* in response to hardware events. DOS plays no part in the transition between the currently executing program and the ISR. Therefore, the individual ISR is responsible for saving the state of the processor before altering that state, and restoring the original state before returning control to the interrupted program. The EMM also has a state, often referred to as a *context*. ISRs using expanded memory must preserve this context before changing it, and must restore it before exiting.

A substantial fraction of the EMS 4.0 function set is devoted to requirements of resident programs, operating systems, and operating environments.

Beside the functions required to save and restore the Expanded Memory Manager's context, EMS 4.0 also introduced several functions specifically designed to provide a cooperative linkage between the operating systems or multitasking environments (OS/Es in EMS parlance) and the EMM. This linkage would allow OS/E software to exploit features that may be incorporated into new EMS hardware designs, such as rapid task switching mechanisms and nonvolatile storage.

With our grasp of the expanded memory concepts presented so far in this chapter, we can now discuss the advanced features of LIM EMS that support resident programs and system-oriented software.

Detecting the Presence of the EMM

Device drivers, which are loaded before DOS is completely initialized, are not supposed to issue DOS file system calls. Most DOS calls are also off-limits to resident programs that do not specifically handle DOS's non-reentrancy problem. Thus, the open handle technique presented earlier in the chapter is an inappropriate means for these programs to detect the presence of expanded memory.

An alternative method that may be used by any program is the *get interrupt vector method*. This method works as follows:

1. The DOS Get Vector function (int 21h, function 35h) is issued to obtain the address of the EMM's software interrupt (67h).

2. The EMM resides within a DOS character device driver, which has a device header at offset zero in the segment returned in the ES register by the previous step. All character device drivers have an 8-character device name field located at offset 0Ah in the device header, which DOS uses to locate the device when file system calls reference it. Compare the device name at offset 0Ah in the segment returned in the ES register in step 1 with the string "EMMXXXX0." (Recall that this device name was referenced in the open call used as part of the open handle technique.) If the strings match, the Expanded Memory Manager is present.

Context Management

If you have already written interrupt service routines for device drivers or TSRs, you are no doubt aware that such programs must save the contents of any of the processor's registers that were altered by the program at entry, and must restore these registers before exit. This concept of saving the processor *state* (the registers, instruction pointer, and flag word constitute its state) must also be applied to the EMM.

Essentially, the state of the EMM, or *context*, is the content of the mapping registers (or simulations thereof). Your program must save the EMM context prior to invoking any functions that would alter it, and must restore the original context before relinquishing control.

The LIM EMS 3.2 specification provided two sets of functions for this purpose. The easiest to use is the function 8/9 pair, called Save Page Map and Restore Page Map. The former, given a handle number, saves the current context in an area internal to the EMM; no storage inside your program is required. The latter function, given the same handle number, restores the context previously stored for that handle in the EMM's internal save area. While they are easy to use, these functions have several limitations that lead to a recommendation to avoid their use in new programs.

The first limitation is that a maximum of one save area is provided for each handle, and some EMMs do not provide a save area for each possible handle. The effect is that your program cannot be fully reentrant if it uses these functions to save and restore the EMM's context, since each save for a given handle must be followed by a restore for that handle before the page map can be saved again using the same handle. Another limitation is that these functions only save or restore the context of the four physical pages defined by LIM EMS 3.2.

To supersede these limitations, LIM EMS 3.2 also provides function 15, Get/Set Page Map. Unlike functions 8 and 9, which save and restore the context from an area inside the EMM, this function saves and restores the context from an area provided by the caller. Subfunction 00h, Get Page Map, stores the EMM context in the user buffer pointed to by registers ES:DI. Subfunction 01h, Set Page Map, loads an EMM context from the user buffer pointed to by registers DS:SI. Subfunction 02h, Get and Set Page Map, does what its name implies, saving the EMM context in the buffer pointed to by ES:DI, and loading a new context from the area pointed to by DS:SI. You should not make any assumptions about the size of the buffer necessary to contain a saved context. Obtain it from the EMM through subfunction 03h, Get Size of Page Map Array. The format of a context save area depends on the internal EMM implementation, and is not designed to be intelligible to your program. Even assuming that you could locate the contents of the page mapping registers inside the context save area, you could not reliably determine which logical pages were mapped into each physical page.

Since the LIM EMS 4.0 supports up to 36 physical pages, the storage overhead of saving and restoring a complete context could be much greater than it was with the 64-Kbyte page frame of LIM EMS 3.2. To reduce this overhead, function 16, Get/Set Partial Page Map, was defined. A program can save the context for only the specific physical pages it will alter, analogous to the ability of the assembly language programmer to save only registers that will be modified by an interrupt service routine. Subfunction 00h, Get Partial Page Map, saves zero or more selected physical page mapping registers in a user-supplied buffer. Subfunction 01h, Set Partial Page Map, restores zero or more such registers. Subfunction 02h, Get Size of Partial Page Map Save Array, returns the size of the save area required to save context consisting of the specified number of physical pages.

Task Switching

Explicit support for task switching using the Expanded Memory Manager was added by LIM EMS 4.0. The set of functions described next are designed for use by operating systems or operating environments (OS/Es), such as Quarterdeck's DESQView or Microsoft's Windows, and should not be used by typical

EMS application programs. Specific details concerning their use exceed the scope of this chapter, but some discussion of their purpose and implementation is appropriate.

These OS/E functions will be able to take advantage of advanced EMS hardware designs. One feature that may be included in new-generation EMS boards is multiple sets of mapping registers. This would allow nearly instantaneous context switching among two or more tasks by dedicating an alternate map register set to each context. Another feature, called DMA Register Sets, would allow a multitasking operating system to switch tasks while another task is waiting for a DMA transfer to complete. Support for multiple context register sets and concurrent DMA transfers is incorporated into nine subfunctions of function 28, Alternate Map Register Sets.

The OS/E software can determine which advanced hardware capabilities are supported by the EMM by issuing function 26, Get Expanded Memory Hardware Information. It returns the number of Alternate Map Register Sets, DMA Register Sets, and an indicator of the ability of the expanded memory hardware to detect when DMA activity is occurring. It also returns the size of the raw pages supported by the EMM.

Hardware incorporating these features is just beginning to appear on the market. To allow multitasking software to be designed and built before new-generation hardware becomes readily available, the LIM EMS 4.0 provides for a software simulation of Alternate Map Register Sets, by saving and restoring context save areas that are provided by, and reside within, the multitasking monitor.

Nonvolatile Storage

Two functions added by LIM EMS 4.0 support the preservation of expanded memory across warm boots. Software that maps memory into mappable conventional memory (memory below 640K) should trap all conditions leading to a warm boot (BIOS int 19h) and issue function 29, Prepare Expanded Memory Hardware for Warmboot. Expanded memory boards with appropriate hardware designs could preserve the contents of mappable conventional memory, as well as the current mapping context across a warm boot. EMMs for existing boards do not implement this option because the boards are dependent on the underlying system's memory refresh circuitry, which is disabled during a warm boot.

Function 19, Get/Set Handle Attribute, allows an application to determine whether the EMM supports the capability to preserve the contents of a handle's pages across a warm boot. If so, the application may request that the EMM either preserve the specified handle's pages across the warm boot by setting its handle attribute to nonvolatile, or allow the EMM to deallocate the handle and discard the contents of its associated pages during a warm boot (a volatile handle). By default, all handles initially have the volatile attribute.

Access Control

An important attribute of the OS/E function set is that the multitasking manager can deny access to operating-system–oriented EMM functions for any program except itself. Function 30, Enable/Disable OS/E Function Set, permits the multitasking manager to disable functions 26, 28, and 30 before it gives control to application software, and to reenable access for its own purposes.

Summary

For many types of applications, expanded memory offers a practical programming solution to PC-DOS's 640K RAM limitation. The LIM EMS 4.0 is the most recent definition of a software interface between the application and a bank-switched memory management mechanism. This software interface is implemented by an Expanded Memory Manager, or EMM, which is typically loaded as a DOS character device driver at boot time. Expanded memory systems may be built by using dedicated EMS hardware, the paging mechanism of the Intel 80386 processor, or mapping registers on certain types of PS/2 memory expansion cards, or expanded memory systems may be completely in software.

Applications issue function requests to the EMM via software interrupt 67h in a style reminiscent of DOS's int 21h interface. Parameters are passed in registers and/or memory resident data structures, a mechanism that is most natural to assembly language programmers. Applications written in high-level languages may also access expanded memory if the language provides ways to issue software interrupts, manipulate the processor's registers, and specify *far* pointers to code and data objects.

The LIM EMS 3.2 defined an 8-megabyte expanded address space, divided into 16-kilobyte pages. Up to 64K of this space could be accessed concurrently through a 64-kilobyte page frame located in the memory space above 640K. It also defined a set of 14 relatively low-level functions that could be used to access and manipulate code and data objects in expanded memory. The 14 functions may be classified into three groups: informational, data management, and context management.

The LIM EMS 4.0 is an upwardly compatible addition to the 3.2 specification, and is now incorporated as a part of MS-DOS version 4.0. It incorporates several features present in the AQA EEMS specification, including a page frame larger than 64K, and the ability to support mapped memory below 640K. It also adds a class of functions designed to directly support rapid task switching by multitasking operating environments. The 4.0 specification increases the expanded memory address space to 32 megabytes and offers a set of functions that manipulate data and code objects at a higher level than was possible with the 3.2 specification.

Both transient and resident applications may use expanded memory. Resident applications must use the context management functions to save and restore the EMM's context, since such programs must save the processor's state at entry and restore that state at exit.

The 4.0 specification's operating system support functions will be able to take advantage of enhanced hardware features that may appear in new expanded memory hardware designs. One such feature is multiple sets of page mapping registers, which would allow a multitasking operating environment to perform nearly instantaneous context switching by dedicating a mapping register set to a task. Another feature, nonvolatile memory, would allow the contents of expanded memory to be retained across a warm boot. Boards providing hardware support for these functions are only now becoming commercially available.

Bibliography

Duncan, Ray. "Lotus/Intel/Microsoft Expanded Memory," *Byte* 11, no. 11, 1986 (Special IBM Edition).
> How to write programs using LIM EMS 3.2. Example portions of RAMDISK program that uses expanded memory.

Hansen, Marion, and John Driscoll. "LIM EMS 4.0: A definition for the Next Generation of Expanded Memory," *MSJ* 3, no. 1, Jan 88.
> A description of the features introduced by LIM EMS 4.0. Sample programs in C and assembly language demonstrate improved methods for screen saving, data sharing between programs, and executing code from expanded memory.

Hansen, Marion, Bill Krueger, and Nick Stuecklen. "Expanded Memory: Writing Programs That Break the 640K Barrier," *MSJ* 2, no. 1, Mar 87.
> A description of LIM EMS 3.2. Sample programs in C and assembly language demonstrate screen saving and executing code from expanded memory.

Lefor, John A., and Karen Lund. "Reaching into Expanded Memory," *PCTJ* 5, no. 5, May 86.
> An application-oriented explanation of the LIM EMS 3.2 and AQA EEMS. Complete sample programs to obtain expanded memory parameters and to dump expanded memory data.

Lotus/Intel/Microsoft. "Lotus/Intel/Microsoft Expanded Memory Specification, Version 4.0," Document number 300275-005, Oct 87.
> The complete specification for the latest version of the expanded memory specification. Includes sample programs in Turbo Pascal and assembly language.

Mirecki, Ted. "Expandable Memory," *PCTJ* 4 no. 2, Feb 86.
> A description of LIM EMS 3.2 and the AQA EEMS. Tests of Intel and AST expanded memory products.

Yao, Paul. "EMS Support Improves Microsoft Windows 2.0 Application Performance," *MSJ* 3, no. 1, Jan 88.
> A technical discussion of the way Windows 2.0 uses LIM EMS 4.0 to manage multiple concurrent applications.

Low-Level Interface Routines and Sample Application

If this chapter has accomplished its mission, you should now have a good idea of how expanded memory works and of how DOS programs can use it to access literally megabytes of additional storage for code and data. Now we'll help you use the power of expanded memory in your own software by providing you with a comprehensive collection of listings written in Microsoft C version 5.0. We'll also provide a sample EMS application that exercises some of the more complex expanded memory functions. Table 7-4 summarizes the listings which you will find at the end of the chapter.

Table 7-4. Low-Level Interface Routines

Listing	File Name	Contents
7-2	EMMCONST.H	Provides *#defines* for general EMS constants, and status codes returned by EMS functions.
7-3	EMMTYPES.H	Contains *typedefs* for data structures passed between the EMS interface functions and the EMS application program.
7-4	EMMERMSG.C	Gives an array of character strings providing a short text description for each nonzero EMS function status code.
7-5	EMMFUNC.C	Has a comprehensive EMS function library. Unless otherwise stated, each EMS function returns the EMS function status code as an integer.
7-6	EMMFUNC.H	Contains function prototypes for each function in EMMFUNC.C. If your compiler supports function prototyping defined in the ANSI C language specification (as does Microsoft's version 5 product), the inclusion of this file in your applications will ensure that the argument types specified in your programs agree with the parameter type expected by the called functions.
7-7	EMMEXIST.H	Contains routines to test for the presence of expanded memory. The "open handle" method is performed by the function *emm_exists* (line 25). The "get interrupt vector" method of testing for the presence of expanded memory is performed by function *emm_exists2* (line 113).
7-8	SNAPSHOT.C	Provides a terminate-and-stay-resident (TSR) program that stores the current contents of the video display screen to a buffer in expanded memory every time the PrtSc key is pressed. The program can store as many screen images as your system has space in expanded memory.
7-9	PLAYBACK.C	Provides a program to copy the screen images stored by the SNAPSHOT program in expanded memory to the DOS standard output file. A program's screen displays could be captured permanently, for example, by redirecting PLAYBACK's standard output to a disk file.
7-10	BEEP.ASM	Has a utility routine to sound an audible tone on the PC's built-in speaker.

About the Sample Application

The sample application consists of two programs: SNAPSHOT.C and PLAY-BACK.C. SNAPSHOT is a terminate-and-stay-resident (TSR) program that stores text screen images in expanded memory by intercepting the print screen interrupt (int 5). This interrupt is invoked every time the PrtSc or Print Screen key is pressed. SNAPSHOT also builds an index data structure in expanded memory that contains the logical page number and byte offset of each screen image stored in expanded memory. PLAYBACK simply reads the index data structure, copying each of the text screens from expanded memory to the DOS standard output file. Figure 7-4 diagrams how expanded memory is used to establish communication between the two independent programs.

In order to demonstrate some of the more advanced expanded memory concepts that were presented in this chapter, this application is necessarily more complicated than an intermediate-level programmer might expect to write as a first expanded-memory project. Developers who are not familiar with TSR and interrupt handler programming in the DOS environment may feel particularly uncomfortable digesting the large portion of code in SNAPSHOT.C that is required to install, manage, and terminate itself.

While SNAPSHOT has more than its share of DOS-related complications, its use of context switching and new LIM EMS 4.0 functions offers a valuable study example of EMS concepts that are not usually demonstrated in EMS programming tutorials. Key EMS features exploited by SNAPSHOT include:

- Expanded memory sharing between programs by using the Named Handle facility (EMS function 20).
- Context switching using Get/Set Page Map (EMS function 15).
- Block moves of data between conventional memory and expanded memory by using the Move/Exchange Memory Region function (EMS function 18).
- Dynamically appending logical pages to a previously allocated EMS handle by using the Reallocate Pages function (EMS function 18).

Note: In order to execute these programs, your Expanded Memory Manager must support the LIM EMS 4.0 specification.

A Few Coding Highlights

The actual work of storing the video display screens in expanded memory is trivial. A single EMS Move/Exchange Memory Region function call at line 175 of SNAPSHOT.C suffices to copy the entire screen image from the video display buffer into expanded memory. Since this takes place inside an interrupt handler, the Get Page Map function on line 110 is required to preserve the EMS mapping context. The Set Page Map function on line 120 restores the EMS mapping context prior to exiting the interrupt handler.

The Set Handle Name function on line 372 of SNAPSHOT.C associates the ASCII name "SNAPSHOT" with the EMS handle that the program allocated for screen storage. By giving the handle a name, the PLAYBACK program can

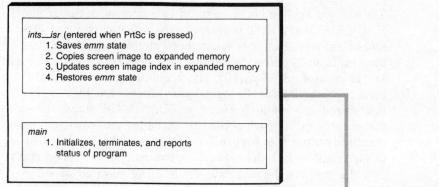

SNAPSHOT.EXE (a TSR)

ints__isr (entered when PrtSc is pressed)
1. Saves *emm* state
2. Copies screen image to expanded memory
3. Updates screen image index in expanded memory
4. Restores *emm* state

main
1. Initializes, terminates, and reports
   status of program

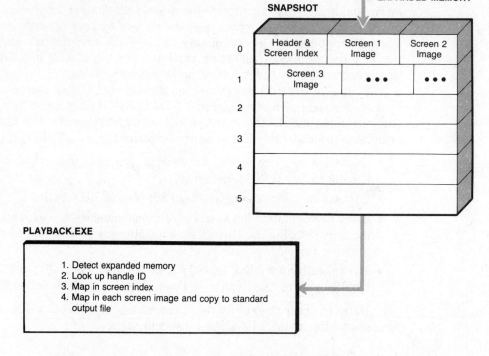

EXPANDED MEMORY

SNAPSHOT

Header & Screen Index	Screen 1 Image	Screen 2 Image

0

| Screen 3
Image | ••• | ••• |

1

2

3

4

5

PLAYBACK.EXE

1. Detect expanded memory
2. Look up handle ID
3. Map in screen index
4. Map in each screen image and copy to standard
   output file

Figure 7-4. Example application—SNAPSHOT/PLAYBACK.

locate and access this region of expanded memory without having to know its
actual handle number, a value that could vary each time SNAPSHOT is started.

Listing 7-2. EMMCONST.H

```
/*
General EMS Constants
*/

#define EMM_INT              0x67        /* expanded memory software interrupt */
#define HANDLE_NAME_LENGTH   8           /* # bytes in handle name */
#define PAGE_FRAMES          4           /* maximum # of physical pages */
#define PAGE_SIZE            16384       /* # bytes in EMS page */
#define EMM_DEVICE           "EMMXXXX0"  /* EMM device driver name */
#define MAX_HANDLE           255         /* maximum # of EMM handles */

/*
Constants for EMS Status Codes
*/

#define FRSTEMERR  0x80    /* first EMM error number */
#define LASTEMERR  0xA4    /* last EMM error number */

#define FUNCCOK    0x00    /* the specified function completed without error */
#define EMDRVSWF   0x80    /* EMM driver software failure */
#define EMDRVHWF   0x81    /* EMM driver detected hardware failure */
#define EMDRVBSY   0x82    /* EMM driver busy (doesn't happen any more) */
#define HANDLNFD   0x83    /* cannot find the specified handle */
#define FUNCCUND   0x84    /* the function code is undefined */
#define HANDLINS   0x85    /* no handles are currently available */
#define MAPCXPRO   0x86    /* mapping context restoration error occurred */
#define TOTPGINS   0x87    /* insufficient total pages for request */
#define UNAPGINS   0x88    /* insufficient unallocated pages for request */
#define LPAGE2SM   0x89    /* zero logical pages have been requested from
                              LIM 3.2 compatible function */
#define LPAGERNG   0x8A    /* logical page out of range for specified handle */
#define PPAGE2BG   0x8B    /* physical page out of range */
#define MRCSAFUL   0x8C    /* mapping register context save area is full */
#define MRCSTDUP   0x8D    /* mapping register context stack already has a
                              context associated with the specified handle */
#define MRCSTNFD   0x8E    /* mapping register context stack does not have a
                              context associated with the specified handle */
#define SFUNCUND   0x8F    /* undefined subfunction was requested */
#define ATTRBUND   0x90    /* the attribute type is undefined */
#define NVSTGUNS   0x91    /* the system does not support nonvolatility */
#define MREGNOVW   0x92    /* partial source overwrite occurred during move
                              region */
#define MREGN2SM   0x93    /* EMS region is too big for specified handle */
```

continued

Listing 7-2. *continued*

```
#define MREGNOVL     0x94    /* conventional memory region and expanded memory
                                region overlap */
#define LPGOF2BG     0x95    /* offset within a logical page exceeds the length of
                                a logical page */
#define MREGN2BG     0x96    /* region length exceed 1-Mbyte limit */
#define MREGNDUP     0x97    /* source and destination expanded memory regions
                                have the same handle and overlap */
#define MREGNUND     0x98    /* undefined/unsupported memory source and
                                destination types */
#define AMRSNFD      0x9A    /* specified alternate map register set does not exist */
#define AMDRSINS     0x9B    /* all alternate map/DMA register sets are in use */
#define AMDRSUNS     0x9C    /* alternate map/DMA register sets are not supported */
#define AMDRSUND     0x9D    /* specified alternate map/DMA register set is not
                                defined, not allocated, or is the current one */
#define DDMACUNS     0x9E    /* dedicated DMA channels are not supported */
#define DDMACNFD     0x9F    /* the specified dedicated DMA channel does not exist */
#define HNDVLNFD     0xA0    /* no corresponding handle value could be found for
                                the specified handle name */
#define HNDNMDUP     0xA1    /* a handle with the specified name already exists */
#define MREGNWRP     0xA2    /* attempt to wrap around 1-Mbyte address space during
                                move or exchange */
#define USRDSFMT     0xA3    /* the contents of the user data structure passed to
                                the function were corrupt or meaningless */
#define OPSYSACC     0xA4    /* the operating system denied access to the function */
```

Listing 7-3. EMMTYPES.H

```
        /*
                Structures used to communicate with EMM
        */

#define PCONTEXT        unsigned char
#define PMAP            unsigned char

typedef struct handle_page {                        /* handle page structure */
        unsignedint     emm_handle;                 /* allocated EMM handle */
        unsignedint     pages_alloc_to_handle;      /* # logical pages belonging
                                                        to handle */
} HANDLE_PAGE;

typedef struct ppmap {                              /* partial context request
```

```
                                             structure */
      unsignedint      seg_cnt;              /* number of mappable segments
                                                to get */
      unsignedint      seg_addr[PAGE_FRAMES]; /* address of mappable segment
                                                to get */
} PPMAP;

typedef struct log_to_phys {                 /* logical to physical
                                                mapping struct */
      unsignedint      log_page_no;          /* logical page number */
      unsignedint      phys_page_no;         /* page frame #/mappable
                                                segment address */
} LOG_TO_PHYS;

typedef struct handle_names {                /* handle name array
                                                element */
      unsignedint      handle_value;         /* handle */
      char             handle_name[HANDLE_NAME_LENGTH]; /* name associated with
                                                handle */
} HANDLE_NAMES;

typedef struct map_phys_page {               /* mappable segment -> phys
                                                page # mapping */
      unsignedint      phys_page_segment;    /* segment address of
                                                physical page */
      unsignedint      phys_page_number;     /* number of physical page */
} MAP_PHYS_PAGE;

typedef struct hardware_info {     /* EMS hardware information structure */
      unsignedint      raw_page_size;        /* # bytes in raw page */
      unsignedint      alt_reg_sets;         /* # alternate map
                                                register sets */
      unsigned int     ctx_savearea_size;    /* # bytes in context save area */
      unsigned int     dma_reg_sets;         /* # DMA register sets */
      unsigned int     dma_chan_op;          /* 0: LIM std. DMA op, 1:
                                                only 1 DMA channel */
} HARDWARE_INFO;

#define CONV_MEM       0    /* conventional memory */
#define EXP_MEM        1    /* expanded memory */

typedef struct mregn {         /* memory region descriptor */
      unsignedchar     memory_type;      /* CONV_MEM / EXP_MEM */
      unsignedint      handle;           /* CONV_MEM: 0, EXP_MEM: handle */
      unsignedint      initial_offset;   /* CONV_MEM:
                                            0 - 65535, EXP_MEM:
```

continued

Listing 7-3. *continued*

```
                                              0 - 16383 */
        unsignedint    initial_seg_page;  /* CONV_MEM: segment address,
                                              EXP_MEM: page # */
} MREGN;

typedef struct move_xchg {  /* move exchange structure */
        long            region_length;     /* 0 - 1 megabyte */
        MREGN                source;       /* source region descriptor */
        MREGN                dest;         /* destination region descriptor */
} MOVE_XCHG;
```

Listing 7-4. EMMERMSG.C

```
/*
Name:        emmermsg.c
Contents:    error messages for LIM EMS Spec 4.0 Error Codes
Reference:   Lotus(r)/Intel(r)/Microsoft(r)
                 Expanded Memory Specification
                 Version 4.0, pp A5 - A10
*/

char    *emmermsg[] = {
        "EMM driver software failure",
        "EMM driver detected hardware failure",
        "EMM driver busy (doesn't happen any more)",
        "Cannot find the specified handle",
        "The function code is undefined",
        "No handles are currently available",
        "A mapping context restoration error has occurred",
        "Insufficient total pages for request",
        "Insufficient unallocated pages for request",
        "Zero logical pages have been requested from LIM 3.2 compatible
            function",
        "Logical page out of range for specified handle",
        "Physical page out of range",
        "Mapping register context save area is full",
        "Mapping register context stack already has a context associated with
            the specified handle",
        "Mapping register context stack does not have a context associated with
            the specified handle",
        "Undefined subfunction was requested",
        "The attribute type is undefined",
```

```
    "The system does not support nonvolatility",
    "Partial source overwrite occurred during move region",
    "Expanded memory region is too big for specified handle",
    "Conventional memory region and expanded memory region overlap",
    "Offset within a logical page exceeds the length of a logical page",
    "Region length exceeds 1-Mbyte limit",
    "Source and destination expanded memory regions have the same handle
        and overlap",
    "Undefined/unsupported memory source and destination types",
    "Error code 0x99 is not used",
    "Specified alternate map register set does not exist",
    "All alternate map/DMA register sets are in use",
    "Alternate map/DMA register sets are not supported",
    "Specified alternate map/DMA register set is not defined, not
        allocated, or is the current one",
    "Dedicated DMA channels are not supported",
    "The specified dedicated DMA channel does not exist",
    "No corresponding handle value could be found for the specified
        handle name",
    "A handle with the specified name already exists",
    "Attempt to wrap around 1-Mbyte address space during move or exchange",
    "The contents of the user data structure passed to the function were
        corrupt or meaningless",
    "The operating system denied access to the function"
    };
```

Listing 7-5. EMMFUNC.C

```
#include<dos.h>
#include"emmconst.h"
#include"emmtypes.h"
#pragma check_stack(off)

#define CONTINUE_COL 32          /* error message continuation column */

static union REGS inregs, outregs;
static struct SREGS segregs;
static int result;
void ShowEMMErr(errcode, lineno, filename)
unsigned int errcode;
unsigned int lineno;
char *filename;
```

continued

Listing 7-5. *continued*

```
{
        unsigned int ec, func, len, line;
        char *bp, *lp, *cp;
        extern char *emmermsg[];

        ec = errcode & 0x00FF;
        func = inregs.x.ax;

        printf("EMM error detected at line(%d) in source file(%s)\n", lineno,
            filename);
        if (ec < FRSTEMERR || ec > LASTEMERR)
                printf("EMM Function (%04X) Error(%02X): Unknown Error
                    Code!\n", func, ec);
        else {
                printf("EMM Function (%04X) Error(%02X): ", func, ec);
                lp = emmermsg[ec - FRSTEMERR];
                line = 0;
                while (*lp) {
                        for (cp = lp, len = 80 - CONTINUE_COL; *cp && len;
                        cp++, len--)
                                if (*cp == ' ')
                                        bp = cp;
                        if (*cp)
                                *bp++ = '\0';
                        if (line++)
                                printf("                            ");
                        printf("%s\n", lp);
                        lp = (*cp) ? bp : cp;
                }
        }
}


EMSGetStatus()  /* tests for presence of working EMM */
{
        inregs.h.ah = 0x40;      /* EMS Get Status function */
        result = (unsigned int) int86(EMM_INT, &inregs, &outregs) >> 8;
        return(result);
}
EMSGetFrameAddr(pfa)                  /* returns far address of EMM page frame */
char far **pfa;
{
        inregs.h.ah = 0x41;      /* EMS Get Page Frame Address function */
        result = (unsigned int) int86(EMM_INT, &inregs, &outregs) >> 8;
        if (!result) {
                FP_SEG(*pfa) = outregs.x.bx;
```

```
                FP_OFF(*pfa) = 0;
        }
        return(result);
}


EMSGetPageCnt(una, tot)          /* returns total and unallocated EMS pages */
unsigned int *una, *tot;
{
        inregs.h.ah = 0x42;      /* EMS Get Unallocated Page Count function */
        result = (unsigned int) int86(EMM_INT, &inregs, &outregs) >> 8;
        if (!result) {
                *una = outregs.x.bx;
                *tot = outregs.x.dx;
        }
        return(result);
}


EMSAllocatePages(handle, pages) /* allocate a handle with 'pages'
   logical pages */
unsigned int *handle, pages;
{
        inregs.h.ah = 0x43;      /* EMS Allocate Pages */
        inregs.x.bx = pages;     /* number of logical pages to allocate */
        result = (unsigned int) int86(EMM_INT, &inregs, &outregs) >> 8;
        if (!result)                             /* function succeeded */
                *handle = outregs.x.dx;          /* EMM handle to use with
                                                    these pages */
        return(result);
}


EMSMapHandlePage(handle, page, frame)    /* map logical page <handle,page>
                                            into 'frame' */
unsigned int handle, page, frame;
{
        inregs.h.ah = 0x44;              /* EMS Map/Unmap Handle Pages */
        inregs.h.al = frame & 0x00ff;    /* target page frame */
        inregs.x.bx = page;              /* logical page number to map in */
        inregs.x.dx = handle;            /* handle to which logical page
                                            belongs */
        result = (unsigned int) int86(EMM_INT, &inregs, &outregs) >> 8;
        return(result);
}


EMSDeallocatePages(handle)       /* deallocate handle 'handle' and all
                                    its pages */
unsigned int handle;
```

continued

Listing 7-5. *continued*

```
{
        inregs.h.ah = 0x45;      /* EMS Deallocate Pages */
        inregs.x.dx = handle;    /* EMM-assigned handle to deallocate */
        result = (unsigned int) int86(EMM_INT, &inregs, &outregs) >> 8;
        return(result);
}

EMSGetVersion(emsver)   /* returns version number of EMM software */
char *emsver;
{
        inregs.h.ah = 0x46;              /* EMS Get Version function */
        result = (unsigned int) int86(EMM_INT, &inregs, &outregs);
        if (!(result & 0xFF00)) {        /* function succeeded */
                emsver[0] = ((result & 0x00F0) >> 4) + '0';
                emsver[1] = '.';
                emsver[2] = (result & 0x000F) + '0';
                emsver[3] = '\0';
        }
        return(result >> 8);
}

EMSSavePageMap(handle)          /* save EMM context in EMM's context
                                    save area */
unsigned int handle;
{
        inregs.h.ah = 0x47;      /* EMS Save Page Map */
        inregs.x.dx = handle;    /* handle to save under */
        result = (unsigned int) int86(EMM_INT, &inregs, &outregs) >> 8;
        return(result);
}

EMSRestorePageMap(handle)       /* restore EMM context from EMM's context
                                    save area */
unsigned int handle;
{
        inregs.h.ah = 0x48;      /* EMS Restore Page Map */
        inregs.x.dx = handle;    /* context area to restore from */
        result = (unsigned int) int86(EMM_INT, &inregs, &outregs) >> 8;
        return(result);
}

EMSGetHandleCnt(hcnt)   /* returns the number of open handles (1 - 255) */
unsigned int *hcnt;
{
```

```
        inregs.h.ah = 0x4B;      /* EMS Get Handle Count */
        result = (unsigned int) int86(EMM_INT, &inregs, &outregs) >> 8;
        if (!result) {           /* function succeeded */
                *hcnt = outregs.x.bx;
        }
        return(result);
}


EMSGetHandlePages(handle, pages)/* returns no. of pages allocated to handle */
unsigned int handle, *pages;
{
        inregs.h.ah = 0x4C;      /* EMS Get Handle Pages */
        inregs.x.dx = handle;    /* handle to which pages supposedly belong */
        result = (unsigned int) int86(EMM_INT, &inregs, &outregs) >> 8;
        if (!result)             /* function succeeded */
                *pages = outregs.x.bx;
        return(result);
}


EMSGetAllHandlePages(hp, hpcnt) /* returns no. of pages allocated to all
                                   open handles */
HANDLE_PAGE *hp;
unsigned int *hpcnt;
{
        segread(&segregs);                  /* fill segment registers */
        inregs.h.ah = 0x4D;                 /* EMS Get All Handle Pages */
        segregs.es = segregs.ds;                    /* segment of HANDLE
                                                       _PAGE array */
        inregs.x.di = (unsigned int) hp;            /* offset of HANDLE
                                                       _PAGE array */
        result = (unsigned int) int86x(EMM_INT, &inregs, &outregs,
            &segregs) >> 8;
        if (!result)                        /* function succeeded */
                *hpcnt = outregs.x.bx;
        return(result);
}


EMSGetPageMap(map)       /* get EMM context in user context save area */
PMAP *map;
{
        segread(&segregs);              /* fill segment registers */
        segregs.es = segregs.ds;        /* use es = ds */
        inregs.x.ax = 0x4E00;           /* EMS Get Page Map */
        inregs.x.di = (unsigned int) map;       /* pointer to map array */
        result = (unsigned int) int86x(EMM_INT, &inregs, &outregs,
            &segregs) >> 8;
```

continued

Listing 7-5. *continued*

```
        return(result);
}


EMSSetPageMap(map)        /* set EMM context from user context save area */
PMAP *map;
{
        segread(&segregs);                /* fill segment registers */
        inregs.x.ax = 0x4E01;             /* EMS Set Page Map */
        inregs.x.si = (unsigned int) map;      /* pointer to map array */
        result = (unsigned int) int86x(EMM_INT, &inregs, &outregs,
            &segregs) >> 8;
        return(result);
}


EMSGetSetPageMap(srcmap, destmap)        /* save EMM context in destmap, and then
                                            set EMM context from srcmap */
PMAP *srcmap, *destmap;
{
        segread(&segregs);                /* fill segment registers */
        segregs.es = segregs.ds;          /* both maps in ds */
        inregs.x.ax = 0x4E02;             /* EMS Get and Set Page Map */
        inregs.x.si = (unsigned int) srcmap;    /* pointer to source map array */
        inregs.x.di = (unsigned int) destmap;   /* pointer to dest map array */
        result = (unsigned int) int86x(EMM_INT, &inregs, &outregs,
            &segregs) >> 8;
        return(result);
}


EMSGetPageMapSize(size) /* get size of user context save area */
unsigned int *size;
{
        inregs.x.ax = 0x4E03;    /* EMS Get Page Map Size */
        result = (unsigned int) int86(EMM_INT, &inregs, &outregs);
        if (!(result & 0xFF00)) /* function succeeded */
                *size = outregs.h.al;
        return(result >> 8);
}


EMSGetPPageMap(pmap, savearea)  /* get partial EMM context in user save area */
PPMAP *pmap;
PCONTEXT *savearea;
{
        segread(&segregs);                /* fill segment registers */
        segregs.es = segregs.ds;    /* use es = ds */
```

```
        inregs.x.ax = 0x4F00;   /* EMS Get Partial Page Map */
        inregs.x.si = (unsigned int) pmap;      /* which frames we want */
        inregs.x.di = (unsigned int) savearea;  /* pointer to map array */
        result = (unsigned int) int86x(EMM_INT, &inregs, &outregs,
            &segregs) >> 8;
        return(result);
}


EMSSetPPageMap(savearea)            /* set partial EMM context from user save area */
PCONTEXT *savearea;
{
        segread(&segregs);      /* fill segment registers */
        inregs.x.ax = 0x4F01;   /* EMS Set Partial Page Map */
        inregs.x.si = (unsigned int) savearea;  /* frames we want to restore */
        result = (unsigned int) int86x(EMM_INT, &inregs, &outregs,
            &segregs) >> 8;
        return(result);
}


EMSGetPPageMapSize(count, size) /* get size of area needed to store */
                                /* EMM context for count page frames */
unsigned int count, *size;
{
        inregs.x.ax = 0x4F02;   /* EMS Get Partial Page Map Size */
        inregs.x.bx = count;    /* number of frames we want to save */
        result = (unsigned int) int86(EMM_INT, &inregs, &outregs);
        if (!(result & 0xFF00)) /* success */
                *size = outregs.h.al;
        return(result >> 8);
}


EMSMapMultPages(handle, map, method, count)     /* map count pages in map for
                                                        handle */
unsigned int handle;    /* handle to map pages for */
LOG_TO_PHYS *map;       /* logical to physical page map */
unsigned int method;    /* use page frame #'s or mappable segment addresses */
unsigned int count;     /* number of entries in map */
{
        segread(&segregs);      /* fill segment registers */
        inregs.h.ah = 0x50;     /* EMS Map Multiple Handle Pages */
        inregs.h.al = (unsigned char) method;
        inregs.x.cx = count;    /* number of pages to map in */
        inregs.x.dx = handle;   /* handle these pages belong to */
        inregs.x.si = (unsigned int) map;       /* pages to map in */
        result = (unsigned int) int86x(EMM_INT, &inregs, &outregs,
            &segregs) >> 8;
```

continued

Listing 7-5. *continued*

```
        return(result);
}


EMSReallocPages(handle, pages)   /* change handle's allocation to pages */
unsigned int handle, *pages;
{
        inregs.h.ah = 0x51;        /* EMS Reallocate Pages */
        inregs.x.bx = *pages;      /* number of logical pages have when done */
        inregs.x.dx = handle;      /* handle to reallocate page for */
        result = (unsigned int) int86(EMM_INT, &inregs, &outregs) >> 8;
        if (!result)               /* function succeeded */
                *pages = outregs.x.bx; /* new number of pages we have */
        return(result);
}


EMSGetHandleAttr(handle, attr)           /* gets handle attribute */
unsigned int handle, *attr;
{
        inregs.x.ax = 0x5200;            /* EMS Get Handle Attribute */
        inregs.x.dx = handle;
        result = (unsigned int) int86(EMM_INT, &inregs, &outregs);
        if (!(result & 0xFF00))          /* function succeeded */
                *attr = outregs.h.al;    /* attribute */
        return(result >> 8);
}


EMSSetHandleAttr(handle, attr)  /* sets handle attribute */
unsigned int handle, attr;
{
        inregs.x.ax = 0x5201;    /* EMS Set Handle Attribute */
        inregs.x.dx = handle;
        inregs.h.bl = attr & 0x00FF;
        result = (unsigned int) int86(EMM_INT, &inregs, &outregs) >> 8;
        return(result);
}


EMSGetAttrCap(cap)               /* get attribute capability */
unsigned int *cap;
{
        inregs.x.ax = 0x5202;    /* EMS Get Attribute capability */
        result = (unsigned int) int86(EMM_INT, &inregs, &outregs);
        if (!(result & 0xFF00)) /* success */
                *cap = outregs.h.al;
        return(result >> 8);
}
```

continued

```
EMSGetHandleName(handle, name)    /* get handle name */
unsigned int handle;              /* handle to get name for */
char *name;                       /* buffer to receive handle name */
{
        segread(&segregs);        /* fill segment registers */
        inregs.x.ax = 0x5300;     /* EMS Get Handle Name */
        segregs.es = segregs.ds;
        inregs.x.di = (unsigned int) name;
        inregs.x.dx = handle;
        result = (unsigned int) int86x(EMM_INT, &inregs, &outregs,
            &segregs) >> 8;
        return(result);
}

EMSSetHandleName(handle, name)    /* set handle name */
unsigned int handle;              /* handle to set name for */
char *name;                       /* buffer with handle name to set */
{
        segread(&segregs);        /* fill segment registers  */
        inregs.x.ax = 0x5301;     /* EMS Set Handle Name */
        inregs.x.si = (unsigned int) name;
        inregs.x.dx = handle;
        result = (unsigned int) int86x(EMM_INT, &inregs, &outregs,
            &segregs) >> 8;
        return(result);
}

EMSGetHandleDir(hnt, hn_cnt)      /* get handle directory */
HANDLE_NAMES *hnt;                /* pointer to handle name table */
unsigned int *hn_cnt;             /* # of entries returned */
{
        segread(&segregs);        /* fill segment registers  */
        inregs.x.ax = 0x5400;     /* EMS Get Handle Directory */
        inregs.x.di = (unsigned int) hnt;
        segregs.es = segregs.ds;
        result = (unsigned int) int86x(EMM_INT, &inregs, &outregs, &segregs);
        if (!(result & 0xFF00)) /* success */
                *hn_cnt = outregs.h.al; /* return # of handle names gotten */
        return(result >> 8);
}

EMSSearchHandleName(name, handle)        /* search for named handle */
char *name;                              /* name to search for */
unsigned int *handle;                    /* returned handle number */
{
        segread(&segregs);               /* fill segment registers  */
```

continued

Listing 7-5. *continued*

```
        inregs.x.ax = 0x5401;    /* EMS Search for Named Handle */
        inregs.x.si = (unsigned int) name;
        result = (unsigned int) int86x(EMM_INT, &inregs, &outregs,
            &segregs) >> 8;
        if (!result)             /* success */
                *handle = outregs.x.dx; /* return handle value */
        return(result);
}


EMSGetTotalHandles(handle_count) /* get total # of handles */
unsigned int *handle_count;
{
        inregs.x.ax = 0x5402;    /* EMS Get Total Handles subfunction */
        result = (unsigned int) int86(EMM_INT, &inregs, &outregs) >> 8;
        if (!result)
                *handle_count = outregs.x.bx;
        return(result);
}


EMSMoveRegion(rp)                 /* Move Region */
MOVE_XCHG *rp;                    /* ptr to region descriptor */
{
        segread(&segregs);       /* fill segment registers */
        inregs.x.ax = 0x5700;    /* EMS Move Region */
        inregs.x.si = (unsigned int) rp;
        result = (unsigned int) int86x(EMM_INT, &inregs, &outregs,
            &segregs) >> 8;
        return(result);
}


EMSExchangeRegion(rp)             /* Exchange Region */
MOVE_XCHG *rp;                    /* ptr to region descriptor */
{
        segread(&segregs);       /* fill segment registers */
        inregs.x.ax = 0x5701;    /* EMS Exchange Region */
        inregs.x.si = (unsigned int) rp;
        result = (unsigned int) int86x(EMM_INT, &inregs, &outregs,
            &segregs) >> 8;
        return(result);
}

EMSGetMapAddrArray(mpaa, mpa_cnt) /* get mappable physical address array */
MAP_PHYS_PAGE *mpaa;              /* ptr to mappable physical address array */
unsigned int *mpa_cnt;           /* # of elements returned */
{
        segread(&segregs);       /* fill segment registers */
```

```
        inregs.x.ax = 0x5800;    /* EMS Get Mappable Physical Address Array */
        inregs.x.di = (unsigned int) mpaa;
        segregs.es = segregs.ds;
        result = (unsigned int) int86x(EMM_INT, &inregs, &outregs,
            &segregs) >> 8;
        if (!result)               /* success */
                *mpa_cnt = outregs.x.cx;   /* return # of mappable
                                              physical pages */

        return(result);
}


EMSGetMapAddrCount(mpa_cnt)      /* get mappable physical address count */
unsigned int *mpa_cnt;           /* # of mappable
                                    physical pages */

{

        inregs.x.ax = 0x5801;    /* EMS Get Mappable Physical Address Count */
        result = (unsigned int) int86(EMM_INT, &inregs, &outregs) >> 8;
        if (!result)               /* success */
                *mpa_cnt = outregs.x.cx;    /* return # of mappable
                                               physical pages */

        return(result);
}
EMSGetHardwareInfo(hwp) /* get EMS hardware info */
HARDWARE_INFO *hwp;              /* ptr to area to receive hardware info */
{

        segread(&segregs);      /* fill segment registers */
        inregs.x.ax = 0x5900;    /* EMS Get EMS Hardware Info */
        inregs.x.di = (unsigned int) hwp;
        segregs.es = segregs.ds;
        result = (unsigned int) int86x(EMM
        _INT, &inregs, &outregs, &segregs) >> 8;
        return(result);
}

EMSGetRawPageCount(rpg_cnt, urpg_cnt)    /* get raw page count, # of
                                            raw pages */
unsigned int *rpg_cnt;           /* # of raw pages */
unsigned int *urpg_cnt;          /* # of unallocated raw pages */
{

        inregs.x.ax = 0x5901;    /* EMS Get Raw Page Count */
        result = (unsigned int) int86(EMM_INT, &inregs, &outregs) >> 8;
        if (!result) {             /* success */
                *rpg_cnt = outregs.x.dx;         /* total # of raw pages */
                *urpg_cnt = outregs.x.bx;        /* # of unallocated raw pages */
}

        return(result);
}
```

continued

Listing 7-5. *continued*

```
EMSAllocateStdPages(handle, pages) /* allocate a handle with 'pages'
   standard pages */
unsigned int *handle, pages;
{
        inregs.x.ax = 0x5A00;   /* EMS Allocate Standard Pages */
        inregs.x.bx = pages;    /* number of logical pages to allocate */
        result = (unsigned int) int86(EMM_INT, &inregs, &outregs) >> 8;
        if (!result)            /* function succeeded */
                *handle = outregs.x.dx;         /* EMM handle to use with
                                                   these pages */

        return(result);
}


EMSAllocateRawPages(handle, pages) /* allocate a handle with 'pages' raw pages */
unsigned int *handle, pages;
{
        inregs.x.ax = 0x5A01;   /* EMS Allocate Raw Pages */
        inregs.x.bx = pages;    /* number of logical pages to allocate */
        result = (unsigned int) int86(EMM_INT, &inregs, &outregs) >> 8;
        if (!result)            /* function succeeded */
                *handle = outregs.x.dx;         /* EMM handle to use with
                                                   these pages */

        return(result);
}


EMSGetAltMapRegSet(set, pmap)    /* get EMS alternate map register set */
unsigned int  *set;              /* current alternate map register set */
PMAP far **pmap;                 /* pointer to context save area pointer */
{
        inregs.x.ax = 0x5B00;   /* get alternate map register set */
        segread(&segregs);
        result = (unsigned int) int86x(EMM_INT, &inregs, &outregs,
            &segregs) >> 8;
        if (!result) {
                *set = outregs.h.bl;     /* currently active set */
                if (*set == 0) {         /* fake alternate register set */
                        FP_OFF(*pmap) = outregs.x.di; /* offset of OS
                                                         context area */
                        FP_SEG(*pmap) = segregs.es;   /* segment of OS
                                                         context area */

                }
        }
        return(result);
}
```

```
EMSSetAltMapRegSet(set, pmap)    /* set EMS alternate map register set */
unsigned int set;        /* new alternate map register set */
PMAP *pmap;              /* pointer to context save area */
{
        segread(&segregs);      /* fill segment registers */
        inregs.x.ax = 0x5B01;   /* set alternate map register set */
        inregs.h.bl = set & 0x00FF;
        if (set == 0) {         /* fake register set */
                inregs.x.di = (unsigned int) pmap;
                segregs.es = segregs.ds;
        }
        result = (unsigned int) int86x(EMM_INT, &inregs, &outregs,
           &segregs) >> 8;
        return(result);
}


EMSGetAltMapArraySize(size)     /* get size of alternate map save array */
unsigned int *size;             /* # of mappable physical pages */
{
        inregs.x.ax = 0x5B02;   /* EMS Get Alternate Map Save Array Size */
        result = (unsigned int) int86(EMM_INT, &inregs, &outregs) >> 8;
        if (!result)            /* success */
                *size = outregs.x.dx;  /* size of array */
                return(result);
}
EMSAllocAltMapRegSet(set)       /* allocate alternate map register set */
unsigned int *set;              /* # of set allocated */
{
        inregs.x.ax = 0x5B03;   /* EMS Allocate Alternate Map
                                   Register Set */
        result = (unsigned int) int86(EMM_INT, &inregs, &outregs) >> 8;
        if (!result)            /* success */
                *set = outregs.h.bl;    /* # of set allocated */
        return(result);
}
EMSDeallocAltMapRegSet(set)     /* deallocate alternate map register set */
unsigned int set;               /* # of set to deallocate */
{
        inregs.x.ax = 0x5B04;   /* EMS Deallocate Alternate Map Register Set */
        inregs.h.bl = set & 0x00FF;
        result = (unsigned int) int86(EMM_INT, &inregs, &outregs) >> 8;
        return(result);
}


EMSAllocDMARegSet(set)          /* allocate DMA register set */
unsigned int *set;              /* # of set allocated */
```

continued

Listing 7-5. *continued*

```
{
        inregs.x.ax = 0x5B05;    /* EMS Allocate DMA Register Set */
        result = (unsigned int) int86(EMM_INT, &inregs, &outregs) >> 8;
        if (!result)        /* success */
                *set = outregs.h.bl;     /* # of set allocated */
        return(result);
}


EMSEnableDMARegSet(set, channel)          /* enable DMA register set */
unsigned int set;         /* # of set to enable */
unsigned int channel;   /* # of DMA channel to associate with map register */
{
        inregs.x.ax = 0x5B06;    /* EMS Enable DMA Register Set */
        inregs.h.bl = set & 0x00FF;
        inregs.h.dl = channel & 0x00FF;
        result = (unsigned int) int86(EMM_INT, &inregs, &outregs) >> 8;
        return(result);
}


EMSDisableDMARegSet(set)          /* disable DMA register set */
unsigned int set;                 /* # of set to disable */
{
        inregs.x.ax = 0x5B07;    /* EMS Disable DMA Register Set */
        inregs.h.bl = set & 0x00FF;
        result = (unsigned int) int86(EMM_INT, &inregs, &outregs) >> 8;
        return(result);
}


EMSDeallocDMARegSet(set)          /* deallocate DMA register set */
unsigned int set;                 /* # of set to deallocate */
{
        inregs.x.ax = 0x5B08;    /* EMS Deallocate DMA Register Set */
        inregs.h.bl = set & 0x00FF;
        result = (unsigned int) int86(EMM_INT, &inregs, &outregs) >> 8;
        return(result);
}


EMSPrepareForWarmboot() /* prepare EMS hardware for warm boot */
{
        inregs.h.ah = 0x5C;    /* EMS Prepare for Warmboot */
        result = (unsigned int) int86(EMM_INT, &inregs, &outregs) >> 8;
        return(result);
}


EMSEnableOSFunc(key)      /* Enable OS Function Set */
```

```
long *key;                /* OS Access key - should be 0 first time used */
{
        inregs.x.ax = 0x5D00;   /* EMS Enable OS Function Set */
        if (*key != 0) {
                inregs.x.bx = FP_OFF(*key);
                inregs.x.cx = FP_SEG(*key);
}

        result = (unsigned int) int86(EMM_INT, &inregs, &outregs) >> 8;
        if (!result) {
                if (key == 0) {
                        FP_OFF(*key) = outregs.x.bx;
                        FP_SEG(*key) = outregs.x.cx;
                }
        }
        return(result);
}


EMSDisableOSFunc(key)      /* Disable OS Function Set */
long *key;                /* OS Access key - should be 0 first time used */
{
        inregs.x.ax = 0x5D01;   /* EMS Disable OS Function Set */
        if (*key != 0) {
                inregs.x.bx = FP_OFF(*key);
                inregs.x.cx = FP_SEG(*key);
        }
        result = (unsigned int) int86(EMM_INT, &inregs, &outregs) >> 8;
        if (!result) {
                if (key == 0) {
                        FP_OFF(*key) = outregs.x.bx;
                        FP_SEG(*key) = outregs.x.cx;
                }
        }
        return(result);
}


EMSReturnAccessKey(key)          /* returns OS access key to the EMM */
long key;                        /* OS access key  */
{
        inregs.x.ax = 0x5D02;   /* EMS Return OS Access Key */
        inregs.x.bx = FP_OFF(key);
        inregs.x.cx = FP_SEG(key);
        result = (unsigned int) int86(EMM_INT, &inregs, &outregs) >> 8;
        return(result);
}
```

Listing 7-6. EMMFUNC.H

```
extern   void ShowEMMErr(unsigned int errcode,unsigned int lineno,char *filename);
extern   int EMSGetStatus(void);
extern   int EMSGetFrameAddr(char far * *pfa);
extern   int EMSGetPageCnt(unsigned int *una,unsigned int *tot);
extern   int EMSAllocatePages(unsigned int *handle,unsigned int pages);
extern   int EMSMapHandlePage(unsigned int handle,unsigned int page,
             unsigned int frame);
extern   int EMSDeallocatePages(unsigned int handle);
extern   int EMSGetVersion(char *emsver);
extern   int EMSSavePageMap(unsigned int handle);
extern   int EMSRestorePageMap(unsigned int handle);
extern   int EMSGetHandleCnt(unsigned int *hcnt);
extern   int EMSGetHandlePages(unsigned int handle,unsigned int *pages);
extern   int EMSGetAllHandlePages(struct handle_page *hp,unsigned int *hpcnt);
extern   int EMSGetPageMap(unsigned char *map);
extern   int EMSSetPageMap(unsigned char *map);
extern   int EMSGetSetPageMap(unsigned char *srcmap,unsigned char *destmap);
extern   int EMSGetPageMapSize(unsigned int *size);
extern   int EMSGetPPageMap(struct ppmap *pmap,unsigned char *savearea);
extern   int EMSSetPPageMap(unsigned char *savearea);
extern   int EMSGetPPageMapSize(unsigned int count,unsigned int *size);
extern   int EMSMapMultPages(unsigned int handle,struct log_to_phys *map,unsigned
             int method,unsigned int count);
extern   int EMSReallocPages(unsigned int handle,unsigned int *pages);
extern   int EMSGetHandleAttr(unsigned int handle,unsigned int *attr);
extern   int EMSSetHandleAttr(unsigned int handle,unsigned int attr);
extern   int EMSGetAttrCap(unsigned int *cap);
extern   int EMSGetHandleName(unsigned int handle,char *name);
extern   int EMSSetHandleName(unsigned int handle,char *name);
extern   int EMSGetHandleDir(struct handle_names *hnt,unsigned int *hn_cnt);
extern   int EMSSearchHandleName(char *name,unsigned int *handle);
extern   int EMSGetTotalHandles(unsigned int *handle_count);
extern   int EMSMoveRegion(struct move_xchg *rp);
extern   int EMSExchangeRegion(struct move_xchg *rp);
extern   int EMSGetMapAddrArray(struct map_phys_page *mpaa,unsigned int
             *mpa_cnt);
extern   int EMSGetMapAddrCount(unsigned int *mpa_cnt);
extern   int EMSGetHardwareInfo(struct hardware_info *hwp);
extern   int EMSGetRawPageCount(unsigned int *rpg_cnt,unsigned int *urpg_cnt);
extern   int EMSAllocateStdPages(unsigned int *handle,unsigned int pages);
extern   int EMSAllocateRawPages(unsigned int *handle,unsigned int pages);
extern   int EMSGetAltMapRegSet(unsigned int *set,unsigned char far * *pmap);
extern   int EMSSetAltMapRegSet(unsigned int set,unsigned char *pmap);
extern   int EMSGetAltMapArraySize(unsigned int *size);
extern   int EMSAllocAltMapRegSet(unsigned int *set);
```

```
extern   int EMSDeallocAltMapRegSet(unsigned int set);
extern   int EMSAllocDMARegSet(unsigned int *set);
extern   int EMSEnableDMARegSet(unsigned int set,unsigned int channel);
extern   int EMSDisableDMARegSet(unsigned int set);
extern   int EMSDeallocDMARegSet(unsigned int set);
extern   int EMSPrepareForWarmboot(void);
extern   int EMSEnableOSFunc(long *key);
extern   int EMSDisableOSFunc(long *key);
extern   int EMSReturnAccessKey(long key);
```

Listing 7-7. EMMEXIST.C

```
#include <stdlib.h>
#include <fcntl.h>
#include <dos.h>
#include <errno.h>
#include "emmconst.h"

#define DOS_INT         0x21        /* DOS function dispatcher */
#define DOS_IOCTL       0x44        /* DOS IOCTL function */
#define IOCTL_GETINFO   0x00        /* IOCTL get device information
                                       subfunction */
#define IOCTL_OUTSTAT   0x07        /* IOCTL get output status subfunction */
#define READY_OUTPUT    0xFF        /* device is ready for output */
#define IS_DEVICE       0x0080      /* handle belongs to a device */

static char device_name[9] = EMM_DEVICE;

        /*
        Checks for the presence of expanded memory using the "open handle"
        method. Sets emm _present to '1' if expanded memory
        is present, '0' if not. The function returns a '0'
        if the presence test completed successfully. Otherwise
        it returns the DOS error code of the DOS function
        call that failed during the presence test.
        */


emm_exists(emm_present)
int *emm_present;                   /* pointer to EMM presence
                                       indicator */
{
        int return_code;            /* file operation return code */
```

continued

Listing 7-7. *continued*

```
        int handle;                             /* file handle */
        unsigned int dev_attr;                  /* device driver attributes */
        unsigned int dev_status;                /* device output status */

        if (_dos_open(device_name, O_RDONLY, &handle)) {
                                                /* couldn't open file */
                if (errno == ENOENT) {          /* file does not exist */
                        return_code = 0;        /* we expected that this might
                                                   happen */
                        *emm_present = 0;       /* EMM is definitely not
                                                   present */
                } else
                        return_code = errno;    /* presence test completed
                                                   unsuccessfully */
        } else                                  /* EMM device name exists */
                if (!(return_code = ioctl_getattr(handle, &dev
                    _attr)))                    /* got attribute */
                        if (!(return_code = ioctl_outstat(handle, &dev_
                            status)))           /* got output status */
                                /* EMM is present if handle belongs to a
                                   device and it is ready for output */
                *emm_present = ((dev_status == READY_OUTPUT) && (dev_attr & IS
                    _DEVICE)) ? 1 : 0;
                close(handle);                  /* close the file handle */
        }

        return(return_code);
}

        /*
                Obtain the DOS attribute word for an open handle
                associated with an open file or device. Returns 0 if
                function completed successfully, otherwise returns
                DOS error code.
        */

ioctl_getattr(handle, attrib)
int handle;                                     /* open file/device handle */
unsigned int *attrib;                           /* -> returned device info */
{
        int rc;
        union REGS regs;

        regs.h.ah = DOS_IOCTL;                  /* DOS I/O control for devices */
        regs.h.al = IOCTL_GETINFO;              /* get device information */
```

```
        regs.x.bx = handle;
        int86(DOS_INT, &regs, &regs);   /* invoke DOS function */
        if (!regs.x.cflag) {            /* if no error occurred */
                *attrib = regs.x.dx;    /*return device/file attributes */
                rc = 0;                 /*function was successful */
        } else
                rc = regs.x.ax;         /*return error code */

        return(rc);
}


        /*
        Obtains the output status of a file or device. A returned status
        of 0 means that the device is not ready for output; a status
        of 0x00FF means the device is ready for output. Returns
        0 if function completed successfully. Otherwise, returns
        DOS error code.
        */

ioctl_outstat(handle, status)
int handle;                             /* open file/device handle */
unsigned int *status;                   /* -> output status word   */
{
        int rc;
        union REGS regs;

        regs.h.ah = DOS_IOCTL;          /* DOS I/O control for devices */
        regs.h.al = IOCTL_OUTSTAT;      /* get output status */
        regs.x.bx = handle;
        int86(DOS_INT, &regs, &regs);   /* invoke DOS function */
        if (!regs.x.cflag) {            /* if no error occurred */
                *status = regs.h.al;    /* return output status */
                rc = 0;                 /* function was successful */
        } else
                rc = regs.x.ax;         /* return error code */

        return(rc);
}


        /*
        Checks for the presence of expanded memory using the "get vector" method.
        Sets emm_present to '1' if expanded memory is present, '0' if not. The
        function always returns a '0';
        */
```

continued

Listing 7-7. *continued*

```
emm_exists2(emm_present)
int *emm_present;
{
        int len;
        char far *dev_name;                     /* character device name
                                                   pointer */

        char *np;
        unsigned int get_int_seg();

        FP_SEG(dev_name) = get_int_seg(EMM_INT); /* EMM device driver segment */
        FP_OFF(dev_name) = 10;                   /* offset of character device
                                                   driver name */

        /* see if EMM name is at offset 10 in EMM_INT's segment */

        for (len = 8, np = device_name; len && *dev_name++ == *np++; len--);

        *emm_present = (len) ? 0 : 1;            /* if all characters matched,
                                                   EMM is present */

        return(0);                               /* always succeeds */
}


        /*
                Returns the segment address of interrupt vector 'intno'
        */

unsigned int get_int_seg(intno)
int intno;
{
  union REGS regs;
  struct SREGS segregs;

  regs.h.al = (unsigned char) intno;
  regs.h.ah = 0x35;                              /* DOS get vector function */
  intdosx(&regs, &regs, &segregs);
  return((unsigned) segregs.es);
}
```

Listing 7-8. SNAPSHOT.C

```c
/*
          Name:            SNAPSHOT.C
          Purpose:         TSR Utility to save text screen images to
                           Expanded Memory.
*/

#include <stdio.h>
#include <stdlib.h>
#include <signal.h>
#include <dos.h>
#include <bios.h>

#include "emmconst.h"                    /* EMM constants */
#include "emmtypes.h"                    /* EMM data structures */
#include "emmerr.h"                      /* EMM error codes */
#include "emmfunc.h"                     /* EMM function declarations */

#define PRTSC_INT          5             /* print screen interrupt */
#define HANDLE_NAME        "SNAPSHOT"    /* expanded memory handle
                                            name */
#define MAX_SCR            500           /* maximum number of screens
                                            to save */
#define MDA_SEG            0xB000        /* monochrome display
                                            adapter buffer segment */
#define CGA_SEG            0xB800        /* color graphics adapter
                                            buffer segment */
#define SCR_ROWS           25            /* assume 25 rows - procedure
                                            to determine */
                                         /* actual # of rows is
                                            adapter-dependent */

#pragma pack(1)                          /* byte align data structures */

#define DisplayError(rc)    ShowEMMErr(rc, __LINE__, __FILE__)

typedef struct bios_video_data {         /* basic BIOS video data */
        unsigned char   crt_mode;        /* display mode */
        unsigned int    crt_cols;        /* number of columns on screen */
        unsigned int    crt_len;         /* length of regen buffer
                                            in bytes */
        unsigned int    crt_start;       /* starting address in regen
                                            buffer */
        unsigned int    cursor_pos[8];   /* cursor position for 8 pages */
```

continued

Listing 7-8. *continued*

```
        unsigned int      cursor_mode;           /* current cursor mode setting */
        unsigned char     active_page;           /* current page
                                                     being displayed */

        unsigned int      addr_6845;             /* base address for active
                                                     display card */

        unsigned char     crt_mode_set;          /* current setting of 3x8
                                                     register */

        unsigned char     crt_palette;           /* current palette setting
                                                     - color card */
} BIOS_VIDEO_DATA;

typedef struct scr {                             /* screen data descriptor */
        unsigned int      scr_page;              /* screen starting expanded
                                                     memory page */

        unsigned int      scr_offset;            /* screen starting expanded
                                                     memory offset */

        unsigned int      scr_width;             /* # cols on the screen */
        unsigned int      scr_len;               /* screen length, in bytes */
} SCR;

typedef struct scr_index {                       /* screen index structure */
        void (interrupt far *scr_int5)();        /* pointer to our interrupt
                                                     service routine */

        unsigned int      scr_count;             /* # of screens currently
                                                     saved */

        unsigned int      scr_max;               /* maximum # of screens to
                                                     save */

        SCR               scr_idx[MAX_SCR];      /* screen index array */
} SCR_INDEX;

        /*
                global data

        */

void (interrupt far *old_int5)();                /* old print screen vector */
PMAP *emm_save;                                  /* EMM context save area
                                                    pointer */

unsigned int emm_tpages,                         /* total expanded memory
                                                    pages */

               emm_apages,                       /* available expanded memory
                                                    pages */

               emm_handle,                       /* expanded memory handle */
               emm_pages,                        /* # pages belonging to
                                                    handle */
```

```
                    isr_status,              /* 0: isr should chain, <>
                                                0: isr should service */

                    terminate_flag;          /* 1: terminate this program */
char            far     *page_frame;         /* far -> to EMS page frame */
SCR_INDEX               far *ip;             /* far -> to screen index */
SCR                     far *sp;             /* far -> to screen
                                                descriptor */


BIOS_VIDEO_DATA far *vp = (BIOS_VIDEO_DATA far *) 0x00400049L;
                                             /* far -> to bios video data
                                                area */



MOVE_XCHG mcb;                               /* move/exchange region
                                                structure */


#pragma check_stack(off)
                                        /* clean up if control-c happens */

void break_handler(sig_type)
int sig_type;
{
        signal(SIGINT, SIG_IGN);        /* disallow control-c during handler */
        cleanup();
        exit(0);
}


        /*
                interrupt handler for print screen interrupt
                Takes a snapshot of conventional memory into expanded memory
        */

void interrupt cdecl far int5_isr(es,ds,di,si,bp,sp,bx,dx,cx,ax,ip,cs,flags)
unsigned es, ds, di, si, bp, sp, bx, dx, cx, ax, ip, cs, flags;
{
        static int rc = 0;      /* keep track of last return code */
        int status;
        if (!isr_status)        /* if interrupt service is not activated,
                                    chain */
                                /* to the previous interrupt handler */

                _chain_intr(old_int5);

        if (rc == 0) {          /* proceed only if no previous errors */

                rc = EMSGetPageMap(emm_save);
```

continued

Listing 7-8. *continued*

```
        if (rc == 0) {  /* context saved successfully */

                        /* take a snapshot of the screen */

                rc = dump_screen();

                        /* restore previous mapping context */

                if (status = EMSSetPageMap(emm_save))
                        rc = status;    /* update error code */
        }
    }

    /* if any failure has occurred, announce it audibly */

    if (rc)
        Beep(32000);
}

dump_screen()
{
    int rc;
    unsigned int overflow, new_offset, scr_size;

    /* map screen index data in logical page 0 into physical page 0 */

    if (rc = EMSMapHandlePage(emm_handle, 0, 0))
        return(rc);     /* failure */
    /* make sure we haven't run out of index entries */

    if (ip->scr_count >= ip->scr_max)
        return(1);      /* index full */

    /* if screen would overflow page, allocate one or more
       additional pages */

    scr_size = vp->crt_cols * SCR_ROWS * 2; /* # bytes on screen */
    new_offset = sp->scr_offset + scr_size; /* new offset in save buffer */

    if (new_offset > PAGE_SIZE) {               /* screen overflows page */

        overflow = new_offset - PAGE_SIZE;      /* amount that
                                                   overflows page */
        emm_pages += (overflow / PAGE_SIZE);    /* # additional
                                                   pages needed */
```

```
        new_offset = overflow % PAGE_SIZE;        /* size of odd
                                                      fragment */
    if (new_offset)                               /* add page for
                                                      odd-size */
            emm_pages++;                          /* fragment if
                                                      necessary */


    if (rc = EMSReallocPages(emm_handle, &emm_pages))
            return(rc);                           /* failure */
}

/* snapshot displayed video screen into expanded memory */

mcb.region_length      = (long) scr_size;        /* # bytes on screen
mcb.source.memory_type        = CONV_MEM;           in conventional
                                                    memory */
mcb.source.handle             = 0;               /* no handle is used */
mcb.source.initial_offset     = vp->crt
                              _start;/* starting screen offset */
mcb.source.initial_seg_page = (vp->crt_mode == 7) ? MDA_SEG : CGA_SEG;
        /* works with color/monochrome text only */
mcb.dest.memory_type                    = EXP_MEM; /* goes into
                                                      expanded memory */
mcb.dest.handle               = emm_handle;      /* handle
                                                    previously
                                                    allocated */
mcb.dest.initial_offset       = sp->scr_offset;  /* next available
                                                      offset */
mcb.dest.initial_seg_page              = sp->scr
                              _page; /* in the current page */

if (rc = EMSMoveRegion(&mcb))                    /* EMS move memory region */
        return(rc);                              /* failure */

Beep(1000);                                      /* issue a short beep to signal
                                                    success */

/* update screen index data (Move Region did not disturb mapping
    context) */

ip->scr_count++;                                 /* increment # of
                                                    screens saved */

sp->scr_len = scr_size;                          /* store # bytes on screen */
sp->scr_width = vp->crt_cols;                    /* store # columns per line */
```

continued

435

Listing 7-8. *continued*

```
        sp++;                              /* point to next index
                                              element */
        sp->scr_len = 0;                   /* new screen not dumped yet */
        sp->scr_width = 0;                 /* so zero length and width */
        sp->scr_page = emm_pages - 1;      /* new screen goes on
                                              last page allocated */
        sp->scr_offset = new_offset;       /* immediately following
                                              previous screen */

        return(rc);                        /* success */
}

        /* deallocate expanded memory, if allocated */

cleanup()
{
        int rc;

        /* ignore return code, since we may be invoked from an error procedure */

        if (emm_handle != -1)
                rc = EMSDeallocatePages(emm_handle);
}

#pragma check_stack(on)

main(argc, argv)
int argc;
char *argv[];
{
        int emm_present, rc;
        unsigned int far *pseg_top;
        char emm_ver[4];

        get_opts(argc, argv);    /* obtain command line switches */

        emm_handle = -1;         /* no expanded memory handle is allocated */

        /* install control-c (break) handler */

        signal(SIGINT, break_handler);

        /* test for presence of expanded memory */
```

```
if (rc = emm_exists(&emm_present)) {     /* emm presence test failed */
        printf("snapshot: EMM presence test failed, rc: %d", rc);
        exit(2);
}

if (!emm_present) { /* expanded memory is not present */
        printf("snapshot: No expanded memory is present");
        exit(1);
}

/* obtain version of EMS supported by the EMM */

if (rc = EMSGetVersion(emm_ver)) {
        DisplayError(rc);
        exit(1);
}

/* make sure it's at least version 4.0 */

if (*emm_ver < '4') {              /* requires LIM EMS 4.0 or greater */
        printf("snapshot: Unsupported EMM version detected: %s, LIM
            EMS 4.0 or greater is required", emm_ver);
        exit(1);
}

/* get pointer to EMS page frame */

if (rc = EMSGetFrameAddr(&page_frame)) {
        DisplayError(rc);
        exit(1);
}

/* look up EMS handle which contains the stored screens */

rc = EMSSearchHandleName(HANDLE_NAME, &emm_handle);

/* error if any return code other than 'normal' or 'handle not found' */

if (rc != 0 && rc != HNDVLNFD) {
        DisplayError(rc);
        exit(1);
}

/* either terminate the TSR, install the TSR, or show its
   current status */
```

continued

Listing 7-8. *continued*

```
if (terminate_flag) {            /* user has requested termination */

        if (rc == 0)             /* handle with our name exists */
                terminate();     /* so try to un-install ourself */
        else {                   /* handle does not exist, so can't
                                        terminate */
                printf("snapshot: can't terminate - not installed");
                exit(1);
        }

} else {                         /* either install or give status */

        /* if a handle named HANDLE_NAME already exists, then */
        /* just report how much EMS memory is currently allocated */
        /* and how many screens are stored in it. Otherwise, install */
        /* an ISR for the print screen interrupt and make the  */
        /* program resident. */

        if (rc == 0)             /* handle with our name already exists */
                show_status();   /* so just show status */
        else {                   /* handle does not exist */
                install();       /* so allocate one and install ISR */

                /* terminate and stay resident */

                FP_SEG(pseg_top) = _psp;  /* ending para. of program
                                                is at psp+2 */
                FP_OFF(pseg_top) = 2;

                printf("snapshot: TSR installing at segment [%04X],
                    size %u  paragraphs\n", _psp, *pseg_top   - _psp);

                _dos_keep(0, *pseg_top - _psp); /* # paragraphs
                                                in program */

        }
    }
}

        /* display the handle id, # of logical pages allocated to that handle */
        /* and the number of screens currently stored in EMS */

show_status()
{
        int rc;
        unsigned int alloc_pages, screens;
```

```
/* look up # of EMS pages allocated to the EMM handle */

if (rc = EMSGetHandlePages(emm_handle, &alloc_pages)) {
        DisplayError(rc);
        cleanup();
        exit(1);
}

/* map in the first logical page, containing the screen index
   into physical page zero */

if (rc = EMSMapHandlePage(emm_handle, 0, 0)) {
        DisplayError(rc);
        cleanup();
        exit(1);
}

/* get addressability to screen index data structure in
   expanded memory */

ip = (SCR_INDEX far *) page_frame;

/* print the current status */

printf("snapshot: status - EMS handle (%d); EMS pages (%d);
   screens (%d)\n",
        emm_handle, alloc_pages, ip->scr_count);

/* unmap the screen index page */

if (rc = EMSMapHandlePage(emm_handle, -1, 0)) {
        DisplayError(rc);
        cleanup();
        exit(1);
}
}


    /* Obtain an EMS handle with one logical page from the EMM, */
    /* and name the handle so that other programs may access it. */
    /* Initialize the screen index data structure, which will be */
    /* located at the start of the first EMS page. Then insert  */
    /* an interrupt service routine for the print screen interrupt */
    /* so that screen images are saved in expanded memory when the */
    /* user presses the PrtSc key. */

install()
```

continued

Listing 7-8. *continued*

```
{
        int rc, context_bytes;

        /* allocate 1 page to start */

        emm_pages = 1;

        if (rc = EMSAllocatePages(&emm_handle, emm_pages)) {
                DisplayError(rc);
                exit(1);
        }

        /* give the handle a name so other programs can find it */

        if (rc = EMSSetHandleName(emm_handle, HANDLE_NAME )) {
                DisplayError(rc);
                cleanup();
                exit(1);
        }

        printf("snapshot: allocated expanded memory handle
           # %d with name '%s'\n",
        emm_handle, HANDLE_NAME);

        /* initialize the data in the screen index page */
        /* which will be stored in logical page 0 */

        if (rc = EMSMapHandlePage(emm_handle, 0, 0)) {
                DisplayError(rc);
                cleanup();
                exit(1);
        }

        /* get addressability to screen index data structure */

        ip = (SCR_INDEX far *) page_frame;

        /* initialize the data therein */

        ip->scr_count = 0;            /* # of screens saved */
        ip->scr_max = MAX_SCR        /* maximum # to save */
        ip->scr_int5 = int5_isr;     /* pointer to our print screen ISR */
        sp = ip->scr_idx;            /* -> 1st index element */
        sp->scr_page  = sizeof(*ip) / PAGE_SIZE;   /* screens begin */
```

```
sp->scr_offset = sizeof(*ip) % PAGE_SIZE;
    /* immediately after index */
sp->scr_len = 0;                            /* initially empty */
sp->scr_width = 0;

/* unmap the screen index page */

if (rc = EMSMapHandlePage(emm_handle, -1, 0)) {
        DisplayError(rc);
        cleanup();
        exit(1);
}

/* allocate an expanded memory context save area for use by the
   print screen interrupt handler */

if (rc = EMSGetPageMapSize(&context_bytes)) {
        DisplayError(rc);
        cleanup();
        exit(1);
}

if ((emm_save = (PMAP *) malloc(context_bytes)) == NULL) {
        printf("snapshot: Couldn't allocate %d bytes for context
            save area", context_bytes);
        cleanup();
        exit(1);
}

/* install an interrupt handler to intercept print screen requests */

old_int5 = _dos_getvect(PRTSC_INT); /* save old interrupt vector */
_dos_setvect(PRTSC_INT, int5_isr); /* install new vector */
printf("snapshot: print screen interrupt handler is installed\n");

isr_status = 1;
/* let new one service interrupts */
printf("snapshot: print screen interrupt handler is activated\n");

}

/* de-install TSR from memory at the request of the user */

terminate()
{
    int rc;
```

continued

Listing 7-8. *continued*

```
unsigned int tsr_psp;              /* program prefix segment of
                                      active TSR */

unsigned int far *envptr;          /* TSR's environment pointer */
void (interrupt far *our
_int5)();                          /* address of installed tsr */

/* suspend processing of print screen interrupts */

isr_status = 0;
printf("snapshot: print screen interrupt handler
    deactivated\n");

/* map in page containing screen index */

if (rc = EMSMapHandlePage(emm_handle, 0, 0)) {
        DisplayError(rc);
        cleanup();
        exit(1);
}

/* get addressability to screen index data structure */
/* so we can obtain the address of the interrupt service */
/* routine we installed when the program started */

ip = (SCR_INDEX far *) page_frame;
our_int5 = ip->scr_int5;                   /* get stored ISR address */

/* release expanded memory */

cleanup();
printf("snapshot: expanded memory handle %d deallocated\n", emm_handle);

/* if no other print screen handler has been installed ahead */
/* of us, then unhook the interrupt service routine and */
/* de-install the program */

if (_dos_getvect(PRTSC_INT) == our_int5) {  /* our ISR is first */

        /* restore the old print screen interrupt vector */

        _dos_setvect(PRTSC_INT, old_int5);
        printf("snapshot: old print screen interrupt handler
            restored\n");

        /* free the TSR's environment strings and program segment */
```

```
        tsr_psp = FP_SEG(our_int5) - 16; /* PSP starts 16 para.
            before code segment */

        printf("snapshot: deallocating TSR at segment [%04X]\n",
            tsr_psp);

        FP_SEG(envptr) = tsr_psp;         /* environment  pointer is
                                              at offset */
        FP_OFF(envptr) = 0x2C;            /* 2Ch in the program
                                              segment prefix */
        _dos_freemem(*envptr);            /* free the environment
                                              strings */
        _dos_freemem(tsr_psp);            /* free the program
                                              segment */

    } else   /* our ISR is not first in chain, cannot de-install TSR */
        printf("snapshot: cannot deallocate TSR - print screen ISR
            is not first in chain\n");
}

    /* process command line switches in the form /L, where 'L' is */
    /* a single character switch identification. Returns index of */
    /* the first element in the ptr array following the switches. */

get_opts(cnt, ptr)
int cnt;
char *ptr[];
{
    int argc;

    terminate_flag = 0;               /* turn terminate flag off */

    argc = 1;
    while ((*++ptr)[0] == '/') {
        switch((*ptr)[1]) {

            case '?':        /* display command and switch usage */
                printf("snapshot: saves text screen images
                    to expanded memory\n");
                printf("usage: snapshot [/X]\n");
                printf("    /X - terminates snapshot");
                exit(0);
                break;

            case 'x':        /* terminate request */
            case 'X':
```

continued

Listing 7-8. *continued*

```
            terminate_flag = 1;
            break;

        default:          /* unknown switch */
            printf("'%c' is an unknown option\n", (*ptr)[1]);
            break;
      }
      argc++;
   }
   return(argc);
}
```

Listing 7-9. PLAYBACK.C

```
/*
        Name: PLAYBACK.C
        Purpose: Dump text screen images saved in expanded memory by the
        SNAPSHOT program to the DOS standard output file.
   */

#include <stdio.h>
#include <stdlib.h>
#include <signal.h>
#include <dos.h>
#include <bios.h>

#include "emmconst.h"               /* EMM constants */
#include "emmtypes.h"               /* EMM data structures */
#include "emmerr.h"                 /* EMM error codes */
#include "emmfunc.h"                /* EMM function declarations */

#define DisplayError(rc)        ShowEMMErr(rc, __LINE__, __FILE__)

#define HANDLE_NAME             "SNAPSHOT"   /* expanded memory
                                                handle name */
#define MAX_SCR                 500          /* maximum number of
                                                screens to save */
#define SCR_COLS                80           /* assume 80 columns - we can
                                                fix this later */


#pragma pack(1)                              /* byte align data structures */
```

```
typedef struct scr {                          /* screen data descriptor */
        unsigned int    scr_page;             /* screen starting expanded
                                                 memory page */
        unsigned int    scr_offset;           /* screen starting expanded
                                                 memory offset */
        unsigned int    scr_width;            /* # cols on the screen */
        unsigned int    scr_len;              /* screen length, in bytes */
} SCR;

typedef struct scr_index {                    /* screen index structure */
        void (interrupt far *scr_int5)();     /* pointer to our interrupt
                                                 service routine */
        unsigned int    scr_count;            /* # of screens currently
                                                 saved */
        unsigned int    scr_max;              /* maximum # of screens to
                                                 save */
        SCR             scr_idx[MAX_SCR];     /* screen index array */
} SCR_INDEX;

        /*
                global data
        */

unsigned int emm_handle,                /* expanded memory handle */
             emm_pages;                 /* # pages belonging to handle */
char far        *page_frame;            /* far -> to EMS page frame */
SCR_INDEX       far *ip;                /* far -> to screen index */
SCR             far *sp;                /* far -> to screen descriptor */

MOVE_XCHG mcb;                          /* move/exchange region
    structure */

main()
{
        unsigned int scan_code;
        int emm_present, rc, current_screen;
        char emm_ver[4];

        /* test for presence of expanded memory */

        if (rc = emm_exists(&emm_present)) {
/* EMM presence test failed */
                printf("replay: EMM presence test failed, rc: %d", rc);
                exit(2);
        }
```

continued

Listing 7-9. *continued*

```
        if (!emm_present) {
/* expanded memory is not present */
                printf("replay: No expanded memory is present");
                exit(1);
        }


        /* obtain version of EMS supported by the EMM */

        if (rc = EMSGetVersion(emm_ver)) {
                DisplayError(rc);
                exit(1);
        }


        /* make sure it's at least version 4.0 */

        if (*emm_ver < '4') {                /* requires LIM EMS 4.0 or greater */
                printf("replay: Unsupported EMM version detected: %s, LIM
                    EMS 4.0 or greater is required", emm_ver);
                exit(1);
        }


        /* get pointer to EMS page frame */

        if (rc = EMSGetFrameAddr(&page_frame)) {
                DisplayError(rc);
                exit(1);
        }


        /* look up handle which contains the stored screens */

        if (rc = EMSSearchHandleName(HANDLE_NAME, &emm_handle)) {
                DisplayError(rc);
                exit(1);
        }


        /* map in the page containing the screen index */

        if (rc = EMSMapHandlePage(emm_handle, 0, 0)) {
                DisplayError(rc);
                exit(1);
        }


        /* get addressability to screen index data structure */

        ip = (SCR_INDEX far *) page_frame;
        sp = ip->scr_idx;                        /* point to first saved screen */
```

```
        if (ip->scr_count == 0)
                printf("replay: no screens have been saved");
        else
                /*
                        dump each stored screen image to standard output
                */

                for (current_screen = 0; current_screen < ip->scr_count;
                    current_screen++) {

                        rc = print_screen(sp++);

                        if (rc) {                    /* an expanded memory error
                                                        has occurred */
                                DisplayError(rc);
                                exit(1);
                        }
                }

                /* unmap the screen index page */

        if (rc = EMSMapHandlePage(emm_handle, -1, 0)) {
                DisplayError(rc);
                exit(1);
        }
}


        /*
                Given a far pointer to a screen descriptor stored in expanded
                memory, write each character of the stored screen image to
                the DOS standard output file.
        */

print_screen(sp)
SCR far *sp;                             /* far -> screen descriptor */
{
        int rc, i, lpages, line, rows;
        char *line_buf[SCR_COLS+1];
        int far *bp;
        struct SREGS segregs;

        /* calculate how many physical pages we need to map in */

        lpages = 1;                     /* at least one page */
```

continued

Listing 7-9. *continued*

```
if (sp->scr_offset + sp->scr_len > PAGE_SIZE)
        lpages++;

/* map logical page(s) which contain the screen image */
/* to physical pages starting with physical page 1 */

for (i = 0; i < lpages; i++)
        if (rc = EMSMapHandlePage(emm_handle, i + sp->scr_page, i + 1))
                return(rc);                    /* failure */

/* get addressability to physical page 1 */

bp = (int far *) page_frame;          /* page frame base
                                          address */
FP_SEG(bp) += (PAGE_SIZE / 16);       /* # paragraphs in
                                          an EMS page */

FP_OFF(bp) = sp->scr_offset;

rows = sp->scr_len / sp->scr_width / 2; /* calculate # lines
                                            per screen */
putchar('[bs]014');                   /* start a new page */

/* write each character on the screen image to standard output */

for (line = 0; line < rows; line++) {
        i = sp->scr_width;
        while (i--)
                putchar(*bp++ & 0xFF);
        putchar('[bs]n');                      /* output a newline
                                                    after each line */

}
return(rc);
}
```

Listing 7-10. BEEP.ASM

```
        TITLE   Beep
_TEXT           SEGMENT           BYTE PUBLIC 'CODE'
_TEXT           ENDS
_DATA           SEGMENT WORD PUBLIC 'DATA'
_DATA           ENDS
CONST   SEGMENT           WORD PUBLIC 'CONST'
```

```
CONST    ENDS
_BSS              SEGMENT           WORD PUBLIC 'BSS'
_BSS              ENDS
DGROUP   GROUP    CONST, _BSS,           _DATA
         ASSUME   CS:_TEXT, DS:DGROUP, SS:DGROUP, ES:DGROUP
_TEXT             SEGMENT
timer    equ      40h
port_b            equ      61h
;----- Emits an audible tone on the IBM PC's internal speaker
;        The length of the tone is controlled by a single integer argument.
;
         PUBLIC   _Beep
         PUBLIC   _Beep
_Beep    PROC     NEAR
         push     bp
         mov      bp,sp
         mov      al,10110110B    ; gen a short beep (long one loses data)
         out      timer+3,al      ; code snarfed from Technical Reference
         mov      ax,533H
         out      timer+2,al
         mov      al,ah
         out      timer+2,al
         in       al,port_b
         mov      ah,al
         or       al,03
         out      port_b,al
         mov      cx,[bp+4]
         mov      bl,1
beep0:   loop     beep0
         dec      bl
         jnz      beep0
         mov      al,ah
         out      port_b,al
         pop      bp
         ret
_Beep             ENDP
_TEXT             ENDS
         END
```

Programming the Serial Port

8

HE serial port in an MS-DOS system provides a gateway to the outside world. The basic purpose of the serial port is to send and receive data over a line in the form of a stream of bits. (Contrast this with a parallel port in which an entire byte is transferred at once.) You can use the serial port to attach a mouse to the system, send data to a printer, or dial out using a modem. Although MS-DOS systems do not need serial ports to function, these ports have become a standard system peripheral.

The serial port on MS-DOS systems is capable of supporting the RS-232C standard for asynchronous communications. Even though the ROM-BIOS, standard on all MS-DOS systems, and MS-DOS itself include some support for programming the RS-232C ports (for example, interrupt number 14h), this support, as we will explain soon, is not adequate for high speed communications. If you want to include efficient serial communications capabilities in an application, you have to access the serial port at the hardware level. This chapter will show you how.

Basics of Asynchronous Serial Communications

In data communications, we are interested in transferring bytes of data from one device to another—say, from the PC to a modem or to a serial printer. If we had eight lines between the two devices, we could let each line correspond to a bit and send the data 1 byte at a time. This would be a *parallel* transfer. The parallel port on the PC works this way, although in addition to the eight data lines there are other signal lines to assist in data transmission.

On the other hand, if we have only a single line, we have to send each byte of data *serially*, one bit at a time. Furthermore, we may also decide to send the data *synchronously* so that every byte is sent at a predetermined time (say, once every *x* seconds), or *asynchronously* at a rate that is not necessarily uniform.

Serial communication is cheaper than parallel because it requires fewer data lines—as few as two for two-way communication. Also, the asynchronous mode of transmission makes much less demand on hardware because there is no need for special hardware to maintain synchronism between the transmitter and the receiver.

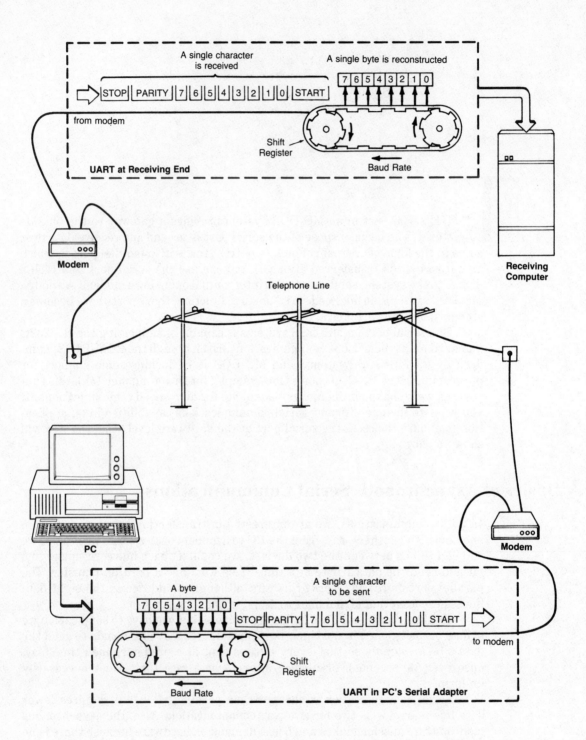

Figure 8-1. Asynchronous serial communication.

Thus, asynchronous serial communication is the preferred solution because of low cost and lower complexity in hardware. Of course, in this mode of data transmission we must have a means to convert each data byte into a series of bits and to indicate to the receiver the beginning and the end of each byte. Figure 8-1 illustrates the concept of asynchronous serial communication.

For the moment let us assume that we have some means of converting each byte into a stream of 1's and 0's, bits that can be transmitted over the communications medium (for example, the telephone line). In fact, the Universal Asynchronous Receiver Transmitter (UART) performs precisely this function, as we will see in the next section. It is normal practice to indicate that a line is "ok" by keeping it at a logical 1 when it is idle, meaning that nothing is being sent over the line. In this case, the line is said to be *marking*. On the other hand, when the line is at a logical 0, it is said to be *spacing*. Thus, logical 1 and 0 are also referred to as MARK and SPACE, respectively.

In asynchronous communication, a change in the condition of the line from MARK to SPACE indicates the start of a character (see Figure 8-2). This is referred to as the *start* bit. Following the start bit is a pattern of bits representing the character and then a bit known as the *parity* bit. Finally, the line changes to its idling MARK condition which represents the *stop* bit and indicates the end of the current character. The number of bits used to represent the character is known as the *wordlength* and is usually either seven or eight. The parity bit is used to perform rudimentary error detection.

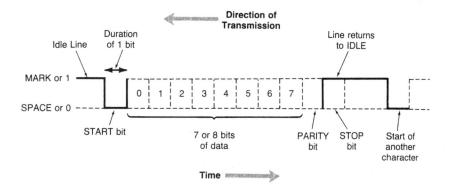

**Figure 8-2. Format of a single character in asynchronous
serial communication.**

How does the transmitter (or the receiver) know how long each bit lasts? In fact, both must have some knowledge of this duration, or the detection of the bits would be impossible. The duration of each bit is determined by data clocks at the receiver and the transmitter. Note, however, that while the clocks at the receiver and the transmitter must have the same frequency, they are not required to be synchronized. The selection of the clock frequency depends on the *baud rate*, which refers to the number of times the line changes state every second. Nominally, a clock rate of "16 times baud rate" is used so that the line is checked often enough to detect the start bit reliably.

There is one particular condition of the line that is sometimes used to gain the attention of the receiver. The normal state of the line is MARK (or 1) and the beginning of a character is indicated by a transition to SPACE (0). If the line stays in the SPACE condition for a period longer than the time it would have taken to receive all the bits of a character, then we say that a BREAK condition has occurred. There is no ASCII representation of BREAK—it is essentially the line "dropping dead" for a short duration of time that constitutes a BREAK.

Parity and Error Detection

Earlier, we mentioned the parity bit as being useful for error detection. For example, when *even parity* is selected, this bit is set so that the total number of 1's in the current word is even (a similar logic applies for odd parity). At the receiving end, the parity is recalculated and compared with the received parity bit. If they disagree, the receiver declares that a parity error has occurred. A major drawback of error detection via parity check is that it can only detect errors that affect a single bit. For example, the bit pattern 0100 0001 0 (ASCII *A*), transmitted with 8-bit wordlength and even parity, may change (due to, say, noise in the line) to 0100 0111 0 (ASCII *G*), but to the receiver everything would seem fine because the parity is still even.

Communicating with the RS-232C Standard

Previously we mentioned sending 1's and 0's over a telephone line. Although in the PC we represent the 1's and 0's by voltage levels, the signals carried in the telephone line are usually tones of different frequencies. The device that sits between the PC's hardware and the transmission line and makes data communication possible is the *modem* (modulator/demodulator). A modem can convert information back and forth between the voltage/no voltage representation of digital circuits and analog signals (for example, tones) appropriate for transmission through the telephone lines. Standards such as the RS-232C (set forth by the Electrical Industry Association, EIA) specify a prescribed method of information interchange between the modem (or in EIA terminology "data communications equipment, DCE") and the PC's communications hardware (or "data terminal equipment, DTE"). A modem can be operated in one of two modes: half duplex or full duplex. *Half duplex* mode can transmit in only one direction at a time, while *full duplex* operation permits independent two-way communications. The RS-232C standard provides control signals such as "Request-To-Send (RTS)" and "Clear-To-Send (CTS)" that may be used to coordinate the transmission and reception of data. The term *handshaking* is used to describe the coordination of transmission and reception of signals. As shown in Figure 8-3, the RS-232C standard is evident in the cable and connectors used to connect the PC to the modem.

Although we have used the modem as an example of data communications equipment (DEC), other devices such as a mouse or a printer with the appropri-

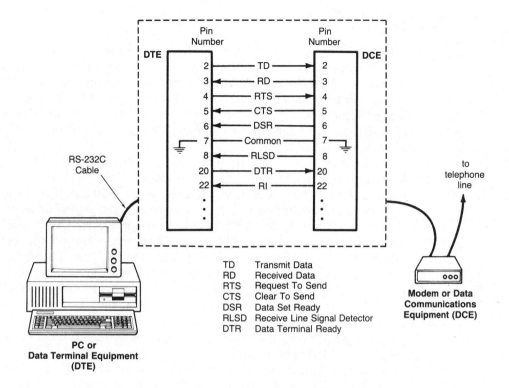

Figure 8-3. The RS-232C connection.

ate circuitry can also exchange data with the PC through the serial port. Thus, all references in this chapter to a modem apply equally to a serial printer or a serial mouse.

Flow Control with XON/XOFF

In addition to the handshaking via the hardware RTS/CTS signals, special ASCII control characters (Control-Q/Control-S or XON/XOFF) are used to achieve flow control in software. Flow control is necessary because sometimes either the transmitter or the receiver may not be able to keep up with the rate of transmission and should be able to inform the other party to stop while it catches up.

Suppose the receiver has a buffer to store incoming characters. As the buffer gets close to full, the receiver can send an XOFF character to the transmitter indicating that transmission should stop. Of course, the transmitter must understand the meaning of XOFF and cease sending characters. Then, when the receiver processes characters (say, puts them in a disk file) and the buffer empties, it can send an XON to indicate that transmission can proceed. This scheme of flow control is widely used because of its simplicity. Most communications programs allow full duplex communication with XON/XOFF flow control.

A Programmer's View of the Serial Port

The serial port hardware on MS-DOS systems is known as the *serial adapter* or *asynchronous communications adapter* (we will refer to it as the serial adapter in the rest of the chapter). This adapter is based on the Intel 8250 UART (Universal Asynchronous Receiver Transmitter), has an RS-232C port for connecting to the modem, and, like the display adapter, is programmable through a set of registers. The registers are accessible to the microprocessor through predefined I/O port addresses.

The Intel 8250 UART is controlled by writing to, or reading from, a set of 8-bit registers. These registers are accessible to the programmer via port addresses. The port addresses are assigned sequentially, so it is enough to know the address of the first port. This is also commonly known as the *base address* of the serial adapter. In the IBM PC, the two serial ports COM1 and COM2 are assigned base port addresses 3F8h and 2F8h respectively. Thus, for the serial adapter COM1, the first register is at 3F8h, the next one at 3F9h, and so on.

There are seven physical registers in the 8250, and these are described in order of increasing offsets from the base address. As Figure 8-4 shows, the base port address has a single register that doubles as the *receive buffer register* and the *transmit holding register* (THR), which is used to store a single character that is being received or transmitted. Next comes the *interrupt enable register*, which is used to enable or disable interrupts that the serial adapter is capable of generating. The third register, called the *interrupt identification register*, contains the UART's report on the identity of an interrupt. Then comes the *line control register*, used to set up various communications parameters such as wordlength, number of stop bits, parity, and baud rate. The fifth register is the *modem control register*, which is used to send signals such as DTR (Data Terminal Ready) and RTS (Request To Send) to the modem. Finally, the last two registers, the *line status register* and the *modem status register* indicate the status of the line and the modem, respectively.

The first two registers are also used in setting baud rates. The baud rate is set by specifying a 16-bit divisor for the clock frequency used by the serial adapter (1.8432 MHz in most MS-DOS systems). The value of the divisor is computed by the formula

$$\text{divisor} = \frac{1,843,200}{16 \times \text{baud rate}}$$

To set the baud rate, you have to follow three steps:

1. Set the most significant bit of the line control register (this is called the *divisor latch access bit* or DLAB) to 1.
2. Load the low and the high bytes of the divisor into the receive buffer and the interrupt enable registers, respectively.
3. Reset DLAB to 0 for normal UART operation.

PORT ADDRESS OF REGISTER

Receive Buffer/Transmit Holding Register

7	6	5	4	3	2	1	0
bit 7 of data							bit 0 of data

Base Address: (COM1-3F8 COM2-2F8)

Interrupt Enable Register

7	6	5	4	3	2	1	0
0	0	0	0	Modem Status	Receive Line Status	Transmit Holding Reg. Empty	Receive Data Available

Base Address +1:

Set bit to 1 to enable

Interrupt Identification Register

7	6	5	4	3	2	1	0
0	0	0	0	0			0 means interrupt pending

Base Address +2:

3-bit Interrupt ID
110 = Line status
100 = Received data
010 = Transmit buffer empty
000 = Modem status

Line Control Register

7	6	5	4	3	2	1	0
Devisor Latch Access Bit	BREAK	Parity 000 = None, 001 = Odd, 011 = Even			Number of Stop Bits 0-1, 1-2	Wordlength 10-7 11-8	

Base Address +3:

1 sets line to SPACE

Modem Control Register

7	6	5	4	3	2	1	0
0	0	0	Loopback Test	OUT2	OUT1	RTS	DTR

Base Address +4:

Must be 1 for interrupt I/0 on PC

Line Status Register

7	6	5	4	3	2	1	0
0	Trans. Empty	Transmit Holding Reg. Empty	BREAK detected	Framing Error	Parity Error	Overrun Error	Receive Data Ready

Base Address +5:

Modem Status Register

7	6	5	4	3	2	1	0
RLSD	RI	DSR	CTS	Delta RLSD	Delta RI	Delta DSR	Delta CTS

Base Address +6:

Figure 8-4. Registers in the 8250 UART.

Using this approach, you can set the baud rate to any value you want. Note that the maximum possible baud rate is ¹⁄₁₆ of the clock frequency, or 115,200 baud (for this baud rate the divisor is 1). This limit stems from the fact that the divisor cannot be less than 1. You can also use BIOS interrupt 14h to set the baud rate. We will discuss the use of BIOS later in the chapter.

Interrupt-Driven Serial I/O

There are two common methods of I/O in any computer system: polled and inter-rupt-driven. *Polling* refers to the repeated checking of the status register of the I/O device to see if the desired transaction can be initiated. In polled I/O, the program requesting an input character repeatedly reads a status register in the I/O device until it indicates that a character is available for input (or until the program decides to "time out"). When the status indicates that there is a character ready, the program reads the character from the appropriate register in the I/O device. A similar sequence of "wait until ready, then write" is used when writing characters out to the I/O device. Thus, the thread of execution of the program is held up until the I/O operation is complete.

A big problem with polled I/O through the communication port is that at baud rates above 300 baud there is hardly any time available for the program to do anything with the received character, even display it on the screen. Consider the following example. Suppose you are reading characters at 300 baud and the communication parameters are 7-bit wordlength, even parity, and one stop bit which, with the start bit, adds up to 10 bits per character. So you expect to receive roughly 30 characters every second. After reading a character, your pro-gram has about ¹⁄₃₀ of a second to do other chores. If you do not want to miss any characters, you must begin polling the port again before this time is up. What happens when the speed is increased to 9600 baud? The time interval between characters is too short to even put the received character on the display, let alone interpret special characters and emulate a terminal.

In the *interrupt-driven* approach, the program enables interrupts from the I/O device, assuming it is capable of signaling interrupts to the CPU, and then it goes about its own business without any concern for the device. When-ever the device is ready for I/O, it signals the CPU via hardware. Upon receiv-ing this signal, the CPU saves its current state and invokes an interrupt service routine whose address is stored in an interrupt vector table. This routine per-forms the I/O, and then it restores the state of the machine and returns to the interrupted program. Consider the case of characters arriving at the communi-cation port of the PC. If you set aside some memory locations to hold characters (a buffer), then you can use a simple interrupt handling routine that quickly reads the character from the communication port and saves it in the next avail-able location in the buffer. As long as the interrupt handler can read and save a character before another one arrives, no characters will be lost. This simple task is easy enough to complete even in the short time interval between characters at 9600 baud. The beauty of this method is that it does not matter how long the main program takes to manipulate the characters saved in the buffer. Of course, there is the risk of filling up the buffer, but this can be remedied by simply increasing the size of the buffer. If this is not good enough, XON/XOFF flow control can be implemented to avoid overflowing the buffer.

From our discussions, it should be clear that an interrupt-driven, buffered communication with XON/XOFF flow control is preferred over a polled implementation.

Interrupts from the Serial Adapter

The serial adapter on the PC can be programmed to interrupt the CPU whenever one of four things happens (see Figure 8-5). The UART assigns a priority to each of these events. Table 8-1 lists the four interrupts.

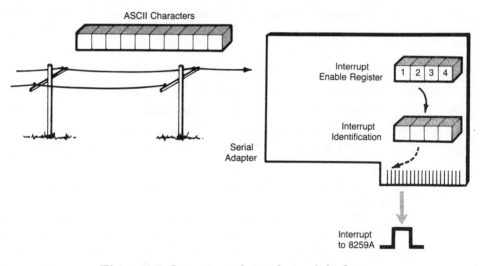

Figure 8-5. Interrupts from the serial adapter.

Table 8-1. Serial Adapter Interrupts

Priority	Interrupt ID
1	Receive line status (RLS)
2	Receive data available (RDA)
3	Transmit holding register empty (THRE)
4	Modem status (MS)

The event with highest priority is the *receive line status* (RLS) interrupt, which is processed by reading the line status register. An RLS interrupt occurs when one of the following happens:

- The line goes dead (logical 0) for a period longer than that necessary to receive a character.

- A character is received before the last one was read (an overrun error).

- There is a parity error.
- No stop bit was found while assembling a character from the received bits (a framing error).

Next comes the *receive data available* (RDA) interrupt, which occurs when a character is ready in the receive buffer register. It can be cleared by reading the character from that register.

The *transmit holding register empty* (THRE) interrupt has the next priority. As the name suggests, it occurs when the register assigned to hold the character to be transmitted (same port address as the receive buffer register) is empty. This interrupt is processed by writing to this register or by reading from the interrupt identification register. The second method of clearing this interrupt is necessary because sometimes, even though the UART interrupts to say the transmit buffer is empty, there may not be anything to transmit.

The lowest priority interrupt is the *modem status* (MS) interrupt. This is caused when the modem:

- Asserts (sends) the "Clear To Send" (CTS) signal.
- Indicates its readiness by setting the "Data Set Ready" (DSR) line.
- Receives a call, setting the "Ring Indicator" (RI) line to a logical 1.
- Detects a carrier signal (that tone you hear when you dial a number and a modem answers) setting the "Receive Line Signal Detect" (RLSD) line to 1.

The modem status interrupt can be cleared by reading the modem status register.

These interrupts may be turned on or off individually by setting appropriate bits in the interrupt enable register. On the IBM Serial/Parallel Adapter (as well as the IBM Asynchronous Adapter), the bit named OUT2 in the modem control register must also be set to 1 before interrupts from the UART can reach the CPU. When interrupts occur, the serial adapter arranges them according to priority and indicates the pending interrupt of highest priority in the interrupt identification register. The adapter stops responding to further interrupts of equal or lower priority until it determines that the current one has been serviced by the interrupt service routine.

The 8259A Programmable Interrupt Controller

In MS-DOS systems, the CPU (the 80x86 microprocessor) does not directly accept interrupts from hardware devices such as the serial adapter. Rather, hardware interrupts are first fielded by an Intel 8259A Programmable Interrupt Controller (PIC) chip. The 8259A acts as the CPU's "receptionist." A programmable device, the 8259A accepts up to eight distinct interrupts and can mask (ignore) interrupts individually. The 8259A responds to each unmasked, or allowed, interrupt and forwards it to the CPU, provided no other interrupt of higher priority is being serviced at that moment.

How does the 8259A assign priorities? Just as the UART has its method of determining priorities of interrupts generated from the serial adapter, the 8259A also has its own scheme of assigning priorities to interrupts. The serial adapter is only one of several hardware devices that can interrupt the 8259A. Each device is hardwired or jumpered to distinct inputs known as the *interrupt request* (IRQ) inputs of the 8259A. That's why it is customary to talk about the IRQ assigned to a hardware interrupt. Another feature is also associated with the IRQ of an interrupt—the *interrupt number* used in referring to that particular interrupt. On the IBM PC this number is eight plus the IRQ. When an interrupt occurs, the CPU uses the interrupt number as an index into a table known as the *interrupt vector table* (located in the beginning of memory), which should contain the address of the interrupt handling routine for that interrupt. Since the 8259A associates higher priorities with lower IRQs, the hardware devices needing maximum attention have lower IRQs. Thus, the system timer gets IRQ0, the keyboard has IRQ1, and so on.

Although MS-DOS 3.3 supports four communication ports, COM1 through COM4, this support is nothing more than the availability of four drivers with these names, each supporting unbuffered, polled I/O only. Since we are interested in interrupt-driven serial I/O, the details of MS-DOS support for the communication ports are not relevant to this discussion.

In the IBM PC, only the first two ports, COM1 and COM2, have designated IRQ numbers and interrupt numbers. Other serial ports such as COM3 and COM4 can be used for interrupt-driven I/O, provided you follow the vendor's instruction during installation of the adapters and assign IRQ numbers by selecting jumpers. Once the IRQ number is known, the steps involved in programming COM3 and COM4 are the same as those for COM1 or COM2. Therefore, in the rest of this chapter, we will focus on COM1 and COM2 only.

The two serial ports COM1 and COM2 are respectively assigned IRQ4 and IRQ3, resulting in interrupt numbers 12 and 11 (decimal). By the way, the interrupt numbers must be known so that DOS function calls (via software interrupt 21h) with function numbers 35h and 25h can be used to get and set interrupt vectors, respectively.

There are a few more details to note before we can talk about programming the serial ports for interrupt-driven I/O. The 80x86 microprocessor automatically disables all interrupts when it transfers control to the service routine for the current interrupt. Although during the servicing of an interrupt the 8259A inhibits further interrupts of the same or lower priority, higher priority interrupts are still acknowledged if the interrupt flag is set. Unless we reenable interrupts immediately, before we begin servicing the interrupt from the serial port, many vital system functions relying on interrupts (such as the system timer, the keyboard, and the disk controller) will **not** be serviced. It is important, therefore, to turn interrupts back on as soon as the service routine gets control by using an STI "SeT Interrupt flag" instruction. This will then allow the timer, the keyboard, and the disk controller to interrupt the serial port's service routine, allowing the other devices to function properly.

How do we tell the 8259A when the serial interrupt processing is complete? Our service routine has to send an *end of interrupt* (EOI) command to the

8259A before returning control to the CPU. Although there are ways of indicating an EOI for a specific IRQ, for the priority scheme used in the PC it is enough to send what is known as a *nonspecific EOI* (code 20h) to the 8259A. This is called nonspecific because it does not specify which interrupt has been serviced. It simply tells the 8259A that the servicing is complete for the highest priority interrupt that has been acknowledged. This reenables acknowledgment of further interrupts at that IRQ or higher.

Programming the 8259A

Interrupt-driven I/O with the serial port requires that you set up the 8259A properly. Otherwise, the interrupts generated by the serial adapter will never be acknowledged by the 80x86 microprocessor. Thus, an important first step is to find out how we can program the 8259A.

Like all hardware in the PC, the 8259A is programmed via two command words (registers). These are located at I/O port adresses 20h and 21h respectively (Figure 8-6). The register at 21h is used solely for masking interrupts. An interrupt is masked (i.e., not acknowledged) if the bit corresponding to its IRQ (counting from right to left with the rightmost bit assigned to IRQ0) is a logical 1. The port at 20h is used to send the end of interrupt command to the 8259A. As we noted earlier, on MS-DOS systems this is done by writing 20h to this port.

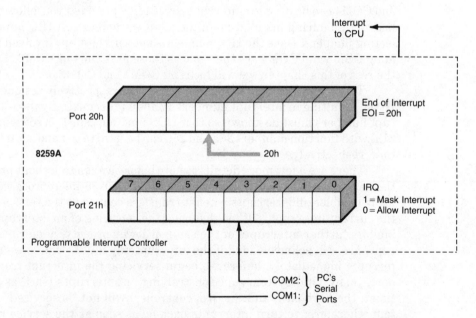

Figure 8-6. The 8259A programmable interrupt controller.

In MS-DOS systems, the first serial port (known as COM1 to MS-DOS) is assigned IRQ4 (interrupt number 12), while the second one (COM2) has IRQ 3 (interrupt 11). As mentioned earlier, ports COM3 and COM4 can be handled in a similar manner provided that you know the IRQ numbers assigned during installation of these ports (only COM1 and COM2 have preassigned IRQs). Thus, the 8259A can be programmed to acknowledge interrupts from COM1 by reading from port 21h and writing back the contents logically ANDed with EFh. Interrupts from COM1 may be masked by repeating the above step but ORing with 10h in place of the logical AND. Thus, the 8259A can be programmed to enable interrupts from COM1 by the code fragment

```
IN     AL,21H      ;get current interrupt mask
AND    AL,EFH      ;enable IRQ4
OUT    21H,AL      ;write it back again
```

When interrupts from COM1 are turned off again, the 8259A can be programmed to mask IRQ4 by

```
IN     AL,21H      ;get current interrupt mask
OR     AL,10H      ;disable IRQ4
OUT    21H,AL      ;write it back again
```

Programming devices in this manner, by first reading the contents of a register and then writing back again with the appropriate bit altered, is recommended because that way we do not disturb any prior bit settings.

In addition to enabling and disabling acknowledgment of interrupts, the 8259A must be informed whenever the processing of a particular interrupt is complete. As described earlier, this is done by sending a 20h to the I/O port address 20h as shown here:

```
MOV    AL,20H      ;end-of-interrupt code
OUT    20H,AL      ;to port 20H of 8259A
```

Using MS-DOS Tools to Program the Serial Port

Once you know the purpose of each register in the serial adapter, programming the serial port involves setting up the registers properly, enabling the interrupts, and installing an interrupt handler. We have already described how to program the programmable interrupt controller. Now we are ready to discuss the rest of the details on programming the serial port.

Driver, TSR, or Stand-alone Program

You have several choices on the approach you adopt to access the serial ports in an MS-DOS system. You can control the serial port through an installable character device driver that performs I/O with the serial port. Chapter 6, "Installable Device Drivers," explains the ins and outs of developing such a driver. The major drawback of this approach is the overhead associated with reaching the driver via DOS. On the plus side, any program that knows about your driver can use it. If you follow this route, you can provide IOCTL capabilities in the driver so that the communications parameters such as baud rate and wordlength can be set by DOS IOCTL calls (DOS function number 44h).

The second approach is to install a TSR (terminate and stay resident) program that takes over the BIOS RS-232C interrupt (14h) and extends its functionality by providing interrupt-driven I/O. This technique will also allow any program to access the serial port through your TSR driver, as long as you document the register settings that are needed when using the new communication functions in the TSR. The access mechanism will be the same as calling the BIOS RS-232C function, which we will describe soon.

The third method is to develop a stand-alone application that includes the interrupt handler for the serial port. In this case, at the start of your application, you can install the serial port's interrupt handler and de-install the handler when the program terminates. This approach creates a self-contained application and is capable of high-speed (9600 baud) serial I/O because there is less overhead than the other two methods.

No matter which approach you adopt, the steps for controlling the serial port will remain the same. Therefore, we will concentrate on these details next.

Using the BIOS for Serial Communications

You are probably wondering if we could have efficient serial I/O through the BIOS. Unfortunately, the answer is no. The BIOS does not provide an efficient way of controlling the serial adapter. The BIOS does have an RS-232C function, accessible via interrupt 14h, to program the serial adapter. Unfortunately, this function supports only polled I/O, which is not much help because of the drawbacks of polling outlined earlier. However, this function is ideal for setting up the parameters of the communication port such as baud rate, wordlength, parity, and stop bits using BIOS interrupt 14h.

Setting Communication Parameters Using the BIOS

Even though serial I/O using the BIOS is not as efficient as the interrupt-driven approach, it is instructive to see how the communications parameters (baud rate, wordlength, parity, and stop bits) can be set by using the BIOS RS-232C functions accessed by interrupt 14h.

Interrupt 14h with a zero in AH sets the parameters of the serial port. The port number should be in DX. A 0 in DX indicates COM1, while a 1 means COM2. The selected communications parameters are passed in the AL register in a packed format, shown in Figure 8-7. The baud rate is specifed by a 3-bit value, the parity by a 2-bit value, the number of stop bits by a single bit, and the wordlength by a 2-bit value. Table 8-2 shows the coded values for each of the communications parameters. Note that the DOS 3.3 COM port drivers can go up to 19,200 baud, but the ROM-BIOS stops at 9600 baud. You can use the baud rate programming capability of the UART, outlined earlier, to achieve baud rates that are not in Table 8-2.

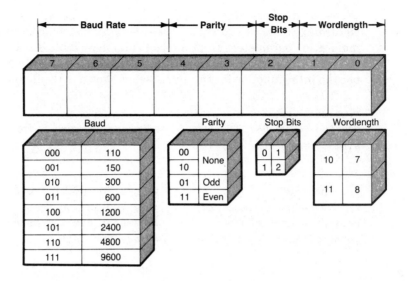

Figure 8-7. Communications parameters packed into a single byte in the format required by BIOS interrupt 14h.

Table 8-2.   Coded Value of Communications Parameters for Interrupt 14h

Parameter Name	Actual Value	Coded Value
Baud Rate	110	0
	150	1
	300	2
	600	3
	1200	4
	2400	5
	4800	6
	9600	7
Parity	None	0 or 2
	Odd	1
	Even	3
Stop Bits	1	0
	2	1
Wordlength	7	2
	8	3

You can prepare the packed form of the parameters easily. For example, if you are using a high-level language such as C, the packed parameters can be obtained by

```
pckd_commparams = (baudrate << 5) | (parity <<3) |
                  (stopbits << 2) | (wordlength);
```

where we have used the bit-shift and bitwise OR operators of C. The variables *baudrate*, *parity*, *stopbits*, and *wordlength* must be coded values of the communication parameters from the last column in Table 8-2. Once the parameters are in this format, you can call the BIOS using an int 14h. In Microsoft C, you can use the **int86** function for this purpose, as shown in the following code fragment:

```
#include <dos.h>
#define  BIOS_RS232 0x14       /* interrupt number for BIOS service */
static union REGS xr, yr;
    .
    .
    .
xr.h.ah = 0;                   /* function no. for BIOS RS-232 call */
xr.h.al = pckd_commparams;     /* communication parameters */
xr.x.dx = port_number;         /* 0 means COM1, 1 means COM2 */
int86(BIOS_RS232, &xr, &yr);   /* make the call */
    .
    .
    .
```

Microsoft C 5.0 makes it even easier to call the BIOS routines: the *_bios_serialcomm* function acts as an interface between your C program and the BIOS interrupt 14h. For example, if you select 8-bit wordlength, 1 stop bit, no parity, and a baud rate of 300, the call

```
_bios_serialcom(_COM_INIT, COM1, (_COM_CHR8 | _COM_STOP1 |
                               _COM_NOPARITY | _COM_300) );
```

will suffice. The *_bios_serialcom* function call

```
status = _bios_serialcomm(service_code, port_number, data);
```

accepts three unsigned integer parameters and returns an unsigned integer status code to indicate the result of the requested operation. The argument *service_code* is used to specify the requested operation, and the *port_number* is either 0 (COM1) or 1 (COM2). The meaning of *data* depends on the service being requested. You can find more details about this function in the *Microsoft C 5.0 Run-time Library Reference*.

Getting the Serial Port's Address

Another useful built-in feature of the BIOS is that, during the *power-on self test* (POST) phase, it checks for the existence of serial adapters COM1 and COM2 (although MS-DOS 3.3 supports ports COM3 and COM4, the BIOS recognizes only COM1 and COM2), and if it finds either, the address of the first register of each adapter is stored in an area of memory beginning at offset zero of segment 40h. Since in the PC a 20-bit physical address equals *10h* ∗ 16-bit segment + 16-bit offset, if your MS-DOS system has a single serial port designated as COM1, then the word at the physical location 400h will contain 3F8h (if COM2 is also present, the next word at 402h will contain 2F8h). Thus, you can get the port address of the serial adapter from this BIOS data area at offset 0 and segment 40h. For example, in Microsoft C, you can set the base port address by

```
#define BIOS_DATA ((short far *)(0x400000L))
static short comport,       /* for base address of port */
            port_number;    /* 0 for COM1, 1 for COM2 */
    .
    .
    .
comport = *(BIOS_DATA + port_number);

if(comport == 0) /* means no serial adapter installed */
{
    printf("Serial port not installed!\n");
    exit(1);
}
```

Once the variable *comport* is initialized, all other registers on the serial adapter can be addressed by adding appropriate offsets to the base address. In C, you can use the *#define* preprocessor directive to set up the addresses of these registers. For example, if you define them as the following, once *comport* is initialized, you can refer to the serial port's registers by the defined names.

```
#define IER    (comport + 1)   /* interrupt enable register */
#define IIR    (comport + 2)   /* interrupt identification */
#define LCR    (comport + 3)   /* line control register */
#define MCR    (comport + 4)   /* modem control register */
#define LSR    (comport + 5)   /* line status register */
#define MSR    (comport + 6)   /* modem status register */
```

Setting Up for Interrupt-Driven Serial I/O

After getting the base address of the port from the BIOS data area, you must set up the serial port and install an interrupt handler before interrupt-driven serial I/O can begin. The interrupt number and IRQ of the serial port interrupt depend on whether you want to use COM1 or COM2. Once you get the interrupt number, you should get the current handler's address and save it. That way, when exiting the program, you can restore the interrupt vector to the original value. MS-DOS functions 35h and 25h, respectively, get and set handlers for a given interrupt number. Microsoft C 5.0 offers the routines *_dos_getvect* and *_dos_setvect* for this purpose. Using C, you can perform this step as follows:

```
short int_number;              /* interrupt number for comm. port */
void interrupt far s_inthndlr(void);  /* handler to be installed */
static  void (interrupt far *old_handler)(); /* place for old one */
    .
    .
```

```
/* get old interrupt vector and save it. */
    old_handler = _dos_getvect(int_number);
/* install the new handler named s_inthndlr
 * disable interrupts when changing handler
 */
    _disable();
    _dos_setvect(int_number, s_inthndlr);
    _enable();
```

In the example we show the handler as a function of type *interrupt*, which is a new keyword introduced in Microsoft C 5.0. The next section shows you how the *interrupt* attribute allows you to write the interrupt handler entirely in Microsoft C 5.0 (Turbo C 1.5 also has a similar facility).

The other point to note is the use of the functions *_disable* and *_enable*. These two functions correspond to the assembly language instructions STI and CLI, respectively. Thus, we are turning interrupts off while switching from one serial interrupt handler to another. Otherwise, an interrupt arriving in the midst of the switch may cause the CPU to jump off to never-never land because the interrupt vector was not the address of any valid handler.

After the interrupt handler is in place, you can set up the communications parameters and enable the serial port to generate interrupts. You must also enable recognition of these interrupts at the 8259A. Once again, you should disable the interrupts until both the port and the 8259A are ready. Here is how we can do this in Microsoft C 5.0.

```
short intmask, int_enable_mask; /* enable mask depends on port */
    .
    .
    .
/* turn on interrupts from comm port . setup 8259A */
    _disable();
/* set up modem control register (port = MCR) */
    outp(MCR, MCRALL);
/* enable all interrupts on serial card (port = IER) */
    outp(IER, IERALL);
/* read 8259A's interrupt mask register and write it
 * back after AND-ing with int_enable_mask
 */
    intmask = inp(P8259_1) & int_enable_mask;
    outp(P8259_1, intmask);
    _enable();
```

At this point, the serial port will begin operating in interrupt-driven mode. The actions that take place will depend on the interrupt handler, which we will discuss next.

Handling the Interrupts from the Serial Port

When the serial port generates an interrupt, our installed handler, *s_inthndlr*, will be called. We must immediately enable acknowledgment of further interrupts by the system so that other higher-priority tasks (such as the timer) can continue to get the attention of the microprocessor.

The next step is to identify the exact cause of the interrupt from the serial port. You have to read the interrupt identification register (IIR) to get this information. Once the cause of the interrupt is determined, you can take the necessary action to handle the interrupt, as outlined in the description of the 8250 UART.

Since the serial port may generate an interrupt while you are in the midst of handling another, you must check bit 0 (least significant bit) of the IIR for this condition. If this bit is 0, another interrupt is waiting and you should process it. On the other hand, if the bit is 1, no more interrupts are pending. In this case you should send an end-of-interrupt to the 8259A and return from the handler. Thus, the handler is an endless loop that keeps processing serial interrupts until there are none waiting. In Microsoft C 5.0, the handler may be implemented as

```
void interrupt far s_inthndlr(void)
{
    int c;
    register int int_id, intmask;

/* enable interrupts immediately */
    _enable();

    while (TRUE)
    {
/* read the interrupt identification register, IIR */
        int_id = inp(IIR);
        if (bit0(int_id) == 1)
        {
/* if bit 0 is 1, then no interrupts pending. send an
 * end of interrupt signal to the 8259A Programmable
 * Interrupt Controller and then return.
 */
            outp(P8259_0, END_OF_INT);
            return;
        }
/* if it is receive data ready interrupt, enable
 * interrupts for "transmit holding register empty"
 */
        if (int_id >= RXDATAREADY)
                    turnon_int(THREINT,intmask);

/* process interrupt according to ID. The following
```

```
 * list is in increasing order of priority.
 */
        switch (int_id)
        {
            case MDMSTATUS:    /* read modem status */
                                .
                                .
                                .
                                break;
            case TXREGEMPTY:   /* send out a character */
                                .
                                .
                                .
                                break;
            case RXDATAREADY:  /* read a character */
                                .
                                .
                                .
                                break;
            case RLINESTATUS:  /* read line status */
                                .
                                .
                                .
                                break;
/* just fall through if ID is none of the above */
        }
    }
}
```

Note that we have used the keyword *interrupt*, introduced in Microsoft C 5.0, which allows us to write the handler entirely in C. This keyword is used as a qualifier for a function that you wish to install as the *interrupt handler* for a specific interrupt number. When the compiler translates a function with the *interrupt* attribute, it generates code to first push the registers AX, CX, DX, BX, SP, BP, SP, SI, DI, DS, and ES. It then sets up the DS register to point to the data segment of that function. After this initial sequence comes the code of the function. Finally, the compiler uses an IRET instruction instead of a normal RET to return from the function. This example is a typical use of the *interrupt* attribute. Turbo C also has this keyword, but the registers are pushed onto the stack in a different order.

When you write the interrupt handler in C, you have to follow the same precautions that apply to assembly language interrupt handlers. For example, you should not call any library routine that calls any DOS function (those accessed by the int 21h instruction). The file I/O routines in C are such functions. On the other hand, routines like the ones in the string manipulation category are safe inside the *interrupt* function.

Queues for the Interrupt Handler

The goal of the handler for serial port interrupts is to save the incoming characters as quickly as possible. This is best done by using a buffer. The application program can retrieve the characters from this buffer at its own pace without worrying about losing any character because it was not processing fast enough. Outgoing characters can also be passed to the interrupt handler through a second buffer.

Conceptually, each of these buffers should behave like a checkout line at the supermarket cash register. The incoming characters line up one after another and the program reading the characters takes the first one in the line and processes it, then it takes the next, and so on. This type of buffer is known as *first-in first-out*, or FIFO, buffer. It is also called a *queue*.

Figure 8-8 shows the conceptual realization of a queue. The queue naturally has a *front* and a *rear*. In an actual implementation the queue size, i.e., the maximum number of characters it can hold, is fixed. It is convenient to think of the storage locations assigned to the queue as a circle so that once we go past the last location we return to the first one. This makes efficient use of the limited space available in the queue. Such an implementation of a queue is described as *circular*.

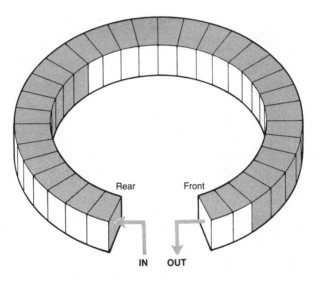

Figure 8-8. A circular FIFO buffer (queue).

Cleaning Up before Closing Shop

When your application no longer needs any more serial I/O, it must restore the port to its original state. This involves setting all the port's interrupt enable register (IER) bits to off and turning off all the modem control signals. Then, the 8259A must be programmed to stop acknowledging interrupts from the serial port. Finally, the interrupt vector for the serial interrupt must be reset to the original value you saved when the port was being initialized for I/O. Here are the steps written in Microsoft C 5.0:

```
      int intmask;
         .
         .
         .
/* Disable interrupts during clean up */
   _disable();
/* First reset Interrupt Enable Register of the port */
   outp(IER, IEROFF);
/* Turn off all bits of the Modem Control Register */
   outp(MCR, MCROFF);

/* Next disable 8259A from recognizing interrupts
   from the serial port */
   intmask = inp(P8259_1) | int_disable_mask;
   outp(P8259_1, intmask);

/* Restore original interrupt vector */
   _dos_setvect(int_number, old_handler);

/* Enable interrupts back on again */
   _enable();
```

A Sample Program

We have described the serial port's hardware and outlined the steps necessary to program the port for efficient interrupt-driven I/O. All that remains is to put the pieces together so that you can see how a complete serial communications program is constructed. We do this in Listing 8-1, which shows a basic communication program written entirely in Microsoft C 5.0.

Listing 8-1. Microsoft C 5.0 Communication Program

```
/*
 * Filename:      S E R I O . C
 * Purpose:       To illustrate programming the serial
 *                port in MS-DOS systems.
 *                This version was developed on an IBM
 *                PC-AT with an IBM Serial Adapter.
 *                DOS version 3.1 was used.
 * Author:        Naba Barkakati, March 1988
 * Language:      Microsoft C 5.0
 * Memory Model:  Large
 * Compile/Link:  CL /AL /Gs serio.c
 */
/*-------------------------------------------------------------*/
#include <stdio.h>
```

```
#include <ctype.h>
#include <dos.h>
#include <bios.h>
#include <conio.h>

#define TRUE 1
#define FALSE 0
#define EOS  '\0'

#define CONTROL(x)  (x-0x40)
#define ESC_KEY      CONTROL('[')

/* Define communications parameters */
#define COM_PARAMS (_COM_CHR8 | _COM_STOP1 | \
                        _COM_NOPARITY |_COM_1200)

/* Define receive and transmit buffer sizes */
#define RXQSIZE 512
#define TXQSIZE 512

/* Definitions for the 8259 Programmable Interrupt
 * Controller
 */
#define P8259_0    0x20     /* int control register */
#define P8259_1    0x21     /* int. mask register */
#define END_OF_INT 0x20     /* Non-specific EOI */

/* Define XON and XOFF ASCII codes */
#define XON_ASCII   (0x11)
#define XOFF_ASCII  (0x13)

/* Address of BIOS data area at 400h */
#define BIOS_DATA   ((int far *)(0x400000L))

/* The address of the comm port is in the short integer
 * 'comport'. This variable is initialized by reading
 * from the BIOS data area at segment 0x40.
 */
#define IER (comport + 1) /* interrupt enable register */
#define IIR (comport + 2) /* interrupt identification */
#define LCR (comport + 3) /* line control register */
#define MCR (comport + 4) /* modem control register */
#define LSR (comport + 5) /* line status register */
#define MSR (comport + 6) /* modem status register */
```

continued

Listing 8-1. *continued*

```
/* Codes to enable individual interrupts */
#define RDAINT   1
#define THREINT  2
#define RLSINT   4
#define MSINT    8

/* Modem Control Register value */
#define MCRALL  15 /* (DTR, RTS, OUT1 and OUT2 = 1) */
#define MCROFF   0  /* everything off */

/* Interrupt Enable Register value to turn on/off int */
#define IERALL  (RDAINT+THREINT+RLSINT+MSINT)
#define IEROFF   0

/* Some masks for turning interrupts off */
#define THREOFF 0xfd

/* Interrupt identification numbers */
#define MDMSTATUS   0
#define TXREGEMPTY  2
#define RXDATAREADY 4
#define RLINESTATUS 6

/* Flags for XON/XOFF flow control */
#define XON_RCVD   1
#define XOFF_RCVD  0
#define XON_SENT   1
#define XOFF_SENT  0

/* Hi and low percentages for xon-xoff trigger */
#define HI_TRIGGER(x)  (3*x/4)
#define LO_TRIGGER(x)  (x/4)

/* Function to get bit 0 of an integer */
#define bit0(i)       (i & 0x0001)

/* Macro to turn on interrupt whose "Interrupt Enable
 * Number" is 'i', in case it has been disabled. For
 * example, the THRE interrupt is disabled when an XOFF
 * is received from the remote system.
 */
#define turnon_int(i,j)  \
        if(((j=inp(IER))&i)==0)outp(IER,(j|i))

#define report_error(s)  fprintf(stderr,s)
```

```
typedef struct QTYPE    /* data structure for a queue */
{
    int  count;
    int  front;
    int  rear;
    int  maxsize;
    char *data;
} QTYPE;

static char  rxbuf[RXQSIZE], txbuf[TXQSIZE];

static QTYPE rcvq = {0, }-1, -1, RXQSIZE, rxbuf},
             trmq = {0, }-1, -1, TXQSIZE, txbuf};

/* Global status indicators */
int  s_linestatus, s_modemstatus;

static  QTYPE *txq = &trmq, *rxq = &rcvq;
static  short comport=0,
              enable_xonxoff = 1,
              rcvd_xonxoff = XON_RCVD,
              sent_xonxoff = XON_SENT,
              send_xon = FALSE,
              send_xoff = FALSE,
              int_number = 12;
              int_enable_mask = 0xef,
              int_disable_mask = 0x10;

/* Functions Prototypes */
int s_sendchar(int);
int s_rcvchar(void);
int s_setup(short, unsigned);
int s_cleanup(void);

char *q_getfrom( QTYPE *, char *);
int   q_puton( QTYPE *, char *);

void interrupt far s_inthndlr(void);

static  void  s_rda(void);
static  void  s_trmty(void);
static  void  (interrupt far *old_handler)();
/*-----------------------------------------------------------*/
main(int argc, char **argv)
{
    int ch, port_number = 0;
```

continued

Listing 8-1. *continued*

```
/* Get port number, if on command line */
    if(argc > 1) port_number = atoi(argv[1]) - 1;
    printf("\nSERIO -- Serial I/O at 1200,8,N,1 \
using port COM%d\n", port_number+1);
    printf("\nConnecting ...\n");

/* First set up the serial port */
    s_setup(port_number, COM_PARAMS);

/* The following endless loop simulates a terminal.
 * Escape key cleans up everything and returns.
 */
    while (TRUE)
    {
        if ((ch = s_rcvchar()) != -1) putch(ch);
        if ( kbhit() != 0)
        {
            ch = getch();
            if (ch == ESC_KEY)
            {
                    s_cleanup();
                    return;
            }
            else
                s_sendchar(ch);
        }       /* end of kbhit() check */
    }
}
/*------------------------------------------------------------*/
/* s _ i n t h n d l r
 * Handler for all serial port interrupts.
 */
void interrupt far s_inthndlr(void)
{
    int c;
    register int int_id, intmask;

/* Enable interrupts immediately */
    _enable();

    while (TRUE)
    {
/* Read the interrupt identification register, IIR */
        int_id = inp(IIR);
```

```
            if (bit0(int_id) == 1)
            {
/* If bit 0 is 1, then no interrupts pending. Send an
 * end of interrupt signal to the 8259A Programmable
 * Interrupt Controller and then return.
 */
                outp(P8259_0, END_OF_INT);
                return;
            }
            if (int_id >= RXDATAREADY)
                            turnon_int(THREINT,intmask);
/* Process interrupt according to ID. The following
 * list is in increasing order of priority.
 */
            switch (int_id)
            {
                case MDMSTATUS:   /* read modem status */
                                  s_modemstatus = inp(MSR);
                                  break;
                case TXREGEMPTY:  s_trmty();
                                  break;
                case RXDATAREADY: s_rda();
                                  break;
                case RLINESTATUS: /* read line status */
                                  s_linestatus = inp(LSR);
                                  break;
/* Just fall through if ID is none of the above */
            }
        }
}
/*------------------------------------------------------------*/
/*  s _ r d a
 *  Process a "receive data available" interrupt
 */
static void s_rda(void)
{
    register int intmask;
    char c;
/* Read from comport */
    c = inp(comport);
    if(enable_xonxoff) {
        if(c == XON_ASCII) {
            rcvd_xonxoff = XON_RCVD;
/* Turn on THRE interrupt if it's off. */
            turnon_int(THREINT,intmask);
```

continued

Listing 8-1. *continued*

```
            return;
        }
        if(c == XOFF_ASCII) {
            rcvd_xonxoff = XOFF_RCVD;
/* Turn off THRE interrupts. */
            intmask = inp(IER);
            if (intmask & THREINT)
                    outp(IER, intmask & THREOFF);
            return;
        }
    }
    q_puton(rxq, &c);
/* Check if queue is almost (75%) full */
    if(enable_xonxoff){
        if(rxq->count >= HI_TRIGGER(RXQSIZE)  &&
            sent_xonxoff != XOFF_SENT ) {
/* Set flag to send XOFF */
            send_xoff = TRUE;
/* Turn on THRE interrupts so we can send the XOFF */
            turnon_int(THREINT,intmask);
        }
    }
}
/*-----------------------------------------------------------------*/
/*  s _ t r m t y
 *  Process "transmit holding register empty" interrupt
 */
static void s_trmty(void)
{
    char c;
    register int ierval;

    if (send_xoff == TRUE) {
        outp(comport, XOFF_ASCII);
        send_xoff = FALSE;
        sent_xonxoff = XOFF_SENT;
        return;
    }
    if (send_xon == TRUE) {
        outp(comport, XON_ASCII);
        send_xon = FALSE;
        sent_xonxoff = XON_SENT;
        return;
    }
```

```
/* Put a character into the transmit holding register */
    if( q_getfrom(txq, &c) != NULL){
        outp(comport, c);
        return;
    }
/* Nothing to send -- turn off THRE interrupts */
    ierval = inp(IER);
    if (ierval & THREINT) outp(IER, ierval & THREOFF);
}
/*------------------------------------------------------------*/
/* s _ s e t u p
 * Sets up everything for communication.
 * Return 1 if setup successful, else return 0.
 */
int s_setup(short port_number, unsigned commparams)
{
    int intmask;

    if (port_number < 0 || port_number > 1)
                report_error("Invalid port number!\n");

/* Get serial port's base address from BIOS data area */
    comport = *(BIOS_DATA + port_number);
    if (comport == 0)
    {
        report_error("BIOS could not find port!\n");
        return(0);
    }

/* Set up masks for 8259A PIC. To enable interrupt from
 * the port this mask is ANDed with the mask register
 * at 21h. To disable, OR the disable mask with the
 * mask register. The interrupt number is 8 + the IRQ
 * level of the interrupt. Com port 1 has IRQ 4, port 2
 * has IRQ 3.
 */
    if (port_number == 0)
    {
        int_enable_mask = 0xef;
        int_disable_mask = 0x10;
        int_number = 12;
    }
    if (port_number == 1)
    {
        int_enable_mask = 0xf7;
        int_disable_mask = 8;
```

continued

Listing 8-1. *continued*

```
        int_number = 11;
    }

/* Get old interrupt vector and save it. */
    old_handler = _dos_getvect(int_number);

/* Install the new handler named s_inthndlr
 * Disable interrupts when changing handler
 */
    _disable();
    _dos_setvect(int_number, s_inthndlr);
    _enable();

/* Set up communication parameters */
    _bios_serialcom(_COM_INIT, port_number, commparams);

/* Initialize XON/XOFF flags */
    rcvd_xonxoff = XON_RCVD;
    if (sent_xonxoff == XOFF_SENT)
        send_xon = TRUE;
    else
        send_xon = FALSE;
    send_xoff = FALSE;

/* Turn on interrupts from comm port + setup 8259A */
    _disable();
/* Set up modem control register (port = MCR) */
    outp(MCR, MCRALL);

/* Enable all interrupts on serial card (port = IER) */
    outp(IER, IERALL);

/* Read 8259A's interrupt mask register and write it
 * back after AND-ing with int_enable_mask.
 */
    intmask = inp(P8259_1) & int_enable_mask;
    outp(P8259_1, intmask);

    _enable();

    return(1);
}
/*-------------------------------------------------------------*/
/* s _ c l e a n u p
 * Cleanup after comm session is done. Turns off all
```

```
 *   interrupts.
 */
int s_cleanup(void)
{
    int intmask;

/* Turn off interrupts from serial card */
    _disable();
/* First reset Interrupt Enable Register on the port */
    outp(IER, IEROFF);

/* Turn off all bits of Modem Control Register */
    outp(MCR, MCROFF);

/* Next disable 8259A from recognizing interrupts
 *   from the serial port
 */
    intmask = inp(P8259_1) | int_disable_mask;
    outp(P8259_1, intmask);

/* Restore original interrupt vector */
    _dos_setvect(int_number, old_handler);

/* Enable interrupts back on again */
    _enable();
}
/*------------------------------------------------------------*/
/* s _ s e n d c h a r
 * Puts a character into transmit queue. Returns 1 if
 * all's ok, 0 if there were problems.
 */
int s_sendchar(int ch)
{
    int retval, intmask;

    _disable();
    retval = q_puton(txq, (char *)&ch);
    _enable();
/* Turn on THRE interrupt if it's off and an XOFF was
 * not received
 */
    if (rcvd_xonxoff != XOFF_RCVD)
                    turnon_int(THREINT,intmask);
    return(retval);
}
```

continued

Listing 8-1. *continued*

```
/*--------------------------------------------------------------*/
/* s _ r c v c h a r
 * Returns a character from the receive queue.
 * Returns -1 if queue is empty.
 */
int s_rcvchar(void)
{
    int ch, intmask;
/* If XOFF sent earlier, we might have to send an XON */
    if(enable_xonxoff)
    {
    if(rxq->count <= LO_TRIGGER(RXQSIZE)  &&
         sent_xonxoff != XON_SENT )
        {
            send_xon = TRUE;
            turnon_int(THREINT,intmask);
        }
    }
    _disable();
    if (q_getfrom(rxq, (char *)&ch) == NULL)
    {
        _enable();
        return(-1);
    }
    else
    {
    _enable();
        return(ch);
    }
}
/*--------------------------------------------------------------*/
/* q _ g e t f r o m
 * Copy next data element in queue to specified
 * location. Also return a pointer to this element.
 */
char *q_getfrom( QTYPE *queue, char *data)
{
    char *current;
    current = NULL;
    if(queue->front == -1) return(current);
/* Else retrieve data */
    current = &(queue->data[queue->front]);
    *data = *current;
    queue->count--;
```

```
        if(queue->count == 0)
        {
/* The queue is empty. Reset front and rear,
 * and the count.
 */
        queue->front = queue->rear = -1;
        return(current);
    }
/* Increment front index and check for wraparound */
    if(queue->front == queue->maxsize-1)
        queue->front = 0;
    else
        queue->front++;
    return(current);
}
/*-------------------------------------------------------------*/
/* q _ p u t o n
 * Put a data element into queue.
 */
int q_puton(QTYPE *queue, char *data)
{
/* First check if queue is full. Return 0 if full. */
    if(queue->count == queue->maxsize) return(0);
/* Else, adjust rear and check for wrap-around */
    if(queue->rear == queue->maxsize-1)
        queue->rear = 0;
    else
        queue->rear++;
/* Save the character in the queue */
    queue->data[queue->rear] = *data;
    queue->count++;
    if(queue->front == -1) queue->front = 0;
    return(1); /* Successfully inserted element */
}
```

Summary

This chapter discussed the hardware features of the serial port in MS-DOS systems and presented techniques for programming the serial port. It also presented a small communications program in Microsoft C 5.0 to illustrate how the techniques can be implemented in practice. The steps involved in programming the serial port for interrupt-driven I/O are as follows:

1. Get the base port address of the selected communication port from BIOS data area at segment 40h and offset 0.

2. Using MS-DOS function 35h, get the address of the old interrupt service routine for the interrupt number corresponding to this adapter and save it.

3. Using MS-DOS function 25h, install our own interrupt service routine for that interrupt number.

4. Set up the communication parameters of the adapter using BIOS function 14h.

5. Set up the receive and transmit queues to hold incoming and outgoing characters.

6. Turn on signals needed by modem (e.g., DTR—Data Terminal Ready, and RTS—Request To Send) in the modem control register.

7. Enable all interrupts from the adapter (by setting bits 0 through 3 of the interrupt enable register to 1).

8. Also turn on bit OUT2 in the modem control register to enable interrupts from the serial adapter.

9. Program the 8259A to recognize interrupts with the IRQ of this adapter (by setting the appropriate bit to zero in the interrupt mask register accessed through the port address 21h).

At some point, when the user decides to terminate the communication session, a "cleanup" routine should be called. The cleaning up involves the following steps:

1. Turn off the interrupts from the serial adapter.

2. Reset the bits in the modem control register.

3. Restore the old interrupt service routine.

4. Mask the interrupts for this IRQ in the 8259A.

Programming the EGA and VGA

THE *Enhanced Graphics Adapter* (EGA) and the newer *Video Graphics Array* (VGA) present a unique set of problems to the developer. The EGA is rapidly becoming the most common graphics card in the MS-DOS world. However, four very different graphics standards are involved in supporting the EGA:

1. CGA-compatible graphics modes
2. Two new EGA graphics modes for 200-line color monitors
3. A new EGA graphics mode for 350-line color monitors
4. A new EGA graphics mode for use with monochrome (text) monitors

The VGA supports all of these modes as well as several new modes. This chapter will discuss programming concepts for each of the new EGA graphics modes as well as the new VGA modes. The CGA-compatible text and graphics modes will not be covered since they are more applicable to the CGA card.

The original EGA from IBM comes with 64K of graphics memory on the card. This may be expanded in 64K increments to 256K. The more EGA memory, the greater the graphics capabilities. EGA-compatible cards from other manufacturers often come with the full 256K memory already installed. VGA cards in most of the new IBM System 2s are essentially attached to the motherboard; for other PCs, the VGA is available as an add-in display card. In either case, the VGA will always have 256K of memory already installed.

Video functions on the IBM PC are called with the BIOS interrupt 10h. These video functions allow a program to set text or graphics modes, read or write single pixels, and place characters on the screen. The EGA has a new BIOS that replaces all the original PC video functions and adds several new functions. The new EGA functions allow new characters to be defined, more control over the palette, and text strings to be printed.[1]

---

1. A complete technical reference manual with an EGA BIOS listing and complete EGA description may be ordered from IBM by calling 1-800-IBM-PCTB (1-800-426-7282). The EGA technical reference is $9.95, part number 6280131. The VGA is documented in the IBM PS/2 technical reference manual, part number 68X2251.

Monitors and EGA Capabilities

The EGA is designed to work with one of three different monitors: the IBM Color Display, the IBM Enhanced Color Display, or the IBM Monochrome Display and their equivalents from other manufacturers. The particular monitor used determines the graphics resolution, the maximum number of colors, the color palette, and the number of pixels that make up each character. The VGA card must be used with an analog monitor, either color or monochrome. Although an analog monitor is functionally different from a digital (or TTL) monitor, from the programmer's perspective it can be treated as a high-resolution digital monitor. The only concern is whether it is monochrome or color.

The IBM Color Monitor has a maximum resolution of 640 x 200 pixels. The Color Monitor is limited to 200 scan lines vertically because it is able to use only one vertical scan rate. The EGA is compatible with all the text and graphics modes of the Color Graphics Adapter when used with the Color Monitor. There are two new graphics modes, modes 13 and 14, that use up to 16 colors with 320 x 200 and 640 x 200 resolution. However, the Color Monitor is limited to a 16-color fixed palette and 200 scan lines vertically. The fixed palette uses the same 16 colors used by the CGA in text mode. The default character box is 8 x 8 pixels. These modes are shown in Table 9-1.

Table 9-1. EGA Used with an IBM Color Monitor

Mode Number	Type	Maximum Colors	Size (Col x Row)	Box Size	Maximum Pages	Buffer Segment	Resolution
0	Text	16	40 x 25	8 x 8	8	B800	320 x 200
1	Text	16	40 x 25	8 x 8	8	B800	320 x 200
2	Text	16	80 x 25	8 x 8	4/8/8*	B800	640 x 200
3	Text	16	80 x 25	8 x 8	4/8/8*	B800	640 x 200
4	Graphics	4	40 x 25	8 x 8	1	B800	320 x 200
5	Graphics	4	40 x 25	8 x 8	1	B800	320 x 200
6	Graphics	2	80 x 25	8 x 8	1	B800	640 x 200
13	Graphics	16	40 x 25	8 x 8	2/4/8*	A000	320 x 200
14	Graphics	16	80 x 25	8 x 8	1/2/4*	A000	640 x 200

*Depends on amount of installed EGA memory.

The Enhanced Color Display

The IBM Enhanced Color Display is compatible with all the modes used with the Color Display, and uses one more high-resolution mode. The Enhanced Color Display is able to use two vertical scan rates, one for 200-line modes and one for 350-line modes. Multisync-type monitors are able to use the two standard EGA-generated vertical scan rates as well as even higher frequencies for higher resolution. The high-resolution mode, mode 16, can be used *only* with the IBM Enhanced Color Display, an equivalent monitor, or a multisync monitor, since the vertical resolution is 350 scan lines and the Color Display can display only 200 lines.

The EGA can display 16 colors from a 64-color palette in most modes when used with the Enhanced Color Display. The 16 colors are available only in mode 16 if there is more than 64K on the EGA card. Modes 4 through 6, the CGA-compatible graphics modes, are limited to the same 16-color fixed palette as the CGA. The text modes on the Enhanced Color Display use 8 x 14 pixels for each character, which gives a higher resolution character than that used on the CGA. The modes for the Enhanced Color Display (and multisync equivalents) are shown in Table 9-2.

Table 9-2. EGA Used with an IBM Enhanced Monitor (or Multisync)

Mode Number	Type	Maximum Colors	Size (Col x Row)	Box Size	Maximum Pages	Buffer Segment	Resolution
0	Text	16 of 64	40 x 25	8 x 14	8	B800	320 x 350
1	Text	16 of 64	40 x 25	8 x 14	8	B800	320 x 350
2	Text	16 of 64	80 x 25	8 x 14	4/8/8*	B800	640 x 350
3	Text	16 of 64	80 x 25	8 x 14	4/8/8*	B800	640 x 350
4	Graphics	4	40 x 25	8 x 8	1	B800	320 x 200
5	Graphics	4	40 x 25	8 x 8	1	B800	320 x 200
6	Graphics	2	80 x 25	8 x 8	1	B800	640 x 200
13	Graphics	16 of 64	40 x 25	8 x 8	2/4/8*	A000	320 x 200
14	Graphics	16 of 64	80 x 25	8 x 8	1/2/4*	A000	640 x 200
16	Graphics	4/16 of 64*	80 x 25	8 x 14	1/2*	A000	640 x 350

*Depends on amount of installed EGA memory.

Monochrome Graphics Modes

The IBM Monochrome Display is used primarily as a text-only display. The text mode is compatible with the IBM Monochrome Adapter. However, there is a new mode that adds 640 x 350 graphics with four "colors," the four colors being black, video, flashing video, and intensified video. If a monochrome monitor is connected to the EGA, the EGA is unable to use any of the color graphics modes, but it may use the new monochrome graphics mode.

The EGA converts the 8 x 14 font used with the Enhanced Color Monitor into an MDA-compatible 9 x 14 font. This is accomplished by extending any line draw characters into the ninth pixel position. Do not confuse an EGA connected to a monochrome monitor with a VGA connected to an analog monochrome monitor. The VGA in this case is treated as if it were connected to either a high-resolution color monitor *or* a digital monochrome monitor, depending on the VGA switch settings.

There is a subtle change to the standard MDA mode 7, the text mode, with the EGA. That change is the addition of multiple video pages. The original Monochrome Adapter uses only one page. The EGA can store up to eight individual video pages, depending on the amount of EGA memory. The page number is specified in the 80x86 register BH when using the BIOS functions for text. If older software uses BH for other data, or fails to initialize it, the final text output may not appear on the desired page.

EGA-compatible cards from other manufacturers may offer a Hercules-compatible graphics mode when used with a Monochrome Display. The two modes for the Monochrome Display are shown in Table 9-3.

Table 9-3.   EGA Used with a Monochrome Monitor

Mode Number	Type	Maximum Colors	Size (Col x Row)	Box Size	Maximum Pages	Buffer Segment	Resolution
7	Text	4	80 x 25	9 x 14	4/8*	B000	720 x 350
15	Graphics	4	80 x 25	8 x 14	1/2*	A000	640 x 350

*Depends on amount of installed EGA memory

IBM offers both monochrome and color analog monitors for use with the VGA. The VGA can be set to treat either analog monitor as if it were a digital monochrome monitor or a digital color monitor. In other words, the VGA can be set to treat the color analog monitor as if it were a digital monochrome monitor, or it can be set to treat a monochrome analog monitor as a high-resolution digital color monitor. This capability exists for backward compatibility with the EGA, and, when set to act as an EGA with a monochrome monitor, the VGA's capabilities are unchanged from the EGA with a monochrome text monitor attached.

The VGA's power-on self-test program calibrates the card to act as either a monochrome adapter or a color adapter when the PC is booted. When calibrated as a monochrome adapter, the modes in Table 9-3 are the only video modes available. When calibrated as a color adapter, the video modes in Table 9-4 are available.

Table 9-4.   Analog Monitor and VGA Configured for Color

Mode Number	Type	Maximum Colors	Size (Col x Row)	Box Size	Maximum Pages	Buffer Segment	Resolution
0	Text	16 of 256K	40 x 25	9 x 16	8	B800	360 x 400
1	Text	16 of 256K	40 x 25	9 x 16	8	B800	360 x 400
2	Text	16 of 256K	80 x 25	9 x 16	8	B800	720 x 400
3	Text	16 of 256K	80 x 25	9 x 16	8	B800	720 x 400
4	Graphics	4	40 x 25	8 x 8	1	B800	320 x 200
5	Graphics	4	40 x 25	8 x 8	1	B800	320 x 200
6	Graphics	2	80 x 25	8 x 8	1	B800	640 x 200
13	Graphics	16 of 256K	40 x 25	8 x 8	8	A000	320 x 200
14	Graphics	16 of 256K	80 x 25	8 x 8	4	A000	640 x 200
16	Graphics	16 of 256K	80 x 25	8 x 14	2	A000	640 x 350
17	Graphics	2 of 256K	80 x 30	8 x 16	1	A000	640 x 480
18	Graphics	16 of 256K	80 x 30	8 x 16	1	A000	640 x 480
19	Graphics	256 of 256K	40 x 25	8 x 8	1	A000	320 x 200

Installation Considerations and Presence Test

The capabilities of the EGA are dependent on the monitor and the amount of memory on the EGA board. The monitor determines which video mode to use for graphics or text, and the amount of EGA memory determines the number of colors and pages available. It is very important for your programs to determine whether there is an EGA present in the PC before you try to use it, and which monitor and memory were used if one is found. The program in Listing 9-1 does just that. The function *get_ega_info(&info)* is called with a pointer to a structure to hold EGA information. The function first retrieves a byte from the BIOS data area. That byte, at 0x40:0x87, has encoded information about the EGA hardware configuration, memory, and monitor. It is one of several status bytes kept by the EGA BIOS for its internal use and to provide information to programs.

We are interested in bits 5 and 6, which indicate total EGA memory; bit 3, which indicates whether the EGA is the active display; and bit 1, which indicates the type of monitor.

The function also calls one of the EGA's new BIOS calls, alternate function 10, which returns EGA information. The EGA is called by placing 0x12 in register AH and 0x10 in BL, and using int 10h. Here is the EGA BIOS call that returns the information:

Return EGA Information

Issue:	Int	0x10
Call with:	AH =	0x12 to select EGA alternate functions
	BL =	0x10 Alternate function for EGA information
Returns:	BH =	0 = Color monitor
		1 = Monochrome monitor
	BL =	Encoded EGA memory:
		0 = 64K
		1 = 128K
		2 = 192K
		3 = 256K
	CH =	Feature bits
	CL =	EGA board switch settings

Since the PC's BIOS does **not** use a video function 0x12, this call can be used as an EGA presence test. The PC's BIOS will safely reject unknown int 10h calls with the registers unchanged. So, if the outgoing registers are unchanged by the call, or, the incoming registers do not match the data in the EGA information byte, then there is simply no EGA present. If there is an EGA, the type of monitor used is determined by reading the installation switch settings. You can safely assume that the user has set the EGA switches properly, and those switches are set to the monitor type.

After detecting an EGA, the function will also test for a VGA. Most registers on the EGA are write only, and read/write on the VGA. A register is set to a value, and then an attempt is made to read that value. If the byte read back does not match the byte written, then the card is an EGA, not a VGA. The register used is the bit mask register, which will be covered in detail later.

The program EGACHECK.C, shown in Listing 9-1, will check for an active EGA display card. (There may be another display card in the system. If another card is active, bit 3 of the byte at 0x40:0x87 will be 1.) If an active EGA card is found, some information about the setup is saved.

The macro *PEEK_BYTE(seg,off)* in Listing 9-1 allows this program to retrieve a byte from anywhere in the PC's memory. It works by shifting the value for the segment left one word (16 bits), and then bit ORing the offset to form a *long* int. This *long* int is then cast to a *far* pointer.

Listing 9-1. Program EGACHECK.C

```c
/* egacheck.c */
/* Checks for an EGA/VGA */
/* If one is found, information is saved */
#include <conio.h>
#include <dos.h>
#include <stdio.h>

#define PEEK_BYTE(seg,off) \
    (*(char far *) ( (long)(seg)<<16 | (off) ) )

struct Ega_info    /* template to hold information about EGA */
{
  char card ;       /* to hold the type of card */
  char monitor ;    /* to hold the type of monitor */
  int memory ;      /* amount of memory: 64, 128, 192, 256K */
  char high_res_graphics ;
  char text_mode ;
} ;


int get_ega_info(struct Ega_info *) ;

main()
{
struct Ega_info info ;

if(get_ega_info(&info))         /* test for EGA */
 {
 if(info.card == 'E')
   {
   printf("\n\nEGA in use.") ;
```

```
   printf("\nConnected to a") ;
   switch(info.monitor)
   {
     case 'C': puts(" Color Monitor") ;
               break ;
     case 'M': puts(" Monochrome Monitor") ;
               break ;
     case 'H': puts("n Enhanced Color Monitor") ;
               break ;
     default:  break ;     /* undefined */
   }
   printf("\n%iK bytes of EGA Memory.", info.memory) ;
   }
   else
     printf("\n\nVGA in use.") ;
   printf("\nMode %#2i is the highest resolution graphics mode.",
           (int)info.high_res_graphics) ;
   printf("\nMode %#2i is the text mode.\n\n",
           (int)info.text_mode) ;
 }
else
 puts("\nNo active EGA.") ;
}                              /* end of main() */


int get_ega_info(info)
struct Ega_info *info ;

/* This function tests if an active EGA is in the system */
{
   union REGS regs ;
   int i, test_mask = 1 ;
/* Get the EGA information byte from the BIOS data area */
   char bios_info = PEEK_BYTE(0x40,0x87) ;

   /* Bit 3 indicates if the EGA is active or not
   ** it is NOT a test for presence */
   if(bios_info & 0x8)
      return (0) ;    /* if bit 3 is 1, EGA is NOT active */

   regs.h.ah = 0x12 ; /* EGA alternate BIOS function */
   regs.h.bl = 0x10 ; /* get info */
   regs.h.bh = 0xFF ; /* an impossible return value */
   int86(0x10, &regs, &regs) ;  /* EGA BIOS video call */

/* bios_info bits 5 + 6 and BL(encoded EGA memory) and */
```

continued

Listing 9-1. *continued*

```c
/* bios_info bit 1 and BH must be equal for an EGA */
if((regs.h.bl != ((bios_info & 0x60) >> 5)) || /* memory */
   (regs.h.bh != ((bios_info & 0x2) >> 1))  || /* monitor */
   (regs.h.bh == 0xFF))                   /* BH must change */
    return(0) ; /* if any test fails, return, no EGA */

/* There is an EGA, save the type of monitor */
/* The monitor type code is:
     'C' for color,
     'M' for mono,
     'H' for highres */
switch(regs.h.cl) /* cl has the EGA switch settings */
{
    case 0:  /* mono primary, EGA color 40x25 */
    case 6:  /* mono second, EGA color 40x25 */
        info->monitor = 'C' ;
        info->high_res_graphics = 0xD ;
        info->text_mode = 0x1 ;
        break ;
    case 1:  /* mono primary, EGA color 80x25 */
    case 2:  /* same as 1 */
    case 7:  /* mono second, EGA color 80x25 */
    case 8:  /* same as 7 */
        info->monitor = 'C' ;
        info->high_res_graphics = 0xE ;
        info->text_mode = 0x3 ;
        break ;
    case 3:  /* mono primary, EGA high res */
    case 9:  /* EGA high res primary, mono second */
        info->monitor = 'H' ;
        info->high_res_graphics = 0x10 ;
        info->text_mode = 0x3 ;
        break ;
    case 4:  /* color 40 primary, EGA mono */
    case 5:  /* color 80 primary, EGA mono */
    case 10: /* EGA mono primary, color 40 second */
    case 11: /* EGA mono primary, color 80 second */
        info->monitor = 'M' ;
        info->high_res_graphics = 0xF ;
        info->text_mode = 0x7 ;
        break ;
    default: /* reserved switch settings */
    return (0) ;
}
```

```
info->memory = 64 * (regs.h.bl + 1) ;

/* Now distinguish between an EGA and a VGA: */
/* This is done by writing a value to a register that is
   read only on the EGA, but read/write on the VGA */
outp(0x3CE, 8) ;          /* EGA/VGA bit mask */
outp(0x3CF, test_mask) ;  /* send the test value */
outp(0x3CE, 8) ;          /* the bit mask again */
if(inp(0x3CF) == test_mask)
   {
   info->card = 'V' ;     /* the register is readable */
   if(info->monitor != 'M')
      {
      info->high_res_graphics = 0x12 ;
      info->text_mode = 0x3 ;
      }
   /* If connected to a Mono, the values already set */
   }
else
   info->card = 'E' ;     /* just an EGA */
outp(0x3CE, 8) ;          /* reset the bit mask */
outp(0x3CF, 0xFF) ;

/* EGA/VGA is active in this system, return the memory */
return(info->memory) ;
}
```

The function prototype for *get_ega_info( )* and the skeleton for the structure *Ega_info* should be added to a new header file called *ega.h*. This function and structure, as well as other functions and macros, will be used by later examples.

Now that we know which mode to use for graphics, we can draw something on the display. The EGA BIOS has the same Write Dot call as the PC BIOS. This call is slow but usable on all IBM graphics cards. Here are the specifics of the EGA BIOS Write Dot:

Write Dot

Issue:	Int	0x10
Call With:	AH =	0xC to select Write Dot function
	BH =	Page
	DX =	Row number
	CX =	Column number
	AL =	Color value
Returns:	Nothing	

Notice the addition of a page value in BH. If you are converting older software to run on the EGA, make sure that the page number is in BH before calling int 10h. Programs written for the monochrome adapter, or the CGA in graphics mode, are especially vulnerable to this oversight.

The BIOS call to switch to a graphics mode is precisely the same as on the PC, namely function 0 of int 10h. *However, the BIOS does not check to make sure that the mode you select will not damage your monitor.* A monochrome monitor, connected to an EGA, may be damaged by a color text or graphics mode signal, so it is important to check for monitor and mode compatibility. The function *get_ega_info(&info)* from the program in Listing 9-1 is used to check the monitor and find the high-resolution mode that is safe to use. The program in Listing 9-2 demonstrates the use of *set_crt_mode( )* to set a graphics mode, and the use of *dot( )*, which uses the BIOS Write Dot function. The program will draw a series of parallel diagonal lines.

Listing 9-2. DIAGONAL.C Program

```
/* diagonal.c */
/* Demonstrates the high res graphics mode */
#include <conio.h>
#include <dos.h>
#include <stdio.h>

void set_crt_mode( char ) ;    /* add this to "ega.h" */
void dot( int, int, int, int ) ;

main()
{
   register i,j ;
   struct Ega_info info ;
   if(get_ega_info(&info))
      set_crt_mode(info.high_res_graphics) ;
   else
      return(1) ;

   for(j = 0; j <= 500; j += 5)
   for(i = 0; i <= 100; ++i)
      dot(i,i+j,13,0) ;
   getch() ;         /* wait for a character to be typed */
   set_crt_mode(info.text_mode) ;
   return(0) ;
}


/*=============================================================*/
void dot(row,col,color,page)
int row, col, color, page;
```

```
{
    union REGS regs ;
    regs.x.dx = row ;
    regs.x.cx = col ;
    regs.h.al = (char)color ;
    regs.h.ah = (char)0xC ;          /* Write Dot call */
    regs.h.bh = (char)page ;
    int86(0x10, &regs, &regs) ;
}

/*============================================================*/
void set_crt_mode(mode)
char mode ;
{
    union REGS regs ;
    regs.h.al = mode ;               /* al = mode to set */
    regs.h.ah = (char)0 ;            /* Set Mode function */
    int86(0x10, &regs, &regs) ;      /* execute BIOS int 10h */
}
/*============================================================*/
```

When you see how slow the BIOS Write Dot function is, you will probably wonder if you can make it faster. To do that requires bypassing the EGA BIOS and putting pixels directly into the EGA's memory. However, first you must understand how the EGA's memory is organized and how to control it.

Memory Organization

The EGA uses two different display memory organizations for graphics. In modes 4 through 6, the EGA uses the same memory organization as the CGA. In these modes, the display memory segment starts at 0xB800 and uses 80 bytes per scan line. Since there are 200 scan lines, 16,000 bytes are used. In the medium-resolution 320 x 200 mode, each byte represents 4 pixels with one of four colors, or two bits per pixel. In mode 6, each byte represents 8 pixels with two colors, or one bit per pixel. If a bit is 1, the corresponding pixel is on; if a bit is 0, the corresponding pixel is off. Additionally, the even-numbered scan lines are in the first 8K of the display memory, and the odd-numbered scan lines are in the second 8K of memory. The split scan line memory requires every pixel's offset to be tested to determine if it is in the even or odd bank.

The display memory for modes 13 through 16 (through mode 18 on the VGA) starts at segment 0xA000 and uses up to 64K of the 80x86 CPU address space. Each byte represents 8 pixels, with the most significant bit being the leftmost. The scan lines are not separated in memory like they are in the CGA modes, so the byte offset of a pixel is easier to calculate. In mode 16, the EGA has a maximum resolution of 640 x 350, or 224,000 pixels. Since there are up to

16 colors, each pixel must use 4 bits to specify the color. Altogether, this represents a total memory usage of (640 x 350 pixels ÷ 8 pixels/byte x 4 bits/pixel) = 109K.

The 80x86 CPU used in the PC can address only a segment of 64K. The EGA fits into the 64K segment limit by dividing 128K of its 256K memory into four 32K bit planes. Each bit plane (or bit map) corresponds to one bit of a pixel's color. Imagine these four bit planes as being stacked on top of each other at the same CPU address. Each CPU display memory address is actually 4 bytes of EGA memory.

In VGA modes 17 and 18, the EGA's memory organization is simply extended for another 130 scan lines. The VGA has a 320x200 resolution mode with 256 colors. This mode, although similar, must be addressed separately later.

Latch Registers

Reading or writing 4 different bytes (one for each bit plane) at the same CPU address presents a problem. To overcome this problem, the EGA has four *latch* registers. The EGA latch registers temporarily hold 1 byte from each of the four bit planes. EGA logic fills each of the four latch registers with a byte from each of the four bit planes at the address last read by the CPU. When the CPU sends a byte to the address last read, each of the four latch register contents may be unchanged, modified, or entirely replaced by the CPU data. The latch register contents are then written back to each of the EGA's bit planes.

When the latch registers are written back to the EGA's bit planes, they are again "stacked," with 1 bit of each of the 4 bytes forming the 4-bit color for 8 pixels. The relationship between the latch registers and the bit planes is shown in Figure 9-1, which shows the state of the EGA's memory and the contents of the four latch registers after the CPU reads the byte at A000:0000. The 8 pixels in the byte contain colors 0 through 7.

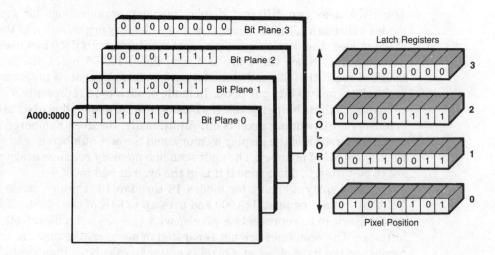

Figure 9-1. EGA bit maps and latch registers.

It is important to understand that the byte returned to the CPU after reading A000:0000 has no use. That byte is read only to establish which pixels to work with (in this case, pixels 0 through 7 in row 0) and to "prime" the latch registers, allowing the individual bytes of the bit planes to be manipulated by CPU data. This allows the 8 pixels contained in the 4 bytes to be modified, replaced, or cleared by the PC's CPU. To work with pixels in a different row or column, the offset from A000 is changed and the new byte containing the pixels is read by the CPU.

Whether the latch registers are modified, replaced, or unchanged by the CPU depends on the settings of several EGA control registers. These registers are accessed through one of five indexed *Very Large Scale Integration* (VLSI) chips on the EGA. These VLSI chips are set by sending an index number corresponding to the function desired, followed by the data for that function. Essentially, the index corresponds to one of many registers internal to the EGA, but mapped to a single PC output port. Data for these registers is sent using the 80x86 OUT instruction or the C library's *outp( )* function.

For example, the EGA has a *bit mask register* that will allow individual bits of the latch registers to be protected from change. Setting a bit to 0 in this register masks out the corresponding bit in the latch registers, and setting a bit to 1 allows that bit to be changed by CPU writes. The bit mask register therefore allows individual pixels to be changed without altering adjacent pixels addressed by the byte.

The bit mask register is function number 8 on the EGA's Graphics 1&2 chip. It is programmed by sending an index of 8 to port 0x3CE, followed by the bit mask data to port 0x3CF. The following C statements would set the bit mask register to protect all bits except bit 2:

```
outp(0x3CE, 8) ;      /* the index of the bit mask */
outp(0x3CF, 0x2) ;    /* all bits, except bit 2, to 0 */
```

But those statements give no clue, except for the comments, to what they do. In a minute, we will cover a C macro to make setting the EGA registers easier.

A second EGA register that affects how the latch register contents are rewritten is the *map mask register*. If any of the four bits of the map mask register are zero, the corresponding bit maps (bit planes) are protected from change. Sending a number between 0 and 15 to the map mask register will allow the color corresponding to that number to be written to the EGA's bit planes. However, the previous contents of the bit planes are not cleared. The previous contents of the bit maps must be cleared *before* setting the map mask to mask for a new color, but *after* setting the bit mask, by writing a zero to the byte containing the pixel to change. The map mask register is part of the EGA's Sequencer chip. It is accessed by sending the index of 2 to port 0x3C4 and sending the map mask to port 0x3C5. The effects of the bit mask and the map mask are shown in Figure 9-2.

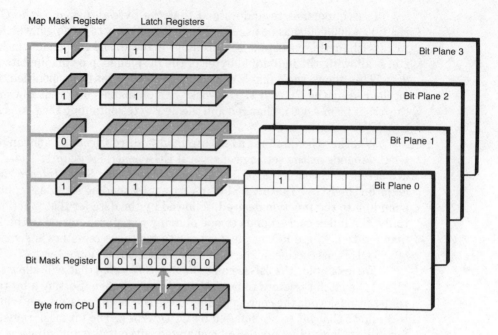

Figure 9-2. The bit mask and map mask registers.

Direct Screen Writing

With the bit mask and map mask registers, and an understanding of the EGA latch registers, we have enough information to create a C routine that will directly write a dot into screen memory. This routine is faster than the same routine in the EGA's BIOS. On an 8-MHz AT, the EGA BIOS will put 2.65 dots on the display in 1 millisecond (2.65 dots/ms). The routine in Listing 9-3 puts 7.55 dots/ms on the display—an increase in speed of 185 percent. The drawback is that *fastdot( )* will work only in EGA-specific graphics modes, and would have to be rewritten for another display card.

The following macros will allow the routine in Listing 9-3 to set the bit mask, the map mask, as well as other internal EGA registers.

```
#define EGA_GRFX(index, value) { outp(OX3CE, index) ; \
                                 outp(0x3CF, value) ;}
#define EGA_SQNC(index, value) { outp(OX3C4, index) ; \
                                 outp(0x3C5, value) ;}
```

The first macro, *EGA_GRFX*, takes as arguments the index number corresponding to the function desired on the Graphics 1&2 controller chip, as well as the value to send to the chip. The EGA's Graphics 1&2 chips control the access to the bit planes. (Although there are actually two chips at the same address, you can treat the Graphics 1&2 chips as one chip.) The address to index the

Graphics 1&2 chip is 0x3CE, and the data address is 0x3CF. The macro expands into two C statements. The first statement sends the index value to the chips, and the second statement sends the data.

The second macro, *EGA_SQNC*, is similar to *EGA_GRFX*. However, *EGA_SQNC* accesses a different chip, the EGA's Sequencer chip, by sending the index and data to different output ports. The Sequencer chip's main interest here is the map mask register.

The next two macros allow the routine to access a segment:offset address anywhere in the PC's address space:

```
#define PEEK_BYTE(s,o) (*(char far *) ( (long)(s)<<16 | (o) ) )
#define PEEK_WORD(s,o) (*(int far *) ( (long)(s)<<16 | (o) ) )
```

The final macros combine the previous macros. The *GET_CRT_COLS( )* macro returns the value to use for the number of bytes per line in the EGA graphics modes. The number of bytes per line is the same as the number of characters per line, and this number is at address 0x40:0x4A in the BIOS data area. The *EGA_BIT_MASK* and *EGA_MAP_MASK* macros set the bit mask and the map mask registers, respectively.

```
#define GET_CRT_COLS()   PEEK_WORD(0x40, 0x4A)
#define EGA_BIT_MASK(mask)      EGA_GRFX(8, mask)
#define EGA_MAP_MASK(mask)      EGA_SQNC(2, mask)
```

Altogether, these macros make it much easier to read and understand code written to manipulate EGA hardware. These macros are used in all the routines in the rest of this chapter.

Most of the EGA registers are write-only. Any program that uses the display needs to make assumptions about the state of the EGA since a write-only register cannot be read. Therefore, the safest state to leave the EGA registers in is the EGA BIOS default state. Additionally, the EGA BIOS assumes that the EGA registers are in the default state when writing characters on the display. If the bit mask register is set to mask bits, the characters will be unreadable. For the bit mask and the map mask, the default is no mask at all, so setting a mask of 0xF and 0xFF in the last two lines of *fastdot()* restores the default state. The majority of the VGA's registers are read/write. (This difference between the EGA and the VGA was used in EGACHECK.C to detect a VGA card.) However, the VGA registers should still be left in the default state.

Be sure that you understand how the byte address of the pixel is calculated in Listing 9-3:

```
char far *rgen = (char far *)(0xA0000000L +
                 (col >> 3) +
                 (row * GET_CRT_COLS()) );
```

The address of the byte is ((*row* × *bytes per row*) + *cols* ÷ 8 bits per byte). For the division of *cols* by 8, C's shift right operator, the >>, is used for greater speed.

Listing 9-3. FASTDOT.C Program

```c
/* fastdot.c */
#include <conio.h>

fastdot(row, col, color)
/* This routine will put a dot in the EGA's display buffer
** Use only in EGA graphics modes (13, 14, 15 or 16)
** and on an EGA with 128K memory or greater
** OR with a VGA in modes 13, 14, 15, 16, 17 or 18
*/
int   row, col, color;
{
char latch ;
/* Establish the address of the byte to change */
/* Buffer byte is A000:((row * bytes/row) + col/8) */
  unsigned char far *rgen = (char far *)(0xA0000000L +
                                (col >> 3)   +
                                (row * GET_CRT_COLS()) ) ;
/* Calculate the bit to change: */
  char bit_mask = (char)(0x80 >> (col & 7)) ;
  EGA_BIT_MASK(bit_mask) ;          /* set the bit mask */
  latch = *(rgen) ;                 /* prime the latches */
  *(rgen) = 0 ;                     /* clear the bit */
  EGA_MAP_MASK(color) ;             /* set the color */
  *(rgen) = 0xFF ;                  /* set the bit */
  EGA_MAP_MASK(0xF) ;               /* reset the map mask */
  EGA_BIT_MASK(0xFF) ;              /* reset the bit mask */
}
```

To find out the number of bytes per row, which can be 40 bytes in video mode 13 or 80 bytes in modes 14 through 16, look at the number of characters per row in the BIOS data area (address 0x40:0x4A). The number of bytes per row and the characters per row are the same in the EGA graphics modes. The result of the total calculation is added to 0xA0000000L, which is the segment of the EGA graphics modes. The entire value is then cast to a *far* pointer.

The bit number in the byte that corresponds to the pixel to change is calculated by *(col~&~7)*. Once the bit number is known, the bit mask is set to 0x80 >> *bit number* (0x80 is 010000000b).

The preceding routine assumes that page 0 is used. To add the ability to address a page other than page 0, insert these lines:

```c
while(page){
  rgen += PEEK_WORD(0x40, 0x4C) ;   /* add page length */
  --page ;}
```

where page is the number of the page to address. The word at 0x40:0x4C contains the length in bytes of the CRT display buffer used by the EGA's BIOS routines.

Try the program in Listing 9-2 after replacing *dot* with *fastdot()*. It is two to three times faster than the BIOS routine.

Lots of Dots

For maximum performance on the EGA, many functions need to be written to take advantage of unique EGA hardware. For example, the *fastdot()* routine sets the bit mask and map mask to the needed values at the beginning of the routine and then resets those registers to the BIOS default state at the end. If a function calls the *fastdot* routine repeatedly, the register reset at the end of the *fastdot* routine is repeated unnecessarily. That slows down the function.

The program in Listing 9-4 includes a line drawing routine that is based on Bresenham's Algorithm. This algorithm was originally used to control digital plotters, but it is equally suited for bit-mapped CRT graphics. The algorithm always increments (or decrements) by 1 in either the X or the Y direction. The X or Y direction is selected by the magnitude of the slope of the line. If the rise (Y direction) is greater, increment (or decrement) Y; if the run (X direction) is greater, increment (or decrement) X. Whether to increment or decrement X and Y is selected by the direction of the line. A cumulative error term is used to decide when to increment or decrement in the perpendicular direction.

Instead of calling the *fastdot()* routine, the dots are placed directly on the display. The EGA registers are reset only once at the end, and the function is much faster than one based on calling *fastdot()*.

Listing 9-4. BRES.C Program

```
/* bres.c */
/* Draws a pattern of lines to demonstrate the line() function */
#include <conio.h>
#include <dos.h>
#include <stdio.h>
#include "ega.h"

void line(int,int,int,int,int) ;   /* add this to ega.h */

main()
{
    int x1, y1, x2, y2 ;
    int step = 10, color = 13, scan_lines ;
    struct Ega_info info ;

    if(get_ega_info(&info) >= 128) /* active EGA? memory? */
```

continued

Listing 9-4. *continued*

```
{
   set_crt_mode(info.high_res_graphics) ;
   scan_lines = (PEEK_BYTE(0x40, 0x84) + 1)
              * PEEK_WORD(0x40, 0x85) ;
   y2 = (scan_lines - 1) - ((scan_lines - 1) % step) ;
   for (y1 = 0, x1 = 0, x2 = 0;
        y1 <= y2;
        y1 += step, x2 += step)
      line(x1,y1,x2,y2,color) ;
   getch() ;        /* wait for a key press */
   set_crt_mode(info.text_mode) ;
   }
   else
   puts("\nEGA adapter not active or not installed.\n") ;
}

void line(x1,y1,x2,y2,color)
int x1,y1,x2,y2,color ;
/* A fast line function - uses Bresenham's algorithm. */
/* Coordinates in row(y's) and col(x's) and assumed not equal */
#define sign(x) (((x) < 0) ? (-1) : (1))
#define qabs(x) (((x) < 0) ? -(x) : (x))
{
int dx = qabs(x2 - x1) ; /* run */
int dy = qabs(y2 - y1) ; /* rise */
int s1 = sign(x2 - x1) ; /* to increment/decrement */
int s2 = sign(y2 - y1) ;
int dx2, dy2, bytes_per_line = GET_CRT_COLS() ;
register error_term, i ;
unsigned char far *rgen = (char far *)(0xA0000000L) ;
unsigned char exchange = (char)0 ;

/* The larger of rise or run determines
** which to increment in the loop
*/
if(dy > dx)
  { int temp = dx; dx = dy; dy = temp; exchange = (char)1;  }

dx2 = (dx << 1) ;      /* used repeatedly, calculate now */
dy2 = (dy << 1) ;
error_term = (dy - dx) << 1 ; /* initialize error_term */
EGA_GRFX(0, color) ;  /* use the EGA's Set/Reset register */
EGA_GRFX(1, 0xF) ;    /* enable all bit planes */
for (i=1; i<=dx; ++i) /* all the pixels along the line */
```

```
{
EGA_BIT_MASK(0x80 >> (x1 & 7) ) ;
rgen[ ((x1 >> 3) + (y1 * bytes_per_line)) ] += 0x1 ;
   while (error_term >= 0)   /* loop until another pixel */
   {
    if (exchange)
        x1 += s1 ;
    else
        y1 += s2 ;
    error_term -= dx2 ;
   }
   if (exchange)
        y1 += s2 ;
   else
        x1 += s1 ;
   error_term += dy2 ;
}
EGA_GRFX(1, 0) ;     /* disable the Set/Reset register */
EGA_BIT_MASK(0xFF) ; /* reset the bit mask */
}
```

To keep the graphic image on the screen, a program should have the height and width of the display in pixels. The width of the display in pixels is given by *GET_CRT_COLS( )* x 8 pixels/byte. The height could be determined exactly with a table containing scan line counts for each mode. However, there is a quicker but less accurate way. Both the number of character rows and the point size (bytes per character) are programmable on the EGA, and therefore either one can change. But the height of the character box in bytes and the number of scan lines determine the number of rows. Since the word at 0x40:0x85 has the bytes per character, and the byte at 0x40:0x84 has the number of rows, they can be used to calculate the number of scan lines for any video mode. The C statement

```
scan_lines = (PEEK_BYTE(0x40, 0x84) + 1)
            * PEEK_WORD(0x40, 0x85) ;
```

calculates the approximate value for total scan lines. The value calculated is approximate, since the number of rows is truncated and may or may not be off by 1. Once the EGA data is known, the program draws a pattern of lines that is independent of the EGA graphics mode used.

Using the Set/Reset Register

The *line()* function in Listing 9-4 uses a different method to specify the color of dots on the display than the *fastdot()* routine. The *fastdot()* routine uses the map mask register to specify the color. But since specifying a mask to the map mask register does not clear the previous dot, the dot must be cleared with the map mask first set to 0xF and then set to the color of the new dot. In other words, both the map mask and the EGA memory must be accessed twice for every dot to set to a specific color.

The *line( )* function uses the set/reset register and the enable set/reset register to specify the color. The set/reset register will set a byte to 0xFF in each EGA bit plane where a bit is on in the set/reset register, and will reset a byte to 0 in each EGA bit plane where a bit is off. Therefore, the previous contents of the latch registers are replaced with the color number corresponding to the value set in the set/reset register. The map mask register has no effect on the set/reset register, but the bit mask register is usable to protect adjacent pixels.

To use the set/reset register, you must first enable it with the enable set/reset register. The set/reset register and the enable set/reset register are part of the EGA's graphics controller. The BIOS default state for the enable set/reset register is 0, which means that the set/reset register is turned off. Each bit of a four-bit value sent to the enable set/reset register corresponds to an EGA bit plane. If a bit in the enable set/reset register is 0, the corresponding bit plane is protected from change by the set/reset register.

The set/reset register is accessed by first sending an index of 0 to port 0x3CE and then sending the four-bit color code to port 0x3CF. The set/reset register affects only the bit planes enabled in the enable set/reset register. The enable set/reset register is accessed by sending an index of 1 to port 0x3CE and then sending the four-bit map mask to port 0x3CF.

Notice the statement *rgen[((x1>>3) + (y1*bytes_per_line))] +@ 0x1 ;* in Listing 9-4. Since the EGA display buffer is linear, it can be easily addressed as an array. The expression inside the brackets calculates the buffer offset of the byte to change. The right side of the statement would seem to be adding 1 to that byte, and that is what the CPU is trying to do. However, the actual purpose is to preserve the adjacent pixels contained in the byte. When the bit mask register is used, the display buffer must be read first to fill the latch registers so that the other bits in the byte may be preserved. Unlike the map mask register method of setting a color, when the set/reset register is used the byte sent by the CPU has no meaning beside establishing the address of the byte to change.

So the *+= 1* accomplishes two things: it reads the display buffer in order to prime the latch registers, and it sends back a byte that triggers the set/reset register. The 1 could be any value as long as the C compiler translates the operation into an 80x86 instruction that first reads and then stores a byte in the EGA's display memory.

Using the EGA Write Modes

The EGA has three write modes: 0, 1, and 2. Changing the EGA write mode changes the way that EGA hardware reacts when the CPU sends a byte to the display buffer. Each write mode is optimized for a different use. Write mode 0 is the general-purpose write mode, write mode 1 is optimized for copying EGA memory regions, and write mode 2 is best used for color fills. Changing the write mode can speed up an operation dramatically.

Write mode 0 is the mode used by the EGA BIOS. It is the most general-purpose write mode. In write mode 0, the color of a pixel may be set by using either the map mask register or the set/reset register. The map mask register is used by the EGA BIOS and by the *fastdot( )* routine. The *line( )* function uses the set/reset register to specify a color. When the map mask register is used, individual pixels may be set by the CPU sending a byte, with the corresponding bits in the byte set to 1. However, adjacent pixels in the byte must be protected with the bit mask register. When the set/reset register is used, the bits in a CPU byte sent to the EGA display do not correspond to pixels. The byte is written only to determine the offset of the pixels to change. The color is specified in the set/reset register, and the bit mask register allows individual control of pixels.

Write mode 2 is the most similar to write mode 0. In write mode 2, the byte sent from the CPU sets the color rather than individual pixels. The bit mask register gives control over individual pixels, and, if the bit mask register is not set, the entire byte of pixels is filled with the color from the CPU. The write mode is specified in bits 0 and 1 of a byte sent to the mode register on Graphics 1&2 chips. The index of the mode register is 5. The program in Listing 9-5 demonstrates write mode 2. The *rect( )* routine uses write mode 2 to fill a rectangle with a given color.

Listing 9-5. RECT.C Program

```
/* rect.c */
/* This program demonstrates write mode 2 */
#include <conio.h>
#include <dos.h>
#include <stdio.h>
#include "ega.h"

void rect(int,int,int,int,char);   /* add to ega.h */

main()
{
int i,j;
struct Ega_info info ;
if(get_ega_info(&info))
   set_crt_mode(info.high_res_graphics) ;
else
   return(1) ;
printf("\nColor #:\n");
for (i=0,j=0;i<16;++i,j+=40)
{
   printf(" %2i  ",i);
   rect(50,j,349,j+39,(char)i);
```

continued

Listing 9-5. *continued*

```
}
getch();
set_crt_mode(3) ;
}

void rect(row1,col1,row2,col2,color)
int col1,row1,col2,row2 ;
char color ;
{ /* This function generates a filled rectangle */
  /* It is assumed that row1 < row2, and col1 < col2 */
unsigned char far *rgen = (char far *)(0xA0000000L) ;
int rows = row2 - row1 ;            /* number of rows */
int cols = (col2 >> 3) - (col1 >> 3) - 1 ; /* total cols */
char left = (char)(0xFF >> (col1 & 7)) ;   /* left mask */
char rght = (char)~(0xFF >> (col2 & 7)) ;  /* right mask */
char next_row ;
char bytes_per_line = (char)GET_CRT_COLS() ;
register x,y ;
char latch ;

if (cols < 0)  /* are col1 and col2 in the same byte? */
    left &= rght, cols = 0, rght = 0 ;
rgen += bytes_per_line*row1 + (col1 >> 3) ;
next_row = bytes_per_line - cols - 2 ;

EGA_GRFX(5,2);            /* set write mode 2 */
for(y = 0 ; y < rows ; y++) /* do every row */
{
  EGA_BIT_MASK(left) ;   /* set the bit mask for left */
  latch = *(rgen) ;      /* latch the EGA bit planes */
  *(rgen++) = color ;    /* set the color, point to next byte */
  EGA_BIT_MASK(0xFF) ;   /* no mask in the center */
  for(x = 0; x < cols; x++) /* do every column */
    {
        latch = *(rgen) ;
        *(rgen++) = color ;
    }
  EGA_BIT_MASK(rght) ;   /* set the right bit mask */
  latch = *(rgen) ;      /* latch the EGA bit planes */
  *(rgen++) = color ;    /* set the color */
  rgen += next_row ;     /* go to the next row */
}
EGA_BIT_MASK(0xFF) ;     /* reset the bit mask */
EGA_GRFX(5,0) ;          /* reset the write mode */

}
```

In Listing 9-5, write mode 2 is set with the macro *EGA_GRFX(5,2)*. You must be careful not to send a value other than 0, 1, or 2 on the EGA (0, 1, 2, or 3 on the VGA), since the other bits of the byte sent to the mode register are significant to the EGA. The map mask and the bit mask registers are effective in write mode 2, but the set/reset register is not usable. Write mode 0, the BIOS default write mode, is set with *EGA_GRFX(5,0)*. The write mode must be reset to 0 before other programs or BIOS calls are used.

Write mode 1 is used to rapidly copy one area of EGA memory to another area. This is most useful for scrolling, animation, or saving and restoring areas of the screen. Write mode 1 allows you to copy the 4 bytes in each of the four bit planes with only one CPU read and write, and is many times faster than reading the 4 individual bytes from the bit planes and then writing the 4 bytes back at the new address.

To copy the 8 pixels, the EGA memory offset containing the 8 pixels is read to prime the latch registers; then the offset containing the destination is written to by the CPU. When the CPU writes a byte, and the write mode is set to 1, the EGA discards the byte from the CPU and copies the latch registers to each of the bit planes. The bit mask register is not usable with write mode 1. All 4 bytes in the latch registers are written to all four bit planes regardless of the setting of the bit mask. The map mask register can be used to protect individual bit planes.

The program in Listing 9-6 demonstrates write mode 1. A pattern of lines is drawn at the top of the screen. That pattern is then copied using write mode 1. Finally, the edge of the pattern is redrawn rapidly to demonstrate the potential for animation.

Listing 9-6. MODEL.C Program

```
/* mode1.c */
/* This program demonstrates EGA write mode 1 */
#include <conio.h>
#include <dos.h>
#include <stdio.h>
#include "ega.h"

void copy( int,int,int,int,int,int ) ;

void main()
{
    register i,j;
    int k = 0;
    set_crt_mode(16) ; /* enhanced monitor only! */
    /* Draw an interesting pattern: */
    for(k = 0; k <= 4; ++k)
    for(j = 0+k; j <= 500+k; j += 5)
```

continued

Listing 9-6. *continued*

```
    for(i = 0+k; i <= 100+k; ++i)
        fastdot(i,i+j,13) ;
    for(k = 0; k <= 3; ++k)
    for(j = 0+k; j <= 500+k; j += 5)
    for(i = 0+k; i <= 100+k; ++i)
        fastdot(i,i+j,3) ;
    /* Copy the pattern 120 rows down: */
    copy(0,0,105,639,    120,0) ;
    while(!kbhit())
    {
/* Copy the edge repeatedly,
** gives the illusion of motion: */
        copy(99,100,106,592,   219,100) ;
        copy(99,100,106,592,   219,108) ;
    }
    set_crt_mode(3) ;
}


void copy(r1_1, c1_1, r2_1, c2_1, r1_2, c1_2)
int     r1_1, c1_1,    /* upper left corner of source */
        r2_1, c2_1,    /* lower right corner of source */
        r1_2, c1_2 ;   /* upper left of destination */
{
/* Copies one screen region to another rapidly. Uses
** write mode 1. Only the upper corner of the destination
** needs to be given.
*/
    char far *source = (char far *)(0xA0000000L) ;
    char far *destination = (char far *)(0xA0000000L) ;
    int rows = r2_1 - r1_1 ;
    int cols = (c2_1 >> 3) - (c1_1 >> 3) ;
    int bytes_per_line = GET_CRT_COLS() ;
    int next_row = bytes_per_line - cols ;
    register x,y ;
    source += bytes_per_line * r1_1 + (c1_1 >> 3) ;
    destination += bytes_per_line * r1_2 + (c1_2 >> 3) ;

    EGA_GRFX(5,1) ;                   /* set write mode 1 */
    for(y = 0 ; y < rows ; y++)
    {
        for(x = 0; x < cols; x++)
            *(destination++) = *(source++) ;
        source += next_row ;
        destination += next_row ;
```

```
    }
    EGA_GRFX(5,0) ;                    /* reset the write mode */
}
```

Since the bit mask register is not usable in write mode 1, the *copy( )* routine will copy all 8 pixels in the source bytes to the destination bytes. In other words, write mode 1 is usable only on bytes rather than pixels. Write mode 1 can be used to save an area of the screen to a nonvisible page. This is useful for implementing pull-down menus. The area under the pull-down menu can be saved to a nonvisible page and then restored after the user has finished with the menu. Write mode 1 can copy only to another part of the EGA's memory. To read a color from EGA memory requires reading the four bit maps individually.

The VGA has one new write mode. Write mode 3 on the VGA is similar to using the set/reset and enable set/reset register pair in write mode 0 on the EGA to set the color (used by *line( )* in Listing 9-4). The difference is that in write mode 3 the enable set/reset register is not used, so that the value in the set/register is not masked by the enable set/reset register.

Reading the Bit Maps

Since each byte of CPU address space reserved for the EGA represents 4 bytes of graphics memory, EGA memory cannot be read by the CPU directly. The EGA will return the byte from the bit plane selected in the read map select register. The map to read must be set before reading the EGA offset containing the pixels you are interested in.

To determine the color of a given pixel requires a separate read from each of the four bit planes. Each bit of the four-bit color value is on one of the four bit planes. The most significant bit of the color value is on bit map 3, and the least significant bit is on bit map 0. The read map select register is index 4 on the EGA's Graphics 1&2 chip. Since each of the EGA's bit maps must be read individually, the value in the read map select register corresponds to only one EGA bit map at a time.

The function in Listing 9-7 returns the color of a pixel on the display. Like *fastdot()*, it is several times faster than the equivalent BIOS routine for reading the color of a dot.

The offset of the byte containing the pixel is determined exactly the same way as in the *fastdot( )* routine. A value for a bit mask is calculated by determining the bit number of the byte to change. But the bit mask value is not sent to the EGA's bit mask register. The EGA's bit mask register has no effect on bytes read from the EGA. The bit mask is used to isolate the pixel from the byte read from the EGA's bit plane. The bits are then added plane by plane to the pixel's color code. The read map select register selects the map to read from. The bit maps are read backwards (map 3, 2, 1, 0), since that makes the color code translation easier. Notice that the read map select register is not reset at the end of

Listing 9-7. Program to Return the Color of a Pixel

```
/* return the color of a pixel */
int readdot(row,col)
int row,col;
{
    register color = 0 ;
    register latch ;
    unsigned char far *rgen = (char far *)(0xA0000000L +
                                (col >> 3)   +
                                (row * GET_CRT_COLS())) ;
    int bit_number = (col & 7)^7 ;
    int bit_mask = (1 << bit_number) ;
    int plane ;
    /* Step through each plane 3,2,1,0 */
    for(plane = 3; plane >= 0; plane--)
    {
        EGA_GRFX(4,plane) ;              /* select plane */
        latch = *(rgen) & bit_mask ;     /* bit from that plane */
        latch >>= bit_number ;           /* right justify */
        color <<= 1 ;                    /* room for new bit */
        color |= latch ;                 /* add the bit */
    }
    return(color) ;
}
```

the routine. The last time through the loop sets the read map select register to 0, which is the default value.

EGA Color Palettes

When used with an Enhanced Color Monitor, the EGA can display any 16 colors from a 64-color palette. It takes 4 bits to represent 16 colors. Each of these bits corresponds to one of the EGA's four bit planes. On the CGA, and with the EGA's default palette, the 4 bits correspond to red, green, blue, and intensity, usually abbreviated as IRGB. But once the EGA palette is changed from the default, the four-bit color code is simply an index to the new palette.

The 64-color palette has the same three basic colors (red, green, blue) as the 16-color palette, but there is no intensity bit. Instead, each color has 2 bits for individual color intensity, giving three intensity levels for each color. The total 64-color palette may thus be represented with 6 bits (3 colors × 2 bits/color). The bits for the lower intensity of the three colors are the most significant bits in the 6-bit value, and are usually abbreviated as lowercase *rgb* for low-intensity red, green, and blue. The least significant 3 bits represent the higher-intensity red, green, and blue, and are abbreviated as an uppercase *RGB*. The total 6-bit value, *rgbRGB*, is used to select 1 of the 64 colors. Once 1 of the 16 displayable colors is set to an *rgbRGB* value, that color may be selected with a 4-bit IRGB value. The bits of an *rgbRGB* value will always indicate the red, green, and blue components of the resulting color, but, with an ECD connected, an IRGB value is simply an index to the current palette.

The *rgbRGB* colors can be used only with an EGA connected to an Enhanced Color Monitor. When the EGA is connected to a Color Display, only the 16 colors from the default palette may be used. In text modes and the EGA graphics modes, individual palette registers may be set to any of the 16 default colors. In the CGA-compatible modes, the palette must be changed by using the CGA-compatible BIOS calls.

The EGA also has an overscan register. The color value sent to the overscan register is displayed as a border. However, the overscan is usable only in the 200 scan line modes.

The EGA's palette registers are most often set with a new EGA BIOS call. The BIOS call can set either 1 of the 16 colors, or all 16 at once. The BIOS call is function 0x10 of interrupt 0x10. There are four subfunctions: 0 sets individual palette registers to any *rgbRGB* value (or any IRGB value if the EGA is not connected to an ECD), 1 sets the overscan register, 2 sets all the palette registers and the overscan register, and 4 toggles between text blinking and intensity. The subfunction is selected in register AL.

Set Palette

Issue: Int   0x10

Call with: AH =   0x10

AL =   0, Set individual palette register

BL =   Color number (IRGB) to change

BH =   *rgbRGB* value to set

AL =   1, Set overscan register

BH =   Color number to set

AL =   2, Set all palette registers and overscan
ES:DX points to a 17-byte table
Bytes 0−15 have the 16 *rgbRGB* values for colors 0−15
Byte 16 is a color number for the overscan register

AL =   3, Toggle intensity/blinking bit
Changes the meaning of bit 7 of the text attribute byte.

BL =   0, Allow background intensity

BL =   1, Allow foreground blinking

Unfortunately, the EGA's palette registers are write only. Normally it is not possible to determine what *rgbRGB* value a given color number represents. The EGA BIOS will check for the existence of a 256-byte table called the *parameter save area* when changing the palette registers. The BIOS will save the *rgbRGB* values in that table if it exists. The creation and maintenance of a parameter save area will not be covered here, but it is important to use BIOS calls to set the palette so that a parameter table will be updated.

The VGA does have read/write palette registers, so individual *rgbRGB* colors may be determined by reading the associated palette register. The VGA also has a more extensive palette, in which any of the 16 colors displayed may be from a palette of 262,144 possible colors. Instead of the 2 bits per color on the EGA, the VGA uses 6 bits per color ($2^6 \times 3$ colors = 262,144 colors).

The program in Listing 9-8 demonstrates the uses of the palette registers. It will work only with an EGA/ECD combination (or VGA). The program will first draw 16 colored rectangles using the *rect( )* function from Listing 9-5. The palette is then continuously changed.

Listing 9-8. PALETTE.C Program

```
/* palette.c */
/* Demonstrates the 64 color palette */
#include <conio.h>
#include <dos.h>
#include <stdio.h>
#include "ega.h"

void set_all_pal(char *) ;
void gotoXY(int,int) ;

main()
{
int i,j,ch = 0;
char palette[17] ;        /* this array holds the palette */
set_crt_mode(16) ;        /* have the right monitor! */

/* Draw some color bars: */
printf("\nColor #:\n") ;
for (i=0,j=0;i<16;++i,j+=40)
{
   printf(" %2i  ",i);
   rect(50,j,300,j+39,i);              /* from listing 9-5 */
   palette[i] = (char)i;               /* initialize array */
}
   gotoXY(15,22) ;
   printf("rgbRGB of color 7") ;
   printf("%c%c%c%c%c%c",205,205,205,205,205,190) ;
```

```
      gotoXY(20,0) ;
      printf("Press Space to single space, Esc to exit") ;

      palette[16] = (char)0 ;
      while(ch != 27)                    /* while not ESC */
         {
         if (kbhit())                    /* if a key is hit, */
            ch = getch() ;               /* get the character */
         for (i = 1; i<=15; ++i)
               {
               palette[i]++;
               if (palette[i] == 64)     /* max rgbRGB value */
                     palette[i] = 1 ;
               }
         set_all_pal(palette) ;          /* set the palette */
         gotoXY(15,23) ;

         /* Convert the rgbRGB value to binary: */
         for(i = 5;i>=0; --i)
            if(palette[7] & 1<<i)
                putchar('1') ;
            else
                putchar('0') ;
         if(ch == 32)                    /* single space mode */
            while(!kbhit());
         }

set_crt_mode(3) ;
}


/*============================================================*/
void set_all_pal(palette)
char *palette ;
/* This function sets the entire palette */
{
union REGS regs ;                   /* the 8086 registers */
struct SREGS segregs ;
char far *fp = (char far *)palette ;
regs.h.ah = 0x10 ;
regs.h.al = 2 ;                     /* function to set all */
segregs.es = FP_SEG(fp) ;          /* ES to segment of palette */
regs.x.dx = FP_OFF(fp) ;           /* DX to offset of palette */
int86x(0x10, &regs, &regs, &segregs) ;
}


/*============================================================*/
```

continued

Listing 9-8. *continued*

```
void gotoXY(x,y)
int x,y ;
/* This function moves the text cursor to x,y */
{
    union REGS regs ;
    regs.h.ah = 2 ;              /* set cursor function */
    regs.h.bh = 0 ;             /* page 0 */
    regs.h.dh = (char)y ;       /* row */
    regs.h.dl = (char)x ;       /* col */
    int86(0x10, &regs, &regs) ; /* call int 0x10 */
}
```

The Data Rotate Register

The data rotate register allows you to select how the data sent by the CPU will be combined with the EGA latch registers. The options are to have the data be ANDed, ORed, XORed, or unmodified with the bytes in the latch registers. Although the data rotate register also has the ability to rotate the byte sent from the CPU, in practice this is of little value. The CPU can be used to rotate the byte more quickly and with less setup. The significant bits of the data rotate register are shown in Figure 9-3, and an example of how to use the data rotate register is shown in Listing 9-9.

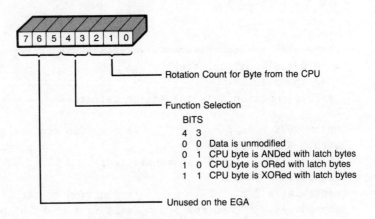

Figure 9-3. The data rotate register.

Listing 9-9. Example Use of Data Rotate Register

```
main()
{
    int i,j, k ;
    for(k=1;k<16;k++)
        {
        set_crt_mode(16) ;
        rect(0,0,200,639,k) ;    /* background */
        EGA_GRFX(3,0) ;          /* reset the DRR */
        for(i=0;i<13;i++)
            printf("\n") ;
        printf("    Unmodified              AND'ed") ;
        printf("    \t OR'ed               XOR'ed") ;
        for(i=0, j=0; i<4; j=160*(i+1),i++)
            {
            switch(i)
                {
                case 1:EGA_GRFX(3,8) ;    /* DRR to AND */
                        break ;
                case 2:EGA_GRFX(3,16) ;   /* DRR to OR */
                        break ;
                case 3:EGA_GRFX(3,24) ;   /* DRR to XOR */
                }
            /* Now draw the rectangles: */
            rect(20,20+j,100,99+j,1) ;
            rect(40,40+j,120,119+j,1<<1) ;
            rect(60,60+j,140,139+j,1<<2) ;
            rect(80,80+j,160,159+j,1<<3) ;
            }
        getch() ;
        }
    set_crt_mode(3) ;
}
```

VGA 256 Color Mode

The VGA has a new video mode, mode 19, that can display 256 colors out of a palette of 262,144 total colors. Mode 19 is conceptually quite easy. Since each pixel is represented by 1 byte of display memory, the calculations to determine the offset of each pixel are simplified. The program in Listing 9-10 is an example VGA mode 19. The entire set of 256 colors is displayed. The first 16 colors are the same palette as the CGA, VGA, and EGA. The next 21 colors are a gray scale. The final 216 colors are three groups of 72 colors. Each group of 72 ranges smoothly from blue to red to green. The three groups correspond to decreasing saturation, or increasing whiteness.

Listing 9-10. Example VGA Mode 19

```
void fast19(int, int, int) ;

main()
{
  register i,j ;
  struct Ega_info info ;
  if(get_ega_info(&info))
    if(info.card == 'V')        /* VGA card? */
      set_crt_mode(19) ;
    else
      return ;
  else
    return ;

  for(i=0x0; i<=0xFF; i++)    /* print the palette */
    for(j=0; j<200; j++)
      fast19(j,i,i) ;
}

void fast19(row,col,color)
int row, col, color ;
{
  /* since each byte is a pixel, the offset of a pixel is
  ** (row * 320 bytes/row) + col
  ** there is also no bit mask */

  unsigned char far *rgen = (char far *)(0xA0000000L +
                            (row * 320) + col) ;

  *rgen = (unsigned char)color ;
}
```

Included in Listing 9-10 is a direct video memory dot routine, *fast19( )*, for the VGA's 256 color mode. Since each pixel uses 1 byte of display memory, the routine can be very direct. There is no need for lengthy memory calculations or bit map or map mask manipulation. A routine to return the value of a pixel is just as straightforward. Simply replace the statement **rgen = color ;* with *return(*rgen) ;*.

Summary

With the EGA, everything is complicated. When IBM designed the EGA, it was locked into supporting two very different previous display standards (the CGA and MDA). The result now is supported in the even more complicated VGA. Your best bet for designing software to run on the EGA or VGA without sacrificing future compatibility is to separate hardware-dependent code into logically independent functions. For example, the *fastdot( )* routine in Listing 9-5 was easy to rewrite for the new VGA 256 color mode. A more complicated plotting routine that calls *fastdot( )* to plot dots would not need to be rewritten as long as *fastdot( )* supports the new mode.

This chapter has developed several basic graphics functions *line( )*, *fastdot( )*, *readdot( )*, and *rect( )*. Many of the EGA peculiarities, such as latch registers, have been examined. The three ways of setting a color on the EGA—the map mask register, the set/reset register, and write mode 2—have also been shown. Although the routines in this paper are fast, there are many improvements that could be made. High-performance graphics routines on the EGA or VGA tend to be found only through exploration.

Programming the Intel Numeric Processing Extension

10

A Programmer's View of the NPX
Using MS-DOS Tools with the NPX
Programming Examples for the NPX with MASM
Summary

HE MS-DOS world belongs exclusively to Intel. That fact provides users of MS-DOS with two benefits. One, programs written for MS-DOS systems are generally portable even at the object code level. Two, most MS-DOS systems have the capability of using the Intel 8087, 80287, or 80387 Numeric Processing Extension chips. Throughout this chapter, we shall refer to the Numeric Processing Extension by the abbreviation "NPX." The NPX's purpose is to provide 8086-family, 80286, and 80386 systems with the ability to perform *fast* floating point calculations.

The NPX supplies the system with instructions for number conversions, basic mathematics, and even some transcendental functions, such as sine, cosine, and log.

The benefits of the NPX are not limited to speed alone. By supplying what amounts to a library of floating-point math routines, the NPX spares the programmer the burden of writing those routines, thus speeding the programming job. In addition, because these routines are contained in the NPX chip rather than in program memory, use of the NPX can result in a smaller program, which can mean a cost savings in some developments.

Unlike earlier math processors, such as the Intel 8231A and 8232, the NPX is accessed with escape sequences that appear to the assembly language programmer as machine language instructions. The NPX does not require the installation of any additional software or hardware (as long as the 8088 or main CPU chip is configured in "max mode"), nor does the NPX require programmed I/O or DMA transfers for access.

Because the NPX is fully compatible with the proposed IEEE (Institute of Electrical & Electronics Engineers) standards for floating point computations, a large and expanding base of advanced numerical calculation software is available. This base conforms with the NPX's way of processing numbers. For a programmer who doesn't have the time to write complicated numerical routines, this software base represents a great savings in time and money.

Use of the 8087 NPX is not limited to the 8086 and 8088 processors. The 8087 NPX can also be used with the 80186 and 80188 processors. For users of the 80286 processor, Intel has provided the 80287 NPX. And for users of the 80386 processor, the 80387 NPX is used. Note that some 80386-based systems provide a socket for the 80287 NPX in addition to, or instead of, an 80387 NPX socket, since the 80287 NPX was cheaper and more readily available than the 80387

NPX when the 80386 was first introduced. Unless otherwise noted, the information presented in this chapter is valid for all of these combinations.

A Programmer's View of the NPX

The following sections discuss aspects of the NPX that are important to keep in mind when you are programming for the NPX. These include data registers, floating-point and other data formats, the NPX instruction set, addressing modes, and the control and status words.

The Data Registers in the NPX

Although it's true that NPX instructions appear as part of the main processor's instruction set, the NPX has no means of accessing the main CPU's registers. Instead, the NPX has its own set of registers and communicates with the main CPU through common memory. That really isn't much of a limitation because the main CPU's registers aren't well suited to real numbers. Instead of the 16-bit or 32-bit registers used in the main CPU, the NPX has eight 80-bit registers and can therefore hold much more information. These registers are shown in Figure 10-1.

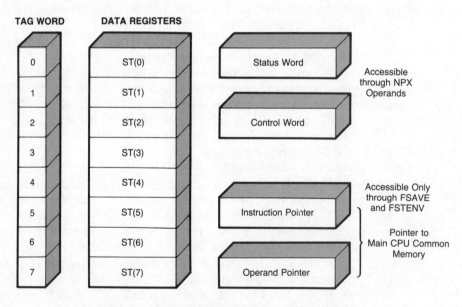

Figure 10-1. Register layout in the NPX.

You should notice that unlike the main CPU, the NPX's data registers don't have unique names but are indexed entries in a stack (for example, ST (1)). Values are loaded into the NPX by pushing them onto this stack, and some values (but not all) are retrieved by popping them from the stack. Many of the

NPX's instructions operate only on the top of the stack, and most of the other instructions default to operating on the stack's top.

The fact that the NPX addresses its registers as a stack is very important because all register addresses are relative to the top of the stack! For example, a value contained in register i is contained in register $i-1$ if the stack is popped and register $i+1$ if a new entry is pushed on the stack.

When programming for the NPX, pay close attention to the behavior of the stack. You can't stuff a value into a register and assume that the value will be in the same place later.

Floating-Point Real Number Representation in the NPX

These registers also differ from the main CPU's registers in that they may hold only one type of number—a floating-point real number (called a *temporary real* in Intel parlance). The topmost format in Figure 10-2 shows what this floating real number looks like in an NPX register. From the picture, you can see that the register is divided into three fields: the *sign bit*, the *biased exponent* (15 bits), and the *significand* (64 bits). Each of these numbers taken by itself is an unsigned binary integer, but when combined they can represent a very large number!

Let's take a closer look at the individual parts of this floating-point real number. The leftmost part (bit 79) is the sign bit. When this bit is a 0, the number is positive. When it's a 1, the number is negative. Simple, but there are two effects to note. Unlike two's complement binary integers (as used in the main CPU), this floating-point real number has exactly as many positive numbers as negative numbers (you'll see why later). The other, more important effect is that this numbering system has two types of 0! This means that 0 can be a positive or a negative number and that 0 doesn't necessarily equal 0. The NPX takes care of this effect, but it's something to be remembered if you attempt to compare real numbers with the main CPU (you shouldn't ever need to because the NPX compares numbers just fine).

Skipping to the right-hand side of the number, we see the significand (bits 0 through 63). This is where the significant digits part of the number is represented. Because each entry can be either positive or negative, the range is exactly the same size for each. You'll also note that bit 63 (the most significant bit of the significand) is shown as a 1. This is because the NPX usually stores numbers in a *normalized* format, which means that the NPX finds the leftmost 1 in a binary number and shifts it up or down until that 1 is in bit 63. (A number with no 1 is 0, and its representation is *all* 0's.) Let's do a short example with the number 10:

```
Decimal:                                                10
Hexadecimal:                                             A
Binary 64 bit integer:    00000000000000...000000000001010
NPX 64 bit real:          10100000000000...000000000000000
```

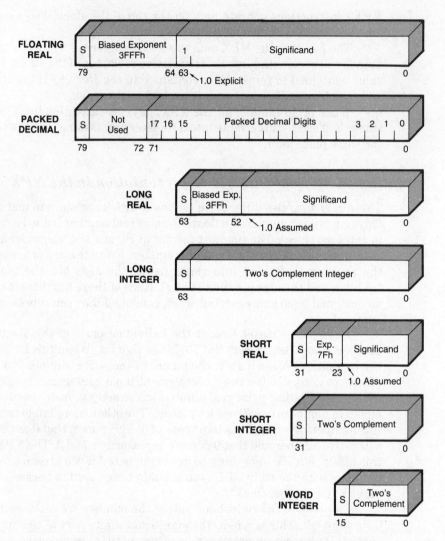

Figure 10-2. Number representations in the NPX.

See how the NPX slid the number to the left? This allows much more room for other digits to be represented, such as 10.1, 10.12, etc. The only problem is that the number shown for the NPX is no longer 10. It's now 10×2^{60}. How does the NPX know that it's really just 10? It uses something called the exponent field (bits 64 through 78).

The NPX always assumes that the number in the significand is between 1 and 2. By itself the number shown above would be 1.01 binary, or 1.25 decimal. (Each binary digit in a fraction is ½ the previous binary digit, so the positions to the right of the decimal point in binary are ½, ¼, ⅛, ¹⁄₁₆, etc.) The NPX remembers in the exponent field how many positions it shifted the original number. For the case of 10, the NPX shifted the decimal point three positions from 1010.0

(binary) to 1.0100 (binary). The value 3 is stored in the exponent field. There is one more trick to the NPX's storage of numbers. Because the exponent is stored as an unsigned integer, if the NPX just put the true exponent in the field, there would be no way to store numbers less than 1 (no negative exponents means no number less than 2^0 or one). So the NPX biases (it adds a bias to) the exponent. The bias used in the NPX is 3FFFh, or 16,383 decimal. For the example of storing the number 10, the biased exponent is 3 plus 3FFFh, or 4002h.

We're all done, so let's look at Figure 10-3 to see what the number 10 looks like inside the NPX. Why must you understand how the NPX stores numbers? Because there are times when you'll want to inspect the contents of NPX registers during debugging, and in order to understand the uses and limitations of some of the more advanced NPX instructions, you must first know the types of data being manipulated.

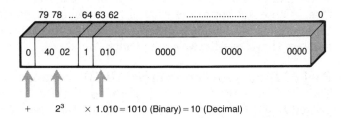

Figure 10-3. NPX representation of the number 10.

Other Data Formats Used with the NPX

Figure 10-2 contains six other data formats in addition to the 80-bit floating-point real number format used internally. What are these representations used for? In addition to the 80-bit real, these forms are those that the NPX can use to read data from or write data to memory. If the data is in one of these formats, it can be understood by the NPX. Otherwise, all bets are off. Three basic types are shown in Figure 10-2. These types are *real*, *integer*, and *packed decimal*.

Short Real and Long Real Data Formats

The short real (32-bit) and long real (64-bit) formats are very similar to the 80-bit floating-point real just discussed. These numbers are capable of representing floating-point real numbers but with less range and accuracy. The differences can be summed up as shown in Table 10-1.

Table 10-1. Differences among Real Data Formats

Data Type	# Bits Significand	# Bits Exponent	Exponent Bias	Leftmost One
80-bit Real	64	15	3FFF (16383)	Explicit
64-bit Real	52	11	3FF (1023)	Assumed
32-bit Real	23	8	7F (127)	Assumed

In addition to their size, the short and long real forms differ from the 80-bit real in that the most significant one bit does not actually appear! Because of their limited space, these forms always assume a 1 at the leftmost position but don't store the 1, and thus they gain another digit position.

Word Integer, Short Integer, and Long Integer Data Formats

The integer forms should be familiar by now. These forms are used by the main CPU to store two's complement integer numbers (although the main CPU can't use the 8-byte long integer format). These numbers have the following ranges:

64-Bit: -9,223,372,036,854,775,808 to 9,223,372,036,854,775,807

32-Bit: -2,147,483,648 to 2,147,483,647

16-Bit: -32,768 to 32,767

These numbers differ from the real numbers in that any value loaded from this form is an exact representation of the number. Also remember that although these are signed numbers and the most significant bit reflects the sign of the number, they are still two's complement numbers.

Packed Binary-Coded Decimal (BCD) Formats

The last form of the NPX is called packed BCD (binary-coded decimal). What is packed BCD? In binary-coded decimal notation, each 4-bit nibble is a separate digit that can have a value between 0 and 9. The entire number has no real meaning other than as a string of digits. In this way, the number is more like an ASCII string. In Figure 10-4, we've taken the number 256 and shown its forms in normal binary and binary-coded decimal. The little calculation attached is shown in decimal base.

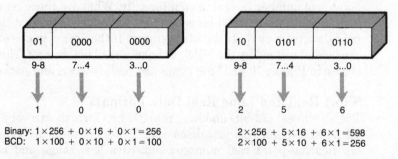

Figure 10-4. Binary-coded decimal number representation.

From Figure 10-4, you can see that in binary-coded decimal we write the number as if it were hexadecimal (one digit every 4-bit nibble) but interpret it as decimal. But why is the data form so important? Because it's a snap to convert between ASCII and packed BCD. Figure 10-5 shows that to convert from BCD to ASCII, you need only unpack the digits (one per nibble) into bytes and add 30 hex to form the ASCII characters 0 through 9 (hex 30 through 39). To convert the other way, subtract 30h from each character and pack them down, two per byte.

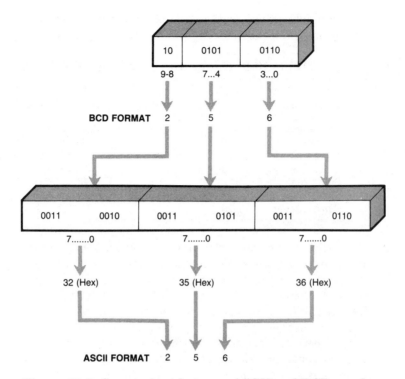

Figure 10-5. Conversions between ASCII and BCD numbers.

This data form is used by the NPX only for loading and storing numbers. None of the arithmetic instructions can use packed BCD form. Even with this limitation, the packed BCD load and store instructions of the NPX are two of the most useful instructions that it possesses. This is because the ability to calculate is worthless without the means to communicate results to the user, and most people use standard decimal notation for floating-point numbers.

The NPX provides for conversion from base 10 to base 2 and back again. The programmer need only take care of the conversions between ASCII strings and packed BCD and of locating the decimal point correctly (we'll see that in the section on converting between decimal and binary floating-point numbers). The NPX takes care of the rest.

Summary of Data Types

In Table 10-2, we've summarized the size of the numbers that can be represented by each data type, along with the approximate decimal resolution (number of significant digits) that each data type supports. In terms of actual use, we can recommend the following: Use packed BCD for converting from ASCII to floating real and back again. Use floating-point real numbers for all calculations and for real number constants in MASM (we'll get to that). And use the smallest integer form that fits a number for integer number constants in MASM. Following these guidelines will give the best possible accuracy with some savings in memory by using the shorter integer forms where possible.

Table 10-2. Range and Precision of NPX Data Types

Data Type	Binary Bits	Decimal Digits	Approximate Range
Floating real	80	19	$3.4 \times 10^{-4932} \le N \le 1.2 \times 10^{4932}$
Packed decimal	80	18	$-10^{18} - 1 \le N \le 10^{18} - 1$
Long real	64	15–16	$4.19 \times 10^{-307} \le N \le 1.67 \times 10^{308}$
Long integer	64	18	$-9 \times 10^{18} \le N \le +9 \times 10^{18}$
Short real	32	6–7	$8.43 \times 10^{-37} \le N \le 3.37 \times 10^{38}$
Short integer	32	9	$-2 \times 10^9 \le N \le +2 \times 10^9$
Word integer	16	4	$-32,768 \le N \le +32,767$

Figure 10-6 shows the range of number representation in the NPX. Note that the NPX stores numbers with greater accuracy internally (80-bit real) than is normally used when loading or storing the NPX's registers (long real). This allows an extra margin of accuracy for calculations. Note also that the spacing between unique representable numbers (the distance between two adjacent numbers that the NPX may represent exactly) decreases towards zero (from either direction), and increases towards infinity (plus or minus). This density of number representation implies that the NPX has more accuracy for processing extremely small numbers than large numbers.

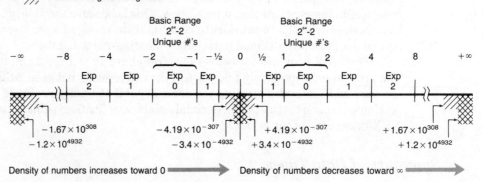

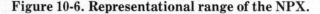

Figure 10-6. Representational range of the NPX.

The Instruction Set of the NPX

The NPX has what is known in the industry as a *rich* instruction set. This doesn't necessarily mean that there are a lot of instructions (although it does have 69 different instructions) but that the instruction set is well suited for the types of operations desired from the NPX. There is an instruction for nearly every purpose, greatly reducing the number of steps (and associated programming difficulties) that might be encountered with a lesser numerical coprocessor.

Table 10-3 lists the 69 instructions. This table is organized by classes of operations rather than alphabetically because you will most likely want to look up an instruction by type rather than by name. Two designations in Table 10-3 need to be explained. First is the (P) mark appearing next to some instructions. This signifies that the associated instruction may be used in a POP form, F*op*P. The POP form tells the NPX to increment the stack pointer and tag the old stack top register as empty, which essentially throws away the stack top. This is all made clearer in the following text.

The FWAIT Prefix

The second designation in Table 10-3 is the (N) mark. The (N) mark means that the associated instruction may be used in a no-wait form, as in FN*op*. Normally the MASM assembler generates an FWAIT prefix for every NPX instruction. The no-wait form tells the MASM assembler not to generate an FWAIT prefix. Now, just what is an FWAIT prefix?

Normally the NPX must wait to finish the current instruction before it can accept a new one. This is accomplished by the FWAIT op-code prefix (9B hex), which is really an 8086 op-code! When the main CPU executes this instruction, the main CPU waits until the TEST pin on the main CPU/NPX interface becomes active. This occurs when the NPX has finished executing and is ready for the next instruction. The main CPU starts executing again and the next NPX instruction is fetched, starting the cycle over again.

The reason that FWAIT is used as a prefix is so that the main CPU waits only when it wants to send the NPX another instruction. Once an NPX instruction has been sent, the main CPU and the NPX can be processing simultaneously, and when the main CPU needs the NPX again, the main CPU must check to ensure that the NPX is ready.

There is one other case where the main CPU must use the FWAIT instruction. Whenever the main CPU needs to read data from the NPX, the main CPU issues the proper NPX instruction to store the data in memory. The main CPU must then wait (via the FWAIT instruction) for the data to become available. In this case, the programmer must explicitly code the NPX instruction FWAIT because MASM doesn't know that the main CPU rather than the NPX is waiting for the instruction to complete.

Table 10-3. List of Intel NPX Instructions and Addressing Forms

Notes	Instruction Mnemonic	Address Modes	Instruction Name
		Data Transfer Instructions (9)	
	FXCH	//d	Exchange registers
	FLD	s	Load real
(P)	FST	d	Store real
	FILD	s	Load integer
(P)	FIST	d	Store integer
	FBLD	s	Load packed BCD
	FBSTP	d	Store packed BCD
		Constant Instructions (7)	
	FLDZ		Load +0.0
	FLD1		Load +1.0
	FLDPI		Load Pi
	FLDL2T		Load $\log_2 10$
	FLDL2E		Load $\log_2 e$
	FLDLG2		Load $\log_{10} 2$
	FLDLN2		Load $\log_e 2$
		Transcendental Instructions (8)	
	FPTAN		Partial tangent
	FPATAN		Partial arctangent
	F2XM1		$2^X - 1$
	FYL2X		$Y \times \log_2 X$
	FYL2XP1		$Y \times \log_2(X + 1)$
	FCOS		Cosine of ST(0) (80387 only)
	FSIN		Sine of ST(0) (80387 only)
	FSINCOS		Sine and cosine of ST(0) (80387 only)
		Comparison Instructions (10)	
(P)	FCOM	//s	Compare real
(P)	FICOM	s	Compare integer
	FCOMPP		Compare & POP twice
	FTST		Test stack top
	FXAM		Examine stack top
	FUCOM		Unordered compare (80387 only)
	FUCOMP		Unordered compare and POP (80387 only)
	FUCOMPP		Unordered compare & POP twice (80387 only)
		Arithmetic Instructions (26)	
(P)	FADD	*	Add real
	FIADD	s	Add integer
(P)	FSUB	*	Subtract real
	FISUB	s	Subtract integer
(P)	FSUBR	*	Subtract real (reversed)
	FISUBR	s	Subtract integer (reversed)

(P)	FMUL	*	Multiply real
	FIMUL	s	Multiply integer
(P)	FDIV	*	Divide real
	FIDIV	s	Divide integer
(P)	FDIVR	*	Divide real (reversed)
	FIDIVR	s	Divide integer (reversed)
	FSQRT		Square root
	FSCALE		Scale
	FPREM		Partial remainder
	FPREM1		Partial remainder (IEEE; 80387 only)
	FRNDINT		Round to integer
	FXTRACT		Extract exponent & significand
	FABS		Absolute value
	FCHS		Change sign

Process Control Instructions (16)

(N)	FINIT		Initialize processor
	FLDCW	s	Load control word
(N)	FSTCW	d	Store control word
(N)	FSTSW	d	Store status word
#(N)	FSTENV	d	Store environment
	FLDENV	s	Load environment
#(N)	FSAVE	d	Save state
	FRSTOR	s	Restore state
	FINCSTP		Increment SP
	FDECSTP		Decrement SP
	FFREE	d	Free register
	FNOP		No operation
	FWAIT		CPU wait
(N)	FDISI		Disable interrupts (8087 only)
(N)	FENI		Enable interrupts (8087 only)
(N)	FCLEX		Clear exceptions

*Instruction operand forms for FADD, FSUB, FSUBR, FMUL, FDIV, FDIVR
   : F<op>   . . . generates F<op>P ST(1),ST
   : F<op> s   . . . generates F<op> ST,<memory>
   : F<op> d,s   . . . d,s registers only
   : F<op>P d,s   . . . d,s registers only

   (P)   F<op> or F<op>P forms
   (N)   F<op> or FN<op> forms
   s   Source
   d   Destination
   //s   None or source
   //d   None or destination
   #   Instruction not self-synchronizing

Addressing Modes of the NPX

Addressing modes in the NPX reflect the stack architecture of the processor. All of the NPX's numeric op-codes, as distinguished from control op-codes, use the top of the stack as at least one operand. Some instructions operate on only the top of the stack, for example, FSQRT and FABS. Others operate on both the top of the stack and the next stack register, for example, FSCALE and F2XM1. The remaining double operand instructions vary according to type. Some take their second operand from another stack register. Others can take their second operand from memory.

Table 10-4 shows the various allowed combinations of operand addressing and NPX instructions. Note that although some math and comparison instructions may use a memory operand as the source, memory operands may never be used as a destination except by the store instructions (FST<P>, FIST<P>, and FBSTP). Note also that the source operand for any integer instruction (FI*op*) must be a memory operand because the NPX's registers always contain real numbers.

Table 10-4. Allowed Types for NPX Numeric Instructions

Example NPX Instructions	SECOND OPERANDS					Math Compare Instructions
	Word	Double Word	Quad Word	Ten Bytes	NPX Register	
FLD source		Yes	Yes	FLD	Yes	Real
FST dest.		Yes	Yes	FSTP		None
FILD source	Yes	Yes	Yes			Int
FIST dest.	Yes	Yes	Yes			None
FBLD source				Yes		None
FBSTP dest.				Yes		None

Some confusion may still exist about how the NPX addresses its operands. A short example should help to clear the fog, so let's take a look at the operation of three NPX op-codes.

```
FLD        <arg1>        ; load 1st argument from  memory
FLD        <arg2>        ; load 2nd argument from  memory
FADD       <arg2>        ; encodes as FADDP ST(1),ST
FSTP       <result>      ; store result into memory
```

This operation uses FLD to read two memory operands into the NPX register stack, adds them using the "classic" form of FADD, and stores the result using FSTP. Remember that when one of the basic arithmetic instructions (FADD, FSUB, FMUL, and FDIV) is coded by itself, MASM generates the classic stack operation with a pop, using the stack top, ST, as the source and the next stack element, ST(1), as the destination.

The operation of the preceding four instructions is graphically displayed in Figure 10-7. We've separated the two parts of the FADD instruction so that you can better see the effects of the pop. Looking at the operation, you can see that the NPX conceptually completes the arithmetic part of the operation—storing the result in ST(1)—then pops the stack, moving the result to the stack top, ST or ST(0).

At the end of our little demonstration, the stack is left exactly as it was when we arrived. Or is it? It is if there was room on the stack for additional arguments. If, however, the stack didn't have enough room to accommodate the new data, the NPX declares an *invalid operation exception* because of stack overflow. (We'll get to exceptions in the following text.) Therefore, before we can do even our tiny example, we must be sure that the NPX can accept the data. Two ways are available to accomplish this.

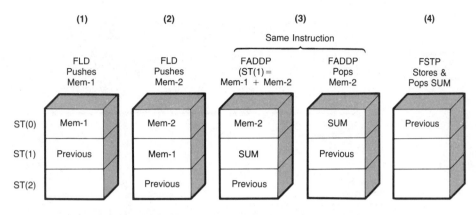

Figure 10-7. Example of NPX stack operations.

The FINIT and FFREE Instructions

The easiest way to prepare the NPX for operations is through the FINIT instruction. This is the first instruction that should be given to the NPX whenever a new program is run. FINIT initializes the NPX as if a hardware reset had occurred, which means that the instruction clears all registers and exceptions and provides a clean slate for the programmer to work with.

The other method of ensuring that the NPX has free registers is with the FFREE instruction. FFREE tags the designated register as empty and allows the programmer to use that register for subsequent calculations. Note that it isn't necessary to clear the registers at the top of the stack. If the bottom of the stack, (ST(7), has enough free room, the upper registers are pushed down into the stack when a new value is loaded.

Controlling the NPX

Besides the eight data registers, the NPX has four other registers that are accessible to the programmer. In Figure 10-1, we can see that these are the *status* word, the *control* word, and the *operand* and *instruction* pointers. The NPX also has another register, called the *tag* word, but it is only used internally by the NPX. (The tag word is where the NPX marks its registers as empty, zero, or not-a-number.) The two pointers, operand and instruction, are useful only during external exception handling, a topic that we'll discuss in forthcoming text. What's left are the control and status words. You will need to understand these two registers to make effective use of the NPX.

The NPX Control Word

The first register that we'll look at is the control word. This 16-bit word defines how the NPX treats the different exception conditions and how it views the numbering system that it uses. We've diagrammed the control word in Figure 10-8, showing the various fields and their effects. Basically, the control word

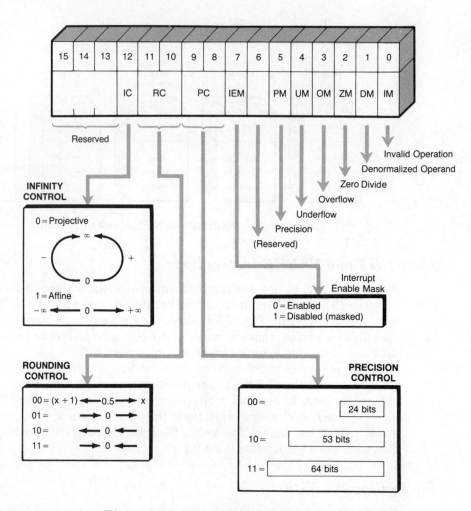

**Figure 10-8. The control word and its effect on
NPX operations.**

contains three control fields and seven flags for use with exceptions. Let's describe the exception flags first.

At this stage in the game, we want to use as much of the built-in facilities of the NPX as possible. Part of this means availing ourselves of the built-in exception handling capabilities of the NPX. You see, the NPX, all by itself, can take care of most of the errors that can occur, either fixing up the number as best it can or returning a special value called *not-a-number*. Because handling these errors ourselves is not easy, we let the NPX do it for us. We do this by masking the exceptions, and we do that by setting the exception masks in the control word. All the exception masks, along with the master interrupt enable mask, are contained in the lower byte of the control word.

To set up the NPX to use its internal error handlers, we set the lower byte to BF (hex), using the load control word instruction FLDCW. We simply define a word in the main CPU memory with a lower byte that has the value BF (hex). Then we load it as follows:

```
    •
    •
    •
cw87    dw      03BFh               ; NPX control word value
        •
        •
        •
        FLDCW   cw87                ; load NPX control word
        •
        •
        •
```

Why did we use the value 3 for the upper byte of the control word? The upper byte contains three fields for determining which number model the NPX uses. These three fields are also shown in the insets in Figure 10-8. Comparing the diagram with our value of 3, you can see that we've chosen 64-bit precision, rounding to the nearest integer, and projective infinity. These values are the ones that Intel recommends and also the ones that the NPX uses as defaults. If you want to change these settings, Figure 10-8 tells you what values to use.

The NPX Status Word

The NPX's status word contains four types of information: (1) a busy indicator; (2) a top-of-stack pointer; (3) condition codes reflecting the results of the FCOM, FTST, and FXAM instructions; and (4) the exception indicators, which signal any errors that may occur. Figure 10-9 gives the positions of the different indicators within the status word.

The busy indicator signals whether the NPX is currently processing an instruction. This indicator really isn't of much use to us because the contents of the status word can't be used until the NPX signals that it is finished storing the status word. At that point, you know that the NPX is idle because the FWAIT instruction finishes.

The top-of-stack pointer, in bits 11 through 13, is useful to the programmer who writes complicated NPX routines that perform successive operations in sequence and store many values on the NPX stack. In these cases, to ensure that enough room is available for the next operation, check the stack depth before proceeding with a routine. If the stack has insufficient room to support the operation, some or all of the registers must be saved in memory to allow the routine to safely execute.

The stack pointer is initialized by FINIT to point to 000 (0), and each successive load operation decrements the stack pointer, wrapping around past 111 (7) until it finally reaches 001 (1). The stack pointer may also be manipulated by the FINCSTP (increment stack pointer) and FDECSTP (decrement stack pointer) instructions. However, because these operations do not mark the registers *empty*, using FDECSTP or FINCSTP could invalidate using the top-of-stack indicator to check for free registers.

The condition codes are needed most often to decide what action to take at a decision point in the program. We'll see in a later section some examples of using the condition codes. Briefly, to check the condition codes, store the status

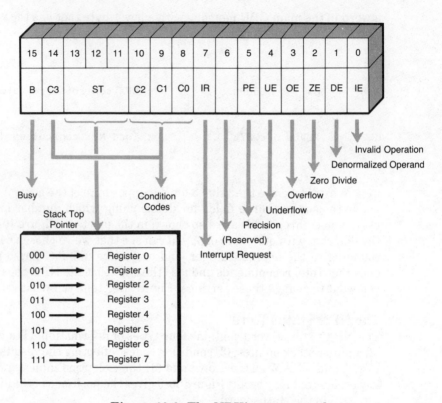

Figure 10-9. The NPX's status word.

word in memory by using the FSTSW instruction; then check the codes with the main CPU. When storing NPX status information for the main CPU to check, remember to add an FWAIT instruction after the store instruction is issued. The following code fragment shows how a comparison sequence might appear.

```
        .
        .
        .
sw87    dw      ?                ; NPX status word space
        .
        .
        .
        FCOM    ST(1)            ; check relationship of ST & ST(1)
        FSTSW   sw87             ; store NPX status word
        FWAIT                    ; wait for NPX to complete
        test    sw87,4000h       ; are operands equal?
        je      are_equal        ; yes ...
        .
        .
        .
```

The meanings assigned to these codes by the various compare instructions are given in Table 10-5. Note that the condition codes do not occur in one group but are split by the stack pointer and that the codes returned by the FCOM and FTST instructions are also split by condition bit C1, which is not used. Note also that NAN means "not a number."

Table 10-5. Status Conditions Set by the FCOM, FTST, and FXAM Instructions

	CONDITION CODES				
Instruction	**C3**	**C2**	**C1**	**C0**	**Result**
F	0	0	D	0	ST > source
C	0	0	O	1	ST < source
O	1	0	N	0	ST = source
M	1	1	'T	1	ST ? source
F	0	0	C	0	ST > 0.0
T	0	0	A	1	ST < 0.0
S	1	0	R	0	ST = 0.0
T	1	1	E	1	ST ? 0.0
F	0	0	0	0	+ Unnormal
X	0	0	0	1	+ NAN
A	0	0	1	0	- Unnormal
M	0	0	1	1	- NAN
	0	1	0	0	+ Normal
	0	1	0	1	+ Infinity
	0	1	1	1	- Infinity
	1	0	0	0	+ Zero
	1	0	0	1	Empty
	1	0	1	0	- Zero
	1	0	1	1	Empty
	1	1	0	0	+ Denormal
	1	1	0	1	Empty
	1	1	1	0	- Denormal
	1	1	1	1	Empty

Exception Handling in the NPX

The lower byte of the status word contains the exception flags. These flags correspond to the exception masks in the control word. When an exception occurs, the NPX sets the proper flag and then checks to see whether that exception is masked or not. Because most operations use the masked response (the NPX's internal error handlers), we summarize their operation in Table 10-6. You should still remember to check periodically for exceptions to ensure the accuracy of the results. If an exception occurs, the proper flag is set and stays set until cleared by initializing the NPX (FINIT) or by using the clear exceptions instruction, FCLEX. Because the flags stay set, they provide a cumulative record of any errors that occur during processing.

The other method of handling exceptions involves unmasking one or more of the exceptions and enabling interrupts in the NPX's control word. In this mode, if the NPX detects an exception, it signals an interrupt and requests the main CPU to process the exception. The NPX, however, is not necessarily tied into the main CPU's interrupt request line! An external interrupt handler circuit is required to field interrupt requests from the NPX. Do not enable the NPX external interrupts unless your system supports them!

Table 10-6. The NPX's Default Exception Response (Exceptions Masked)

Exception	Masked Response
Precision	Return rounded result.
Underflow	Denormalize result.
Overflow	Return signed infinity.
Zero-divide	Return infinity signed with exclusive-or of operand signs.
Denormal operand	If memory operand, ignore. If register operand, convert to "unnormal" and reevaluate.
Invalid operation	If one operand NAN, return it. If both are NANs, return one with larger absolute value. If neither is NAN, return *indefinite*.

If your system supports external interrupts and you enable them, you must provide an exception handler when the NPX interrupts the main CPU. The main CPU routine should read the NPX's status word to determine the nature of the problem. If you desire, your exception handler can also determine the instruction and operand that caused the problem by examining the NPX's instruction and operand pointers. To obtain this information, the exception handler must issue one of the NPX instructions FSTENV or FSAVE. These instructions write into the main CPU memory at least the contents of the five NPX control registers (status word, control word, tag word, instruction pointer, and operand pointer). The exception handler can retrieve this information from memory and process it. If you would like a more detailed picture of these registers, Listing 10-1 in the section "Programming Examples for the NPX with MASM" contains a sample program that dumps and then decodes this information.

Using MS-DOS Tools with the NPX

The only difference between writing programs for the NPX and writing them without is that with the coprocessor there are more instructions to use for numeric operations. Because the difference is visible only at the instruction level, the MS-DOS tools that need to know about the NPX are MASM and DEBUG. All of the other tools, LINK, LIB, and CREF, remain ignorant of the NPX's presence.

Using MASM and the NPX

When using MASM with the NPX, the programmer simply enters NPX instructions in the same manner as the main CPU instructions. Instructions for the NPX have the same fields as the main CPU instructions: labels, op-codes, operands, and comments. The only difference in encoding instructions is that NPX operands may be only NPX registers or memory, and main CPU operands may be only main CPU registers or memory. In the case of memory operands, the two forms are not different. NPX instructions may use any of the five basic memory forms shown here:

–Displacement Only	FSTSW	mem_word
–Base or Index Only	FIADD	word ptr [bx]
–Displacement + Base or Index	FSTP	base[di]
–Base + Index	FLDCW	[bp][si]
–Displacement + Base + Index	FILD	[bp]table[di]

CAUTION

MASM version 1.25 has an error that causes it to exchange the op-codes FSUB with FSUBR or FDIV with FDIVR and vice versa if any of these are used in "classic" form (without specifying the operands). If you are using an older version of MASM, explicitly specify the operands and type for these instructions, as in:

```
FSUBP      ST(1),ST
FDIVRP     ST(1),ST
```

Remember that the classic form always uses the pop form of the instruction.

MASM's NPX Switches—/r and /e

Once the program has been entered into a file, MASM must be used to assemble the program. If the standard MASM command line is used, every NPX instruction encountered produces a **Syntax Error**. This is because in the normal mode of operation MASM doesn't know anything about the NPX. To actually assemble NPX instructions, use the command line switch /r (real mode) to tell MASM that the source file contains NPX instructions:

```
A:>masm test.asm test.obj test.lst test.crf/r
```

This lets MASM know that the program being assembled is intended for execution on a real NPX. MASM then generates the proper NPX op-codes, prefixed with the FWAIT op-code unless one of the FN<*op*> instructions is used. (Note, however, that although the NPX's no-operation instruction, FNOP, begins with FN, it generates an FWAIT prefix.)

MASM has yet another switch that instructs it to assemble NPX instructions. This is the /e (emulation mode) switch. The /e mode switch is nearly identical to the real mode switch, except that no-wait instructions (FN<*op*>) are not assembled. The purpose of this switch is for users who have emulation libraries that can replace the NPX op-codes with main CPU CALLs to emulation subroutines. Because MASM does not provide such an emulation library and because there is no point in using the library if you have a real NPX, we don't provide further information on this topic.

NPX Data Types in MASM

You now know that the NPX supports seven different data types: word; short and long integer, short and long real; packed binary-coded decimal; and floating-point real. To use these types, the proper storage locations must be defined in memory. Table 10-7 shows the correspondence between the NPX's data types and the methods used in MASM to define and reference them.

Storage locations are allocated by using the define data (*dw*, *dd*, *dq*, or *dt*) MASM directives, followed by a question mark (?). This format tells MASM to reserve the space but not initialize it. In order to initialize the reserved location to a particular real number value, MASM provides three different forms: the scientific notation without an exponent, the scientific notation with an exponent, and the real (R) form. Each of these forms may be used with any of the larger "define data" directives, as follows:

```
double   dd 3.14159               ; scientific without exponent
quad     dq 1.23456E + 03         ; scientific with exponent
tenbyte  dt 0123456789ABCDEF0123R ; real
```

Table 10-7. A Comparison of Data Types for the NPX and MASM

NPX Data Type	Main CPU Data Type	Size in Bytes	MASM Directive	Operand Name	NPX Compatible
Word integer	Word	2	*dw*	*word ptr*	Yes
Short integer	Double word	4	*dd*	*dword ptr*	Yes
Short real	Double word	4	*dd*	*dword ptr*	No
Long integer	Quad word	8	*dq*	*qword ptr*	Yes
Long real	Quad word	8	*dq*	*qword ptr*	No
Packed BCD	Ten byte	10	*dt*	*tbyte ptr*	"R" form
Floating real	Ten byte	10	*dt*	*tbyte ptr*	Yes

Defining real numbers with the define byte (*db*) or define word (*dw*) directives isn't possible. Real numbers may only be initialized to integer values.

The scientific notations are evaluated into a floating-point format (sign, exponent, and significand), whereas the real notation is used on a digit-per-nibble basis so that the real notation's hexadecimal representation exactly corresponds to its definition.

Note that although MASM has the ability to define real numbers in both 4- and 8-byte lengths, the format used to initialize these numbers is not compatible with the NPX! Figure 10-10 shows how Microsoft implemented real numbers for these sizes. By comparing them with Figure 10-2, you can see that they are quite different. If you must use these formats (for compatibility with existing software, for example), you can write conversion routines to change from one format to the other.

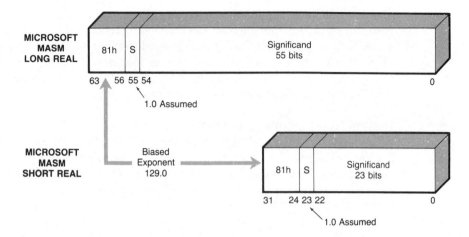

Figure 10-10. Microsoft MASM real number formats.

Using DEBUG with the NPX

DEBUG always knows about NPX instructions. This explains why when you sometimes attempt to "unassemble" memory, DEBUG lists strange instructions. (One common technique used in debugging is to fill unused memory with the hex word DEAD. This distinctive pattern allows the programmer to quickly see what memory is being altered. However, DEBUG disassembles this as FISUBR WORD PTR [DI + ADDE].)

Even though DEBUG is always in NPX mode, so to speak, DEBUG doesn't recognize all the NPX instructions. It doesn't display, nor allow you to assemble, any of the FN<*op*> form instructions. The rationale behind this is that DEBUG recognizes the FWAIT as a separate instruction from the NPX opcode, which it really is. So, DEBUG decodes an FN<*op*> instruction as a standard instruction that doesn't happen to be prefixed by FWAIT.

The reverse is that unlike MASM, DEBUG does not automatically insert the FWAIT prefix on standard NPX instructions. You must remember to manually assemble the FWAIT when entering NPX instructions in DEBUG.

You should remember also that when specifying memory operands in DEBUG, you must always tell DEBUG what size the operand is, as in the form:

```
FLD      TBYTE PTR [200]
```

The brackets are required to inform DEBUG that the number is an address rather than an immediate value.

Debugging the NPX's Registers

One of the things that DEBUG cannot do is display the status of the NPX or the contents of any of its registers. If you desire to examine any of the NPX's registers, you first must have the NPX write the data into common memory.

To help you in debugging your NPX programs, we have provided the *dump87* routine in the following section, "Programming Examples for the NPX with MASM." This routine uses the FSAVE instruction to store the entire state of the NPX and then displays it in more understandable form on the console display. The routine may be put in a library or included at the time of assembly and called whenever you need to check on the state of an NPX calculation. The routine itself is described more fully in the next section.

Instruction Encoding Formats

When hexadecimal dumps are being read, NPX instructions may be recognized in code by the presence of either the FWAIT op-code (9B) or by their distinctive escape codes, D8 through DF (hex). Figure 10-11 shows the different forms that an NPX instruction may take, but all instructions start with the 11011 bit pattern.

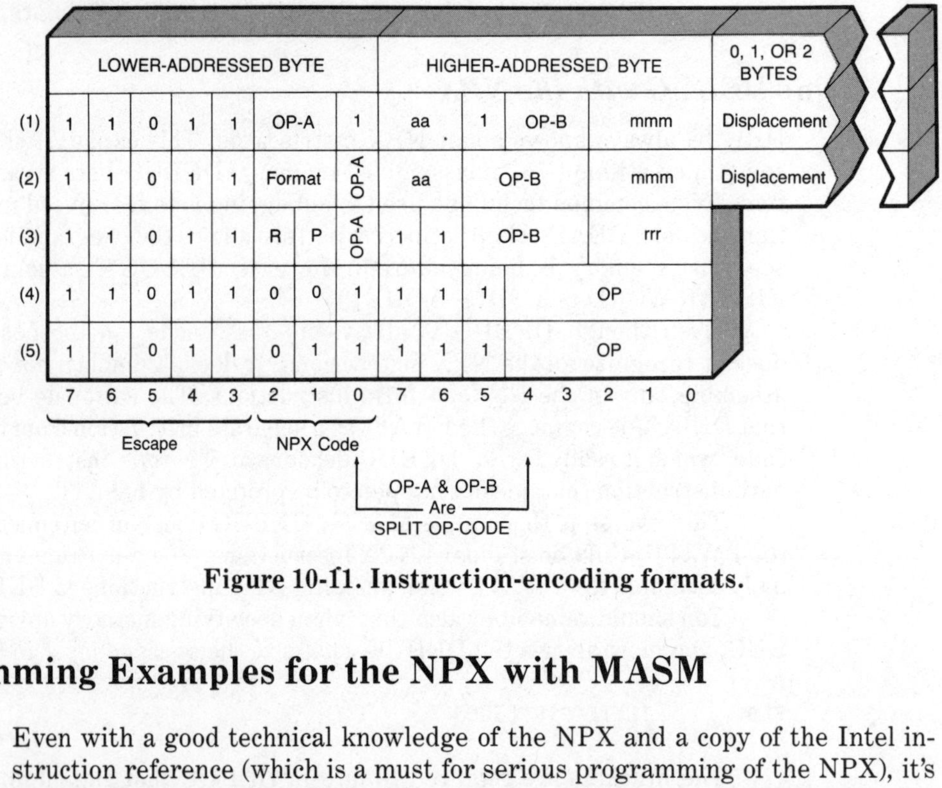

							LOWER-ADDRESSED BYTE			HIGHER-ADDRESSED BYTE				0, 1, OR 2 BYTES
(1)	1	1	0	1	1	OP-A	1	aa	1	OP-B	mmm			Displacement
(2)	1	1	0	1	1	Format	OP-A	aa	OP-B		mmm			Displacement
(3)	1	1	0	1	1	R P	OP-A	1 1	OP-B		rrr			
(4)	1	1	0	1	1	0 0 1	1 1 1	OP						
(5)	1	1	0	1	1	0 1 1	1 1 1	OP						

```
       7  6  5  4  3  2  1  0   7  6  5  4  3  2  1  0
       └────────┘  └──────┘
        Escape      NPX Code
                        │
               OP-A & OP-B
                  ── Are ──
               SPLIT OP-CODE
```

Figure 10-11. Instruction-encoding formats.

Programming Examples for the NPX with MASM

Even with a good technical knowledge of the NPX and a copy of the Intel instruction reference (which is a must for serious programming of the NPX), it's hard to understand the NPX without some hands-on experience. Because we can't give you an actual computer and NPX, we do the next best thing. We present here a number of nontrivial programming examples that should give you a better understanding of the NPX's mode of operation and provide a starting place for building your own library of NPX routines.

The FWAIT and FINIT Instructions

Let's stress once again that if the main CPU intends to use results from the NPX, it must first ensure that the NPX is finished by issuing an FWAIT.

Another point that must be understood is that the NPX must be initialized with the FINIT instruction at the start of the program. It is very important to force the NPX into a known state before proceeding with operations.

DUMP87 Routine

We previously pointed out that the DEBUG program is unable to examine the contents or state of the NPX, and we promised to give you some help in that situation. Listing 10-1 provides a routine to dump the contents of the NPX and examine them.

Listing 10-1.   DUMP87 NPX Debugging Aid

```
PAGE    60,132          ; wide listing
#.8087                  ; allow assembly of 8087 NPX instructions
;==================================================================
;       L I B R A R Y   I M P L E M E N T A T I O N
;
        PUBLIC  dump87          ; defined library routine
;
#MODEL  SMALL
;
#.CODE
        EXTRN   bin2hex:NEAR    ; called library routine
;==================================================================
;       D U M P 8 7   -   8 0 8 7   D E B U G G I N G   T O O L
;
; This procedure dumps the entire state of the Intel Numeric
; Processor Extension (NPX) (8087, 80287, or 80387) onto the
; stack and then formats and outputs said state to the screen.
;
; Setup Requirements: NONE
; Stack Requirements: 108 bytes free on the stack
;
; ...wd -- Word Defines for bit fields within various words
; The defined structures take advantage of the fact that the
; SW and CW interrupt structures match.
;------------------------------------------------------------------
;       M A C R O   D E F I N I T I O N S
;
;; Display a character (from DL)
```

continued

Listing 10-1. *continued*

```
@DisChr MACRO   char
        push    ax
        push    dx
        mov     dl,&char
        mov     ah,02h
        int     21h
        pop     dx
        pop     ax
        ENDM
;;
;; Display a String by Label
@DisStr MACRO   string
        push    ax
        push    dx
        mov     dx,offset &string
        mov     ah,09h
        int     21h
        pop     dx
        pop     ax
        ENDM
;
;; Display a String (from DS:DX)
@Display MACRO
        mov     ah,09h
        int     21h
        ENDM
;
#.DATA
;----------------------------------------------------------------
;       S T R U C T U R E   D E F I N I T I O N S
;
intrpt  record  master:1,nul0:1,pr:1,un:1,ov:1,zd:1,de:1,inv_op:1
control record  infc:1,rndc:2,prec:2
status  record  busy:1,c3:1,stp:3,c2:1,c1:1,c0:1
tag     record  onetag:2
ipwd    record  ipseg:4,nul2:1,opcode:11 ; op-code & instruction
                                         ; ... pointer
opwd    record  opseg:4,nul3:12          ; operand pointer segment
expwd   record  sign:1,exp:15            ; sign & exponent
;
; Basic Environment Structure:
enviro  STRUC
cw87    dw      ?                        ; control word
sw87    dw      ?                        ; status word
```

```
tw87     dw       ?                         ; tag word
ipo87    dw       ?                         ; instruction pointer offset
ips87    dw       ?                         ; IP segment & op-code
opo87    dw       ?                         ; operand pointer offset
ops87    dw       ?                         ; OP segment
enviro   ENDS
;
; Register Structure:
fltreg   STRUC
man87    dq       ?                         ; mantissa (significand)
exp87    dw       ?                         ; exponent & sign
fltreg   ENDS
;
; Entire State Save Structure:
state87  STRUC
         db       size enviro dup (?)       ; environment header
reg87    db       size fltreg * 8 dup (?) ; 8 data registers
state87  ENDS
;
dump87s  STRUC                              ; stack format for
;                                           ; ... dump 87
rec87    db       size state87 dup (?)      ; space for NPX state
; oldbp dw       ?                         ; entry base pointer
dump87s  ENDS
;
BASE     EQU      [bp - size dump87s]       ; Structure Index
;
#.CODE
;----------------------------------------------------------------
;        B E G I N   P R O G R A M   C O D E
;
dump87   PROC     NEAR
         push     bp                ; save entry BP
         pushf                      ; save caller's flags
         push     ds                ; save caller's data segment
         mov      bp,sp             ; and set up index
         sub      sp,size dump87s ; allocate space for
                                    ; ... local store
         push     ax                ; save caller's registers
         push     bx
         push     cx
         push     dx
         push     di
         push     si
;
         mov      ax,cs             ; set DS to point to this
```

continued

Listing 10-1. *continued*

```
        mov     ds,ax           ; ... routine's data area
;
; Get copy of the NPX's internal state:
        pushf                   ; save caller's interrupt state
        cli                     ; don't allow interrupts
                                ; ... while saving
        FSAVE   BASE.rec87      ; save state of NPX
        FRSTOR  BASE.rec87      ; restore state that was just
                                ; ... saved
        FWAIT                   ; wait to complete restore
        popf                    ; reenable interrupts?
;
; Now that we have a copy of the NPX's state, decode it and
; present it to the user on the terminal.
;
;       Presentation consists of the following items:
;
;       ===================== NPX DUMP =============================
;       Infinity: Affine    Round....... near       Precision: 64
;       Inst Addr: x:xxxx   Oper Addr: x:xxxx       Opcode:  Dxxx
;
;               INT PRE UND OVR ZER DEN IOP         C3 C2 C1 C0
;       Enable: x   x   x   x   x   x   x           x  x  x  x
;       Signal: x   x   x   x   x   x   x <-- "x" means unmasked
;                                                  or signaled
;               exponent     significand
;       ST(x)   + xxxx   xxxx xxxx xxxx xxxx  #0   tag
;         .
;         .
;         .
;       ------------------------------------------------------------
;
; Infinity, Rounding, and Precision Control:
        @DisStr LINE1                   ; start display
        mov     al,byte ptr BASE.cw87+1 ; get control word
        and     al,mask infc            ; infinity control
        mov     cl,infc
        shr     al,cl                   ; condition #
        mul     inf_siz ; condition offset
        add     ax,offset inf_cnd       ; condition address
        mov     dx,ax
        @Display
;
        @DisStr rnd_lab
        mov     al,byte ptr BASE.cw87+1 ; get control word
        and     al,mask rndc            ; rounding control
```

```
        mov     cl,rndc
        shr     al,cl           ; condition #
        mul     rnd_siz         ; condition offset
        add     ax,offset rnd_cnd ; condition address
        mov     dx,ax
        @Display
;
        @DisStr pre_lab
        mov     al,byte ptr BASE.cw87+1 ; get control word
        and     al,mask prec    ; precision control
        mov     cl,prec
        shr     al,cl           ; condition #
        mul     pre_siz         ; condition offset
        add     ax,offset pre_cnd ; condition address
        mov     dx,ax
        @Display
;
; Instruction & Operand Pointers, and Opcode
        @DisStr LINE2           ; next line
        mov     ax,BASE.ips87   ; instruction pntr.
        and     ax,mask ipseg   ; segment
        mov     cl,ipseg
        shr     ax,cl           ; digit
        mov     ch,1            ; display 1
        call    bin2hex
        @DisChr ':'
        mov     ax,BASE.ipo87   ; instruction pntr.
        mov     ch,4            ; offset
        call    bin2hex
;
        @DisStr opadr           ; operand pointer
        mov     ax,BASE.ops87   ; segment
        and     ax,mask opseg
        mov     cl,opseg
        shr     ax,cl           ; digit
        mov     ch,1            ; display 1
        call    bin2hex
        @DisChr ':'
        mov     ax,BASE.opo87   ; operand pntr.
        mov     ch,4            ; offset
        call    bin2hex
;
        @DisStr ocode           ; opcode
        mov     ax,BASE.ips87
        and     ax,mask opcode
        or      ax,0800h        ; add OPCODE assumed bit
```

continued

Listing 10-1. *continued*

```
        mov     ch,3                    ; 3 digits
        call    bin2hex                 ; display
;
; Interrupt / Exception - Enable Flags:
        @DisStr LINE3                   ; next line
        mov     al,byte ptr BASE.cw87   ; exception enable flags
        call    exception_flags         ; show status
;
; Condition Codes:
        @DisStr space10
        mov     ah,byte ptr BASE.sw87+1 ; condition codes
        push    ax                      ; (save codes)
        mov     al,30h                  ; (ASCII "0")
        and     ah,mask c3              ; C3
        sub     ah,mask c3              ; 0 -> CY, 1 -> NC
        cmc                             ; 0 -> NC, 1 -> CY
        adc     al,0                    ; 0 -> "0", 1-> "1"
        @DisChr al                      ; display
        pop     ax                      ; (save codes)
;
        mov     ch,c2 + 1               ; # of codes to display
next_cc:
        @DisStr SPACE2
;
        mov     al,30h                  ; (ASCII "0")
        and     ah,mask c2 + mask c1 + mask c0
        sub     ah,mask c2              ; 0 -> CY, 1 -> NC
        cmc                             ; 0 -> NC, 1 -> CY
        adc     al,0                    ; 0 -> "0", 1-> "1"
        @DisChr al                      ; display
;
        shl     ah,1                    ; next code
        dec     ch                      ; 1 less to go ...
        jnz     next_cc                 ; ... until all done
;
; Interrupt / Exception - Status Flags:
        @DisStr LINE6
        mov     al,byte ptr BASE.sw87   ; exception signal flags
        call    exception_flags         ; show status
;
; Data Register Display:
        @DisStr CRLF
        mov     dh,8                    ; # of reg. to display
        mov     si,0                    ; start with reg #0
```

```
;
register_display:
        @DisStr LINE8                        ; registers status
        push    dx                           ; save count
        mov     al,8                         ; calculate register #
        sub     al,dh
        add     al,30h                       ; convert to ASCII
        @DisChr al                           ; and display
        pop     dx
;
; Sign of Data Register:
        @DisStr paren                        ; sign comes next
        mov     ax,word ptr BASE.reg87[si].exp87
        test    ax,mask sign                 ; what is it?
        jnz     sign_minus
        @DisStr plus
        jmp     show_exponent
sign_minus:
        @DisStr minus
;
; Exponent Portion of Data Register:
show_exponent:
        and     ax,mask exp                  ; obtain exponent
        xor     cx,cx                        ; four characters
        call    bin2hex                      ; and display
        @DisStr space3
;
        mov     di,si                        ; base of register
        add     di,offset exp87              ; location of mantissa
        mov     dl,4                         ; 4 words per register
;
; Display Significand Portion of Data Register:
show_significand:
        sub     di,2                         ; point at word start
        mov     ax,word ptr BASE.reg87[di]
        call    bin2hex                      ; and display
        @DisStr SPACE1
        dec     dl                           ; another word gone
        jnz     show_significand
;
; True Register Number:
        @DisStr truenum
        mov     al,byte ptr BASE.sw87+1 ; get stack pointer
        and     al,mask stp
        mov     cl,stp
        shr     al,cl                        ; have stack pointer
```

continued

Listing 10-1. *continued*

```
;
        mov     cl,8                    ; convert counter to ...
        sub     cl,dh                   ; ... 0 through 7
        add     al,cl                   ; current reg. #
        and     al,07H
;
        push    ax                      ; save register number
        add     al,30h                  ; convert to ASCII
        @DisChr al                      ; and display
;
        @DisStr SPACE2                  ; now for the TAG field
;
; Tag Word Status:
        mov     ax,BASE.tw87            ; get tag word
        pop     cx                      ; get register number
                                        ; ... in CL
        shl     cl,1                    ; multiply by 2
        shr     ax,cl                   ; and get proper tag word
        and     ax,mask tag
;
        push    dx
        mul     tag_siz                 ; condition offset
        add     ax,offset tag_cnd       ; condition address
        mov     dx,ax
        @Display                        ; show tag status
        pop     dx
;
; All Done for That Register!
        add     si,size fltreg          ; next register
        dec     dh                      ; 1 less
        jz      finished
        jmp     register_display        ; until all gone
;
; All Done for All Registers!
;
finished:
        @DisStr LINE9                   ; all done!
;
; Restore the main CPU to the way it was and return
; Start w/ saved registers
        pop     si                      ; restore caller's registers
        pop     di
        pop     dx
        pop     cx
        pop     bx
```

```
        pop     ax
        mov     sp,bp           ; restore stack
        pop     ds              ; restore data segment
        popf                    ; restore caller's flags
        pop     bp              ; restore entry BP
        ret                     ; return when finished
;
;----------------------------------------------------------------
; Display Subroutine for displaying MASK & SIGNAL status of
; exceptions.
; Test byte in AL for bits corresponding to exception flags
;
exception_flags PROC    NEAR
        test    al,mask master          ; master control
        call    mark_it
;
        mov     cl,pr                   ; next is PR flag
        ror     al,cl                   ; move to 1's position
        inc     cl                      ; count 1 > bit #
;
test_exception:
        test    al,1            ; is flag set?
        call    mark_it
        rol     al,1            ; next flag
        dec     cl              ; keep track of count
        jnz     test_exception  ; continue until done
        ret
;
;----------------------------------------------------------------
; Mark result according to flags set on entry
;
mark_it PROC    NEAR
        jz      mark_space
        @DisStr marky
        ret
mark_space:
        @DisStr markn
        ret
mark_it ENDP
;
exception_flags ENDP
;
#.DATA
;----------------------------------------------------------------
; D U M P 8 7   L O C A L   C O N S T A N T   S T O R A G E
```

continued

Listing 10-1. *continued*

```
;
;          ----- this section read only -----
;
; "_lab" - label for section
; "_cnd" - condition for label
; "_siz" - number of bytes in condition
;
@CRet   MACRO                            ;; new line macro
        db      0Dh,0Ah
        ENDM
;
LINE1   EQU     $
        @CRet
        db '====================NPX DUMP ======================
        db '==='
        @CRet
        db      'Infinity: $'
rnd_lab db      '   Round:....... $'   ; label
pre_lab db      '    Precision: $'     ; label
inf_siz db      7
inf_cnd db      'Proj. $'              ; infinity state
        db      'Affine$'              ; infinity state
rnd_siz db      5
rnd_cnd db      'near$'                ; round state
        db      'down$'                ; round state
        db      'up  $'                ; round state
        db      'chop$'                ; round state
pre_siz db      3
pre_cnd db      '24$'                  ; "ret" precision state
        db      '**$'                  ; "ret" precision state
        db      '53$'                  ; "ret" precision state
        db      '64$'                  ; "ret" precision state
;
LINE2   EQU     $
        @CRet
        db      'Inst Addr: $'         ; "x:xxxx"
opadr   db      '   Oper Addr: $'      ; "x:xxxx"
ocode   db      '   Opcode:  D$'       ; "xxx","ret","ret"
;
LINE3   EQU     $
        @CRet
        @CRet
```

```
            db      '          INT PRE UND OVR ZER DEN IOP'
            db      '                  C3 C2 C1 C0'
            @CRet
            db      'Masked:$'
;                   condition codes                     "ret"
LINE6       EQU     $
            @CRet
            db      'Signal:$'               ; "ret"
marky       db      ' x  $'
markn       db      '    $'
;
LINE8       EQU     $
            @CRet
            db      'ST($'                   ; "x"
paren       db      ')  $'
plus        db      '+ $'
minus       db      '- $'                    ; "xxxx"
space10 db  '          '                     ; 10 space
SPACE2      EQU     $ + 1                     ; 2 space
SPACE1      EQU     $ + 2                     ; 1 space
space3      db      '   $'                    ; 3 space
                                             ; "xxxx " 4 times
truenum db  ' #$'                            ; " #x", then "  "tag
tag_siz db  6
tag_cnd db  'Valid$'                         ; tag state
            db      'Zero $'                 ; tag state
            db      'Spec.$'                 ; tag state
            db      'Empty$'                 ; tag state
;
LINE9       EQU     $
            @CRet
            db      '--------------------------------------------------'
            db      '--------'
CRLF        EQU     $
            @CRet
            db      '$'
;
#.CODE
;
dump87  ENDP
;===============================================================
        END              ; end of routine(s)
```

DUMP87 obtains the information to display by using the NPX FSAVE instruction. This instruction saves the entire state of the NPX in 94 bytes in the format shown in Figure 10-12. However, FSAVE also initializes the NPX as if an FINIT had been performed. This allows a numeric subroutine to save the state of the NPX and then initialize it in one instruction, which is analogous to pushing the registers and clearing them on entry to a main CPU subroutine. Because we wish to continue processing without disruptions, we must follow the FSAVE with the FRSTOR instruction, which reloads the NPX from the saved information.

From Figure 10-12, you can also see that the first 14 bytes of the saved information are identical to that saved by the FSTENV (store environment) instruction. FSTENV does not reinitialize the NPX; rather, it is intended to allow the programmer access to the information required in exception handling: the status word and the instruction and operand pointers. Like FSAVE, FSTENV

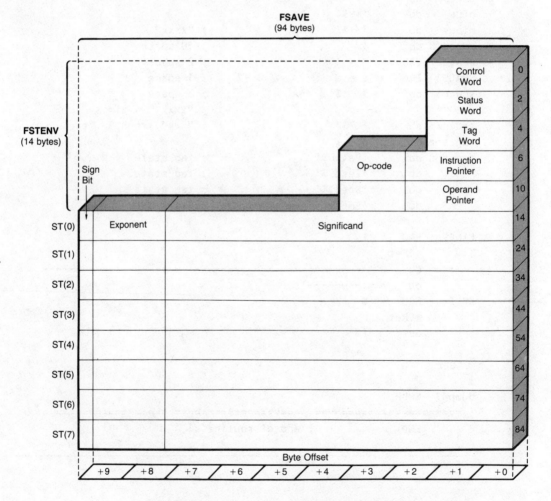

Figure 10-12. FSAVE and FSTENV memory structure.

has a corollary instruction called FLDENV that can reload the environment from stored information.

Using the DUMP87 Routine

The remainder of the program has nothing to do with the NPX. Instead, the rest of the program uses MASM structure and record definitions to break down the information returned by FSAVE and present it to the user. The format used to present the information is documented in the routine's header section. The listing as presented is suitable for assembly and inclusion in a library file. If you follow this procedure, DUMP87 may be included in any other file by matching DUMP87's segment and class names, by declaring it external, and by providing the external routine BIN2HEX. One variation for using DUMP87 is as follows:

```
code    segment para public 'code'    ; library segment
        assume  cs:code,ds:code,es:code,ss:code
        extrn   dump87:near            ; LIBRARY ROUTINE
        ORG     0100h                  ; .COM FORMAT
main    proc    far
start:
        FINIT                          ; initialize NPX
        .
        .
        .
        call    dump87                 ; analyze NPX
        .
        .
        .
```

DUMP87 requires in excess of 120 bytes on the CPU stack. In return, the program does not use any data storage, which allows greater freedom of placement and use. As mentioned, DUMP87 requires a routine called BIN2HEX. BIN2HEX appears in Appendix A.

Using the NPX for Binary to Decimal to Binary Conversions

Now that we are equipped to check on what the NPX is up to, we can turn to some more serious programming. The first necessity for using the NPX is to provide some means to get data into and out of the NPX in a form that humans can understand. And that means decimal representation.

Integer Operations

Performing integer to binary conversions on the NPX is a snap, thanks to the FBLD and FBSTP packed BCD load and store instructions. All that is needed is a simple main CPU routine to pack and unpack the BCD digits from and to ASCII strings. To convert from decimal to binary, load the decimal number with FBLD and store it as a binary integer with FIST. To convert in the other direction use an FILD followed by the decimal store instruction, FBSTP.

Note that as long as the numbers being converted are small enough to fit within a 16-bit (or 32-bit register in an 8038) register, it is not worth using the NPX to convert from decimal to binary. The overhead associated with packing the digits and executing an FBLD-FIST sequence is greater than that which is involved with the standard "shift-multiply" conversion routine as follows:

```
; Assume number being accumulated is in AX and the new digit is
; in the CL register.
        shr     ax,1                ; existing number x 2
        mov     bx,ax               ; save
        shr     ax,1                ; number x 4
        shr     ax,1                ; number x 8
        add     ax,bx               ; (# x 8) + (# x 2) = # x 10
        xor     ch,ch               ; prepare for 16-bit add
        add     ax,cx               ; next digit added in
```

For small numbers (one to three decimal digits), the NPX takes about twice as long to convert from decimal to binary, including the time necessary to create the packed BCD vector from an ASCII string.

When numbers get larger than 16 binary bits, the main CPU begins to slow down because it must continuously check for carries, possible overflows or underflows, etc. In the range of 16 to 64 binary bits, the NPX really makes the conversions fly!

As long as the numbers are no longer than 18 decimal digits (which is hard to exceed!), no NPX operations beyond the load and store instructions are required. Once numbers begin to exceed 18 digits, they must be scaled, and we enter the realm of floating-point real numbers.

Floating Point Operations

Handling conversions between decimal and binary numbers in the floating point world is mainly a matter of scaling. That is, we can use the FBLD and FBSTP instructions to get the basic numbers in and out of the NPX, but then we need to adjust the numbers by some power of ten. To understand how these operations take place, let's review some basic mathematical identities of number conversions.

1. $10^X = 2^{X * \log_2 10}$
2. $E^X = 2^{X * \log_2 E}$
3. $Y^X = 2^{X * \log_2 Y}$
4. $\log_{10} X = \log_{10} 2 * \log_2 X$
5. $\log_E X = \log_E 2 * \log_2 X$

Fortunately, the NPX knows how to calculate some of these operations and can provide constants for others. The pertinent instructions that we need to accomplish our conversions are

A. F2XM1 calculates $2^X - 1$
B. FLDL2T constant $\log_2 10$
C. FLDL2E constant $\log_2 E$
D. FYL2X calculates $Y * \log_2 X$

E. FLDLG2 constant $\log_{10}2$

F. FLDLN2 constant $\log_E 2$

We know that once an integer number has been loaded, we must either multiply it by a power of ten for a number with a positive base-ten exponent or divide it by a power of ten for a number with a negative base-ten exponent. From rule number 1, we can see that the first step toward obtaining a power of 10 is calculating 2 to some power X.

The 2^X Calculation

Generally, 2 can be raised to a power through a simple shift, and this is indeed what the NPX accomplishes with its FSCALE instruction. Unfortunately, that is not the entire solution because integer powers of 10 don't correspond to integer powers of 2. Some fractional part of the power of 2 needs to be calculated. This is where the NPX instruction F2XM1 applies (see rule A).

F2XM1 has the capability of calculating 2 to the Xth power for a value of X from 0.0 through 0.5, inclusive. Given an arbitrary number X, we can separate it into its fractional and integer parts by evaluating the expressions:

$$\text{integer } (X) = \text{FRNDINT } (X)$$
$$\text{fractional } (X) = \text{FSUB } X - \text{integer } (X)$$

The integer portion of X is used in FSCALE to raise 2 to an integer power, and the fractional portion becomes the input for F2XM1. We can use two successive operations because we know that for any Y and Z the following holds true:

$$2^{(Y + Z)} = 2^Y * 2^Z$$

The absolute value of the fractional part of X is held within the range of 0.0 to 0.5 by ensuring that the NPX's rounding control is set to nearest, which ensures a maximum fraction of 0.5.

We may then calculate the total result by applying F2XM1, adding 1 back to the result, and using FSCALE on that. Of course, if the fractional part is negative, we must make sure that we use its absolute value and use the identity

$$2^{(Y - Z)} = 2^Y/2^Z$$

for the correct result. This is essentially the sequence of events that takes place in the routine EXP2, which appears near the end of the next listing (Listing 10-2).

The 10^X Calculation

Now that we have determined how to calculate 2 to the Xth, we have accomplished the major part of calculating 10 to the Xth. From rule number 1, we know that

$$10^X = 2^X * \log_2 10$$

which means that all we need to find is the value

$$X * \log_2 10$$

in order to be able to use the 2 to the Xth routine just developed. From looking at rule B, we see that the NPX can supply us with the value for the base 2 log of 10. Calculating 10 to the Xth then becomes the operation FLDL2T, followed by the multiplication FMUL and finishing with a call to EXP2. These are the instructions that appear in the routine EXP10, also contained in Listing 10-2.

By changing identities from base 2 log of 10 to base 2 log of e to base 2 log of X, we can calculate the values of 10 to the Xth, e to the Xth, and Y to the Xth, all with the EXP2 routine.

The Decimal to Real Scaling Function

Once we have the value of 10 to the Xth, what do we do with it? We wanted this number so that we could use scientific notation in the NPX. Given a packed BCD number and a word integer X for the exponent, we can convert the parts to a floating-point real number by loading the packed BCD significand with FBLD. We calculate 10 to the absolute value of X and then either multiply the result by the significand for positive X (FMUL) or divide the significand by the resulting 10 to the Xth for negative exponents (FDIV). As you've probably guessed, that's what the routine DEC2FLT does in Listing 10-2. This routine looks larger than it is because we needed to keep track of and adjust for the sign of the exponent.

The resulting package of routines, EXP2, EXP10, and DEC2FLT, can take a two-part number (packed BCD significand and integer exponent), which the main CPU can generate, and turn it into a floating-point real number inside of the NPX.

The Real to Decimal Scaling Function

Once we have numbers inside the NPX, we can calculate with them to our hearts content. If we run out of room, we can always store them in common memory as temporary reals (the FSTP instruction does that). But what about when it is time to see the results? How do we go about turning a floating-point real number into a two-part integer number?

The answer is that we must play with the NPX's biased exponent so that the NPX can give us an integer significand. You see, when storing a number as a packed BCD string, the FBSTP instruction first rounds the number to the nearest integer. If the number is too large to be represented by a packed BCD string, the NPX is unable to store that number. If the number is too small, significant precision is lost when the number is rounded. In order to use the FBSTP instruction, we must first make sure that the number stored in the register is in the proper range.

We can tell that a number is in the proper range because its biased exponent (a sort of binary decimal point) has a value less than 64 (otherwise, the number is too large) and greater than the number of significant binary digits (otherwise, we lose precision). Typically, we choose a number that we know gives us good precision. For a number that we wish to be accurate to 10 decimal digits, a true exponent of 32 is a good number. That means that the binary decimal point is on bit 32, about halfway through the floating point. Not too large and not too small.

Now what if the number has an exponent that's not in that range? We have to change the exponent. The first step is to determine what the exponent really is. We use the FXTRACT instruction, which splits an NPX data register into two, one holding the significand with an exponent of zero (ST) and the other holding the original number's true exponent as a real number (ST(1)). The part that we're interested in is ST(1).

The first step of this calculation is to determine how many binary decimal places we're off. Another way of saying this is that we wish to determine the distance between the desired exponent and the existing exponent. FSUB can tell us that pretty quickly.

Once we have the distance, can't we just apply it as a scaling factor (with FSCALE) to the original exponent? No, because when we display the number, we're going to tell the user what the exponent is in scientific notation, as in:

$$+1.2345600000E + 00$$

and we won't be able to do that if the exponent is a power of 2. The idea of this exercise is to have the NPX produce an integer number and then know how many powers of 10 that number was shifted to make it an integer. Straight-up scientific notation.

What we have to do is somehow convert the distance, which is currently in powers of two, into a distance of integer powers of 10. As it turns out, the relationship between the two values is expressed by the rule

$$2^X = 10^{X * \log_{10}2}$$
$$2^X = 10^{X / \log_2 10}$$

The second relationship results from the identity stating that

$$\log_a b = 1/\log_b a$$

Either way we calculate, we have determined the value of X (for the expression 10 to the Xth) required to create the proper scaling factor. Creating the factor can be accomplished through the FLDLG2 (load base 10 log of 2) followed by an FMUL or through FLDL2T (load base 2 log of 10) followed by an FDIV. However, these methods give us an exact number of X for 10 to the Xth, and we need the closest integer. So we apply FRNDINT to round the number, and we have our base 10 exponent.

Given the exponent, we have but a moment's work to calculate 10 to the Xth (with EXP10), and we have the scaling factor to turn the real number into an integer (with FMUL). We return the exponent of 10 via FIST (store integer) and the significand portion with FBSTP (store packed BCD). Everything except the BCD store is contained in FLT2DEC in Listing 10-2.

Another useful trick is that once the packed BCD number is stored in memory, we can use a binary to hexadecimal display routine (such as BIN2HEX) to display the digits because they look exactly like a hexadecimal number.

We've been talking about Listing 10-2, and it finally follows. Notice that, like the DUMP87 listing, this one is formatted to be used as a library also. In addition, all operations take place on the main CPU stack or in locations specified by the caller, so there should be no problem with portability.

Listing 10-2. DE2FLT, FLT2DEC, and the Exponent Routines EXP2, EXP10, EXPE, and EXPY

```
PAGE    60,132  ; wide listing
#.8087          ; allow the assembly of 8087 NPX instructions
;
        PUBLIC  dec2flt   ; declare library routine
        PUBLIC  flt2dec   ; declare library routine
        PUBLIC  exp10     ; declare library routine 10**x
        PUBLIC  expE      ; declare library routine  e**x
        PUBLIC  expY      ; declare library routine  y**x
        PUBLIC  exp2      ; declare library routine  2**x
;
;=================================================================
;       I M P L E M E N T A T I O N
;
#.MODEL  SMALL
;
#.CODE
;
;*****************************************************************
; DEC2FLT - Convert decimal integer with exponent to floating
;       point real number. Accept exponent and pointer to
;       packed BCD string on stack. Return result in ST(0)
;
; Use:  push    offset (tbyte ptr packed_BCD)
;       push    exponent
;       call    dec2flt
;
; Requirements: 3 stack locations
; Notation:    N ...... exponent for 10**N
;              S ...... significand portion of loading real
;-----------------------------------------------------------------
;
#.DATA
D2FLTD  STRUC
d2fltbp dw      ?                        ; old base pointer
```

```
        dw      ?                       ; return address
d2fltex dw      ?                       ; exponent
d2fltpd dw      ?                       ; pointer to packed BCD
D2FLTD  ENDS
;
#.CODE
dec2flt PROC    NEAR
        push    bp
        mov     bp,sp                   ; address parameters
        cmp     word ptr [bp].d2fltex,0 ; check sign of exponent
        jz      d2flt_nxp               ; if zero, no 10**N
                                        ; ... needed
        pushf                           ; save sign of exponent
        jg      d2flt_pos               ; if positive start 10**N
        neg     word ptr [bp].d2fltex   ; else make exp positive
d2flt_pos:
        FILD    word ptr [bp].d2fltex   ; get exponent of 10
        call    exp10            ; calculate 10**N
d2flt_nxp:                              ; enter here if exp is 0
        push    si
        mov     si,[bp].d2fltpd ; get   pointer to packed BCD
        FBLD    tbyte ptr [si]  ; ST => S;   ST(1) = 10**N
        pop     si
        popf                            ; restore exponent.s sign
        jz      d2flt_end       ; done if exp is 0
        jl      d2flt_neg       ; if negative do divide
        FMUL                    ; ST => significand * 10**N
        jmp     d2flt_end       ; and done
d2flt_neg:
        FDIVR                   ; ST => significand / 10**N
d2flt_end:
        pop     bp              ; restore bp
        ret     4
dec2flt ENDP
;
;*******************************************************************
; FLT2DEC - Convert floating point real to decimal integer with
;        exponent. ST(0) contains number to be converted.
;        Stack contains number of binary digits desired and
;        pointer to 10's exponent location.
;        Returns with ST(0) converted to an integer and writes
;        the 10's exponent to the designated location.
;
; Use:  push    sig_digits
;       push    offset (word ptr to exponent)
```

continued

Listing 10-2. *continued*

```
;       call    flt2dec
;
; Requirements: 4 stack locations
; Notation:     R ...... Real number to display
;               N ...... Exponent of 10 to convert R to integer
;               I ...... Integer portion of resultant number
;               n(N).... nearest integer of N
;------------------------------------------------------------------
;
#.DATA
F2DECD  STRUC
f2deccw dw      ?                ; original control word
f2decbp dw      ?                ; old base pointer
        dw      ?                ; return address
f2decex dw      ?                ; pointer to exponent
f2decsd dw      ?                ; number of signif. binary digits
F2DECD  ENDS
;
#.CODE
; *** check rounding control at this point - use other ?? ***
F2DECCT EQU     03BFh   ; new control word - round nearest
;
flt2dec PROC    NEAR
;
; Set up the NPX's control word and open storage
; on the stack:
        push    bp               ; save old base pointer
STKADJ1 EQU     f2decbp-F2DECD
        sub     sp,STKADJ1       ; make storage on the stack
        mov     bp,sp            ; address new structure
        push    ax               ; save AX
        mov     ax,F2DECCT       ; push new control word on stack
        push    ax
        FSTCW   word ptr [bp].f2deccw
        FLDCW   word ptr [bp-4] ; set to round to nearest int
        pop     ax               ; clean up stack
        pop     ax               ; restore AX
;
; Find N for 10**N to convert to integer:
        FLD     ST(0)            ; duplicate R (preserve until
                                 ; ... end)
        FXTRACT                  ; ST(1) => exponent portion of R
```

```
            FSTP    ST(0)               ; ST => exponent portion of R
            FISUBR  word ptr [bp].f2decsd ; sigdig - exp = # of
                                        ; ... scale digits
            FLDL2T                      ; ST => log2 (10), ST(1) => scale
            FDIV                        ; ST => scale / log2 (10) = N
            FRNDINT                     ; ST => n(N)
;
; Store nint (N) as exponent & calculate 10**nint(N):
            push    si
            mov     si,[bp].f2decex ; get pointer to exponent
            FIST    word ptr [si]   ; store base 10 scale
            FWAIT
            neg     word ptr [si]   ; direction to move dec. point
            pop     si
            call    exp10           ; calculate 10**N (scale)
;
; ST(1) now has R (the original real #) - scale it:
            FMUL                        ; ST => R * 10**N = Integer
            FLDCW   word ptr [bp].f2deccw ; restore control word
STKADJ2 EQU         f2decbp-F2DECD
            add     sp,STKADJ2      ; resize stack to original
            pop     bp              ; restore BP
            ret     4               ; clear stack on return
flt2dec ENDP
;
;********************************************************************
; EXP10 - Calculate 10 to the power of ST(0)
;         Return result in ST(0)
;
; Uses formula: 10**N = 2**(N*log2(10))
;
; CALLS:        EXP2
;
; Requirements: 3 stack locations
; Notation:     N ...... exponent for 10**N
;               X ...... equivalent exponent for 2**X
;               n(x) ... nearest integer of X
;               f(x) ... fractional part of X
;-------------------------------------------------------------------
exp10   PROC    NEAR
            FLDL2T                      ; ST > log2 (10); ST(1) => N
            FMUL                        ; ST => N * log2 (10) => X
            call    exp2            ; raise 2 to ST power
            ret                         ; ... for 10 ** N
exp10   ENDP
```

continued

Listing 10-2. *continued*

```
;
;*********************************************************************
; EXPE - Calculate E to the power of ST(0)
;        Return result in ST(0)
;
; Uses formula: E**N = 2**(N*log2(E))
;
; CALLS:        EXP2
;
; Requirements: 3 stack locations
; Notation:     N ...... exponent for E**N
;               X ...... equivalent exponent for 2**X
;               n(x) ... nearest integer of X
;               f(x) ... fractional part of X
;-------------------------------------------------------------------
expE    PROC    NEAR
        FLDL2E                     ; ST > log2 (e); ST(1) => N
        FMUL                       ; ST => N * log2 (e) => X
        call    exp2               ; raise 2 to ST power
        ret                        ; ... for E ** N
expE    ENDP
;
;*********************************************************************
; EXPY - Calculate Y [ST(0)] to the power of N [ST(1)]
;        Return result in ST(0)
;        ST(1) (value of N) is lost!
;
; Uses formula: Y**N = 2**(N*log2(Y))
;
; **** NOTE: Y MUST BE POSITIVE ****
;
; CALLS:        EXP2
;
; Requirements: 3 stack locations
; Notation:     N ...... exponent for Y**N
;               X ...... equivalent exponent for 2**X
;               n(x) ... nearest integer of X
;               f(x) ... fractional part of X
;-------------------------------------------------------------------
expY    PROC    NEAR
        FYL2X                      ; ST => N * log2 (Y) => X
        call    exp2               ; raise 2 to ST power
        ret                        ; ... for Y ** N
expY    ENDP
```

```
;
;****************************************************************
; EXP2 - Calculate 2 to the power of ST(0)
;        Return result in ST(0)
;
; Requirements: 3 stack locations
; Notation:     X ...... exponent for 2**X
;               n(x) ... nearest integer of X
;               f(x) ... fractional part of X
;---------------------------------------------------------------
;
#.DATA
EXP2D   STRUC
exp2cc  dw      ?               ; condition codes
exp2cw  dw      ?               ; original control word
exp2bp  dw      ?               ; old base pointer
        dw      ?               ; return address
EXP2D   ENDS
;
#.CODE
EXP2CT  EQU     03BFh   ; new control word - round nearest
exp2    PROC    NEAR
;
; Set up the NPX's control word and open storage
; on the stack:
        push    bp              ; save old base pointer
STKADJ3 EQU     exp2bp-EXP2D
        sub     sp,STKADJ3      ; make storage on the stack
        mov     bp,sp           ; address new structure
        push    ax              ; save AX
        mov     ax,EXP2CT       ; push new control word on stack
        push    ax
        FSTCW   word ptr [bp].exp2cw
        FLDCW   word ptr [bp-4] ; set to round to nearest int
        pop     ax              ; clean up stack
        pop     ax              ; restore AX
;
; Start processing the number now:
        FLD     ST(0)           ; ST => ST(1) => X for 2**X
        FRNDINT                 ; ST => n(X); ST(1) => X
        FXCH                    ; ST => X; ST(1) => n(X)
        FSUB    ST,ST(1)        ; ST => f(X); ST(1) = n(X)
        FTST                    ; set condition codes
        FSTSW   word ptr [bp].exp2cc        ; store CC's
        FWAIT
        and     byte ptr [bp+1].exp2cc,45h ; mask all but CC's
```
continued

Listing 10-2. *continued*

```
        cmp     byte ptr [bp+1].exp2cc,1  ; test for negative
        ja      exp2_err          ; NAN or infinity -> error
        je      exp2_neg          ; fractional part is minus
;
        F2XM1             ; ST => (2**f(X)) - 1; ST(1) = n(X)
        FLD1              ; ST => 1; ST(1) => (2**f(X))-1;
                          ; ... ST(2) = n(X)
        FADD              ; ST => 2**f(X); ST(1) => n(X)
        FSCALE            ; ST => 2**(X) => 2**(N*log2(?)) => ?**N
        FSTP    ST(1)     ; ST => ?**N; ST(1) => restored
        jmp     exp2_mer ; merge
;
exp2_neg:
        FABS              ; ST => 1-f(x); ST(1) = n(X) + 1
        F2XM1             ; ST => (2**(1-f(x)))-1; ST(1) = n(X) + 1
        FLD1              ; ST => 1; ST(1) => (2**(1-f(x)))-1
        FADD              ; ST => 2**(1-f(x)); ST(1) => n(X) + 1
        FXCH              ; ST => n(X) + 1; ST(1) => 2**(1-f(x))
        FLD1              ; ST => 1; ST(1) = n(X) + 1
        FSCALE            ; ST => 2**(n(x) + 1);
                          ; ... ST(2) => 2**(1-(f(x))
        FDIVRP  ST(2),ST ; ST(1) => 2**(n(X) + 1)/2**(1 - f(x))
        FSTP    ST(0)     ; ST => 2**(n(x) + 1 - 1 + f(x) => 2**(X)
;
exp2_mer:
        clc                               ; no errors
exp2_out:
        FLDCW   word ptr [bp].exp2cw ; restore control word
STKADJ4 EQU     exp2bp-EXP2D
        add     sp,STKADJ4                ; resize stack to original
        pop     bp                        ; restore BP
        ret
exp2_err:
        stc                               ; errors occurred
        jmp     exp2_out
exp2    ENDP
;***************************************************************
        END                               ; end of routines
```

Summary

By providing these example routines for debugging and I/O, we hope that we have given you an understanding of how the NPX works and what is possible with it and that we have encouraged you to develop your own applications for the NPX. Equipped with this boost, you should be able to branch out into whatever field interests you. Trigonometric analysis, Fourier transforms—all are much easier when the power of the NPX can be brought to bear. Good luck and happy numeric coprocessing!

RECOVERY PART III

Disk Layout and File Recovery

11

F you've been using MS-DOS for a while, you probably have inadvertently deleted or accidentally lost a file that you later realized you needed. The ERASE (or DEL) command in MS-DOS is very useful and powerful and, by its very nature, is a destructive command. Its destructiveness, of course, is essential for it to accomplish its task, but when you're careless, it can become more destructive than you want it to be.

The only safeguard against inadvertently deleting files with the ERASE or DEL command is displayed when you specify that all files on a disk be deleted by entering *erase *.**. A prompt asks whether you're sure you want the operation executed. If you enter *n* (for no), the command's execution is stopped. But when you use the command to delete a particular file or group of files, the only other safeguard is to discipline yourself to freeze your fingers before pressing the Return (or Enter) key and to carefully examine the file-delete command sequence you've just typed. Even then, no matter how certain you are that the file or files you specified for deletion are the ones you ultimately want deleted, at some point we all make a mistake. Because computers are designed to obey your commands to the letter, your request for deleting files is executed immediately after you've pressed the Return or Enter key following the command sequence.

A file can also be erased by a program that you are currently running. Word processors and other programs providing file-management facilities can be instructed, either directly or indirectly, to erase files. Additionally, files can be erased by an equipment malfunction, a power interruption, or a quirky feature in a program.

So what do you do when a file that hasn't been backed up is accidentally deleted? Fortunately, the MS-DOS file system was designed so that, under certain conditions, restoring a file isn't difficult. As a result of this design, several utilities have been developed to recover erased files. Some of these are in the public domain. Others are commercially available products. Of the commercial products available, the Norton Utilities and Mace Utilities are popular examples. A similar product called Ultra Utilities consists of a set of utilities in the "freeware" category and is currently available through various channels of public-domain software distribution.

In this chapter we discuss how to recover erased files and how to use the MS-DOS utilities CHKDSK and RECOVER for recovering damaged and lost files. We also discuss the use of other file recovery methods, including the commercial program Norton Utilities and the user-supported program Ultra Utilities.

Before we do this though, you must understand how the MS-DOS file system works so that you understand the limitations of these file-recovery utilities. Note that both Norton Utilities and Ultra Utilities operate only on IBM Personal Computers or close compatibles. Starting with version 2.01, Norton Utilities also supports the recovery of files on hard disks (10-megabyte hard disks on the IBM PC or compatible environment), and Norton Utilities version 3.0 includes support for both the IBM AT's 20-megabyte hard disk and high-capacity floppy format (under MS-DOS version 3.0 or later). Norton Utilities version 4.0 includes the ability to deal with any disk media running under MS-DOS, provided the disk media is formatted according to standard MS-DOS conventions.

Although file-recovery utility packages are extremely useful in the environments for which they were designed, they may not work properly in your particular MS-DOS environment, especially if your system is not an IBM PC or not sufficiently compatible with the IBM PC. For this reason, this chapter includes a program that you can try if the other utilities fail or if you decide they are not appropriate for your machine. The program, RESCUE, is simple in design, and can be expanded and customized with new features. RESCUE is designed to support any disk format, both removable and fixed-disk media, provided the disk's format adheres to standard MS-DOS formatting conventions. Before we show you how to use Norton and Ultra Utilities and the alternate program RESCUE, let's review the basics of the MS-DOS disk storage system and file recovery.

Principles of File Recovery

You probably are wondering how it is possible to restore a file that's been erased. It would seem, initially, that if a file is erased, it must have been wiped off the face of the disk forever. This initial assumption is partially correct because, after a file is erased, it is no longer visible or accessible by any of the standard MS-DOS commands.

Each file stored by MS-DOS on a disk, however, consists of the following three parts:

- The file's directory entry
- The file's space allocation
- The data sectors containing the file data

When a file is erased, only the first two parts of the file, the directory entry and the space allocation, are affected. These two parts act as control points for MS-DOS to reference the file's data sectors. The data sectors of the file, however, are not erased, which is why it is possible to recover a file if you know something about the first two parts of the file. We'll talk about the space allocation and directory sections in more detail a little further on, but first we'll cover the layout of disks that have been formatted in various ways under MS-DOS.

The following paragraphs describe the formats of standard floppy disk formats as well as hard (fixed) disk formats. Note that in some systems all 40-track formats supported by MS-DOS also can be used with 3½-inch floppy disks. In such systems, the 3½-inch floppy drive must be treated by the system hardware as if it were a 40-track, 5¼-inch floppy drive, as is often the case when 3½-inch floppy drives are connected to existing floppy disk controllers in IBM PC, XT, and AT systems. However, the 80-track formats supported by MS-DOS are normally not interchangeable between 3½-inch and 5¼-inch floppy disks.

Layouts of 5¼-Inch, 40-Track, Single-Sided Floppy Disks

Figure 11-1 shows the basic layout of a 5¼-inch, 40-track, single-sided disk. It shows the tracks and sectors and provides an example of how file data can be arranged on a disk. The first part shows the layout of a disk formatted to eight sectors per track. The portion to the right shows the difference on track 0 of a disk formatted to nine sectors per track.

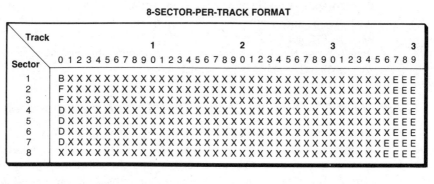

Figure 11-1. Information layout on a single-sided, 40-track, 5¼-inch floppy disk.

The first part of Figure 11-1 shows the simplest disk format under MS-DOS. Because all standard disk formats under MS-DOS support a sector size of 512 bytes, we can easily verify the information in Figure 11-1 by calculating the total capacity of the disk as follows:

40 tracks × 8 sectors × 512 bytes = 163,840 bytes (160 Kbytes) total capacity

The total disk capacity can be checked against the results displayed when the FORMAT or CHKDSK command is used.

A disk formatted to nine sectors per track (MS-DOS versions 2.0 and above only) is similar to an 8-sector-per-track disk except that a ninth sector is added at the end of each track, thereby increasing total disk space. This can be verified with the following formula and checked against the results displayed by the FORMAT or CHKDSK command:

40 tracks × 9 sectors × 512 bytes = 184,320 bytes (180 Kbytes) total capacity

Another difference between 8- and 9-sector-per-track disks is the number of FAT (file allocation table) sectors. Although both formats have one boot sector and four directory sectors, the number of FAT sectors is greater in the 9-sector-per-track format. Eight-sector-per-track disks have two FAT sectors (sectors 2 and 3 of track 0). Nine-sector-per-track disks have four FAT sectors (sectors 2 through 5 of track 0). The extra number of FAT sectors in 9-sector-per-track disks is necessary because of the extra file space permitted by the 40 extra sectors (one per track).

Layouts of 5¼-Inch, 40-Track, Double-Sided Floppy Disks

Double-sided, 40-track floppy disks formatted under MS-DOS are assigned the same number of FAT sectors (proportionally) as single-sided disks, but more directory sectors are provided to increase the total number of files that can be stored on a disk. In both 8- and 9-sector-per-track double-sided formats, seven sectors are assigned as directory sectors. The layouts of the two double-sided, 40-track disk formats supported by MS-DOS are shown in Figure 11-2. The part at left shows the layout in the 8-sector-per-track format. The part at right shows the layout in the 9-sector-per-track format.

The layout of the disk in Figure 11-2 is very similar to the one in Figure 11-1. Notice, however, that on all double-sided floppy disks formatted under MS-DOS, storage information on a track always begins at side 0, sector 1; moves to the last sector of the track; continues from side 1, sector 1 to the last sector of the track; then reverts back to side 0, starting with the first sector on the next track; and so on until the last sector on the last track of side 1 is reached. Also note that the arrangement of directory sectors and FAT sectors differs from that of single-sided disks. Both double-sided formats have one boot track and have proportionally the same number of FAT sectors as single-sided disks. However, the number of directory sectors for both double-sided formats is increased to seven. Again, by comparing the results of the following calculations with the results of the CHKDSK program, we can verify the total capacity of the two 40-track, double-sided floppy disk formats:

40 tracks × 8 sectors × 512 bytes × 2 sides =
327,680 bytes (320 Kbytes) total capacity

40 tracks × 9 sectors × 512 bytes × 2 sides =
368,640 bytes (360 Kbytes) total capacity

8-SECTOR-PER-TRACK FORMAT

```
     Track
              ...      3
 Sector    0 1 2 ... 6 7 8 9

        1  B X X ... X X X X
        2  F X X ... X X X X
        3  F X X ... X X X X
 SIDE   4  D X X ... X X X X
   0    5  D X X ... X X X X
        6  D X X ... X X X X
        7  D X X ... X X X X
        8  D X X ... X X X X
        1  D X X ... X E E E
        2  D X X ... X E E E
        3  X X X ... X E E E
 SIDE   4  X X X ... X E E E
   1    5  X X X ... X E E E
        6  X X X ... X E E E
        7  X X X ... E E E E
        8  X X X ... E E E E
```

9-SECTOR-PER-TRACK FORMAT

```
     Track
              ...      3
 Sector    0 1 2 ...    9

        1  B X X ...
        2  F X X ...
        3  F X X ...
 SIDE   4  F X X ...
   0    5  F X X ...
        6  D X X ...
        7  D X X ...
        8  D X X ...
        9  D X X ...
        1  D X X ...
        2  D X X ...
 SIDE   3  D X X ...
   1    4  X X X ...
        5  X X X ...
        6  X X X ...
        7  X X X ...
        8  X X X ...
        9  X X X ...
```

B = Boot Record   For example purposes only:
D = Directory Entry   X = Sectors containing file data
F = File Allocation Table E = Empty sectors

**Figure 11-2. Information layout on a double-sided, 40-track,
5¼-inch floppy disk.**

Layouts of 5¼-Inch, 80-Track, Double-Sided Floppy Disks

MS-DOS version 3.0 introduced a new 5¼-inch floppy disk format commonly known as the *high-capacity* format. This format provides a data storage capacity of 1.2 million bytes and requires a special 80-track, 5¼-inch floppy disk drive and appropriate disk controller (introduced on the IBM AT system). This particular high-capacity format is not available for 3½-inch floppy disks.

The structure of this format is very similar to the older formats we've just described. The format's higher capacity depends on the use of floppy disks with double the number of tracks (80) and the formatting of more sectors (15) per track. Figure 11-3 illustrates the layout of this format and shows the higher number of directory and FAT sectors needed to support the extended capacity.

The following formula can be used to verify the results displayed by the CHKDSK program when it is used with an 80-track, 5¼-inch floppy disk:

80 tracks × 15 sectors × 512 bytes × 2 sides =
1,228,800 bytes (1,200 Kbytes or 1.2 Mbytes) total capacity

MS-DOS version 3.20 introduced support for 3½-inch floppy diskettes. The 3½-inch diskettes can be formatted to the same single- or double-sided, 8- or

15-SECTOR-PER-TRACK FORMAT (5¼" DISKETTES)

```
        Track
                    ...  7
Sector        0 1 2 ... 7 8 9
         1    B X X ... X E E
         2    F X X ... X E E
         3    F X X ... X E E
         4    F X X ... X E E
         5    F X X ... X E E
         6    F X X ... X E E
         7    F X X ... E E E
SIDE     8    F X X ... E E E
0        9    F X X ... E E E
        10    F X X ... E E E
        11    F X X ... E E E
        12    F X X ... E E E
        13    F X X ... E E E
        14    F X X ... E E E
        15    F X X ... E E E
         1    D X X ... E E E
         2    D X X ... E E E
         3    D X X ... E E E
         4    D X X ... E E E
         5    D X X ... E E E
         6    D X X ... E E E
         7    D X X ... E E E
SIDE     8    D X X ... E E E
1        9    D X X ... E E E
        10    D X X ... E E E
        11    D X X ... E E E
        12    D X X ... E E E
        13    D X X ... E E E
        14    D X X ... E E E
        15    X X X ... E E E
```

9-SECTOR-PER-TRACK FORMAT (3½" DISKETTES)

```
        Track
                    ...  7
Sector        0 1 2 ... 8 9
         1    B X X ... X X
         2    F X X ... X X
         3    F X X ... X X
SIDE     4    F X X ... X X
0        5    F X X ... X X
         6    F X X ... X X
         7    F X X ... X X
         8    D X X ... X X
         9    D X X ... X X
         1    D X X ... X X
         2    D X X ... X X
         3    D X X ... X X
SIDE     4    D X X ... X X
1        5    D X X ... X X
         6    X X X ... X X
         7    X X X ... X X
         8    X X X ... X X
         9    X X X ... X X
```

18-SECTOR-PER-TRACK FORMAT (3½" DISKETTES)

```
        Track
                    ...  7
Sector        0 1 2 ... 8 9
         1    B X X ... X X
         2    F X X ... X X
         3    F X X ... X X
         4    F X X ... X X
         5    F X X ... X X
         6    F X X ... X X
         7    F X X ... X X
SIDE     8    D X X ... X X
0        9    D X X ... X X
        10    D X X ... X X
        11    D X X ... X X
        12    D X X ... X X
        13    D X X ... X X
        14    D X X ... X X
        15    D X X ... X X
        16    F X X ... X X
        17    F X X ... X X
        18    F X X ... X X
         1    F X X ... X X
         2    F X X ... X X
         3    F X X ... X X
         4    F X X ... X X
         5    F X X ... X X
         6    F X X ... X X
         7    F X X ... X X
         8    F X X ... X X
SIDE     9    F X X ... X X
1       10    F X X ... X X
        11    F X X ... X X
        12    F X X ... X X
        13    F X X ... X X
        14    F X X ... X X
        15    F X X ... X X
        16    X X X ... X X
        17    X X X ... X X
        18    X X X ... X X
```

B = Boot Record
D = Directory Entry
F = File Allocation Table

For example purposes only:
X = Sectors containing file data
E = Empty sectors

Figure 11-3. Information layout of high-capacity, double-sided, 80-track, 5¼-inch and 3½-inch floppy disks.

9-sector-per-track formats as used for 40-track, 5¼-inch diskettes, provided that the *physical* name of the drive is specified with the FORMAT command. A double-sided, 80-track, 9-sector-per-track format for 3½-inch diskettes was also introduced in MS-DOS version 3.20. The layout for this format is shown in Figure 11-3. This format yields a total storage capacity of 720 Kbytes:

$$80 \text{ tracks} \times 9 \text{ sectors} \times 512 \text{ bytes} \times 2 \text{ sides} =$$
$$737{,}280 \text{ bytes (720 Kbytes) total capacity}$$

The 3½-inch diskettes are formatted to the 720K format by specifying a logical drive name with the FORMAT command, without any format-specific parameters. The logical drive used, which is expressly created for formatting 720K floppy diskettes, is created at boot time if the following string is included in the CONFIG.SYS file,

DEVICE=DRIVER.SYS /D:*x*

where *x* is the physical number of the 80-track, 3½-inch drive (0 = A:, 1 = B:, etc.). The DRIVER.SYS file is a device driver provided with MS-DOS version 3.2 and higher versions. When the system is booted, DRIVER.SYS creates a logical drive using the next available drive letter, and maps it to the specified physical drive number. Once a disk has been formatted to the 720K format, it can be read and written to by using the physical drive name as well as the corresponding logical drive name.

MS-DOS version 3.30 introduced yet another 3½-inch, high-capacity format, consisting of 80 tracks, each formatted to 18 sectors (see Figure 11-3). This format yields a total capacity of 1.44 megabytes, using disks that have been tested to 2 megabytes. Special 3½-inch disk drives, first introduced in the IBM PS/2 systems, are required to support this format. The 1.44-megabyte drive also supports the 720K format.

80 tracks × 18 sectors × 512 bytes × 2 sides =
1,474,560 bytes (1.44 Mbytes) total capacity

The Boot Sector

The very first sector on a disk formatted under MS-DOS is always defined as the boot record. It contains a short program that is automatically loaded into memory when the disk is used to load the MS-DOS operating system after system power-up or reset. This program then instructs the computer where to look on the disk for the files that contain the MS-DOS operating system. Once the files are found, the boot program loads the files into memory and transfers control to MS-DOS. Because the number of MS-DOS files and the way in which they are stored may differ according to the type of implementation (IBM PC, COMPAQ, CompuPro, for example), the contents of the boot record may vary. For the sake of consistency, the boot sector is always defined first on a formatted disk, regardless of whether you intend to make the disk a "boot" disk or a "data-only" disk.

The first 3 bytes of the boot record always contain a jump instruction. At boot-up, the jump instruction tells the system to jump past the first part of the record to the boot code. With the introduction of MS-DOS 2.00, the 27 bytes of the boot record between the initial jump instruction and the boot code contain information about the disk format. By examining this block of data, programs can obtain nearly all the formatting information needed for the disk. Table 11-1 shows the contents of the format information block in the boot record.

The formatting information in the boot record can prove to be very valuable in determining the format of a disk. The boot record is initially created when the disk is formatted by using the FORMAT command for floppy disks, or the FDISK command for hard disks. The "OEM and Version" part of the formatting information in the boot record usually contains the implementation and version number of the MS-DOS used to create the boot record. For example, if IBM DOS version 3.3 was used to format the disk, this field will contain the

Table 11-1. The Boot Record Formatting Information

Offset (dec)	(hex)	Size	Contents						
0	00	3 bytes	Near JMP to boot code*						
3	03	8 bytes	OEM name and version						
11	0B	1 word	Bytes per sector	B	P	B		F	I
13	0D	1 byte	Sectors per cluster	I	A	L		O	N
14	0E	1 word	Number of reserved sectors	O	R	O		R	F
16	10	1 byte	Number of FAT tables	S	A	C		M	O
17	11	1 word	Number of directory entries**		M	K		A	R
19	13	1 word	Number of logical sectors		E			T	M
21	15	1 byte	Media descriptor byte***		T			T	A
22	16	1 word	Number of FAT sectors		E R			I	T I
24	18	1 word	Sectors per track					N	O
26	1A	1 word	Number of heads		27 bytes			G	N
28	1C	1 word	Number of hidden sectors						
30	1E	416 bytes	Boot code						
446	1BE	16 bytes	Partition information****		482 bytes				
462	1CE	50 bytes	Rest of boot code						

*For MS-DOS version 2.X = 3-byte near jump.
For MS-DOS version 3.X = 2-byte short jump plus NOP.
**Total entries of root directory.
***Media descriptor bytes are not always valid as of MS-DOS 2.00.
****Bootable hard (fixed) disks only; this area is not used on floppy disks.

information "IBM 3.3". The rest of the items in the boot record's formatting information are a superset of the BIOS Parameter Block (BPB) (see Chapter 6) as it existed when the disk was formatted. The last three items of the formatting information (sectors per track, number of heads, and number of hidden sectors) are calculated and inserted in the boot record when the disk is formatted.

The READFMT program, shown in Listing 11-1, provides a method by which the formatting information of the boot record is read from the disk and displayed on the screen. In addition to the formatting items that exist in the boot record, READFMT also calculates several other format items, such as total system storage, total data storage, and total disk storage capacities, and displays them on screen.

Listing 11-1. READFMT Program

```
PAGE    50,132
TITLE   READFMT.ASM/.EXE
.SALL           ; supress macro expansion listing
.8086           ; use 8086/8088 instructions only
;****************************************************************
;** READFMT Version 1.00
```

```
;**
;** This program reads the boot sector of any disk, decodes the
;** BIOS Parameter Block (BPB) found in the boot record, and
;** displays the information on the screen along with some other
;** calculated information.
;**
;** NOTE: When this program is created the LINK switch "/CP:1"
;** must be used so that only the amount of memory actually
;** needed by the program at load time is allocated. The default
;** maximum memory allocation if "/CP:1" is not specified is all
;** memory above the program's load point, which will cause the
;** program to exit with an error message because it won't be
;** able to do any additional run-time allocation of memory.
;******************************************************************
;
; INCLUDES:
;
INCLUDE         stdequ.inc      ; include standard equates file
INCLUDE         stdmac.inc      ; include standard macros file
INCLUDELIB      stdlib.lib      ; include STDLIB.LIB library at
                                ; link time
;
; Declarations for external library routines in STDLIB.LIB:
EXTRN    dosv2con:NEAR   ; get & display current DOS ver.
EXTRN    dosver:NEAR     ; get current DOS version
EXTRN    bin2dec2:NEAR   ; display DX:AX in ASCII decimal digits
                         ; (if DX = 0, AX is treated as unsigned;
                         ; CH = minimum digits to display)
;
;----- INITIALIZATION -------------------------------------------
;
.MODEL  SMALL                   ; small model
.STACK  2048                    ; create 2K stack
;
;******************************************************************
; MAIN PROGRAM
;
.DATA
;
;----------------------------------------------------------------
; References to boot record components read from disk and stored
; in block of memory referenced via ES. Only the components of
; the "BIOS Parameter Block" (BPB) are referenced; the
; first 3 bytes and all data after the BPB area of the boot
; record are ignored.
;
```

continued

Listing 11-1. *continued*

```
bootrecord      STRUC
BootJump        db      3 DUP (?)  ; initial jump instruction
OEMstring       db      8 DUP (?)  ; OEM & version of DOS used to
                                   ; ... format disk
SectorBytes     dw      ?          ; bytes per sector
ClusterSec      db      ?          ; sectors per cluster
ReservedSec     dw      ?          ; reserved sectors
FATcopies       db      ?          ; number of FAT copies
DirEntries      dw      ?          ; number of root directory
                                   ; ... entries
TotalSectors    dw      ?          ; total disk sectors
                                   ; ... (100% of disk)
MediaDescrip    db      ?          ; media descriptor
FATsectors      dw      ?          ; number of sectors occupied
                                   ; ... by 1 FAT
TrackSectors    dw      ?          ; number of sectors per track
Heads           dw      ?          ; number of heads
HiddenSectors   dw      ?          ; number of hidden sectors
bootrecord      ENDS
;
;
.CODE                              ; begin code segment
;
; Local data storage (keep these definitions in the code
; segment):
;
DSsave          dw      seg DGROUP    ; storage for DS register
;
.DATA
PSPseg          dw      ?             ; PSP segment
.CODE
;
main    PROC    NEAR                  ; begin main process
;****************************************************************
; Start of program
;****************************************************************
        mov     ds,DSsave             ; initialize DS
        mov     ax,es                 ; get PSP seg. address
        mov     word ptr PSPseg,ax    ; ... and save it
;
;----------------------------------------------------------------
; Display startup message
;----------------------------------------------------------------
        @DisStr Start1_Msg            ; display startup msg.
```

```
;
;-----------------------------------------------------------------
; Get disk drive number/name:
;-----------------------------------------------------------------
        mov     di,80h                    ; ES:DI = command-line
        cmp     byte ptr es:[di],0        ; are there parameters?
        je      get_default_drive         ; no, get default drive
        cmp     byte ptr es:[di+3]],':'   ; is colon present?
        jne     get_default_drive         ; no, get default drive
;
get_disk_drive:                           ; get drive in cmd. line
        xor     ah,ah                     ; clear out AH
        mov     al,byte ptr es:[di+2]     ; get specified drive
        cmp     al,">"                    ; was redirection used?
        je      get_default_drive         ; yes, get default drive
        cmp     al,61h                    ; is drive in uppercase?
        jge     convert_upper             ; yes, convert from
                                          ; ... uppercase ASCII
        sub     al,40h                    ; else, convert from
                                          ; ... lowercase ASCII
        jmp     short test_drive          ; and continue
convert_upper:
        sub     al,60h                    ; convert uppercase ASCII
test_drive:
        cmp     al,1                      ; is number below 1?
        jl      bad_drive                 ; yes, exit to error msg.
        dec     al                        ; else, make A: = 0;
                                          ; ... B: = 1, etc.
        cmp     al,25                     ; is it >25 ( >Z: )?
        jg      bad_drive                 ; yes, exit error msg.
        jmp     short drive_used          ; else, save drive
                                          ; ... specified
get_default_drive:
        mov     ah,19h                    ; get default drive
        @DosCall
drive_used:
        mov     byte ptr DiskDrive,al     ; store drive
        jmp     short drive_end           ; and continue
bad_drive:
        @DisStr BadDrive_Msg              ; else, display error msg
                                          ; ... (syntax error)
        jmp     terminate                 ; and exit to DOS
drive_end:
;
;-----------------------------------------------------------------
; Read boot sector information into memory
```

continued

Listing 11-1. *continued*

```
; On return ES:DI (ES:0) points to memory block containing
; boot record.
;--------------------------------------------------------------
.DATA
BootSeg dw      ?           ; storage of segment address of memory
                            ; block containing copy of boot record
.CODE
        mov     bx,40h              ; alloc. 1024 bytes (64 paras.)
        call    memalloc            ; allocate the block
        jnc     read_boot           ; continue if no error
        call    mem_err_handler     ; else, deal with error
        jmp     terminate           ; and exit to DOS
;
read_boot:
        mov     word ptr BootSeg,ax     ; save the seg. address
        push    ax                      ; and save it
        mov     al,byte ptr DiskDrive   ; get drive to read
        xor     ah,ah                   ; clear AH

        pop     ds                 ; get seg. addr. of new block
        mov     dx,0               ; read logical sector 0
        mov     cx,1               ; read in one sector
        mov     bx,0               ; store data at DS:0
        int     25h                ; read the disk
        jc      read_boot_error    ; exit if error
        popf                       ; clear flags pushed by int 25h
        mov     ds,DSsave          ; reinitialize DS
        mov     ax,word ptr BootSeg ; get boot seg. address
        mov     es,ax              ; and initialize ES to it
        xor     di,di              ; with offset of 0
        jmp     end_read_boot      ; and continue
;
read_boot_error:
        popf                       ; clear flags pushed by int 25h
        mov     ds,DSsave          ; reinitialize DS
        @DisStr ReadError_Msg      ; exit with error
        jmp     terminate          ; ... message
;
end_read_boot:
;
;--------------------------------------------------------------
; Verify that the boot record read contains the information we
; need. If the disk is a 160K or 320K floppy, the boot record
; will not contain the BPB information we need (may be true
```

```
; with some nonstandard disk formats as well), in which case
; the FAT table must be read to get the format ID byte. This byte
; is needed to determine whether the disk is 160K (DOS 1.0) or
; 320K (DOS 1.1) format.
;----------------------------------------------------------------
;
        mov     bx,20h              ; allocate 512 bytes
                                    ; ... (32 paras.)
        call    memalloc            ; allocate memory block
        jnc     read_fat            ; continue if no error
        call    mem_err_handler     ; else, go to error handler
        jmp     terminate           ; and exit to DOS
;
read_fat:
.DATA
FATSeg  dw      ?                   ; seg. address of FAT information
.CODE
        mov     word ptr FATseg,ax  ; save FAT seg. address
        push    ax                  ; and save it
        mov     al,byte ptr DiskDrive  ; get drive to read
        xor     ah,ah               ; clear AH
        pop     ds                  ; get seg. address of new block
        mov     dx,1                ; read logical sector 1
        mov     cx,1                ; read in one sector
        mov     bx,0                ; store data at DS:0
        int     25h                 ; read the disk
        jnc     process_FAT         ; continue if no error
        popf                        ; else, clear flags
        mov     ds,DSsave           ; reinitialize DS
        @DisStr ReadError_Msg       ; exit with error
        mov     ax,word ptr FATSeg  ; get boot seg. address
        call    memfree             ; deallocate the block
        jnc     end_fat_err         ; exit if no error
        call    mem_err_handler     ; else, display error msg.
end_fat_err:
        jmp     terminate           ; exit to DOS
;
process_FAT:
        popf                        ; clear flags pushed by int 25h
        mov     ds,DSsave           ; reinitialize DS
        mov     ax,word ptr FATSeg  ; get boot seg. address
        mov     es,ax               ; and init. ES to it
        xor     di,di               ; with offset of 0
.DATA
FAT_ID  db      ?                   ; ID byte from the FAT
.CODE
```

continued

Listing 11-1. *continued*

```
        mov     al,byte ptr es:[di] ; get FAT entry 0
        mov     byte ptr FAT_ID,al  ; and save it as a byte
        call    memfree             ; deallocate FAT seg.
                                    ; ... (address is in ES)
        jnc     comp_byte_id        ; continue if no error
        call    mem_err_handler     ; else, display error msg.
        jmp     terminate           ; exit to DOS
;
comp_byte_id:
        mov     ax,word ptr BootSeg ; point to boot segment
        mov     es,ax               ; ES:0 points to ...
        xor     di,di               ; ... boot record
        mov     al,byte ptr FAT_ID  ; get FAT ID byte
        cmp     al,byte ptr es:[di].MediaDescrip ; and compare
                                    ; with ID byte in boot record
        jne     chk_dos1_fmt        ; if different, then resolve
        jmp     end_read_fat        ; else, continue
chk_dos1_fmt:
        cmp     al,0FEh             ; is it a 160K floppy?
        je      init_dos1_fmt       ; yes, initialize boot record
        cmp     al,0FFh             ; else, is it a 320K floppy?
        je      init_dos1_fmt       ; yes, initialize boot record
.DATA
UnknownMedia db "Unable to determine disk format--possible "
        db   "non-MS-DOS disk.",CR,LF,"$"
.CODE
        @DisStr UnknownMedia        ; display error message
        jmp     terminate           ; and exit to DOS
;
init_dos1_fmt:
        ; Initialize format items that are the same between
        ; the 160K and 320K formats:
        mov word ptr es:[di+3],"D"      ; spell out "DOS 1.X"?
        mov word ptr es:[di+4],"O"      ; ... in OEM and DOS
        mov word ptr es:[di+5],"S"      ; ... version field
        mov word ptr es:[di+6]," "      ; ... of boot record
        mov word ptr es:[di+7],"1"
        mov word ptr es:[di+8],"."
        mov word ptr es:[[b]di].SectorBytes,512 ; bytes per sec.
        mov word ptr es:[di].ReservedSec,1 ; reserved sectors
        mov byte ptr es:[di].FATcopies,2   ; number of FAT copies
        mov word ptr es:[di].FATsectors,1  ; # FAT sectors
        mov word ptr es:[di].TrackSectors,8 ; # of sec. per track
        mov word ptr es:[di].HiddenSectors,0 ; # of hidden sec.
```

```
        cmp     al,0FEh         ; is it a 160K floppy?
        je      init_160K       ; yes, initialize boot record
        cmp     al,0FFh         ; else, is it a 320K floppy?
        je      init_320K       ; yes, initialize boot record
;
init_160K:
        mov word ptr es:[di.9],"0"      ; "DOS 1.0"?
        mov word ptr es:[di.10],"?"
        mov byte ptr es:[di].ClusterSec,1 ; sectors per cluster
        mov word ptr es:[di].DirEntries,64 ; # of dir. entries
        mov word ptr es:[di].TotalSectors,320 ; total disk sect.
        mov byte ptr es:[di].MediaDescrip,0FEh ; media descriptor
        mov word ptr es:[di].Heads,1         ; number of heads
        jmp     end_read_fat
;
init_320K:
        mov word ptr es:[di.9],"1"              ; "DOS 1.1"?
        mov word ptr es:[di.10],"?"
        mov byte ptr es:[di].ClusterSec,2   ; sectors per cluster
        mov word ptr es:[di].DirEntries,112 ; # of dir. entries
        mov word ptr es:[di].TotalSectors,640 ; total disk sec.
        mov byte ptr es:[di].MediaDescrip,0FFh ; media descriptor
        mov word ptr es:[di].Heads,2         ; number of heads
        jmp     end_read_fat
;
end_read_FAT:
;
;----------------------------------------------------------------
; Calculate values not available in the BIOS Parameter Block
; NOTE: ES:DI (offset 0) must point to boot record read into
; memory. All calculated results are stored in the data segment.
;----------------------------------------------------------------
get_new_values:
        xor     di,di                   ; clear out DI
;
; Calculate total sectors used for all copies of the FAT
        xor     ah,ah                   ; clear out AH
        mov     al,byte ptr es:[di].FATcopies ; get FAT copies
        xor     dx,dx                   ; clear out DX
        mov     bx,word ptr es:[di].FATsectors ; get FAT sectors
        mul     bx                      ; multiply by it
        mov     word ptr TotalFATSec,ax ; save the 1-word result
;
; Calculate total sectors used by all directory entries
        mov     ax,word ptr es:[di].DirEntries  ; get total root
                                        ; ... directory entries
```

continued

Listing 11-1. *continued*

```
        mov     bx,word ptr DirEntBytes ; get dir. entry bytes
        xor     dx,dx                   ; clear out DX
        mul     bx                      ; multiply
        mov     bx,word ptr
    es:[di].SectorBytes; get sector bytes
        xor     dx,dx                   ; clear out DX
        div     bx                      ; divide
        mov     word ptr DirSectors,ax  ; save the 1-word result
;
; Calculate total cylinders
        mov     ax,word ptr es:[di].TotalSectors ; get total sec.
        mov     bx,word ptr es:[di].TrackSectors ; get sec./track
        xor     dx,dx                   ; clear out DX
        div     bx                      ; and divide by it
        mov     bx,word ptr es:[di].Heads ; get number of heads
        xor     dx,dx                   ; clear out DX
        div     bx                      ; and divide by it
        cmp     word ptr es:[di].HiddenSectors,0 ; hidden secs.?
        je      store_cyl               ; no, we now have total
                                        ; ... cylinders
        mov     cx,word ptr es:[di].HiddenSectors ; else, hidden
                                        ; ... sectors = 1
        cmp     cx,word ptr es:[di].TrackSectors; ... cylinder?
        je      add_cyl                 ; yes
        mov     ax,0                    ; else, we have an error
        jmp     short store_cyl         ;
add_cyl:
        add     ax,1                    ; add an extra cylinder
store_cyl:
        mov     word ptr Cylinders,ax   ; save result
;
; Get total number of bytes on all (100%) of disk
        mov     ax,word ptr es:[di].TotalSectors ; get total sec.
        xor     dx,dx                   ; clear out DX
        mov     bx,word ptr es:[di].SectorBytes ; get sec. bytes
        mul     bx                      ; and multiply by it
        mov     word ptr TotalBytes,ax  ; & save 2-word result
        mov     word ptr TotalBytes.2,dx ; ... from AX and DX
;
; Get total number of data sectors (where files can be stored)
        mov     ax,word ptr es:[di].TotalSectors ; get total sec.
        xor     dx,dx                   ; clear out DX
        sub     ax,word ptr es:[di].ReservedSec ; sub. reser. sec.
        sub     ax,word ptr TotalFATSec ; sub. total FAT sectors
```

```
                                         ; ... (all copies of FAT)
        sub     ax,word ptr DirSectors  ; sub. root dir. sectors
        mov     word ptr DataSectors,ax ; and save result
;
; Get number of bytes per cluster
        xor     ah,ah                    ; clear out AH
        mov     al,byte ptr es:[di].ClusterSec ; get cluster sec.
        xor     dx,dx                    ; clear out DX
        mov     bx,word ptr es:[di].SectorBytes ; get sec. bytes
        mul     bx                       ; and multiply by it
        mov     word ptr ClusterBytes,ax ; and save result
;
; Get total number of clusters
        mov     ax,word ptr DataSectors ; get data sectors
        xor     bh,bh                    ; clear out BH
        mov     bl,byte ptr es:[di].ClusterSec ; get cluster sec.
        xor     dx,dx                    ; clear out DX
        div     bx                       ; div. by sectors/cluster
        mov     word ptr TotalClusters,ax ; and save word result
;
; Get number of bits in a FAT entry
; Always 12 bits if total clusters = 4,085 or below;
; always 16 bits if total clusters is above 4,085
        cmp     word ptr TotalClusters,4085 ; total clusters
                                         ; ... above 4085?
        jle     got_entry_size           ; no, use 12-bit default
        mov     al,16                    ; else, it's 16 bits
        mov     byte ptr FATentryBits,al ; and save value
got_entry_size:
;
; Get total number of data bytes (usable bytes)
        mov     ax,word ptr DataSectors ; get total data sectors
        xor     dx,dx                    ; clear out DX
        mov     bx,word ptr es:[di].SectorBytes ; get sec. bytes
        mul     bx                       ; and multiply by it
        mov     word ptr DataBytes,ax    ; & save 2-word result
        mov     word ptr DataBytes.2,dx  ; from AX and DX
;

; Calculate size of disk in kilobytes or megabytes
        mov     ax,word ptr TotalBytes   ; get total disk bytes
        mov     dx,word ptr TotalBytes.2 ; ... (double word)
        mov     cx,1024                  ; set up divisor
        div     cx                       ; and get kilobytes
        mov     word ptr Kbytes,ax       ; save value
        cmp     ax,1000                  ; calculate megabytes?
```

continued

Listing 11-1. *continued*

```
        jl      dis_info              ; no, we're done
        mov     bx,1000               ; else, set up divisor
        xor     dx,dx                 ; clear out DX
        div     bx                    ; and get megabytes
        mov     word ptr Mbytes,ax    ; save main value
        mov     word ptr Mbytes2,dx   ; & save fraction, if any
        cmp     dx,0                  ; is there a fraction?
        je      megabytes_end         ; no, we're done
        mov     ax,dx                 ; else, set up dividend
        mov     bx,10                 ; set up divisor
        xor     dx,dx                 ; and clear out DX
;
; Delete-trailing-zeros loop
compress_loop:
        div     bx                    ; divide AX by 10
        cmp     dx,0                  ; is there a remainder?
        jne     megabytes_end         ; yes, we're done
        mov     word ptr Mbytes2,ax   ; else, save new
                                      ; ... compressed value
        jmp     short compress_loop   ; and go through again
megabytes_end:
;
;-----------------------------------------------------------------
; Display disk format information:
;-----------------------------------------------------------------
dis_info:
        @DisStr Start2_Msg            ; display first part of
                                      ; ... drive msg
        xor     ah,ah                 ; clear out AH
        mov     al,byte ptr DiskDrive ; and display drive name
        inc     al                    ; make it a usable number
        add     al,40h                ; convert it to uppercase
                                      ; ... ASCII letter
        @DisChr al                    ; and display it
        @DisChr ':'                   ; followed by a colon
        @NewLine
;
        @DisStr OEM_Msg               ; display OEM message
        push    di                    ; save DI
        mov     di,bootrecord.OEMstring ; point to OEM string
        mov     cx,8                  ; set up char. count
more_char:                            ; enter display loop
        mov     al,byte ptr es:[di]   ; get character
        @DisChr al                    ; display character
```

```
        inc     di                  ; point to next character
        dec     cx                  ; dec. character count
        cmp     cx,0                ; all done?
        jg      more_char           ; no, output next char.
        @NewLine                    ; else, we're done
        pop     di                  ; restore DI
;
        @DisStr MediaDescrip_Msg    ; display media descrip.
        xor     ah,ah               ; clear out AH
        mov     al,byte ptr es:[di].MediaDescrip ; read byte val.
        @DisNum ax,16,2             ; display 2 hex digits
        cmp     byte ptr es:[di].MediaDescrip,0F8h ; fixed disk?
        je      fixed_disk          ; yes, display message
        @DisStr RemovableMedia_Msg  ; else, it's removable
        jmp     short media_size    ; and now do KB/MB size
fixed_disk:
        @DisStr FixedMedia_Msg      ; display fixed media msg
media_size:
        cmp     word ptr Mbytes,0   ; show megabytes?
        je      show_kilobytes      ; no, kilobytes instead
        mov     ax,word ptr Mbytes  ; yes, get megabytes
        @DisNum ax,10,1,0           ; output unsigned dec. #
        cmp     word ptr Mbytes2,0  ; is there a fraction?
        je      done_mbytes         ; no, we're done
        @DisChr '.'                 ; else, display decimal
                                    ; ... point
        mov     ax,word ptr Mbytes2 ; get megabytes fraction
        @DisNum ax,10,1,0           ; output unsigned dec. #
done_mbytes:
        @DisChr 'M'                 ; display meg. symbol
        jmp     short done_media    ; and we're done
show_kilobytes:
        mov     ax,word ptr Kbytes  ; get kilobytes value
        @DisNum ax,10,1,0           ; output unsigned dec. #
        @DisChr 'K'                 ; display kilobytes
                                    ; ... symbol
done_media:
        @DisStr Media_Msg           ; and display end of msg
        @NewLine
;
        @DisStr Cylinders_Msg       ; display total
                                    ; ... cylinders (tracks)
        cmp     word ptr Cylinders,0 ; was there an error?
        jne     show_cyl            ; no, display total
                                    ; ... cylinders
        @DisChr '?'                 ; else, display unknown
```

continued

Listing 11-1. *continued*

```
        jmp     short end_cyl           ; and end
show_cyl:
        mov     ax,word ptr Cylinders   ; get value
        @DisNum ax,10,1,0               ; and display it
end_cyl:
        @NewLine
;
        @DisStr Heads_Msg               ; display number of heads
        mov     ax,word ptr es:[di].Heads       ; get word value
        @DisNum ax,10,1,0               ; output unsigned dec. #
        @NewLine
;
        @DisStr TrackSectors_Msg        ; display # of sectors
                                        ; ... per track
        mov     ax,word ptr es:[di].TrackSectors ; get word value
        @DisNum ax,10,1,0               ; output unsigned dec. #
        @NewLine
;
        @DisStr SectorBytes_Msg         ; disp. bytes per sector
        mov     ax,word ptr es:[di].SectorBytes ; get word value
        @DisNum ax,10,1,0               ; output unsigned dec. #
        @NewLine
;
        @DisStr HiddenSectors_Msg       ; display number of
                                        ; ... hidden sectors
        mov     ax,word ptr es:[di].HiddenSectors ; get word val.
        @DisNum ax,10,1,0               ; output unsigned dec. #
        cmp     word ptr es:[di].HiddenSectors,0 ; are there any
                                        ; ... hidden sectors?
        je      hidden_done             ; no, we're done
        @DisStr PartitionInfo_Msg       ; else, indicate
                                        ; ... partition info.
hidden_done:
        @NewLine
;
        @DisStr TotalSectors_Msg        ; display total disk
                                        ; ... sectors
        mov     ax,word ptr es:[di].TotalSectors ; get word value
        @DisNum ax,10,1,0               ; output unsigned dec. #
        @NewLine
;
        @DisStr TotalBytes_Msg          ; display total bytes of
                                        ; ... disk
        mov     ax,word ptr TotalBytes  ; get 2-word value and
```

```
        mov     dx,word ptr TotalBytes.2 ; put it into AX and DX
        call    bin2dec2                 ; and display result from
                                         ; ... DX:AX
@NewLine
;
@DisStr ReservedSec_Msg                  ; display number of
                                         ; ... reserved sectors
        mov     ax,word ptr es:[di].ReservedSec ; get word value
@DisNum ax,10,1,0                        ; output unsigned dec. #
@NewLine
;
@DisStr FATsectors_Msg                   ; display number of
                                         ; ... sectors in 1 FAT
        mov     ax,word ptr es:[di].FATsectors  ; get word value
@DisNum ax,10,1,0                        ; output unsigned dec. #
@NewLine
;
@DisStr FATcopies_Msg                    ; display number of
                                         ; ... FAT copies
        xor     ah,ah                    ; clear out AH
        mov     al,byte ptr es:[di].FATcopies   ; get byte value
@DisNum ax,10,1,0                        ; output unsigned dec. #
@NewLine
;
@DisStr TotalFATsectors_Msg              ; display total sectors
                                         ; ... for all FATs
        mov     ax,word ptr TotalFATSec  ; get word value
@DisNum ax,10,1,0                        ; output unsigned dec. #
@NewLine
;
@DisStr DirEntries_Msg                   ; display number of root
                                         ; ... directory entries
        mov     ax,word ptr es:[di].DirEntries  ; get word value
@DisNum ax,10,1,0                        ; output unsigned dec. #
@NewLine
;
@DisStr DirSectors_Msg                   ; display total root
                                         ; ... directory sectors
        mov     ax,word ptr DirSectors   ; get word value
@DisNum ax,10,1,0                        ; output unsigned dec. #
@NewLine
;
@DisStr DataSectors_Msg                  ; display total data
                                         ; ... sectors
        mov     ax,word ptr DataSectors  ; get word value
@DisNum ax,10,1,0                        ; output unsigned dec. #
```

continued

Listing 11-1. *continued*

```
        @NewLine
;
        @DisStr ClusterSectors_Msg        ; display number of
                                          ; ... sectors per cluster
        xor     ah,ah                     ; clear out AH
        mov     al,byte ptr es:[di].ClusterSec  ; get byte value
        @DisNum ax,10,1,0                 ; output unsigned dec. #
        @NewLine
;
        @DisStr ClusterBytes_Msg          ; display bytes per
                                          ; ... cluster
        mov     ax,word ptr ClusterBytes  ; get word value
        @DisNum ax,10,1,0                 ; output unsigned dec. #
        @NewLine
;
        @DisStr Totalclusters_Msg         ; display total clusters
        mov     ax,word ptr TotalClusters ; get word value
        @DisNum ax,10,1,0                 ; output unsigned dec. #
        @NewLine
;
        @DisStr FATentrySize_Msg          ; display size of each
                                          ; ... FAT entry
        xor     ah,ah                     ; clear out AH
        mov     al,byte ptr FATentryBits  ; get byte value
        @DisNum ax,10,1,0                 ; output unsigned dec. #
        @DisStr Bits_Msg                  ; indicate that value is
                                          ; ... in bits
        cmp     byte ptr FATentryBits,12  ; find out how many
                                          ; ... bytes there are
        jg      dis_two_bytes
        @DisStr SmallFAT_Msg              ; FAT entry = 1.5 bytes
        jmp     short show_fat_done
dis_two_bytes:
        @DisStr LargeFAT_Msg              ; FAT entry = 2 bytes
show_fat_done:
        @NewLine
;
        @DisStr DataBytes_Msg             ; display total data
                                          ; ... bytes of disk
        mov     ax,word ptr DataBytes     ; get 2-word value & put
        mov     dx,word ptr DataBytes.2   ; ... it into AX and DX
        call    bin2dec2                  ; and display it
        @NewLine
;
```

```
        push    es                      ; save current ES
        mov     ax,word ptr BootSeg     ; get seg. address of
                                        ; ... allocated block
        mov     es,ax                   ; and assign ES to it
        call    memfree                 ; deallocate block
        pop     es                      ; restore ES
;
terminate:
        @ExitToDOS                      ; terminate program
;
;*****************************************************************
; End of program
;*****************************************************************
main    ENDP                            ; end of main process
;
;*****************************************************************
; Start of routines
;*****************************************************************
;
;+++++++++++++++++++++++++++++++++++++++++++++++++++++++++++++++++
; MEM_ERR_HANDLER: Memory allocation/deallocation/resize error
; handler.
; ENTRY:          AX = error code
;                 BX = maximum memory block available
;                      (if error code 8)
;                 ES = segment address of allocated block
;                      (if error code 9)
;
; EXIT:           None (all registers are restored).
;
; CALLED ROUTINES:        None.
;----------------------------------------------------------------
mem_err_handler PROC     NEAR
;
        cmp     ax,7                    ; trashed memory control
                                        ; ... blocks?
        jne     mem_error8              ; no, continue checking
.DATA
TrashedMemErr_Msg db    "Memory allocation failure: memory "
                  db    "control blocks destroyed.",CR,LF,"$"
.CODE
        @DisStr TrashedMemErr_Msg       ; yes, exit with message
        ret                             ; return
;
mem_error8:
        cmp     ax,8                    ; insufficient memory?
```

continued

Listing 11-1. *continued*

```
        jne     mem_error9              ; no, continue checking
.DATA
InsuffMemErr_Msg  db      "Memory allocation failure: "
                  db      "insufficient memory",CR,LF
                  db      "Largest block of memory available = $"
.CODE
        @DisStr InsuffMemErr_Msg        ; yes, exit with message
        @DisNum bx,10,1,0               ; ... is available
        @NewLine                        ; display blank line
        ret                             ; return
;
mem_error9:
        cmp     ax,9                    ; invalid memory block
                                        ; ... address?
        jne     mem_err_unknown         ; no, unknown cause
.DATA
IncorrSegAddr_Msg db "Incorrect segment address for "
                  db "resize/deallocation.",CR,LF
                  db "Segment address = $"
.CODE
        @DisStr IncorrSegAddr_Msg       ; display error message
        @DisNum es,16,4                 ; display seg. address
        @NewLine                        ; display blank line
        ret                             ; return
;
mem_err_unknown:
.DATA
UnknownMemErr_Msg db "Unknown memory allocation/resize/"
                  db "deallocation error.",CR,LF,"$"
.CODE
        @DisStr UnknownMemErr_Msg       ; display message
        ret
;
mem_err_handler ENDP
;
;;++++++++++++++++++++++++++++++++++++++++++++++++++++++++++++++++++
; MEMALLOC: Allocates a block of memory of the specified size
; in paragraphs (16 bytes).
;
; ENTRY:          BX = size, in 16-byte paragraphs,
;                      of requested block
;
; EXIT:           SUCCESS if Carry flag = 0, with
;                      AX = segment address of allocated
```

```
;                              memory block
;                              (BX is restored)
;
;                    FAILURE if Carry flag = 1, with
;                            AX = error code
;                                   7 = memory control blocks
;                                        destroyed
;                                   8 = insufficient memory
;                            BX = largest memory block available
;                                   in paragraphs
;
; CALLED ROUTINES:      None.
;------------------------------------------------------------------
memalloc        PROC    NEAR
;
        push    bp              ; save base pointer
        push    bx              ; save BX
        mov     bp,sp           ; initialize base pointer
;
        xor     al,al           ; clear out AL
        mov     ah,48h          ; load allocate memory function
        @DosCall                ; execute memory allocation
        jnc     end_memalloc    ; exit if no error with
                                ; ... seg. address in AX
                                ; else, exit with carry flag set,
        mov     word ptr [bp],bx ; max. size block (BX),
                                ; and error code in AX
;
end_memalloc:
        pop     bx              ; restore BX
        pop     bp              ; restore base pointer
        ret
memalloc        ENDP
;
;
;;++++++++++++++++++++++++++++++++++++++++++++++++++++++++++++++++++
; MEMFREE: Deallocates a block of memory previously allocated by
; the MALLOC routine.
;
; ENTRY:        ES = segment address of allocated memory block
;
; EXIT:         SUCCESS if Carry flag = 0
;                       (ES is restored)
;
;               FAILURE if Carry flag = 1, with
;                       AX = error code
```

continued

Listing 11-1. *continued*

```
;                                 7 = Memory control blocks
;                                     destroyed
;                                 9 = Invalid address
;                         (ES is restored)
;
; CALLED ROUTINES:       None.
;--------------------------------------------------------------------
memfree PROC     NEAR
;
        push     bp                ; save base pointer
        push     es
        push     ax                ; save AX
        mov      bp,sp             ; initialize base pointer
;
        xor      al,al             ; clear out AL
        mov      ah,49h            ; load deallocate mem. function
        @DosCall                   ; execute memory deallocation
        jnc      end_memfree       ; exit if no error
                                   ; else, exit with carry flag set,
        mov      word ptr [bp],ax  ; and error code (AX)
;
end_memfree:
        pop      ax                ; restore AX
        pop      es
        pop      bp                ; restore base pointer
        ret
;
memfree ENDP
;
;
;********************************************************************
; End of routines
;********************************************************************
;
.DATA                             ; switch to data segment
;********************************************************************
; Start of data storage
;********************************************************************
;
; Variables:
;
DiskDrive        db  0            ; disk drive to operate on
                                  ; (initial value=default drive)
;--------------------------------------------------------------------
```

```
; Rest of (calculated) disk format parameter variables:
Cylinders       dw   ?    ; total cylinders
TotalBytes      dd   ?    ; total disk capacity in bytes
TotalFATSec     dw   ?    ; total FAT sectors (all copies)
DirEntBytes     dw   32   ; number of bytes in a directory entry
DirSectors      dw   ?    ; sectors occupied by root directory
DataSectors     dw   ?    ; total data sectors for file storage
ClusterBytes    dw   ?    ; bytes per cluster
TotalClusters   dw   ?    ; total clusters
FATentryBits    db   12   ; number of bits in a FAT entry
DataBytes       dd   ?    ; total data bytes (for file storage)
Kbytes          dw   ?    ; total kilobytes (all of disk)
Mbytes          dw   0    ; total megabytes (all of disk)
Mbytes2         dw   0    ; and total megabytes fraction
;
;----------------------------------------------------------------
; Text messages:
;
Start1_Msg      db   "MS-DOS Disk Format Identifier "
                db   "-- Version 1.00",CR,LF,"$"
Start2_Msg      db   "BPB = Value extracted from boot record; "
                db   "CAL = Calculated value",CR,LF,CR,LF
                db   "Format information for drive $"
;
OEM_Msg                 db      "BPB: Formatted by:       $"
SectorBytes_Msg         db      "BPB: Bytes per sector:   $"
ClusterSectors_Msg      db      "BPB: Sectors per cluster: $"
ReservedSec_Msg         db      "BPB: Reserved sectors:   $"
FATcopies_Msg           db      "BPB: FAT copies:         $"
DirEntries_Msg          db      "BPB: Root dir. entries:  $"
TotalSectors_Msg        db      "BPB: Total disk sectors: $"
MediaDescrip_Msg        db      "BPB: Media descriptor:   $"
FATsectors_Msg          db      "BPB: FAT sectors (1 FAT): $"
TrackSectors_Msg        db      "BPB: Sectors per cylinder: $"
Heads_Msg               db      "BPB: Heads:              $"
HiddenSectors_Msg       db      "BPB: Hidden sectors:     $"
;
TotalFATsectors_Msg     db      "Cal: Total FAT sectors:  $"
DirSectors_Msg          db      "Cal: Directory sectors:  $"
TotalBytes_Msg          db      "Cal: Total disk bytes:   $"
Cylinders_Msg           db      "Cal: Total cylinders:    $"
DataSectors_Msg         db      "Cal: Total data sectors: $"
Totalclusters_Msg       db      "Cal: Total clusters:     $"
ClusterBytes_Msg        db      "Cal: Bytes per cluster:  $"
FATentrySize_Msg        db      "Cal: FAT entry size:     $"
DataBytes_Msg           db      "Cal: Total data bytes:   $"
```

continued

Listing 11-1. *continued*

```
;
FixedMedia_Msg          db      " (fixed $"
RemovableMedia_Msg      db      " (removable $"
Media_Msg               db      " media)$"
Bits_Msg                db      " bits$"
Bytes_Msg               db      " bytes$"
SmallFAT_Msg            db      " (1.5 bytes)$"
LargeFAT_Msg            db      " (2 bytes)$"
CurrPartition_Msg       db      " (within current partition)$"
PartitionInfo_Msg       db      " (partitioning information)$"
;
;-------------------------------------------------------------
; Error messages:
NonDOSerr_Msg   db      "Disk could not be read."
                db      "Probable non-DOS disk.",CR,LF,"$"
BadDrive_Msg    db      "Syntax error or the drive specified is "
                db      "not allowed.",CR,LF,"$"
ReadError_Msg   db      "General error in reading disk."
                db      CR,LF,"$"
UnknownErr_Msg  db      "Unknown error -- terminating.",CR,LF,"$"
;
;
;****************************************************************
; End of data storage
;****************************************************************
        END     main                    ; end of program
```

Hard Disk Partition Tables

With the introduction of support for hard, or "fixed," disks under MS-DOS version 2.00, a new item was added to a disk's formatting information: the disk partition table. The *disk partition table* is used to describe how a disk is divided into sections, and is almost always used only on fixed (nonremovable) hard disks with capacities of 10 megabytes or more. The disk partition table consists of 16 bytes of information starting at offset 01BE hex in the boot record (first sector of the disk). The layout of the disk partition table is shown in Table 11-2.

When the hard disk is partitioned into one or more partitions with the FDISK command, a new boot record with partition table is stored in the first sector of each partition. Thus, a disk with one partition contains a master partition table (in the boot record stored in the very first sector of the disk) and a second partition table in its boot record stored in the first sector of the partition itself. Additional partitions also contain their own boot record and partition table. The master partition table is updated each time FDISK is used to change partitions, and the *partition status field* of each individual partition is updated to reflect its active/inactive state.

Table 11-2.   Disk Partition Table Layout

Offset (dec)	(hex)	Size	Name	Contents
0	00	1 byte	Partition status	0 = Inactive 80h = Bootable, active
1	01	1 byte	Starting head	Integer
2	02	1 word	Starting sector and cylinder	See note*
4	04	1 byte	Partition type**	1 = DOS with 12-bit FAT 4 = DOS with 16-bit FAT 5 = Extended DOS***
5	05	1 byte	Ending head	Integer
6	06	1 word	Ending sector and cylinder	See note*
8	08	2 words	Starting absolute sector	Integer****
12	0C	2 words	Number of sectors	Integer****

*The partition table begins at offset 01BE hex in the initial boot record (1st absolute sector of the hard disk). The partition table contains the starting head, cylinder, and sector number of the boot record of the active partition.

**Additional partition types are used by some manufacturers to identify their system or to identify large-capacity disks divided into several logical drives.

***The extended DOS partition is supported only under MS-DOS versions 3.30 and above.

****Cylinder and sector are stored in bit-position—coded notation, as applied to the starting and ending cylinder and sector.

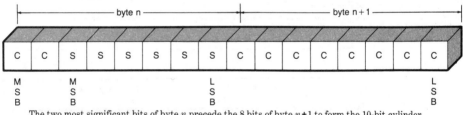

The two most significant bits of byte *n* precede the 8 bits of byte *n*+1 to form the 10-bit cylinder number. The 6 least-significant bits of byte *n* form the sector number.

Although the FAT sectors are next in the sequence of sectors on the disk, we're going to skip them and instead talk about the directory sectors. You must understand the contents of the directory sectors in order to understand what is stored on the rest of the disk.

The Directory Sectors

The *directory sectors* store the directory information for all files in the root directory of the disk. The information for files contained in subdirectories is stored in the *subdirectory file*, the entry for which is stored in its parent directory (root or other subdirectory). When you issue the DIR command, the information is obtained from the directory sectors if reading from the root directory or is obtained from the subdirectory file describing the current subdirectory. Because a sector is usually 512 bytes long, we can easily deduce that each directory entry is 32 bytes long. The total number of root directory entries depends on how many directory sectors are defined. For example, single-sided floppy disks have a total of 64 root directory entries, whereas double-sided, 40-track disks have a total of 112, and double-sided, 80-track, 5-¼-inch disks have a total of 224. In most hard disks, the total number of directory entries depends on how the disk is formatted: each hard disk partition will have a maximum number of root directory entries according to the partition's size. The total number of root directory entries determines the maximum number of files that can be stored in the root directory. This restriction, however, does not exist for subdirectories. Because the directory entries that correspond to files stored in subdirectories are themselves stored in the *subdirectory description file*, there is no limit to the number of files stored in a subdirectory; the subdirectory description file can continue to grow as needed.

The information contained in a directory entry is divided into six components, four of which are directly or indirectly relevant to recovering erased files. Figure 11-4 shows the components of a directory entry, the length of each component, and how each is defined.

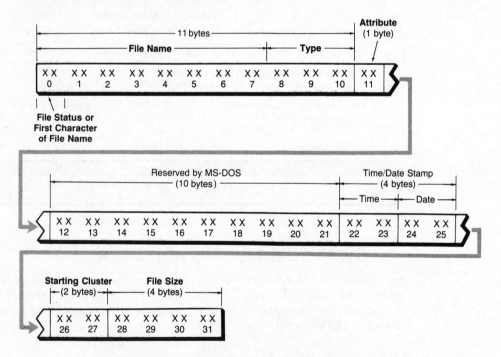

Figure 11-4. Components of a directory entry.

The four parts of a directory entry with which we need to be concerned, as shown in Figure 11-4, are the file name and type, the attribute(s), the starting cluster, and the file size.

File Name, File Type, and File Status
The file name and type consist of 11 bytes, representing the name of the file to which the directory entry corresponds. Each byte contains an ASCII character.

In MS-DOS versions 2.0 and above, the file name in a directory entry always refers to a file in the root directory. Because subdirectory names are treated as files by MS-DOS, they also have their own entries in the directory sectors. A subdirectory name, however, contains information in its directory entry that is slightly different from normal files. We'll cover these differences in later sections of this chapter.

Note also that under MS-DOS versions 2.0 and above, the maximum number of files or directory entries that a floppy disk can accommodate (64, 112, and 224) corresponds only to the root directory. Because all files stored in a subdirectory have directory entries in the subdirectory "file" itself, there is effectively no limit to the number of files that can be stored on a disk within the space provided by the particular type of disk and format. We'll talk about subdirectories and file recovery in more detail later in this chapter.

When a file is erased, two things happen to the disk. The first item affected is the first character of the file name in the directory entry. As shown in Figure 11-4, the first byte in a directory entry can either indicate the file's status or represent the first ASCII character of the file's name. If a directory entry has not been used since the disk was last formatted, this first byte is always set to 00. In this way, MS-DOS needs to read only the first byte of a directory entry to determine whether it can be used. When a file is created, the first byte is changed to represent the first character of the file's name. When the file is later erased, the first byte is changed to a hexadecimal value of E5. The rest of the information in the erased file's directory entry is left intact. When you examine the disk's sectors for the information on the erased file's directory entry, this value is your first clue that the desired directory entry has been found.

The second clue, of course, is the presentation of the rest of the file's name and type in ASCII format. But the first character of hex value E5 tells you that the directory entry represents an erased file. The byte is set to this value so that MS-DOS knows that the directory entry is free to be overwritten with new file information should the space be needed. Thankfully, the designers of MS-DOS saw fit to implement file deletion in this manner. Because they did, we are able (most of the time) to restore a file that has just been erased.

Attribute

The *attribute byte* contains information about the file's storage attributes. Attributes indicate how MS-DOS treats the file. Table 11-3 shows the definitions of each attribute and the respective hexadecimal values that can be stored in the attribute byte. Each bit in the byte defines a specific attribute and is set to 1 when the attribute is assigned to the file.

Notice that a file can have more than one attribute. For example, if a file is assigned the read-only (hex 01) and hidden (hex 02) attributes, the resulting value in the attribute byte is the sum of both attribute values—hex 03. Information contained in the attribute byte may or may not be useful when recovering a file. For example, it's unlikely that we'd try to recover a file assigned the read-only attribute, unless we were trying to recover a damaged disk. Normally, we wouldn't care what the file's attributes are. However, if we're recovering a file with the hidden attribute assigned to it, we would want to change the attribute

Table 11-3. File Attribute Definitions

Bit	Hex Value	Attribute
1st	80	Not defined (in MS-DOS version 3.0 and below)
2nd	40	Not defined (in MS-DOS version 3.0 and below)
3rd	20	*Archive status*: Set when the file has been opened and closed and is used by some hard disk backup and restore utilities
4th	10	*Subdirectory entry*: Indicates that the directory entry pertains to a subdirectory "file"
5th	08	*Volume label*: Indicates that the directory entry contains a volume label (DOS 2.0 and above only); rest of entry contains no useful information
6th	04	*System status*: Used to indicate system files, such as those used for booting the system. The MS-DOS boot files (e.g., IBMDOS.COM and IBMBIO.COM) must have this attribute set.
7th	02	*Hidden status*: File is excluded from normal directory searches
8th	01	*Read-only status*: File cannot be erased

because otherwise we wouldn't be able to see the file listed when we used the DIR command to verify that the file was recovered. Another reason we may want to reference the file's attribute byte is if we try to recover a subdirectory name.

Starting Cluster

A *starting cluster* is a 2-byte, 16-digit binary number that represents the first section of the disk occupied by the file. This section of the disk is referred to as a *cluster*. Although Figure 11-1 portrayed a formatted disk in terms of tracks and sectors, MS-DOS actually views the disk in terms of clusters of sectors rather than individual sectors. The starting cluster is the initial "pointer" to the file's first data sector as well as to subsequent pointers in the FAT sectors. Having read this initial pointer in the directory entry, MS-DOS proceeds to read the rest of the pointers to the file's data sectors in the FAT sectors. We talk about FAT sectors next, but for now note that referencing the starting cluster is one of the most important first stages in the restoration of an erased or damaged file.

File Size

A file's size is represented by a 4-byte binary number, the first byte of which represents the least significant part of the file's size. The fourth byte is the most significant part of the file size, and we use that value to determine the exact length of a file and thus determine the number of sectors that an erased file occupies or is supposed to occupy.

Now that the essential portions of the directory entry have been defined, we move on to the FAT sectors. The information in these sectors provides additional clues about how an erased or damaged file can be recovered.

The "." and ".." Directory Entries

The directory information just described is valid for all files stored under MS-

DOS, with the exception of two special types of directory entries: the "." and ".." directory entries found in all subdirectories. The "." directory entry contains information for the current subdirectory, and the ".." entry contains information on the parent directory of the current directory. Table 11-4 describes the contents of each field of the directory entries for the "." and ".." directories.

Table 11-4.   Contents of the "." and ".." Directory Entries

"." (Current) Directory

Field	Contents
Name/type	1st byte = 2E hex; the rest = 00
Attribute	Directory status only (10 hex)
Time	Time created
Date	Date created
Starting cluster	Cluster number of current directory
Size	Blank (size is in parent's directory entry for this directory)

".." (Parent) Directory

Field	Contents
Name/type	1st and 2nd bytes = 2E hex; the rest = 00
Attribute	Directory status only (10 hex)
Time	Time created
Date	Date created
Starting cluster	Cluster number of *parent* directory, only if *parent* is not the root directory
Size	Blank

File Allocation Table (FAT) Sectors

The sectors containing the FAT are used by MS-DOS to determine the locations on the disk of each part of every file. Unlike some operating systems that always store files consecutively and utilize sectors in a contiguous manner, MS-DOS is capable of storing files and parts of each file in a random manner. A system that always stores files contiguously keeps track of files more easily and can thus access the files more quickly. To recover a file that is stored contiguously, we need only locate the beginning and end of the file. All the data in-between pertains to the file.

But contiguous file storage is less efficient when a file stored between several files is deleted and replaced by a larger file. For if the free space made available by the deleted file is not large enough to accommodate the new file, sufficient contiguous space for the new file must be allocated toward the end of the string of files. If the disk doesn't contain sufficient space for the file, the disk is considered full. This can pose a real problem when using floppy disks with fairly low storage capacity because a lot of storage space can go to waste.

MS-DOS and similar disk-based microcomputer operating systems were designed to allow random storage as well as contiguous or sequential storage. The information in the FAT sectors permits MS-DOS to accomplish this feat.

When a disk is first formatted under MS-DOS and several files are copied to that disk, information stored in the FAT sectors is used by MS-DOS to determine the location of each part of a file. Files are referenced by the FAT in terms of clusters. A file always occupies at least one cluster and, if it is large enough, is divided into several clusters. A cluster is really a section of allocation and consists of one data sector in single-sided floppy disks and two data sectors in double-sided floppy disks. Some hard disks use clusters that each consist of as many as eight sectors. The entire data storage area of a disk (except for the boot, FAT, and directory sectors) is divided equally into clusters, and the entire range of clusters is mapped out by the FAT. Figures 11-5 and 11-6 show how single- and double-sided, 40-track floppy disks, in both the 8- and 9-sector formats, are mapped in terms of clusters. Figure 11-7 shows how the 80-track, high-capacity floppy disk is mapped out.

8-SECTOR-PER-TRACK FORMAT						**9-SECTOR-PER-TRACK FORMAT**					
Track						**Track**					
Sector	0	1	2	...	39	**Sector**	0	1	2	...	39
1	Boot	3	11	...	.	1	Boot	2	11	...	.
2	FAT 1	4	12	...	.	2	FAT 1	3	12	...	.
3	FAT 2	5	13	...	309	3	FAT 1	4	13	...	346
4	Dir	6	14	...	310	4	FAT 2	5	14	...	347
5	Dir	7	15	...	311	5	FAT 2	6	15	...	348
6	Dir	8	16	...	312	6	Dir	7	16	...	349
7	Dir	9	.	...	313	7	Dir	8	17	...	350
8	2	10	.	...	314	8	Dir	9	.	...	351
						9	Dir	10	.	...	352

**Figure 11-5. Cluster numbers in single-sided,
40-track floppy disks.**

Notice that in the previous three figures the FAT sectors are either numbered one or two. They're shown this way because the designers of the MS-DOS file system reserved twice as many FAT sectors as are actually necessary to map out the disk. A possible reason for this design was to allow room for the FAT to grow with larger-capacity floppy disks. In versions of MS-DOS up to 3.3, however, the extra set of sectors is used to store an exact copy of the first set of FAT sectors. Having redundant sets of the FAT can prove to be convenient if the first set is damaged for some reason. Repairing a damaged FAT can be very tedious and complicated. When recovering files, however, you normally need to reference only the first FAT.

Each cluster on the disk has a corresponding FAT entry. The FAT entry that corresponds to the first cluster of a file contains the number of the next cluster occupied by that file. By looking in the FAT entry corresponding to this "next" cluster, we find either that the end of the file has been reached or that the entry contains the number of yet another cluster occupied by the file. Thus, the

8-SECTOR-PER-TRACK FORMAT

Track Sector	0	1	2	...	39	
SIDE 0 1	Boot	5	13	...	.	
2	FAT 1					
3	FAT 2	6	14	...	.	
4	Dir					
5	Dir	7	15	...	311	
6	Dir					
7	Dir	8	16	...	312	
8	Dir					
SIDE 1 1	Dir	9	17	...	313	
2	Dir					
3	2	10	18	...	314	
4						
5	3	11	19	...	315	
6						
7	4	12	.	...	316	End
8		.				

Start of Data Sectors → (SIDE 1, sector 3)

9-SECTOR-PER-TRACK FORMAT

Track Sector	0	1	2	...	39	
SIDE 0 1	Boot	5	14	...	.	
2	FAT 1					
3	FAT 1	6	15	...	.	
4	FAT 2					
5	FAT 2	7	16	...	349	
6	Dir					
7	Dir	8	17	...	350	
8	Dir					
9	Dir	9	18	...	351	
SIDE 1 1	Dir					
2	Dir	10	19	...	352	
3	Dir					
4	2	11	20	...	353	
5						
6	3	12	.	...	354	
7						
8	4	13	.	...	355	End
9						

Start of Data Sectors → (SIDE 1, sector 4)

**Figure 11-6. Cluster numbers in double-sided,
40-track floppy disks.**

FAT entries effectively contain pointers both to the clusters occupied by the file and to subsequent FAT entries that correspond to additional clusters occupied by the file. Because the total number of entries in the FAT sectors exceeds the total number of clusters on the disk, the entire disk can be easily mapped even when it has reached maximum storage capacity. In Figures 11-5, 11-6, and 11-7, the numbering of clusters begins with 2. This is because clusters are numbered the same as FAT entries (to allow for quick indexing into the FAT), and FAT entries 0 and 1 are used for other purposes. To make up for the reserved FAT

15-SECTOR-PER-TRACK FORMAT

Sector \ Track		0	1	2	...	79
	1	Boot	3	33	...	.
	2	FAT 1	4	34	...	.
	3	FAT 1	5	35	...	1166
	4	FAT 1	6	36	...	1167
	5	FAT 1	7	37	...	1168
	6	FAT 1	8	38	...	1169
SIDE 0	7	FAT 1	9	39	...	1170
	8	FAT 1	10	40	...	1171
	9	FAT 2	11	.	...	1172
	10	FAT 2	12	.	...	1173
	11	FAT 2	13	.	...	1174
	12	FAT 2	14	.	...	1175
	13	FAT 2	15	.	...	1176
	14	FAT 2	16	.	...	1177
	15	FAT 2	17	.	...	1178
	1	Dir	18	.	...	1179
	2	Dir	19	.	...	1180
	3	Dir	20	.	...	1181
	4	Dir	21	.	...	1182
	5	Dir	22	.	...	1183
	6	Dir	23	.	...	1184
SIDE 1	7	Dir	24	.	...	1185
	8	Dir	25	.	...	1186
	9	Dir	26	.	...	1187
	10	Dir	27	.	...	1188
	11	Dir	28	.	...	1189
	12	Dir	29	.	...	1190
	13	Dir	30	.	...	1191
	14	Dir	31	.	...	1192
	15	2	32	.	...	1193

Start of Data Sectors → (points to Side 1, Sector 15)

Figure 11-7. Cluster numbers in double-sided, 80-track floppy disks.

entries, the clusters are numbered from 2 to the number of the last FAT entry. The number of clusters on a disk is thus equal to the number of the last FAT entry minus 1. Because the boot, FAT, and directory sectors do not have cluster numbers, cluster 2 contains the first data sector(s) on the disk. The example in Figure 11-8 illustrates how FAT entries can be referenced.

Decoding the FAT Entries

The value in FAT entry 0 always indicates the format of the disk. Entry 1 is always set to (F)FFF to act as a barrier or filler between entry 0 and entry 2. Table 11-5 shows the different values for each format supported under MS-DOS versions 1.0 through 3.3.

All subsequent FAT entries are used for mapping the disk. Each of these entries contains one of four types of information:

- The next cluster number of a file
- The end-of-file marker

- An unused cluster
- A cluster that is marked as reserved or bad

Table 11-6 lists the values that can exist in FAT entries.

Directory Entry for File 1
Starting cluster number
points to FAT Entry 2
(1st part of file is in cluster 2)

Directory Entry for File 2
Starting cluster number
points to FAT Entry 5
(1st part of file is in cluster 5)

0	FFD	Double-sided, 9-sector-per-track floppy disk
1	FFF	(Filler)
2	003	Next part of File 1 points to Entry/Cluster 3
3	004	Next part of File 1 points to Entry/Cluster 4
4	008	Next part of File 1 points to Entry/Cluster 8
5	006	Next part of File 2 points to Entry/Cluster 6
6	007	Next part of File 2 points to Entry/Cluster 7
7	FFF	End of File 2
8	009	Next part of File 1 points to Entry/Cluster 9
9	010	Next part of File 1 points to Entry/Cluster 10
10	FFF	End of File 1
11	000	Not used — Allocated as Free Space
12	000	Not used — Allocated as Free Space
13	000	Not used — Allocated as Free Space

Figure 11-8. Sample FAT.

Table 11-5.   Disk Type Values in FAT Entry 0

At Entry 0 (hex value)	Type of Disk and Format
(F)FF0	3½-inch, 1.44-Mbyte diskette (MS-DOS 3.30 and above) *or* Other nondefined format (MS-DOS 3.30 and above
(F)FF8	Fixed disk (IBM PC, XT, and AT hard disks with MS-DOS 2.0 and above)
(F)FF9	Removable media. Normally represents: 5¼-inch, 1.2-Mbyte, high-capacity floppy diskette format (MS-DOS 3.0 and above) *or* 3½-inch, 720-Kbyte diskette format (MS-DOS 3.20 and above)
(F)FFC	Removable media. Normally represents: 5¼-inch, 180-Kbyte floppy diskette (MS-DOS 2.00 and above)
(F)FFD*	Removable media. Normally represents: 5¼-inch, 360-Kbyte floppy diskette (MS-DOS 2.00 and above) *or* 8-inch, 501-Kbyte (double-sided, single-density) floppy disk
(F)FFE*	Removable media. Normally represents: 5¼-inch, 160-Kbyte floppy diskette (MS-DOS 1.00 and above) *or* 8-inch, 250-Kyte (single-sided, single-density) floppy disk *or* 8-inch, 1.232-Mbyte (double-sided, double-density) floppy disk
(F)FFF	Removable media. Normally represents: 5¼-inch, 320-Kbyte floppy diskette (MS-DOS 1.10 and above)

*Note: Some implementations of MS-DOS support 8-inch, soft-sectored floppy disks. Although custom device drivers must be written for the particular type of 8-inch disk drives used in the system, "generic" MS-DOS supports four 8-inch disk formats: two single-sided, single-density (128 bytes per sector) formats; one double-sided, single-density format; and one double-sided, double density (1,024 bytes per sector) format. The only difference between the two single-sided, single-density formats is that one has a single reserved sector for the boot record and the other has four sectors. The disk format definition value in FAT entry 0 for both the single-density format with one reserved sector and the double-density format is FFE (hex). For the single-density format with four reserved sectors, the value is FFD. Sharing the same value with 5¼-inch disks is no problem because MS-DOS, through its device driver, knows when it is accessing 8-inch disks. However, in order for MS-DOS to distinguish 8-inch formats when it encounters FFE in FAT entry 0, it first reads the disk assuming it is single density and subsequently tries to read the single-density address mark in the first sector. If no error occurs, it continues reading the disk knowing that it is in single-density format. If an error occurs, MS-DOS assumes that the disk is formatted to double density and, expecting a double-density format, returns to the beginning to read the data. If your system is equipped with 8-inch floppy disk drives, the MS-DOS manual accompanying your particular MS-DOS implementation should have the necessary technical information about 8-inch disk formats.

As shown in Tables 11-5 and 11-6, all FAT entries contain either a three- or a four-digit hexadecimal number. This means that a FAT entry contains either a 12-bit or a 16-bit value. All disks containing 4,085 or fewer clusters (most floppy disks and other removable media) use 12-bit FAT entries, whereas all disks having more than 4,085 clusters (most fixed hard disks and some removable media) use 16-bit FAT entries.

Table 11-6. FAT Entry Values Controlling File Allocation

FAT Entry Hex Value	Meaning
(0)000	Cluster is unused and is available for new file storage
(F)FF0 through (F)FF6	Reserved cluster (not available for normal file storage)
(F)FF7	Cluster is marked as bad by MS-DOS and is not used for file storage
(F)FF8 through (F)FFF	Last cluster occupied by a file
(X)XXX	Any other value indicates a cluster number in the chain defining how a file is stored

Why are there two different FAT formats? Before the support for hard disks under MS-DOS was introduced (MS-DOS version 2.0), the designers of MS-DOS saw fit to minimize the amount of space needed to store the FAT table. Since the maximum number of clusters stored on a floppy disk is below 4,085 (2,847 clusters on a 1.44-megabyte 3½-inch disk), disk space would be wasted if 16-bit FAT entries were used, and the maximum cluster number that could be mapped with 8-bit entries would be 255, which would be inadequate. So, in order to decode the entries in the FAT table, the total number of clusters on the disk must first be determined.

Processing 12-Bit FAT Entries

The MS-DOS scheme of storing numbers that are 1½-bytes wide in FAT entries on floppy disks may seem strange. But MS-DOS is designed to be able to decode these bytes easily. The way MS-DOS stores FAT information is to scramble FAT entries into pairs in which two 1½-byte entries are interweaved into a tidy 3-byte pair. If we want to determine the cluster number in FAT entry 2, we also need to look at FAT entry 3. If we want to look at the cluster number in FAT entry 3, we have to look back to FAT entry 2. FAT entries 4 and 5 would be paired together in the same manner as well as entries 6 and 7, 8 and 9, and so on. Figure 11-9 illustrates how two cluster numbers are encoded into a pair of FAT entries when viewing the numbers as they are presented in DEBUG. Figure 11-10 shows how two cluster numbers can be decoded from a pair of FAT entries.

If only three digits are extracted from the cluster number, why is the second most significant digit of the first cluster number swapped with the least significant digit of the second cluster? The swapping scheme operates faster in terms of how the machine itself decodes bytes and extracts information. The digits *appear* swapped only when humans read the FAT in DEBUG.

To decode the information in 12-bit FAT entries on paper or in a program, use the following formula.

1. Multiply FAT entry or cluster number by 1½ bytes. (Multiply the number by 3; then divide by 2.)

2. Use the result as an offset into the FAT, pointing to the entry that maps the cluster just used. That entry contains the number of the next cluster occupied by the file.

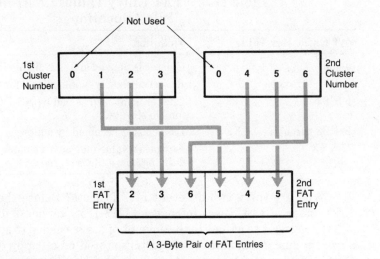

Figure 11-9. Encoding two cluster numbers into a pair of 12-bit FAT entries.

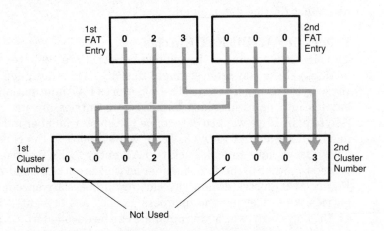

Figure 11-10. Decoding a pair of 12-bit FAT entries into two cluster numbers.

3. Load the word (a 2-byte number) located at that offset into a register.

4. There are now four hexadecimal digits in the register. Because we need only three digits for a three-digit FAT entry, determine whether the FAT entry number is even or odd.

5. If the entry number is even, keep the low-order three digits in the register by ANDing it with 0FFF. If the number is odd, keep the high-order three digits by shifting the register right four bits with the SHR instruction.

6. If the resulting three digits represent a number from FF8 through FFF, you have reached the end of the file. Otherwise, the three digits represent the number of the next cluster occupied by the file.

Processing 16-Bit FAT Entries

Dealing with cluster numbers and FAT entries on disks that use 16-bit FAT entries is considerably easier than it would be for those with 12-bit FAT entries because all FAT entries are *word bound*; that is, each FAT entry can be read and written as a complete word without having to worry about its neighboring FAT entries.

To decode the information in 16-bit FAT entries on paper or in a program, use the following formula:

1. Obtain the starting cluster of the file from its directory entry.
2. Multiply the cluster number used by 2 (bytes; 1 word).
3. Use the result as an offset into the FAT table, pointing to the entry that maps the cluster just used. That entry contains the number of the next cluster occupied by the file.
4. Load the word (2 bytes) located at that offset into a register.
5. If the resulting 4 digits represent a number from FFF8 through FFFF, you have reached the end of the file. Otherwise, the four digits represent the number of the next cluster occupied by the file.

Converting Clusters to Logical Sectors

If you write a program that accesses the data storage area of disks, you will find that MS-DOS facilities such as int 25h (Absolute Disk Read) and int 26h (Absolute Disk Write) as well as the DEBUG program require that you specify logical sector numbers. Although the disk layout illustrations (see Figures 11-2 and 11-3) identify the first sector of a disk as side 0, track 0, sector 1, the first sector actually equates to logical sector 0. All subsequent logical sectors are sequential offsets of 0. Thus, logical sector 1 would be side 0, track 0, sector 2; and logical sector 2 would be side 0, track 0, sector 3. Because each FAT entry, according to the results in the preceding formula, always produces a cluster number, the following formula shows you how to convert a cluster number to a logical sector number:

1. Subtract 2 from the cluster number.
2. Multiply the result by the number of sectors used in a cluster, as follows:
   a. For all single-sided floppy disk formats or for the double-sided, 80-track, 5¼-inch (high capacity) format, multiply by 1.
   b. For all double-sided, 40-track, 5¼-inch floppy disks, multiply by 2.
   c. For double-sided, double-density, 8-inch floppy disks, multiply by 4.
   d. For hard disks, use one of the above values or another number depending on the disk format.

3. Add the result to the logical sector number of the beginning of the data storage area.

By applying the proper formulas in the right order, you can now go from a directory entry to a FAT entry to the cluster number to the logical sector number. Given this, who needs MS-DOS? You could read the files yourself, a sector at a time!

An Overview of Recovery Procedures

When a file on a disk has been damaged in some way, three basic approaches to correcting the problem are possible. The first approach is to use one of MS-DOS's built-in facilities, such as CHKDSK or RECOVER. These programs can isolate damaged areas of the disk so that you can recover some or all of a damaged file.

The second approach is to use DEBUG, which allows you to do anything that you want in attempting to recover a damaged or erased file. Unfortunately, DEBUG offers little intelligence to aid you in this goal and is often the "court of last resort." A similar approach is to write your own recovery program, such as the RESCUE program presented later in these chapter. The information presented in the preceding section on decoding the disk's directory and FAT is essential to writing your own recovery programs.

The last approach, and a more comfortable one if your pocketbook can stand it, is to use one of the available off-the-shelf utilities, such as Norton Utilities or Ultra Utilities. These utilities are like a toolbox, providing all the capabilities of the above methods, including decoding the FAT, inspecting individual sectors on the disk, repairing damaged files, and restoring erased files.

Recovering Damaged Files Using CHKDSK and RECOVER

Understanding how a disk is laid out under MS-DOS can be very useful if a file or part of a disk appears to be damaged. Fortunately, the operating system contains several functions that not only call attention to damaged parts of a disk but also allow you to recover data that is otherwise not accessible. When faced with file storage problems or defective disks, MS-DOS automatically isolates the problem part of the disk when the system attempts to access it. Although MS-DOS doesn't necessarily tell you exactly what has happened, you probably get an error message indicating that the part of the disk from which you wanted to read cannot be accessed properly. If this happens, use the DIR command to examine the directory of the disk. If the DIR command shows the directory as normal, the recovery of the file(s) should be more or less straightforward: use the RECOVER command on the file or files.

If the directory entries are not in the directory, use the CHKDSK command, initially without any parameters. You will probably get a message stating that a certain number of clusters are lost on the disk, which is a good sign because it indicates that you can again use the CHKDSK command, this time accompanied by the /F parameter. This parameter causes CHKDSK to read all "lost" clusters and store them in one file. Sometimes CHKDSK cannot recover all the lost data in one pass. Use CHKDSK as many times as is necessary until the *lost clusters* message disappears. CHKDSK creates a new file each time the command is used to recover lost data. Once the new file(s) is created, copy it to a new disk, and then look at the contents of the file just created by CHKDSK.

If the recovered data corresponds to text files, you can open the file with a text editor or word processor and sort out the information. If, however, the recovered data corresponds to files that are not in a readable text format (such as object code or machine code), you have to use DEBUG or some other utility to look at the information and sort it out. In either case, do not be surprised if a small part of the data is missing. The part of the disk on which the data was stored may have been so badly damaged that it can't be read. Most of the time, data that isn't recoverable consists of increments of 512 or 1,024 bytes, depending on the format of the disk (one 512-byte sector in one cluster for single-sided floppies or two 512-byte sectors in one cluster for double-sided floppies). The reason MS-DOS can't recover this data is that the cluster(s) in question already has been isolated in the corresponding FAT entries and each entry contains a value of (F)FF7, indicating that the clusters are bad and that no program is to use them under any circumstances. You could try to read these clusters with DEBUG, but they may be so badly damaged that even DEBUG cannot read them.

The following section shows how to use DEBUG to read portions of a disk on a sector-by-sector basis.

Recovering Erased Files

Fortunately, when a file is erased under MS-DOS, only part of the file's directory entry is modified: the first character of the file name is changed to a hexadecimal E5. This value is used as a flag. When MS-DOS scans the directory sectors for a free spot to store a new file's directory information, the system finds and uses the first entry that begins either with hex E5 (erased file) or with 00 (directory entry hasn't been used yet). The rest of the information in the directory entry is left intact. If all we had to do was change E5 to the value of the first character of the erased file name, recovering erased files would be very easy. Unfortunately, however, MS-DOS is much more efficient in erasing the information stored in the FAT sectors. Although MS-DOS doesn't touch the information stored in the data sectors or clusters occupied by a file, the system sets to 000 all FAT entries corresponding to these clusters. MS-DOS does this because that's the only way the system can quickly scan the disk for blank space when it wants to store new files. Thus, our task of recovering an erased file is a little more involved than it might seem at first. Some basic guidelines to recovering erased files are described next.

The Basics

There are many ways to lose files. Maybe you inadvertently used the ERASE or DEL command. Or perhaps your hardware malfunctioned or power was lost during an edit session. After scanning the disk, you discovered that the file you were editing could not be found.

Generally, a file is only truly "erased" (with the first character in the file's directory entry equaling hex E5) if it is erased with the ERASE or DEL command or by another program that performs the same function. If you lose a file because of a hardware malfunction or power loss, the file probably isn't truly erased. It's simply lost on the disk if the program you are using didn't have time to close the file properly. In such a case, you can use the MS-DOS disk recovery programs RECOVER and CHKDSK to recover the lost data.

CAUTION

When recovering files, the first thing you should do is make an exact duplicate of the disk by using the disk copy program. Do not store any new files on the disk until you've made an attempt to recover the lost or erased files.

The preceding caution is very important because storing new data to the disk probably makes file recovery difficult if not impossible. And by first making an exact copy of the disk, you avoid the possibility of corrupting certain parts of the disk (thereby guaranteeing permanent data loss) as a result of improper file recovery. Thus, if things don't go right the first time, you still have the original disk from which you can copy the data and the file recovery process can begin again.

The best way to determine whether a file is truly erased or is merely lost is to use the CHKDSK program without any parameters. If the file is lost, the CHKDSK program displays the message, *Lost clusters found*. This message is displayed if CHKDSK finds a break in the chain of clusters described in the FAT—if, for example, the last cluster in the chain doesn't point to a FAT entry that contains an end of file marker—(F)FF8 through (F)FFF). When this happens, you should reenter CHKDSK with the /F parameter to recover all lost clusters and store the data into a file that is created by CHKDSK.

This is where the initial step of making an entire copy of the original disk may prove to be a blessing. For if you also had other files that were truly erased on the disk, the CHKDSK/F command sequence quite likely stores the file containing the recovered data *over* the area containing the erased files! File recovery, no matter what the circumstances, should be approached in a methodical and careful manner.

Once it is clear that a file has been truly erased, and if no additional files have been stored on the disk since the file was erased, you know three things with certainty: First, the file's directory entry is intact, except for the first character, which is hex E5. Second, the clusters or sectors in the data area of the disk originally used by the file still contain the file's data. Third (sadly), the FAT entries originally used to map out the clusters occupied by the file each contain (0)000.

To recover an erased file, the following steps should be taken.

1. Search through the directory entries until you find an entry that begins with hexadecimal E5 at byte 00. Look at the characters of the rest of the file name in bytes 1 through 10 and verify that it's the file you want to recover.

2. Look at the starting cluster number (bytes 26 and 27). Use the starting cluster number as a pointer to the first cluster in the data area of the disk occupied by the file as well as to the first FAT entry originally used.

3. Look at the file's size (bytes 28 through 31, the last 4 bytes in the directory entry). Knowing the file's size is important if the file takes up more than one cluster in the data area of the disk and especially important if parts of the file are scattered at different parts of the disk.

4. Having determined the cluster number occupied by the beginning of the file, examine the contents of that cluster. Search for an ASCII *Control-Z* character (hex 1A) in the cluster. If you know that the file contains text (ASCII) and if one or more Control-Z characters are found, recover the file as follows. (Otherwise, proceed to Step 5.)

   a. If one or more Control-Z characters were found, you know that the file occupies only one cluster. Begin recovering the file by storing any number from (F)FF8 through (F)FFF in the FAT entry corresponding to the cluster.

   b. Change the hex E5 in the directory entry to whatever you think the first character of the file's name should be.

   c. Back at the MS-DOS prompt, use the DIR command to verify that the file is listed. Open the file with a text editor or word processor to verify that the contents are intact. You're done! Stop here and ignore the following steps.

5. If the end of the file wasn't found, search through the subsequent FAT entries (sequentially) until one containing 000 is found. Look at the contents of the cluster that is numbered the same as the FAT entry. If the contents appear to be part of the erased file, make note of the cluster number and continue the search through the FAT entries and the equivalent clusters until you think the end of the file has been reached. The amount of searching you do depends on several things, as described in the next step.

6. Determine from the size of the file extracted from the directory entry how many clusters the file *should* occupy. Also keep in mind that if you're recovering an ASCII text file, the presence of a Control-Z character (hex 1A) in a cluster indicates the end of the file. Therefore, loop back to step 5 until you reach the maximum number of clusters occupied by the file.

Make note of each cluster number that contains data you think is part of the erased file. If you find a Control-Z in a cluster but haven't yet examined a sufficient number of clusters matching the file's size, be careful: The cluster with the Control-Z on it could mark the end of another erased file. Search through subsequent directory entries for erased files and make note of their starting clusters as well as their file sizes. It's possible that two or more erased files have interweaving paths for any given sequence of clusters.

7. Once you're reasonably certain about the clusters occupied by the file and how they're chained together and you're fairly certain you've found the end of the file, reconstruct the FAT. Beginning with the first cluster, go to the equivalent FAT entry and store the number of the next cluster occupied by the file. Then go to this next FAT entry and store the number of the subsequent cluster. Continue this operation until the last cluster is reached, storing in the corresponding FAT entry any number from (F)FF8 through (F)FFF to mark the end of the file. Next, go to the file's directory entry, and change the first character of hex E5 to the ASCII equivalent (in hexadecimal) of whatever you think the first character of the file should be.

8. That's it! When you're back at the MS-DOS prompt, use the DIR command to verify that the file is listed. If the recovered file is a text file, open the file with a text editor or word processor to verify its contents. If it's some other type of file, such as an .EXE or a .COM file, load the file as a program to verify that it works correctly.

The previous steps might suggest that the procedure for recovering a file is fairly straightforward. Depending on the tools you have at your disposal, however, actually looking at the data on the disk and writing information to the disk can be a bit cumbersome. Notice also that Steps 6 and 7 provide cautions about the possibility that several erased files might be interwoven through a sequence of clusters. Recovering data that is interwoven in this way can be very tedious and at times rather mind-boggling. But with patience (possibly quite a bit) and by forcing yourself to be methodical, you can untangle the files.

Now that you have an idea of the effort that it takes to recover erased files, this is a good time to point out that the fastest way to recover erased files is to copy them off your backup disk. You should try to get into the habit of backing up your work frequently, and always use a *copy* of your purchased or private software, never the original disk(s).

Recovering Erased Files the Hard Way

If all you have at your disposal is the DEBUG program for recovering files, and you don't have the time or the patience to type and assemble the program RESCUE described in this chapter, the following tips may prove useful to you. The four DEBUG functions or commands of interest are L (Load), D (Display), E (Enter), and W (Write). Once you make a copy of the disk with the erased file on it, load DEBUG. At the DEBUG prompt, enter the L command to load data from the part of the disk you're interested in looking at.

```
L <address> <drive> <start sector> <end sector>
```

In this case, *<address>* represents the beginning address in memory where the data is to be loaded, *<drive>* is the drive number (for example, 0 for A, 1 for B, 2 for C), and *<start sector>* and *<end sector>* indicate the range of logical sectors (hexadecimal numbers only) that you want to load. To load the contents of all the directory sectors on a double-sided, 40-track, 5¼-inch diskette formatted to nine sectors per track and inserted in drive B, enter the following:

```
A>DEBUG
-L 0 1 5 B
```

When the information is loaded, you can use the D command to display the contents in memory and the E command to change individual bytes as needed. Once you note the information you need and make any changes, the data can be written back to the disk using the W command. The W command uses the exact same syntax as the L command. Make sure that you specify the same parameters as you did with the L command. This ensures that only the correct part of the disk is overwritten.

The only time you need to write information to the disk is when you change the first character of an erased file name in its directory entry or when you modify the contents of the FAT entries that correspond to the file. When examining the contents of the clusters occupied by the actual file, you don't have to write the information back to the disk unless you're doing some tricky repair work that could otherwise not be accomplished. Refer to the *MS-DOS User's Manual* (or your system's equivalent manual) for more information on how to use DEBUG and its commands.

Using the RESCUE Program

The program described in Listing 11-4 is very straightforward and easy to use. The command RESCUE is typed, followed by the file name of the erased file. RESCUE will accept only the name of the file, so the default drive and directory containing the erased file must be set with the CHDIR or CD command before running RESCUE. The file to be erased may be any file: normal, hidden, system, read-only, or subdirectory. If you're unerasing a file in a subdirectory that is also erased or if you wish to rescue the entire directory tree below an erased subdirectory, you must first unerase the subdirectory by name with RESCUE, make the newly rescued subdirectory the default directory (using the CHDIR or CD command), and then manually unerase the file(s) in the subdirectory with RESCUE.

If the name of the file is found in the directory (root directory or subdirectory "file"), an attempt is made to recover the file by analyzing and writing information to the FAT. If the file was not found or was found to be not deleted, a message is displayed to that effect. As explained earlier, the allocation path taken through the FAT for a given file can be sometimes complex. If RESCUE cannot resolve the allocation path of a file (maybe it was interwoven with a path of another file), the program terminates and no information is written to the disk. An important factor in the way the program works is that it won't write any information to the disk until all aspects of the file have been resolved. It accomplishes this by reading all directory and FAT sectors into memory where all of the modifications to the file's directory entry and its FAT entries are made. When all modifications have been made, RESCUE writes the entire directory and FAT back to the disk. If difficulties are encountered in analyzing the data and making the modifications, RESCUE terminates and the disk is left untouched.

As noted earlier, RESCUE is designed so that it can deal with any disk format that adheres to standard MS-DOS formatting conventions. It uses the undocumented MS-DOS function 32h, Get Disk Parameter Block, to obtain the necessary information about the disk's format. It also makes extensive use of functions contained in the Microsoft C Run-Time Library. If you adapt this program to another language or compiler, you will have to find or write substitutes for these functions.

The RESCUE program is intentionally simple, both to aid in understanding and to enable us to fit it in the book. There are a number of enhancements that you may want to add to make RESCUE more useful. You may want to allow the user to specify the drive and directory of the erased file on RESCUE's command line, or you may want to allow wildcard specifications of the erased files by using the * or ? standards. A very useful addition would be one that checked to see if the user is trying to restore a file whose name already exists (which can be done by judicious use of the existing routines).

Another modification that you may wish to do is to allow RESCUE to work with hard disks that have partitions larger than 32 megabytes, as introduced in MS-DOS 4.0. These extended-size partitions use 32-bit sector numbers instead of the 16-bit sector numbers used in partitions of 32 megabytes or smaller. In order to avoid having to deal with 32-bit FAT entries, the sector-to-cluster ratio is increased in extended-size partitions so that 16-bit FAT entries can still be used. However, the maximum size of the FAT table (one copy) has been increased from 64K (MS-DOS version 3.3) to 128K (in MS-DOS version 4.0). MS-DOS applications are shielded from the extended-size partition cluster and sector-mapping scheme provided that only standard MS-DOS file functions or absolute cluster referencing is used. However, absolute sector references using interrupts 25h and 26h require different calling conventions between partitions that are 32 megabytes or less and partitions that are more than 32 megabytes. The following listings show the two calling conventions in MS-DOS 4.0 for interrupt 25h (Absolute Disk Read) and interrupt 26h (Absolute Disk Write):

With some modifications, RESCUE can be turned into a very capable application, able to deal with any type of disk media, regardless of the implementation and version of MS-DOS.

Listing 11-2. Calling Convention for Absolute Disk Read/Write (Int 25h/26h) on Disk Partitions 32 Mbytes or Less (All Versions of MS-DOS)

```
ENTRY:    AL = Drive number (0 = A, 1 = B, etc.)
          CX = Number of sectors to read (int 25h) or
               write (int 26h)
          DX = Beginning logical sector number
          DS:BX = Transfer address

RETURN:   Carry Flag = 0 (successful transfer), or
                     = 1 (unsuccessful transfer):
                       AL = Error code
                       AH = Type of error
NOTE:     AX is returned with 0207h if an attempt is made
          to read or write a partition larger than 32 megabytes.
```

Listing 11-3. Calling Convention for Absolute Disk Read/Write (Int 25h/26h) on Disk Partitions Larger than 32 Mbytes (MS-DOS Versions 4.0 and Higher Only)

```
ENTRY:    AL = Drive number (0 = A, 1 = B, etc.)
          BX = Pointer to parameter list
          CX = -1 (indicates extended (>32MB) format)

RETURN:   Carry Flag = 0 (successful transfer), or
                     = 1 (unsuccessful transfer)
                       AL = Error code
                       AH = Type of error

NOTE:     POP AX (error code) on return. Error codes the same
          as above.

          Parameter list structure:

          rba       dd   ?   ; first sector (32-bits, 0 origin) to
                             ; read/write
          count     dw   ?   ; number of sectors to read/write
          buffer    dd   ?   ; data buffer
```

Listing 11-4. RESCUE Program

```
/*********************************************************************
     FILE:   RESCUE2.C    Rescue File Utility Version 2.00

Enhancements: Rescuing a file in subdirectories
              Rescuing an erased subdirectory
              Handles any type of MS-DOS disk media
              (floppies, fixed disks, removable cartridges)

Compile with Microsoft C Compiler:

    cl /c /Zp1 /AS /GO /Ze /Ot rescue2.c

Link with Microsoft Linker:

    link /DOSSEG/MA/LI/CPAR:1/STACK:4096 rescue2,rescue2.exe,
        rescue2.map,slibce;
**********************************************************************/

/*  I N C L U D E   F I L E S  */

#include  <stdio.h>      /* for printf() and much more */
#include  <conio.h>      /* for getch() */
#include  <dos.h>        /* for intdos(), int86(), and so forth */
#include  <malloc.h>     /* for _fmalloc () & malloc */
#include  <string.h>     /* for memory "mem...()" and "str..." */
#include  <ctype.h>      /* for toupper() and "is...()" */
#include  <direct.h>     /* for getcwd() */

/*  C O N S T A N T    D E F I N I T I O N S   */

#define FALSE           0           /* these definitions are to */
#define TRUE            1           /* make the program more */
#define AND             &&          /* readable and understandable */
#define OR              ||
#define EQ              ==
#define NE              !=
#define LE              <=

#define ABS_READ        0x25        /* read disk interrupt */
#define ABS_WRITE       0x26        /* write disk interrupt */

                                    /* DOS int 21h functions: */
#define DFUNC_RESETDSK  0x0D        /* reset drive */
#define DFUNC_GETDISK   0x19        /* get current drive */
```

```
#define DFUNC_GETDPB    0x32    /* get disk parameter block */
#define DFUNC_GETCD     0x47    /* get current directory */


                                /* DOS file attribute bits: */
#define FATR_NONE       0x00    /* matches ANY */
#define FATR_READ       0x01    /* READ Only */
#define FATR_HIDDEN     0x02    /* Hidden */
#define FATR_SYSTEM     0x04    /* System File */
#define FATR_VOLUME     0x08    /* Volume Label */
#define FATR_SUBDIR     0x10    /* Sub-Directory */
#define FATR_ARCHIV     0x20    /* Archived File */


#define CL_OFF          2       /* first cluster number is 2 */
#define TENMB           20740L  /* maximum # of sectors ... */
                                /* ... supported by 12-bit FAT */
#define CHAIN_END       1       /* used by "get_cluster()" ... */
                                /* ... to indicate end-of-file */
#define FILE_END        0xfff8  /* FAT entry for end-of-file */


                                /* match() routine match types */
#define NO_MATCH        0       /* no match */
#define IS_MATCH        1       /* did match */
#define IS_ERASED       2       /* match on erased files */
#define IS_UNIQUE       4       /* match on unerased files */


#define DNAME_SIZE      80      /* maximum directory name size */

/*  S T R U C T U R E   &   T Y P E   D E F I N I T I O N S  */

typedef unsigned int  BOOL ;
typedef unsigned char BYTE ;
typedef unsigned int  WORD ;
typedef unsigned long DWORD ;
typedef union {
        BYTE far * ptr ;
        struct {
            WORD off ;
            WORD seg ;
            } a ;
        } LONGPTR ;

typedef struct dpbbuf {         /* disk parameter block buffer */
    BYTE   PhysDrive ;          /* drive number */
    BYTE   DriverUnit ;         /* unit number within drive */
    WORD   BytesSector ;        /* bytes per sector */
    BYTE   SectorsCluster ;     /* sectors per cluster -1 */
```

continued

Listing 11-4. *continued*

```
        BYTE  ClusterShift ;      /* cluster shift */
        WORD  Reserve ;           /* number reserved sectors */
        BYTE  NumberOfFATs ;      /* FAT table copies */
        WORD  DirEntries ;        /* number root directory entries */
        WORD  DataSect ;          /* first data sector */
        WORD  TotClust ;          /* total clusters + 1 */
        BYTE  nFATsec ;           /* number of FAT sectors (1 FAT) */
        WORD  DirSect ;           /* sector number of directory */
        DWORD DevHeaderAddr ;     /* address of device header */
        BYTE  MediaByte ;         /* media descriptor byte */
        BYTE  DiskAccFlag ;       /* disk access flag */
        DWORD NextBlockAddr ;     /* address of next disk block */
        } DPB ;

typedef struct dirbuf {           /* disk directory entry */
        char    name [8] ;        /* name */
        char    ext [3] ;         /* extension */
        BYTE    attrib ;          /* attribute */
        BYTE    reserved [10] ;
        WORD    time ;            /* time: hhhhh mmm - mmm sssss */
        WORD    date ;            /* date: yyyyyyy m - mmm ddddd */
        WORD    cluster ;         /* starting cluster */
        DWORD   fsize ;           /* total size in bytes */
        } DENTRY ;


/*  G L O B A L   V A R I A B L E S    */

DPB     far * DPBPtr ;            /* pointer to DPB */
WORD    ClUnit ;                  /* sectors per cluster */
                                  /* (also size of directory buffer) */
WORD    BytClust ;                /* number of bytes per cluster */
DWORD   TotSect ;                 /* total number of sectors on disk */
WORD    FATSize ;                 /* number of bytes in FAT table */
WORD    far * FatAnchor ;         /* FAT table buffer address */
DENTRY  near * DirAnchor ;        /* directory buffer address */
DENTRY  near * AltAnchor ;        /* alternate directory buf address */
char    default_sname [] = {"*.*"} ;    /* default search name */

/*  P S E U D O - S U B R O U T I N E   D E F I N E S      */

#define diskread(d,s,c,b)   diskaccess(ABS_READ,d,s,c,b)
#define diskwrite(d,s,c,b)  diskaccess(ABS_WRITE,d,s,c,b)

#define sector_of(cl)    (DPBPtr->DataSect+(cl-CL_OFF)*ClUnit)
#define cluster_of(sec)  (CL_OFF+(sec-DPBPtr->DataSect)/ClUnit)
```

```
/* S U B R O U T I N E    P R E - D E C L A R A T I O N S */

WORD     get_cluster () ;          /* get cluster entry value */
void     put_cluster () ;          /* store value in cluster */
BOOL     savefile () ;             /* restore file.s FAT & DIR */
DENTRY   near * findf () ;         /* search directory buffer */
DPB      far * getdpb () ;         /* get disk param block addr */
void     diskaccess () ;           /* absolute disk read/write */
BOOL     match () ;                /* match spec. name with file */


/* ***************************************************** */
/*                                                       */
/*            M A I N    E N T R Y    P O I N T          */
/*                                                       */
/* ***************************************************** */

main (argc, argv, envp)
int argc ;
char   * argv [] ;
char   * envp [] ;
    {
    char    near * sspec ;              /* search specifier */
    char    dname [DNAME_SIZE] ;        /* directory name buffer */
    char    * pptr ;                    /* pointer to dir name */
    WORD    dnum ;                      /* drive number (origin 0) */
    WORD    snum ;                      /* directory sector number */
    WORD    savenum ;                   /* used to store snum */
    DENTRY  near * dptr ;               /* current directory entry */

    printf ("\nRESCUE, Version 2.00\n\n") ;

    if (argc < 2) {                     /* if no parameters ... */
        printf ("*** Filename not specified ***\n") ;
        exit (1) ;
        } ;

    sspec = argv [1] ;                  /* file to restore */
    getcwd (dname, DNAME_SIZE) ;        /* get default drive & dir */
    if (*(char *)((WORD)dname + strlen(dname) - 1) NE '\\')
        strcat (dname, "\\") ;          /* pathname ends with "\" */
    pptr = dname + 3 ;                  /* init path name pointer */
    dnum = *dname - 'A' ;               /* extract drive number */

/* Determine various global values from Disk Parameter Block, ...
... including FAT size, bytes per cluster, total sectors, etc. */
```

continued

Listing 11-4. *continued*

```
DPBPtr = getdpb (dnum) ;           /* get disk param block */

if (dnum NE DPBPtr->PhysDrive) {
    printf ("Drive %c: is SUBSTituted\n",(dnum+'A')) ;
    printf ("RESCUE will work only on physical drives\n") ;
    exit (1) ;
    } ;


FATSize = DPBPtr->BytesSector * DPBPtr->nFATsec ;
ClUnit = DPBPtr->SectorsCluster + 1 ;
TotSect = (DWORD) DPBPtr->TotClust * (DWORD) ClUnit
    + (DWORD) DPBPtr->DataSect ;
BytClust = DPBPtr->BytesSector * ClUnit ;

/* Allocate memory for directory buffers and FAT tables */

    if (((DirAnchor=(DENTRY near *) malloc(BytClust)) EQ NULL) OR
        ((AltAnchor=(DENTRY near *) malloc(BytClust)) EQ NULL) OR
        ((FatAnchor=(WORD far *) _fmalloc(FATSize)) EQ NULL)) {
        printf ("*** Can't Allocate Working Memory ***\n") ;
        exit (1) ;
        } ;

/* Read in initial FAT table */

    diskread (dnum,DPBPtr->Reserve,DPBPtr->nFATsec,FatAnchor) ;

/* Follow chain of directory entries to match dname path */

    snum = DPBPtr->DirSect ;           /* first directory sector */
    while (*pptr NE '\0')              /* while dir path non-null */
        if ((dptr = findf (dnum, &snum, pptr, DirAnchor,
            NULL, FATR_SUBDIR, IS_UNIQUE)) NE NULL) {
            snum = sector_of (dptr->cluster) ;
            while ((*pptr NE '\0') AND (*pptr NE '\\'))
                pptr++ ;
            if (*pptr EQ '\\') pptr++ ;
        } else {
            printf ("*** Can't Find Directory %s ***\n", pptr) ;
            exit (1) ;
            } ;

/* Abort if the file to restore is not erased. */

    savenum = snum ;                        /* save direc sector */
```

```
      if (findf (dnum, &snum, sspec, DirAnchor,
        NULL, FATR_NONE, IS_UNIQUE) NE NULL) {
        printf ("*** %s%s is not erased ***\n", dname, sspec) ;
        exit (1) ;
        } ;

/* If file is erased sub-directory or file then un-erase it */

      snum = savenum ;                        /* restore dir sector */
      if ((dptr = findf (dnum, &snum, sspec, DirAnchor,
        NULL, FATR_NONE, IS_ERASED)) NE NULL) {
        if (get_cluster (dptr->cluster) NE 0)
            printf ("Unerased file %s%s can't be restored\n",
              dname, sspec) ;
          else {
            if (savefile (dnum,dptr,snum,toupper(*sspec))) {
                if (dptr->attrib & FATR_SUBDIR)
                    printf ("Subdirectory %s%s restored\n",
                      dname, sspec) ;
                  else
                    printf ("File %s%s restored\n",
                      dname, sspec) ;
              } else {
                printf ("Failed to restore %s%s\n",
                  dname, sspec) ;
                diskread (dnum,DPBPtr->Reserve,
                  DPBPtr->nFATsec,FatAnchor) ;
                } ;
            } ;
        } else {
          printf ("Can't locate unerased file %s%s\n",
            dname, sspec) ;
          } ;
      } ;

/* **** FIND NEXT CLUSTER IN A CHAIN *****************************
```

This routine retrieves the value of a FAT entry. This is
equivalent to chaining the FAT cluster. This routine returns
either a cluster's value (the next cluster in a DOS file
chain) or the value NULL if there are no more clusters in
the chain.

If the disk is 10 Mbytes or less, then 12-bit FAT entries
(clusters) are used. If the disk is larger, then 16-bit FAT
entries are used.

continued

Listing 11-4. *continued*

```
Cluster values: (0)000 ................ free cluster
                (0)001 ................ undefined
                (0)002 - (F)FEF ....... next cluster
                (F)FF0 - (F)FF6 ....... reserved
                (F)FF7 ................ bad cluster
                (F)FF8 - (F)FFF ....... end of chain
*/


WORD    get_cluster (clust)
    WORD clust ;                        /* cluster number */
    {
    union { WORD FAR }* w ;             /* pointer to FAT table */
        BYTE far * b ;
        } fatptr ;
    WORD    value ;                     /* cluster content */

    if (TotSect > TENMB) {
        fatptr.b = (BYTE far *)
          ((DWORD) FatAnchor + (DWORD) (clust * 2)) ;
        value = *fatptr.w ;
      } else {
        fatptr.b = (BYTE far *)
          ((DWORD) FatAnchor + (DWORD) (clust * 3/2)) ;
        value = *fatptr.w ;
/* Odd-numbered clusters are left-shifted 4 bits in the word */
        if (clust & 0x01) value >>= 4 ;
        value &= 0x0fff ;
        } ;
    if ((value & 0x0ff0) EQ 0xff0) return (CHAIN_END) ;
      else return (value) ;
    } ;


/* **** STORE CLUSTER VALUE *************************************

    This routine stores a value into a cluster entry in the FAT.
    If the disk is 10 Mbytes or less, then 12-bit FAT entries
    (clusters) are used. If the disk is larger, then 16-bit FAT
    entries are used.
*/

void put_cluster (clust,value)
    WORD clust ;                        /* cluster number */
    WORD value ;                        /* new cluster value */
    {
```

```
      union { WORD FAR }* w ;              /* pointer to FAT Table */
         BYTE far * b ;
         } fatptr ;
      WORD    cur_val ;                    /* current cluster value */

      if (TotSect > TENMB) {
         fatptr.b = (BYTE far *)
           ((DWORD) FatAnchor + (DWORD) (clust * 2)) ;
         *fatptr.w = value ;               /* patch FAT */
        } else {
         fatptr.b = (BYTE far *)
           ((DWORD) FatAnchor + (DWORD) (clust * 3/2)) ;
         cur_val = *fatptr.w ;
/* Odd-numbered clusters are left-shifted 4 bits in the word */
         if (clust & 0x01)
             *fatptr.w = (cur_val & 0x000f) | (value << 4) ;
           else
             *fatptr.w = (cur_val & 0xf000) | (value & 0x0fff) ;
        } ;
     } ;


/* *** FIND A FILE'S CLUSTER, AND SAVE THE FILE'S DIR & FAT ***

   This routine restores an erased file, if possible. It
   calculates the number of clusters the file should occupy, and
   looks for those clusters in the FAT.

   This routine assumes that the starting cluster number of the
   file to be restored has been checked, and its value is zero.
*/

BOOL savefile (dnum,dptr,sect,ch)
     WORD    dnum ;                        /* operative drive */
     DENTRY  near * dptr ;                 /* directory entry to save */
     WORD    sect ;                        /* dir "cluster" sector # */
     BYTE    ch ;                          /* 1st char of file name */
     {
     DENTRY  far  * writeptr ;             /* pointer to dir buffer */
     WORD    filecls ;                     /* file size (in clusters) */
     WORD    last ;                        /* last cluster number */
     WORD    current ;                     /* current cluster number */
     WORD    next ;                        /* next cluster in chain */
     WORD    fatsect ;                     /* FAT sector number */
     union { WORD FAR }* w ;               /* pointer to FAT Table */
         BYTE far * b ;
         } fatptr ;
```

continued

Listing 11-4. *continued*

```
        if (dptr->attrib & FATR_SUBDIR) /* If file is a sub-dir */
            filecls = 0 ;                 /* no additional needed */
          else
            filecls = (WORD) ((dptr->fsize + (DWORD) BytClust - 1L) /
              (DWORD) BytClust) - 1 ;
        current = last = dptr->cluster ;         /* 1st cluster */

        /* Patch the FAT */

        while (filecls) {
            if (++current > DPBPtr->TotClust) {
                printf ("\n*** Unable to Restore File ***\n") ;
                return (FALSE) ;
                } ;
            if (get_cluster(current) EQ 0) {    /* blank cluster */
                put_cluster (last,current) ;     /* part of chain */
                last = current ;
                filecls-- ;
                } ;
            } ;
        put_cluster (last, FILE_END) ;          /* end chain */

        *(dptr->name) = ch ;                     /* save 1st char */

/* Preparation complete - write out the FAT and Directory
   sectors */

        writeptr = DirAnchor ;
        fatsect = DPBPtr->Reserve ;
        diskwrite (dnum,fatsect,DPBPtr->nFATsec,FatAnchor) ;
        fatsect += DPBPtr->nFATsec ;
        diskwrite (dnum,fatsect,DPBPtr->nFATsec,FatAnchor) ;
        diskwrite (dnum,sect,ClUnit,writeptr) ;
        bdos (DFUNC_RESETDSK,NULL,NULL) ;
        return (TRUE) ;
        } ;


/* **** FIND SPECIFIED ENTRY IN THIS DIRECTORY ************** */

DENTRY  near * findf (dnum, sect, pptr, dbuf, bptr, sattr, mtype)
    WORD    dnum ;                      /* operative drive */
    WORD    * sect ;                    /* current direc sector */
    char    near * pptr ;               /* path name pointer */
    DENTRY  near * dbuf ;               /* directory buffer */
    DENTRY  near * bptr ;               /* another buffer pointer */
```

```
BYTE    sattr ;                     /* search attribute */
int     mtype ;                     /* type of match desired */
{
int     i ;                         /* loop counter */
WORD    cluster ;                   /* used for chaining */
DENTRY  near * dirptr ;             /* directory buf pointer */
DENTRY  far  * readptr ;            /* directory buf pointer */
DENTRY  near * dirend ;             /* address of buffer end */

readptr = dbuf ;
dirend = (DENTRY near *) ((WORD) dbuf + BytClust - 1) ;

while (TRUE) {
    if (bptr NE NULL) {             /* continue from ... */
        dirptr = ++bptr ;           /* ... where left off */
        bptr = NULL ;
    } else {                        /* else start at begining */
        diskread (dnum,*sect,ClUnit,readptr) ;
        dirptr = dbuf ;
        } ;
                                    /* any matching files ? */
    while (dirptr < dirend) {
        if (((dirptr->attrib & sattr) EQ sattr) AND
            (match (pptr,dirptr->name,mtype)))
            return (dirptr) ;
        dirptr++ ;
        } ;

/* all entries in this "cluster" checked, get another */

if (*sect >= DPBPtr->DataSect) {    /* sub-directory */
        cluster = cluster_of (*sect) ;  /* next cluster */
        if ((cluster = get_cluster (cluster)) LE CHAIN_END)
            return (NULL) ;
          else *sect = (sector_of (cluster)) ;
      } else                        /* root directory */
        if (*sect >= DPBPtr->DirSect) {
            *sect += ClUnit ;       /* next sectors */
            if (*sect >= DPBPtr->DataSect) return (NULL) ;
          } else return (NULL) ;
    } ;
  } ;

/* **** GET BIOS PARAMETER BLOCK FOR SPECIFIED DRIVE ******** */

DPB far *getdpb (dnum)              /* return pointer to DPB */
```

continued

Listing 11-4. *continued*

```
WORD      dnum ;                      /* operating drive number */
{
union REGS inregs, outregs ;
struct SREGS segregs ;
LONGPTR farptr ;

inregs.h.ah = DFUNC_GETDPB ;
inregs.h.dl = dnum + 1 ;
intdosx (&inregs, &outregs, &segregs) ; /* get DPB */
if (outregs.x.cflag) {
    if (outregs.h.al EQ 0xff)
        printf ("*** Drive %c Invalid ***\n", (dnum + 'A')) ;
      else
        printf ("*** Can't Read Drive %c Paramters ***\n",
          (dnum + 'A')) ;
    exit (1) ;
    } ;
farptr.a.off = outregs.x.bx ;
farptr.a.seg = segregs.ds ;
return ((DPB far *) farptr.ptr) ;
} ;

/* **** DIRECT DISK READ / WRITE ****************************** */

void diskaccess (function, dnum, sector, count, buffer)
    BYTE function ;              /* interrupt function */
    BYTE dnum ;                  /* physical drive number */
    WORD sector ;                /* sector number */
    WORD count ;                 /* sector count */
    BYTE far * buffer ;          /* buffer */
    {
    union REGS inregs, outregs ;
    struct SREGS segregs ;
    LONGPTR farptr ;

    farptr.ptr = buffer ;
    inregs.h.al = dnum ;
    inregs.x.dx = sector ;
    inregs.x.cx = count ;
    inregs.x.bx = farptr.a.off ;
    segregs.ds = farptr.a.seg ;
    int86x (function, &inregs, &outregs, &segregs) ;
    if (outregs.x.cflag) {
        if (function EQ ABS_READ)
            printf ("*** Error During Disk Read ***\n") ;
```

```
            else
              printf ("*** Error During Disk Write ***\n") ;
            exit (1) ;
            } ;
        } ;
/* **** CHECK NAMES FOR MATCH ******************************** */

/* Note that the name arrays are accessed unsigned, so that the
   compare to 0xE5 will be carried out properly */

BOOL match (sname, fname, mtype)
    BYTE    near *sname ;              /* search match name */
    BYTE    near *fname ;              /* file or directory name */
    int     mtype ;                   /* type of match desired */
    {
    int     i ;                       /* index */
    char    near *fext ;              /* file or dir extension */

    fext = fname + 8;                 /* file extension */

/* Check the file status (erased/unerased) against search type */

    if ((((*fname NE 0xe5) AND (mtype EQ IS_ERASED)) OR
        ((*fname EQ 0xe5) AND (mtype NE IS_ERASED)))
        return (NO_MATCH) ;

    if (*fname EQ 0xe5) {              /* ignore 1st character ...*/
        fname++ ;                     /* ... of an erased file */
        sname++ ;
        } ;

    while (fname < (fext+3)) {
        if (*fname EQ toupper(*sname)) {
            fname++ ;
            sname++ ;
            } else                     /* if names differ ... */
            switch (*sname++) {        /* ... find out why */
                case '.':
                    if ((*fname EQ ' ') OR (fname EQ fext)) {
                        fname = fext ;      /* extension check */
                        break ;
                        } ;                 /* else ... */
                    return (NO_MATCH) ;
                case '\\':
                case '\0':
                    if (*fname EQ ' ')       /* end of sname */
```

continued

Listing 11-4. *continued*

```
                        return (IS_MATCH) ;
                default:
                        return (NO_MATCH) ;
                } ;
        } ;
        return (IS_MATCH) ;
    } ;


/*  End of FILE RESCUE.C    */
```

Using Norton Utilities

Norton Utilities are very easy to use, especially when you know something about how MS-DOS disks are laid out. In versions of Norton Utilities prior to 3.0, the DL (DiskLook) and UE (UnErase) programs are the most useful for file recovery. DiskLook examines sector by sector any part of the disk, showing hexadecimal data on the left side of the screen and the ASCII equivalent on the right side. Smart enough to recognize the disk format as well as the type of sectors being read (such as boot, FAT, directory, or data area), the program displays this information on the screen. The program is also capable of displaying a simple map of the disk, similar to the disk layout illustrations in this chapter, showing what each sector or cluster is used for on a per-track basis. It also shows which parts of the disk contain files and which are empty.

The UnErase program is similar to DiskLook. However, UnErase has difficulties if it encounters the types of problems discussed in this chapter, problems such as incomplete files that have been overwritten with new information or several files with complex interwoven chains.

To some extent, the value of Norton Utilities depends on how well you understand the layout of MS-DOS disks and what you know about FAT sectors and directory sectors, and where they begin and end. Even so, you may find using the programs very educational because of the clear and detailed manner in which they display disk data. Another advantage is that safeguards are built into the programs to prevent you from doing any damage to disks.

In version 3.0 of Norton Utilities, the functions of both DiskLook and UnErase are combined in the program NU (Norton Utilities). The functions in this implementation have been improved and include more detailed text interpretations of what is on the disk instead of relying mostly on cryptic hexadecimal data. Only versions 3.0 and higher are capable of working with the 80-track, double-sided, 5¼-inch (high capacity) floppy disks as well as with the 20-megabyte hard disk in the IBM PC AT and compatibles. None of the versions (up to 3.0) are capable of working with 8-inch floppy disks formatted under MS-DOS nor can they work with hard disks that have formats different from those used in

IBM XT and IBM AT systems. Only Norton Utilities version 4.0 is capable of dealing with all disk formats that adhere to standard MS-DOS formatting conventions. Additionally, because of the fancy way in which these programs display information on the screen, they operate only with display equipment compatible or closely compatible with equipment used in IBM systems. However, if you use an IBM PC or compatible system, you'll find Norton Utilities are effective and entertaining because they deal very well with the topics described in this chapter.

Using Ultra Utilities

Ultra Utilities are a set of file recovery programs similar to Norton Utilities. Ultra Utilities are "user-supported" programs, also sometimes known as "freeware," and can be obtained through various channels of public-domain software distribution. Ultra Utilities include a notice to the user that if the programs are found to be useful, a suggested fee be paid to the originators, in return for which the user becomes a registered user and is eligible for future software updates.

Three programs are provided on the main Ultra Utilities disk: U-ZAP, U-FORMAT, and U-FILE. U-ZAP is similar to the Norton Utilities DiskLook program and provides extensive capabilities for modifying any of the contents of a disk. U-FORMAT is a very special program because it provides the capability of formatting individual tracks on a disk. U-FORMAT can even reformat a track without destroying any MS-DOS data stored on it. This can prove very useful on troublesome disks with formatting problems so severe that even MS-DOS can't recover inaccessible data. The U-FILE program has many capabilities of displaying and modifying files on the disk, including recovering erased files.

Ultra Utilities are a fine alternative to Norton Utilities if you are cost-conscious. And don't be dissuaded by the semi-free aspect of this package-Ultra Utilities are very fine programs designed by professionals who use low-cost methods of distribution.

Summary

This chapter has focused on disk layout and file recovery under MS-DOS. The information in this chapter has shown that, if equipped with the necessary information, you can recover erased, damaged, and lost files. Even though the various tools mentioned for recovering files provide varying degrees of simplicity and disk file accessibility in their use, the basic sequence of file recovery outlined in this chapter remains the same.

The next chapter presents a similar topic: recovering data lost in memory. Understanding disk layouts and file storage will help you understand the information in the next chapter.

Recovering Data Lost in Memory

12

LMOST every computer user has at some point lost valuable data in RAM (random access memory). Losing data that's currently in memory can be caused by operator error, hardware malfunction, an elusive bug in a program, or a power failure. In many cases, some if not all of the data lost in memory can be recovered and stored safely to a disk if you're willing to do some patient investigating. Before taking any drastic measures, like resetting the system, any problem short of a power failure or an automatic system reset is worth investigating.

Of course, it's a good idea to experiment with data recovery and explore the memory of your system before something goes wrong. Word processing programs and BASIC interpreters are good starting points in experimenting with data recovery. Note that the procedures for recovering lost data are appropriate only if the malfunction was not severe enough to lock up the entire system. If, however, the MS-DOS prompt returns and you're able to enter commands, you can start searching for the lost data.

Recovering from Word Processing/Test Editing Failures

Probably the easiest way to explore your system memory is to simulate a problem. Load your favorite word processor or test editor, create a short, simple text file, and then exit normally to MS-DOS. Immediately afterwards, load the DEBUG program, and using the D (Display) command, start scanning the contents of memory. DEBUG always assumes memory offset 0100h as the beginning point. Don't worry about setting the segment address (DEBUG defaults to one anyway) but make note of what that address is in case you need to return to it later.

For this exercise, we used the WordStar word processing program on an IBM Personal Computer. If you use a different word processor or a different system, don't worry. Although no two word processing programs utilize memory in exactly the same way (there are even differences between the various WordStar versions), the very nature of the way MD-DOS loads programs aids us in our endeavor. Nearly all word processors or text editors load the program first and use the memory *above* the program to store the text. When we load DEBUG into the system, more often than not DEBUG will overlay the program portion of the word processor or text editor, allowing us to scan upward in memory looking for our lost text. If by chance your favorite text editor is smaller than DEBUG (in terms of code space used), some data may be lost, but on average-sized files the majority of the data will still be there, above DEBUG.

The following examples begin with a sample text file, followed by a description of the contents of memory after loading WordStar and the text file, and then exiting back to MS-DOS.

Load WordStar and create the following TEST.TXT file:

```
xxxx1xxxx2xxxx3xxxx4xxxx5xxxx6xxxx7xxxx8xxxx9x10
xxx11xxx12xxx13xxx14xxx15xxx16xxx17xxx18xxx19x20
xxx21xxx22xxx23xxx24xxx25xxx26xxx27xxx28xxx29x30
xxx31xxx32xxx33xxx34xxx35xxx36xxx37xxx38xxx39x40
xxx41xxx42xxx43xxx44xxx45xxx46xxx47xxx48xxx49x50
xxx51xxx52xxx53xxx54xxx55xxx56xxx57xxx58xxx59x60
xxx61xxx62xxx63xxx64xxx65xxx66xxx67xxx68xxx69x70
xxx71xxx72xxx73xxx74xxx75xxx76xxx77xxx78xxx79x80
xxx81xxx82xxx83xxx84xxx85xxx86xxx87xxx88xxx89x90
xxx91xxx92xxx93xxx94xxx95xxx96xxx97xxx98xxx99100
```

The contents of the file TEST.TXT may look a little strange at first, but the purpose of the text arrangement becomes clear when you see it (or part of it) in memory. This file consists of 100 5-character or 5-byte words. Each word is numbered 1 through 100, which enables us to count the number of portions or words of text we actually see in memory. Note that the last "words" on each line (x10, x20, . . . 100) consist of only three characters. Because we have to accommodate the carriage return and line feed characters at the end of each line, these three-character words become five-character words. Note that some word processor and text editor programs insert only a carriage return character when the Return or Enter key is pressed. Such programs execute the line feed function automatically without actually inserting it in the text. In such cases, expand the last words on each line to four characters (xx10, xx20, . . . x100).

Now exit WordStar by saving the file using Control-KX command (or Control-KD, then X). Immediately load DEBUG and start searching through memory for the lost text. Use the D (Display) command to dump the contents of memory on the screen until you see the sought-after text on the right side of the display. The following code shows what our sample file looked like when we finally found it on our system. (Note that the actual addresses will quite likely be different on your system.)

```
A>debug
-d 7e10
68F8:7E10  00 00 00 00 00 00 00 00-B9 00 78 78 78 78 31 78   ........9.xxxx1x
68F8:7E20  78 78 78 32 78 78 78 78-33 78 78 78 78 34 78 78   xxx2xxxx3xxxx4xx
68F8:7E30  78 78 35 78 78 78 78 36-78 78 78 78 37 78 78 78   xx5xxxx6xxxx7xxx
68F8:7E40  78 38 78 78 78 78 39 78-31 30 0D 0A 78 78 78 31   x8xxxx9x10..xxx1
68F8:7E50  31 78 78 78 31 32 78 78-78 31 33 78 78 78 31 34   1xxx12xxx13xxx14
```

```
68F8:7E60    78 78 78 31 35 78 78 78-31 36 78 78 78 31 37 78    xxx15xxx16xxx17x
68F8:7E70    78 78 31 38 78 78 78 31-39 78 32 30 0D 0A 78 78    xx18xxx19x20..xx
68F8:7E80    78 32 31 78 78 78 32 32-78 78 78 32 33 78 78 78    x21xxx22xxx23xxx
-d
68F8:7E90    32 34 78 78 78 32 35 78-78 78 32 36 78 78 78 32    24xxx25xxx26xxx2
68F8:7EA0    37 78 78 78 32 38 78 78-78 32 39 78 33 30 0D 0A    7xxx28xxx29x30..
68F8:7EB0    78 78 78 33 31 78 78 78-33 32 78 78 78 33 33 78    xxx31xxx32xxx33x
68F8:7EC0    78 78 33 34 78 78 78 33-35 78 78 78 33 36 78 78    xx34xxx35xxx36xx
68F8:7ED0    78 33 37 78 78 78 33 38-78 78 78 33 39 78 34 30    x37xxx38xxx39x40
68F8:7EE0    0D 0A 78 78 78 34 31 78-78 78 34 32 78 78 78 34    ..xxx41xxx42xxx4
68F8:7EF0    33 78 78 78 34 34 78 78-78 34 35 78 78 78 34 36    3xxx44xxx45xxx46
68F8:7F00    78 78 78 34 37 78 78 78-34 38 78 78 78 34 39 78    xxx47xxx48xxx49x
-d
68F8:7F10    35 30 0D 0A 78 78 78 35-31 78 78 78 35 32 78 78    50..xxx51xxx52xx
68F8:7F20    78 35 33 78 78 78 35 34-78 78 78 35 35 78 78 78    x53xxx54xxx55xxx
68F8:7F30    35 36 78 78 78 35 37 78-78 78 35 38 78 78 78 35    56xxx57xxx58xxx5
68F8:7F40    39 78 36 30 0D 0A 78 78-78 36 31 78 78 78 36 32    9x60..xxx61xxx62
68F8:7F50    78 78 78 36 33 78 78 78-36 34 78 78 78 36 35 78    xxx63xxx64xxx65x
68F8:7F60    78 78 36 36 78 78 78 36-37 78 78 78 36 38 78 78    xx66xxx67xxx68xx
68F8:7F70    78 36 39 78 37 30 0D 0A-78 78 78 37 31 78 78 78    x69x70..xxx71xxx
68F8:7F80    37 32 78 78 78 37 33 78-78 78 37 34 78 78 78 37    72xxx73xxx74xxx7
-d
68F8:7F90    35 78 78 78 37 36 78 78-78 37 37 78 78 78 37 38    5xxx76xxx77xxx78
68F8:7FA0    78 78 78 37 39 78 38 30-0D 0A 78 78 78 38 31 78    xxx79x80..xxx81x
68F8:7FB0    78 78 38 32 78 78 78 38-33 78 78 78 38 34 78 78    xx82xxx83xxx84xx
68F8:7FC0    78 38 35 78 78 78 38 36-78 78 78 38 37 78 78 78    x85xxx86xxx87xxx
68F8:7FD0    38 38 78 78 78 38 39 78-39 30 0D 0A 78 78 78 39    88xxx89x90..xxx9
68F8:7FE0    31 78 78 78 39 32 78 78-78 39 33 78 78 78 39 34    1xxx92xxx93xxx94
68F8:7FF0    78 78 78 39 35 78 78 78-39 36 78 78 78 39 37 78    xxx95xxx96xxx97x
68F8:8000    78 78 39 38 78 78 78 39-39 31 30 30 0D 0A 1A 1A    xx98xxx99100....
-d
68F8:8010    1A 1A 1A 1A 1A 1A 1A 1A-1A 1A 00 E8 EC 01 E8 C2    ..........hl.hB
68F8:8020    ......
```

Write down the address where you found the test. In our case this was 68F8:7E10 (hex). Now, continue scanning memory until you no longer see the text you wish to recover and write down the last address (68F8:8019 in our example).

We see in the preceding screen that the entire file is still resident in memory. If we have created a file that is larger than the available memory, only the part of the file last edited is resident in memory. By scanning the memory beyond the limits shown in the preceding screen, we found that on our system 19,449 bytes of text may be retained in memory. If we could recover that many bytes of text from memory, we could avoid a lot of retyping! In the previous example, however, we know we've reached the end of text at location 8019 because that's where the string of Control-Z (ASCII 1A hex) values end. These values are required by Word Star as end-of-file markers, so these values are written to the disk when the file is saved.

The following shows how text stranded in memory can be saved to the disk while you are still in DEBUG.

```
-n test.sav
-h 8019 7e1a
FE33  01FF
-r bx
BX 0000
:
-r cx
CX 0000
:1ff
-r
AX = 0000 BX = 0000 CX = 01FF DX = 0000 SP = FFEE BP = 0000 SI = 0000 DI = 0000
DS = 68F8 ES = 68F8 SS = 68F8 CS = 68F8 IP = 0100   NV UP DI PL NZ NA PO NC
68F8:0100 C9           DB      C9
-w 7e1a
Writing 01FF bytes
-q
A>dir test.sav
 Volume in drive A has no label
 Directory of A:\
TEST    SAV      522   4-09-85 11:03a
        1 File(s)    188416 bytes free
A>
```

The first step in this example is to specify a file name that DEBUG uses for disk read and write operations by using the N (Name) command. A new file name should be used, such as TEST.SAV. Next, use the offset address of the beginning of text (7E1A) and the ending address (8019) to calculate how many bytes should be written to the disk. DEBUG's built-in H ("hexarithmetic") command is a useful tool for calculating the result we need. When specifying the address values after the H command, make sure you specify the ending address before the starting address because the difference must be a positive integer. In the preceding screen, the result on the left is the sum of the two hexadecimal address values. The difference between the two address values (on the right) represents the number of bytes that we want to write to the disk. Load this value into the CX register in preparation for the W (Write) command. Note that the BX register is also used with CX for values greater than FFFF (otherwise it should contain zero). We then write the data to the disk specifying the starting address.

When the file is saved and you've returned to MS-DOS, type the file to the screen to verify its contents. You can later combine this file with other parts of the recovered file by using your word processor.

But what do we do when not all of the lost text can be found in RAM memory? WordStar, like most other word processing programs, constantly shuffles text in and out of memory as you move around in the text being edited. If you've been editing an existing file, say TEST.TXT, WordStar creates a file called TEST.$$$, which is used to store the new edited text. When you finish editing and save the edit session to disk, the program renames TEST.TXT to TEXT.BAK (overwriting the old TEST.BAK if it exists) and renames TEST.$$$ to TEST.TXT. Thus, in normal operation, TEST.$$$ is never seen in the directory when you return to MS-DOS. However, if the program fails abnormally, you find TEST.$$$ listed in the directory. If not all the text can be found in memory using DEBUG, check the contents of the $$$ file for the rest of the text. If the status of your file is not immediately obvious by looking at the directory listing, you may have to resort to a disk utility (such as Norton Utilities or Ultra Utilities described in the previous chapter) that shows hidden information on the disk. Before doing so, however, check the status of the disk with the CHKDSK program. This lets you know whether there are any stranded clusters on the disk. If stranded clusters are introduced to the disk after the failed edit session, part of the lost text may be in these lost clusters. You can recover them by specifying the /F parameter with CHKDSK but do so only after you've examined the contents of RAM memory and have saved stranded text to the disk.

As mentioned previously, the ways in which various word processing and text editing programs utilize memory differ greatly. All have different locations in memory for their work space. Some have larger work spaces than others. Some programs have multiple areas of memory for text manipulation, sometimes called buffers, which can complicate things even further. However, if you've never before tried to recover stranded data from memory, the previous examples illustrate some useful tools and techniques.

Recovering BASIC Programs from Memory

Have you ever done extensive work on a program using a BASIC interpreter only to discover that, after testing the program, a "Return to MS-DOS" command embedded in the program terminated the interpreter before you had a chance to save the program to the disk? If the program is short (20 lines or fewer), this is a minor frustration. If the program is long, unexpected termination of the interpreter is disastrous.

Just as we were able to recover lost text from memory, we also should be able to recover "lost" BASIC programs because they must reside in memory in their entirety for the convenience of the interpreter. And for those interpreters that always deal with normal ASCII program text, the techniques described previously for recovering text from memory can be applied. But this is not the case with interpreters that deal with programs in "protected" mode or programs that are *tokenized*. A tokenized program, as seen by the interpreter, is a series of hexadecimal instruction values and absolute integer values. An ASCII program, on the other hand, consists of a series of two-digit ASCII values for each character or number, thus increasing the size of the file considerably.

Microsoft BASIC and IBM BASIC are the most popular examples of interpreters that deal with tokenized programs. Although these interpreters can read programs in standard ASCII format, they default to the tokenized state. They convert an ASCII program to its tokenized equivalent when it's loaded by the interpreter. The problem with trying to recover a lost tokenized BASIC program in memory is that it is virtually impossible to decipher with DEBUG's D (Display) command. So a slightly different approach must be taken.

The following example shows how to recover a program using Microsoft/IBM BASIC on the IBM Personal Computer. A variation of this procedure is required for other BASIC interpreters or different machines, but the following example provides some tips on how to approach the problem of program recovery on other machines.

Immediately after losing the program, the first step is to load DEBUG. According to the technical manual for the system, the address of the BASIC segment (where the beginning of our program is) can be found by examining location 0050:0010. Use the D command to display the first two values at this location. These values vary depending on the version of MS-DOS, the version of the BASIC interpreter, and the amount of memory installed in your system. Study the following program code and explanation.

```
A>debug
-d 0050:0010 l2
0050:0010 73 6B          ←BASIC segment address
-d 6b73:30 l2            ←examine the segment (reverse the bytes) at offset 0030
6B73:0030 EF 11          ←this is the beginning address of the lost program
-f 6b73:11ee l1 ff       ←enter an FF at the beginning address of the lost program at
                            offset−1 (again, reverse the two beginning−address bytes)
-d 6b73:358 l2           ←locate the ending address of the lost program at offset 0358
6B73:0358 88 12          ←this is the ending address
-h 1288 11ee             ←calculate the number of bytes used by the program (reverse the
                            2-byte ending address as well)
2476 009A                ←the second number is the difference, and therefore the
                            program's length
-r cx                    ←load the program's length into the
CX000                      CX register
-n %test.bas             ←establish the file specification in which the program is to be
                            stored
-w 6b73:11ee             ←write the bytes starting at the program's beginning address
Writing 009A bytes
-q                       ←return to MS-DOS
A>
```

When you return to the MS-DOS prompt, check the recovered file by loading it in the BASIC interpreter and listing it to the screen. The contents of the file are tokenized, so it can't be read any other way. The contents of the file should be intact.

Summary

This chapter shows some of the techniques that can be used to recover data stranded in memory. The two types of programs covered, Word Processors/Text Editors and BASIC Interpreters, are the most likely to be involved when data is lost in memory. Similar problems with other programs, such as database managers, for example, or communications programs, can often be approached using these techniques. If you lose important data in memory because of any circumstance other than a power failure or system reset, spending your time to investigate recovery techniques is well worth the effort.

COMPATIBILITY PART IV

Differences between MS-DOS Versions

13

S INCE the introduction of the first version of MS-DOS in 1981, the operating system has been enhanced to accommodate new hardware environments, fix problems, and generally improve its operation. Although many of these enhancements resulted in more powerful capabilities, they have also caused a few headaches because the new functions have not been compatible with older versions of MS-DOS. In order to keep the value of these enhancements in proper perspective, this chapter has information that will help you determine the compatibility among the different versions of MS-DOS. The information in this chapter is especially useful if you're using assembly language to develop your programs.

Except for those commands that are, by design, tools for programmers, such as the debugger (DEBUG) and linker (LINK), new and enhanced MS-DOS commands are of relatively little use to programmers. Changes that are of special interest to a programmer include MS-DOS interrupts, function calls, error codes, floppy and hard disk formats, and file manipulation. These areas can be dealt with fairly easily because topics such as function calls exist in all implementations of a given MS-DOS version.

Other areas, such as memory mapping, cannot be dealt with generically because they often vary according to the hardware environment for which an implementation of MS-DOS is targeted. This is the case with the IBM Personal Computer and close compatibles. Systems with radically different hardware architectures have different memory mapping schemes specific to the implementation of MS-DOS. Even among some of the more "standard" areas, such as interrupts, critical differences exist.

Therefore, a programmer needs to know the dos and don'ts when developing an application program. The differences are especially important if you're developing a program that is intended to have as wide a distribution as possible. Remember that there are different machine-specific versions of MS-DOS and that there are also lots of machines with different hardware architectures and implementations of MS-DOS. Simply following the *MS-DOS Technical Manual* can be very misleading if you're developing a program that is intended to run under *all* implementations of MS-DOS.

This chapter is not meant to replace the *MS-DOS Technical Manual*. Its intent is rather to present an overview of the differences between the versions of MS-DOS and thus complement the technical manuals of all versions of MS-DOS.

The information is divided into topics by which the differences between all the versions (from 1.0 through 4.0) are presented. Where appropriate, this chapter includes specific technical information and tips about suggested procedures and things to avoid, depending on the nature of the application program you're developing.

General Compatibility Recommendations

Various degrees of compatibility are available to a programmer. In most cases, the goal is total compatibility. However, because we generally like to design "slick" programs, we often take advantage of the "new and improved" functions built into our implementation of MS-DOS, such as fancy screen functions or special-purpose interrupts, and frequently forget the consequences of noncompatibility. Choosing a degree of compatibility is often the compromise we make. If we must achieve total compatibility, the following rules are useful.

1. Do not under any circumstances use any 8086-family INT (interrupt) instruction, except those that are designated as *MS-DOS interrupts*.
2. Never write data to any absolute memory location outside of your program. Let MS-DOS handle memory usage.
3. Never use the 8086-family IN and OUT instructions.
4. Avoid using instructions that are provided only by the 80188, 80186, 80286, and 80386 microprocessors, as follows:

   PUSH *immediate* (push immediate)
   PUSHA (push all registers)
   POPA (pop all registers)
   SHR >1 (shift right with immediate value greater than 1)
   SHL >1 (shift left with immediate value greater than 1)
   IMUL *dest.-reg.,source,immediate* (multiply immediate signed integer)
   INS *source-string,port* (in string)
   OUTS *port,dest.-string* (out string)
   ENTER (enter procedure)
   LEAVE (leave procedure)
   BOUND (detect value out of range)

   Avoid using the instruction POP CS because it functions properly only with the 8088 and 8086 microprocessors. Be aware of all the other differences in operation between the various processors in the 8086 family.

   Avoid all 80286/80386 instructions:

   LGDT, LIDT, and LLDT (load descriptor table)
   INSB (input from port using bytes)
   OUTSB (output string to port using bytes)
   ARPL (adjust requested privilege level—protected mode)
   CLTS (clear task switched flag—protected mode)
   LAR (load access rights—protected mode)

LMSW (load machine status word—protected mode)
LSL (load segment limit—protected mode)
LTR (load task register—protected mode)
SGDT, SIDT, and SLDT (store descriptor table—protected mode)
SMSW (store machine status word—protected mode)
STR (store task register—protected mode)
VERR and VERW (verify read or write—protected mode)

Avoid all 80386-only instructions:

MOV *special-registers* (move to/from special registers)
MOVSX (move with sign extend)
MOVZX (move with zero extend)
OUTSW (output string to port using words)
BSF and BSR (bit scan)
BT, BTC, BTR, and BTS (bit tests)
CWDE (convert word to extended double)
INSW (input from port using words)
LFS, LGS, and LSS (load far pointer)
POPAD (pop all into 32-bit registers)
POPFD (pop flags into 32-bit flags register)
PUSHAD (push all 32-bit registers)
PUSHFD (push 32-bit flags register)
SET *condition* (set conditionally)
SHLD and SHRD (double-precision shift)

5. If the machine you're using to develop a program has routines stored in ROM, never call these routines. Don't even attempt to read them.

6. For absolute compatibility, never use an MS-DOS function call that is supported only in MS-DOS versions above 1.0. However, since versions of MS-DOS prior to 2.0 are no longer supported by Microsoft and IBM, setting the minimum version to 2.0 provides you with more flexibility.

7. Always make sure that information written to the screen consists only of standard ASCII characters (00 through 7F hexadecimal). Avoid using any other characters, such as those in the extended character set of IBM PCs and compatibles.

If you find that you must break any of the first five rules, you might as well break rule 6 because your first option would be to write a device driver targeted for a machine that would otherwise be incompatible. And because installable device drivers are supported only under MS-DOS version 2.0 and above, you'll find yourself using function calls not supported by MS-DOS versions 1.0 and 1.1. If you need (or want) to break rule 7, write a device driver for the target machine or a "universal" installation program that can be used to customize the application program for a variety of terminals and monitors. The installation program must, of course, at least follow rule 7.

Because one solution to incompatibility might be a device driver, we find ourselves already breaking rule 6, which introduces another level of compatibility that needs to be considered. In many cases, you will want to break rule

6 intentionally because not all versions of MS-DOS provide a particular function call that you like or need to use. For example, if your application program made extensive use of tree-structured directories, you probably would want to use function calls 39 through 3B, in which case the level of compatibility would be restricted to MS-DOS versions 2.0 and higher and would exclude versions 1.0 and 1.1. Similarly, if your program needs to make use of the networking functions supported by MS-DOS 3.1, the program would not be compatible with MS-DOS versions 1.0 through 2.1.

Never forget to state plainly the compatibility restrictions of your program, either in the source code or in the documentation (preferably both). If your program is to be made commercially available, make sure that compatibility restrictions (or the lack of restrictions!) are clearly stated both in the packaging and in advertisements.

If you develop a program that is designed to operate under any version of MS-DOS but that contains some routines which can be optionally executed if a particular version of MS-DOS is being used, use function 30h (Get DOS Version Number) to control whether or not certain routines are executed. Although this function is provided only in MS-DOS versions 2.0 and higher, it can be executed using versions 1.0 and 1.1 without ill effects as long as the precautionary steps described under *Invoking DOS Functions* in your MS-DOS manual are followed.

To use this function, load 30h into the AH register. When int 21h is executed, the major version number is returned in register AL and the minor version in register AH. If AL contains 00, you can assume that the version of MS-DOS is either 1.0 or 1.1. Any other number in AL indicates the version number. For example, if you are using MS-DOS version 2.00, 02 is found in AL and 00 is found in AH. If you are using MS-DOS version 3.10, you will find 03 in AL and 10 in AH. Even if you don't need to control the optional execution of certain routines, this function allows you to control the display of a friendly message if a user attempts to run the program under an incompatible version of MS-DOS. The routine in Listing 13-1 can be implemented in your programs to accomplish this function.

Listing 13-1. Routine to Determine the MS-DOS Version

```
; ROUTINE TO DETERMINE THE VERSION OF MS-DOS UNDER WHICH
; THE PROGRAM CONTAINING THIS ROUTINE IS RUNNING
;
; NOTE: Make sure that the following statements are defined
; either in the data segment or in the data area of the
; code segment in your program:
;
;       majver db ?     ; major version number (hex)
;       minver db ?     ; minor version number (hex)
;
;
getdosver       proc    near    ; change to far if needed
```

```
;
        push    ax                  ; save registers
        push    bx
        push    cx
;
        mov     ah,30h              ; get the function number ready
        int     21h                 ; execute the MS-DOS function call
;
        cmp     al,0                ; see whether it's pre-version 2.0
        jnz     dos2plus            ; if not, it's version 2.00 or above
        mov     al,1                ; major version is 1.00 (because we
        mov     ah,0                ; know AH still contains the function
                                    ; number (30h), we won't be able
                                    ; to find out what the minor version
                                    ; is, so we assume the worst case:
                                    ; version 1.00)
;
dos2plus:
        mov     majver,al           ; save major version
        mov     minver,ah           ; save minor version
;
        pop     cx                  ; restore registers
        pop     bx
        pop     ax
;
        ret                         ; return
;
getdosver       endp
```

In the previous subroutine, you can do several things with the version number stored in the two variables *majver* and *minver*. Each number can be converted to decimal ASCII for output to the screen with a message, or you can use these variables to control whether or not certain parts of the program are to be executed.

High-Level Language Considerations

If you're writing a program with a high-level language, be aware of the specifications of the particular compiler or interpreter being used. If the product specifications state that your compiler or interpreter runs only under a particular version of MS-DOS, your compiled or interpreted programs probably don't function under an earlier version. This is especially true for BASIC interpreters, such as Microsoft/IBM BASIC and GWBASIC because new versions of these interpreters are often released to complement new versions of MS-DOS.

MS-DOS Interrupts

The software interrupts defined for use by MS-DOS are consistent among all versions except interrupt 2Fh, which has been added to version 3.0. Table 13-1 lists the interrupts.

Table 13-1. MS-DOS Interrupts

Interrupt		MS-DOS Version								
Int	**Description**	**1.0**	**1.1**	**2.0**	**2.1**	**3.0**	**3.1**	**3.2**	**3.3**	**4.0**
20	Program Terminate									
21	Function Request									
22	Terminate Address									
23	Ctrl/Break Exit Address									
24	Critical Error Handler Vector					Yes				
25	Absolute Disk Read									
26	Absolute Disk Write									
27	Terminate But Stay Resident									
28	Reserved				(Used internally by MS-DOS)					
29 – 2E	(Reserved)					(Reserved)				
2F	Multiplex Interrupt			No			Yes			
30 – 66	Reserved					(Reserved)				
67	Expanded Memory System Interface	No			(see Note 1)					Yes
68 – 6F	Reserved					(Reserved)				

Note 1: The Expanded Memory System (EMS), as defined by both the Lotus/Intel/Microsoft (LIM) and AST/Quadram/Ashton-Tate (AQA) specifications, is accessible through int 67h in all versions of MS-DOS beginning with version 2.0. However, only MS-DOS versions 4.0 and higher have int 67h officially reserved specifically for accessing EMS. See Chapter 7 for information on EMS int 67h functions.

Many machines have several interrupts not listed in Table 13-1. These interrupts are defined for special uses, such as accessing the BIOS (basic input/

output system) routines or communicating with serial communications ports. Don't confuse these interrupts with those defined for use with MS-DOS. Only those interrupts described in your *MS-DOS Technical Manual* are true MS-DOS interrupts. In order to maintain compatibility with all implementations of MS-DOS, avoid using any interrupts that are not true *MS-DOS interrupts*. Refer to Appendix B for information on undocumented interrupts.

Function Calls

The use of function calls is probably the most important compatibility factor when programming in assembly language. Because almost all operations normally performed by MS-DOS can be initiated by function calls, you can avoid the use of interrupts (except int 21) and BIOS calls. By using MS-DOS function calls, you also eliminate any need to include in your programs certain types of routines, such as those that manipulate files. If blindingly fast execution of your programs is not crucial, it's worthwhile to let MS-DOS perform all standard operations by means of function calls. MS-DOS performs function calls fast enough for most situations.

Performing Function Calls the Standard Way

When the first version of MS-DOS was introduced, two methods were provided to perform function calls. The first is recommended for use with all versions of MS-DOS and the procedure is as follows:

1. Save the contents of the AX, BX, CX, and DX registers as appropriate by pushing them onto the stack.
2. Place the function number in the AH register.
3. Place other data in the registers specified for the particular function to be executed if and when appropriate.
4. Execute the int 21h instruction.
5. Depending on the function executed, variable data is returned in specified registers that can be later read and used by your program. Some functions don't return anything.
6. Perform the desired operation, if needed, based on the returned data from the function just executed.
7. Restore the original contents of the registers.

The previous procedure is recommended for all versions of MS-DOS. The second method is described next.

Performing Function Calls in Compatibility Mode

The second method that MS-DOS provides for compatibility with other operating systems applies specifically to CP/M-80 and CP/M-86. This method doesn't really provide the capability of running CP/M programs under MS-DOS. It only simplifies the conversion of CP/M programs to MS-DOS by not always requiring the redefinition of the function call process. You will, however, probably have to change many of the function numbers. This method works only with MS-DOS functions 0 through 24h. You might also encounter difficulties with register usage of some function calls, so this method should be avoided unless you want to test a program before it has been fully converted. MS-DOS requires that function calls using this second method be made by using the following procedure:

1. Save the contents of the AX, BX, CX, and DX registers as appropriate by pushing them onto the stack.

2. Place the function number in the CL register. (Only function numbers 0 through 24h may be used.)

3. Place other data in the registers specified for the particular function to be executed as desired.

4. Make an intrasegment call to location 5 in the current code segment. This location contains a long call to the MS-DOS function dispatcher.

5. Depending on the function executed, variable data is returned in specified registers that can be later read and used by your program. Some functions don't return anything. *Note:* This procedure always wipes out the contents of the AX register. All other registers, however, are affected in the same manner as when the standard function call procedure is followed.

6. Restore the original contents of the registers.

And Yet Another Method (MS-DOS Versions 2.00 and Higher Only)

A third method for making function calls was introduced in MS-DOS version 2.00. This method can be used with higher versions as well, but it doesn't operate correctly with any previous versions. The third method is accomplished in the following manner.

1. Save the contents of the AX, BX, CX, and DX registers as appropriate by pushing them onto the stack.

2. Place the function number in the AH register.

3. Place other data in the registers specified for the particular function to be executed.

4. Make a long call to offset hex 50 in the program segment prefix.

5. Depending on the function executed, variable data is returned in specified registers that can be later read and used by your program. Some functions don't return anything.

6. Restore the original contents of the registers by POPping the stack.

With the release of MS-DOS version 3.10, both Microsoft and IBM have recommended that this method not be used. Why then was it introduced? One possible use of the method may explain why it was introduced. Offset 50 hex in the PSP (program segment prefix) usually contains an int 21h instruction. By using the method described previously, the programmer has channeled all MS-DOS function code accesses (excluding other interrupts) through one location. By altering the instruction located at offset 50 hex, you can redirect all of the program's MS-DOS accesses. Was this an abandoned attempt of Microsoft's to implement multitasking? Only Microsoft knows for sure.

Functions Supported in Different Versions

Table 13-2 lists all the MS-DOS functions supported in versions 1.0 through 3.1 and indicates which functions are new for certain versions.

Table 13-2. MS-DOS Functions

Function		MS-DOS Version								
Num Hex	Description	1.0	1.1	2.0	2.1	3.0	3.1	3.2	3.3	4.0
0	Program Terminate									
1	Keyboard Input									
2	Display Output									
3	Auxiliary Input									
4	Auxiliary Output									
5	Printer Output									
6	Direct Console I/O									
7	Direct Console Input Without Echo									
8	Console Input Without Echo				Yes					
9	Print String									
A	Buffered Keyboard Input									
B	Check Standard Input Status									
C	Clear Keyboard Buffer and Invoke Keyboard Function									
D	Disk Reset									
E	Select Disk									

continued

Table 13-2. *continued*

Function		MS-DOS Version								
Num **Hex**	**Description**	**1.0**	**1.1**	**2.0**	**2.1**	**3.0**	**3.1**	**3.2**	**3.3**	**4.0**
F	Open File									
10	Close File									
11	Search for First Entry									
12	Search for Next Entry									
13	Delete File				Yes					
14	Sequential Read									
15	Sequential Write									
16	Create File									
17	Rename File									
18	(Reserved)	///								
19	Current Disk									
1A	Set Disk Transfer Address									
1B	Allocation Table Information				Yes					
1C	Allocation Table Information Specific Device									
1D– 20	(Reserved)	/// /// ///								
21	Random Read									
22	Random Write									
23	File Size									
24	Set Relative Record Field				Yes					
25	Set Interrupt Vector									
26	Create New Program Segment									

Function			MS-DOS Version								
Num Hex	**Description**		**1.0**	**1.1**	**2.0**	**2.1**	**3.0**	**3.1**	**3.2**	**3.3**	**4.0**
27	Random Block Read		Yes								
28	Random Block Write										
29	Parse Filename										
2A	Get Date										
2B	Set Date										
2C	Get Time										
2D	Set Time										
2E	Set/Reset Verify Switch										
2F	Get Disk Transfer Address (DTA)		No		Yes						
30	Get DOS Version Number										
31	Terminate but Remain Resident										
32	(Reserved)		///								
33	Ctrl/Break Check		No		Yes						
34	(Reserved)		///								
35	Get Vector		No		Yes						
36	Get Disk Free Space										
37	(Reserved)		///								
38	Country Dependent Information	Get	No		Yes						
		Set			No		Yes				
39	Create Subdirectory (MKDIR)		No		Yes						
3A	Remove Subdirectory (RMDIR)										

continued

Table 13-2. *continued*

Num Hex	Description	1.0	1.1	2.0	2.1	3.0	3.1	3.2	3.3	4.0
	Function				**MS-DOS Version**					
3B	Change Current Directory (CHDIR)									
3C	Create a File (CREAT)					Yes				
3D	Open a File (normal)									
3D	Open a Network File	No	No			Yes				
3E	Close a File Handle									
3F	Read from a File or Device									
40	Write to a File or Device									
41	Delete a File from a Specified Directory (UNLINK)									
42	Move File Read/Write Pointer (LSEEK)									
43	Change File Mode (CHMOD)					Yes				
44	I/O Control for Devices (IOCTL)									
	00 Get Device Information									
	01 Set Device Information									
	02 Read from Character Device									
	03 Write to Character Device									
	04 Read from Block Device									
	05 Write to Block Device									

Function		MS-DOS Version								
Num Hex	**Description**	**1.0**	**1.1**	**2.0**	**2.1**	**3.0**	**3.1**	**3.2**	**3.3**	**4.0**
44	06 Get Input Status	No		Yes						
	07 Get Output Status									
	08 Is Block Device Changeable?	No				Yes				
	09 Is Logical Device Local or Remote?	No					Yes			
	0A Is Handle Local or Remote?									
	0B Change Sharing Retry Count	No				Yes				
	0C Generic IOCTL Handle Request (code page switching)	No								Yes
	0D Block Device Generic IOCTL Request	No						Yes		
	0E Get Logical Device									
	0F Set Logical Device									
45	Duplicate a File Handle (DUP)	No		Yes						
46	Force a Duplicate of a Handle (CDUP)									
47	Get Current Directory									
48	Allocate Memory									
49	Free Allocated Memory									
4A	Modify Allocated Memory Blocks (SETBLOCK)									

continued

Table 13-2. *continued*

Function		MS-DOS Version								
Num Hex	**Description**	**1.0**	**1.1**	**2.0**	**2.1**	**3.0**	**3.1**	**3.2**	**3.3**	**4.0**
4B	Load or Execute a Program (EXEC)	No				Yes				
4C	Terminate a Process (EXIT)									
4D	Get Return Code of a Sub-Process (WAIT)									
4E	Find First Matching File (FIND FIRST)									
4F	Find Next Matching File									
50– 53	(Reserved)	///								
54	Get Verify Setting	No		Yes						
55	(Reserved)	///								
56 57	Rename a File Get/Set a File's Date and Time									
58	(Reserved)	///								
59	Get Extended Error	No				Yes				
5A	Create Temporary File									
5B	Create New File									
5C	Lock/Unlock File Access									
5D	(Reserved)	///								
5E	Lock/Unlock File Access	No					Yes			
	00 Get Machine Name									
	02 Set Printer Setup									

Function		MS-DOS Version								
Num Hex	Description	1.0	1.1	2.0	2.1	3.0	3.1	3.2	3.3	4.0
5E	03 Get Printer Setup	No					Yes			
5F	02 Get Redirection List Entry	No					Yes			
	03 Redirect a Device									
	04 Cancel Redirection									
60 61	(Reserved)	///								
62	Get Program Segment Prefix (PSP) Address	No				Yes				
63 64	(Reserved)	///								
65	Get Extended Country Information	No							Yes	
66	Get/Set Global Code Page									
67	Set Handle Count									
68	Commit File									
69– 6B	(Reserved)	///								
6C	Extended Open/Create	No								Yes

In view of how MS-DOS functions are defined in the various versions as shown in Table 13-2, the range of functions can be divided into "functional" groups, which, incidentally, tend to define boundaries between different versions of MS-DOS, but not always. These groups are described in the following paragraphs.

Program Terminate Group

The only function in this group is function 0. This function is almost identical to the int 20h interrupt. Although int 20h is defined as Program Terminate in almost all implementations of MS-DOS, you should use function 0 instead so that the use of the INT instruction is avoided. You should be aware that the manuals for MS-DOS versions 2.0 and higher recommend that function 4Ch (Terminate a Process, also known as EXIT) be used as the "preferred" method to terminate a program. However, function 4Ch doesn't exist in versions prior to 2.00.

Following the manual's advice for terminating a program is a good idea. We highly recommend that you always use function 4Ch to terminate your programs for MS-DOS versions 2.00 and higher. If you want your programs to run under all versions, use the Get DOS Version function (30h) to determine which program terminate code to use: Use function 0 for MS-DOS versions 1.0 and 1.1, and use function 4Ch for all other versions.

Standard Character Device Input/Output Group (01h – 0Ch)

This group includes functions 01 through 0Ch. They are used for input from the keyboard, and output to the console display, output to the printer, and as input and output to and from the auxiliary (logical) devices. These functions operate the same way throughout all versions of MS-DOS and are similar in nature to the equivalent range of functions in CP/M.

Standard File Management Group (0Dh – 24h, 27h – 29h)

This group includes functions 0Dh through 24h and 27h through 29h. Using these functions to manipulate files allows compatibility with all versions of MS-DOS. Some of these functions are similar to the equivalent range of functions used in CP/M. Although some fancier functions for file manipulation were introduced in MS-DOS 2.00 (described next), carefully consider the compatibility implications when using them. The section on file manipulation towards the end of this chapter also contains some important information that you should know about when deciding which group of functions to use.

Standard Nondevice Functions (25h, 26h, 2Ah – 2Eh)

This group includes functions 25h, 26h, and 2Ah through 2Eh. Note that function 2Eh is the highest function supported in MS-DOS versions prior to 2.00. These functions perform a variety of different tasks that aren't related to devices: retrieving and setting the current time and date, setting the interrupt vector, creating a new program segment, and setting or resetting the verify switch. All of these functions are specific to MS-DOS, and equivalents are not found in CP/M. All of these functions perform well in all versions of MS-DOS, but special attention should be given to function 25h (Set Interrupt Vector). This function requires two things before it is executed: the address of the interrupt handling routine must be loaded into the DX register and the data segment (DS:DX), and the interrupt number must be loaded into the AL register. Because this function deals with interrupts, be careful with its use because it may make your program incompatible with other implementations of MS-DOS and hardware environments.

Extended (General) Function Group (2Fh − 38h, 4Ch − 4Fh, 54h − 57h, 59h − 5Fh, 62h)

This group of functions crosses the boundaries of MS-DOS versions 2.00 through 3.10. Functions 59h through 5Ch and 62h exist only in versions 3.00 and higher, and functions 5Eh and 5Fh exist only in versions 3.10 and higher. None of these functions are available under MS-DOS versions below 2.00. Additionally, as of MS-DOS version 3.10, functions 32h, 34h, 37h, 50h through 53h, 55h, 58h, 5Dh, 60h, and 61h are reserved (not defined for use). Functions existing in all versions also work consistently among them, with the following exceptions.

1. ***Function 38h (Country Dependent Information).*** Under MS-DOS versions 3.00 and higher, this function can be used to set country-dependent information as well as to retrieve the information. However, in versions starting with 2.00 up to (but not including) 3.00, the function can be used only to retrieve information.

2. ***Function 44h (I/O Control for Devices) [IOCTL].*** Has two new additional parameters in MS-DOS version 3.00 to support device drivers (AL = 08h to check for removable media and AL = 0Bh to change the sharing retry count on a block device). In MS-DOS 3.10, two more parameters were added to check for redirection on a network (AL = 09h checks devices, whereas AL = 0Ah checks file or device handles).

3. ***Functions 5Eh and 5Fh.*** These functions are supported only under versions 3.1 and higher and are used only in network environments. Each is subdivided into several subfunctions. They are loaded into the AX register as four-digit hexadecimal (16-bit) function numbers, with the last two digits representing the specific function (or subfunction). Function 5E00h is used to retrieve the name of a machine connected to the same network as the machine making the function call. Function 5E02h is used to initialize a printer connected to a network that is shared by several computers. Functions 5F02h through 5F04h are used to control redirection of data throughout a network: 5F03h redirects a device, 5F02h retrieves redirection information, and 5F04h cancels redirection.

Directory Group (39h − 3Bh, 47h)

This group consists of functions 39h through 3Bh and 47h, provided under MS-DOS versions 2.00 and higher. These functions complement the subdirectory commands: 39h creates a subdirectory (MKDIR or MD), 3Ah removes a directory (RMDIR or RD), and 3Bh changes the current directory (CHDIR or CD). Function 47h is used to retrieve the current-directory information (as if the CD command were entered without any parameters).

Memory/Process Management Group (48h − 4Bh)

Several functions added to MS-DOS version 2.00 can be used for the management of processes and memory. Most of the functions in this group deal with controlling memory allocation. The last function, 4Bh, is useful for programs that call and load other programs or overlays. Note that function 4Ch, Terminate a Process (EXIT), should always be used in programs that are called and loaded by function 4Bh.

By now it is clear that maintaining a total or reasonable degree of compatibility can be complex and rather frustrating. It's always good practice to decide beforehand what level of compatibility you want to achieve and then make note of the MS-DOS functions you can use.

Error Codes

The errors generated by MS-DOS, their types, and the way they're handled have changed considerably from earlier versions of MS-DOS. Not only have new error codes been introduced in later versions, but new mechanisms of error reporting have been introduced as well. The following paragraphs describe the differences in error handling among the versions of MS-DOS.

Critical or Hard Error Codes (via Int 24h)

In MS-DOS version 1.0, the process of returning error codes is handled exclusively by the int 24h interrupt vector. All of these error codes represent errors that are hardware-related and are considered serious or critical in nature. These same codes and their reporting mechanism are supported in all later versions, although some new error codes were introduced in MS-DOS version 2.0.

For an application program to respond to this error-reporting mechanism, the program's initialization code should save the int 24h vector and replace the vector with one pointing to the program's custom error routine. Before the program terminates, the original int 24h vector should be restored to its original state. Up to seven codes can be returned through this mechanism under MS-DOS version 1.0, up to 13 codes under MS-DOS version 2.0, and up to 16 codes under MS-DOS versions 3.0 and higher.

Table 13-3 lists the codes and indicates which are supported only in MS-DOS versions 2.00 and higher. The critical error codes shown in Table 13-3 can also be retrieved through another error-reporting mechanism introduced in MS-DOS version 2.0. Under this version, certain function calls return error codes when an error condition occurs. This mechanism is described in the paragraph following the table.

Function Call Error-Return Codes (MS-DOS Versions 2.0 and Higher Only)

Beginning with version 2.0, some function calls return error codes in certain registers if an error results after the function executes. If an error occurs, the carry flag is set, and the appropriate register can be examined (if supported by the function) for the error code. If the carry flag is clear, you can assume no error occurred. The critical or hard errors described previously (determined via the int 24h mechanism) are also presented through this mechanism, although different code values are used. Under versions of MS-DOS from 2.0 to 3.1, the following functions return an error code in the AX register if the carry flag is set after execution: 38h through 4Bh, 4Eh, 4Fh, 56h, 57h, 5Ah through 5Ch, and 5E00h through 5E04h. The AL half of AX should always be examined for the error code because some functions return other information in AH. For all of these functions, the presence of 0 in AL indicates that no error occurred.

Table 13-4 lists all of the error codes that can be returned after a function call is made. The version(s) of MS-DOS under which each code is supported is indicated. Note also that error codes 19 through 31 correspond on a one-to-one basis to int 24h type error codes 0 through Ch, and error code 34 corresponds to int 24h type error code Fh.

Table 13-3.   Critical Error Code (via Int 24h)

Error Code	Description	MS-DOS Version			
		1.XX	2.XX	3.XX	4.XX
0	Write attempt on write-protected disk	Yes			
1	Unknown unit	No			
2	Drive not ready	Yes			
3	Unknown command	No			
4	Data error (CRC)	Yes			
5	Bad request structure length	No			
6	Seek error	Yes		Yes	
7	Unknown media type	No			
8	Sector not found	Yes			
9	Printer out of paper	No			
A	Write fault	Yes			
B	Read fault	No			
C	General failure	Yes			
D	Not defined	//////	//////	//////	//////
E	Not defined	//////	//////	//////	//////
F	Invalid disk change	No		Yes	

continued

Table 13-4. Function Call Error Codes
(MS-DOS Versions 2.0 and Higher Only)

Error Code (hex)	Description	MS-DOS Version						
		2.0	2.1	3.0	3.1	3.2	3.3	4.0
1	Invalid function number							
2	File not found							
3	Path not found							
4	Too many open files							
5	Access denied							
6	Invalid handle							
7	Memory control blocks destroyed							
8	Insufficient memory							
9	Invalid memory block address							
A	Invalid environment							
B	Invalid format							
C	Invalid access code							
D	Invalid data				Yes			
E	(Reserved)							
F	Invalid drive specified							
10	Remove attempt of current directory							
11	Not the same device							
12	No more files							
13	Int 24h error 0 (Table 13-3)							
14	Int 24h error 1 (Table 13-3)							
15	Int 24h error 2 (Table 13-3)							
16	Int 24h error 3 (Table 13-3)							
17	Int 24h error 4 (Table 13-3)							
18	Int 24h error 5 (Table 13-3)							
19	Int 24h error 6 (Table 13-3)							
1A	Int 24h error 7 (Table 13-3)							

Table 13-4. *continued*

Error Code (hex)	Description	MS-DOS Version						
		2.0	2.1	3.0	3.1	3.2	3.3	4.0
1B	Int 24h error 8 (Table 13-3)	Yes						
1C	Int 24h error 9 (Table 13-3)							
1D	Int 24h error A (Table 13-3)							
1E	Int 24h error B (Table 13-3)							
1F	Int 24h error C (Table 13-3)							
20	Sharing violation	No		Yes				
21	Lock violation							
22	Int 24h error F (Table 13-3)							
23	FCB unavailable							
24	Sharing buffer overflow	///////	///////	///////	///////	///////	Yes	
25−41	(Reserved)	///////	///////	///////	///////	///////	///////	///////
42	Network request not supported	No		Yes				
43	Remote computer not listening							
44	Duplicate name on network							
45	Network name not found							
46	Network busy							
47	Network device no longer exists							
48	Network BIOS command limit exceeded							
49	Network adapter hardware error							
4A	Incorrect response from network							
4B	Unexpected network error							
4C	Incompatible remote adaptor							
4D	Print queue full							

continued

Table 13-4. *continued*

Error Code (hex)	Description	MS-DOS Version						
		2.0	2.1	3.0	3.1	3.2	3.3	4.0
4E	Queue not full	No			Yes			
4F	Not enough space to print file							
50	Network name was deleted							
51	Access denied							
52	Network device type incorrect							
53	Network name not found							
54	Network name limit exceeded							
55	Network BIOS session limit exceeded							
56	Temporarily paused							
57	Network request not accepted							
58	Print/disk redirection paused							
59–5F	(Reserved)	///////	///////	///////	///////	///////	///////	///////
60	File exists	No		Yes				
61	(Reserved)	///////	///////	///////	///////	///////	///////	///////
62	Cannot make <*function*>	No			Yes			
63	Failure on Int 24h							
64	Out of structures	No						Yes
65	Already assigned							
66	Invalid password							
67	Invalid parameter							
68	Network write fault							

Function Call Extended Error Information (MS-DOS Versions 3.0 and Higher Only)

Because of concerns about compatibility between all versions of MS-DOS, it wasn't possible to add error-return information handling to all new and existing function calls in later versions. Therefore, in order to enhance MS-DOS's error handling capabilities, a new mechanism called the Extended Error Code was introduced under MS-DOS version 3.0. Under 3.0 and all subsequent versions, when a function executes and either the carry flag is set or the AL register contains FFh, additional detailed error information can be retrieved by immediately loading 0 into the BX register and then issuing function call 59h (Get Extended Error). The information returns as shown in Table 13-5.

Table 13-5.   Extended Error Return Information

Register	Contents
AX	Error code (see Table 13-4)
BH	Error class
BL	Suggested action
CH	Locus

Error Code
The error code returned in the AX register can be any one of those listed in Table 13-4, depending on the version of MS-DOS.

Error Class
One of the values in Table 13-6 is returned in the BH register and indicates the general category of the error. This can help determine the actual cause of the error because the same error code could occur twice from different causes.

Table 13-6.   Error Classes

Value	Definition
1	Out of resource (no more space, channels, etc.)
2	Temporary situation (problem may go away, such as a locked file)
3	Authorization (denied access)
4	Internal (MS-DOS determined that error was caused by an internal bug, not by the user or the system)
5	Hardware failure (problem not caused by user program)
6	System failure (serious failure of system software, although may not be directly the fault of the user program—such as missing or faulty configuration files)
7	Application program error (such as inconsistent requests)
8	Not found (file or other item not found)
9	Bad format (file or item of incorrect format)
10	Locked (file or item is interlocked)
11	Media (media failure such as incorrect disk, CRC error, incorrect disk in drive, or damaged media surface)
12	Already exists (collision with existing item such as a file name or machine name)
13	Unknown (error not categorized or is inappropriate)

Suggested Action

One of the values in Table 13-7 is returned in the BL register and suggests a course of action to recover from the error condition.

Table 13-7.   Suggested Error-Recovery Actions

Value	Definition
1	Retry (retry a few times and if failure persists, prompt user to determine whether program should continue or be aborted)
2	Delay retry (same as retry but pause first to determine whether error recovers itself)
3	User (prompt user to reenter input-incorrect text may have been typed)
4	Abort (terminate the program normally after cleanup)
5	Immediate exit (terminate the program abnormally, skipping cleanup)
6	Ignore (the error can be ignored)
7	Retry after user intervention (continue operation after user interaction, such as replacing a disk

Locus

The values in Table 13-8 are returned in the CH register and provide additional information about where the problem is located.

Table 13-8.   Locus of Error

Value	Definition
1	Unknown (nonspecific or not appropriate)
2	Block device (related to disk storage media)
3	Network
4	Serial device (error is related to a serial link or device)
5	Memory (error is related to RAM memory)

Because of the changes made in error handling in newer versions of MS-DOS, programmers face difficult choices. The new "extended error" information technique is obviously the most useful for designing error-trapping routines in your programs. But its price is noncompatibility. If you must include this technique in your programs and also must maintain some form of downward compatibility with older versions of MS-DOS, the Get MS-DOS Version routine (described earlier in this chapter) could prove useful. For MS-DOS versions below 2.0, you would check only for those error codes supported by the version. For versions 2.0 and 2.1, you would expand the error-handling capability and provide for the detection of more error codes. And for versions 3.0 and higher, you could expand error-handling even further with the Get Extended Error Information function call.

Disk Formats

As pointed out in Chapter 11, "Disk Layout and File Recovery," several disk formats are supported by the various versions of MS-DOS. Tables 13-9 and 13-10 provide summaries of the specifications of all the standard 3½-inch, 5¼-inch, and 8-inch floppy disk formats supported by MS-DOS up to version 4.0. For more detailed information, however, refer to Chapter 11.

Although other formats and types of disks are supported under some implementations of MS-DOS, Table 13-9 shows only those floppy disk formats that are officially supported by MS-DOS as of the printing of this book. Similarly, specifications of hard disks are not covered because many variations are product or system specific. The support for hard disks is generally contained in the ROM-BIOS of the system; many types and sizes of hard disks can be used, depending on the version and manufacturer of the ROM-BIOS. Special types of media, such as the Bernoulli Box, often require special disk controllers and installable device drivers in order to contend with the lack of support in most implementations of the ROM-BIOS. MS-DOS versions 2.0 through 3.30 support many hard disk formats, with partitions reaching a maximum size of 32 megabytes.

MS-DOS versions 2.0 through 3.2 support only one DOS partition per hard disk, whereas version 3.3 supports several DOS partitions per hard disk, each with a maximum size of 32 megabytes and each assigned a drive name. MS-DOS version 4.0 (and COMPAQ MS-DOS version 3.31) supports extended-size partitions that may be as large as 512 megabytes. Extended-size partitions are optional under MS-DOS 4.0: a large hard disk can still be formatted with several DOS partitions that are 32 megabytes or smaller in size. Note that 32-megabyte or smaller partitions use 16-bit sector numbers, and extended-size partitions use 32-bit sector numbers. This can cause incompatibility problems with many applications that reference a disk's file allocation table (FAT) and that reference sectors with 16-bit values. See Chapter 11 for more information on disk formats.

Table 13-9.   MX-DOS Floppy Disk Formats

Specifi-cations	MS-DOS Version							See Note 1		
	1.0	1.1	2.0	2.1	3.0	3.2	3.3			
Size	5¼"	5¼"	5¼"	5¼"	5¼"	3½"	3½"	8"	8"	8"
Format byte	FFE	FFF	FFC	FFD	FF9	FF9	FF0	FFE	FFD	FFE
Sides	1	2	1	2	2	2	2	1	2	2
Tracks per side	40	40	40	40	80	80	80	77	77	77
Sections per track	8	8	9	9	15	9	18	26	26	8
Bytes per sector	512	512	512	512	512	512	512	128	128	1024

Specifications	MS-DOS Version							See Note 1		
	1.0	1.1	2.0	2.1	3.0	3.2	3.3			
Sections per cluster	1	2	1	2	1	2	1	4	4	1
Boot sectors	1	1	1	1	1	1	1	1	4	1
Sectors per FAT	1	1	2	2	7	3	9	6	6	2
Number of FATs	2	2	2	2	2	2	2	2	2	2
Root directory sectors	4	7	4	7	14	7	14	17	17	6
Root directory entries	64	112	64	112	224	112	224	68	68	192
Total sectors	320	640	360	720	2400	1440	2880	2002	4004	1232
Data sectors	313	630	351	708	2371	1426	2857	1972	3940	1221
Total clusters	313	315	351	354	2371	713	2857	493	985	1221
Total capacity	160 Kbytes	320 Kbytes	180 Kbytes	360 Kbytes	1.2 Mbytes	720 Kbytes	1.44 Mbytes	501 Kbytes	250.25 Kbytes	1.232 Mbytes
Total data capacity	156.5 Kbytes	315 Kbytes	175.5 Kbytes	354 Kbytes	1.1855 Mbytes	713 Kbytes	1.4285 Mbytes	246 Kbytes	492.5 Kbytes	1.221 Mbytes

1. The format descriptor byte values used to identify the format of 8-inch disks are the same as those used for some of the 5¼-inch disks. The distinction is handled either within the BIOS of the particular implementation of MS-DOS or within a device driver. Most implementations of MS-DOS, especially in those systems that have the BIOS stored in ROM, do not have the necessary routines within the BIOS for 8-inch disks. Thus, support is usually handled with a special device driver. Because the first single-density, 8-inch format has the same descriptor byte value (FFE) as the last (double-density) format, MS-DOS makes the distinction when it tries to read the disk: The system first assumes that the disk is formatted to single density. If no error occurs after reading the first sector, MS-DOS continues treating the disk as a single-density disk. If an error occurs after first reading the disk, MS-DOS assumes that the disk is formatted to double density and tries to read the first sector again. Note also that some systems support a double-density format for single-sided, 8-inch disks, which yields a total disk capacity approximately half that of double-sided disks (610 Kbytes).

File Manipulation

When dealing with different MS-DOS versions, consider the way in which files are handled in your programs. When MS-DOS was first released, it provided file-handling capabilities similar to those used under the CP/M (control program for microcomputers) operating system. This similarity was intentional because it provided programmers with a relatively painless method to convert both 8-bit and 16-bit programs from CP/M to MS-DOS. In order to maintain compatibility, all versions of MS-DOS up to version 3.1 have the same file-handling capabilities. A new method, however, was introduced under version 2.0 that represents a major departure from CP/M-style file handling. This method is very similar to the file-handling method used in the XENIX operating system. Although much easier to use, the new method is not, however, compatible with the older method and therefore requires cautious attention. The following paragraphs describe the differences between these two methods.

Using File Control Blocks (FCBs)

Function calls 0Fh through 29h, introduced in the first version of MS-DOS, are used in conjunction with an FCB (file control block) to create, modify, and delete a file. An FCB is a segment of code written to memory that defines the parameters of a program-manipulated file. MS-DOS and the application program use the FCB parameters to ascertain the file's location, name, size, and other pertinent information. However, because no function call was provided to actually create an entire FCB, the FCB must already be defined before any of the file-related function calls are used in a program. In all cases, each of the file-related function calls (0Fh through 29h) requires that the location of the FCB in memory be loaded into the DS:DX register pair prior to executing the function. This means that the application program must first create an FCB and load it to a known location in either the data segment or the data area of the code segment of memory (whichever is initially defined by the program).

When MS-DOS loads a program, the system creates and formats two FCBs in the program's PSP (program segment prefix). The location of these FCBs in the PSP, as well as the means of accessing the PSP, are described in Chapter 3. The file name fields are filled in from information typed on the command line when the program is entered (as with "A>MUNG infile outfile"). However, if a file specification contains a path name, only the drive number in the FCB is valid. Additionally, no redirection directives appear in the FCB. Finally, note that if the program opens the first FCB in the PSP, the second FCB is overwritten.

Table 13-10 shows the structure of an FCB and indicates both the size and the offset location in memory for each parameter within the FCB. Notice that not all parameters within an FCB are controlled by the application program. Some are modified only by MS-DOS itself, and others can be modified by both the program and MS-DOS. In either case, space must be allotted for all parameters when an FCB is created.

In Table 13-10, fields with negative offsets are used under MS-DOS versions 2.0 and higher to turn the FCB into an *extended FCB*, which allows the use of the file attribute parameter in offset –1. 0FFh must be at offset –7 to denote the FCB as an extended FCB.

Table 13-10.   MS-DOS FCB Format

Offset Byte	Size	Description	Modified by
-7	1	0FF hex	Program
-6	6	Reserved (must be zero)	Program
-1	1	File attribute	Program/MS-DOS
0	1	Drive number (0 through 16)	Program/MS-DOS
1	8	File or device name	Program
9	3	File extension or type	Program
12	2	Current block	Program
14	2	Record size in bytes	Program
16	4	File size in bytes	MS-DOS
20	2	Date	MS-DOS
22	10	Reserved	MS-DOS
32	1	Current record	Program/MS-DOS
33	4	Random record number	Program/MS-DOS

Both offset and size values are in decimal.

MS-DOS File Handles

MS-DOS version 2.0 provided a much easier method for the manipulation of files. Instead of painstakingly defining and creating an FCB whenever a file is created or opened, several function calls can be used that require only that you specify a single ASCII string describing the entire file specification and terminated by a zero. Called an *ASCIIZ string*, it can be as long as 64 bytes to accommodate long path names, and it follows the same syntax as a normal file specification:

drive:\path\filename.extension

When either function call 3Ch (Create a File) or function 3Dh (Open a File) is executed, MS-DOS creates a *file handle*, based on the information contained in the ASCIIZ string. Function calls 3Ch through 57h are all file-related functions that involve the use of file handles. These include three new functions (5Ah through 5Ch) introduced in MS-DOS version 3.0.

Because MS-DOS creates and controls file handles, the application program no longer needs to keep track of where the file information is located in memory. Simply referencing the ASCIIZ string is sufficient to inform MS-DOS about what the program is doing according to the functions being used. This built-in facility also has another benefit: Several file handles can exist at one time because MS-DOS always keeps track of where they're located in memory.

The only disadvantage with file handles is that they're not supported by versions of MS-DOS prior to 2.0. So if a program must be compatible with all versions of MS-DOS, avoid the use of file handles. Note, however, that with the introduction of file handles, as well as many other features, MS-DOS versions 2.0 through 3.1 have proven to be stepping stones of sorts between older operating systems (such as CP/M) and the more advanced XENIX operating system.

Almost all of the new MS-DOS file-related function calls are directly compatible with those under XENIX, as are other features such as path names, tree-structured directories, and redirection. Thus, upward compatibility should also be considered, especially when one realizes that current versions of XENIX do not support the old FCB method of file handling.

MS-DOS and the IBM Personal Computer and IBM Personal System 2 Series

The IBM Personal Computer (IBM PC) undoubtedly has been the most popular of all the computers installed with MS-DOS. Indeed, the high popularity of MS-DOS has been due to the unprecedented success of the IBM Personal Computer series and compatible machines. How does MS-DOS, as it is implemented on the IBM PC, compare with the implementations described in this chapter and in this book? When reading the MS-DOS manual for the IBM PC and IBM PS/2 (in which MS-DOS is called DOS or IBM PC-DOS) and the MS-DOS manual published by Microsoft, you notice both similarities and significant differences. The similarities involve parts of MS-DOS that are standard or "generic" to all implementations of MS-DOS. The differences represent features of MS-DOS that are often unique to particular implementations. The goal of this book is to cover programming in the MS-DOS environment from the generic point of view and the focus is thus on items of programming that are applicable to all implementations of MS-DOS. However, because MS-DOS on the IBM PC is the most popular implementation, the similarities and differences must be made clear. Having this information helps you make crucial compatibility design decisions for your programs.

Similarities

The following generic aspects of MS-DOS are the same throughout all implementations of MS-DOS for any version.

- *DOS (disk operating system) program.* This program *is* MS-DOS and is stored in a hidden file on the boot disk. On the IBM PC, this file is called IBMDOS.COM. Although it may be called something else on other machines, this file is always the same for a given version and can be broken down into the following parts.

  1. Operating system executive
  2. Function calls
  3. Memory management (not memory layout) up to 640K
  4. BIOS interface (not the BIOS itself)

- *The BIOS interface program.* The BIOS (basic input/output system) interface program acts as an interface or translator between MS-DOS and the BIOS. In the IBM PC, this interface is stored on the boot disk in a hidden file called IBMBIO.COM. The input part of the program is the same for any version of MS-DOS, but the output depends on the particular machine (IBM PC, IBM PC*jr*, IBM PC Portable, IBM PC XT, IBM AT, or IBM PS/2). DOS for IBM PC-compatible machines has a similar file, but it is called something else. In some implementations of MS-DOS, such as MS-PRO and PC-PRO for the CompuPro (Viasyn) computers, this file is replaced by the entire BIOS itself.

- *Command interpreter (COMMAND.COM).* This nonhidden file exists on all boot disks. It is normally the same for all implementations, but you occasionally encounter some differences. It provides the interface between MS-DOS and the user, displays prompts, and provides built-in commands and functions, such as DIR, COPY, RENAME, ERASE, and redirection.

- *External commands.* A set of external commands is standard throughout all implementations of MS-DOS. However, some external commands unique to particular implementations of MS-DOS are often added. For example, the commands COMP and DISKCOMP are unique to the IBM PC series. Most other implementations of MS-DOS have equivalent commands, but they're slightly different and normally called something else.

Differences

The following parts of MS-DOS are implementation-specific:

- *BIOS.* On the IBM PC series, as well as almost all IBM PC-compatible machines, the BIOS is stored in ROM. The BIOS contains routines that act as extensions of MS-DOS to control the hardware. Because the hardware is always based on the proprietary design of the computer's manufacturer, the design of the BIOS must also be proprietary unless it is purchased from another manufacturer. The following general aspects of the BIOS are often machine-specific:

  1. Hardware and software interrupt handlers
  2. Routines for disk controllers and disk drivers
  3. Routines for the console, printer, and communications ports
  4. Other miscellaneous functions, such as graphics controllers and game adapters

- *BIOS interface program.* On all machines containing a BIOS interface file (such as IBMBIO.COM on the IBM PC series), the input part of the program is the same so that it can accept generic data from the MS-DOS operating system. The output part of this file, however, is different because it has to be able to communicate with the proprietary BIOS.

- *Device drivers.* In order to control certain unique aspects of the system's hardware, many systems now include device drivers as part of MS-DOS. In the IBM PC series, the device driver called ANSI.SYS adds extended functions to the monitor system. A similar file is provided with some IBM PC-compatible machines but is rarely provided for non-IBM PC-compatible machines.

- *External commands.* Special nonstandard external commands are often included in implementations of MS-DOS.

Generally, the most important difference between MS-DOS implementations involves the BIOS itself because the BIOS contains the routines required by the unique hardware (such as disk controllers, monitors or terminals, and keyboards) of the machine. Thus, when making design decisions about a program, the intended level of program compatibility should be carefully considered. If you want your program to be compatible with all implementations of MS-DOS, never access the BIOS directly and never use system-specific functions, such as interrupts. If system-specific functions are necessary but across-the-board compatibility is still required, such functions should be handled either in device drivers or, if accompanied by an installation program that can make machine-specific modifications, in the program itself.

Even within the series of IBM PCs, compatibility issues arise. For example, the capabilities of BIOS programs stored in ROM vary among the IBM PC, IBM PC XT, and IBM AT. Although the BIOS functions in the IBM PC also exist in the IBM PC XT, the XT provides additional functions. Comparable differences exist between the IBM PC XT and the IBM AT. If you're unsure about the differences, refer to the *IBM Technical Reference* (hardware) manuals for each machine. The entire listing of the BIOS is provided in each manual.

Compatibility with Other Operating Systems

As mentioned earlier in this chapter, MS-DOS is in various ways similar to other operating systems. The first version of MS-DOS, from both the programmer's and the user's standpoints, is similar to the CP/M operating system. Although many features of MS-DOS do not exist in CP/M, the basic structure and command usage (such as the DOS > prompt and .COM command files) are virtually identical. MS-DOS version 2.00, however, introduced several features and functions derived from a much more advanced operating system called XENIX, also from Microsoft. (XENIX is a variation of the popular minicomputer and mainframe operating system called UNIX.) Functions such as file and device redirection, pipes, device drivers, and file handles are derivations of similar functions provided by XENIX. With several versions of MS-DOS now available, some of the newer operating systems offer MS-DOS compatibility. Probably the best known examples are Concurrent PC DOS and Concurrent DOS286 from Digital Research, Inc. (the original designers of CP/M). The following paragraphs give an overview of the similarities and differences among MS-DOS and these compatible and pseudo-compatible operating systems.

CP/M-80

After examining the architecture and capabilities of MS-DOS, you will know that the designers got their ideas from the CP/M operating system for 8080, 8085, and Z80 microprocessor-based machines. Before the introduction of the IBM PC with MS-DOS, CP/M was considered the *de facto* standard operating system for microcomputers. CP/M still remains the most popular operating system for 8-bit machines. When computer manufacturers began to entertain plans for designing 16-bit computers using the then recently introduced 8086 microprocessor from Intel, many of them had to wait because a 16-bit version of CP/M (now called CP/M-86) was not available. A company called Seattle Computer Products went ahead and designed their own operating system, which they called QDOS (Quick 'n Dirty Operating System) and which, after several improvements, they later renamed 86-DOS.

The architecture of 86-DOS was very similar to that of CP/M, but Seattle Computer Products improved on many functions and added some new ones. 86-DOS was then sold to Microsoft and was renamed MS-DOS. This first version of MS-DOS (which was essentially an unchanged 86-DOS) was adopted for use by IBM on their newly released personal computer, the IBM PC. Microsoft then made several enhancements to MS-DOS, which resulted in MS-DOS version 2.00. MS-DOS 2.0 retained most of the functions of the first version. Thus, the similarity to CP/M was maintained, which was of great benefit to programmers because most CP/M programs could be easily converted to MS-DOS. From the programmer's point of view, the following similarities are important:

- *Function calls.* Most of the function calls in the first version of MS-DOS, especially those related to file functions, are very similar to those provided by CP/M versions 2.2 and 3.0. Although register usage differs considerably between the 8-bit 8080/Z80 and the 16-bit 8086 family of microprocessors, the way in which the functions are set up and return information is very similar. Even some of the function call numbers themselves are the same. MS-DOS functions that are virtually identical to those of CP/M include functions 0 through 24 hex. These functions and their operation have been retained in later versions of MS-DOS up to version 3.1.

- *FCBs.* The only way the first version of MS-DOS could create, open, change, or delete a file was through the use of an FCB. The format of an FCB under MS-DOS and the way in which it is set up is almost identical to FCB usage under CP/M. Because file handling is crucial in most DOS-based operating systems, the similarities between FCB usage in CP/M and in MS-DOS are invaluable to programmers. Although a new file-handling mechanism was introduced in MS-DOS version 2.00, all versions up to version 3.1 still retain, for compatibility purposes, the "old" FCB method.

- *Commands.* The use of built-in commands and external program commands is very similar in both operating systems. CP/M has its built-in commands in what is called the CCP (console command processor), which is part of the operating system when loaded into memory. MS-DOS handles built-in commands in much the same way, except that its command processor exists in a disk file called COMMAND.COM. MS-DOS also has an 8-bit compatibility mode for external commands and thus handles .COM files in a manner almost identical to the way they are handled by CP/M. Under MS-DOS, .COM files use only a 64-Kbyte segment of memory, thereby emulating the memory usage of an 8080 or Z80 microprocessor-based system. The .EXE command format under MS-DOS, however, is used only in machines with 8086-family microprocessors and therefore is not compatible with CP/M.

CP/M-86 and Concurrent CP/M-86

The CP/M-86 operating system is the 16-bit counterpart of the original CP/M for the 8086 family of microprocessors. Many of its features, carried over from the 8-bit CP/M version, are similar to MS-DOS. For example, FCBs and file-related function calls (excluding file handles) are referenced in CP/M-86 much like the methods used in MS-DOS.

Shortly after the introduction of CP/M-86, a new version was introduced called Concurrent CP/M-86, which added multitasking and windowing features to CP/M-86. Special versions of both operating systems were released for the IBM PC, which made special use of these features. Most of the functions of CP/M-86 were carried over to Concurrent CP/M-86, but many of them were further complicated by the multitasking features of the newer operating system.

Concurrent PC-DOS and Concurrent DOS-286

With the emergence of MS-DOS as the *de facto* standard operating system for the 16-bit 8086 family of microcomputers (especially the IBM PC and compatible machines), the makers of CP/M realized that they would have to provide some form of compatibility with MS-DOS because of the large user-base of MS-DOS systems. Digital Research, Inc., released an enhanced version of Concurrent CP/M-86 called Concurrent PC-DOS, which, in its initial release, provided MS-DOS version 1.0 compatibility. Version 3 of Concurrent PC-DOS was enhanced yet again to include MS-DOS version 2.00 compatibility. This operating system is capable of running both CP/M-86 and MS-DOS programs concurrently and accepts all of the function calls supported under the equivalent versions of MS-DOS.

Another variation of Concurrent PC-DOS called Concurrent DOS286 is planned for machines with the Intel 80286 microprocessor. This operating system is designed for use with the 80286 processor in "virtual" (also called "protected") mode, providing a memory-addressable range of 16 megabytes. This operating system is also capable of running in the "real" mode (8086-compatibility mode) concurrently with the virtual mode so that both MS-DOS and CP/M-86 programs can be run. Concurrent DOS286 provides the same MS-DOS compatible features as Concurrent PC-DOS. Caution should be exercised when dealing with the compatibility of this operating system because its correct operation depends heavily on the version of the 80286 processor used in the system (earlier versions of the processor had problems switching and communicating between the virtual and real modes).

XENIX and UNIX

As indicated previously, later versions of MS-DOS (beginning with version 2.0) incorporated some features found in XENIX, another Microsoft operating system. Most of the features introduced in MS-DOS version 2.0, such as device drivers, redirection, piping, and file handles, are features based on those found in XENIX, which in turn is based on the UNIX operating system from AT&T. Thus, although you should pay attention to downward compatibility issues (MS-DOS and CP/M), upward compatibility should also be a consideration because the XENIX-like features of MS-DOS represent an indication of what's in store for future versions of MS-DOS.

OS/2

MS-DOS programs are not in any way compatible with the 80286/80386 protected-mode operation of the OS/2 operating system. OS/2 does, however, provide a "compatibility box" in which most MS-DOS programs can run, unmodified, under an MS-DOS emulator. The compatibility box of OS/2 runs in the 8086-family real mode (1 megabyte of addressable memory, of which 640K is usable under MS-DOS) and provides MS-DOS emulation compatible with MS-DOS version 3.3. However, because the compatibility box does not actually run MS-DOS but rather emulates it, compatibility is not 100 percent. For example, programs using timing interrupts will most likely not run in the compatibility box. Furthermore, some of the undocumented int 21h function calls may not operate the same as they do under the real MS-DOS. The locations of some of the data structures in MS-DOS may not be the same in the compatibility box. In general, so-called well-behaved programs will run in the compatibility box without needing any modifications.

Because OS/2 is designed primarily for the 80286 processor, OS/2 runs on the 80386 processor in "80286 protected mode." Consequently, OS/2 supports only one compatibility box at a time despite its multitasking capabilities. The 80386 processor is capable of running many real mode "boxes" at once when the processor is placed in the 80386 protected mode. Multiple compatibility boxes will not be possible under OS/2 until an 80386-specific version of OS/2 is released.

Summary

Many things—more than can be covered in one chapter—must be considered when you develop programs intended to be compatible with all or most versions and implementations of MS-DOS. The information presented here should provide a good basis for starting to investigate the many compatibility issues you're likely to encounter. Most manufacturers of computers that run MS-DOS have published technical information about how MS-DOS is implemented on their machines. If you're writing a program targeted for a particular machine (or intended to be compatible with a particular machine), these manuals can help you considerably.

APPENDIXES  PART V

Development Tools

A

Using Batch Files to Automate the Assembly Process
Using the Microsoft MAKE Facility
Using Templates to Create .COM and .EXE Programs
Using Library Routines

HIS appendix describes some tools that can simplify and enhance the process of using assembly language to develop application programs. The following text describes: automating the program development process with batch files, using the Microsoft MAKE facility, creating .EXE and .COM programs with templates, and using *include* files and library routines.

Using Batch Files to Automate the Assembly Process

The MS-DOS batch processor is often one of the least appreciated facilities in the operating system. This facility can, however, be a very useful tool when you use the MASM macroassembler. Listings A-1, A-2, and A-3 provide the sources for three batch files: MASM2EXE.BAT, MASM2COM.BAT, and MK.BAT. MASM2EXE.BAT is used to automate the process of assembling and linking .EXE programs. MASM2COM.BAT is a modification of the first file and includes the process of converting an .EXE file to a .COM file. Both files are designed to work with Microsoft MASM versions 1.00 through 4.00 and most versions of the linker LINK. MK.BAT (Listing A-3) is a significantly enhanced development batch file for use with MASM versions 5.0 and higher and LINK versions 3.00 and higher. MK.BAT can be used to create .EXE, .COM, or .OBJ (linkable object-code) files by using command-line parameters.

Using Batch Files for Versions of MASM Prior to Version 5

The MASM2EXE.BAT and MASM2COM.BAT batch files shown in Listings A-1 and A-2 are appropriate for use with versions of MASM from 1.00 to 4.00 and LINK 1.00 to 2.00.

Modifications to the batch files for later versions of MASM and LINK are provided in the remarks in the listings. Both files require that a second file called AUTOLINK be present. This file contains four carriage return/line feeds and is used to deal with the problem that LINK (up to version 2.00) has: It cannot accept null parameters on the command line for the listing (.MAP) and library (.LIB) options. AUTOLINK is submitted to LINK by adding the file name on the command line and preceding it with an @ sign. The @ sign is used for compatibility with MS-DOS versions prior to version 2.00 because the earlier versions don't support command-line redirection.

Using the batch files is very simple. Simply enter the name of the batch command followed by the name of the file to be assembled. Do not include the extension, as .ASM is assumed. If you're using MS-DOS version 2.00 or above and the PATH is set correctly, the drives on which any of the related files are stored don't have to be specified.

Listing A-1. MASM2EXE.BAT

```
echo off
if not exist %1.asm goto NOFILERR
rem
masm %1 %1 nul nul
rem
rem Use the above only with versions of MASM below 2.00
rem Use "masm %1.asm,,;" for MASM version 2.00 and above
rem
link %1 @a:autolink
rem
rem Use the above only with versions of LINK below 2.20
rem Use "link %1.obj,,nul;" for LINK version 2.20 and above
rem
echo Deleting %1.obj
del %1.obj >nul:
echo Done!
dir %1.*
goto END
rem
:NOFILERR
echo The file %1.asm was not found.
:END
```

Listing A-2. MASM2COM.BAT

```
echo off
if not exist %1.asm goto NOFILERR
rem
masm %1 %1 nul nul
rem
rem Use the above only with versions of MASM below 2.00
rem Use "masm %1.asm,,;" for MASM version 2.00 and above
rem
link %1 @a:autolink
```

```
rem
rem Use the above only with versions of LINK below 2.20
rem Use "link %1.obj,,nul;" for LINK version 2.20 and above
rem
echo Deleting %1.obj
del %1.obj >nul:
echo Creating %1.com from %1.exe (and deleting %1.exe)
exe2bin %1.exe %1.com >nul:
del %1.exe >nul:
echo Done!
dir %1.*
goto END
rem
:NOFILERR
echo The file %1.asm was not found.
:END
```

Note that some of the lines in Listings A-1 and A-2 terminate with output redirection parameters. If you're using a version of MS-DOS prior to version 2.00, these parameters should be stripped.

Using Batch Files for MASM Versions 5 and Higher

If you are using MASM version 5 and LINK version 3, or higher versions, the batch file MK.BAT, shown in Listing A-3, may be used. MK.BAT may be used to create either .EXE, .COM, or .OBJ files by specifying the correct parameter on the command line. For example, if you wish to assemble a file called TEST1.ASM to create TEST1.EXE, simply enter *MK TEST1 EXE*. Conversely, if the target file is TEST1.COM, enter *MK TEST1 COM*, or enter *MK TEST1 OBJ* to create an .OBJ-linkable object-code file. MK.BAT also makes use of return codes generated by MASM and LINK. If a return code other than 0 is returned by either MASM or LINK, MK.BAT stops processing and exits with an error message. MK.BAT's error checking is useful, for example, when MASM detects an error at assembly time—MK.BAT is prevented from continuing to link time until the error in the source file is fixed.

Listing A-3. MK.BAT

```
@ECHO off
REM Use the above line to prevent "ECHO off" from being
REM displayed, but only if running DOS 3.3 or above. Otherwise,
REM use the next two lines with ANSI.SYS loaded.
REM ("^[" = ASCII ESCape character).
REM    ECHO off
```

continued

Listing A-3. *continued*

```
REM    ECHO ^[[s^[[1A^[[K^[[u
REM
  IF (%1)==() goto :NOPARM
  IF not exist %1.asm goto :NOFILE
  SET F1=%1
  IF (%2)==() goto :ASKTYPE
  SET TYPE=%2
  IF (%3)==() goto :CHKTYPE
  SET MASMS=
  SET LINKS=
  IF (%3)==(m) SET MASMS=%4
  IF (%3)==(M) SET MASMS=%4
  IF (%3)==(mo) SET MASM=%4
  IF (%3)==(mO) SET MASM=%4
  IF (%3)==(Mo) SET MASM=%4
  IF (%3)==(MO) SET MASM=%4
rem
  IF (%3)==(l) SET LINKS=%4
  IF (%3)==(L) SET LINKS=%4
  IF (%3)==(lo) SET LINK=%4
  IF (%3)==(lO) SET LINK=%4
  IF (%3)==(Lo) SET LINK=%4
  IF (%3)==(LO) SET LINK=%4
rem
  IF (%5)==(m) SET MASMS=%6
  IF (%5)==(M) SET MASMS=%6
  IF (%5)==(mo) SET MASM=%6
  IF (%5)==(mO) SET MASM=%6
  IF (%5)==(Mo) SET MASM=%6
  IF (%5)==(MO) SET MASM=%6
rem
  IF (%5)==(l) SET LINKS=%6
  IF (%5)==(L) SET LINKS=%6
  IF (%5)==(lo) SET LINK=%6
  IF (%5)==(lO) SET LINK=%6
  IF (%5)==(Lo) SET LINK=%6
  IF (%5)==(LO) SET LINK=%6
rem
  GOTO :CHKTYPE
:ASKTYPE
  ECHO ^H
  ANSWER Enter type of file to be created: OBJ, COM, or EXE:
  ECHO ^H
:CHKTYPE
  IF (%TYPE%)==(o)    SET TYPE=OBJ
```

```
    IF (%TYPE%)==(o)   SET TYPE=OBJ
    IF (%TYPE%)==(ob)  SET TYPE=OBJ
    IF (%TYPE%)==(Ob)  SET TYPE=OBJ
    IF (%TYPE%)==(oB)  SET TYPE=OBJ
    IF (%TYPE%)==(OB)  SET TYPE=OBJ
    IF (%TYPE%)==(obj) SET TYPE=OBJ
    IF (%TYPE%)==(Obj) SET TYPE=OBJ
    IF (%TYPE%)==(oBj) SET TYPE=OBJ
    IF (%TYPE%)==(obJ) SET TYPE=OBJ
    IF (%TYPE%)==(OBj) SET TYPE=OBJ
    IF (%TYPE%)==(oBJ) SET TYPE=OBJ
    IF (%TYPE%)==(OBJ) goto :DOASM
rem
    IF (%TYPE%)==(e)   SET TYPE=EXE
    IF (%TYPE%)==(E)   SET TYPE=EXE
    IF (%TYPE%)==(ex)  SET TYPE=EXE
    IF (%TYPE%)==(Ex)  SET TYPE=EXE
    IF (%TYPE%)==(eX)  SET TYPE=EXE
    IF (%TYPE%)==(EX)  SET TYPE=EXE
    IF (%TYPE%)==(exe) SET TYPE=EXE
    IF (%TYPE%)==(Exe) SET TYPE=EXE
    IF (%TYPE%)==(eXe) SET TYPE=EXE
    IF (%TYPE%)==(exE) SET TYPE=EXE
    IF (%TYPE%)==(EXe) SET TYPE=EXE
    IF (%TYPE%)==(eXE) SET TYPE=EXE
    IF (%TYPE%)==(EXE) goto :DOASM
rem
    IF (%TYPE%)==(c)   SET TYPE=COM
    IF (%TYPE%)==(C)   SET TYPE=COM
    IF (%TYPE%)==(co)  SET TYPE=COM
    IF (%TYPE%)==(Co)  SET TYPE=COM
    IF (%TYPE%)==(cO)  SET TYPE=COM
    IF (%TYPE%)==(CO)  SET TYPE=COM
    IF (%TYPE%)==(com) SET TYPE=COM
    IF (%TYPE%)==(Com) SET TYPE=COM
    IF (%TYPE%)==(cOm) SET TYPE=COM
    IF (%TYPE%)==(coM) SET TYPE=COM
    IF (%TYPE%)==(COm) SET TYPE=COM
    IF (%TYPE%)==(cOM) SET TYPE=COM
    IF (%TYPE%)==(COM) goto :DOASM
rem
  GOTO :ASKTYPE
:DOASM
  IF (%MASM%)==() SET MASM=/S/P/V/L%MASMS%
  IF not (%MASM%)==() ECHO MASM command-line switches: %MASM%
```

continued

Listing A-3. *continued*

```
    ECHO on
    MASM %F1%.asm;
    @ECHO off
    IF errorlevel 1 goto :NOASSEM
REM
    IF (%TYPE%)==(OBJ) goto :LSTFILES
    IF (%LINK%)==() SET LINK=/I/CP:1%LINKS%
    IF not (%LINK%)==() ECHO Link command-line switches: %LINK%
    ECHO on
    LINK %F1%.obj,%F1%.exe;
    @ECHO off
    IF errorlevel 1 goto :NOLINK
    IF exist %F1%.obj DEL %F1%.obj >nul:
REM
    IF (%TYPE%)==(COM) EXE2BIN %F1%.exe %F1%.com >nul:
    IF (%TYPE%)==(COM) goto :DEL_EXE
    GOTO :LSTFILES
:DEL_EXE
    IF exist %F1%.exe DEL %F1%.exe >nul:
:LSTFILES
    IF exist %F1%.bak DEL %F1%.bak >nul:
    DIR %F1%.*
    GOTO :END
:NOPARM
    ECHO No parameter was specified!
    GOTO :END
:NOFILE
    ECHO The file "%F1%.ASM" does not exist!"
    GOTO :END
:NOASSEM
    ECHO Assembly error!
    GOTO :END
:NOLINK
    ECHO Linking error!
:END
    SET F1=
    SET TYPE=
    SET MASM=
    SET LINK=
    SET MASMS=
    SET LINKS=
```

Note that MK.BAT makes use of some nonprintable ASCII characters: ASCII ESC (escape) shown as ^[and ASCII BS (backspace) shown as ^H. When creating this file, the editor or word processor you use must provide a way for you to insert these characters in the text. The beginning of the listing shows the use of the MS-DOS version 3.3 *@ECHO off* command, which causes echoing to be turned off without *ECHO off* being displayed. However, if you're using a version of MS-DOS prior to 3.3, the ANSI escape sequence shown on the next few lines of the listing can be used. The ANSI escape sequence works only if the ANSI.SYS device driver is loaded when the system booted. The ASCII backspace character is used to cause MS-DOS to display a blank line when the file executes: the statement *ECHO ^H* causes a blank line to be displayed in all versions of MS-DOS.

MK.BAT makes use of a public-domain program called ANSWER.COM. This program is used to display a prompt of your choice, and, in response to the prompt, any text entered is assigned to the environment variable ANSWER. The entry to the prompt can then be tested in the batch file by using %ANSWER% in a statement.

Using the Microsoft MAKE Facility

The Microsoft Program Maintenance Utility called MAKE can be used to significantly enhance the automation of program development. MAKE is used to automatically update an executable file whenever changes are made to one or more of its source or object files, and it can update any file whenever changes are made to other, related files. In order to use MAKE, a *description file* must be created that contains instructions to MAKE on how a particular project is built. For example, if you want to create a program called TEST1.EXE using MAKE, the MAKE description file might contain the statements shown in Listing A-4.

Listing A-4. Example MAKE Description File

```
#  Standard command line text macro definitions
f1=test1                  # name of file to be created
msm=masm /S /P /V /L      # MASM command-line switches
lnk=link /CP:1 /I         # LINK command-line switches
#
#  The ASM File List
$(f1).obj: $(f1).asm
    $(msm) $(f1).asm;
#
$(f1).exe: $(f1).obj
    $(lnk) $(f1).obj,$(f1).exe;
    DEL $(f1).obj
```

A MAKE description file generally has the same name as the executable file but without an extension. Thus, if the executable file is called TEST1.EXE, then the MAKE description file used to create TEST1.EXE is called simply TEST1. To create or update TEST1.EXE, simply enter *MAKE TEST1*.

The MAKE description file shown in Listing A-4 has the following characteristics:

- Any text that begins with the # character is a comment and is ignored by MAKE during processing.

- *Text=* represents a *text macro* that is assigned a string of text, allowing for that text to be represented symbolically throughout the description file. The example in Listing A-4 shows that the text macro *f1* is assigned the name of the program file that is to be processed; *f1* is then used throughout the rest of the description file to represent the program file in the form of *$(f1)*. If you need to change the name of the program file, it is changed in only one place, where *f1* is first assigned.

- *$(f1).OBJ* is the name of the first target file, called the *outfile*, and *$(f1).ASM* (which translates to *test1.ASM* in the example) is the name of the source file, called the *infile*. The infile is the file required to create the outfile. The outfile is always entered first, followed by a colon, and then followed by one or more infiles required to create the outfile. If the outfile does not exist or if it is stamped with a time and date earlier than the associated infile(s), the next line in the description file is executed as an MS-DOS command (*$(msm) $(f1);*, which would translate to *masm /S /P /V /L test1;* in the example). If the infile does not exist, then MAKE stops processing at that point and exits with an error message.

- *$(f1).EXE* is the name of the final outfile, and *$(f1).OBJ* is the required infile. Again, if *$(f1).EXE* (which translates to *test1.EXE*) does not exist or if it is stamped with a time and date earlier than *$(f1).OBJ*, then the next line is executed (*$(lnk) $(f1;*, which translates to *link /CP:1 /I test1;* in the example). If *$(f1).OBJ* does not exist, then MAKE stops processing and exits with an error message.

- The description file may contain any MS-DOS command. At the end of the example, the command *DEL $(f1).obj* causes the *$(f1).obj* (which translates to *test1.obj*) to be deleted, but only if the linking process was successful.

The MAKE facility is capable of responding to error codes returned by MS-DOS commands in the description file. For example, if MASM returned an "error level" above 0 (*$(msm) $(f1).asm;* in the example), MAKE would stop processing the description file at that point and display an error message on the screen. If MASM is successful in assembling the file, but LINK returned an error, then the command to delete the object file (*DEL $(f1).obj*) would not be processed.

The MAKE facility is an excellent tool for building program projects, especially large ones. The MAKE description file may contain rules for many source files and object files, and can specify the use of several different assemblers, compilers, linkers, and other tools, as well as several instances of the same tools. When all the files of a large project are backed up or archived, the

MAKE description file for building the project can be archived as well, so that, when the project is rebuilt, it can be easily accomplished by simply running MAKE and specifying the description file.

Using Templates to Create .COM and .EXE Programs

Listings A-5, A-6, and A-7 can be useful when you create programs initially. Listing A-5 shows the format for an .EXE program with gaps for you to write your code. Listing A-6 shows the format for a .COM file. Listing A-7 contains some macros that can be useful when writing either .EXE or .COM programs. The macros either can be embedded in your program source file or can permanently reside in a separate file which is "included" in your source file during the assembly process (by embedding the MASM INCLUDE directive in the source file).

Listing A-5. .EXE Program Template

```
PAGE    60,132                                  ; wide listing
;-----------------------------------------------------------------
FALSE   EQU     0                               ; FALSE compare
TRUE    EQU     0FFFFh                          ; TRUE compare & mask
;
;       < INCLUDES FOR EQUATES AND MACROS GO HERE >
;
;---- INITIALIZATION ---------------------------------------------
_TEXT   SEGMENT WORD PUBLIC 'CODE'      ; code segment
_TEXT   ENDS
_DATA   SEGMENT WORD PUBLIC 'DATA'      ; data segment
_DATA   ENDS
STACK   SEGMENT PARA STACK 'STACK'      ; stack segment
STACK   ENDS
;
DGROUP  GROUP   _DATA, STACK
;
        ASSUME  cs:_TEXT, ds:DGROUP, ss:DGROUP, es:DGROUP
;
_TEXT   SEGMENT                         ; begin code segment
; Local data storage (keep these definitions in the code
; segment):
DSsave          dw      seg DGROUP      ; storage for DS register
;
_TEXT   ENDS
_DATA   SEGMENT
PSPseg          dw      ?               ; PSP segment
_DATA   ENDS
```

continued

Listing A-5. *continued*

```
_TEXT    SEGMENT
;
main     PROC    NEAR                        ; begin main process
         mov     ds,DSsave                   ; initialize DS
         mov     ax,es                       ; get PSP seg. address
         mov     word ptr PSPseg,ax          ; ... and save it
;
;
;        < MAIN ROUTINE GOES HERE >
;
;
         mov     ax,4C00h                    ; terminate program
         int     21h
;
main     ENDP
;
;-------------------------------------------------------------------
;
;        < THE REST OF YOUR ROUTINES GO HERE >
;
;-------------------------------------------------------------------
_TEXT    ENDS
_DATA    SEGMENT
;
;        < INSERT DATA HERE >
;
_DATA    ENDS
_TEXT    SEGMENT
;------------------------------------------------------------------
_TEXT    ENDS
         END     main
```

Listing A-6. .COM Program Template

```
PAGE    60,132                              ; wide listing
;------------------------------------------------------------------
FALSE   EQU     0                           ; FALSE compare
TRUE    EQU     0FFFFh                       ; TRUE compare & mask
;
;       < INCLUDES FOR EQUATES AND MACROS GO HERE >
;
;---- INITIALIZATION ----------------------------------------------
code    SEGMENT
```

```
        ASSUME  cs:code, ds:code, ss:code, es:code
;
main    PROC    NEAR
;
entry:  ORG     0100h
;
        mov     sp,offset top_of_stack  ; set new stack
;
;
;       < MAIN ROUTINE GOES HERE >
;
;
        mov     ax,4C00h                ; terminate program
        int     21h
;
main    ENDP
;
;-------------------------------------------------------------
;
;       < THE REST OF YOUR ROUTINES GO HERE >
;
;-------------------------------------------------------------
;
;       < INSERT DATA HERE >
;
;-------------------------------------------------------------
; Optional stack - CAUTION - You *must* use function 4Ch
; to terminate the program if you use a local stack !
;
        db      32 DUP ('stack   ')     ; 256 byte stack
top_of_stack    EQU     $
;
;-------------------------------------------------------------
code    ENDS                            ; end code segment
        END     entry
```

Listing A-7. Useful Macros (STDMAC.INC)

```
;-------------------------------------------------------------
; MACRO DEFINITIONS INCLUDE FILE
;-------------------------------------------------------------
; STANDARD EQUATES:
;
TRUE    EQU     OFFFFh                  ; TRUE
```

continued

Listing A-7. *continued*

```
FALSE    EQU     0                    ; FALSE
;
; Standard nonprintable ASCII characters:
NUL      EQU     00000000b            ; null
BEL      EQU     00000111b            ; bell
BS       EQU     00001000b            ; backspace
HT       EQU     00001001b            ; horizontal tab
LF       EQU     00001010b            ; line feed
FF       EQU     00001100b            ; form feed
CR       EQU     00001101b            ; carriage return
SUBST    EQU     00011010b            ; substitute
ESCAPE   EQU     00011011b            ; escape
SPACE    EQU     00100000b            ; space
COLON    EQU     00111010b            ; colon
SCOLON   EQU     00111011b            ; semicolon
;
; IBM Extended characters:
SLINE    EQU     11000100b            ; horizontal line
;
;-------------------------------------------------------------
..XLIST                               ; suppress listing macro defs.
;;.LALL                               ; list everything
;;
;;
;;** @Model ***************************** GENERAL PURPOSE MACRO **
;; Set up segments according to memory model.
;; This macro emulates the MASM 5.X .MODEL
;; directive for use with earlier versions of
;; of MASM.
IF1       ;; assemble only during Pass 1
@Model MACRO memory_model,code_name,stack_size
        ;; NOTE: "code_name" is used only with medium,
        ;;       large, and huge memory models.
        IFNB <memory_model>       ;; was memory model specified?
        ;;
          IF memory_model EQ 0
            @TinyModel stack_size
          ELSE
            IF memory_model EQ 1
              @SmallModel stack_size
            ELSE
              IF memory_model EQ 2
                @MediumModel code_name,stack_size
              ELSE
                IF memory_model EQ 3
```

```
                     @CompactModel stack_size
                 ELSE
                   IF memory_model EQ 4
                     @LargeModel code_name,stack_size
                   ELSE
                     IF memory_model EQ 5
                       @LargeModel code_name,stack_size
                     ELSE
                      .ERR
                       %OUT @Model macro: unknown memory model
                     ENDIF ;; end of huge model check
                   ENDIF ;; end of large model check
                 ENDIF ;; end of compact model check
               ENDIF ;; end of medium model check
             ENDIF ;; end of small model check
           ENDIF ;; end of tiny model check
         ;;
         ELSE      ;; memory model was not specified
          .ERR            ;; terminate with error message
          %OUT @Model macro error: Memory model not specified.
         ENDIF     ;; end of memory-model parameter check
         ;;
         ENDM      ;; end of macro definition
ENDIF     ;; end of pass execution
;;
;;** @Tiny **************************** GENERAL PURPOSE MACRO **
;; Direct macro to set up TINY memory model (.COM type programs)
;; (This macro is called via "@Model 0".
;; This macro may also be called directly.)
;; Note that this macro, unlike the other memory-model macros,
;; does not make use of the @Stack macro, since alternate
;; stacks in .COM programs must be defined at the end of
;; of the program. To define an alternate stack in a .COM
;; program, execute the @Stack macro at the appropriate position
;; in the source code.
IF1       ;; assemble only during Pass 1
@TinyModel MACRO
         MEMODEL = 0
         _TEXT SEGMENT BYTE PUBLIC 'CODE' ; code segment
         _TEXT ENDS
         ;; Assign physical segments:
         ASSUME  cs:_TEXT, ds:_TEXT, ss:_TEXT, es:_TEXT
         ;;-------------------------------------------------
         ;; Insert the following code manually after @Model 0:
         ;;
         ;; _TEXT  SEGMENT
```

continued

Listing A-7. *continued*

```
;; main   PROC near
;; entry: ORG   0100h
;;           jmp   start
;;           ; <insert data here if desired>
;; start:
;;           ; <insert program code here>
;; main   ENDP
;;           ; <insert routines here>
;;           ; <Insert optional stack here>
;;           ; <insert data at the end if desired>
;; _TEXT ENDS
;;           END   entry
;;-----------------------------------------------
;;
      ENDM   ;; end of macro definition
ENDIF    ;; end of pass execution
;;
;;** @Small *************************** GENERAL PURPOSE MACRO **
;; Direct macro to set up SMALL memory model
;; (This macro is called via "@Model small".
;; This macro may also be called directly.)
IF1      ;; assemble only during Pass 1
@SmallModel MACRO stack_size
      MEMODEL = 1
      _TEXT SEGMENT BYTE PUBLIC 'CODE'   ; code segment
      _TEXT ENDS
      _DATA SEGMENT WORD PUBLIC 'DATA'   ; data seg. (DGROUP)
      _DATA ENDS
      CONST SEGMENT WORD PUBLIC 'CONST' ; constants segment
      CONST ENDS                        ; ... (DGROUP)
      _BSS  SEGMENT WORD PUBLIC 'BSS'   ; uninitialized data
      _BSS  ENDS                        ; ... segment (DGROUP)
      STACK SEGMENT PARA STACK 'STACK'  ; stack seg. (DGROUP)
      STACK ENDS
      ;;
      IFNB <stack_size>
            @Stack stack_size
      ENDIF
      ;;
      DGROUP GROUP _DATA,CONST,_BSS,STACK ; data seg. grouping
      ;;
      ;; Assign physical segments:
      ASSUME  cs:_TEXT, ds:DGROUP, ss:DGROUP, es:DGROUP
      ;;
```

```
            ENDM     ;; end of macro definition
    ENDIF  ;; end of pass execution
    ;;
    ;;** @Medium *********************** GENERAL PURPOSE MACRO **
    ;; Direct macro to set up MEDIUM memory model
    ;; (This macro is called via "@Model medium".
    ;; This macro may also be called directly.)
    IF1      ;; assemble only during Pass 1
    @MediumModel MACRO code_name,stack_size
            MEMODEL = 2
            code_name_TEXT SEGMENT BYTE PUBLIC 'CODE' ; named code
            code_name_TEXT ENDS                    ; ... segment
            _DATA SEGMENT WORD PUBLIC 'DATA'  ; data segment (DGROUP)
            _DATA ENDS
            CONST SEGMENT WORD PUBLIC 'CONST' ; constants segment
            CONST ENDS                        ; ... (DGROUP)
            _BSS  SEGMENT WORD PUBLIC 'BSS'   ; uninitialized data
            _BSS  ENDS                        ; ... segment (DGROUP)
            STACK SEGMENT PARA STACK 'STACK'  ; stack seg. (DGROUP)
            STACK ENDS
            ;;
            IFNB <stack_size>
                    @Stack stack_size
            ENDIF
            ;;
            DGROUP GROUP _DATA,CONST,_BSS,STACK ; data seg. grouping
            ;;
            ;; Assign physical segments:
            ASSUME  cs:_TEXT, ds:DGROUP, ss:DGROUP, es:DGROUP
            ;;
            ENDM     ;; end of macro definition
    ENDIF    ;; end of pass execution
    ;;
    ;;** @Compact ********************** GENERAL PURPOSE MACRO **
    ;; Direct macro to set up COMPACT memory model
    ;; (This macro is called via "@Model compact".
    ;; This macro may also be called directly.)
    IF1      ;; assemble only during Pass 1
    @CompactModel MACRO stack_size
            MEMODEL = 3
            _TEXT SEGMENT BYTE PUBLIC 'CODE' ; code segment
            _TEXT ENDS
            FAR_DATA SEGMENT PARA 'FAR_DATA' ; private far data
            FAR_DATA ENDS                    ; ... segment (DGROUP)
            FAR_BSS  SEGMENT PARA 'FAR_BSS'  ; private far unini-
            FAR_BSS  ENDS              ; ... tialized data seg. (DGROUP)
```

continued

Listing A-7. *continued*

```
        _DATA SEGMENT WORD PUBLIC 'DATA' ; data segment (DGROUP)
        _DATA ENDS
        CONST SEGMENT WORD PUBLIC 'CONST' ; constants segment
        CONST ENDS                        ; ... (DGROUP)
        _BSS  SEGMENT WORD PUBLIC 'BSS'   ; uninitialized data
        _BSS  ENDS                        ; ... segment (DGROUP)
        STACK SEGMENT PARA STACK 'STACK'  ; stack seg. (DGROUP)
        STACK ENDS
        ;;
        IFNB <stack_size>
                @Stack stack_size
        ENDIF
        ;;
        DGROUP GROUP _DATA,CONST,_BSS,STACK ; data seg. grouping
        ;;
        ;; Assign physical segments:
        ASSUME  cs:_TEXT, ds:DGROUP, ss:DGROUP, es:DGROUP
        ;;
        ENDM    ;; end of macro definition
ENDIF   ;; end of pass execution
;;
;;** @Large ************************** GENERAL PURPOSE MACRO **
;; Direct macro to set up LARGE memory model
;; (This macro is called via "@Model large".
;; This macro may also be called directly.)
IF1     ;; assemble only during Pass 1
@LargeModel MACRO code_name,stack_size
        MEMODEL = 4
        code_name_TEXT SEGMENT BYTE PUBLIC 'CODE' ; named code seg.
        code_name_TEXT ENDS
        FAR_DATA SEGMENT PARA 'FAR_DATA'  ; private far data
        FAR_DATA ENDS                     ; ... segment (DGROUP)
        FAR_BSS  SEGMENT PARA 'FAR_BSS'   ; private far unini-
        FAR_BSS  ENDS             ; ... tialized data seg. (DGROUP)
        _DATA SEGMENT WORD PUBLIC 'DATA'  ; data segment (DGROUP)
        _DATA ENDS
        CONST SEGMENT WORD PUBLIC 'CONST' ; constants segment
        CONST ENDS                        ; ... (DGROUP)
        _BSS  SEGMENT WORD PUBLIC 'BSS'   ; uninitialized data
        _BSS  ENDS                        ; ... segment (DGROUP)
        STACK SEGMENT PARA STACK 'STACK'  ; stack seg. (DGROUP)
        STACK ENDS
        ;;
        IFNB <stack_size>
```

```
              @Stack stack_size
          ENDIF
          ;;
          DGROUP GROUP _DATA,CONST,_BSS,STACK ; data seg. grouping
          ;;
          ;; Assign physical segments:
          ASSUME  cs:_TEXT, ds:DGROUP, ss:DGROUP, es:DGROUP
          ;;
          ENDM     ;; end of macro definition
  ENDIF   ;; end of pass execution
  ;;
  ;;** @Huge **************************** GENERAL PURPOSE MACRO **
  ;; Direct macro to set up HUGE memory model
  ;; (This macro is called via "@Model huge".
  ;; This macro may also be called directly.)
  ;; The HUGE memory model is currently set up the
  ;; same as the LARGE memory model.
  IF1      ;; assemble only during Pass 1
  @HugeModel MACRO code_name,stack_size
          MEMODEL = 5
          @LargeModel code_name,stack_size
          ENDM     ;; end of macro definition
  ENDIF    ;; end of pass execution
  ;;
  ;;** @Stack **************************** GENERAL PURPOSE MACRO **
  ;; Direct macro to establish the size of the stack
  IF1      ;; assemble only during Pass 1
  @Stack MACRO stack_size,prog_type
          ;;
          IFB <prog_type> ;; if prog_type parameter is blank ...
            IF MEMODEL EQ 0
              PROGTYPE = 0
            ELSE
              IF MEMODEL EQ 1
                PROGTYPE = 1
              ELSE
                IF MEMODEL EQ 2
                  PROGTYPE = 1
                ELSE
                  IF MEMODEL EQ 3
                    PROGTYPE = 1
                  ELSE
                    IF MEMODEL EQ 4
                      PROGTYPE = 1
                    ELSE
```

continued

709

Listing A-7. *continued*

```
        IF MEMODEL EQ 5
          PROGTYPE = 1
        ELSE
            .ERR
            %OUT @Stack macro: The memory model or
            %OUT program type was not established.
        ENDIF ;; end of huge model check
      ENDIF ;; end of large model check
     ENDIF ;; end of compact model check
    ENDIF ;; end of medium model check
   ENDIF ;; end of small model check
  ENDIF ;; end of tiny model check
ELSE ;; prog_type parameter was specified
  IF prog_type EQ 0      ;; set up for .COM type program
    PROGTYPE = 0
  ELSE
    IF prog_type EQ 1
      PROGTYPE = 1
    ELSE
      .ERR        ;; exit with error message
      %OUT @Stack macro: Incorrect prog. type specified.
    ENDIF ;; end of .EXE type check
  ENDIF ;; end of .COM type check
ENDIF ;; end of "prog_type" parameter check
;;
IFNB <stack_size>
;;
  IF PROGTYPE EQ 0
        ; Optional stack. CAUTION! You MUST use
        ; function 4Ch to terminate the program
        ; when using a local stack!
                db      stack_size DUP ('stack    ')
        top_of_stack    EQU       $
  ELSE ;; prog. type is .EXE
        STACK SEGMENT
                db      stack_size DUP ('stack    ')
        STACK ENDS
  ENDIF ;; end of PROGTYPE check
;;
ELSE ;; "stack_size" parameter wasn't specified
;;
  IF PROGTYPE EQ 0
        ; Optional stack. CAUTION! You MUST use
        ; function 4Ch to terminate the program
```

```
                ; when using a local stack!
                    db      32 DUP ('stack   ')
            top_of_stack    EQU     $
      ELSE ;; prog. type is .EXE
            STACK SEGMENT
                        db          32 DUP ('stack    ')
                STACK ENDS
            ENDIF ;; end of PROGTYPE check
            ;;
            ENDIF   ;; end of "stack_size" check
            ;;
            ENDM    ;; end of macro definition
ENDIF   ;; end of pass execution
;;
;;** @SwapNewStack ******************** GENERAL PURPOSE MACRO **
;; Switch stack to a new stack
IF1     ;; assemble only during Pass 1
@SwapNewStack MACRO tos
        LOCAL   bypass
        ;;
        jmp     bypass          ;; skip data area
old_stk_seg dw      ?           ;; space for caller's stack segment
old_stk_ptr dw      ?           ;; space for caller's stack pointer
new_stk_seg dw      ?           ;; space for new stack segment
new_stk_ptr dw  offset tos ;; space for new stack pointer
        ;;
bypass:
        mov     cs:new_stk_seg,cs ;; set new stack segment
        mov     cs:old_stk_seg,ss ;; save old stack values
        mov     cs:old_stk_ptr,sp ;; save old stack pointer
        mov     ss,cs:new_stk_seg ;; get new stack values
        mov     sp,cs:new_stk_ptr ;; get new stack pointer
        @PushAll                  ;; save flags and all registers
        ENDM    ;; end of macro definition
ENDIF   ;; end of pass execution
;;
;;** @SwapOldStack ******************** GENERAL PURPOSE MACRO **
;; Switch from new stack to the original stack.
        @PopAll                   ;; restore flags and all regs.
        mov     ss,cs:old_stk_seg ;; restore old stack values
        mov     sp,cs:old_stk_ptr
        ENDM    ;; end of macro definition
ENDIF   ;; end of pass execution
;;
;;** @DosCall *********************** GENERAL PURPOSE MACRO **
;; Call an MS-DOS function
```

continued

Listing A-7. *continued*

```
IF1        ;; assemble only during Pass 1
@DosCall MACRO
        int     21h
        ENDM    ;; end of macro definition
ENDIF   ;; end of pass execution
;;
;;** @DirConCharIO ****************** GENERAL PURPOSE MACRO **
@DirConCharIO MACRO              ; check keyboard status & read
        push    dx              ; save DX
        mov     dl,OFFh         ; no character to output
        mov     ah,06h
        @DosCall
        pop     dx              ; restore DX
        ENDM
;;
;;** @ReadCon_NoEcho ***************** GENERAL PURPOSE MACRO **
@ReadCon_NoEcho MACRO
        mov     ah,08h          ; read keyboard without echo
        @DosCall
        ENDM
;;
;;** @ReadBuffInput ****************** GENERAL PURPOSE MACRO **
@ReadBuffInput MACRO buffname   ; read buffered keyboard input
        mov     dx,offset bufname
        mov     ah,OAh
        @DosCall
        ENDM
;;
;;** @DisChr ************************* GENERAL PURPOSE MACRO **
;; Display an immediate character
IF1        ;; assemble only during Pass 1
@DisChr MACRO   char
        IFNB <char>     ;; was character argument specified?
                        ;; yes, so insert code
        push    ax      ;; save registers used
        push    dx
        mov     dl,char ;; load character
        mov     ah,02h  ;; load func. number
        @DosCall        ;; call MS-DOS
        pop     dx      ;; restore registers
        pop     ax
        ELSE            ;; otherwise
        .ERR            ;; generate error and output message
        %OUT @DisChr macro: "char" argument not supplied.
```

```
          ENDIF
          ;;
          ENDM     ;; end of macro definition
   ENDIF     ;; end of pass execution
   ;;
   ;;** @DisStr ************************* GENERAL PURPOSE MACRO **
   ;; Display a string from memory with default "$"
   ;; end-of-string terminator or with a specified
   ;; terminator.
   ;; (Calls @DisStr1 or @DisStr2 internal macros.)
   IF1               ;; assemble only during Pass 1
   @DisStr MACRO   string,terminator
          IFNB <string>    ;; was string argument specified?
                           ;; yes, so ...
            IFB <terminator> ;; was terminator specified?
                  ;; no, so insert default code for "$" terminator
                  @DisStr1 string
            ELSE  ;; otherwise, a terminator was specified
                  @DisStr2 string,terminator
            ENDIF ;; end "terminator" check
          ELSE    ;; otherwise, "string" was not specified
          .ERR    ;; generate error and output message
          %OUT @DisStr macro: "string" argument not supplied.
          ENDIF
          ENDM     ;; end of macro definition
   ENDIF   ;; end of pass execution
   ;;
   ;;** @DisStr1 ****************************** SUPPORT MACRO **
   ;; Called by @DisStr to display a string from memory with
   ;; default "$" end-of-string terminator.
   IF1      ;; assemble only during Pass 1
   @DisStr1 MACRO  string
          push    ax        ;;save registers used
          push    dx
          mov     dx,offset ds:string ;; point to string
                                      ;; in memory
          mov     ah,09h ;; load func. number
          @DosCall          ;; call MS-DOS
          pop     dx        ;; restore registers used
          pop     ax
          ENDM     ;; end of macro definition
   ENDIF   ;; end of pass execution
   ;;
   ;;** @DisStr2 ****************************** SUPPORT MACRO **
   ;; Called by @DisStr to display a string from memory with a
   ;; specified end-of-string terminator.
```

continued

Listing A-7. *continued*

```
IF1      ;; assemble only during Pass 1
@DisStr2 MACRO   string,terminator
         LOCAL   strloop,strloopdone ;; create local labels
         push    si                  ;; save registers
         push    ax
         push    bx
         push    dx
         xor     bh,bh           ;; clear BX
         mov     bl,terminator   ;; get the terminator
         mov     si,offset string ;; point to string
         xor     dx,dx
strloop:
         mov     dl,byte ptr [si] ;; get next char.
         cmp     dl,bl           ;; is it the terminator?
         je      strloopdone     ;; yes, we're done
         mov     ah,02h          ;; load output-char. function
         @DosCall                ;; and call DOS
         inc     si              ;; point to next char.
         jmp     short strloop   ;; and go thru again
strloopdone:
         pop     dx              ;; restore registers
         pop     bx
         pop     ax
         pop     si
         ENDM    ;; end of macro definition
ENDIF   ;; end of pass execution
;;
;;** @TypeStr ************************* GENERAL PURPOSE MACRO **
;; Display an immediate string (string defined on the fly)
;; NOTE: "string" must be presented within quotes so that
;; it is treated as a single argument to the macro and to
;; ensure that the data is encoded correctly.
IF1      ;; assemble only during Pass 1
@TypeStr MACRO   string              ;; define and display a string
         LOCAL   TypeStrAddr         ;; set up a local label
         ;;
         IF MEMODEL NE 0             ;; if not .COM type
_TEXT    ENDS                        ;; end code segment
_DATA    SEGMENT                     ;; change to data segment
         ENDIF
TypeStrAddr DB  string,'$'           ;; define string in data segment
         IF MEMODEL NE 0             ;; if not .COM type
_DATA    ENDS                        ;; end data segment
_TEXT    SEGMENT                     ;; return to code segment
```

```
          ENDIF
          ;;
          @DisStr TypeStrAddr      ;; display string
          ENDM    ;; end of macro definition
ENDIF     ;; end of pass execution
;;
;;** @TypeStrCR *********************** GENERAL PURPOSE MACRO **
;; Display an immediate string terminated with a CR/LF
IF1       ;; assemble only during Pass 1
;; "string" must be presented within quotes so that it is
;; treated as a single argument to the macro.
@TypeStrCR MACRO string
          @TypeStr string          ;; define and display string
          @NewLine                 ;; terminate with a CR/LF
          ENDM    ;; end of macro definition
ENDIF     ;; end of pass execution
;;
;;** @NewLine *********************** GENERAL PURPOSE MACRO **
;; Display a carriage return and linefeed
IF1       ;; assemble only during Pass 1
@NewLine MACRO
          IFNDEF  EXT_NEWLINE      ;; was EXT_NEWLINE symbol defined?
          EXTRN   newline:NEAR     ;; no, insert EXTRN only once
          EXT_NEWLINE EQU 0        ;; and define equate only once
          ENDIF               ;; (the above 2 lines won't be inserted
                              ;; in subsequent calls of the macro)
          call    newline ;; call NEWLINE procedure
          ENDM    ;; end of macro definition
ENDIF     ;; end of pass execution
;;
;;** @DisNum *********************** GENERAL PURPOSE MACRO **
;; Display a binary number in ASCII decimal or hexadecimal
IF1       ;; assemble only during Pass 1
@DisNum MACRO number,type,digits,sign
          ;;
          ;; Test for required parameters first
          IFB <number>    ;; was number parameter specified?
          .ERR            ;; no, exit with error message
          %OUT @DisNum macro: "number" parameter not specified.
          ENDIF
          ;;
          IFNB <type>     ;; was type of output specified?
          ;;
            IF type EQ 10          ;; decimal conversion specified?
              IFNDEF EXT_BIN2DEC   ;; was EXT_BIN2DEC defined?
              EXTRN bin2dec:NEAR   ;; no, insert EXTRN declaration
```

continued

Listing A-7. *continued*

```
        EXT_BIN2DEC EQU 0    ;; and equate only once
        ENDIF
        ;;
        ELSE
        ;;
     IF type EQ 16           ;; hex. conversion specified?
      IFNDEF EXT_BIN2HEX      ;; was EXT_BIN2HEX defined?
      EXTRN    bin2hex:NEAR   ;; no, insert EXTRN declara-
      EXT_BIN2HEX EQU 0       ;; tion and equate only once
      ENDIF
    ;;
    ELSE
    ;;
      .ERR
      %OUT @DisNum Macro: Illegal "type" specified.
      ENDIF    ;; end check for 16
  ;;
  ENDIF ;; end check for 10
;;
ELSE     ;; otherwise, parameter is blank
;;
.ERR     ;; exit with error message
%OUT @DisNum macro: "type" parameter not specified.
ENDIF    ;; end check for blank parameter
;; End test for required parameters
;;
;; Begin code insertion
push    ax          ;; save registers
push    cx
push    dx
;;
mov     ax,number ;; put number in AX
;;
IFNB <digits>       ;; was digits argument specified?
mov     ch,digits ;; yes, put value in CH
ELSE                ;; otherwise
mov     ch,1        ;; default to disp. at least 1 digit
ENDIF
;;
IFNB <sign>         ;; was the sign argument specified?
mov     dx,sign   ;; yes, so put it in DX
ELSE                ;; otherwise
mov     dx,0        ;; default to unsigned
ENDIF
```

```
;;
IF type EQ 10      ;; decimal conversion specified?
call    bin2dec
ELSE
        IF type EQ 16     ;; hex. conversion specified?
                call    bin2hex
                ENDIF    ;; end of base 16 check
        ENDIF   ;; end of base 10 check
        ;;
        pop     dx        ;; restore registers
        pop     cx
        pop     ax
        ;;
        ENDM     ;; end of macro definition
ENDIF    ;; end of pass execution
;;
;;
;;** @GetDate ************************** GENERAL PURPOSE MACRO **
;; Get the system date
IF1      ;; assemble only during Pass 1
@GetDate MACRO
        mov     ah,2Ah  ;; load func. number
        @DosCall          ;; call MS-DOS
        ENDM     ;; end of macro definition
ENDIF    ;; end of pass execution
;;
;;** @GetTime ************************** GENERAL PURPOSE MACRO **
;; Get the system time
IF1      ;; assemble only during Pass 1
@GetTime MACRO
        mov     ah,2Ch  ;; load func. number
        @DosCall          ;; call MS-DOS
        ENDM     ;; end of macro definition
ENDIF    ;; end of pass execution
;;
;;** @DiskRead ************************* GENERAL PURPOSE MACRO **
;; Read from logical sector(s)
IF1      ;; assemble only during Pass 1
@DiskRead MACRO
        int     25h       ;; execute absolute disk-read interrupt
        ENDM     ;; end of macro definition
ENDIF    ;; end of pass execution
;;
;;** @DiskWrite ************************ GENERAL PURPOSE MACRO **
;; Write to logical sector(s)
IF1      ;; assemble only during Pass 1
```

continued

Listing A-7. *continued*

```
@DiskWrite MACRO
          int     26h      ;; execute absolute disk-write interrupt
          ENDM    ;; end of macro definition
ENDIF     ;; end of pass execution
;;
;;** @GetDOSVersion ****************** GENERAL PURPOSE MACRO **
;; Get DOS Version number
IF1       ;; assemble only during Pass 1
@GetDOSVersion MACRO
          push    bx       ;; save registers destroyed
          push    cx
          mov     ah,30h   ;; load func. number
          @DosCall         ;; call MS-DOS
          pop     cx       ;; restore registers
          pop     bx
          ENDM    ;; end of macro definition
ENDIF     ;; end of pass execution
;;
;;** @GetDOSVer ********************* GENERAL PURPOSE MACRO **
;; Get DOS Version number
IF1       ;; assemble only during Pass 1
@GetDOSVer MACRO
          IFNDEF  EXT_GDOSV     ;; was symbol defined?
          EXTRN   GETDOSV:NEAR  ;; no, insert EXTRN only once
          EXT_GDOSV EQU 0       ;; and define equate only once
          ENDIF                 ;; (the above 2 lines won't be inserted
                                ;; in subsequent calls of the macro)
          call    dosver        ;; call library routine
          ENDM    ;; end of macro definition
ENDIF     ;; end of pass execution
;;
;;** @DisDOSVer ********************* GENERAL PURPOSE MACRO **
;; Get and display DOS Version number
IF1       ;; assemble only during Pass 1
@DisDOSVer MACRO
          IFNDEF  EXT_DDOSV     ;; was symbol defined?
          EXTRN   DOSV2CON:NEAR ;; no, insert EXTRN only once
          EXT_DDOSV EQU 0 ;; and define equate only once
          ENDIF                 ;; (the above 2 lines won't be inserted
                                ;; in subsequent calls of the macro)
          call    dosv2con ;; call library routine
          ENDM    ;; end of macro definition
ENDIF     ;; end of pass execution
;;
```

```
;;** @ChangeCase ********************** GENERAL PURPOSE MACRO **
;; Change case of character
IF1      ;; execute only on pass 1
@ChangeCase MACRO char,type
        IFB <char>       ;; was char to be converted specified?
        .ERR             ;; no, generate error and output message
        %OUT @ChangeCase macro: "char" parameter not defined!
        ELSE             ;; otherwise
        mov     al,char ;; load char into AL
        ENDIF
        ;;
        IFB <type>       ;; was type of conversion specified?
        mov     ah,0     ;; no, so load 0 into AH
        ELSE
        mov     ah,type ;; load type of conversion into AH
        ENDIF
        ;;
        IFNDEF  EXT_CHGCASE    ;; was EXT_CHGCASE symbol defined?
        EXTRN   CHGCASE:NEAR   ;; no, insert EXTRN only once
        EXT_CHGCASE EQU 0      ;; and define equate only once
        ENDIF                  ;; (the above 2 lines won't be inserted
                               ;; in subsequent calls of the macro)
        ;;
        call    chgcase ;; call change-case library procedure
        ENDM    ;; end of macro definition
ENDIF   ;; end of pass execution
;;
;;** @Case *************************** GENERAL PURPOSE MACRO **
;; CASE macro for assembly language
@Case   MACRO   key,case_list,jmp_labels
        ??tmp_1 = 0
        IRP     match,<&case_list>        ;; sequence through cases
          ??tmp_1 = ??tmp_1 + 1           ;; set index number
          cmp   key,&&match               ; case match?
          ??tmp_2 = 0
          IRP   retl,<&jmp_labels>        ;; sequence through jumps
            ??tmp_2 = ??tmp_2 + 1         ;; ... until index matches
            IF  (??tmp_1 EQ ??tmp_2)
              je  &&retl                  ; yes!
              EXITM
            ENDIF          ;; end condition check
          ENDM            ;; end 2nd IRP block
        ENDM            ;; end 1st IRP block
        ENDM            ;; end macro definition
;;
;;
```

continued

Listing A-7. *continued*

```
;;********************************************************************
;; Use the @PushAll and @PopAll macros instead of the
;; PUSHA and POPA instructions supported by the
;; 80186/80188/80286/80386 processors to maintain
;; compatibility with the 8086/8088 processors.
;;
;;** @PushAll ************************* GENERAL PURPOSE MACRO **
;; Push all registers
IF1                          ;; execute only during pass 1
@PushAll MACRO               ;; save all registers onto the stack
        push    ax
        push    bx
        push    cx
        push    dx
        push    bp
        push    di
        push    si
        ENDM    ;; end of macro definition
ENDIF   ;; end of pass execution
;;
;;** @PopAll ************************* GENERAL PURPOSE MACRO **
;; Pop all registers
IF1     ;; execute only during pass 1
@PopAll MACRO                ;; restore all registers off of the stack
        pop     si
        pop     di
        pop     bp
        pop     dx
        pop     cx
        pop     bx
        pop     ax
        ENDM    ;; end of macro definition
ENDIF   ;; end of pass execution
;;
;;** @ExitToDos *********************** GENERAL PURPOSE MACRO **
;; Terminate process with optional ERRORLEVEL settings
IF1     ;; execute only during pass 1
@ExitToDOS MACRO errorcode
        IFB <errorcode>  ;; was an errorcode specified?
        mov     ax,4C00h ;; no, load func. & errorlevel 0 into AX
        ELSE             ;; otherwise
        mov     ah,4Ch   ;; load function
        mov     al,errorcode ;; and errorlevel separately
        ENDIF
```

```
        ;;
        @DosCall          ;; call MS-DOS
        ENDM    ;; end of macro definition
ENDIF   ;; end of pass execution
;;
;;*********************************************************************
;; END OF MACRO DEFINITIONS
;;*********************************************************************
.LIST                           ; restore listing back to normal
; End of macro definitions include file.
```

Using Library Routines

If you use a standard set of unmodified routines in all your programs, you may find it practical to put these routines in a library file that is always linked with your programs. Using this method simplifies the assembly and linking process and reduces the size of your program source files. A library file is created by assembling the file containing your routines and then processing the .OBJ file with the LIB program included on the MASM disk. The LIB program produces a correctly formatted object code file with the extension .LIB. The external references to the routines should be declared within the source code of the program that is to call these routines. These are written in the format:

    EXTRN *routine:distance*

where EXTRN is the directive that informs MASM that *routine* will be included at link time, from either another object file or a library file. The *distance* parameter is either *near* or *far*, depending on how the referenced routine was declared. For .COM type programs, *distance* is always *near*. Once the external routines have been declared, they can be called like any other routine.

Listing A-8 provides a complete source to the library file STDLIB.LIB, as discussed in previous chapters.

Listing A-8. Source for STDLIB.LIB Library File

```
PAGE 60,132
TITLE   stdlib.asm/.obj → .lib
.8086                   ; allow only 8086/8088 instructions
.SALL                   ; suppress macro expansion listing
;-----------------------------------------------------------------
;
;------ EQUATES AND MACRO DEFINITIONS ------------------------------
;
INCLUDE stdmac.inc      ; include standard macro library and equates
```

continued

Listing A-8. *continued*

```
;
;----- INITIALIZATION ----------------------------------------
;
; The following initialization is a subset of (and compatible
; with) the ".MODEL SMALL" directive in MASM 5.0 and higher
; versions.
;
_TEXT    SEGMENT  WORD PUBLIC 'CODE'       ; code segment
_TEXT    ENDS
;
_DATA    SEGMENT  WORD PUBLIC 'DATA'       ; data segment
_DATA    ENDS
;
DGROUP   GROUP   _DATA                     ; define segment group
;
ASSUME   cs:_TEXT, ds:_DATA                ; assign physical segments
;
;
;*******************************************************************
; BEGIN LIBRARY ROUTINES
;*******************************************************************
;
_TEXT    SEGMENT                           ; begin code segment
;
;+++++++++++++++++++++++++++++++++++++++++++++++++++++++++++++++++++
; NEWLINE - Displays a new line (carriage return + linefeed).
;
; INPUT:        None
;
; OUTPUT:       AX and DX are restored;
;               no other registers are used.
;
; ROUTINES CALLED: None
;-----------------------------------------------------------------
PUBLIC   NEWLINE                           ; library routine
;
newline PROC    NEAR
        push    ax                        ; save registers
        push    dx
;
        mov     dl,CR                     ; display carriage return
        mov     ah,02h
        @DosCall
        mov     dl,LF                     ; display linefeed
```

```
          mov     ah,02h
          @DosCall
;
          pop     dx        ; restore registers
          pop     ax
          ret
;
newline ENDP
;
;
;++++++++++++++++++++++++++++++++++++++++++++++++++++++++++++++++++++++
; CSAVE: Performs an automatic saving and restoral of the
; BX, CX, DI, and SI registers within a called subroutine.
; It is called from within another called routine, as follows:
;
;- - - - - - - - - - - - - - - - - - - - - - - - - - - - - - - - -
; LOCALSIZE    EQU     10h
; routine PROC  NEAR     ; FAR if medium, large, or huge model
;
;          push    bp
;          mov     bp,sp
;          sub     sp,LOCALSIZE
;          call    csave
;          :
;          (routine's code)
;          :
;          ret                ; always goes to $cret
;
; routine ENDP
;- - - - - - - - - - - - - - - - - - - - - - - - - - - - - - - - -
;
; INPUT:        See description above.
;
; OUTPUT:       See description above.
;
; REGISTERS USED: BX, CX, DI, & SI are saved;
;                 AX & DX aren't touched.
;
; ROUTINES CALLED: Calls "calling" routine, until its RET returns
; to this routine, whereupon this routine's RET returns to the
; original calling location.
;-----------------------------------------------------------------
PUBLIC  CSAVE              ; library routine
;
csave   PROC    NEAR
          push    bp        ; set up stack addressing
```

continued

723

Listing A-8. *continued*

```
        mov     bp,sp
        xchg    bx,[bp+2]       ; save BX and obtain return
                                ; ... address of calling routine
        pop     bp              ; restore current return address
        push    cx              ; save remainder of registers
        push    si
        push    di
        call    bx              ; resume processing in calling
                                ; ... routine
;
; Arrive here after calling routine's RET
$cret:  pop     di              ; restore saved registers
        pop     si
        pop     cx
        pop     bx
        mov     sp,bp           ; discard local variables
        pop     bp
        ret                     ; returns to where calling
                                ; ... routine's RET would
                                ; ... normally return
;
csave   ENDP
;
;
;++++++++++++++++++++++++++++++++++++++++++++++++++++++++++++++++++++++++
; BIN2DEC - BINary to DECimal conversion. Displays a 16-bit
; signed or unsigned number on the screen in decimal.
; Finds the rightmost digit by division. Repeat until all found.
; A minimum number of digits to be displayed can be specified:
; if minimum number of digits specified is greater than the
; actual number of digits, the output number is padded with
; leading zeros.
;
; INPUT:        AX = number to be displayed
;               CH = minimum number of digits to be displayed
;               DX = 0 if number is to be processed as unsigned,
;                    or 1, if signed.
;
; OUTPUT:       None (AX, CX, and DX are restored)
;
; ROUTINES CALLED: None
;----------------------------------------------------------------------
PUBLIC  BIN2DEC                 ; library routine
;
bin2dec PROC    NEAR
```

```
        push    ax                  ; save registers
        push    bx
        push    cx
        push    dx
        mov     cl,0                ; clear digit count
        mov     bx,10               ; set divisor = 10
        cmp     dx,0                ; always display # as positive?
        je      more_dec            ; yes, skip negative check
;
; Check for negative number. If negative, make number positive.
        or      ax,ax               ; is number positive?
        jnl     more_dec            ; yes, skip "negate"
        neg     ax                  ; make number positive
        @DisChr '-'                 ; display minus sign
;
; Main Division Loop - Get Decimal Digit
; Repeat as long as digits are remaining
more_dec:
        xor     dx,dx               ; cleanup
        div     bx                  ; divide by 10
        push    dx                  ; save remainder
        inc     cl                  ; digit counter + 1
        or      ax,ax               ; test quotient
        jnz     more_dec            ; continue if more
;
; Main Digit Print Loop - Reverse Order
        sub     ch,cl               ; min. number of digits reached?
        jle     morechr             ; yes - begin display
        xor     dx,dx               ; no - start pushing "0"s
morezero:
        push    dx
        inc     cl                  ; digit counter + 1
        dec     ch                  ; check if matched yet
        jnz     morezero            ; no - keep pushing it
morechr:
        pop     dx                  ; restore last digit
        add     dl,30h              ; convert to ASCII
        @DisChr dl                  ; output digit
        dec     cl                  ; digits count - 1
        jnz     morechr             ; continue if more
;
        pop     dx                  ; restore registers
        pop     cx
        pop     bx
        pop     ax
        ret
```

continued

Listing A-8. *continued*

```
;
bin2dec ENDP
;
;
;++++++++++++++++++++++++++++++++++++++++++++++++++++++++++++++++++++++
; BIN2DEC2 - BINary to DECimal conversion. Displays a 32-bit
; signed number. Creates two decimal numbers which are displayed
; through calls to BIN2DEC.
; A minimum number of digits to be displayed can be specified:
; if minimum number of digits specified is greater than the
; actual number of digits, the output number is padded with
; leading zeros.
;
; NOTE: The register pair containing the number is split by
; division by 10,000. Since, at most, the least significant
; portion is 9,999, it will never be displayed as a
; negative number.
;
; INPUT:         DX:AX = number to be displayed
;                CH = minimum number of digits to be displayed
;
; OUTPUT:        None (AX:DX and CX are restored)
;
; ROUTINES CALLED: BIN2DEC (output 16-bit number in decimal)
;-------------------------------------------------------------------
PUBLIC   BIN2DEC2                      ; library routine
;
bin2dec2 PROC    NEAR
;EXTRN   bin2dec:NEAR                  ; reference BIN2DEC routine
         push    ax                    ; save registers
         push    bx
         push    cx
         push    dx
;
; Check for negative number. If negative, make number positive.
         or      dx,dx                 ; is number positive?
         jnl     bd2_pos               ; yes, skip "negate"
         not     ax                    ; make number positive
         not     dx
         add     ax,1                  ; 2's complement the hard way
         adc     dx,0
         push    dx
         push    ax
         @DisChr '-'
```

```
        pop     ax
        pop     dx
;
; Now split the number to be printed into manageable parts
bd2_pos:
        mov     bx,10000        ; set divisor = 10,000
        div     bx              ; split number into pairs
        cmp     dx,0            ; quit if most significant number
        je      bd2_2big        ; ... is too large
        or      ax,ax           ; find out if most significant
                                ; ... number is zero
        jz      bd2_nosig       ; there is no most significant
                                ; ... number
;
; Print the most significant number first (leftmost number)
        push    dx
        sub     ch,4            ; four digits will be printed from
                                ; ... least significant part
        jnc     bd2_cntok       ; asked for more than 4, so count
                                ; ... is valid
        mov     ch,0            ; otherwise go until run out of
                                ; ... digits
bd2_cntok:
        call    bin2dec         ; print the most significant
                                ; ... portion
        pop     dx              ; recover least significant
                                ; ... portion
        mov     ch,4            ; four digits in least
                                ; ... significant number
;
; Print the least significant portion (rightmost number)
bd2_nosig:
        mov     ax,dx           ; print the DX portion (least
                                ; ... significant) first
        call    bin2dec         ; print least significant number
bd2_done:
        pop     dx              ; restore registers and exit
        pop     cx
        pop     bx
        pop     ax
        ret
bd2_2big:
        @DisStr Bin2BigErrMsg
        jmp     short bd2_done  ; return from routine
;
_TEXT   ENDS
```

continued

Listing A-8. *continued*

```
_DATA   SEGMENT
Bin2BigErrMsg   db        "BIN2DEC2 error: Number is too large.$"
_DATA   ENDS
_TEXT   SEGMENT
;
bin2dec2 ENDP
;
;
;+++++++++++++++++++++++++++++++++++++++++++++++++++++++++++++++++++++++++
; BIN2HEX - BINary to HEXadecimal conversion. Displays a 16-bit
; number in hexadecimal.
; A minimum number of digits to be displayed can be specified:
; if minimum number of digits specified is greater than the
; actual number of digits, the output number is padded with
; leading zeros.
;
; INPUT:        AX = number to display
;               CH = minimum number of digits to display
;                    (1 to 4)
;                    (If CH = 0, digit count defaults to 4.)
;
; OUTPUT        None (AX and CX are restored)
;
; CALLED ROUTINES: None.
;-----------------------------------------------------------------
PUBLIC  BIN2HEX                     ; library routine
;
bin2hex PROC    NEAR
        push    ax                  ; save registers
        push    bx
        push    cx
        push    dx
;
        mov     bx,ax               ; use BX as temporary holding
        cmp     ch,0                ; count already set?
        jne     align_left          ; yes, so continue
        mov     ch,4                ; else, set character count to 4
;
; Align the number on the leftmost side of the AX
; (rotate left by (4 - CH) * 4 bit positions
align_left:
        mov     cl,4                ; find number of digits to shift
        sub     cl,ch
        shl     cl,1                ; multiply by 4
        shl     cl,1
```

```
                rol     bx,cl               ; align on left side
                mov     cl,4                ; and set minor rotate count
        ;
        ; Main loop - repeat N times ... Print the leftmost digit
        more_hex:
                rol     bx,cl               ; left digit to right
                mov     al,bl               ; move to AL
                and     al,0Fh              ; right digit only
                add     al,90h              ; sneaky conversion
                daa                         ; ... to ASCII hex characters
                adc     al,40h
                daa
        ;
        ; Display digit
                @DisChr al
                dec     ch                  ; digits count - 1
                jnz     more_hex            ; continue if more
        ;
                pop     dx                  ; restore registers
                pop     cx
                pop     bx
                pop     ax
                ret
        ;
        bin2hex ENDP
        ;
        ;
        ;++++++++++++++++++++++++++++++++++++++++++++++++++++++++++++++++++
        ; CHGCASE - CHanGe CASE of character. Changes the case of an
        ; ASCII character. Type of case conversion is specified:
        ;
        ; 1. Forced upper-to-lower case conversion
        ; 2. Forced lower-to-upper case conversion
        ; 3. Toggle case (if lower, then upper; if upper, then lower)
        ;
        ; INPUT:          AL = ASCII alphabetic character to be converted
        ;                 AH = type of conversion:
        ;                         "L" or "l"     = force char. to lowercase
        ;                         "U" or "u"     = force char. to uppercase
        ;                         any other value = toggle case
        ;
        ; OUTPUT:         AL = converted ASCII character
        ;                 AH = character's status:
        ;                         "L" = lowercase
        ;                         "U" = uppercase
        ;                          0  = if character in AL wasn't an
```

continued

Listing A-8. *continued*

```
;                              ASCII alpha character
;                   All other registers are restored.
;
; ROUTINES CALLED:        None
;----------------------------------------------------------------
PUBLIC   CHGCASE                  ; library routine
;
chgcase PROC     NEAR
         push    dx               ; save registers
;
; Determine if AL contains an ASCII alpha character
; and if a valid character, determine its case.
         cmp     al,"A"      ; is char. below 1st uppercase let.?
         jl      error       ; yes, it isn't an ASCII alpha char.
         cmp     al,"Z"      ; is char. below last uppercase let.?
         jle     is_upper    ; yes, char. is uppercase.
         cmp     al,"a"      ; is char. below 1st lowercase let.?
         jl      error       ; yes, it isn't an ASCII alpha char.
         cmp     al,"z"      ; is char. below last lowercase let.?
         jle     is_lower    ; yes, char. is lowercase.
         jmp     short error ; else, it isn't an ASCII alpha char.
;
is_upper:
         mov     dl,"U"          ; flag character as uppercase
         jmp     short convert_type ; and continue
is_lower:
         mov     dl,"L"          ; flag character as lowercase
         jmp     short convert_type ; and continue
error:
         mov     ah,0            ; flag char. as not an ASCII
                                 ; ... alpha char.
         jmp     short done      ; and exit procedure
;
convert_type:
         cmp     ah,"l"          ; convert to lowercase?
         je      to_lower        ; yes, so convert character
         cmp     ah,"L"          ; convert to lowercase?
         je      to_lower        ; yes, so convert character
         cmp     ah,"u"          ; convert to uppercase?
         je      to_upper        ; yes, so convert character
         cmp     ah,"U"          ; convert to uppercase?
         je      to_upper        ; yes, so convert character
;
; Else, toggle character's case
```

```
        cmp     dl,"L"          ; is character lowercase?
        je      to_upper        ; yes, convert it to uppercase
                                ; ... else, it is uppercase,
                                ; ... so make it lower
;
to_lower:
        mov     ah,"L"          ; set the case flag for return
        cmp     dl,ah           ; is char. already lowercase?
        je      done            ; yes, so we're done
        add     al,20h          ; else, convert to lowercase
        jmp     short done      ; and exit procedure
;
to_upper:
        mov     ah,"U"          ; set the case flag for return
        cmp     dl,ah           ; is char. already uppercase?
        je      done            ; yes, so we're done
        sub     al,20h          ; else, convert to uppercase
;
done:
        pop     dx              ; restore registers
        ret
;
chgcase ENDP
;
;
;++++++++++++++++++++++++++++++++++++++++++++++++++++++++++++++++++
; DOSVER: Gets the version of MS-DOS and return "major" and
; "minor" versions. Returns "1.00" if DOS version is currently
; 1.00 or 1.10.
;
; INPUT:          None
;
; OUTPUT:         AL = major version
;                 AH = minor version (= 00 if pre-DOS 2.00)
;                 (all other registers are restored)
;
; ROUTINES CALLED:       None
;-----------------------------------------------------------------
PUBLIC  DOSVER                  ; library routine
;
dosver  PROC    NEAR
        push    bx              ; save registers
        push    cx
        push    dx
;
        xor     ax,ax           ; clear out AX
```

continued

Listing A-8. *continued*

```
        mov     ah,30h              ; load "get DOS Version" function
        @DosCall
        cmp     al,0                ; is it pre-version 2.00?
        jg      dos2plus            ; no, we're done
        mov     al,1                ; else, it's version 1.XX
        mov     ah,0                ; set minor version to 00
;
dos2plus:
        pop     dx                  ; restore registers
        pop     cx
        pop     bx
        ret
;
dosver  ENDP
;
;
;++++++++++++++++++++++++++++++++++++++++++++++++++++++++++++++++++++++++
; DOSV2CON: Obtains and displays the version of MS-DOS currently
; running, and returns version to calling routine.
;
; INPUT:          None
;
; OUTPUT:         AL = major version
;                 AH = minor version
;                 (all other registers are restored)
;
; ROUTINES CALLED:        DOSVER (gets version of MS-DOS)
;                         BIN2CON (displays numbers in decimal)
;-----------------------------------------------------------------------
PUBLIC  DOSV2CON                    ; library routine
;
dosv2con PROC   NEAR
;
;EXTRN  dosver:NEAR                 ; get version of MS-DOS
;EXTRN  bin2dec:NEAR                ; displays numbers in decimal
;
        push    bx                  ; save registers
        push    cx                  ;
        push    dx                  ;
;
        call    dosver              ; get version of MS-DOS
        push    ax                  ; save returned version
        push    ax                  ; and save it again
        xor     ah,ah               ; output major version in AL
```

```
        mov     ch,1                ; display at least 1 digit
        call    bin2dec             ; output number
        @DisChr '.'                 ; separator character
        pop     ax                  ; restore minor version number
        cmp     al,1                ; is it version 1.XX?
        je      ver1xx              ; yes, display "XX" as minor ver.
        xchg    ah,al               ; else, put minor version in AL
        xor     ah,ah               ; clear upper
        mov     ch,2                ; display at least two digits
        call    bin2dec             ; output number
        jmp     short end_ver       ; and end
;
ver1xx:
        @DisChr 'X'                 ; output an X
        @DisChr 'X'                 ; and again
;
end_ver:
        pop     ax                  ; restore version for return to
                                    ; ... main routine
        pop     dx                  ; restore rest of registers
        pop     cx
        pop     bx
        ret
;
dosv2con ENDP                       ; end of routine
;
;
;+++++++++++++++++++++++++++++++++++++++++++++++++++++++++++++++++++++++
; MEMALLOC: Allocates a block of memory of the specified size
; in paragraphs (16 bytes).
;
; INPUT:          BX = size, in 16-byte paragraphs,
;                      of requested block
;
; OUTPUT:         Carry flag = 0 if SUCCESS, with
;                      AX = segment address of allocated
;                           memory block
;                      (BX is restored)
;
;                 Carry flag = 1 if FAILURE, with
;                      AX = error code
;                              7 = memory control blocks
;                                  destroyed
;                              8 = insufficient memory
;                      BX = largest memory block available
;                           in paragraphs
```

continued

Listing A-8. *continued*

```
;
; CALLED ROUTINES:      None.
;----------------------------------------------------------------
PUBLIC  MEMALLOC                  ; library routine
;
memalloc PROC     NEAR
         push     bp              ; save base pointer
         push     bx              ; save BX
         mov      bp,sp           ; initialize base pointer
;
         xor      al,al           ; clear out AL
         mov      ah,48h          ; load allocate memory function
         @DosCall                 ; execute memory allocation
         jnc      end_memalloc    ; exit if no error with
                                  ; ... seg. address in AX
                                  ; else, exit with carry flag set,
         mov      word ptr [bp],bx; max. size block (BX),
                                  ; and error code in AX
;
end_memalloc:
         pop      bx              ; restore BX
         pop      bp              ; restore base pointer
         ret
;
memalloc ENDP
;
;
;++++++++++++++++++++++++++++++++++++++++++++++++++++++++++++++++++
; MEMSIZE: Changes the size of a block of memory previously
; allocated via the MEMALLOC routine. The block's address and
; the requested size (in 16-byte paragraphs) is specified.
;
; INPUT:       ES = segment address of allocated memory block
;              BX = new size, in 16-byte paragraphs
;
; OUTPUT:      Carry flag = 0 if SUCCESS, with
;                       (all registers are restored)
;
;
;              Carry flag = 1 if FAILURE, with
;                       AX = error code
;                            7 = memory control blocks
;                                destroyed
;                            8 = insufficient memory
;                            9 = invalid block address
```

```
;                               BX = largest memory block available
;                                    in paragraphs if AX = 8;
;                                    else, it is restored.
;                               (ES is restored)
;
; CALLED ROUTINES:      None.
;---------------------------------------------------------------
PUBLIC  MEMSIZE                         ; library routine
;
memsize PROC    NEAR
        push    bp                      ; save base pointer
        push    es                      ; save memory block address
        push    ax                      ; save AX
        push    bx                      ; save BX
        mov     bp,sp                   ; initialize base pointer
;
        xor     al,al                   ; clear out AL
        mov     ah,4Ah                  ; load "change block size" func.
        @DosCall
        jnc     end_memsize             ; exit if no error
                                        ; else, exit with carry flag set
        pushf                           ; save flags
        cmp     ax,8                    ; insufficient memory?
        jne     memsize_err             ; no, continue
        mov     word ptr [bp],bx        ; else, save max. size available
memsize_err:
        mov     word ptr [bp+2],ax      ; save error code
        popf                            ; restore flags
;
end_memsize:
        pop     bx                      ; restore registers
        pop     ax
        pop     es
        pop     bp                      ; restore base pointer
        ret
;
memsize ENDP
;
;
;+++++++++++++++++++++++++++++++++++++++++++++++++++++++++++++++++
; MEMFREE: Deallocates a block of memory previously allocated by
; the MALLOC routine.
;
; ENTRY:        ES = segment address of allocated memory block
;
; EXIT:         Carry flag = 0, if SUCCESS
```

continued

Listing A-8. continued

```
;                    (ES is restored)
;
;                    Carry flag = 1, if FAILURE, with
;                              AX = error code
;                                      7 = Memory control blocks
;                                            destroyed
;                                      9 = Invalid address
;                              (ES is restored)
;
; CALLED ROUTINES:     None.
;--------------------------------------------------------------
PUBLIC  MEMFREE                       ; library routine
;
memfree PROC    NEAR
        push    bp              ; save base pointer
        push    es              ; save block address
        push    ax              ; save AX
        mov     bp,sp           ; initialize base pointer
;
        xor     al,al           ; clear out AL
        mov     ah,49h          ; load deallocate mem. function
        @DosCall                ; execute memory deallocation
        jnc     end_memfree     ; exit if no error
                                ; else, exit with carry flag set,
        mov     word ptr [bp],ax ; and error code (AX)
;
end_memfree:
        pop     ax              ; restore AX
        pop     es              ; restore block address
        pop     bp              ; restore base pointer
        ret
;
memfree ENDP
;
;
;++++++++++++++++++++++++++++++++++++++++++++++++++++++++++++++++++
; MERRHNDL: Memory allocation/deallocation/resize error
; handler.
;
; INPUT:        AX = error code
;               BX = maximum memory block available
;                    (if error code 8)
;               ES = segment address of allocated block
;                    (if error code 9)
```

```
;
; OUTPUT:          None (all registers are restored)
;
; CALLED ROUTINES:       BIN2DEC (via @DisNum macro)
;------------------------------------------------------------------
PUBLIC   MERRHNDL               ; library routine
;
merrhndl PROC    NEAR
;
        cmp     ax,7            ; trashed memory control blocks?
        jne     mem_error8      ; no, continue checking
        @DisStr TrashedMemErr_Msg ; yes, exit with message
        ret                     ; return
;
mem_error8:
        cmp     ax,8            ; insufficient memory?
        jne     mem_error9      ; no, continue checking
        @DisStr InsuffMemErr_Msg ; yes, exit with message
        @DisNum bx,10,1,0       ; ... and largest block available
        @NewLine                ; display blank line
        ret                     ; return
;
mem_error9:
        cmp     ax,9            ; invalid memory block address?
        jne     mem_err_unknown ; no, unknown cause
        @DisStr IncorrSegAddr_Msg ; display error message
        @DisNum es,16,4         ; display seg. address
        @NewLine                ; display blank line
        ret                     ; return
;
mem_err_unknown:
        @DisStr UnknownMemErr_Msg ; display message
        ret
;
_TEXT    ENDS                   ; end code segment
_DATA    SEGMENT                ; start data segment
TrashedMemErr_Msg db "Memory allocation failure: memory "
                  db "control blocks destroyed.",CR,LF,"$"
InsuffMemErr_Msg  db "Memory allocation failure: "
                  db "insufficient memory",CR,LF
                  db "Largest block of memory available = $"
IncorrSegAddr_Msg db "Incorrect segment address for "
                  db "resize/deallocation.",CR,LF
                  db "Segment address = $"
UnknownMemErr_Msg db "Unknown memory allocation/resize/"
                  db "deallocation error.",CR,LF,"$"
```

continued

Listing A-8. *continued*

```
_DATA    ENDS                  ; end data segment
_TEXT    SEGMENT               ; start code segment
;
merrhndl ENDP
;
;
;*********************************************************************
; END LIBRARY ROUTINES
;*********************************************************************
_TEXT    ENDS
         END
```

As you can see in the listing, all routines must be declared PUBLIC in the source file in order to make them available to other programs. Any label (which is what a routine's name is) that is to be used in another program must be declared this way.

If the routines are to be included in an .EXE file, all that's needed is to use the EXTRN directive, placed *outside the segment definition*. LINK finds the reference in the library and places the referenced routine in its own segment in the final program. However, if the routines are to be included in a .COM type file, both the segment name and the "class" name used for the .COM program must match those used in the library routine. To use either the BIN2DEC or BIN2HEX routines, the .COM program must use the segment definition:

```
code    segment para public "code"
```

Note that the segment definition must also be declared PUBLIC. In this case both the segment name (code) and the class name ('code') are the same to help in remembering the names. In addition, the EXTRN directives must be placed inside of the segment definition to let MASM know that the external routines are part of the same segment. (PUBLIC and EXTRN labels are given the same segment attributes as the segment that encloses their definitions.)

Additional information about libraries, PUBLIC, and EXTRN may be found in the Microsoft MASM and LINK reference manuals.

Undocumented MS-DOS Interrupts and Functions   **B**

Undocumented MS-DOS Interrupts
Undocumented Interrupt 21h (33) Function Calls

THIS appendix provides descriptions of some of the undocumented features of MS-DOS. In particular, MS-DOS interrupts and functions associated with interrupts are covered. *Undocumented* refers to features that are not described in any detail and are simply referred to as "reserved" or "unused" in the *MS-DOS Technical Reference Manual* (Microsoft) or *DOS Technical Reference Manual* (IBM). Although some of the *reserved* features are indeed reserved and appear to have no functionality associated with them, others have had their functionality revealed over the years by dedicated and curious programmers. The features described next are a compendium of undocumented interrupts and interrupt-functions that have been analyzed by the authors and by other people who have submitted their findings through various electronic bulletin boards as public-domain information.

It should be stated that the authors and the publisher do not make any warranties whatsoever as to the validity and accuracy of the information presented in this appendix. Since all the interrupts and functions described in this appendix are labeled as reserved in the technical reference documentation from Microsoft and IBM, it is reasonable to assume that the originators of MS-DOS could, conceivably, change the definitions of these interrupts and functions in future versions of MS-DOS. Therefore, anyone wishing to use any of the described interrupts or functions in programs does so at his or her own risk. Only some of the interrupts and functions have gained popular acceptance for their use in certain types of programs (e.g., terminate-and-stay-resident (TSR) programs). The majority of the features described are presented only to satisfy the curiosity that we all have and to further our understanding of how the MS-DOS operating system works.

Undocumented MS-DOS Interrupts

As of MS-DOS 3.3, MS-DOS interrupts 28 through 2E (hex) are declared as reserved in the MS-DOS documentation. Of these interrupts, 28, 29, and 2E (hex) are described in the following paragraphs.

Interrupt 28h (40): DOS Safe Interrupt

Interrupt 28h is commonly called the *DOS safe interrupt* or *keyboard busy loop* interrupt. It is used internally by the MS-DOS Get Input from Keyboard routine, if and only if it is safe to use interrupt 21h functions 0Ch and above. Int 28h is used primarily by terminate-and-stay-resident programs, including MS-DOS's PRINT.COM. When a program has called the MS-DOS Get Input from Keyboard routine and is waiting for a key to be pressed, MS-DOS ceases calling int 28h as a signal to other applications that may be loaded that no int 21h functions (0Ch and above only) should be called. Once a key is pressed and the routine has terminated, int 28h is called to signal other applications that may be loaded that the system is sitting idle and it is safe to execute int 21h functions. Generally, int 28h is used in conjunction with int 21h function 34h (Get DOS Busy Flag): MS-DOS calls or releases int 28h as appropriate, and the application calls the Get DOS Busy Flag function to determine the idle state of the system.

Interrupt 29h (41): Console Device Output

Interrupt 29h, often referred to as *console device output* or FAST PUTCHAR, is called internally by MS-DOS output routines if output is going to a device rather than a file, and if the attribute word of the device's device driver has bit 3 (04h) set to 1. Int 29h can be regarded as a back door to the console output device driver: the character in the AL register is output to the console when this interrupt is executed.

Interrupts 2Ah (42) through 2Dh (45): MS-DOS Internal Routines

Interrupts 2Ah through 2Dh are MS-DOS internal interrupts. Their vectors all point to an IRET op-code. Int 2Ah is used for network control in systems installed with MSNET and other Microsoft network software.

Interrupt 2Eh (46): Back Door to COMMAND Processor

The EXEC function (int 21h function 4Bh) is normally used for executing a command through the command processor COMMAND.COM. However, interrupt 2Eh provides an alternative, quick and dirty method of accomplishing the same function. To execute an MS-DOS command, first shrink the memory to make room for the new program (as in int 21h function 4Bh), then make the DS:SI register point to the parameter string for the command, and finally execute int 2Eh. The first byte in the command's parameter string is the length of the string, followed by the string itself (e.g., CHKDSK C:), and is terminated by a carriage return (0Dh). The terminating carriage return is counted as part of the string's length. After int 2Eh has been executed, it is important to reset the stack, since int 2Eh may not have saved the SS and SP registers.

Interrupts 30h (48) through FFh (255)

Interrupts 30h through FFh are marked as reserved beginning with MS-DOS version 3.30. However, some of these interrupts are used by add-on hardware and software. For example, int 67h is the interrupt reserved for use by the

Lotus/Intel/Microsoft (LIM) Expanded Memory System (EMS) specification. It is through this interrupt (implemented in the EMS device driver) that all the LIM EMS functions are executed (see Chapter 7 for more information on EMS). Other types of add-on hardware and software make use of these interrupts, such as Microsoft and IBM network adapters and BIOS routines, the EGA and VGA adapters, and others.

Undocumented Interrupt 21h (33) Function Calls

The following interrupt int 21h function calls are labeled as "reserved" or "unused" in the Microsoft and IBM *DOS Technical Reference Manual* (as of MS-DOS version 3.30): 18h, 1Dh through 20h, 32h, 34h, 37h, 50h through 53h, 55h, 58h, 5Dh, 60h, 61h, 63h, 64h.

The highest int 21h function defined (as of MS-DOS version 3.30) is 68h. Reserved functions beyond 68h, if any, remain to be discovered.

The following paragraphs describe in more detail the undocumented int 21h functions with uncovered operations.

Functions 18h (24), 1Dh (29), 1Eh (30), 20h (32h): Dummy Functions for Compatibility with CP/M

Many of the lower-numbered functions of MS-DOS have an equivalent CP/M counterpart. Not all of the CP/M functions were implemented in MS-DOS, but many of them have "blank slots" in order to ease the porting of CP/M programs to MS-DOS. These functions do not return anything when they are executed.

Function 1Fh (31): Locate Disk Block Information for Default Drive

Function 1Fh is used to return a pointer to the *disk block information table* for the default drive. Table B-1 shows the format of this table and what its contents are.

Entry: AH = 1Fh

Return: DS:BX contains the address of the first entry in the disk block of the default drive.

Notes: Function 1Fh is the same as function 32h, except that function 32h returns the disk block information for a specified drive. Under MS-DOS versions 2.0 and higher, this function simply executes int 21h function 32h with AL = 0.

Table B-1.   MS-DOS Disk Block Layout

Offset	Type	Data
00	Byte	Drive: 0 = A, 1 = B, etc.
01	Byte	Unit within driver (0, 1, 2, etc.)

continued

Table B-1. *continued*

Offset	Type	Data
02	Word	Bytes per sector
04	Byte	Sectors per cluster − 1
05	Byte	Cluster to sector shift
06	Word	Number of reserved (boot) sectors
08	Byte	Number of FAT tables
09	Word	Number of root directory entries
0B	Word	Sector number of Cluster 2 (1st data sector)
0D	Word	Number of clusters + 1 (or last cluster number)
0F	Byte	Sectors for FAT
10	Word	Sector number of directory
12	Dword	Address of device header
16	Byte	Media descriptor byte
17	Byte	Zero if disk has been accessed
18	Dword	Address of next DOS disk block (FFFF if last one in chain)

Function 32h (50): Locate Disk Block Information for Specified Drive

Function 32h is the same as function 1Fh, except that the pointer to the disk block information table for a specified drive may be specified.

Entry: AH = 32h
         DL = Number of disk drive (0 = default, 1=A, etc.)

Return: AL = 00 if drive exists; FFh for invalid drive.
          DS:BX contains the address of the first entry in the DOS disk block.

Notes: Function 32h is the same as function 1Fh, except that function 1Fh only returns the disk block information for the default drive.

Function 34h (52): Get MS-DOS Busy Flag

Function 34h returns a pointer to the DOS busy flag (also called the DOS critical section flag). The DOS busy flag is a byte that is set to zero when it is safe to interrupt MS-DOS, and is set to a nonzero value when it is not safe to interrupt MS-DOS. This function is used in conjunction with interrupt 28h: the interrupt sets the DOS busy flag, and int 21h function 34h points to the location of the flag (refer to the earlier discussion on undocumented interrupts).

Entry: AH = 34h

Return: ES:BX points to the DOS busy flag.

Notes: There are some peculiarities regarding the DOS busy flag in various versions of MS-DOS. Under MS-DOS 2.10, the byte immediately after the DOS busy flag must be set to 00 to permit the PRINT.COM interrupt to be called. For MS-DOS

3.0 and 3.1 (except COMPAQ DOS 3.0), the byte before the DOS busy flag must be zero; for COMPAQ DOS 3.0, the byte 01AAh before it must be zero.

Function 37h (55): Get/Set Switch Character

Function 37h is used to change the character that is used for switches on MS-DOS command lines. The default switch character is a slash (/), but it can be changed by using function 37h to something else, like the − (hyphen) character, which is the default in the UNIX operating system. This function was fully documented in the MS-DOS documentation before MS-DOS version 3.0 was released, as was a command that could be placed in the CONFIG.SYS startup file (SWITCHAR = /). References to both this function and the CONFIG.SYS SWITCHAR command were removed from the MS-DOS documentation as of MS-DOS version 3.0. However, as of MS-DOS version 3.30, int 21h function 37h operates as it did before.

> **Entry:** AH = 37h
> AL = 0 (Read switch character (returned in DL)
> AL = 1 (Set switch character (new character in DL)
> AL = 2 (MS-DOS 2.X only: Read device availability)
> AL = 3 (MS-DOS 2.X only: Set device availability, where DL = 0 if /DEV/ must precede device names, and DL < > 0 if /DEV/ need not precede device names
>
> **Return:** DL = Switch character (if AL = 0 or 1 on entry)
> DL = Device availability flag (if AL = 2 or 3 on entry)
> AL = 0FFh if error (value in AL on entry was not 0 through 3)

Function 50h (80): Set PSP Segment

Function 50h is used to set the segment for a new program segment prefix (PSP).

> **Entry:** AH = 50h
> BX = Segment address of new PSP
>
> **Return:** None
>
> **Notes:** Under MS-DOS 2.X, this function cannot be invoked inside an int 28h handler without a prior call to int 21h function 5Dh.

Function 51h (81): Get PSP Segment

Function 51h is used to return the segment address of the current program segment prefix (PSP).

> **Entry:** AH = 51h
>
> **Return:** BX = Segment address of current PSP

Function 52h (82): Get Address of the MS-DOS List of Lists

Function 52h returns a pointer to the MS-DOS "list of lists," which contains various types of information, including pointers to other lists of information. Tables B-2 and B-3 show the layout of the MS-DOS list of lists.

Entry:　AH = 52h

Return:　ES:BX contains the address of the MS-DOS list of lists.

Notes:　The list of lists pointed to is different between MS-DOS versions 2.XX and 3.XX. See Tables B-2 and B-3 for the differences. Although the list of lists table pointed to after function 52h is invoked contains information on the first disk block, it does not cause the drive to be accessed, so the information in the disk block may not be accurate. Functions 1Fh or 32h, however, do cause the drive to be accessed, automatically updating the disk block if the disk changed.

Table B-2.　MS-DOS 2.XX List of Lists

Offset	Type	Data
-02	Word	Segment of first memory control block
00	Byte	Null
01	Word	Pointer to first disk block (see function 36h)
04	Byte	Not known; pointer to first resident driver?
08	Word	Pointer to CLOCK$ device driver
0C	Word	Pointer to actual CON: device driver
10	Byte	Number of logical drives in system
11	Word	Maximum bytes per block of any block device
13	Byte	Unknown
17	Byte	Beginning (not a pointer) of the NUL device driver

Table B-3.　MS-DOS 3.XX List of Lists

Offset	Type	Data
-02	Word	Segment of first memory control block
00	Byte	Null
01	Word	Pointer to first disk block (see function 36h)
04	Byte	Not known; pointer to first resident driver?
08	Word	Pointer to CLOCK$ device driver
0C	Word	Pointer to actual CON: device driver
10	Word	Maximum bytes per block of any block device
12	Byte	Unknown (possibly a pointer to current directory block)
16	Byte	Unknown (possibly an array of drive information)
1A	Byte	Unknown
20	Byte	Number of block devices
21	Byte	Value of LASTDRIVE command in CONFIG.SYS (default = 5)
22	Byte	Beginning (not a pointer) of the NUL device driver

Function 53h (83): Translate BIOS Parameter Block (BPB) to Disk Block

Function 53h translates the BIOS Parameter Block (BPB) of a given disk into the DOS *disk block* format and places information at the specified location (see Table B-4).

Entry: AH = 53h
DS:SI = Pointer to BIOS Parameter Block (BPB) for disk
ES:BP = Pointer to area in which to store the DOS disk block

Return: Disk block layout information stored in area originally pointed to by ES:BP.

Table B-4.   MS-DOS Disk Block Layout Information Returned from Function 53h

Offset	Type	Data
00	Word	Bytes per sector
02	Byte	Sectors per cluster
03	Word	Reserved sectors
05	Byte	Number of FATs
05	Byte	Cluster to sector shift
06	Word	Number of root directory entries
08	Word	Total number of sectors
0A	Byte	Media descriptor byte
0B	Word	Number of sectors per FAT

Function 55h (85): Create PSP Block

Function 55h is used to create a *child* program segment prefix (PSP). It is similar to int 21h function 26h except that a new PSP is created instead of copying the current PSP.

Entry: AH = 55h
DX = Segment address in which to set up the PSP

Return: None

Function 58h (88): Get/Set Memory Allocation Strategy

Entry: AH = 58h
AL = Function code
AL = 0 to get allocation strategy
AL = 1 to set allocation strategy
BL = Strategy Code
BL = 0 if first fit (use first memory block large enough to fit)
BL = 1 if bet fit (use smallest memory block large enough to fit)
BL = 2 if last fit (use high part of last usable memory block)

Return: Carry Flag = 1 if error, with error code in AX. Carry Flag = 0 if no error, with strategy code in AX.

Note: The set subfunction accepts any value in BL: 2 or greater means "last fit." The subfunction returns the last value set, so programs should check to see whether the value is equal to or greater than 2, and not just equal to 2.

Function 60h (96): Resolve Path String to Fully Qualified Path String

Function 60h takes a path string that is pointed to and returns a fully qualified version of the same path.

Entry: AH = 60h
DI:SI = Pointer to path string
ES:DI = Pointer to area in which to store the returned fully qualified path string

Return: Fully qualified path string is returned in area originally pointed to by ES:DI. There are no known returned error codes.

Function 63h (99): Get Lead Byte Table

Entry: AH = 63h
AL = Subfunction
AL = 0 to get system lead-byte table
AL = 1 to set or clear interim console flag
    DL = 0 to clear flag
    DL = 1 to set flag
AL = 2 to get interim console flag

Return: DS:SI = pointer to lead byte table (if called with AL = 0)
DL = interim console flag (if called with AL = 2).

Bibliography

C

HE following books and articles are ones used by the authors as references. You may wish to consult these texts for further information on specific topics.

Books

Abel, P. *Programming Assembler Language*. 2d ed. Reston, VA: Reston, 1984.

Allworth, S.T. *Introduction to Real-Time Software Design*. New York: Springer-Verlag, 1981.

Angermeyer, J., R. Fahringer, K. Jaeger, and D. Shafer. *Tricks of the MS-DOS Masters*. Indianapolis: Howard W. Sams, 1987.

DeMarco, T. *Structured Analysis and System Specification*. New York: Yourdon, 1978.

Disk Operating System. Boca Raton, FL: International Business Machines, 1982 (for DOS 1.10), 1983 (for DOS 2.00), 1983 (for DOS 2.10), 1984 (for DOS 3.00), 1984 and 1985 (for DOS 3.10).

Disk Operating System Technical Reference. Boca Raton, FL: International Business Machines, 1983 (for DOS 2.10), 1984 (for DOS 3.00), 1984 and 1985 (for DOS 3.10).

Duncan, Ray. *Advanced MS-DOS*. Redmond, WA: Microsoft Press, 1986.

Hyman, Michael. *Memory Resident Utilities, Interrupts, and Disk Management with MS & PC DOS*. Portland, OR: MIS Press, 1986.

IAPX 86/88, 186/188 *User's Manual: Programmer's Reference*. Santa Clara, CA: Intel, 1983.

Kane, G., D. Hawkins, and L. Leventhal. *68000 Assembly Language Programming*. Berkeley, CA: Osborne/McGraw-Hill, 1981.

Kernighan, Brian, and Dennis Ritchie. *The C Programming Language*. Englewood Cliffs, NJ: Prentice-Hall, 1978.

Lafore, R. *Assembly Language Primer for the IBM PC and XT*. New York and Scarborough, Ontario: New American Library, 1984.

Lai, S. Robert. *Writing MS-DOS Device Drivers*. New York: Addison-Wesley, 1987.

Lattice 8086/8088 C Compiler Manual. New York: Lifeboat Associates, 1982.

Microsoft C Compiler: User's Guide. Bellevue, WA: Microsoft, 1984 and 1985 (for C 3.00).

Microsoft C: Run-Time Library Reference. Bellevue, WA: Microsoft, 1984 and 1985 (for C 3.00).

Microsoft Macro Assembler User's Manual. Bellevue, WA: Microsoft, 1981 and 1983 (for MASM 2.00), 1984 and 1985 (for MASM 4.00).

Microsoft MS-DOS Programmer's Reference. Bellevue, WA: Microsoft, 1981 and 1983 (for MS-DOS 2.10).

Morgan, C. L. *Bluebook of Assembly Language Routines for the IBM PC & XT*. New York and Scarborough, Ontario: New American Library, 1984.

Morgan, C.L., and M. Waite. *8086/8088 16-Bit Microprocessor Primer*. Peterborough, NH: BYTE/McGraw-Hill, 1982.

Norton, P. *Inside the IBM PC*. Bowie, MD: Robert J. Brady Co., 1983.

Savitzky, Stephen. *Real-Time Microprocessor Systems*. New York: Van Nostrand Reinhold, 1985.

Simrin, Steven. *The Waite Group's MS-DOS Bible*. rev. ed. Indianapolis: Howard W. Sams, 1988.

Tausworthe, R.C. *Standardized Development of Computer Software*. Pt. I. Englewood Cliffs, NJ: Prentice-Hall, 1977.

Turbo Pascal Reference Manual Version 2.0. Scotts Valley, CA: Borland International, 1984.

Turbo Pascal Reference Manual Version 3.0. Scotts Valley, CA: Borland International, 1983, 1984, and 1985.

Waite Group, The. *The Waite Group's MS-DOS Papers*. Indianapolis: Howard W. Sams, 1988.

Yourdon, E.U., and L.L. Constantine. *Structured Design*. Englewood Cliffs, NJ: Prentice-Hall, 1977.

Yourdon, E.U. *Techniques of Program Structure and Design*. Englewood Cliffs, NJ: Prentice-Hall, 1975.

Articles

Duncan, Ray. "Lotus/Intel/Microsoft Expanded Memory," *Byte* 11, no. 11, 1986 (Special IBM Edition).
> How to write programs using LIM EMS 3.2. Example portions of RAMDISK program that uses expanded memory.

Hansen, Marion, and John Driscoll. "LIM EMS 4.0: A Definition for the Next Generation of Expanded Memory," *MSJ* 3, no. 1, Jan 88.
> A description of the features introduced by LIM EMS 4.0. Sample programs in C and assembly language demonstrate improved methods for screen saving, data sharing between programs, and executing code from expanded memory.

Hansen, Marion, Bill Krueger, and Nick Stuecklen. "Expanded Memory: Writing Programs That Break the 640K Barrier," *MSJ* 2, no. 1, Mar 87.
> A description of LIM EMS 3.2. Sample programs in C and assembly language demonstrate screen saving and executing code from expanded memory.

Lefor, John A., and Karen Lund. "Reaching into Expanded Memory," *PCTJ* 5, no. 5, May 86.
> An application-oriented explanation of the LIM EMS 3.2 and AQA EEMS. Complete sample programs to obtain expanded memory parameters and to dump expanded memory data.

Lotus, Intel, Microsoft. "Lotus/Intel/Microsoft Expanded Memory Specification, Version 4.0," Document number 300275-005, Oct 87.
> The complete specification for the latest version of the expanded memory specification. Includes sample programs in Turbo Pascal and assembly language.

Mirecki, Ted. "Expandable Memory," *PCTJ*, no. 2, Feb 86.
> A description of LIM EMS 3.2 and the AQA EEMS. Tests of Intel and AST expanded memory products.

Yao, Paul. "EMS Support Improves Microsoft Windows 2.0 Application Performance," *MSJ* 3, no. 1, Jan 88.
> A technical discussion of the way Windows 2.0 uses LIM EMS 4.0 to manage multiple concurrent applications.

ASCII Cross-Reference and Number Conversions D

Nonprintable ASCII Character Definitions
Hexadecimal to Decimal Conversion
Decimal to Hexadecimal Conversion

ABLE D-1 cross-references terminal keys with their decimal (base 10), hexadecimal (base 16), octal (base 8), and ASCII (American Standard Code for Information Interchange) assignments. The key sequences that consist of **Control-** are typed by simultaneously pressing the Control key and the key indicated. These sequences are based on those defined for most standard terminals, such as the Diablo 1640 keyboard and the Televideo series of terminals, and may be defined differently on other keyboards.

Table D-1.   ASCII Cross-Reference

DEC X_{10}	HEX X_{16}	OCT X_8	ASCII	IBM Graphics Char.	Terminal Key*
0	00	00	NUL		\<Ctrl-@\>
1	01	01	SOH	☺	\<Ctrl-A\>
2	02	02	STX	☻	\<Ctrl-B\>
3	03	03	ETX	♥	\<Ctrl-C\>
4	04	04	EOT	♦	\<Ctrl-D\>
5	05	05	ENQ	♣	\<Ctrl-E\>
6	06	06	ACK	♠	\<Ctrl-F\>
7	07	07	BEL	●	\<Ctrl-G\>
8	08	10	BS	▫	\<Ctrl-H\>
9	09	11	HT	○	\<Ctrl-I\>
10	0A	12	LF	■	\<Ctrl-J\>
11	0B	13	VT	♂	\<Ctrl-K\>
12	0C	14	FF	♀	\<Ctrl-L\>
13	0D	15	CR	♪	\<Ctrl-M\>
14	0E	16	SO	♫	\<Ctrl-N\>
15	0F	17	SI	☼	\<Ctrl-O\>
16	10	20	DLE	►	\<Ctrl-P\>
17	11	21	DC1	◄	\<Ctrl-Q\>
18	12	22	DC2	↕	\<Ctrl-R\>
19	13	23	DC3	‼	\<Ctrl-S\>
20	14	24	DC4	¶	\<Ctrl-T\>
21	15	25	NAK	§	\<Ctrl-U\>
22	16	26	SYN	—	\<Ctrl-V\>
23	17	27	ETB	↨	\<Ctrl-W\>
24	18	30	CAN	↑	\<Ctrl-X\>
25	19	31	EM	↓	\<Ctrl-Y\>

continued

Table D-1. *continued*

DEC X_{10}	HEX X_{16}	OCT X_8	ASCII	IBM Graphics Char.	Terminal Key*
26	1A	32	SUB	→	\<Ctrl-Z\>
27	1B	33	ESC	←	\<Esc\>
28	1C	34	FS	∟	\<Ctrl-\\>
29	1D	35	GS	↔	\<Ctrl-` \>
30	1E	36	RS	▲	\<Ctrl-=\>
31	1F	37	US	▼	\<Ctrl- -\>
32	20	40	SP		(Space) \<SPACE BAR\>
33	21	41	!	!	! (Exclamation mark)
34	22	42	"	"	" (Quotation mark)
35	23	43	#	#	# (Number sign or Octothorpe)
36	24	44	$	$	$ (Dollar sign)
37	25	45	%	%	% (Percent)
38	26	46	&	&	& (Ampersand)
39	27	47	'	'	' (Apostrophe or acute accent)
40	28	50	(	(	((Opening parenthesis)
41	29	51	)	)	) (Closing parenthesis)
42	2A	52	*	*	* (Asterisk)
43	2B	53	+	+	+ (Plus)
44	2C	54	,	,	, (Comma)
45	2D	55	-	-	- (Hyphen, dash, or minus)
46	2E	56	.	.	. (Period)
47	2F	57	/	/	/ (Forward slant)
48	30	60	0	0	0
49	31	61	1	1	1
50	32	62	2	2	2
51	33	63	3	3	3
52	34	64	4	4	4
53	35	65	5	5	5
54	36	66	6	6	6
55	37	67	7	7	7
56	38	70	8	8	8
57	39	71	9	9	9
58	3A	72	:	:	: (Colon)
59	3B	73	;	;	; (Semicolon)
60	3C	74	<	<	< (Less than)
61	3D	75	=	=	= (Equals)
62	3E	76	>	>	> (Greater than)
63	3F	77	?	?	? (Question mark)
64	40	100	@	@	@ (Commercial at)
65	41	101	A	A	A
66	42	102	B	B	B
67	43	103	C	C	C
68	44	104	D	D	D
69	45	105	E	E	E
70	46	106	F	F	F
71	47	107	G	G	G
72	48	110	H	H	H
73	49	111	I	I	I
74	4A	112	J	J	J
75	4B	113	K	K	K

DEC X_{10}	HEX X_{16}	OCT X_8	ASCII	IBM Graphics Char.	Terminal Key*
76	4C	114	L	L	L
77	4D	115	M	M	M
78	4E	116	N	N	N
79	4F	117	O	O	O
80	50	120	P	P	P
81	51	121	Q	Q	Q
82	52	122	R	R	R
83	53	123	S	S	S
84	54	124	T	T	T
85	55	125	U	U	U
86	56	126	V	V	V
87	57	127	W	W	W
88	58	130	X	X	X
89	59	131	Y	Y	Y
90	5A	132	Z	Z	Z
91	5B	133	[	[	[(Opening bracket)
92	5C	134	\	\	\ (Reverse slant)
93	5D	135	]	]	] (Closing bracket)
94	5E	136	^	^	^ (Caret or circumflex)
95	5F	137	—	—	— (Underscore or underline)
96	60	140	`	`	` (Grave accent)
97	61	141	a	a	a
98	62	142	b	b	b
99	63	143	c	c	c
100	64	144	d	d	d
101	65	145	e	e	e
102	66	146	f	f	f
103	67	147	g	g	g
104	68	150	h	h	h
105	69	151	i	i	i
106	6A	152	j	j	j
107	6B	153	k	k	k
108	6C	154	l	l	l
109	6D	155	m	m	m
110	6E	156	n	n	n
111	6F	157	o	o	o
112	70	160	p	p	p
113	71	161	q	q	q
114	72	162	r	r	r
115	73	163	s	s	s
116	74	164	t	t	t
117	75	165	u	u	u
118	76	166	v	v	v
119	77	167	w	w	w
120	78	170	x	x	x
121	79	171	y	y	y
122	7A	172	z	z	z
123	7B	173	{	{	{ (Opening Brace)
124	7C	174	¦	¦	¦ (Vertical bar; logical OR)

continued

Table D-1. *continued*

DEC X_{10}	HEX X_{16}	OCT X_8	ASCII	IBM Graphics Char.	Terminal Key*
125	7D	175	}	}	} (Closing brace)
126	7E	176	~	~	~ (Tilde)
127	7F	177	DEL	DEL	\<Del\>

Nonprintable ASCII Character Definitions

ACK (ACKNOWLEDGMENT)—A communication control character that serves as a general "yes" answer to various queries but also sometimes indicates "I received your last transmission and I'm ready for your next."

BELL (BELL)—A general-purpose control character that activates a bell, beeper, or other audible alarm on the device to which it was sent.

BS (BACKSPACE)—A format effector control character that moves the carriage, print head, or cursor back one space or position.

CAN (CANCEL)—A general-purpose control character that indicates that the material in the previous transmission is to be disregarded. The amount of material is decided by the user.

CR (CARRIAGE RETURN OR RETURN)—A format effector control character that moves the carriage, print head, or cursor on a terminal back to the beginning of the line. On most terminals, the Return key causes both a CR and an LF (line feed).

DC1–DC4 (DEVICE CONTROLS)—General-purpose control characters that control the user's terminal or similar devices. No standard functions are assigned, except that DC4 frequently means *stop*. The CCITT (Comité Consultatif International Télégraphe et Téléphone [International Telegraph and Telephone Consultative Committee]) suggests a number of possible assignments. In general, CCITT prefers using the first two controls for *on*, and the last two for *off*, and DC2 and DC4 to refer to the more important device. In some systems, these codes are labeled XON, TAPE, XOFF, and NO TAPE, respectively. X means *transmitter*, and TAPE and NO TAPE mean *tape on* and *tape off*. These labels are found on the keytops of some terminals.

DEL (DELETE)—A general-purpose control character that deletes a character. Called RUBOUT on some terminals, DEL is not strictly a control character because it is not grouped with the other ASCII control characters. The DEL function has a binary all-ones bit pattern (1111 1111, base 2). The reason is historic: The only way to erase a bit pattern punched into paper tape was to punch out all the holes so that the resulting pattern was equivalent to a null. ASCII still considers DEL equivalent to a null, although many operating systems use DEL to erase the preceding character.

DLE (**DATA LINK ESCAPE**)—A communications control character that uses a special type of escape sequence specifically for controlling the data line and transmission facilities.

EM (**END OF MEDIUM**)—A general-purpose control character that indicates the end of paper tape (or other storage medium) or is the end of the material on the medium.

ENQ (**ENQUIRY**)—A communications control character that usually is used for requesting identification or status information. In some systems, this code is WRU (who are you?).

EOT (**END OF TRANSMISSION**)—A communications control character that marks the end of a transmission after one or more messages.

ESC (**ESCAPE**)—A general-purpose character that marks the beginning of an escape sequence. An escape sequence consists of a series of codes, which as a group have a special meaning, usually a control function. On some terminals, ESC is called ALT MODE.

ETB (**END OF TRANSMISSION BLOCK**)—A communications control character that is used when you want to break up a long message into blocks. ETB marks block boundaries. The blocks usually have nothing to do with the format of the message being transmitted.

EXT (**END OF TEXT**)—A communications control character that marks the end of a text. See SOH. This code was originally called EOM (end of message) and may be labeled as such on some terminals.

FF (**FORM FEED**)—A format effector control character that causes the carriage, print wheel, or cursor to advance to the top of the next page.

FS, GS, RS, US (**FILE, GROUP, RECORD AND UNIT SEPARATOR**)—A set of information separator control characters that delimit portions of information. No standard usage exists, except that FS is expected to refer to the largest division and US to the smallest.

HT (**HORIZONTAL TAB**)—A format effector control character that tabs the carriage, print wheel, or cursor to the next predetermined stop on the same line. The user usually decides where the horizontal tab stops are positioned.

LF (**LINE FEED**)—A format effector control character that moves the carriage, print head, or cursor down one line. Most systems combine CR (carriage return) with LF, and the new line is called NL (new line).

NAK (**NEGATIVE ACKNOWLEDGMENT**)—A communications control character that indicates *no* in answer to various queries. Sometimes it is defined as "I received your last transmission, but it had errors and I'm waiting for a retransmission."

NUL (**NULL**)—A general-purpose control character that mainly is used as a space filler. *See also* SYN.

SI (**SHIFT IN**)—A general-purpose control character that is used after an SO code to indicate that codes revert to normal ASCII meaning.

SO (SHIFT OUT)—A general-purpose control character that indicates the following bit patterns have meanings outside the standard ASCII set and will continue to do so until SI is entered.

SOH (START OF HEADING)—A communications control character that marks the beginning of a heading when headings are used in messages along with text. Headings usually state the name and location of an addressee. This code was originally called SOM (start of message).

STX (START OF TEXT)—A communications control character that is used as a marker for the beginning of text and end of heading (if used). This code was originally called EOA (end of address).

SUB (SUBSTITUTE)—A general-purpose control character indicating a character that is to take the place of a character known to be wrong.

SYN (SYNCHRONOUS IDLE)—A communications control character used by some high-speed data communications systems that use synchronized clocks at the transmitter and receiver ends. During idle periods, when there are no bit patterns to enable the receiver's clock to track the transmitter's, the receiver may drift out of sync. Every transmission following an idle period therefore is replaced by three or four SYN characters. The SYN code has a bit pattern that enables the receiver not only to lock onto the transmitter's clock but also to determine the beginning and end points of each character. SYN characters may also be used to fill short idle periods to maintain synchronization, hence the name.

VT (VERTICAL TAB)—A format effector control character that tabs the carriage, print head, or cursor to the next predetermined stop (usually a line).

Hexadecimal to Decimal Conversion

Figure D-1 shows how the hexadecimal number 5F9D is converted to its decimal equivalent.

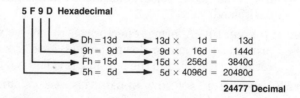

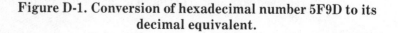

Figure D-1. Conversion of hexadecimal number 5F9D to its decimal equivalent.

Each hexadecimal digit is always 16 times greater than the digit immediately to the right.

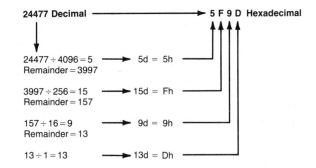

Figure D-2. Decimal number 24477 converted back to its hexadecimal equivalent.

Decimal to Hexadecimal Conversion

The conversion process is reversed when converting decimal numbers to hexadecimal. Start by selecting the leftmost digit and determine its significance in the number (thousands, hundreds, etc.). The decimal is then divided by the hexadecimal value of the first digit's relative position. If, for example, the first digit is in the thousands position, divide by 4,096 (hexadecimal equivalent of 1,000 decimal). The result is the first hexadecimal digit. The remainder is divided by the hexadecimal value of the next digit's relative position (that is, divide the hundreds digit by 256 because 256 is the hexadecimal equivalent of 100 decimal). Figure D-2 shows how the decimal number derived in the previous example is converted back to hexadecimal.

Table D-2.   IBM Extended Cross-Reference

Binary X_2	OCT X_8	DEC X_{10}	HEX X_{16}	Ext. ASCII
1000 0000	200	128	80	Ç
1000 0001	201	129	81	ü
1000 0010	202	130	82	é
1000 0011	203	131	83	â
1000 0100	204	132	84	ä
1000 0101	205	133	85	à
1000 0110	206	134	86	å
1000 0111	207	135	87	ç
1000 1000	210	136	88	ê
1000 1001	211	137	89	ë
1000 1010	212	138	8A	è
1000 1011	213	139	8B	ï
1000 1100	214	140	8C	î

continued

Table D-2. *continued*

Binary X₂	OCT X₈	DEC X₁₀	HEX X₁₆	Ext. ASCII
1000 1101	215	141	8D	ì
1000 1110	216	142	8E	Ä
1000 1111	217	143	8F	Å
1001 0000	220	144	90	É
1001 0001	221	145	91	æ
1001 0010	222	146	92	Æ
1001 0011	223	147	93	ô
1001 0100	224	148	94	ö
1001 0101	225	149	95	ò
1001 0110	226	150	96	û
1001 0111	227	151	97	ù
1001 1000	230	152	98	ÿ
1001 1001	231	153	99	Ö
1001 1010	232	154	9A	Ü
1001 1011	233	155	9B	¢
1001 1100	234	156	9C	£
1001 1101	235	157	9D	¥
1001 1110	236	158	9E	P_t
1001 1111	237	159	9F	ƒ
1010 0000	240	160	A0	á
1010 0001	241	161	A1	í
1010 0010	242	162	A2	ó
1010 0011	243	163	A3	ú
1010 0100	244	164	A4	ñ
1010 0101	245	165	A5	Ñ
1010 0110	246	166	A6	ª
1010 0111	247	167	A7	º
1010 1000	250	168	A8	¿
1010 1001	251	169	A9	⌐
1010 1010	252	170	AA	¬
1010 1011	253	171	AB	½
1010 1100	254	172	AC	¼
1010 1101	255	173	AD	¡
1010 1110	256	174	AE	«
1010 1111	257	175	AF	»
1011 0000	260	176	B0	░
1011 0001	261	177	B1	▒
1011 0010	262	178	B2	▓
1011 0011	263	179	B3	│
1011 0100	264	180	B4	┤
1011 0101	265	181	B5	╡
1011 0110	266	182	B6	╢
1011 0111	267	183	B7	╖
1011 1000	270	184	B8	╕
1011 1001	271	185	B9	╣
1011 1010	272	186	BA	║
1011 1011	273	187	BB	╗
1011 1100	274	188	BC	╝
1011 1101	275	189	BD	╜
1011 1110	276	190	BE	╛
1011 1111	277	191	BF	┐
1100 0000	300	192	C0	└

Binary X_2	OCT X_8	DEC X_{10}	HEX X_{16}	Ext. ASCII
1100 0001	301	193	C1	⊥
1100 0010	302	194	C2	⊤
1100 0011	303	195	C3	╟
1100 0100	304	196	C4	—
1100 0101	305	197	C5	+
1100 0110	306	198	C6	╞
1100 0111	307	199	C7	╟
1100 1000	310	200	C8	╙
1100 1001	311	201	C9	╒
1100 1010	312	202	CA	╨
1100 1011	313	203	CB	╤
1100 1100	314	204	CC	╟
1100 1101	315	205	CD	=
1100 1110	316	206	CE	╬
1100 1111	317	207	CF	╧
1101 0000	320	208	D0	╨
1101 0001	321	209	D1	╤
1101 0010	322	210	D2	╥
1101 0011	323	211	D3	╙
1101 0100	324	212	D4	╘
1101 0101	325	213	D5	╒
1101 0110	326	214	D6	╓
1101 0111	327	215	D7	╫
1101 1000	330	216	D8	╪
1101 1001	331	217	D9	┘
1101 1010	332	218	DA	┌
1101 1011	333	219	DB	■
1101 1100	334	220	DC	▬
1101 1101	335	221	DD	▌
1101 1110	336	222	DE	▐
1101 1111	337	223	DF	▬
1110 0000	340	224	E0	α
1110 0001	341	225	E1	β
1110 0010	342	226	E2	Γ
1110 0011	343	227	E3	π
1110 0100	344	228	E4	Σ
1110 0101	345	229	E5	σ
1110 0110	346	230	E6	μ
1110 0111	347	231	E7	τ
1110 1000	350	232	E8	Φ
1110 1001	351	233	E9	Θ
1110 1010	352	234	EA	Ω
1110 1011	353	235	EB	δ
1110 1100	354	236	EC	∞
1110 1101	355	237	ED	ϕ
1110 1110	356	238	EE	ϵ
1110 1111	357	239	EF	$\cap$
1111 0000	360	240	F0	$\equiv$
1111 0001	361	241	F1	$\pm$
1111 0010	362	242	F2	$\geq$
1111 0011	363	243	F3	$\leq$

continued

Table D-2. *continued*

Binary X_2	OCT X_8	DEC X_{10}	HEX X_{16}	Ext. ASCII
1111 0100	364	244	F4	⌠
1111 0101	365	245	F5	⌡
1111 0110	366	246	F6	÷
1111 0111	367	247	F7	≈
1111 1000	370	248	F8	°
1111 1001	371	249	F9	•
1111 1010	372	250	FA	·
1111 1011	373	251	FB	√
1111 1100	374	252	FC	η
1111 1101	375	253	FD	2
1111 1110	376	254	FE	▪
1111 1111	377	255	FF	(blank)

* Those key sequences consisting of "<Ctrl->" are typed in by pressing the CTRL key, and while it is being held down, pressing the key indicated. These sequences are based on those defined for the IBM Personal Computer series keyboards. The key sequences may be defined differently on other keyboards.

IBM Extended ASCII characters can be displayed by pressing the <Alt> key and then typing the decimal code of the character on the keypad.

Abbreviations:
DEC   = Decimal (Base 10)
HEX   = Hexadecimal (Base 16)
OCT   = Octal (Base 8)
ASCII = American Standard Code for Information Interchange

Index

A

Absolute addressing, 91
Absolute Disk Read function, 230, 293, 297–298, 625, 660
Absolute Disk Write function, 230, 293, 297–298, 625, 660
@Accept macro for parameter passing, 82–83
ACK character, 760
Addresses
    as operands, 25–26
    passing parameters by, 85–86
Addressing
    of expanded memory, 390–392
    with NPX, 535–536
Adjust_temp program, 267–268
Allocate Alternate Map Register Set EMM function, 376
Allocate DMA Register Set EMM function, 376
Allocate Memory function, 106, 108, 667, 671–672
Allocate Pages EMM function, 369, 389
Allocate Standard/Raw Pages EMM function, 375
Allocate Table Information function, 664
Alt key, 196
Alter Page Map and Call EMM function, 373, 397
Alter Page Map and Jump EMM function, 373, 397
Alternate Map Register Set EMM function, 376, 401
Ampersands (&) with macro arguments, 8–9, 20, 29–30
AND operator, 24
Angle brackets (<>) operators for macros, 17, 20, 55
ANSWER.COM program, 699
AQA EEMS, 119, 362–363, 366–367

Arguments, 76
    C, on stack, 102
    FORTRAN, passing of, 104
    macro, 7–9, 16–18, 20, 27–35
    PASCAL, passing of, 104
Arithmetic NPX instructions, 534–535
Arrays
    bounds checking for, 112–113
    C, passing of, 102
Articles, bibliography of, 752–753
ASCII characters, 197
    and BCD, 530–531
    cross reference for, 757–759, 763–765
    macro to display binary numbers as, 715–717
ASCII programs, recovery of, 647–648
ASCIIZ strings in environment block, 129
Assembly language programs
    batch files for, 693–699
    compared to high-level, 5–6
    compatibility issues with, 661
    conditional assembly of, 18–25
    for expanded memory, 380–385
    macros for, 6–18
    modular programs for, 75–89
    STRUC directive for, 64–68
    structured control statements in, 35–50
ASSIGN command, 193–194, 291
ASSUME macro directive, 13, 107, 112
Asynchronous BIOS requests, TSRs for, 194
Asynchronous communication. *See* Serial communication port
Asynchronous communications adapter, 458
AT computer, multitasking with, 276–277
Attributes
    character, 199
    for device headers, 301–305
    file storage, 607–608
AUTOEXEC.BAT files, 119–121
Automatic variables, 96
    in C, 102

MS-DOS STRUCTURES

Directory Structure

```
Time RECORD    Hour:5, Minute:6, Second:5
               ; F E D C B A 9 8 7 6 5 4 3 2 1 0
               ;     | | | | | | | | | | | | | | |
               ;     | | | | | | | | | | |  Seconds/2
               ;     | | | | | |  Minutes
               ;     |  Hours

Date RECORD    Year:7, Month:4, Day:5
               ; F E D C B A 9 8 7 6 5 4 3 2 1 0
               ;     | | | | | | | | | | | | | | |
               ;     | | | | | | | | | |  Day 1-31
               ;     | | | | | |  Month 1-12
               ;     |  Year + 1980

dir       STRUC
dir_stat    db  1 dup (?)      ; file name's actual first character or:
                              ;    00h = file name never used
                              ;    05h = first character is really E5h
                              ;    E5h = file has been erased
                              ;    2Eh = file is a subdirectory
dir_name    db  7 dup (?)      ; rest of file name characters
dir_ext     db  3 dup (?)      ; extension
dir_attr    db  1 dup (?)      ; attributes:
                              ;  7 6 5 4 3 2 1 0
                              ;  | | | | | | | |
                              ;  | | | | | | |  Read only
                              ;  | | | | | |  Hidden
                              ;  | | | | |  System
                              ;  | | | |  Volume label
                              ;  | | |  Subdirectory
                              ;  | |  Archive
                              ;  |  Unused
dir_resv    db 10 dup (?)      ; reserved
dir_time    Time < >          ; time stamp (2 bytes)
dir_date    Date < >          ; date stamp (2 bytes)
dir_first   db  2 dup (?)      ; starting cluster number of file
dir_size    db  4 dup (?)      ; file size in bytes (1st word holds low-
                              ;   order size)
dir       ENDS
```

BIOS Parameter Block (BPB)

```
bpb        STRUC              ; Offset--Description
bpb_sec_size   dw  ?          ;  0--number of bytes per sector
bpb_clust_sec  db  ?          ;  2--number sectors per cluster
bpb_resv_sec   dw  ?          ;  3--number of reserved sectors
bpb_fats       db  ?          ;  5--number of FATs (copies)
bpb_dir_ents   dw  ?          ;  6--number of root directory entries
bpb_secs       dw  ?          ;  8--total number of sectors
bpb_media      db  ?          ; 10--media descriptor byte
bpb_fat_secs   dw  ?          ; 11--number of sectors per FAT
bpb        ENDS
```

continued

MS-DOS STRUCTURES
continued

File Control Block (FCB) Layout

```
Date        RECORD     year:7, month:4, day:5

fcb         STRUC                  ; MAIN PART OF FCB
                                   ; Offset--Description
fcb_drive      db    1 dup (0)     ;  0--drive number (0 = default drive
                                   ;      before open)
fcb_name       db    8 dup (" ")   ;  1--file name or device name;
left-                              ;      left-justified; no colon
fcb_ext        db    3 dup (" ")   ;  9--file extension; left-justified
fcb_cur_blk    dw    ?             ; 12--current block relative to start of file
fcb_rec_size   dw    80h           ; 14--logical record size in bytes
fcb_filsiz_lo  dw    0             ; 16--file size in bytes; low word
fcb_filsiz_hi  dw    0             ; 18--file size in bytes; high word
fcb_date       Date  < >           ; 20--date file was created or last
                                   ;      updated (see directory structure)
fcb_resv1      db    10 dup (?)    ; 22--reserved
fcb_curr_rec   db    ?             ; 32--current relative record within
                                   ;      current block
fcb_rndm_rec_l dw    ?             ; 33--relative record from start of
                                   ;      file; low word
fcb_rndm_rec_h dw    ?             ; 35--relative record from start of
                                   ;      file; high word
fcb         ENDS
fcb_exten STRUC                    ; EXTENDED PART OF FCB
                                   ; Offset--Description
fcb_ext_flag   db    0FFh          ; -7--flag containing FFh indicates
                                   ;      extended FCB
fcb_resv2      db    5 dup (0)     ; -6--reserved
fcb_attr       db    ?             ; -1--attributes (see directory structure)
fcb_struc      FCB   <>            ;  0--reference main FCB structure
fcb_exten ENDS
```

Program Segment Prefix (PSP) Layout

```
psp         STRUC                  ; Offset--Description
psp_int20      db    0CDh,020h     ;   0--int 20h instruction
psp_top        dw    ?             ;   2--top of memory in paragraph form
psp_reserv1    db    6 dup (?)     ;   4--reserved
psp_termIP     dw    ?             ;  10--terminate address IP
psp_termCS     dw    ?             ;  12--terminate address CS
psp_ctlbrkIP   dw    ?             ;  14--Ctrl-Break exit address IP
psp_ctlbrkCS   dw    ?             ;  16--Ctrl-Break exit address CS
psp_critIP     dw    ?             ;  18--critical error exit address IP
psp_critCS     dw    ?             ;  20--critical error exit address CS
psp_reserv2    db    22 dup (?)    ;  22--reserved
psp_environ    dw    ?             ;  44--environment segment address
psp_reserv3    db    34 dup (?)    ;  46--reserved
psp_dos        db    0CDh,021h     ;  80--MS-DOS int 21h function call
psp_reserv4    db    10 dup (?)    ;  82--reserved
psp_fcb1       db    16 dup (?)    ;  92--unopened standard FCB 1
psp_fcb2       db    20 dup (?)    ; 108--unopened standard FCB 2
psp_parmlen    db    ?             ; 128--number of characters in parameter list
psp_parms      db 127 dup (?)      ; 129--command parameters
psp         ENDS
```